THE
SOVIET
UNION

A BIOGRAPHICAL
DICTIONARY

THE SOVIET UNION

A BIOGRAPHICAL
DICTIONARY

Edited by

Archie Brown

Weidenfeld and Nicolson
London

George Weidenfeld and Nicolson Ltd
91 Clapham High Street, London SW4 7TA

ISBN 0 297 82010 9

Printed in Great Britain by Butler & Tanner Ltd,
Frome and London

Contents

Preface

Given the speed of change in the Soviet Union in recent years, this has not been an easy book to write and it would have been an impossible one for a single author. I am, accordingly, enormously grateful to the specialists in various fields of Soviet studies drawn from different parts of the English-speaking world – Britain, the United States, Australia, Canada and New Zealand – who have been my co-contributors.

Special thanks are due to several friends and colleagues. Gerry Smith, Professor of Russian at Oxford University, was a constant source of valuable advice on Russian writers as well as of encouragement to the editor in the course of a project which took several years between its beginning and ending. Jackie Willcox, the Secretary and Librarian of the Russian Centre of St Antony's College, gave important and highly efficient help, especially at the earliest stage of drawing up a list of candidates for inclusion. At a late stage in the compilation of the volume, Martha Merritt – at that time a graduate student at St Antony's, now a lecturer in the Department of Government of the University of Texas at Austin – provided invaluable (and unfailingly cheerful) editorial assistance. To them and to all the contributors (especially those who, like John Miller, sent updated or new entries at short notice) I offer my warmest thanks.

My greatest debt of all is to my wife Pat, who has taken charge of the copy-editing of the book and most of the tasks of production editor. Her technical editorial experience (on the *Slavonic and East European Review*) and methodical approach have helped to impose order on the chaos which I at times created. Our desks have made a sharp contrast in tidiness, but in spite of this apparent incompatibility – as well as the strains involved in catching up with a moving target – we are still together!

There were times – as new institutions and new public figures emerged almost overnight in the Soviet Union – when I wondered whether I had done the right thing in responding positively to Lord Weidenfeld's invitation to me to edit this book. It was from the outset George Weidenfeld's idea and at the end of the process I am again convinced, as I was at the beginning, that it was a good one and that a book of this nature constitutes a worthwhile project. It is also still a timely one, even though the work has taken longer than either my publisher or I expected. I am grateful to Juliet Gardiner, Christopher Falkus, Nick Williams and Benjamin Buchan to whom I successively reported at Weidenfeld and Nicolson, for their patience and continuing enthusiasm for the volume. I also appreciate the publisher's commitment to speedy production following submission of the manuscript.

A book of this kind is of necessity highly selective, although it is naturally my hope that the choice of entries will prove to be both interesting and useful for a broad readership as well as for those who are concerned with the Soviet Union professionally. I have sought, and been much influenced by, the advice of other specialist contributors in the selection of entries in their areas of expertise. But I accept sole responsibility for the final list and for the areas of concentration of the book in the full knowledge that this is something on which no two specialists on the Soviet Union would be likely wholly to agree.

St Antony's College, Oxford   Archie Brown
1990

The Contributors

MARK ADAMS   **MBA**
Professor of History and Sociology of Science at the University
of Pennsylvania, Philadelphia

ROY ALLISON   **RA**
Lecturer in Soviet Defence Policy and International Security
at the Centre for Russian and East European Studies, University of Birmingham

JOHN BARBER   **JB**
Fellow of King's College, Cambridge and Lecturer in Politics
at Cambridge University

JOHN E. BOWLT   **JEB**
Professor in the Department of Slavic Languages and Literatures, University of Southern California, Los Angeles

ARCHIE BROWN   **AHB**
Professor of Politics at Oxford University and Fellow of St
Antony's College, Oxford

MARY BUCKLEY   **MB**
Lecturer in Politics at Edinburgh University

WILLIAM E. BUTLER   **WEB**
Professor of Law at University College, University of London

KATERINA CLARK   **KC**
Associate Professor of Comparative Literature and Slavic at
Yale University

SELMA JEANNE COHEN   **SJC**
Editor, *International Encyclopedia of Dance*

JULIAN COOPER — **JMC**
Lecturer in Soviet Technology and Industry at the Centre for Russian and East European Studies, University of Birmingham

JULIE CURTIS — **JAEC**
Fellow of Robinson College, Cambridge

ROBERT W. DAVIES — **RWD**
Professor and former Director of the Centre for Russian and East European Studies, University of Birmingham

JOHN ERICKSON — **JE**
Professor and Director of Defence Studies at the University of Edinburgh

BARBARA HELDT — **BH**
Professor of Russian in the Department of Slavonic Languages and Literatures at the University of British Columbia, Vancouver

DAVID HOLLOWAY — **DH**
Professor of Political Science at Stanford University, California

GEOFFREY HOSKING — **GAH**
Professor of Russian History at the School of Slavonic and East European Studies, University of London

MICHAEL KASER — **MCK**
Reader in Economics at Oxford University, Fellow of St Antony's College, Oxford, and Director of the Oxford University Institute of Russian, Soviet and East European Studies

ROBERT MCNEAL — **RHMcN**
Late Professor of History at the University of Massachusetts, Amherst

MARTHA MERRITT — **MM**
Lecturer in Government at the University of Texas at Austin

JOHN H. MILLER — **JHM**
Senior Lecturer in Politics at La Trobe University, Melbourne

MICHAEL NICOLSON — **MAN**
Fellow of University College, Oxford, and Lecturer in Russian at Oxford University

The Contributors

NORMA C. NOONAN
NN
Professor of Political Science at Augsburg College, Minneapolis

RIITTA H. PITTMAN
RHP
Research Fellow at St Antony's College, Oxford

PETER REDDAWAY
PBR
Professor of Political Science at George Washington University, Washington, DC

JAMES RIORDAN
JWR
Professor of Russian Studies at the University of Surrey

MICHAEL ROWE
MR
Keston College, Kent

GERALD SEAMAN
GS
Associate Professor, School of Music, University of Auckland

ROBERT SERVICE
RS
Reader in Soviet History and Politics at the School of Slavonic and East European Studies, University of London

HAROLD SHUKMAN
HS
Fellow of St Antony's College, Oxford, and Director of the Russian and East European Centre at St Antony's College

GERALD S. SMITH
GSS
Professor of Russian at Oxford University and Fellow of New College, Oxford

SUSAN COOK SUMMER
SCS
Slavic Cataloger, Columbia University Libraries, New York

RICHARD TAYLOR
RT
Senior Lecturer in Politics and Russian Studies at the University College of Swansea

WILLIAM J. TOMPSON
WJT
Corpus Christi College, Oxford

STEPHEN WHITE
SLW
Reader in Politics at the University of Glasgow

FAITH C. M. WIGZELL
FCMW
Senior Lecturer in Russian Language and Literature at the School of Slavonic and East European Studies, University of London

Introduction

The Soviet Union is today going through a period of dramatic change, and interest in it has seldom, if ever, been higher in the West. The aim of this book is to provide readers with easily digestible information – much of it difficult to obtain elsewhere – on some of the most prominent figures in Soviet public life from 1917 to the present day. Apart from being the most up-to-date book of its kind, this work differs from other single-volume biographical dictionaries in being written by a variety of specialists in different aspects of Soviet life, whether literature, art and architecture, the military, sport or cinema.

Special attention has, however, been paid to politics and politicians. The great majority of people who have ever been members of the Politburo or Secretariat of the Communist Party of the Soviet Union between 1917 and 1990 have been included, for until 1990 – when this began to change – these office-holders were the most powerful politicians in the land. Substantial biographical essays are devoted to the major Soviet leaders from Lenin to Gorbachev.

Although key makers of Soviet history from the earlier post-revolutionary years are included – and attention is, for example, devoted to leading figures in the rapid industrialization of the Soviet Union – there is a certain bias, and a quite deliberate one, towards the most recent period. Since 1989 major new political institutions have emerged and there are, accordingly, biographies of all of the members of the Presidential Council formed in March 1990 as well as of a number of the major figures in the Congress of People's Deputies and Supreme Soviet elected in 1989.

Increasingly, Soviet citizens outside the formal power structure – not least, innovative economists and other social scientists – are exercising important political influence. Attention is, accordingly, paid to them and more generally to some of the boldest exponents of *glasnost'* and key figures of the era of *perestroika*.

The speed of change, including personnel change, in the Soviet Union in recent years has made this an exceptionally difficult volume to complete.

Introduction

Some people have changed their jobs or status several times over between the conception of the book and its delivery. The advent of competitive elections in the Soviet political system in 1989 has brought about changes forced from below as well as change engineered from above in the incumbency of many political offices.

The increasingly radical demands of a number of the Soviet Union's national groups – in some cases for outright secession – has also posed editorial problems as new politicians who were totally unknown outside their own republics two years ago became well-known names within the Soviet Union as a whole and also in the outside world. Every effort has been made to keep pace with such developments, although there is no way in which that endeavour could be wholly successful, given that the Soviet Union is going through a period of remarkable transformation and uncertainty – a time which many have called a 'second revolution'.

Even the past does not stay the same. Quite a few of the people who died long ago and whose biographies appear in this volume have been rehabilitated in the Soviet Union only within the past two years and new information on some of them has come to light. This has, however, been but a minor problem for the contributors to this volume since they did not rely on the biased accounts in Soviet reference books on the victims of Stalin; it has been more a matter of Soviet writing on those who in the past fell foul of the system coming closer in the most recent period to assessments such as those included here.

The contributors to this volume have, of course – like the authors of all reference books on the Soviet Union – made some use of Soviet published sources. But although the best Soviet journals and newspapers cast aside in the second half of the 1980s many of the constraints of censorship and self-censorship which previously led to the deliberate suppression of facts deemed politically sensitive, the major Soviet encyclopaedias and biographical dictionaries predate *glasnost'* . It is of some importance, therefore, that the authors of the pages that follow have expertise in the particular sphere of activity on which they are writing and that this volume is, accordingly, less dependent on Soviet compilations than a number of its predecessors.

In many cases the entry here is the first on that person to appear in an English-language reference book. Some of the information has been based on interviews with the subjects of the biography and in a number of those cases and in certain other entries there is information included which is published in this volume for the first time in any language.

The style of the book also differs from a number of its predecessors. It is not that of a *Who's Who*, but of entries written in continuous prose. Moreover, in many instances they contain not only factual information but also evaluations and interpretative comment. The intention is to make this a book in which it will be interesting to browse as well as a helpful work of reference.

The entries are of very different sizes. Some have been kept deliberately short in order to make room for quite lengthy entries on those who have wielded great power or influence and in other ways played a major role in Soviet life.

The number of entries – approximately 1,400 – is large enough to contain much information that no single reader of the book is likely already to know. It is also short enough to guarantee that every reader already well informed about the Soviet Union will find some people omitted whom he or she feels strongly should have been included. If, however, the entries had been expanded to several thousand (as could easily, in principle, have been done), the book would either have become too large and expensive for most individuals and even many libraries to buy or, alternatively, there would have been no space for the extended treatment of major figures – whether Stalin or Solzhenitsyn, Trotsky or Zhukov – which this book contains.

One criterion for inclusion in the volume should be made explicit. This is not a book concerned with all people of Russian or Soviet birth. Emigrants from the Soviet Union are included only if they made a mark within the USSR prior to their departure. The focus of the book is on Soviet history, politics and society. Accordingly, even when a personality is included who spent part of his or her life in exile, more attention is paid to that person's activity within the Soviet Union.

Authors' initials are appended to each entry and the key to the identity of those authors immediately precedes this introduction. The book also has four appendices. The first lists the people included in the volume by their profession or broad area of activity. A number of the subjects of biographies appear under more than one heading, for there have, for example, been many 'in-and-outers' in Soviet politics – people who at one time worked in the Central Committee apparatus and at another as journalists or as social scientists in academic institutes. The second appendix is a key to acronyms and abbreviations used in the text. The third is a brief guide to the changing Soviet institutional structure, so that references to the Chairmanship of Sovnarkom, to the Presidium of the Supreme Soviet or to the first sec-retaryship of a union republican party organization, may become more meaningful. The last appendix consists of a short list of suggested further reading.

Transliteration of Russian words and proper names into English poses a dilemma in a book of this nature between technical consistency, on the one hand, and recognizability and readability, on the other. Accordingly, the transliteration scheme adopted is the British Standard one (which is used also by a number of important American publications) but it has been modified in several respects which are worth mentioning. The Russian 'E' is rendered as an English 'E' with, however, the exception of the initial letter in proper names. That means that one of the most prominent Soviet poets

Introduction

who first acquired nationwide fame in Khrushchev's time will be found under Yevtushenko rather than Evtushenko and the Soviet politician who was in May 1990 elected Chairman of the Supreme Soviet of the Russian republic appears as Yel'tsin rather than El'tsin; this has the advantage of being closer to the Russian pronunciation as well as to the form in which these names have become familiar to many Western readers.

For similar reasons the 'skiy' ending in Russian proper names has been simplified to 'sky', as in Burlatsky. There is also an occasional deviation from strict consistency in transliteration when a word is particularly well known in English with a different spelling. Thus, for example, we have avoided *perestroyka* (the rendering of the Russian word for reconstruction according to the British Standard system) and have used *perestroika* which has become so familiar in that form to British and American newspaper readers as to be by now almost part of the English language.

Archie Brown

A

ABALKIN, Leonid Ivanovich (b. 1930) The chairman of the State Commission for Economic Reform, Director of the Institute of Economics of the Academy of Sciences of the USSR and a deputy chairman of the Council of Ministers, Abalkin is one of the Soviet Union's most serious and influential economic reformers. He made a predominantly academic career until 1989, although over the previous two years he was increasingly in the public eye as an advocate of far-reaching reform.

Abalkin taught at the Plekhanov Institute of National Economy in Moscow (1971–77) before moving to the Academy of Social Sciences (a Communist Party institution) where he became head of the department of political economy in 1985. In 1986 he was appointed Director of the Institute of Economics and in 1987 he was elected to membership of the Academy of Sciences.

Chosen as a member of the Congress of People's Deputies in March 1989, he became chairman of the new State Commission of Economic Reform and a member of the government in June of that year which necessitated his resigning his seat as a deputy.

Abalkin has favoured a faster rate of economic reform than that advocated by the Chairman of the Council of Ministers, Nikolay Ryzhkov, and than was pursued in the Soviet Union up until the Spring of 1990. In addition to his academic and political activities, Abalkin heads the Soviet Chess Federation. AHB

ABDRASHITOV, Vadim Yusupovich (b. 1945) Film director. Abdrashitov began his film-making career as a pupil of Romm and a protégé of Raizman and is best known for his partnership with Aleksandr Mindadze. Their films include *Speech for the Defence* (1977), *The Turning-Point* (1979), *The Fox Hunt* (1980) and *The Parade of the Planets* (1984). Their drama *The Train Has Stopped* (1982) attracted a great deal of controversy as one of the first films to broach the subject of petty corruption in everyday Soviet life. *Plumbum, or a Dangerous Game* (1986) was attacked for its portrayal of the seamier side of Soviet life and its pessimism about the younger generation and its sense of responsibility. RT

ABRAMOV, Fedor Aleksandrovich (1920–1983) A novelist who first became known through a 1954 article attacking the over-optimistic portrayal of collective farm life common in post-war literature. In his trilogy on the villagers of his native Arkhangel'sk province (published together as *The Pryaslins*, 1974) he practised what he preached, presenting a frank picture of their poverty and of the arbitrary and inefficient agricultural administration, to which he counterposed the innate resilience of the peasant community. In his last years he worried that the latter was being undermined by the coming of both greater prosperity and urban customs, which he described in *Home* (1978). GAH

ABULADZE, Tengiz Yevgen'evich (b. 1924) Film director. Abuladze has had a considerable career in Georgian cinema and theatre but shot to international prominence with his remarkably imaginative film essay on Stalinism and its excesses, *Repentance*. This was completed in 1984 but kept 'on the shelf' – in this case concealed by the director himself – until its release as the trail-blazer of *glasnost'* in 1986, when it was seen by seventeen million people in three weeks! RT

AFANAS'EV, Viktor Grigor'evich (b. 1922) Until recently a leading Soviet journalist and political writer, Afanas'ev – who is of Russian nationality – was born in Aktanysh in the Tatar autonomous republic. He acquired positions of prominence and influence in the Brezhnev era which he succeeded in retaining until well into the age of *perestroika*.

After service in the Soviet Army, Afanas'ev held teaching and administrative posts first at the Chelyabinsk Pedagogical Institute (1953–60) and then at the Academy of Social Sciences of the party Central Committee in Moscow (1960–68). After spells on *Voprosy filosofii* (the main Soviet philosophical journal) and *Pravda*, he became editor of the party's theoretical journal, *Kommunist*, in 1974

before becoming editor-in-chief of *Pravda* in 1976, a post he retained until 1989 when he was succeeded by Ivan Frolov. From 1976 to 1990 he was also Chairman of the Soviet Union of Journalists.

In his writings on economic management and ideology in the Brezhnev years, Afanas'ev projected an image of the cautious reformer, but the reforms of the Gorbachev era revealed that his caution greatly exceeded his reformism. Although Afanas'ev paid lip-service to *perestroika*, *Pravda*'s support for radical change was much less than wholehearted so long as he occupied the editorial chair.

Afanas'ev was a full member of the Central Committee of the Soviet Communist Party from 1976 to 1990 and was elected to full membership of the Academy of Sciences of the USSR in 1981. AHB

AFANAS'EV, Yuriy Nikolaevich (b. 1934) One of the most active and radical reformers in the contemporary Soviet Union, Yuriy Afanas'ev is a historian by profession who has become a major public figure during the period of *perestroika*. Born in the town of Ulyanovsk, Afanas'ev has had a varied career in scholarship, political journalism and politics. After studying history at Moscow University, he became a secretary of a local Komsomol organization in Krasnoyarsk in Siberia, joining the Communist Party in 1961. He worked for a time in the 1960s in the Komsomol Central Committee in Moscow, but took up academic pursuits again in 1968, studying French history at the Academy of Social Sciences of the Communist Party Central Committee.

From heading the section on foreign cultures at the Institute of World History of the Academy of Sciences,

Afanas'ev moved in 1980 to the journal, *Kommunist*, as head of its history section. In 1986 he became Rector of the Moscow State Historical Archival Institute and it is from that time that he has become a major and outspoken figure on the Soviet political scene. Afanas'ev became a forthright proponent of applying the principle of *glasnost'* to Soviet history and became himself more radical as his campaign proceeded, extending his critique of Stalin and Stalinism to embrace in due course Lenin and Leninism.

Elected a member of the Congress of People's Deputies in 1989 (winning a large majority over the party apparatus-backed candidate in the town of Noginsk, near Moscow), Afanas'ev became one of the leaders of the Inter-Regional Group of Deputies when it was formed in the summer of 1989. A frequent speaker at demonstrations, he became one of the Communist Party members most respected by non-party members including Academician Andrey Sakharov, with whom he collaborated closely. Some party reformers, however, began to regard him as too much of a maximalist, impatient of the delays and compromises forced upon Gorbachev by the balance of political forces within the power structures. Afanas'ev, for his part, became increasingly disillusioned with the Communist Party and finally resigned from it in April 1990.

Afanas'ev has played an important role in giving substance to the development of a civil society in the Soviet Union and he became one of the leaders of the Memorial society, an anti-Stalinist pressure group set up to build a memorial to the victims of Stalin and to combat attempts to cover up acts of state repression in the Stalinist or more recent past. Afanas'ev's writings in the era of *perestroika* have been on Soviet history and politics, rather than French history. In 1988 he edited what was the most radical critique of the Soviet system and society published up to that time in Moscow, *Inogo ne dano* (There is No Other Way). AHB

AFINOGENOV, Aleksandr Nikolaevich (1904–1941) A playwright born in Ryazan' Province, Afinogenov became a party member in 1922, and obtained a journalism degree the same year he published his first play (1924). In the twenties he was a member and later director of the *Proletkul't*'s theatre, but in the late twenties he turned away from the *Proletkul't*'s influence to write more psychological works and became in the early thirties the chief drama theoretician of RAPP. He wrote twenty-six plays but is best known for *Fear* (1931) and *Mashenka* (1941). His work was attacked in 1936 and he was expelled from the party in 1937 but was never purged and was rehabilitated in 1938 to continue writing until his death in a German air raid. KC

AGADZHANOVA-SHUTKO, Nina Ferdinandovna (1889–1974) Scriptwriter. Agadzhanova-Shutko was the author of *The Year 1905* from which Eisenstein's *The Battleship Potemkin* (1926) derived, and of the scripts for *The Two Buldis* (1930, with Osip Brik), which she co-directed with Kuleshov, and Pudovkin's *The Deserter* (1933). RT

AGANBEGYAN, Abel Gazevich (b. 1932) One of the most prominent Soviet economists and an especially influential one in the early stages of *perestroika*, Aganbegyan, who is of mixed Armenian and Hungarian extraction, was born in the Georgian capital, Tbilisi. He graduated from the State Institute of Economics in Moscow in 1955 and between then and 1961 he worked as an economist at the State Committee for Labour and Wages. Aganbegyan joined the Communist Party in 1956.

From 1961 until 1985 he was attached to the Siberian Academy of Sciences, working in the Institute of Economics and Organization of Industrial Production at Novosibirsk – from 1967 to 1985 as Director of that Institute. Aganbegyan also edited the journal of the Institute, EKO, which during the 1970s and first half of the eighties was the most reform-oriented of Soviet social scientific journals and one of the liveliest.

Aganbegyan first met Gorbachev through his former colleague in Novosibirsk, Tat'yana Zaslavskaya, who had been brought into Gorbachev's circle of advisers in 1982. A serious reformer, although not the most radical, Aganbegyan had by the end of the 1980s ceased to be the most influential Soviet economist in the reform process. He remained, however, a member of numerous key committees, several of which he chaired. Since 1985 he has been Chairman of a Committee on Productive Forces and from 1987 to 1989 he headed the Economics division of the Academy of Sciences of the USSR. He is currently Director of the Academy of National Economy.

Aganbegyan, who has been a frequent visitor to the West as a speaker and conference participant in recent years, has also been a prolific writer. His works appear in many Soviet publications and his books, *The Challenge: Economics of Perestroika* and *Moving the Mountain: Inside the Perestroika Rev-*

olution were published in English in 1988 and 1989 respectively. AHB

AGOL, Izrail' Iosifovich (1891–1937) Marxist physician, philosopher of biology, geneticist. Son of a Jewish carpenter from Vilna, Agol trained in philosophy and wrote extensively on the philosophical dimensions of evolutionary theory, embryology, and heredity, including his book *Vitalism and Marxism*. He was an active Bolshevik after the revolution and earned a medical degree from Moscow University in 1923. After studying embryology at the Communist University with B. M. Zavadovsky, Agol switched to genetics in 1928 and did important work with A. S. Serebrovsky on the 'step-allelism' theory of gene structure in *Drosophila melanogaster*. In 1929 he was appointed head of the Timiryazev Institute and helped bring it under the control of the Communist Academy. He studied with H. J. Muller in Texas in 1931. Upon his return, he became vice-president of the All-Ukrainian Association of Marxist-Leninist Scientific Research Institutes. After his election to the Ukrainian Academy of Sciences in 1934, he headed the new genetics division of its Institute of Zoology and Biology. An outspoken Deborinite, Agol was arrested in December 1936 as a 'Menshevizing idealist', a 'Trotskyite bandit', and an enemy of the people and was shot on 10 March 1937. MBA

AIRIKYAN, Paruir Arshavirovich (b. 1949) Armenian nationalist leader often jailed for advocating an independent Armenian state. From the late 1960s he played a leading role in the National United Party of Armenia. He has been in captivity for nationalist activity of various kinds (1969–73, 1974–87 and 1988–). His last arrest followed protest demon-

strations by hundreds of thousands of Armenians in Yerevan in early 1988.
PBR

AKHMADULINA, Bella Akhatovna (b. 1937) A talented poet and glamorous personality, born in Moscow. Akhmadulina is the most eminent female in the generation that entered Soviet literature during the Khrushchev period. She specializes in the intimate personal lyric and the celebration of comradeship, has a keen eye for interior and external settings, and a colloquially-tinged style. She has travelled and been published a good deal abroad; her apoliticism hampered official endorsement at home until the Gorbachev period. GSS

AKHMATOVA, Anna Andreevna (1889–1966) Poet, born near Odessa and brought up in Tsarskoe Selo (now Pushkin), just outside St Petersburg. In the short love lyrics written in her twenties she 'taught women to speak', presenting them in intimate, dramatic personal situations usually as victims, but not passive, not innocent, and not conventionally virtuous. The six collections published between 1912 (*Evening*) and 1922 (*Anno domini MCMXXI*) established her as a major poet. The First World War brought a civic resonance to her work. She demonstratively refused to emigrate, but then fell into an unproductive silence until the eve of the Second World War, when the retrospective *From Six Books* appeared. Along with Mikhail Zoshchenko she was publicly condemned in the notorious Leningrad speech of Zhdanov in 1946, which declared her work to be un-Soviet and imposed a further silence. In this second, enforced period of withdrawal, she was creatively active, turning now mainly to epic: *Poem without a Hero* (1940–62, published abroad in 1960) deals somewhat enigmatically with life in Petersburg on the eve of war and revolution; and *Requiem* (1935–40, published abroad in 1963, Moscow in 1987) is her memorial to the victims of Stalin's purges, written out of her own experience as mother of the arrested Lev Gumilev, her son by the poet Nikolay Gumilev. In her late work there is a mystical element that is absent from her early lyrics, which tend to use religious concepts and terms and deny their metaphysical associations. Akhmatova returned to Soviet literature after the death of Stalin, with collections in 1950 (*Poems*) and 1965 (*The Course of Time*). She travelled to Italy to receive the Taormina Prize in 1964 and to Oxford for an honorary doctorate in 1965. As the last survivor of the Silver Age she was an important presence for the younger Leningrad poets who emerged in the late fifties. GSS

AKHROMEEV, Sergey Fedorovich (b. 1923) First Deputy Minister of Defence – Chief of General Staff, Sergey Akhromeev is one of the few Soviet military officials who currently maintains an international reputation and standing. As a prominent exponent of Soviet military thinking on arms control under the Gorbachev leadership he remains a key adviser and spokesman on military affairs. His meetings with Western officials have confirmed his reputation as a military intellectual, although initially he was conservative in his interpretation of the new 'defensive' military doctrine proclaimed by the Soviet leadership in 1987. Recognition of his talents contributed to his retention in the military command despite the removal of many of his peers when Gorbachev came to power.

Akhromeev first joined the Red Army in 1940 and gained command of a tank battalion on the Fourth Ukraine Front by the end of the war. His career moved through a series of command posts from 1946 to 1972. He was a graduate of the Military Academy of Tank Troops (1952) and the Military Academy of the General Staff (1967). The latter provided the basis for subsequent senior staff appointments: First Deputy Commander – Chief of Staff, Far East military district (1972–74); Deputy Chief General Staff (1974–79); First Deputy Chief General Staff (1979–84). Military and political honours ensued; the Lenin Prize, candidate membership of the CPSU Central Committee in 1981, full membership in 1983, and the rank of Marshal of the Soviet Union in the same year. His caution in an apparent party-military debate over military doctrine in the early 1980s earned its reward in September 1984 when he replaced Nikolay Ogarkov as Chief of the General Staff. Ogarkov had been a strong advocate of new conventional military technologies. In the climate of budgetary restraints and arms control under Gorbachev, Akromeev's emphasis has been more on constraining Western advances in military technology and fostering military detente. No implicit criticism of the economic priorities set by the civilian leadership can be detected in the writings of Akhromeev. He was critical, however, of the idea of unilateral Soviet conventional force cuts (1987–88), and he resigned as Chief of General Staff when Gorbachev announced such cuts in December 1988. He was replaced by the relatively unknown Colonel-General Mikhail Moiseev. Nevertheless, Akhromeev remains influen-

tial as a special adviser to Gorbachev on arms control and as a spokesman on Soviet defence policy. He addressed the United States Congress during a visit to Washington in July 1989. RA

AKIMOV, Nikolay Pavlovich (1901–1968) Born in Khar'kov, a stage, book and poster designer active mainly in Leningrad. Influenced by the artists of the World of Art group, Akimov was known especially for his surrealistic designs of the 1920s and early 1930s. He decorated many productions at the Academic Theatre of Drama (Leningrad), the Leningrad Theatre of Satire where he was chief designer (1945–49 and 1955–68), the Vakhtangov Theatre in Moscow, and also for the State Circus. JEB

AKSENOV, Aleksandr Nikiforovich (b. 1924) A party and state official for most of his working life, Aleksandr Aksenov was born in Belorussia and was educated at the Higher Party School in Moscow before serving in the Soviet Army during the Second World War. He joined the CPSU in 1945 and then held a number of Komsomol and governmental positions in Belorussia, becoming first secretary of the Vitebsk regional party committee in 1966, second secretary of the Belorussian Central Committee in 1971, and Belorussian prime minister from 1978 to 1983. He was Soviet Ambassador to Poland (1983–85), and has since then served as chairman of the USSR State Committee for Television and Radio. SLW

AKSENOV, Nikolay Fedorovich (1928–1985) A party member from 1954 and latterly a local party official, Nikolay Aksenov served as a secretary in the Altay territorial committee of the CPSU from 1961 to 1973, when he became chairman of the territorial executive committee. In 1976 he became first secretary of the Altay territorial party committee, holding the position until his death. He became a USSR Supreme Soviet deputy in 1974 and was elected a full member of the CPSU Central Committee in 1981. SLW

AKSENOV, Vasiliy Pavlovich (b. 1932) A leading novelist of the youth school, whose early novels (*Colleagues*, 1960; *A Ticket to the Stars*, 1961; *Oranges from Morocco*, 1963) treated elders and superiors irreverently, whilst each ending with a youthful re-dedication to the goals of communism. His use of a variety of narrative viewpoints, and of a language drawn from pop-music, sport and technology, drew him into an experimentation which intensified with his discovery of western literature and of the semi-suppressed Russian avant-garde of the early twentieth century. His attempt to encourage the emergence of a succeeding generation of youth writers by editing an unauthorized almanac, *Metropol* (1979), led to his final break with the authorities and emigration to America in 1980. Here he published *The Burn* (1980), a fantasmagoric re-examination of his childhood (when his father was executed and his mother, Yevgeniya Ginzburg, spent many years in labour camps) and of the increasing cultural repression of the late 1960s. GAH

AKULOV, Ivan Aleksandrovich (1888–1939) An old Bolshevik. Akulov, who held a great variety of government and party posts, was born in St Petersburg, the son of an office-worker and small trader, who died when he was eight. He went to trade school, becoming a member of the RSDLP in 1907 on the Bolshevik side. He suffered arrest and exile. He worked as a party official during the Civil War, became involved in trade union and party work in the 1920s, and was appointed Deputy Chairman of Rabkrin from December 1929 to July 1931, then First Deputy Chairman of OGPU in July 1931. Akulov was sent to the Donbass during the coal crisis of 1932, and made Procurator of the USSR from June 1933 to March 1935, having served in the Party Central Committee between 1927 and 1930. RWD

ALABYAN, Karo Semenovich (1897–1959) Architect. Born in Kirovabade, Alabyan was one of the principal practitioners of Socialist Realism in architecture. After studying in Tiflis (Tbilisi) and Moscow (graduating from Vkhutein in 1929), he designed various buildings in Yerevan and Moscow, including the Theatre for the Red Army (1934) and the Armenian pavilion for the 'All-Union Agricultural Exhibition' (1936–37) (both held in Moscow). He also supervized the construction of the Soviet pavilion at the New York World's Fair in 1939. Whether administrative or residential, most of his projects extended the 'Stalin style' – eclectic and decorative with a particular emphasis on the classical tradition. JEB

ALEKSANDROV, Aleksandr Danilovich (b. 1912) Mathematician, relativity theorist, philosopher of science, and administrator. After his graduation from Leningrad University in 1933, Aleksandrov served as a professor of mathematics there to 1964, working concurrently in the Leningrad branch of the Institute of Mathematics of the USSR Academy of Sciences. His work on theoretical geometry led to a government prize in 1942 and election to the academy as a corresponding member in 1946. Beginning with Lysenko's triumph in

1948, broad areas of science came under renewed ideological attack. In 1951 Aleksandrov joined the party and, in the mid 1950s, played an active role in the Academy of Sciences in defending relativity theory and reforming the philosophy of science. As rector of Leningrad University (1952–64), he played a key role in the de-Stalinization of the university, the resistance to Lysenkoism, and the reestablishment of Soviet genetics. As a result of his efforts, beginning in 1957 the university became the earliest to reestablish genetics, subsequently publishing M. E. Lobashev's *Genetika* (1963), the first modern Soviet genetics textbook. Elected a full member of the academy in 1964, Aleksandrov moved to the science city at Novosibirsk where he joined the staff of its Mathematics Institute, became a professor at Novosibirsk University, and continued his work on geometry, relativity, and the philosophy of science and his support of genetics and academic freedom. MBA

ALEKSANDROV, Grigory Vasil'evich (1903–1984) Film director and scriptwriter. It was Aleksandrov who assisted Eisenstein on his first four films, accompanied him to Western Europe, the United States and Mexico, and returned to the USSR to make musical comedy films and virtually found the genre in Soviet cinema. His major films, which all starred his wife, Lyubov' Orlova, and all enjoyed enormous popular success, were: *The Happy Guys* (also known as *The Jolly Fellows*) (1934), *The Circus* (1936), *Volga-Volga* (1938) and *Springtime* (1947). Consistently underrated by film theorists, Aleksandrov has exerted a major influence on the formation of a popular Soviet cinema. RT

ALEKSANDROV, Ivan Gavrilovich (1875–1936) Leading electrical engineer. A major figure in the design of the Dniepr Dam in the mid-1920s and other hydro-electric projects, Aleksandrov advocated the use of advanced technology to pull the USSR up to world levels, and was also an enthusiast for regional planning. Educated at Moscow Higher Technical School and School of Railway Engineering, he graduated in 1901 and began work on the design of bridges in 1904. In 1920 he was a leading figure in GOELRO (the State Commission for the Electrification of Russia). He also served intermittently on the presidium of Gosplan (1923–32), and was elected as a full member of the Academy of Sciences in 1932. RWD

ALEKSEEV, Mikhail Nikolaevich (b. 1918) 'Village prose' writer and author of war novels. Alekseev was born into a poor peasant family in the village of Monastyrskoe in the Saratov region of the Russian Republic. Both his parents perished in the famine of 1933. He entered the Atkarsk Pedagogical Institute for teacher training but his studies were interrupted in 1938 when he was called up for army service, and during the war was in the midst of heated military action. In summer 1943 he was appointed a deputy editor of a divisional newspaper. He began to keep a diary of his war-time experiences which later became incorporated into his fiction. Alekseev has been a member of the CPSU since 1942. He is a secretary of the Moscow Writers' organization, of the RSFSR and the USSR Writers' Unions, and also the head of the USSR Writers' Union committee on Ukrainian literature. He was appointed the Chief Editor of the literary monthly *Moskva* in 1968. During the Gorbachev era Alekseev has spoken out against cosmopolitanism and issued warnings against the reformist 'demagogues' of the age, but despite his personal views and reactionary outlook the journal *Moskva* has published such controversial works as Nabokov's novel *The Defence*, Chudakova's biography of Mikhail Bulgakov and the mammoth history of Russia by the Tsarist historian, Nikolay Karamzin. RHP

ALEKSEEV, Mikhail Pavlovich (1896–1981) A literary historian and specialist in comparative literature of extraordinarily broad range and erudition, Alekseev was one of the most outstanding of Soviet scholars in the humanities. Up until the early 1980s – and his death at the age of eighty-five – he was a living embodiment of the education and values of the best of the pre-revolutionary Russian intelligentsia. Born in Kiev, he became a professor in Leningrad University in 1932, a corresponding member of the Academy of Sciences of the USSR in 1946 and a full Academician in 1958. For many years a leading figure at the Institute of Russian Literature (Pushkinsky Dom) in Leningrad, Alekseev was Chairman of the Soviet and International Committee of Slavists and of the Pushkin Commission of the Academy of Sciences. He was widely regarded as the world's leading authority on links between Russian and British culture. His remarkably numerous publications in his lifetime ranged over that broad field (and many others), but his *magnum opus*, on which he worked for some thirty years, was published posthumously. That was his *Russian-English Literary Links (The Eighteenth Century and the First Half of the Nineteenth Century)* (1982).

Among Alekseev's honorary doctorates were ones from Oxford University and the Sorbonne. AHB

ALEKSEEV, Sergey Sergeevich (b. 1924) A leading legal philosopher of the Brezhnev and Gorbachev periods. Alekseev's writings have been concerned with the practical minutiae of a rule-of-law state and means of measuring the effectiveness of law. Elected a corresponding member of the USSR Academy of Sciences (1987), Alekseev has been the acknowledged leader of a dynamic group of legal theorists at the Sverdlovsk Juridical Institute. He is Chairman of the Committee for Supervision of the USSR Constitution as well as Chairman of the USSR Supreme Soviet Committee on Legislation, Legality, and Law and Order. WEB

ALEKSEEV, Vasiliy (b. 1942) Weightlifter. The most remarkable of all Soviet postwar weightlifters, he set an unsurpassed seventy-nine world records in the superheavy division and was the first man to break the 600 kg barrier in the combined lift, press and jerk, doing so in March 1970. During his ten-year reign as world strongman, he was twice Olympic champion (1972 and 1976), six times world and Soviet champion, and eight times European champion. Born in the village of Pokrovo-Shishkino in the Ryazan' Region and a mining engineer by trade, he retired from competitive weightlifting in 1982, undefeated in competition, and took up coaching in the mining town of Shakhty. In the age of superheavies, he was certainly one of the world's largest weightlifters: his heaviest competitive weight was 162 kg. His other statistics were height 186 cm, neck 53, biceps 50, chest 140, waist 122, thigh 80 and calf 45 cm. JWR

**ALEKSI (Simansky, Sergey Vladim-
irovich), Patriarch of Moscow**
(1877–1970) Russian Orthodox
Patriarch in the post-war years.
Consecrated Bishop of Tikhvin in
1913, Aleksi served in various dioceses until in 1933 he was made Metropolitan of Leningrad. Though he
served a brief term of exile in Central
Asia, he was one of the very few hier-
archs to remain in office during the
1930s. He earned considerable respect
at the time of the siege of Leningrad
when he remained in the city, and
was extremely active in encouraging
believers to support the war effort.
Aleksi was elected Patriarch at a
Council held in 1944. From that time
he was assiduous in defending Soviet
foreign and religious policies abroad in
an attempt to gain limited concessions
for the church at home. MR

ALESHIN, Georgiy Vasil'evich (b.
1931) A Russian electrical engineer
and party official from Krasnoyarsk.
Trained in Tomsk, he moved in 1954
to Novosibirsk (where he must have
encountered Yegor Ligachev) and
rose to be First Secretary of Novosibirsk *obkom* from 1979 to 1985. He
retired in 1990 after four years as
Second Secretary of the Estonian
Communist Party. JHM

ALIEV, Geydar Alievich (b. 1923) An
Azeri who was promoted to full membership in the Politburo by Andropov
in 1982 and then removed by Gorbachev in 1987, Aliev has the kind of
law-and-order background that made
him a useful ally when the emphasis
was on shaking up the party apparatus
rather than restructuring it. His career
was in the police (MVD) and KGB
apparatuses until 1969 when, following a vigorous anti-corruption
campaign, he moved abruptly from
the chairmanship of the Azerbaydzhan KGB to become republican
first secretary. He was made a full
member of the CPSU Central Committee in 1971, deputy chairman of
one of the chambers of the Supreme
Soviet from 1974 to 1979, and a candidate member of the Politburo from
1976 to 1982.

Aliev is more likely to have been
squeezed out of Gorbachev's Politburo
by the difference between mild and
radical approaches to reform than
because of the charges of corruption
which continue to cloud his name
(probably stemming from his three
years as deputy chairman of the Azerbaydzhan KGB under Brezhnev crony
Tsvigun). He suffered the further
indignity of 'voluntary' retirement
from the Central Committee in April
1989 and used the opportunity for one
last public denunciation of his detrac-
tors. MM

ALIGER, Margarita Iosifovna (b.
1915) A poet. Aliger was born in
Odessa, studied at the Gor'ky Institute, began publishing in the thirties,
and was most prolific in the forties.
Her collection *Year of Birth* (1938) celebrates the First Five-Year Plan. In
1942 she joined the party and published *Zoya* which is about a Moscow
schoolgirl who became a partisan
martyr. She participated in the independent almanac *Literary Moscow*
(1956), but recanted in 1957. KC

AL'MEDINGEN, Boris Alekseevich
(1887–1960) A stage designer in the
realist tradition, Al'medigen was
associated in the 1920s with the Constructivists. His production designs
included: *The Death of Tarelkin* (1918)
and numerous operas from Verdi's *La
Traviata* (1923 and 1952) for the Leningrad Malyy Opera to Wagner's *Die
Meistersinger* (1926) in Khar'kov. RT

AL'TMAN, Natan Isaevich (1889–1970) Artist. Born in Vinnitsa, Al'tman – a younger member of the avant-garde – achieved his initial reputation for his Cubist landscapes and portraits, for example, his portrait of Anna Akhmatova (1914). Welcoming the Revolution, he played a major role in the reorganization of artistic life in Petrograd, participating in the Petrograd affiliation of the Institute of Artistic Culture, designing Vladimir Mayakovsky's *Mystery-Bouffe* (1921), contributing to the May Day celebrations, etc. After a residence in Paris (1929–35), Al'tman returned to Leningrad where, in spite of harsh criticism of his 'formalist' tendencies, he continued to work as a painter, illustrator and designer. JEB

ALTUNIN, Aleksandr Terent'evich (b. 1921) Former Chief of Civil Defence. Altunin was deputy commander of a regiment from 1941 to 1945. After a number of staff and command posts in the post-war period he was assigned command of the North Caucasus Military District (1968–70). He assumed the position of Head of Cadre Administration in the Soviet Ministry of Defence (1970–72) and was subsequently appointed Deputy Minister of Defence and Chief of Soviet Civil Defence. He became an Army General in 1977 and a member of the CPSU Central Committee in 1976. Altunin was replaced as Chief of Civil Defence by Army General Govorov in June 1986 after the Chernobyl' disaster. RA

AMAL'RIK, Andrey Alekseevich (1938–1980) Dramatist and historian, who was exiled to Siberia in 1965 as a 'parasite' when his historical research became too independent for the authorities. He published an account of his experience in *Involuntary Journey to Siberia* (1970). Intelligent, perceptive and not easily classifiable in outlook, his essay *Will the Soviet Union survive till 1984?* proved wrong in prophecy, but asked some fundamental questions which preoccupied dissenters in the 1970s. He died in a motor accident after emigration. GAH

AMBARTSUMOV, Yevgeniy Arshakovich (b. 1929) Born in Moscow, Ambartsumov is the son of an Armenian father and Russian mother. He is one of the most erudite of Soviet social scientists and journalists who began as a historian but is now among the ablest political analysts of developments in present-day Europe and the Soviet Union. He has, however, continued to write also on historical themes (chosen for their contemporary relevance) and among his books translated into English are *How Socialism Began: Russia under Lenin* (1978) and *NEP: A Modern View* (1988). Ambartsumov graduated from the Moscow Institute of International Relations in 1951 and has for many years been head of the department of politics within what was until 1990 called the Institute of Economics of the World Socialist System. Like a number of prominent reformers within the Soviet Communist Party, Ambartsumov spent some years in Prague (on the *World Marxist Review*) and even before Gorbachev became General Secretary he was arguing for radical reform of the Soviet system. As recently as 1984, the Central Committee journal, *Kommunist*, devoted an entire article to an attack on his views. He was elected to the Congress of People's Deputies of the RSFSR in 1990. AHB

AMFITEATROV, Aleksandr Valentinovich (1862–1938) Born into the family of a Moscow priest, Amfiteatrov was a journalist in the late nineteenth-century tradition. In the 1880s he wrote *feuilletons* for *New Time* and travelogues for other journals, and was one of the founders of the journal *Russia* in 1889. Exiled in 1902 for a satire on the royal family, he emigrated to Paris in 1905, where he published the journal *Red Banner*. He returned to Russia in 1916 as an editor of *The Russian Will* but, unable to support the Soviet regime, he left again in 1921. He wrote a number of fictional works, including novels about the intelligentsia at the end of the nineteenth century. KC

ANDRIANOV, Nikolay (b. 1952) Gymnast. Andrianov competed in a record three Olympic Games (1972–80), at which he won seven gold, five silver and three bronze medals at gymnastics. At the 1976 Olympics he was also all-round gymnastics champion. Besides his remarkable Olympic success, he was three times world champion, eight times European champion and winner of the World Cup gymnastics competitions (1975–77). Born in Vladimir, he had the honour of having the premier Soviet gymnastics school named after him and established in his home town; he took up coaching there upon retirement from active gymnastics in 1981.
JWR

ANDRIANOV, Vasiliy Mikhaylovich (b. 1902) Born to a peasant family in the Bryansk province, Vasiliy Andrianov began his career working on the railways at the age of thirteen and later gravitated into party work, first in Moscow (where he was a university student) and from 1937 in Stalingrad, Sverdlovsk and elsewhere. From 1949 to 1953 Andrianov was first secretary of the Leningrad city and regional party committee; he was

elected a full member of the Central Committee in 1939 and 1952 and was a member of the CPSU Presidium (now Politburo) from 1952 to 1953. SLW

ANDROPOV, Yuriy Vladimirovich (1914–1984) A complex character who was actually a respected leader in the Soviet Union during his fifteen months as General Secretary, in spite of having served for fifteen years as Chairman of the KGB, Andropov played a significant part in changing the Soviet political agenda after the death of Brezhnev. He brought new people into the party leadership and attempted to introduce greater discipline in Soviet society, while beginning at the same time to point to the need for reform of the economic system.

Andropov was born, the son of a white-collar railway employee, at the railway station of Nagutskaya in the Stavropol' region of southern Russia. A Russian of partly-Greek ancestry, he left school at the age of sixteen in 1930 and over the next two years worked as a telegraph boy, as a cinema projectionist and on boats on the Volga before entering a technical institute in Rybinsk to study water transportation.

It was as a shipyard organizer for the Komsomol (Young Communist League) which he had first joined when he was sixteen that Andropov in 1936 embarked on a full-time political career. In the late 1930s he was a secretary and then first secretary of the Komsomol in Yaroslavl' and in 1940 he became first secretary of the Komsomol in what was then called the Karelo-Finnish republic. Among the valuable contacts this work gave Andropov was that with Otto Kuusinen, the Finnish Communist who was a leading figure in the Comintern and who was later to be a member of Khrushchev's Politburo. During the war Andropov was involved in organizational work, rather than military combat, on the Karelian front.

Andropov supplemented his earlier limited education with part-time study at Petrazavodsk University and at the Higher Party School, and prominent Soviet party intellectuals who worked with him later in the Central Committee apparatus in Moscow were impressed both by the extent of his private reading and his intelligence.

Between 1953 and 1957 Andropov was in diplomatic work, from 1954 as Soviet Ambassador to Hungary. The Hungarian revolution of 1956 revealed more than one side of Andropov's character. On the one hand, he demonstrated his capacity for ruthlessness by playing his part in the suppression of that revolution. On the other, Andropov is known to have warned Khrushchev of the dangers of 'counter-revolution' in Hungary before the uprising took place and he advised him that Matyas Rakosi should be removed from the leadership of the Hungarian Communists. Andropov was a strong supporter of Janos Kadar and remained an ally of his during Kadar's long subsequent period as Hungarian leader, including times when Kadar's reforms were being called into question by dogmatic Soviet critics.

Khrushchev was sufficiently impressed by Andropov to put him in charge of a new department of the Central Committee established in 1957 (and abolished in 1988) – the Department for Relations with Communist and Workers' Parties of Socialist Countries. It was during the ten years

that he headed that department (with, from 1962, the rank of Secretary of the Central Committee) that Andropov acquired the reputation of being the most reform-minded member of the Soviet leadership.

The testimony of party reformers who worked with him then and the very fact that he accepted these particular people as his advisers lends substance to that view. Among those who were his full-time consultants during his period as a department head in the Central Committee were Fedor Burlatsky, Georgiy Shakhnazarov, Aleksandr Bovin, Oleg Bogomolov and Georgiy Arbatov.

Andropov had good relations with Khrushchev who appeared to be grooming him as a potential successor to Mikhail Suslov with similar major responsibilities for ideology within the Secretariat. Relations between Suslov and Andropov were cool, for Andropov was much less rigid in his ideological outlook than Suslov and significantly more of an anti-Stalinist. It was Suslov who proposed Andropov for the Chairmanship of the KGB, as he wanted to get him out of the Secretariat and believed that the KGB chairmanship would put Andropov out of the running for subsequent party promotion. The proposal was supported by the Chairman of the Council of Ministers, Aleksey Kosygin. Although there was no personal animosity between Kosygin and Andropov, Kosygin was anxious to improve relations with China and he believed that Andropov – who had been head of the Socialist Countries Department of the Central Committee when the split with China took place – was an obstacle to these improved relations.

It is not accidental that it was at the

13

first Central Committee meeting after the death of Suslov in January 1982 that Andropov returned to the Secretariat of the Central Committee and immediately became a prime contender for the succession to Brezhnev. It is clear that all of Suslov's considerable authority would have been deployed in an attempt to prevent Andropov becoming party leader if the order in which Suslov and Brezhnev died in 1982 had been reversed. Brezhnev himself played a mediatory role in 1967 and agreed to Andropov's move from the Secretariat on condition that no loss of political standing was involved. This was to be indicated by Andropov's elevation to candidate membership of the Politburo at the same time as he became head of the KGB, thus preserving the right, which he had enjoyed as a Secretary of the Central Committee, to attend Politburo meetings.

Even while Andropov was head of the KGB, those who had worked closely with him in the Central Committee apparatus continued to suggest that he was the most reform-minded member of Brezhnev's Politburo. This may well have been so, for at least until Gorbachev became a full member in 1980 the competition for that accolade was far from intense, but Andropov's moral reputation was seriously undermined by KGB persecution of Soviet dissidents during the years in which he headed the State Security Committee. The only defence that reformers among his supporters could offer for this was that under anyone else's chairmanship in Brezhnev's time the KGB would have been worse.

Andropov's years as KGB chief did help to gain him support from constituencies other than reformist ones. The KGB under Andropov was, in terms of Soviet norms, one of the most efficient organizations in the country both as a body engaging in domestic surveillance and controls and as one conducting foreign intelligence. By the end of the Brezhnev era, the scope and significance of overt dissent within the Soviet Union had been much reduced by the adoption of a differentiated policy towards dissidents, ranging from labour camp incarceration through deprivation of employment to involuntary deportation and permission for voluntary emigration. Andropov's years as KGB chief meant that he had supporters not only among a section of party reformers (who preferred to remember his earlier years in the Central Committee apparatus) but also among those whose principal demands were for 'discipline' and 'order' in every branch of Soviet life, including economic life.

Following Suslov's death at the beginning of 1982, Andropov moved back to the party apparatus from the KGB, becoming a Secretary of the Central Committee in May of that year while retaining the full membership of the Politburo which he had been granted in 1973. He immediately launched an anti-corruption drive which implicated several people close to Brezhnev and, not entirely coincidentally, helped to undermine the position of Brezhnev supporters, including Konstantin Chernenko – Brezhnev's favourite for the succession – who had long-standing ties with the corrupt Sergey Medunov (sacked as regional party first secretary for Krasnodar at Andropov's instigation in August 1982) as well as with the Minister of Interior, Nikolay Shchelokov. His removal from office was completed only after Andropov had actually defeated a strong challenge from Chernenko – backed by the Brezhnev clients within the Politburo – and become General Secretary of the Central Committee on 12 November 1982, two days after Brezhnev's death.

Andropov came to power committed to stamping out complacency and corruption, determined to impose discipline, more receptive to ideas of economic reform than his predecessor, and conscious of the need for a rejuvenation of the party and state apparatus. In that he differed sharply from the policy pursued by Brezhnev as he also did in giving preference not only to comparative youth but to professional competence as distinct from long-standing acquaintanceship which counted for much with Brezhnev. Andropov's brief period at the top was characterized both by his emphasis on discipline, including an anti-alcohol campaign, and by his cautious placing of economic reform on the political agenda. There were few, if any, hints that Andropov was contemplating radical political, as distinct from economic, change and he continued to make a sharp distinction between 'within-system' reformers, who were given more encouragement than they had received for twenty years, and dissidents who continued to be severely repressed.

As early as February 1983 Andropov's health began to fail. It was revealed only after his death in February 1984 that for the whole of the previous year he had been receiving treatment for a chronic kidney complaint and that he had long suffered from diabetes and latterly also from cardiovascular deficiency. Andropov's last meeting with foreigners was in August 1983 with a group of American senators who confirmed reports of his physical frailty while commenting on his mental alertness.

Andropov attempted a number of foreign policy initiatives, including an effort to improve relations with China and a campaign to woo West European opinion away from the Reagan administration's position on arms control. This policy suffered a number of setbacks, one of which was the victory of Helmut Kohl and the Christian Democrats in the March 1983 German general election and another was the aftermath of the shooting-down at the beginning of September of the same year of a Korean civilian airliner – with the loss of 269 lives – by Soviet defence forces who apparently mistook it for a military aircraft. This episode damaged the Soviet Union's international standing and put the ailing Andropov on the defensive.

At a man-on-the-street level Andropov remained popular in the Soviet Union. He corresponded to traditional hankerings after a strong leader and he was regarded as intelligent and untainted by corruption. To a limited extent he helped to pave the way for the much more radical reforms that were to be introduced under Gorbachev. In retrospect, it is clear that one of his most important acts was to increase Gorbachev's powers and responsibilities within the Central Committee Secretariat and to bring into the Secretariat such new men from the provinces as Nikolay Ryzhkov and Yegor Ligachev who were to play important political roles in the Gorbachev era.

Andropov himself reached the top too late to fulfil much of the promise that some of his supporters had long held out for him. Even in foreign affairs, about which he was unusually well-informed, he could make little positive impact. Neither his health nor the international climate at the time permitted him to have even one summit meeting with his American counterpart and he remained to the end more highly regarded at home than abroad. AHB

ANIKUSHIN, Mikhail Konstantinovich (b. 1917) A sculptor born in Leningrad. After studying there under Matveev and Viktor Sinaisky, Anikushin rapidly became a leading exponent of Socialist Realism in sculpture. Favouring a heroic, monumental style, he produced many statues and busts, for example, the statue to Pushkin in the foyer of Moscow University (1957). He also designed reliefs and tombstones. From 1947 he has been teaching at the Repin Institute, Leningrad. JEB

ANTOKOL'SKY, Pavel Grigorievich (1896–1978) Poet, born in St Petersburg, educated in Moscow. Antokol'sky was active in the Moscow theatre after the Revolution. Largely traditional in style, his early poetry dealt with culturological and historical themes. The long poem *My Son* (1943), mourning the son killed on active service, became a Soviet classic. He was a party member from 1943, but a notable liberal presence during the 1960s. GSS

ANTONOV, Aleksey Innokent'evich (1896–1962) Former Chief of General Staff. Antonov held a series of senior wartime staff posts which included Chief of Staff Southern Army Group (from August 1941) and Chief of Staff of the North Caucasian, then Transcaucasian Army Groups (from July 1942). He was appointed Chief of Operations of the General Staff in December 1942, and simultaneously served as First Deputy Chief of the General Staff from April 1943. He was promoted to Chief of the General Staff for the period February 1945 to March 1946. He was once again First Deputy Chief of Staff (1946–48). From 1955 until his death he retained the position of Chief of Staff of the Warsaw Pact Forces. This was a formative period in the evolution of the Warsaw Pact military structure. RA

ANTONOV, Aleksey Konstantinovich (b. 1912) An engineer and state official and a graduate of Leningrad Polytechnical Institute, Aleksey Antonov joined the CPSU in 1940 and worked in industry before heading Leningrad Economic Council from 1961 to 1965, when he became USSR Minister of the Electrical Engineering Industry. In 1980 he was appointed a vice-chairman of the USSR Council of Ministers and in 1985 he became the USSR's permanent representative in CMEA or Comecon. He retired from both positions in September 1988. SLW

ARAKISHVILI, Dmitriy Ignat'evich (1873–1953) Composer and ethnomusicologist. Dmitriy Arakishvili (real name Arakchiev) was born in Vladikavkaz (Georgia) and died in Tbilisi. In 1901 he graduated from the Moscow Philharmonic Society School of Music and Drama, where he studied composition under Aleksandr Il'insky, taking composition with Aleksandr Grechaninov at a later date (1910–11). He was also a graduate of the Moscow Archaeological Institute in 1917. In 1901 he was a member of the Moscow University Musical-Ethnographic Commission and was one of the organizers of the Moscow People's Conservatory in 1906. He edited the Moscow journal *Music and Life* (1908–12). From 1901 to 1908 he travelled frequently to Georgia to write down folk music, his researches giving rise to several publications. In 1918 he moved to Georgia. He was active as a composer, writing one of the first Georgian national operas *The Tale of Shota Rustaveli* (première, Tbilisi, 1919) and a host of attractive songs. He was made a People's Artist of the Georgian SSR in 1929. GS

ARBATOV, Georgiy Arkad'evich (b. 1923) The Director of the Institute for the Study of the USA since its foundation in 1967 (renamed Institute for the Study of the USA and Canada in 1974), Arbatov – who is of Russian-Jewish origin – was born in the Ukrainian town of Kherson. He served in the Soviet army during the Second World War and attended military schools and academies. After the war he graduated from the Institute of International Relations in Moscow in 1949. In his subsequent career he worked as a journalist, in the party apparatus and then as head of one of the most policy-oriented of research institutes.

Between 1949 and 1960 Arbatov worked on the journals, *Voprosy filosofii* (Problems of Philosophy), *Novoe vremya* (New Times) and *Kommunist*, and from 1960 to 1962 in Prague on the journal, *World Marxist Review*. From 1962 to 1964 he was a section head at the Institute of World Economy and International Relations (IMEMO) before moving in 1964 into the apparatus of the Central Committee. There he became the leader of a group of consultants to Yuriy Andropov who at that time headed the Department of the Central Committee for Liaison with Communist and Workers' Parties of Socialist Countries.

Upon his appointment to the Directorship of the Institute for the Study of the USA, Arbatov became an influential adviser of the Soviet leadership on American politics and played an important role in building up a team of Americanists – who included some very able and well-informed specialists – within that institute. As a defender of the Soviet foreign policy line at any given time on his visits to the United States, Arbatov was often regarded there as no more than a propagandist. At home, however, he was an advocate of detente and – within safe limits – of reform. Some of his Institute staff became more outspoken reformers and the Institute emerged in the Gorbachev era as one of the major centres of the 'New Political Thinking'. Arbatov himself, however, by the end of the 1980s had lost some of his earlier more exclusive access to the top leadership as an interpreter of the United States as a wider range of institutions and individuals began to make an impact on Soviet foreign policy. Although a strong supporter of Gorbachev, he had to face the criticism that he had made too successful a career in Brezhnev's time. AHB

ARBUZOV, Aleksey Nikolaevich (1908–1986) A playwright and from 1928 theatre director in Moscow and Leningrad, his plays have been some of the most often performed on the Soviet stage. His first play written for the Moscow *Proletkul't* Theatre was *Class* (1930). The majority of his works concern the problems encountered by young people in their spiritual growth into adulthood. The best known include *Tanya* (1938, revised 1947) about the heroine's development from schoolgirl into a responsible doctor, and a classic of post-Stalin drama, *The Irkutsk Story* (1959) which tells of a love triangle on a Siberian construction project. KC

ARISTOV, Averkiy Borisovich
(1903–1973) A party and diplomatic
official for most of his working life,
Averkiy Aristov joined the CPSU in
1921 and became a Central Committee Secretary from 1952 to 1953
and from 1955 to 1960, at the same
time serving as a member of the ruling
party Presidium (now Politburo). He
became Soviet Ambassador to Poland
in 1961 and was then Ambassador to
Austria (1971–73). He was a full
member of the party Central Committee from 1952 to 1971. SLW

**ARKHIPOVA, Irina Konstant-
inovna** (b. 1925) Mezzo-soprano.
Irina Arkhipova was born in Moscow. After first studying at the
Moscow Architectural Institute, from
which she graduated in 1948, she
entered the Moscow Conservatory,
where her teacher was Leonid Sar-
vansky. On completing her course in
1953, the years 1954 to 1956 were
spent as a soloist with the Opera and
Ballet Theatre of Sverdlovsk, after
which she was engaged by the Moscow
Bol'shoy. She became a member of the
party in 1963 and was made a People's
Artist of the USSR in 1966. She is also
a Deputy of the Upper Soviet. The
possessor of a voice of exceptional richness and warmth, she has made several
tours abroad. GS

**ARMAND, Inessa (Yelizaveta Fye-
dorovna)** (1875–1920) A noted
woman revolutionary and the first
head of Zhenotdel, Armand was born
Elizabeth d'Herbenville in Paris. Her
father was French. After her parents'
death, she travelled to Russia to live
with an aunt who worked for a
wealthy industrial family, the
Armands. Inessa was raised as a
member of the family. She married
A. E. Armand, a son of the family,
with whom she had five children. She

resided for a time on the family estate,
establishing a school for children
there. Initially a Tolstoyan, Inessa
became a socialist about 1901. Her
marriage ended in 1903, but she and
her husband remained friends, and he
supported her financially. Inessa
Armand had a lengthy love affair
with her brother-in-law, Vladimir
Armand, who died in 1909. While
living abroad in 1904, she first became
acquainted with Lenin's work and
decided to join the Bolshevik Party,
thus establishing herself as one of
Lenin's earliest supporters, although
the exact date is uncertain.

She returned to Russia in 1905 and
worked for the Bolsheviks. Over the
next few years she was twice arrested
and exiled. From 1909 to 1912, she
lived abroad in Brussels and Paris.
While in Paris she was active among
the Paris Bolsheviks and met Lenin.
Upon her return to Russia in 1912,
she worked in the Bolshevik organization in Petrograd prior to her
arrest. Released because of her husband's intervention, she moved to
Cracow and worked for *Rabotnitsa*, the
journal of the Russian women Communists.

There has been much speculation
about her personal relationship with
Lenin. Armand was a close friend of
both Krupskaya and Lenin, and, in
comparison with the homely Krupskaya, a glamorous woman, much like
Kollontai. Lenin found her to be
attractive as well as intelligent, but
there is no evidence of a liaison. Kollontai fuelled these rumours after
Lenin's death with the publication of
her novel *A Great Love*, whose leading
characters are reminiscent of Lenin,
Armand and Krupskaya. Although
Armand and Lenin disagreed on specific points, she was, apart from Krup-

skaya, his closest female friend and one whose views he valued on issues pertaining to women. Prior to the revolution, she performed numerous responsible assignments for the Bolsheviks.

Armand was abroad during the First World War and returned to Russia together with Lenin and other Bolsheviks in April 1917. After the Bolshevik Revolution, she worked in the Moscow Provincial Party Committee and chaired the Moscow Provincial Sovnarkhoz. She also participated in the First and Second Congresses of the Comintern. Actively involved in planning the first Congress of Women in 1918, in 1919 Armand was chosen as the first head of Zhenotdel, the Women's Department of the communist Party, over the more controversial Alexandra Kollontai. Her selection as head of Zhenotdel was not surprising, since she was one of the senior women Bolsheviks and a long-time activist on women's issues, as well as a close associate of Lenin. As a Bolshevik, she had a longer record than did Kollontai. Her work with Zhenotdel during its formative period was significant, cut short by her untimely death from cholera in 1920. She was responsible for establishing the network of local *zhenotdely* so important both in recruiting women to the Bolshevik cause and in addressing women's problems. Much of the work performed by Zhenotdel during the civil war could be described as 'war relief'. Armand worked herself to exhaustion and was ordered to go to the Caucusus for a rest cure. There she contracted cholera and died. An extremely able and dedicated revolutionary, her life was cut short by the conditions of the civil war. Her ashes are preserved in the Kremlin

Wall with those of other prominent revolutionaries. NN

ARNSHTAM, Leo Oskarovich (b. 1905) Arnshtam is a Leningrad-based film director and critic who trained with Yutkevich and Ermler and directed *The Girlfriends* (1936). RT

ARTEM'EV, Pavel Artem'evich (1897–1979) A soldier in the First World War and Civil War, and a communist from 1920, Artem'ev became an officer in the uniformed NKVD troops. Early in the Great Fatherland War he transferred to the regular army and was made commander of the Moscow Military District (1941–47) and 1949–53). He became a candidate member of the Central Committee in 1952, but was then removed to obscure jobs during 1953, which suggests that his earlier NKVD connections had not been forgotten. JHM

ARTYUKHINA, Aleksandra Vasil'-evna (1889–1969) A party activist and leader of Zhenotdel, Artyukhina also served on the Central Committee of the Russian Communist Party from 1925 to 1930. The daughter of a weaver, Artyukhina worked in the textile industry prior to the Bolshevik revolution. She joined the RSDLP in 1910 and worked in the Textile and Metal Workers' Union in Petrograd. She was arrested and deported several times.

After the Bolshevik Revolution, she worked in several government positions until assuming the position of deputy head of Zhenotdel under Klavdya Nikolaeva, replacing Nikolaeva as head in 1927. During these years she also edited the women's journal, *Rabotnitsa*, and briefly served on the Orgburo (1926–27) and as a candidate member of the Secretariat of the Communist Party. Artyukhina was the head of Zhenotdel when the party decided to eliminate the department in 1930. Publicly at least, she supported the party's decision.

In the 1930s she worked for a time in the Workers and Peasants' Inspection of the Central Control Commission, then as a union official in the Textile Union's Central Committee (1934–38). Prior to retirement in 1951, she served as chairman of several textile factories. In her later years, she received numerous awards including three Orders of Lenin and Hero of Socialist Labour. NN

ARUTYUNYAN, Suren Gurgenovich (b. 1939) An Armenian who spent the years 1970 to 1986 in Moscow and was, therefore, a useful, non-aligned choice in May 1988 for the position of Party First Secretary in Armenia after the agitation over the Nagorno-Karabakh region had begun. Trained in Yerevan as a veterinarian, Arutyunyan became a Komsomol official there and in Moscow, and worked in the central apparatus of the CPSU. From 1986 to 1988 he was First Deputy Chairman of the Armenian Council of Ministers. He resigned from the post of First Secretary in April 1990 and was succeeded by V. M. Movsisyan. JHM

ARVATOV, Boris Ignatievich (1896–1940) A Polish-born literary critic, Arvatov was a political commissar during the Civil War and joined the Communist Party in 1919. In the twenties he wrote for the *Prolekul't* and *LEF*, and became a leading theoretician of 'left art'. He contended that art should not be independent of production, but should be fused with it to become 'production art'. KC

ARYUTYUNYAN, Aleksandr Grigor'evich (b. 1920) Armenian composer. Aleksandr Aryutyunyan (Harut'unyan) was born in Yerevan.

After first studying piano and composition at the Yerevan Conservatory, graduating in 1941, the years 1946 to 1948 were spent in further study in Moscow at the House of Armenian Culture under Genrikh Litinsky. In 1954 he became artistic director of the Armenian Philharmonic. A member of the party since 1952, he was made a People's Artist of the USSR in 1970. Best known in the Western world for his Concertos for Piano (1941) and Trumpet (1950), his music is strongly influenced by the rhythms and intonations of Armenian folk music. GS

ASAF'EV, Boris Vladimirovich (1884–1949) Musicologist and composer. Boris Asaf'ev was born in St Petersburg and died in Moscow. While attending the Faculty of History and Philology of the University of St Petersburg, from which he graduated in 1908, he also studied composition under Lyadov at the Petersburg Conservatory, graduating in 1910. The same year he was appointed as a ballet coach at the Imperial Mariinsky Theatre, which served as an impetus for his own composition. In 1914 he began to write regularly for the journal *Muzyka* (Music), using the pen-name Igor' Glebov. He taught at the Institute of the History of Arts in Petrograd (1919–30), and was also a teacher at the Leningrad Conservatory (1925–43). He edited the journal *Novaya muzyka* (New Music) (1924–28). In 1943 he moved to Moscow as Head of the Research Section of the Conservatory, becoming an Academician the same year. He was made a People's Artist of the USSR in 1946. His book, *Glinka*, was, it seems, the only book on music ever to receive a Stalin Prize (1947). He is remembered primarily for his musicological writings and for a few ballets, especially *The Fountain of Bakhchisaray* (1934). GS

ASEEV, Nikolay Nikolaevich (1889–1963) Poet, born near Kursk, educated in Moscow. A leading Futurist, and a dedicated supporter of Bolshevism, Aseev was the author of political verse in the 1920s (especially *Budenny*, 1923; *The Twenty-Six*, 1924); his best work, the long poem *Mayakovsky Begins* (1937–40) draws on his friendship with the poet. GSS

ASHKENAZY, Vladimir (b. 1937) Pianist. Vladimir Ashkenazy was born in Gor'ky. Raised in a musical background (both parents were excellent pianists), he first studied at the Central Music School, Moscow, then at the Moscow Conservatory where he was a pupil of Lev Oborin. In 1956 he was awarded first place in the Queen Elizabeth International Competition, Belgium. He made a tour of the United States in 1958 and in 1962 gained first place jointly with John Ogden in the International Tchaikovsky Contest. He married the Icelander, Sofia Johannsdottir, in 1961 and since 1963 has lived in the West. Apart from his work as a performer and recording artist, in recent times he has taken up conducting and in 1981 was guest conductor of the Philharmonia Orchestra, London. GS

ASKOLDOV, Sergey (Sergey Alekseevich Alekseev) (1871–1945) The Neo-Kantian philosopher and religious thinker, son of A. A. Kozlov, whose philosophy influenced his work. He was primarily an epistemologist, but is also known for his writings on Dostoevsky, Bely and Akhmatova. His *Thought and Reality* (1914) links philosophic thought to religious experience and mystic revelation, and also explores the dualism of thought and matter. Dismissed from Petrograd University in 1922, he lived in internal exile in the thirties and left for Germany during the war. KC

ASTAF'EV, Viktor Petrovich (b. 1924) A prose writer of Siberian peasant origins who fought in the Second World War. Astaf'ev trained at the Gor'ky Institute and began publishing in the fifties, and emerged in the sixties and seventies as a leading writer of Village Prose noted for his use of Siberian dialects and folk imagery. A favourite theme is the ethical and ecological problems caused by technological advance in rural Siberia. His best known work of this period is *The King Fish* (1976). In *The Sad Detective* (1986), Astaf'ev turned to the topic of modern urban life, painting a very black picture of violence, indifference and drunkenness. KC

ASTAKHOVA, Anna Mikhaylovna (1886–1971) Folklorist, and Head of the Folklore Archives in the Institute of Russian Literature in Leningrad (1931–56). A specialist in the study of the folk epos (the *byliny*), Astakhova is best known for two major studies, one on the evolution of the *bylina* in the Russian North (1948), the other a major reassessment of the study of the genre (1966). FCMW

ASTAUROV, Boris L'vovich (1904–1974) Animal cytogeneticist and embryologist. A student of N. K. Kol'tsov, Astaurov was a member of the Chetverikov group that pioneered the development of population genetics. In 1930 he switched to silkworm research and subsequently developed techniques for artificial parthenogenesis, intraspecific and interspecific androgenesis, and the production of the first artificially created polyploid animal species. As a corresponding (1958) and then full

(1966) member of the USSR Academy of Sciences, he played a central role in combating Lysenkoism and reestablishing genetics as a legitimate science in the Soviet Union. Except for the period when he worked in Central Asia (1930–35), Astaurov spent his entire career at the Kol'tsov institute and became its director in 1967 when it was transformed into the Institute of Developmental Biology. He died of a stroke in the midst of a major dispute with his rival, N. P. Dubinin, over the hereditarian view of human characteristics, which Astaurov supported. MBA

ATLANTOV, Vladimir Andreevich (b. 1939) Tenor. Vladimir Atlantov was born in Leningrad. The son of a singer, he entered the Leningrad Conservatory, where he studied under Natal'ya Bolotina. On graduating in 1963 he joined the Leningrad Kirov Theatre, remaining there for two years. The period 1963 to 1965 was spent in Italy at the La Scala Opera School, Milan, improving his vocal technique. After winning the Tchaikovsky Competition in 1966 and the International Contest for Young Opera Singers in Sofia in 1967, he was appointed a soloist with the Moscow Bol'shoy. He became a member of the party in 1966 and was made a People's Artist of the RSFSR in 1972. He has toured abroad and has made a number of recordings. GS

AVERBAKH, Leopold Leonovich (1903–1939) Born in Saratov and during the twenties a literary critic and leader of the most militantly 'proletarian' literary organization, Averbakh was a founding member of VAPP, general secretary of RAPP 1926 to 1932 and editor of their principal organs *On Guard* and *On the Literary Guard*. RAPP demanded hegemony in Soviet literature for itself as the only truly 'proletarian' (Party) literary group. Its sectarianism and hostility toward Fellow Travellers came to be branded as 'Averbakhism' upon RAPP's dissolution in 1932. Although he held a position in the newly-formed Writers Union, his career declined thereafter. He was accused of Trotskyism in 1937 and executed in 1939. KC

AVETISYAN, Minas Karapetovich (1928–1975) Painter and designer, born in Dazhadzhur. After studying at the Yerevan Art Institute and then the Repin Institute in Leningrad (1960), Avetisyan soon became one of Armenia's primary painters, known for his bright colours and national motifs. His themes concerned the popular traditions of Armenia as, for example, in *Baking Lavash* (1972). He was also active as a stage designer, especially of operas by Prokof'ev, Ravel and Rossini. JEB

AYTMATOV, Chingiz Torekulovich (b. 1928) Born in a small settlement (Sheker) in Kirghizia, Aytmatov is one of the most popular and prominent prose writers in the Soviet Union. Originally trained in animal husbandry, he earned national and international prominence with his 'Dzhamilia' (1958) which concerns the right of a Kirghiz woman to marry according to the dictates of her heart rather than those of the tribe. Since then, he has been awarded many Lenin and State Prizes for his works, and has enjoyed high office (on the governing board of the *Literary Gazette* and *New World*, head of the Kirghiz Cinematographers Union for twenty years and from 1986 of their Writers' Union, a delegate to five Party Congresses, and a member of the Supreme Soviet). A frequent speaker to delegations from the Third World or East Bloc peace conferences, under Gorbachev he organized the Issyk-Kul Forum, an international gathering of concerned intellectuals to discuss urgent problems of the modern world. His early works were written in Kirghiz, but since 1966 he has written them first in Russian, although most are set primarily in his native Kirghizia or neighbouring Kazakhstan. His work bears some resemblance to Village Prose in that it is nostalgic and anti-urban. Aytmatov has been influenced by Marquez and frequently interpolates into his narrative material purported to be ancient myths of the Turkic peoples of Soviet Central Asia, used both as parables about modern life and in urging closer links between past and present. His recurrent themes include the confrontation of the innocent with evil (especially in *The White Steamship* of 1970), Stalinism and the purges (especially in *Farewell, Gul'sary!* of 1966 and the play *The Ascent of Mt. Fuji* of 1973 which he wrote together with Kaltai Mukhamedzhanov). His fiction of the eighties uses multiple settings in time and place. *The Day Longer Than an Age Doth Last* (1980) extols the Muslim traditions of the Kazakh people, but also includes material on East-West tensions and a utopian civilization on a remote galaxy. *The Executioner's Block* (1986) treats such topics as the ecology, the economic reforms, alchoholism and drugs, and includes among its protagonists an expelled, God-seeking Russian Orthodox seminarian who is himself crucified by a drunken 'Stalinist' zealot.

Aytmatov was elected to the Congress of People's Deputies and to the reformed Supreme Soviet in 1989 and the following year was appointed by Gorbachev to membership of the new Presidential Council. KC

B

BABADZHANYAN, Arno Harutyuni
(1921–1983) Armenian composer and
pianist. Arno Babadzhanyan was born
in Yerevan and died in Moscow. After
graduating from the Yerevan Conservatory in composition in 1947, he
went on to the Moscow Conservatory,
where he studied piano under Konstantin Igumnov, graduating in 1948.
At the same time (1946–48) he took
classes in composition at the Armenian
Cultural Centre with Genrikh Litinsky. In 1950 he joined the faculty of
the Yerevan Conservatory. A member
of the party since 1956, he was made
a People's Artist of the USSR in 1971.
His Piano Trio, with its strong
national colouring, was awarded a
USSR State Prize in 1953. GS

BABAKHANOV, Ziyautdin (1908–
1982) Leading Islamic cleric active in
the international arena. From a long
line of Islamic scholars, Babakhanov
studied at Islamic institutes in the
USSR and Egypt. In 1957 he succeeded his father as Mufti of the
Central Asian Muslim Religious
Board. Mufti Babakhanov travelled
widely in the Islamic world defending
and propagating Soviet foreign and
religious policies. He was succeeded
as Mufti of Central Asia by his son
Shamsutdin. MR

BABEL', Isaak Emmanuilovich
(1894–1941?) Babel' was first published in 1916 in Gor'ky's *Chronicle*. In
1917 he took Gor'ky's advice to 'go
among the people' and was a type-
setter, reporter, participant in grain
requisitions, Chekist, and commissar
in Budenny's First Cavalry during the
Russo-Polish War; the latter was the
basis for a series of stories, first published in *LEF* in 1923, which would
become *Red Cavalry* (1926). At the
same time he wrote a series of tales
based on the lives of Jewish criminals
in his native Odessa which became
Odessa Tales (1931). His stories are distinguished by their compactness, vivid
imagery, and language usage – Communist slogans, distorted Biblical references, and illiterate peasant speech
appear side by side. The intensely
realist depiction of the Cossack
soldiers in *Red Cavalry* earned him
Budenny's rebuke, but Babel''s works
were quite popular in the twenties.
During the late twenties and thirties,
he wrote not especially successful plays
and film scenarios, was working on a
novel on the Cheka, and travelled a
great deal in an apparently fruitless
search for new material. His long love-
affair with the secret police seems to
have been the cause for his arrest in
1937. He was posthumously rehabilitated and his selected works published
in 1957. KC

BABOCHKIN, Boris Andreevich (1904–1975) Stage and screen actor. Babochkin was associated with a wide range of stage roles and theatres but famous for his title role in the film *Chapayev* (1934). RT

BAEV, Aleksandr Aleksandrovich (b. 1904) Biochemist, molecular biologist. A 1927 graduate of Kazan' University, Baev worked in the biochemistry department of the Kazan' Medical Institute until 1935, when he joined the staff of the Biochemical Institute of the USSR Academy of Sciences in Moscow. In 1959 he moved to V. A. Engel'gardt's new Institute of Radiation and Physicochemical Biology (later renamed the Institute of Molecular Biology). In the 1960s he studied transfer RNA and established the primary structure of the tRNA coding for valine (1967), which led to his election to the division of biophysics, biochemistry, and the chemistry of physiologically active compounds of the USSR Academy of Sciences as a corresponding member (1968), a full member (1970), and academician-secretary of the division (from 1971). In this post, he oversaw the rapid expansion of Soviet research in molecular biology and genetic engineering. MBA

BAGIROV, Mir Dzhafar Abassovich (1896–1956) Azerbaydzhani political leader. M. D. Bagirov began his revolutionary career as an activist in Azerbaydzhan in 1915. He spent the Civil War years engaged in military-political work in the Red Army. During the 1920s he ran the Cheka-OGPU in Azerbaydzhan and from 1933 to 1953 he was the first secretary of the Azerbaydzhan party. A long-standing client of L. P. Beria, he became a candidate member of the Presidium of the Central Committee in March 1953 when his patron's star was rising. When Beria fell, Bagirov was removed from his party and state posts. In 1956 he was tried and executed for dictatorial and arbitrary use of his power and for propagating a cult of personality in Azerbaydzhan. WJT

BAGRITSKY, Eduard Georgievich (Dzyubin) (1895–1934) Poet. Born in Odessa, he saw active service with the Red Army, and presented a heroic, romantic vision of the Civil War in the lyrics of *South-West* (1928) and the long ballad *The Lay of Opanas* (1926). Influential in Moscow as teacher of young writers before dying of chronic asthma, Bagritsky is revered as an idealistic, thoroughly Soviet poet. GSS

BAKATIN, Vadim Viktorovich (b. 1937) Appointed a member of Gorbachev's Presidential Council when it was created in March 1990, Vadim Bakatin has been Minister of Internal Affairs since 1988. His background before he became head of the Soviet ordinary police (as distinct from the KGB) was in party work – both in the Central Committee apparatus and as a regional party first secretary in Kirov (1985–87) and Kemerovo (1987–88).

Bakatin, who is Russian by nationality, was educated at the Novosibirsk Engineering and Construction Institute and at the Academy of Social Sciences attached to the Central Committee of the Communist Party. Before entering the party apparatus he worked in construction. AHB

BAKH (Bach), Aleksey Nikolaevich (1857–1946) Russian revolutionary, chemist, and a founder of Soviet biochemistry. Bakh entered Kiev University in 1875 but in 1878, because of political activity, he was expelled and exiled for three years to Belozersk and subsequently became involved in the revolutionary 'People's Will' party. He emigrated to Europe in 1885, worked for a decade in Paris, and settled in Geneva in 1894, establishing a biochemical laboratory in his home. There Bakh gained an international reputation in medical and agricultural chemistry for his work on catalysis and photosynthesis and for his 'peroxide theory' of oxidation. He returned to Russia in 1917. In 1918 he founded the Central Chemical Laboratory (renamed the Karpov Physiochemical Institute in 1922) and directed it throughout his life. In the 1920s he helped to organize chemical technology in various food industries. After joining the party in 1927, he rose rapidly in administrative power, serving as a member of the government's Central Executive Committee (from 1927), the organizer of the All-Union Association of Scientists and Technicians (VARNITSO) (1928), a member of the USSR Academy of Sciences (from 1929), and the perpetual president of the All-Union Chemical Society (from 1932). In 1935 he organized the academy's new Biochemistry Institute, became its director, and created one of the world's first biochemistry journals, *Biokhimicheskiy Zhurnal*. He was a deputy of the Supreme Soviet beginning in 1937 and, following the academy reorganization of 1939, served as head of its division of chemical sciences. MBA

BAKHTIN, Mikhail Mikhaylovich (1895–1975) Born in Orel, a thinker, literary scholar and philosopher of language, Bakhtin completed classical studies at Petrograd University in 1918, moving to Nevel and Vitebsk, where in the first of several 'Bakhtin circles' he discussed German Neo-

Kantian philosophy and new developments in literary theory. During these years he wrote a number of works on the phenomenology of self/other relations (extant only as fragments, the longest of which, 'Author and Hero', was published in *The Aesthetics of Verbal Creation*, 1979). In 1924 Bakhtin moved back to Leningrad where he published several books and articles under the names of his friends (*Freudianism*, 1927; and *Marxism and the Philosophy of Language*, 1929, under Voloshinov's name; and *The Formal Method in Literary Study*, 1928, under the name of Medvedev). In 1929 his *Questions of Dostoevsky's Poetics* appeared, just as he was arrested for suspected participation in an underground religious group. During the thirties and forties he lived in Kustanay (Kazakhstan), Savyolovo (near Moscow) and Saransk in Mordovia, but he continued working on the theory of the novel. The work he did during these years could appear only later, in the anthology *Questions of Literature and Aestheticsm* (1975), and *The Work of Francois Rabelais and Popular Culture of the Middle Ages* (1965). After the war, Bakhtin taught at the Mordovian State University in Saransk until his retirement in 1961. In 1972, now a greatly revered figure, he moved to Moscow where he later died of a respiratory disease. Many of Bakhtin's most influential categories were developed in his work on the theory of the novel, such as his concept of polyphony in Dostoevsky (whose novels are characterized by the absence of any single, monologic point of view) or carnival in Rabelais (joyful opposition to official restraints, that manifests itself in celebration of the body's physicality and the timelessness of common bonds among the folk).

But these categories are only particular instances of a more general philosophy, dialogism, that stresses social interdependence and the collective, non-immanent nature of the human subject. KC

BAKLANOV (Fridman), Grigoriy Yakovlevich (b. 1923) A Voronezh-born prose writer and war veteran who joined the Communist Party in 1942. Initially an author of minor fiction on kolkhoz themes, he attained prominence with his controversial *An Inch of Soil* (1959) which questions the assumption of previous Soviet war fiction that a mere 'inch of soil' gained is worth any amount of human loss. *July 1941* (1965) alternates scenes of the Soviet retreat with those of the purges of the thirties. Recent fiction such as *Friends* (1975), about bureaucratic corruption, and *The Youngest of the Brothers* (1981), about a Moscow professor, has taken up contemporary themes. Baklanov has been chief editor of the journal *Znamya* since 1986. KC

BAKLANOV, Oleg Dmitrievich (b. 1932) The Secretary of the Central Committee of the Soviet Communist Party who supervises military industry, Oleg Baklanov has a background of work in that sector of the economy. When he became a Central Committee Secretary in 1988, this was his first party post.

Ukrainian by nationality, Baklanov was born in Khar'kov and trained as an electrical engineer. A party member since 1953, he is very much a technocrat. After receiving steady promotion in industry (by 1975–76 he was general manager of a large production association), he became a deputy minister in the USSR Ministry of General Machine Building in 1976, later First Deputy Minister (1981–83)

and Minister of General Machine Building (1983–88). He became a full member of the Central Committee in 1986 and since 1988 he has been one of the few representatives of the military-industrial complex in the party's top leadership with responsibilities which now include the conversion of many military factories to civilian use. AHB

BAKSHEEV, Vasiliy Nikolaevich (1862–1958) Painter, born in Moscow. Although he achieved his reputation as a landscapist before the Revolution, studying at the MIPSA and exhibiting with the Association of Travelling Exhibitions, Baksheev quickly ajusted his Realist style to Soviet society. In the 1920s he interpreted Revolutionary scenes such as *May Day Demonstration* (1927) and, in the 1930s, did a series of collective farm scenes. To some extent, Baksheev's work was a model for the young Socialist Realist artists of the 1930s. JEB

BALAKSHIN, Pyotr P. (b. 1898) A Russian born in China, Balakshin wrote primarily journalistic and historical pieces. After fighting under Kolchak during the Civil War, he travelled to America and settled in San Francisco, contributing in the twenties and thirties to several Russian émigré periodicals. He produced autobiographical short stories and a long history of the Russian emigration to China. KC

BALANCHINE, George (Balanchivadze) (1904–1983) Dancer and one of the foremost choreographers in the history of ballet. The creator of more than 200 major ballets, Balanchine used his training in classical ballet and music as the basis for creating an entirely new formalist aesthetic. He developed the dance element into an independent, self-sufficient art and produced a new form of ballet. His career began in Russia, continued in Europe, and flourished in the United States, where he became co-founder and artistic director of the New York City Ballet.

The son of a Georgian composer, Balanchine entered the Imperial School of Ballet in 1914 and graduated in 1921. He also studied piano and composition at the Petrograd Conservatory (1920–23). From 1921 to 1924 he danced with the Academic Theatre of Opera and Ballet (formerly the Maryinsky).

In 1921 he founded the Young Ballet (Molodoy balet), for which he staged a number of experimental works (1922–24). With a group called Soviet State Dancers, Balanchine embarked on a European tour in 1924. While abroad, he decided not to return to the Soviet Union and joined Serge Diaghilev's Ballets Russes.

Balanchine created ten ballets for the Diaghilev company, many of which were fundamental to the development of his choreography. They included: *Barabau* (1925), *La Pastorale* (1926), *Jack in the Box* (1926), *La Chatte* (1927), *Apollon Musagète* (1928), *Le Bal* (1929), and *Prodigal Son* (1929).

In 1932 he was ballet master of René Blum's Ballets Russes de Monte Carlo and the next year he established his own *Les Ballets 1933* for which he choreographed *Mozartiana*, *Les Songes*, and *L'Errante*.

Later in 1933 Balanchine moved to the United States where he and Lincoln Kirstein founded the School of American Ballet (1934) and the company American Ballet (1935). He choreographed several works for this company, including *Serenade* (1935), *Le Baiser de la fée* (1936), and *Card Party* (1937). He also staged ballets for numerous operas at the Metropolitan Opera and introduced ballet to Broadway musicals, staging *Slaughter on Tenth Avenue* (1936), *I Married an Angel* (1938), and *Keep off the Grass* (1940). He choreographed dances for the films *On Your Toes* (1939) and *I Married an Adventuress* (1940). In 1942 he created *Ballet of the Elephants* for the circus.

In 1946 Balanchine and Kirstein founded the Ballet Society (renamed the New York City Ballet in 1948), for which he choreographed *The Four Temperaments* (1946) and *Theme and Variations* (1947).

In the 1950s and 1960s Balanchine was receiving wide recognition and created a number of his greatest works. These included many abstract, concentrated, plotless ballets with which he became so identified. His works from this period included *La Valse* (1951), *Scotch Symphony* (1952), *Allegro Brilliante* (1956), *Agon* (1957), and *Stars and Stripes* (1958). In 1964 the company moved to the New York State Theater. Balanchine's career was at its peak and he began to create some works with more plot and spectacle. These included *Harlequinade* (1965), the three-act ballet *Don Quixote* (1965), *Jewels* (1967), and his romantic ballet *Robert Schumann's Davidsbündlertänze* (1980). In 1972 Balanchine created a Stravinsky festival followed by a Ravel festival (1975), a Tchaikovsky festival (1981), and a second Stravinsky festival (1982).

Balanchine toured the Soviet Union with the New York City Ballet in 1962 and 1972. Part of his *Symphony in C* was performed at the Kirov Theatre in the 1960s. The Georgian Ballet's production of *Serenade* in 1984 was the first staging of a full-length Balanchine ballet in the Soviet Union. scs

BALANCHIVADZE, Andrey Melitonovich (b. 1906) Composer and teacher. Andrey Balanchivadze was born in St Petersburg. The son of a distinguished Georgian composer, he studied at the Tbilisi Conservatory, where his teachers included Ippolitov-Ivanov, graduating in 1927, then at the Leningrad Conservatory until 1931. In 1935 he joined the staff of the Tbilisi Conservatory, becoming a professor in 1942, and served as artistic director of the Georgian State Symphony Orchestra (1941–48). From 1953 onwards he has held various posts with the Georgian Composers' Union. He was made a People's Artist of the USSR in 1968. His work *The Heart of the Mountains* (1936) was the first Georgian ballet, while his nationally coloured First Symphony (USSR State Prize, 1944) is regarded as the first Soviet Georgian symphony of significance. His brother was the American choreographer George Balanchine. GS

BARDIN, Ivan Pavlovich (1883–1960) The most prominent Soviet iron and steel engineer. His father was a 'pugnacious village tailor' near Saratov. Educated in artisan and agricultural schools, Bardin graduated from Kiev Polytechnic in 1910. He worked in various capacities before the Revolution, spending some time in the United States at the Gary works. He supported the Russian cause in the First World War, and decided to stay with the Bolsheviks during the Civil War. He worked in various iron and steel works in the 1920s. From 1929 onwards he was a major figure in the construction and operation of the Kuznetsk iron and steel works, which played a crucial role in the armaments industry during the Second World War. He was given the special post of 'chief of blast-furnaces' in the People's Commissariat for Heavy Industry. He held senior posts in the Commissariat/Ministry of Iron and Industry from 1939. He was made a full member of the Academy of Sciences from 1932, and its Vice-President in 1942. He headed the Institute of Metallurgy and its successor from 1939. RWD

BARKHIN, Grigoriy Borisovich (1880–1969) Architect, born in Perm'. Barkhin graduated from the Academy of Arts, before working for Roman Klein's firm in Moscow (1909–14). After the Revolution, Barkhin supported the Constructivist style, as is demonstrated by his design for the *Izvestiya* building in Moscow (1925–27). From 1928 to 1930 he was editor of the *Ezhegodnik Moskovskogo arkhitekturnogo obshchestva* and in the 1930s designed a number of sanatoria. JEB

BARNET, Boris Vasil'evich (1902–1965) Film actor and a much underrated director. Barnet studied with Kuleshov and acted in his *The Extraordinary Adventures of Mr West in the Land of the Bolsheviks* (1924). Among the films he directed were: *The Girl with the Hatbox* and *Moscow in October* (1927), *The House on Trubnaya* (1928), *The Outskirts* (also known as *Okraina*) (1933) and *By the Deep Blue Sea* (1936). His *The Exploits of an Intelligence Agent* (1947) served as a popular model for subsequent spy thrillers and all his films are remarkable for their originality and lightness of touch. He committed suicide in 1965. RT

BARSHAY, Rudol'f Borisovich (b. 1924) Conductor and viola player. Rudol'f Barshay was born in the village of Labinskaya, near Krasnodar'. After completing his viola studies under Vadim Borisovsky at the Moscow Conservatory in 1948, he gained fame as a soloist and ensemble player. His most outstanding achievement was the founding in 1956 of the Moscow Chamber Orchestra, the first group of its kind in the USSR. In 1976 he left the Soviet Union, and was leader of the Israel Chamber Orchestra up to 1981, then conductor of the Bournemouth Symphony Orchestra from 1982. He has travelled extensively. GS

BARSOVA, Valeriya Vladimirovna (1892–1967) Coloratura soprano. Valeriya Barsova was born in Astrakhan' and died in Sochi. Her real name was Vladimirova. She received her first singing lessons from her sister, and then entered the Moscow Conservatory where she studied with Umberto Mazetti, graduating in 1919. She was a soloist at the Moscow Bol'shoy Theatre (1920–48), as well as fulfilling many other engagements. From 1950 to 1953 she held a teaching post at the Moscow Conservatory. She was made a People's Artist of the USSR in 1937. A party member from 1940, she was also a Deputy of the Supreme Soviet of the RSFSR. Barsova was generally acclaimed for the distinctive 'silvery' quality of her voice. She toured Britain and Western Europe in 1929. GS

BARUZDIN, Sergey Alekseevich (b. 1926) Born in Moscow, Baruzdin saw service during the Second World War, and joined the Communist Party in 1949. He published a large number of best-selling poems and stories for children. He has been Chief Editor of the journal *Druzhba narodov* since 1966, publishing many important works before and during the period of *glasnost'*, and he has held high offices in the Union of Writers. GSS

BARYSHNIKOV, Mikhail (b. 1948) An outstanding dancer, Baryshnikov studied ballet in Riga before entering Leningrad Ballet School in 1964. There he studied with the celebrated teacher Aleksandr Pushkin and made his début in the *pas de deux* from *Don Quixote*.

He joined the Kirov troupe in 1967, soon becoming a leading soloist with a wide repertoire of major roles in ballets including *Giselle*, *Swan Lake*, and *Sleeping Beauty*. He received particular notice for his portrayals of Mercutio in *Romeo and Juliet* (1969), the Toreador in *Fiesta* (1971), and Adam in *The Creation of the World* (1971). In addition, Baryshnikov received numerous awards at international ballet competitions including gold medals in Varna and in Moscow, and toured widely.

Baryshnikov defected to the West in 1974 and has danced in a wide variety of roles with the New York City Ballet and the American Ballet Theater. He has appeared in a number of ballets by choreographers including Balanchine, Frederick Ashton, Antony Tudor, and Twyla Tharp. He has also appeared in several films and television programmes, such as *That's Dancing*, *Baryshnikov on Broadway* and *The Turning Point*. From 1980 to 1989 he served as Artistic Director of the American Ballet Theater, for which he staged ballets including *The Nutcracker*, *Don Quixote*, and *Giselle*. SCS

BASHKIROV, Dmitriy Aleksandrovich (b. 1931) Pianist and teacher. Bashkirov was born in Tbilisi. After studying initially at the *desyatiletka* (specialist children's music school) attached to the Tbilisi Conservatory, he entered the Moscow Conservatory in 1950. His piano professor for the following four years was

Aleksandr Gol'denveyzer. In 1955 he was awarded second prize in the Marguerite Long-Jacques Thibaud Competition in Paris and in 1970 won the Schumann Prize in Zwickau for the best performance of that composer's work. Since 1957 he was taught at the Moscow Conservatory and has toured abroad on several occasions. He was made an Honoured Artist of the RSFSR in 1968. GS

BATALIN, Yuriy Petrovich (b. 1927) The Chairman of the State Committee for Construction (Gosstroi) and a member of the Central Committee of the Communist Party (1986–89) (when he went into retirement), Batalin was one of a number of members of the Soviet government with a background in industrial administration. A graduate of the Ural Polytechnic Institute in Sverdlovsk, he joined the Communist Party in 1956 and after working as chief engineer in several large industrial enterprises, he held a series of appointments as deputy minister in the gas and petroleum industries. From 1983 to 1985 he was Chairman of the State Committee for Labour and Social Problems and from 1986 Chairman of Gosstroi. From 1985 to 1989 he was a deputy chairman of the Council of Ministers and a member of its Presidium. AHB

BATALOV, Aleksey Vladimirovich (b. 1928) Actor. Batalov is a Moscow Art Theatre actor who went into films. He is best known for the roles of Boris in Kalatozov's *The Cranes Are Flying* (1957), Gusev in Romm's *Nine Days of One Year* (1962) and, more recently, for his appearance in *Moscow Does Not Believe in Tears* (1979). RT

BATALOV, Nikolay Petrovich (1899–1937) Actor. Batalov was a Moscow Art Theatre actor whose film roles included: the Red Army soldier in Protazanov's *Aelita* (1924), Pavel in Pudovkin's *The Mother* (1926), the cuckolded husband in Room's *Third Meshchanskaya* (1927), Sergeyev in Ekk's *A Path to Life* (1931) and the title role in Kuleshov's *Gorizont* (1933). Batalov's acting was notable for its understatement. RT

BATITSKY, Pavel Fedorovich (b. 1910) Former Commander-in-Chief of Anti-Aircraft Defence Forces (PVO). Batitsky, a Ukrainian, entered the Soviet Army in 1924 and commanded an artillery corps during the Second World War. After the war he was appointed Chief of Staff of the Moscow anti-aircraft defence region (1948–50), and promoted to Chief of Staff and Deputy Commander-in-Chief of the Soviet Anti-Aircraft Defence Forces (1950–53). For eleven years he commanded the Moscow Anti-Aircraft Defence System (1954–65) and was briefly First Deputy Chief of the General Staff of the Soviet Armed Forces (1965–66). In 1966 he was named Commander-in-Chief of the Soviet Anti-Aircraft Defence Forces and Deputy Minister of Defence. This position, which he held until 1978, also placed him in charge of the Warsaw Pact Air Defence Forces. He gained the rank of Marshal of the Soviet Union. RA

BAUMAN, Karl Yanovich (1892–1937) A Latvian whose promising party career was cut short by the Stalinist purges, Karl Bauman was born into a peasant family in the Baltic provinces. He studied at Pskov agricultural college and later at the Kiev Business Institute. In 1907 he joined the Social Democratic party, adhering to its Bolshevik wing. In 1916 he helped to organize the Latvian section of the Kiev Social Democratic organization; after the October revolution of 1917 he became a deputy to the Kiev Soviet and held a series of governmental positions, usually in the area of banking and finance. In the summer of 1923 Bauman came to Moscow to work as deputy head of the Organization Department of the Central Committee apparatus, subsequently (in 1928) becoming head of the party's Rural Work department. Later the same year Bauman became second secretary of the Moscow regional party organization and in April 1929 First Secretary; his meteoric rise continued when in the same month he became a candidate member of the Politburo and a member of the Secretariat. Criticized for excessive zeal in implementing collectivization, he lost his Moscow post in April 1930 and was removed from the Politburo soon afterwards. In 1931 Bauman was named as head of the Central Committee's Central Asian Bureau and in 1934 became head of the Science Department of the central party apparatus, losing his Secretariat position at the same time. A full Central Committee member from 1925 and a member for many years of the Central Executive Committee, the Soviet Union's quasi-parliament at this time, Bauman was nonetheless arrested during the purges and died in imprisonment. SLW

BAZAROV (Rudnev), Vladimir Aleksandrovich (1874–1939) Leading economist and theorist in Gosplan in the 1920s. Bazarov was born in Tula, and studied chemistry at Moscow University. He was close to the Bolsheviks from 1905, but was criticized by Lenin for 'Machism'. He then became a 'liquidator' (1910–11) and later moved closer to the Mensheviks. He edited the Menshevik paper in Khar'kov which was anti-Bolshevik territory in 1919. He was a close associate of Groman in Gosplan (1922–29). He favoured industrialization which concentrated on industries where the USSR could achieve economies of scale. He was arrested for alleged counter-revolutionary activities in 1930, but was not put on open trial. RWD

BAZHBEUK-MELIKYAN, Aleksandr Aleksandrovich (1891–1966) Painter, born in Tiflis. One of Georgia's leading artists, Bazhbeuk-Melikyan studied at the Tiflis Art Institute (1906–10), before enrolling in the Academy of Arts in 1911. Known for his colourful, stylized female portraits and circus scenes, he also responded to political reality, painting collective farm and war scenes such as *Fruit Harvest* (1935) and *A Gift to the Front* (1945). During the 1920s and thirties he taught at the Toidze Studio, Tiflis, and at the Tbilisi Academy of Arts. JEB

BEK, Aleksandr Alfredovich (1902–1972) Born in Saratov, a prose writer best known for the war novel *The Volokolamsk Highway* (1943–44). In 1956 Bek participated in the independent almanac *Literary Moscow*. His *The New Appointment* about corruption in the upper government hierarchy was published posthumously in 1986. KC

BEKHTEEV, Vladimir Georgievich (1878–1971) Painter, designer, and graphic artist. Born in Moscow, Bekhteev received his training in Paris and Munich before the Revolution, before becoming artistic director of the First State Circus in Moscow in 1921. In the 1930s he concentrated on book illustration, while maintaining a simple, figurative style of painting. JEB

BEKHTEREV, Vladimir Mikhay-lovich (1857–1927) Psychiatrist, a founder of Russian psychology. After graduating from the Medico-Surgical Academy of St Petersburg (1878), Bekhterev studied abroad (1884) and returned as head of psychiatry at Kazan' University, where he created one of the first Russian laboratories of psychophysiology. In 1893 he was called back to Petersburg to chair psychiatry and neuropathology at the academy and, after 1897, at the Women's Medical Institute. In the next decade he published several classic works, including *Foundations of Brain Function* (7 vols, 1903–7). In 1908 he created the world-famous Psychoneurological Institute. Through his theory of reflexology, for which he is principally remembered, Bekhterev sought to create a unified scientific psychology of mind that explained behaviour in terms of the physiology of the human brain and spinal cord. Within this framework, his studies ranged broadly, encompassing sexual behaviour in children, alchoholism, hypnosis, eugenics, criminality, and schizophrenia. In 1918 he became director of the new Institute of the Brain and Psychic Activity. He died suddenly in Moscow shortly after commenting at a reception that Stalin's behaviour was that of a classic paranoid schizophrenic; rumours persist that he was poisoned. MBA

BEK-NAZAROV, Amo (Ambartsum) Ivanovich (1892–1965) Film director. Bek-Nazarov was the first Armenian film director of any distinction. His films included *Namus* (1926), the first Armenian film and *Pepo* (1935), the first Armenian sound film. He also acted and wrote scripts. RT

BELASHOVA, Yekaterina Fedorovna (1906–1971) Sculptor. Born in St Petersburg, after graduating from the Leningrad Vkhutein, Belashova devoted herself to monuments (including tombstones) and statues, especially of women, supporting a heroic, romantic style. This is evident, for example, in her famous war monument called *Unconquerable* (1945). JEB

BELOUSOV, Igor' Sergeevich (b. 1928) A Leningrad-born Russian, Belousov has been Chairman of the Military-Industrial Commission of the Presidium of the Council of Ministers of the USSR since 1988. His background is in ship building and military industry and he held a variety of appointments as chief engineer before becoming a deputy minister of the Ship Building Industry in 1969. He was First Deputy Minister (1976–84) and between 1984 and 1988 Minister of the Ship Building Industry. He joined the Communist Party in 1955 and became a full member of its Central Committee in 1986. AHB

BELOUSOVA, Ludmila Yevgen'evna (b. 1935) (and Protopopov, Oleg Alekseevich (b. 1932)) Figure skaters. The husband and wife pair will long be remembered in pairs figure skating for their lyrical skating to classical music, particularly Beethoven. Ludmila, born in Ulyanovsk, and Oleg, born in Leningrad, came together as a figure-skating pair in 1955 and won the Soviet pairs title from 1965 to 1968, being the first Soviet figure skaters to win the European, world and Olympic titles. They won their Olympic titles at Innsbruck in 1964 and Grenoble in 1968, and held the world title from 1965 to 1968. The pair defected to the West in 1970 and performed in Swiss ice-skating revues. JWR

BELOV, Vasiliy Ivanovich (b. 1932) A native of Vologda province, he played a leading role in the revival of rural fiction in the late 1960s. His character Ivan Afrikanovich (from *That's How Things Are*, (1966) represented for many critics the ideal Russian peasant figure, whose way of life was threatened by bureaucracy and encroaching urbanism. He gave this vision deeper roots in *On the Eve* (1972–88), which portrays an integrated peasant community being destroyed by the first stages of the collectivization of agriculture. GAH

BELOVA, Yelena (b. 1947) Fencer. Elena Belova (née Novikova) was the first Soviet woman to win the Olympic individual fencing competition, in 1968. She won a total of four gold medals, a silver and a bronze medal between the 1968 and 1976 Olympic Games. Born in the Soviet Far East, she transferred to Minsk, graduating from the Minsk Pedagogical Institute and later becoming a Candidate of Pedagogical Sciences. Upon retirement from active sport at the age of thirty-four, she became head of Psychology at the Belorussian Physical Culture Institute in Minsk. JWR

BELOZERSKY, Andrey Nikolaevich (1905–1972) Plant biochemist. A 1927 graduate of the Central Asian University in Tashkent, Belozersky went to Moscow to study plant biopolymers with A.R. Kisel' and after 1930 worked in his department of plant biochemistry at Moscow University (MGU), where he spent the remainder of his career, winning his doctorate in 1943 for work on nucleic acids in bacteria. In 1946 he became professor at MGU and established a laboratory at the Institute of Biochemistry of the USSR Academy of Sciences. Following the publication of the Watson-Crick double-helix model of DNA in 1953, which explained gene characteristics in terms of structural chemistry, he rose rapidly in prominence as the leading Soviet expert on nucleic acids. Elected a corresponding member of the academy in 1958, he came to international recognition for research, performed between 1957 and 1959 with his student A. S. Spirin, that demonstrated disparities between base frequencies of DNA and RNA in a range of bacterial species, later seen as evidence of the existence of transfer-RNA. As chairman of the department of plant biochemistry at MGU (from 1960), a full member of the USSR Academy of Sciences (from 1962), and its vice-president (1971–72) in charge of chemistry and biology, he orchestrated the rapid expansion of Soviet molecular biology. MBA

BELSKY, Igor' Dmitrievich (b. 1925) A leading dancer, choreographer and teacher. People's Artist of the RSFSR (1966). Belsky was a student of Aleksey Pisarev and Andrey Lopukhov, graduating from Leningrad Ballet School in 1943. He joined the Kirov troupe in 1942, while still a student, during the company's evacuation to Perm. For his official debut in 1943, Belsky danced the Chief Warrior in the Polovtsian Dances from *Prince Igor*. He also studied at the Institute for Theatrical Arts, graduating from the Acting Department in 1957.

Belsky was a leading soloist at the Kirov from 1942 to 1963. He particularly excelled in character roles, performing brilliant interpretations of such parts as the Gypsy Dance in *Don Quixote* and the Hindu Dance in *La Bayadère*. He danced major roles in a wide variety of ballets, including Tybalt in Leonid Lavrovsky's *Romeo and Juliet*, Izmail in *Gayané*, and Severyan in *The Stone Flower*. He created the lead role in *Shurale* (1951) and the role of Mako in *The Path of Thunder* (1955).

Belsky was a major choreographer from the 1960s to the 1970s. He was chief choreographer at the Maly Theatre (1962–73), at the Kirov Theatre (1973–77), and at the Leningrad Music Hall (1979–).

His first major work was the two-act ballet *The Coast of Hope* (1959), a choreographic symphony based on the themes of patriotism and faithfulness. This was followed in 1961 by *The Leningrad Symphony*, to the first movement of Shostakovich's Seventh Symphony and on the subject of the Second World War and the siege of Leningrad. Belsky's later works included his own version of *The Humpbacked Horse* (1963), to music by Rodion Shchedrin; his own version of *Swan Lake* (1965); *The Gadfly* (1967); and *Icarus* (1974).

He taught character dance at the Leningrad Ballet School (1946–56) and taught in the choreography department of the Leningrad Conservatory (1962–64 and 1966–). He was appointed a professor in 1982. Belsky was awarded the State Prize of the USSR in 1951. scs

BELY, Andrey (pseud. of Bugaev, Boris Nikolaevich) (1880–1934) Poet, novelist, memoirist, literary critic and historian, born and educated in Moscow. A key figure in Russian Symbolism before the First World War, Bely was widely regarded as the most talented and intellectually gifted man of his generation. Uncontrollably prolific, driven and undermined by a quixotic, mercurial personality, Bely published several volumes of verse (1904–9), the key modernist novel *Petersburg* (1916), turned to Anthroposophy and lived at

Dornach (1914–15). He greeted the Revolution with the long poem *Christ is Risen* (1918). He experimented with emigration in Berlin, returning to Russia in 1923, where he plunged into educational activity. He continued publishing novels and memoirs until his death, struggling to reconcile his questing religious intellect with the rise of Soviet reality. gss

BELYAEV, Dmitriy Konstantinovich (1917–1985) Geneticist and mink breeder. The younger brother of N.K. Belyaev, Dmitriy Belyaev graduated from the Ivanovsky Agricultural Institute in 1938. For the next two decades, except for the war years, he worked on the genetics of mink at the State Scientific Research Institute of the Breeding of Fur-Bearing Animals. In 1959 he became director of the new Institute of Cytology and Genetics of the Siberian Division of the USSR Academy of Sciences in the science city at Novosibirsk, where he worked until his death. Under his leadership, even during Lysenkoist times, the institute became the preeminent Soviet centre of genetics research and teaching. MBA

BELYAEV, Nikolay Il'ich (1903–1966) Russian political figure. Trained as an agronomist, N.I. Belyaev occupied posts in agricultural cooperatives from 1925 until 1940 and subsequently worked as a regional party secretary. In 1955 he entered the Secretariat of the Central Committee of the CPSU with responsibility for agriculture. Belyaev was made a Presidium member in 1957, but failures in the Virgin Lands soon damaged his reputation and in early 1960 he was demoted to First Secretary of the Stavropol' regional party organization. In June of that year, he lost even that post and disappeared from view. WJT

BELYAEV, Nikolay Konstantinovich (1899–1937) Geneticist. After graduation from Moscow University in 1925, Belyaev worked at N. K. Kol'tsov's Institute of Experimental Biology where he joined the group on drosophila genetics, headed by Sergey Chetverikov, that initiated the first studies of the genetic structure of natural populations of fruitflies, thereby originating 'experimental' or 'ecological' population genetics. After the group was dispersed in 1929 Belyaev took up studies of silkworms at the Central Asian (1929–32) and Transcaucasian (1932–37) institutes of sericulture. In 1937 he was arrested and shot. MBA

BELYAKOV, Oleg Sergeevich (b. 1933) The head of the Department of the Defence Industry of the Central Committee of the Soviet Communist Party since 1985, Belyakov formerly worked in the Leningrad party organization and had associations with the former Leningrad party chief and rival of Gorbachev, Grigoriy Romanov. Since 1972 he has worked in the apparatus of the Central Committee in Moscow, between 1983 and 1985 as one of the personal assistants of Romanov. AHB

BERG, Lev Semenovich (1876–1950) Ichthyologist, geographer, and evolutionary theorist. After graduating from Moscow University in 1898, Berg was put in charge of fishes at the Zoological Museum of the Petersburg Academy of Sciences (1904–13) and subsequently held ichthyological posts at the Moscow Agricultural Institute (1914–18), the Institute of Practical Agronomy (1922–34), and the Zoological Institute of the Academy of Sciences (1934–50), concurrently

serving as professor of physical geography at Petrograd (Leningrad) University (1916–50). He won early fame for *Nomogenesis* (1922), a book that mobilized his considerable knowledge of systematics and biogeography to set forth an influential non-Darwinian theory of evolution as a lawful process in which natural selection played no major role. The work led to his election to the Academy of Sciences in 1928 as a corresponding member, but it was strongly attacked by Marxists on ideological grounds in the late 1920s and early 1930s. Thereafter, he moved into less controversial areas, publishing treatises on the major land zones (based on geology, geography, climate, and animal and plant distribution) and on fish systematics. He was elected president of the prestigious Geographical Society in 1940 and a full member of the USSR Academy of Sciences in 1946. During his final years, he completed important works on the history of Russian geography. MBA

BERGGOL'TS, Ol'ga Fedorovna (1910–1975) Poet and prose writer. Known primarily as a writer of the siege of Leningrad, she established her reputation in the thirties with prose and children's tales, but began to write her best poetry in 1942. Her radio broadcasts to Leningraders in the blockade are collected in *Leningrad Speaks* (1946). Her work *Day Stars* (1959) is a lyric diary recalling the past. She is a moral writer, speaking at once for the self and humanity. BH

BERIA, Lavrentiy Pavlovich (1899–1953) Georgian politician and security official. One of the most notorious of Stalin's courtiers, L. P. Beria began his career in the Communist Party in the Russian army in 1917. In 1920 he was deported from Georgia for attempting to start an uprising against the Mensheviks. In 1921 he joined the Cheka (later the OGPU). He spent the next decade rising through its ranks and by 1931 he was in charge of the security organs in all of Transcaucasia. Beria was elected First Secretary of the Georgian republic in 1931 and the following year became First Secretary for Transcaucasia, a region he was to rule either directly or through clients until 1953. Constantly ingratiating himself with Stalin, Beria became the dictator's chief informer and inquisitor in the region. In 1938 Stalin appointed him USSR Commissar of Internal Affairs, a post he held until 1945.

After the war, Beria continued to manage his internal security empire through his client Abakumov. A close ally of Malenkov throughout this period, Beria played a key role in the Leningrad affair of 1949 which sealed the defeat of the Zhdanovites. After 1951, however, he lost Stalin's favour and found himself under attack: his clients were purged from key posts in the security services and the Georgian party, and he himself was the intended victim of the 'Doctors' Plot' of 1953. Saved by Stalin's death, he managed the initial succession in cooperation with his ally Malenkov but the two soon fell out. Beria then attempted to challenge Malenkov from his power base in the security services and among the non-Russian cadres of certain republics. In June 1953, however, others in the leadership concluded that he was too great a threat to be tolerated; he was arrested, charged with a preposterous array of anti-state activities rather than with his real crimes, and executed in December. WJT

BERKLAV, Eduard Karlovich (Berklavs, Eduards) (b. 1914) A Latvian who joined the Communist Party in 1939, Berklavs became Secretary of the Latvian Komsomol in 1940. By 1955 he was Deputy Chairman of the Latvian Council of Ministers and, from 1956 to 1958, First Secretary of Riga *gorkom* and member of the Bureau of the Latvian Communist Party. In 1959 he was dismissed (among many others) for nationalism and became a cinema manager in the Russian city of Vladimir! Berklavs returned to Latvia in 1968, and during 1988 emerged as a prominent figure in the Popular Front of Latvia and the Latvian National Independence Movement, the formation of which was influenced by memories of the 1959 purge. He was elected to the 1990 Supreme Soviet in Latvia. JHM

BERMAN, Lazar Naumovich (b. 1930) Pianist. Lazar Berman was born in Leningrad. At the Moscow Conservatory, from which he graduated in 1953, he was a student of Aleksandr Gol'denveyzer. In 1956 he was awarded fifth prize at the Queen Elizabeth International Competition, Belgium, and also gained third place in the International Liszt Contest in Budapest the same year. He toured Italy in 1970 and achieved great success in the United States in 1976. GS

BESSMERTNOVA, Natal'ya Igorevna (b. 1941) Outstanding ballerina. People's Artist of the USSR (1976). A student of Mariya Kozhukova and Sofiya Golovkina, Bessmertnova graduated from the Bol'shoy Ballet School in 1961. She joined the Bol'shoy troupe upon graduation and soon became one of the company's foremost dancers. With her long, expressive arms and melancholic expression, she became a leading ballerina of the romantic repertoire. In addition, she has performed in numerous modern ballets, many of them choreographed by her husband, Yuriy Grigorovich.

Bessmertnova made her début in the seventh waltz from *Chopiniana* in 1961 and, two years later, captivated audiences with her sensitive, elusive portrayal of the title role in *Giselle*.

Her other major roles have included the creations of Leili in Kasyan Goleyzovsky's *Leili and Madjnun* (1964), Shirin in Goleyzovsky's *Legend of Love* (1965), Phrygia in Grigorovich's *Spartacus* (1968), Odette-Odile in Grigorovich's new version of *Swan Lake* (1969), and Juliet in Grigorovich's *Romeo and Juliet* (1979).

In addition to her affiliation with the Bol'shoy Theatre, where she has been a frequent partner of Mikhail Lavrovsky, Bessmertnova has also appeared as a guest artist with the Kirov Theatre. At the Kirov she was often partnered by Mikhail Baryshnikov, until his emigration in 1974.

Bessmertnova has received numerous prizes, including at the International Ballet Competition at Varna (1965) and the Anna Pavlova Prize (1970). She has also toured abroad, most recently in a 1989 tour to the United States with the Stars of the Bol'shoy Ballet. scs

BESSMERTNYKH, Aleksandr Aleksandrovich (b. 1933) A career diplomat whose speciality has been the United States, Bessmertnykh's career has flourished especially strongly since Eduard Shevardnadze became Soviet Foreign Minister in 1985. In 1986 Bessmertnykh was appointed a deputy foreign minister, in October 1988 he became First Deputy Foreign Minister, while remaining in charge of the United States and Canada department, and in 1990 he was appointed Soviet Ambassador to Washington.

Earlier in his career, Bessmertnykh served as a translator in the United Nations Secretariat (1960–62), in the UN Department of Political and Security Council Affairs (1962–66), in the Ministry of Foreign Affairs in Moscow (1966–70) and in the Soviet Embassy in Washington from 1970 to 1983, latterly as Minister-Counsellor. AHB

BEZYMENSKY, Aleksandr Il'ich (1898–1973) Poet, born in Zhitomir. Bezymensky was a party member from 1916, prominent in official literary circles throughout his life, and sedulous versifier of the evolving party line in innumerable lyrics and long poems; he is the author of the Komsomol anthem (1922, revised 1962). GSS

BIKKENIN, Nail' Barievich (b. 1931) The chief editor of the theoretical journal of the Communist Party, *Kommunist*, since June 1987 and Central Committee member since 1990, Bikkenin is a Tatar born in Kazan'. A member of the party since 1955, he studied at Moscow University and took a doctorate in philosophy. He is a Corresponding Member of the Academy of Sciences of the USSR. From 1963 to 1966 he worked on the journal, *Kommunist*, but then moved into the apparatus of the party's Central Committee. From 1966 to 1983 he was an official in the Department of Propaganda and from 1983 to 1985 head of a group of consultants in the Department of Science and Educational Institutions of the Central Committee. In 1985 he became a deputy head of the Department of Propaganda, from where he moved to his present post. Under Bikkenin, *Kom-*

munist has retained the more open-minded character it acquired under his immediate predecessor, Ivan Frolov, and embraces a much greater diversity of viewpoints than in the past. AHB

BILL'-BELOTSERKOVSKY, Vladimir Naumovich (1884–1970) Bill'-Belotserkovsky worked as a stevedore in America before the Revolution but returned to Russia in 1917. He was a naturalistic playwright, noted for his polemical plays on behalf of the Bolshevik cause including: *The Storm* (1925), *The Calm* and *The Moon from the Left* (both 1927), *The West is Nervous* (1931), *Life is Calling* (1934) and the anti-American *Skin Colour* (1947). RT

BIRMAN, Serafima Germanovna (1890–1976) Actress and director associated with the Moscow Art Theatre, Serafima Birman created a number of major roles especially in the plays of Afinogenov. She also directed and acted in Gor'ky's *Vassa Zheleznova* (1936) and played Yefrosinia Staritskaya in Eisenstein's *Ivan the Terrible* (1943–46), the role for which she is best remembered by a wider public. RT

BIRMAN, S.P. (?–1937) A prominent industrial manager in the 1930s. Birman was noted for the independence of his views. Born in Hungary, chairman of the Budapest soviet during the abortive Communist revolution of 1918, he was exchanged for a Hungarian officer in 1921. Employed as manager of the iron and steel trust Yugostal' in the 1920s, he then occupied various posts in the 1930s, as director of a major iron and steel works, for example, and as a senior official in the Commissariat where he was for a time in charge of industrial statistics. RWD

BIRYUKOVA, Aleksandra Pavlovna (b. 1929) A Soviet party and state official, Biryukova is the highest ranking woman in the Soviet administration until her retirement in 1990. During the Gorbachev period, she was promoted from trade union official to the Central Committee Secretariat (1986) and from the Secretariat to Deputy Premier in the Council of Ministers, (1988). She was also a candidate member of the Politburo (1988–90).

Biryukova was born into a peasant family in the Moscow region. She graduated from the Moscow Textile Institute in 1952 and during the 1950s worked as a foreman and shop supervisor at the First Printed Fabric Cotton Works in Moscow. She joined the Communist Party in 1956 at the age of twenty-nine. From 1959 to 1963 she served as an official in the textile and knitware industries of the Moscow City Economic Council (*Mosgorsovnarkhoz*). In 1963 Biryukova was appointed the chief engineer of a Moscow cotton combine (*Trekhgornaya manufaktura*). She served as Secretary and member of the Presidium of the Central Council of Trade Unions (1968–86) and was appointed Deputy Chairman of the Central Trade Union Council in 1985. She was elected a candidate member of the CPSU Central Committee in 1971 and a full member in 1976.

Although she had travelled in the West, Biryukova was generally unknown outside the USSR until 1986. At the Twenty-seventh Congress of the CPSU in 1986, the first party congress after Gorbachev became General Secretary, Biryukova was appointed to the Central Committee Secretariat. The first woman in the Secretariat in twenty-five years, she served as Secretary for light industry and consumer goods production, areas in which she had considerable expertise. Biryukova was also a deputy to the USSR Supreme Soviet (Eleventh Convocation) and to the Supreme Soviet of the RSFSR where she chaired the Commission on Working and Living Conditions of Women, Mothers and Childcare.

In October 1988 Biryukova was one of several officials whose portfolios were changed. At the 1 October plenum of the Central Committee, she was elected a candidate member of the Politburo, the first woman to serve in the Politburo since Furtseva in the Khrushchev years. Shortly afterwards at the session of the Supreme Soviet which elected Gorbachev Chairman of the Presidium of the Supreme Soviet, Biryukova was selected as a Deputy Premier in the Council of Ministers and Chairman of its Bureau of Social Development. In 1989 she was sent on a well-publicized shopping trip to London to buy scarce consumer goods for the Soviet people. In her position as Deputy Premier she also emerged as a spokesperson on women's issues. NN

BIRYUZOV, Sergey Semenovich (1904–1964) Former Chief of the General Staff. Biryuzov, who was of worker origin, entered the Red Army in 1922. During the war he was Commander of the Forty-Eighth Army in the Voronezh sector in 1942 and Chief of Staff of the Second Guards Army in the Stalingrad counter-offensive (1942–43). He also became Chief of Staff of several other army groups in the battles for the Ukraine and Crimea and the conquest of Romania and Bulgaria (1943–44). He was appointed Deputy Head of the Allied Control Commission in Bulgaria for two

periods between 1944 and 1947. He held command of the Far Eastern Military District (1947–53), working with Marshal Malinovsky in this region during the tense period of the Korean War. He was briefly Commander-in-Chief of Soviet forces in Hungary (1953–54). Biryuzov acquired the rank of Marshal of the Soviet Union and served for seven years as Commander-in-Chief of the Soviet Anti-Aircraft Defence Forces (1955–62) before he was placed in charge of the Strategic Rocket Forces (1962–63). He was appointed Chief of the General Staff and First Deputy Minister of Defence in March 1963, but died a year and a half later in an air crash. RA

BISHER, Il'mar Ol'gertovich (Bisers, Ilmars) (b. 1930) One of the two deputy chairmen of the Soviet of Nationalities of the Supreme Soviet of the USSR, Bisher is a Latvian by nationality and represents a Latvian territorial constituency in the Congress of People's Deputies of the USSR, to which he was elected in 1989. A professor of law in Riga, he is a member of the Constitutional Commission of the Congress of People's Deputies and was also a member of its Commission set up to investigate the activities of the Investigation Group headed by Gdlyan at the office of the Procurator General of the USSR. Bisher is a member of the Latvian Popular Front. AHB

BISTI, Dmitriy Spiridonovich (b. 1925) Graphic artist and designer. Born in Sevastopol', Bisti studied at the Moscow Polygraphical Institute under Andrey Goncharov, whose style exerted an appreciable influence on him. Romantic by inclination, Bisti has achieved a sound reputation as an illustrator of various authors, includ-

ing Byron, Homer and Mayakovsky.
JEB

BITOV, Andrey Georgievich (b. 1937) A Leningrad writer of 'youth prose', distinguished from his colleagues by his precise and fastidious descriptions of everyday life, his 'stream of consciousness' technique, and his early awareness of both Russian and western modernism. His principal novel, *The Pushkin House* (1978 – referring to the principal literary archive in Leningrad) explores the question of responsibility for the degradation of the cultural heritage in Soviet Russia. GAH

BLOK, Aleksandr Aleksandrovich (1880–1921) Born in St Petersburg, a Symbolist poet, dramatist and essayist, Blok began publishing in 1903. His early works are dominated by the theme of the Beautiful Lady, a version of the Eternal Feminine influenced by the philosopher Solov'ev's 'Sophia' (the female spirit of Wisdom), or are set in a Petersburg characterized as a black hell. His main formal innovation was in his use of the *dol'nik*, accentual verse previously not used in high literature. After 1905 he took up the theme of Russia and also began his series of outspoken essays about the role of the intelligentsia. He initially welcomed the Revoluton as the passionate cataclysm that would overturn the tyranny of a dark order, and served it conscientiously (primarily as a functionary in the Drama Section of the Commissariat of Culture). His main literary responses to the Revolution, *The Twelve* (1918) and *The Scythians* (1918), also mark the end of his major output. *The Twelve* describes twelve Red Guards advancing through revolutionary Petrograd; controversy continues as to why Christ appears at the end as their leader. *The Scythians*

describes Russia as an Asiatic sphinx looming over Europe; Blok was associated with the Scythian Movement, founded by Ivanov-Razumnik. KC

BLOKHIN, Oleg (b. 1953) Oleg Blokhin was one of the most skilful and productive of all Soviet soccer players, scoring over 200 goals for his club, Dinamo Kiev, over ten years up to 1985 – the first Soviet footballer to do so. During that period he was a regular member of the Soviet national team and helped his club to several national league titles. In 1975 he received the Golden Boot award as Europe's highest-scoring soccer player.

Born in the Ukraine, he gained a soccer coaching diploma from the Kiev Physical Culture Institute and graduated in law from Kiev University in 1983. He retired from soccer at the end of the 1985–86 season at the age of thirty-three. JWR

BLYUKHER, Vasiliy Konstantinovich (1890–1938) Early Red Army commander. Blyukher began his working life as a metal craftsman in Petrograd and the Moscow vicinity, and was decorated as a junior officer during the First World War. After the February Revolution of 1917 he was drawn into political work in the army; in March 1918 he became chairman of the Soviet at Chelyabinsk. He rose to prominence after the mutiny of the Czechoslovak corps when he led a daring raid through the Urals and became the first to be awarded the Order of the Red Banner. Blyukher took part in action against the forces of the White leader Kolchak as an infantry division commander and as assistant commander of the Third Army. He contributed to important military successes later in the Civil War and was appointed Minister of War (1921–22). Under his command the Red Army of the newly created Soviet Republic of the Far East finally defeated White and Japanese forces in this region.

Blyukher was involved in the reorganization of the Red Army after the Civil War and was attached to the Chinese revolutionary government as its primary military adviser (1924–27). He was placed in command of the special Far Eastern Army in the period 1929 to 1938 and directed Red Army operations during the Soviet-Chinese conflict of 1929. Through the creation of the so-called Kolkhoz Corps Blyukher attempted the military colonization of the Manchurian frontier. As Commander-in-Chief of the Far Eastern Front he was also responsible for a Soviet victory in a military clash with the Japanese in July 1938 at Lake Khasan. At his moment of triumph, however, he was arrested and executed as part of a broader purge of the Far Eastern Staff. RA

BLYUMENTAL'-TAMARINA (née Klimova), Maria Mikhaylovna (1859–1938) Blyumental'-Tamarina was an actress in Korsh's Comedy Theatre from 1921 to 1933 and then in the Maly Theatre until her death. She also played the old woman in Ermler's film *Counterplan* (1932). RT

BOBYSHEV, Dmitriy Vasil'evich (b. 1936) Poet and essayist. He published poems in Soviet periodicals, then emigrated in 1979, when his first book *Gapings* was published in Paris. His long poem 'Russian Tercets' (1977–81), begun in Leningrad and completed in Milwaukee, mixes biblical intonation with colloquial phrasing, focusing on Russia from an indeterminate present. BH

BOGATYREV, Pyotr Grigor'evich (1893–1971) A folklorist, Bogatyrev was a founder of the (Formalist) Moscow Linguistic Circle; he lived in Czechoslovakia as a member of the Soviet diplomatic mission for nearly twenty years where he participated in the Prague School. Bogatyrev collaborated with Roman Jakobson on many articles, particularly on the origin of folk creations. He is best known for his writings on puppet theatre and folk costume which are regarded as important contributions to semiotic theory. He returned to the Soviet Union in 1940; his later work helped give rise to Soviet semiotics in the sixties. KC

BOGDANOV (Malinovsky), Aleksandr Aleksandrovich (1873–1928) A philosopher, party activist and literary theorist, along with Gor'ky and Lunacharsky, Bogdanov formed the Party School on Capri (1908–17). In 1917 he helped found the *Prolekul't*, an organization aimed at developing a distinctive proletarian culture. In theoretical works such as *Art and the Working Class* (1918), he argued that the party's role is to organize the workers' consciousness and the unions to organize the economy; cultural development, on the other hand, must come from the workers themselves. Hence the *Prolekul't* actively recruited workers and tried to make of them artists, writers and actors. He also argued that art should not merely amuse, but should serve to unify the collective. Trained as a physician, Bogdanov valued science highly; he was a pioneer of systems thinking, illustrated not only in his theoretical works such as *Tectology* (1922), but also in his two utopian novels, *Red Star* (1908) and *Engineer Menni* (1912), which describe a superior socialistic society on Mars. After the *Prolekul't* was merged with the Trade Unions in 1925, Bogdanov became director of the Blood Transfusion Institute where he died during a transfusion experiment. KC

BOGDANOV, Petr Alekseevich (1882–1939) An old Bolshevik who occupied leading posts in the economy in the early post-revolutionary years. Bogdanov, whose father had been a rich Moscow merchant, joined the Bolsheviks in 1905. Graduating from the Moscow Higher Technical Institute in 1909, he was later employed as an engineer in Moscow local government and dropped out of political activity. He worked in VSNKh from 1917, as chairman (1921–23), then as chairman of VSNKh of the RSFSR (1923–25), followed by various less important posts, which included the position of head of the Soviet trading agency in the United States (Amtorg). RWD

BOGOLYUBOV, Nikolay Ivanovich (1899–1980) Actor. Bogolyubov was a Meyerkhol′d Theatre actor whose films include: Protazanov's *Tommy* (1932), Barnet's *The Outskirts* (1933), Ermler's *Peasants* (1935) and *A Great Citizen* (1938–39) and the role of Voroshilov in Romm's *Lenin in 1918* (1939). RT

BOGOMOLETS, Aleksandr Aleksandrovich (1881–1946) Pathologist, physiologist, and administrator. A 1906 graduate of Novorossiysk University in Odessa, Bogomolets worked there as a pathologist and after a year's study in Paris (1911) was professor at Saratov University (1911–25), head of pathology at the Second Moscow Medical Institute (1925–31), and director of the Institute of Transfusion (1928–31). A physiologist and pathologist of broad profile, he worked on blood transfusion, rejuvenation, and gerontology under the influence of A. A. Bogdanov (Malinovsky) but

played his major role as a scientific organizer. Elected to the Ukrainian Academy of Sciences in 1929, he served as its president from 1930 until his death, organizing and directing its Institue of Clinical Physiology (from 1934) as well as the Institute of Experimental Biology and Pathology of the health ministry of the Ukraine (from 1930). He was elected to the USSR Academy of Sciences in 1932 and served as its vice-president during the war years (1942–46). In addition, he was a member of the Central Executive Committee of the USSR, the Supreme Soviet of the USSR, and the Supreme Soviet of the Ukrainian SSR, serving as president of the Ukrainian Supreme Soviet (1944–46). MBA

BOGOMOLOV, Oleg Timofeevich (b. 1927) Economist. As the principal academic concerned with East European economies in the 1970s and 1980s he assiduously spread the lessons of their reforms and their inefficiencies among the higher officials of the party until the opportunities came for Soviet reform under Andropov and Gorbachev, to both of whom he has been an adviser. Born in Moscow he graduated from the Moscow Institute of Foreign Trade in 1949. After a short period in the Ministry of Foreign Trade he was assigned to the Council for Mutual Economic Assistance (Comecon), when the agency was being reactiviated after quiescence under Stalin (1954–56). Successively on the staff of the State Planning Commission and the Party Central Committee where he was one of Andropov's consultants in the Socialist Countries department, he became Director of the Institute of Economics of the World Socialist System of the USSR Academy of Sciences in 1969. While most of his writings have been on economic relations within Comecon, he turned to domestic economic shortcomings in the Gorbachev era, being one of the first to study 'hidden inflation' (1987). Bogomolov was elected to the Congress of People's Deputies of the USSR in 1990. MCK

BOGORODSKY, Fedor Semenovich (1895–1959) Painter. Born in Nizhniy Novgorod, Bogorodsky joined AKhRR in 1925 after studying at Vkhutemas. Close in style to Osmerkin and Riazhsky, Bogorodsky interpreted the new reality (Red Army sailors, NEPmen, and *bezprizorniki* [homeless children]), and in the 1930s became a prominent exponent of Socialist Realism – exemplified by his major painting *Glory to the Fallen Heroes* of 1945. JEB

BOGUSLAVSKY, Mark Moiseevich (b. 1924) A specialist on private international law, international economic law, intellectual property, an arbitrator, a professor, and senior research associate at the Institute of State and Law of the USSR Academy of Sciences. Influential in shaping Soviet joint enterprise legislation, Boguslavsky is the author of a standard text on private international law translated into English in 1988. WEB

BOLDIN, Valeriy Ivanovich (b. 1935) The head of the General Department of the Central Committee which works especially closely with the General Secretary and prepares the Politburo agenda and accompanying papers, Boldin has long-standing links to Mikhail Gorbachev. A graduate of the Timiryazev Agricultural Academy in Moscow and former head of the agricultural section of *Pravda*, Boldin became an aide to Gorbachev in 1981 when Gorbachev was still the Secretary of the Central Committee responsible for agriculture. He

remained on Gorbachev's personal staff during Gorbachev's first two years as General Secretary before becoming head of the General Department in 1987. Boldin became a candidate member of the Central Committee in 1986 and a full member in 1988. Since March 1990 Boldin has been one of the sixteen members of Gorbachev's Presidential Council. AHB

BONCH-BRUEVICH, Vladimir Dmitrievich (1873–1955) A close colleague of Lenin and organizer of the party archives in Geneva (1904). From early on in his career Bonch-Bruevich showed special interest in the problems facing religious sectarians in Tsarist Russia and pointed out their revolutionary potential. In 1930 he was appointed Director of the State Literature Museum and in 1946 Director of the Museum of the History of Religion and Atheism. In 1950 he instigated publication of the Museum's annual *Problems of the History of Religion and Atheism*. MR

BONDAREV, Yuriy Vasil'evich (b. 1924) Born in Orsk near Orienburg, a prose writer, war veteran and Communist Party member since 1944. His first literary successes, *The Battalions Request Fire* (1957) and *The Last Salvoes* (1959), became part of a trend for 'revisionist' war fiction which dispenses with simplistically pure heroes and vile villains and emphasizes the human cost of the war. His *The Silence* (1962), set in 1949, became a landmark in the thaw of 1962 as the first work to depict a citizen (a war veteran) wrongly sentenced to the camps. *The Burning Snow* (1970), considered his best war novel, concentrates more on characterization than his previous war fiction. His fiction since the mid-seventies such as

The Shore (1975) and *The Choice* (1980) looks at the past (including the war) from the perspective of the present; it is distinctly anti-Western and pre-occupied with a perceived moral and spiritual degeneration in the modern day. *The Game* (1985) continues this trend but also presents apocalyptic scenarios of what will happen to the world if technological progress and the arms build up continue at their present pace; it chastises the Russian intelligentsia for failing to meet their unique mission to save the world, and advances Avvakum as a martyred emblem of intelligentsia virtue. KC

BONNER, Yelena Georgievna (b. 1923) Doctor, human rights activist, and writer. A nurse during the war, she was wounded, losing much of her eye-sight, but still became a Lieutenant. Despite her disabled status she was a practising doctor from 1953 to retirement age. From 1965 to 1972 Bonner was a party member. In 1970 she became a dissident, and met and married Andrey Sakharov. In 1976 she was a founder and core member of the Moscow group to monitor observation of the 1975 Helsinki accords. From 1980 to 1984 she regularly brought news of Sakharov to Moscow from Gor'ky, where he was exiled. In 1984 she received a five-year exile sentence herself. She was released in 1986 and wrote her memoirs, *Alone Together* (1986). PBR

BORISYAK, Aleksey Alekseevich (1872–1944) Paleontologist. A graduate of the Petersburg Mining Institute, Borisyak headed its department of historical geology from 1911 and was elected corresponding member of the Academy of Sciences in 1921 and a full member in 1929, serving as head of the paleontology section of the Geological Committee until 1932. His publications on Tertiary mammals and Jurassic molluscs established him as one of the leading Soviet paleontologists of his day, and he did much to organize the discipline by creating and directing both the Institute of Paleontology of the USSR Academy of Sciences (1930–44) and the department of paleontology of Moscow University (1939–42). MBA

BORZOV, Valeriy (b. 1949) Athlete. He had the distinction of being the greatest of all Soviet sprinters: he competed in two Olympics, winning both the 100 and the 200 m at the 1972 Olympic Games, taking a silver medal in the 4 x 100 m relay, and winning two bronze medals (in 100m and the 4 × 100m relay) at the 1976 Olympics. Born in the Ukraine, he studied at the Kiev Physical Culture Institute and returned there with his wife, the gymnast Ludmila Turishcheva, to engage in sports biological research in 1979. JWR

BOTVINNIK, Mikhail Moiseevich (b. 1911) Chess player. He has been the greatest influence on the Soviet chess school and was the first Soviet chess player to win the world title in 1948, retaining it until 1957 when he lost to Smyslov, and holding it from 1958 to 1960, then losing to Tahl, and from 1961 to 1963, losing to Petrosyan. Born in Repino, he beat the then world champion Capablanca at the age of fourteen when Capablanca was giving an exhibition in Moscow of simultaneous play. And in the first Soviet sporting venture abroad against 'bourgeois' opposition, he drew with the world champion Flohr in 1933. Three years later his tie for first place with the Cuban Capablanca at the Nottingham world championship merited a picture and full-length article on *Pravda*'s front page. He

became the first Soviet player to gain the Soviet grandmaster award in 1935 and was awarded the international grandmaster title in 1950. Besides his chess interest he became Doctor of Technical Sciences in 1951 and subsequently gained a professorship.
JWR

BOVIN, Aleksandr Yevgenevich (b. 1930) One of the ablest and best-known Soviet journalists, Aleksandr Bovin has been for many years the principal political columnist of the newspaper, *Izvestiya*, writing particularly on foreign affairs, as well as a popular presenter of television programmes. Even in Brezhnev's time, he was able to maintain a certain independence of judgement (in comparison, for example, with his *Pravda* counterpart, Yuriy Zhukov).

Bovin, who was born in Leningrad, graduated in law from Rostov University in 1953. His first job, surprisingly, was as a judge in the Krasnodar region of southern Russia. But within a few years he decided to return to university – this time to Moscow University in the Philosophy Faculty where he completed his graduate studies in the late 1950s. He worked on the journal, *Kommunist* (1959–63), and then – at the invitation of Fedor Burlatsky – joined Yuriy Andropov's group of consultants in the Central Committee of the Communist Party. He succeeded Georgiy Arbatov as head of that advisory group, Arbatov having, in turn, succeeded its first head, Burlatsky.

Bovin stayed in the Central Committee apparatus until 1972 when he moved to *Izvestiya*. His political influence increased when Andropov became General Secretary, but he lost some ground under Chernenko. During the Gorbachev era he has sought to end the taboo on criticism by Soviet journalists of Soviet foreign policy and has played a significant part in the extension of *glasnost'* into the discussion of international affairs.
AHB

BRATUS', Sergey Nikitich (b. 1904) A major figure in Soviet legal theory and civil law, an arbitrator, active in COMECON legal affairs, a consultant to the USSR Supreme Court and State *Arbitrazh*, and sometime chairman of the USSR Foreign Trade Arbitration Commission. Director of the Institute of Soviet Legislation of the USSR Ministry of Justice, and author of more than 200 works on civil law and legal theory, Bratus' has been a champion of the civil (as opposed to the economic) law approach to Soviet economic management. In 1961 he chaired the working commission which prepared the USSR Fundamental Principles of Civil Legislation.
WEB

BRAUN, Andrey Georgievich (b. 1937) Currently the highest-ranking Soviet official of German nationality. Born in the Ukraine, he was brought up in Kazakhstan (whither most Soviet Germans were deported in 1941), and educated in Omsk. He has been director of a state farm and a party and government official in Tselinograd and Kochetav provinces, serving since 1986 as First Secretary of Tselinograd *obkom*. JHM

BRAZAUSKAS, Al'girdas-Mikolas Kazevich (Brazauskas, Algirdas-Mikolas) (b. 1932) A Lithuanian construction engineer, Brazauskas was Minister of the Construction Materials Industry (1965–66) and First Deputy Chairman of Gosplan (1966–77) in Lithuania. From 1977 he was Secretary for Industry, and from October 1988, First Secretary of the Lithuanian Communist Party with the daunting task of maintaining communist appeal and unity in competition with the Lithuanian Restructuring Movement (Sajudis). For a few weeks in early 1990 he was also Chairman of the Presidium of the Lithuanian Supreme Soviet, and then Deputy Premier in the Sajudis government. JHM

BRESIS, Vilnis-Edvin Gedertovich (Bresis, Vilnis-Edvins) (b. 1938) Bresis graduated in Riga and Leningrad and became a Komsomol and party official. He was First Secretary of the Latvian Komsomol from 1970 to 1973, moved into economic planning and emerged as head of Latvia's *Gosagroprom* in 1987. Since October 1988 he has been Chairman of the Latvian Council of Ministers. JHM

BREZHNEV, Leonid Il'ich (1906–1982) Leonid Brezhnev, who was top leader in the Soviet Union for a longer period than anyone other than Stalin, was born into a Russian working-class family in the Ukrainian town of Dneprodzerzhinsk (then called Kamenskoye). When he died on 10 November 1982 he had been leader of the Soviet Communist Party for over eighteen years and titular head of state for more than seven years.

Brezhnev worked in agriculture as well as industry as a youth and in 1927 qualified as a land surveyor. He spent several years working in Kursk province, in Byelorussia and in the Urals before returning to the Ukraine and employment in the Dneprodzerzhinsk iron and steel plant where he had begun his working life. His ambition led him into both political work and part-time study. He had joined the Komsomol (Young Communist League) when he was sixteen and eight years later (in 1931) he became

a Communist Party member. While working as a fitter after his return to Dneprodzerzhinsk, he studied at a metallurgical institute and became chairman of its trade union committee and then secretary of its party committee.

After graduating from that institute as a qualified engineer in 1935, Brezhnev became a shift leader in his factory, but was soon called up for military service which he completed as a political instructor of a tank company. Soon after his return to Dneprodzerzhinsk in 1936, Brezhnev's political career developed in earnest. He became deputy chairman of the city soviet in 1937 and in 1938 was recruited into the party apparatus. With the worst years of Stalin's purges just coming to an end, there were many dead men's shoes to fill and promotion could be fast for ambitious newcomers.

By February 1939 Brezhnev was already propaganda secretary of the Dnepropetrovsk regional party committee (*obkom*). He remained in that *obkom* apparatus until after the Nazi invasion of the Soviet Union in 1941 when he became a political officer in the armed forces. He served as deputy chief of the Southern Front's political department and subsequently as chief of the political department of the Eighteenth Army and of the fourth Ukrainian front. Political officers, whose tasks included the maintenance of troops' morale and the issue of cards to new party members, had much better chances of survival than the fighting soldiers. Many Soviet accounts of Brezhnev as a war hero were to be published much later, at the time when he also happened to be the most powerful politician in the Soviet Union. They contained numerous exaggerations, though it seems probable that Brezhnev in wartime already displayed some organizational skills. During the last part of his war service he participated in the sovietization of former Czechoslovak and Romanian territories in the Carpathian Military District. Brezhnev left the army in 1946 with the rank of Major-General.

It was to Brezhnev's lasting benefit that he had already made a good impression on Nikita Khrushchev who from 1938 until 1949 (with the exception of a brief period in 1947) was party First Secretary in the Ukraine. It was Khrushchev's patronage which was to take him to the highest echelons of the Soviet party and state. Brezhnev returned to the Ukraine on demobilization from the army and was given the significant party post of First Secretary of an *obkom* – of the Zaporozhe regional committee (less than a hundred miles from his native Dneprodzerzhinsk). The high-speed reconstruction of industry in this region which had been devastated by the war enhanced Brezhnev's standing and before the end of 1947 he was promoted to the First Secretaryship of his native region, the larger one of Dnepropetrovsk, and to membership of the Central Committee of the Ukrainian Communist Party.

Both before and after the war, Brezhnev established many friendships and political alliances which were to retain an importance during his later political life. Many of these people were to form the so-called 'Dnepropetrovsk group' (or 'Dnieper mafia') in Moscow during Brezhnev's years as party leader and some of them continued to hold high office several years after Brezhnev's death.

Soon after Brezhnev's patron,

Khrushchev, left Kiev for Moscow at the end of 1949, Brezhnev was given important assignments outside the Ukraine. In 1950 he spent several months in the Central Committee apparatus in Moscow and in that same year became party First Secretary in Moldavia. With an energy which impressed his Moscow superiors, he completed the sovietization of a republic in which most people identified with neighbouring Romania. Brezhnev waged war on 'bourgeois nationalism' and greatly increased party membership and the number of party organizations in the republic.

Brezhnev brought with him to Moldavia one of his Dnepropetrovsk colleagues, Nikolay Shchelokov, later (when Brezhnev was General Secretary of the Central Committee of the CPSU) to become Minister of Internal Affairs for the Soviet Union. He also established particularly good personal and political relations with the head of the department of propaganda and agitation of the Moldavian Central Committee, Konstantin Chernenko, for whom Brezhnev's arrival in Moldavia was to be of as decisive importance for his future promotion as Khrushchev's patronage was for Brezhnev.

In the last year of Stalin's life, Brezhnev achieved a spectacular promotion. At the Nineteenth Party Congress in 1952, he was elected not only to membership of the Central Committee, but to two of its inner bodies – to a Secretaryship of the Central Committee and to candidate membership of a new and enlarged Presidium which replaced the Politburo. Brezhnev was part of an influx of younger people into the highest party posts which may well have been part of Stalin's plan to undertake a purge of some of his more senior lieutenants.

Though Brezhnev's career suffered a temporary setback in the immediate aftermath of Stalin's death when he lost his seat on both of the Central Committee's inner bodies and became first deputy head of the political administration of the Ministry of Defence with responsibilities for the navy, he was restored to an important party post within a year. Khrushchev was looking for a reliable ally to look after his 'Virgin Lands' scheme – a highly ambitious plan to grow grain on a vast scale on hitherto unused land – and Brezhnev accordingly was appointed in 1954 second secretary of the second largest Soviet republic, Kazakhstan. A year later he was First Secretary. Though the 'Virgin Lands' scheme was by no means an unqualified success, and though it had its strong opponents within the party, it did nevertheless, on the whole, make a useful contribution to Soviet agricultural production and Brezhnev had earned a share in the credit for organizing a difficult enterprise. Later, when he was party leader, he was to be accorded more than his share, for in reality the driving force behind the 'Virgin Lands' venture had been Khrushchev.

From 1956 Brezhnev was back in Moscow and was to be close to the centre of power in the Soviet system for the rest of his life. In February 1956 he was elevated to the Secretariat of the Central Committee and became a candidate member of the Politburo (at that time still called the Presidium of the Central Committee). After Khrushchev's victory over the 'anti-party group' of Malenkov, Molotov and others in June 1957, Brezhnev became a full Politburo member. In 1960 he suffered what at the time could be considered a slight demotion. While retaining his Politburo membership, he ceased to be a Secretary of the Central Committee, becoming instead Chairman of the Presidium of the Supreme Soviet. As such, he was formal head of the Soviet state, and though the Supreme Soviet had never been much of a power base, he was able to put his experience there to good use by making fifteen foreign visits within three years and learning more about the outside world.

Khrushchev, in the meantime, was losing some support within the highest party and state echelons as a result of his increasingly high-handed actions. Initially, this strengthened not Brezhnev, but one of Khrushchev's opponents within the leadership, Frol Kozlov. When, however, Kozlov suffered an incapacitating stroke in April 1963, Brezhnev's career blossomed. In June 1963 he became a Secretary of the Central Committee again and for a year he combined Politburo membership not only with his Secretaryship of the Central Committee but with the Chairmanship of the Presidium of the Supreme Soviet, though he relinquished the latter post in June 1964 to concentrate on his work in the Secretariat where he was in day-to-day charge of the party organization.

From that position of considerable power, he took part in the removal of his own patron, Khrushchev, in October 1964 and was accorded the more important of the two major offices which Khrushchev held – the First Secretaryship (in 1966 renamed General Secretaryship) of the Central Committee of the party, while Aleksey Kosygin was appointed Chairman of the Council of Ministers. Brezhnev's colleagues apparently took the view that Brezhnev would be a leader who would respect their collective wishes and interests in a manner Khrushchev had not. In this expectation they were, on the whole, correct.

In his attitude both to policy and to personnel changes, Brezhnev displayed caution and patience where Khrushchev had been bold and impulsive. Where a premature attempt to remove former or potential rivals from the leadership might have led to dangerous confrontation, Brezhnev was content to tolerate their presence in the Politburo until it was clearly safe to act against them. While he obviously yearned to play a prominent part on the world stage, he allowed Kosygin to represent the Soviet Union in numerous discussions with foreign leaders during the 1960s rather than seem to be following in Khrushchev's footsteps by taking too much upon himself.

The political changes which took place in Czechoslovakia in 1968, saw Brezhnev play a major and discreditable part in the crushing of the Prague Spring. Since they involved another ruling Communist Party, the events of 1968 helped to propel Brezhnev into the position of principal spokesman for the Soviet Union on international policy. That role was expanded in the 1970s when Brezhnev devoted more attention to Western countries and saw himself as the architect of détente. Brezhnev's more active part in the conduct of Soviet foreign policy began in 1970 and 1971 with talks with West German Chancellor Willy Brandt, with whom Brezhnev established a certain rapport. The political basis for improved relations was provided in 1970 with the signing of an agreement recognizing the frontiers of the two Germanies and of Poland.

Brezhnev was also well to the fore in the attempt to develop relations with the United States, with a view to keeping the arms race within bounds and to securing access to American high technology. Brezhnev received President Richard Nixon in Moscow in May 1972 and paid a return visit to Washington in June 1973. In 1974 Brezhnev received two American Presidents – Nixon in July and his successor, Gerald Ford, in Vladivostok in November. In these years a series of treaties on arms control and trade were signed, though the USSR-USA Trade Agreement of 1972 was abrogated by the Soviet Union in January 1975 in response to Senator Jackson's public claim that the easing of restrictions on Jewish emigration was part of the package of the agreement.

Brezhnev invested considerable prestige in the search for a new European security settlement based on recognition of the territorial division established at the end of the Second World War. This eventually resulted in the Helsinki Agreement of 1975 which was, however, at best a partial success for Brezhnev, since in order to secure the agreement the Soviet side had to make significant concessions in principle on human rights and dissemination of information, and that part of the accord was to cause the Soviet authorities some subsequent embarrassment.

Brezhnev's last 'summit talks' with the head of the other superpower were with President Carter in Vienna in 1979 when the two leaders signed an agreement on strategic arms limitation (SALT II) which was not subsequently ratified by the USA. The American President was already having difficulties with the Senate over this when the Soviet military intervention in Afghanistan in December 1979 put paid to the chances of ratification and exacerbated already deteriorating US-Soviet relations (as compared with the early or mid-1970s). With President Reagan in the White House during Brezhnev's last two years of life, relations became still cooler, though as long as Brezhnev was alive the theme of détente with the West was stressed.

Domestically, Brezhnev adopted a conservative Communist policy, one which was neither Stalinist nor anti-Stalinist. It is characteristic of his General Secretaryship that during this period attacks on Stalin and on the Stalin period were virtually outlawed, but Stalin himself was not fully rehabilitated. Large-scale administrative re-organizations, as favoured by Khrushchev, and meaningful economic reform, which Kosygin in the mid-1960s regarded with more favour, were equally eschewed by Brezhnev, for whom giving security from disruption or dismissal to the great mass of party and state officials not only accorded with his conservative political instincts but was also part of his strategy for consolidating power.

In his domestic policy, Brezhnev laid great stress on the need to improve the performance of Soviet agriculture. As early as March 1965 he delivered a major report to the Central Committee which reversed a number of Khrushchev's agricultural policies and his last plenary session of the Central Committee – in May 1982 – was devoted to a much-heralded 'Food Programme'. By supporting greater investment in agriculture, Brezhnev helped to bring about some improvement in this sector of the economy, but his unwillingness to countenance greater autonomy for farmers or economically realistic prices for foodstuffs helped to ensure that the progress made was limited and uneven.

Though cautious in his personnel policy, Brezhnev gradually succeeded in replacing a number of senior party and state leaders whom he had inherited by people with whom he had close ties. Even those whose relations with Brezhnev appeared to be cool survived for some years in his Politburo, and Brezhnev moved against them only when it was evidently safe to do so. Thus, Shelest' and Voronov were dropped from the leadership in 1973, to be followed by Shelepin in 1975 and Podgorny in 1977. The removal of Podgorny was connected with Brezhnev's desire to have a high state office to complement his party leadership. The Central Committee plenum of October 1964 which had removed Khrushchev had determined that the offices of General (then First) Secretary of the Central Committee and Chairman of the Council of Ministers would be kept separate. Brezhnev, looking for an alternative, thus became the first Soviet party leader to be also head of state, assuming in 1977 the Chairmanship of the Presidium of the Supreme Soviet which had been held by Podgorny since 1965.

Such an enhancement of Brezhnev's authority had been made possible by the gradual changes in the composition of the Politburo and Secretariat of the Central Committee which he had engineered. Among his strong supporters in high positions were Kulakov, Kunaev and Shcherbitsky who entered the Politburo in 1971 and Konstantin Chernenko who, in successive years between 1976 and 1978, became a Central Committee Secretary, candidate member of the

Politburo and full member of the Politburo. When Kosygin was forced by ill-health to resign from the Chairmanship of the Council of Ministers in October 1980, he was replaced by Brezhnev's friend of long standing, Nikolay Tikhonov.

From the mid-1970s onwards, something of a cult of Brezhnev's personality (albeit on a minor scale in comparison with Stalin's) was promoted. This was reflected in numerous references to the wisdom and inspirational value of Brezhnev's utterances and in the presentation to him of a series of awards which were within the gift of the Soviet top leadership. These reached ever-higher levels of absurdity – from the International Lenin Peace Prize in 1973 to the highest military award, the Order of Victory, in 1978, and the highest writers' award, the Lenin Prize for Literature, in 1979 for his ghosted memoirs.

In 1982, when Brezhnev's health (which had been in decline for several years) was visibly failing, the struggle for the succession intensified and Brezhnev's authority – and that of his allies – was somewhat undermined by rumours of corruption and economic crime on the part of party and state officials who had been close to him or close to members of his family. A number of arrests were made and the point was conveyed by those who wished to prevent Brezhnev from being able to nominate his successor that there were limits to his powers. In fact, it was Brezhnev's sensitivity to these limits which had allowed him to lead the Soviet Union for so long and to die in office just a little over a month short of his seventy-sixth birthday. AHB

BRODSKY, Iosif Aleksandrovich (b. 1940) Poet. Brodsky was born and brought up in Leningrad, surviving the blockade. He left school at fifteen and worked at a variety of menial jobs. He was the brightest star in the renaissance of Leningrad poetry that began in the late 1950s. Brodsky published a small number of poems in periodicals, and had achieved an immense underground reputation by 1964, when he was arrested and sent into administrative exile as a 'parasite'. He was released after the intervention of powerful cultural figures. He emigrated in 1972, and has been an American citizen since 1977. Brodsky has become the most internationally prestigious Russian poet ever. He was awarded the Nobel Prize for Literature in 1987, and his work began to appear in leading Soviet periodicals soon after. He has been widely translated. He has published six substantial collections of poetry in Russian, and a book of essays in English, *Less than One* (1987). GSS

BRODSKY, Isaak Izraelevich (1884–1939) Painter. Born in Sofievka, Brodsky – one of the foremost supporters of Socialist Realism – received acclaim as a portrayer of Lenin and Stalin. He received his traning at the Odessa Art Institute (1896–1902) before enrolling at the Academy of Arts where he studied under Il'ya Repin. The guiding force of AKhRR, Brodsky sought documentary, almost photographic accuracy in his paintings and drawings; and he developed the principles of Russian Realism to accommodate Soviet themes, exemplified by his famous renderings of Lenin at the Second and Third Cominterns and his portraits of Gor'ky and Stalin. Brodsky was also an art collector and his Leningrad apartment is now a museum. JEB

BROMLEY, Yulian Vladimirovich (1921–1990) Historian and ethnographer. From 1966 until 1989 (when he became Honorary Director on his semi-retirement), Bromley was Director of the Institute of Ethnography of the Academy of Sciences. He graduated from Moscow University's History Faculty in 1950 and his earliest research was on sixteenth-century Croatia. He became a prominent specialist on ethnicity, with particular reference to both Yugoslavia and the USSR. Though he held administrative appointments in first the History division of the Academy of Sciences and then its Presidium between 1966 and 1986, in addition to his Institute directorship, Bromley published a number of ethnographical works and at the end of the 1980s was a contributor to the growing debate on national relations within the USSR, favouring greater cultural autonomy for the various nationalities but opposing advocates of confederal solutions to the problems of the Soviet multi-ethnic state. AHB

BRUMEL, Valeriy Nikolaevich (b. 1942) Athlete. Born in Razvedka, near Chita in Siberia, he was one of the world's most outstanding high jumpers until he severely fractured his right leg in a motor-bike accident in 1965. He first made a name for himself at the age of eighteen during the 1960 Rome Olympics when he jumped the same height (216 cm) as the winner Robert Shavlakadze, but took the silver medal. Then came the Brumel era: he broke the world record six times between 1961 and 1963, his 228 cm record lasting seven years, and he won the Olympic high-jumping title in 1964. During that period he was named the world's top athlete three years in a row and awarded top international prizes – the Helms World Trophy and the Golden Caravel. On retirement, he became a professional writer on sporting themes for books and films. JWR

BRUNI, Lev Aleksandrovich (1894–1948) Painter and graphic artist. Born in Malaya Vishera, a graduate of the Academy of Arts in 1912, Bruni, like Al'tman, experimented with Cubism in his early work. In 1923 he moved to Moscow and became a member of the Four Arts group, teaching at Vkhutemas-Vkhutein from 1923 to 1928. He is remembered for his lyrical landscapes in watercolour and for his portraits, for example, of Nikolay Klyuev (1920). JEB

BRYUKHANOV, Nikolay Pavlovich (1878–1942) An old Bolshevik. Bryukhanov was a leading figure in the running of the economy in the first thirteen years after the revolution. Born in Simbirsk, where his father was a land measurer, gardener, and fisherman, he studied history at Moscow University. He was exiled in 1899, joined the RSDLP in 1902, and was thereafter in and out of exile until the revolution. A major figure with responsibility for food supplies (1918–23), he also served as Deputy People's Commissar of Finance (May 1924–January 1926), People's Commissar (January 1926–October 1930), but was dismissed for alleged responsibility for inflation. He was later appointed Deputy People's Commissar for Supplies (internal trade) (1931–33), and deputy chairman of the commission for determining (or rather falsifying) the harvest (1933–38). He was a candidate member of the Party Central Committee (1927–34). RWD

BRYUSOV, Valeriy Yakovlevich
(1873–1924) Poet, novelist, translator.
Born and educated in Moscow,
Bryusov became a precocious and talented Symbolist poet, energetic and
able editor, and determined self-pro-
moter if not opportunist. He was a
dominant figure in Russian literary life
during the decade before the First
World War. His poetry notably
includes the collection *Urbi et Orbi*
(1903), his novels *The Fiery Angel*
(1908). He joined the party after the
Revolution and plunged into administrative and educational work. GSS

BUBKA, Sergey (b. 1964) Athlete. He
was the first pole vaulter to clear 6 m,
in July 1985 in Paris; he revolutionized
pole-vaulting style in the 1980s with
his high pole grip, late thrust and long
pole (5.3 m; Bubka's height – 184 cm).
Born in Donetsk in the Ukraine, he
and his elder brother Vasiliy began
pole vaulting when Sergey was ten and
Vasiliy twelve. He won a gold medal
at the 1988 Seoul Olympics. Sergey
was one of the first Soviet field athletes
to reap the new financial benefits for
athletes in the 1980s, appearing in
many international sports spec-
taculars. JWR

BUBNOV, Andrey Sergeevich (1883–
1940) Andrey Bubnov, a party and
state offical during the inter-war
period, was born in Ivanovo-Voznesensk. He was educated locally and
at the Moscow Agricultural Institute,
from which he was expelled for political activity. He became a member
of the Social Democratic party in 1903
and, according to his autobiography,
a 'convinced Bolshevik' from this date
onwards. Bubnov was an active party
organizer and propagandist in
Moscow and central Russia during the
pre-revolutionary period, suffering
thirteen arrests and spending four

years in prison. In August 1917 he was
elected to the party Central Committee; he played an active part in the
October revolution as a member of the
Politburo and of the Military-Revolutionary Council, and was prominently involved in the Civil War,
particularly in the Ukraine.

Bubnov was a left-wing Communist
during the early post-revolutionary
period: he voted against the conclusion of the Brest-Litovsk treaty with
Germany in 1918 and was later a
member of the 'Democratic Centralist'
opposition and, with Trotsky, a sig-
natory of the 'Declaration of the 46'
in 1923. From this point onwards,
however, Bubnov associated himself
with the majority position and was
entrusted with a variety of important
party posts over the subsequent
period. He was a member of the
party's central Secretariat from 1925,
and from 1924 until 1929 headed the
Political Directorate of the Red Army.
From 1929 until 1937 he was education commissar of the RSFSR, and
he was also a full member of the party
Central Committee. Bubnov's oppositional past finally caught up with
him 1937: he was arrested and died in
prison three years later. SLW

**BUCHMA, Amvrozy Maksimil-
yanovich** (1891–1957) Ukrainian
actor of stage and screen. Buchma's
many appearances included the films
Shchors (1939) and *Ivan the Terrible*
(1943–46). RT

BUDENNY, Semen Mikhaylovich
(1883–1973) Civil War and Second
World War commander. Budenny
occupies an honoured place in Soviet
military history as a Civil War hero.
Budenny, who was of peasant origin,
was drafted into the tsarist army in
1903 and served in the cavalry until
the Revolution. He fought in the

Russo-Japanese War and in the First World War as a non-commissioned officer before entering the Red Army. Budenny was poorly educated but he was an experienced tactician and able to exercise authority. He became one of the founders of the Red Cavalry, commanded the First Cavalry Army during the Civil War and became Inspector of the Red Cavalry during the 1920s. Like Voroshilov Budenny developed an association with Stalin during the Civil War which ensured him high rank and immunity from the purges in the future Stalinist state. In the early 1920s Budenny sided with a number of other successful Civil War field commanders who believed that they had developed a new doctrine of war and opposed Trotsky over the organization of the Red Army. In 1935 he became one of the five Marshals of the Soviet Union. Stalin expressed his trust in Budenny by appointing him Commander of Moscow Military District (1937–39), and Deputy, then First Deputy, People's Commisar for Defence (1939–41). Budenny was entrusted with high command during the Second World War: Commander-in-Chief of the South-Western Strategic Sector, Commander of the Reserve Army Group (1941), and Commander of the Transcaucasian Army Group (1942). He performed poorly as a military commander in these positions, but remained in the military high command in charge of the Soviet Cavalry for the period 1943 to 1953.

RA

BUGAEV, B. N. *see* BELY, A.

BUKHARIN, Nikolay Ivanovich (1888–1938) One of the leading Bolshevik politicians, Bukharin was born in Moscow. Both his parents were school-teachers, and his early life was comfortable despite recurrent financial difficulties. Bukharin was a brilliant pupil at school. In 1905 he became involved in the student disturbances which accompanied the contemporary political turmoil. He also joined the Russian Social-Democratic Labour Party in 1906 and sided with the Bolsheviks. He was politically active among students at Moscow University. The city's Bolsheviks, moreover, included several who would later become leaders of the left wing of post-revolutionary Bolshevism. Bukharin found their company congenial. He was short, red-haired, intellectually-dynamic and highly sociable. Throughout his life he had a talent for friendship, and – fatally in Stalin's case – strove to believe the best of his associates.

Some of Bukharin's associates before 1914 supported Bogdanov against Lenin in the rivalry for the faction's leadership. Bukharin developed a loyalty to Lenin; but this did not stop him from pursuing an interest in Bogdanov's ideas after the collapse of the 1905 to 1906 revolution. The quest for a universal science of man and nature was strong in Bukharin as in Bogdanov. He was attracted, too, by technical work on current economic theory (wherein he was akin to Lenin); but, unlike Lenin, he openly acknowledged that his explorations might benefit from the insights of non-Marxist scholarship. Countering Lenin's continuing castigation of his delight in twentieth-century sociology, Bukharin argued that his vital and underlying objective was to refute attacks on Marxism. He also shared with Bogdanov a concern with the cultural components of revolutionary change, and he recognized the influence of the ideological underpinnings of capitalist society.

Bukharin's involvement with the social-democrats brought him into his first direct contact with working-class life and exposed him to the dangers of underground activism. In 1909 he was arrested but soon released. In 1910 he was re-arrested and sentenced to exile in Arkhangel'sk province. He escaped in 1911 and moved abroad, where he was welcomed as a fellow theoretician of Bolshevism by Lenin. The two met in Galicia, and Bukharin was exasperated by Lenin's refusal to accept the damning nature of evidence against the police agent Roman Malinovsky. Bukharin thereafter resided in Vienna, continuing his economic studies and giving special attention to debates among Austrian scholars. His intellectual range widened.

After the outbreak of the First World War, Bukharin was deported to Switzerland. He settled in the village of Baugy with other Bolshevik leftists who had private funds at their disposal. Relations with Lenin had become tense. Bukharin and his friends vehemently opposed all support for the war effort in any belligerent country; but, in contrast with Lenin, they wanted Russian social-democrats to utilize the political possibilities of the pro-peace movement in Europe. They also disliked Lenin's baiting of Trotsky, and objected to his proclamation of the principle of national self-determination; for they felt that global capitalism had nearly reached its *apogée* and that the possibility of the dismemberment of large multinational states was a reactionary scheme. For a while the disagreements were containable, and Lenin wrote an (admittedly half-hearted) introduction to Bukharin's *The World Economy and Imperialism*.

Difficulties increased when Bukharin moved to Scandinavia in 1915 and became linkman in the chain of Bolshevik communications between Switzerland and Russia. Lenin was annoyed by his lack of deference to him. He also felt that Bukharin's radicalism, involving a call to smash the capitalist state once socialists took power, was virtual anarchism. Irritated in his turn, Bukharin left for New York: an early example of his lack of will and of tactical acumen.

Yet he was already a Bolshevik of considerable stature, and he contacted other prominent Russian Marxists in the USA like Trotsky. When the February Revolution occurred in Petrograd, his main problem was how to arrange to get back home. Eventually, in May, he arrived in Moscow; and in July-August 1917, when several other major Bolshevik leaders were in prison or in hiding, he gave one of the Central Committee reports to the Sixth Party Congress. He was a force on the left of Bolshevik politics in his native Moscow. An ultra-utopian on most issues, he nevertheless was not without perspicacity. For example, he had a keener sense than Lenin about the obstacles posed by German working-class patriotism to the advance of European socialism.

Meanwhile Lenin in *The State and Revolution* moved closer to Bukharin by affirming the Marxian authenticity of the view that the capitalist state could not simply be inherited but should be smashed. Both men now agreed on this. Bukharin was also an ardent supporter of Lenin's advocacy of the need for a rapid seizure of power. On the other hand, he had a negligible impact on the Central Committee's decisions before the October Revolution and contributed little of practical sig-

nificance to the establishment of a Bol-
shevik-led administration in Moscow.
His main importance lay in newspaper
journalism and in Marxist theoretical
discussions.

Soon after the October Revolution,
the pace of transition to a fully socialist
economy was a topic dividing Lenin
and Bukharin; and, even more importantly, Bukharin (despite having con-
ceded at the Sixth Party Congress that
an offensive revolutionary war was
beyond a Russian socialist regime's
capacity to wage) refused to accept
the need to sign a separate peace with
Germany and Austria-Hungary in
1918. He wanted a defensive military
strategy to be adopted on the grounds
that a separate peace would involve
Bolsheviks in conniving at the pro-
longation of capitalist imperialism.

Bukharin and the so-called Left
Communists were a variegated group,
and Bukharin by no means shared all
the ideas of his associates. His walk-
out from the Central Committee in
March 1918 after Lenin won the vote
on peace and war was anyway short-
lived. The intensification of the Civil
War and the Bolshevik party's surge
towards socio-economic policies of
comprehensive governmental intervention and control, which had been
demanded by Bukharin all along,
secured a reconciliation with Lenin.
Bukharin not only became editor of
Pravda but also joined the Politburo as
a candidate member in 1919. Bukharin's propagandistic activities continued during military hostilities and,
with E.A. Preobrazhensky, he
produced one of the early Soviet textbook classics, *The ABC of Communism.*
It was as a theorist, an editor and a
counsellor on policy that he was influential in the Civil War.

Bukharin did not help to instigate

the NEP (New Economic Policy) in
1921; and indeed, in the so-called
trade union controversy of 1920 to
1921, he adhered to a political stance
to the left of Lenin. But he was among
the NEP's heartiest advocates after its
inception. His revolutionary zeal had
been dampened by the failure of the
economics of War Communism, and
he accepted the need for a relaxation
of the regime's pressures on society.
This, Lenin contended, could be
achieved only through the temporary
acceptance of private ownership in
sectors of the economy and especially
the permission for peasants to keep a
portion of the annual harvest for
private trade.

Bukharin took up the NEP's cause
with alacrity. In 1922 his enthusiasm
led him into conflict even with Lenin,
who opposed the repeal of the state
foreign-trade monopoly. And yet
Bukharin also remained personally
close to Lenin; he was almost an adop-
tive son. Bukharin felt that the NEP
launched by Lenin should be viewed
not as a retreat but as a bridgehead
towards socialism. He claimed, after
Lenin's death in 1924, that Lenin had
confided similar thoughts to him.
There is no proof of the veracity of the
claim; and, even if it were to have
been true, there is no certainty that the
strategically-flexible and politically-
impulsive Lenin would have held fast
to such a perspective. Be that as it
may, Bukharin's political star was on
the rise. In 1924 he had become a full
Politburo member. He was a principal
harrier and vilifier of oppositionist
groups in the Bolshevik party hostile
to the NEP. And, despite his breadth
of learning in non-Marxist scholarship, he was indefatigable in his harassment of academics who opposed his
Marxism (just as he was animated by

a desire to create a robustly pro-Bolshevik Institute of Red Professors).

As Trotsky and then Kamenev and Zinov'ev went into opposition, the Stalin-Bukharin axis was consolidated. Bukharin's confidence was such in 1925 as to induce him to urge peasants simply to 'enrich' themselves. He was seen as the peasant's friend in the Politburo. But his support in the party was waning as frustration with the moderate economic progress of the NEP and the continuing crisis in foreign policy, industrial investment, and food supplies, annoyed Bolshevik officials at central and local levels.

When Stalin in 1925 to 1926 began to undermine the agrarian pillars of the NEP, Bukharin was powerless to resist. The problem was not only Stalin's control of the bureaucratic levers of authority but also the contemporary ideological face of Bolshevism. Bukharin was in any case not entirely opposed to the squeezing of the incomes of so-called *kulaks*. The repercussions, however, were disastrous for food supplies in 1927. Bukharin's supporters wanted a return to the old ways of the NEP and were appalled by Stalin's campaign of forced requisitioning in 1928. A compromise was worked out, and Bukharin's proposals were adopted for a while. But economic success did not ensue. Nor did Bukharin try, even then, to accumulate a strong cohort of supporters throughout the party to form a faction of opposition to Stalin. Forcible mass collectivization of agriculture occurred from 1929, and the break-neck pace of the industrializing drive of the First Five-Year Plan (1928–33) ensured its apparent completion a year ahead of schedule.

In 1929 Bukharin lost his seat in the Politburo and there was a witchhunt against his Right Deviation – his supporters were so few and disorganized that they were not designated a Right Opposition. In the 1920s he had taken an increasingly important part in the discussions of the Communist International, and in the early 1930s he perceived the Nazi danger more acutely than Stalin. He was also horrified by the collectivization drive. He at last indicated to former oppositionists his mistake in trusting Stalin; but in public he kept calm and sought readmission to the portals of influence.

It seemed that his loyalty would be rewarded. A certain relaxation of the regime's policies occurred from 1932, and the Seventeenth Party Congress in 1934 confirmed that this was to be the general party line. Bukharin was even elected to the Central Committee at the Congress. A dreadful period ensued with Kamenev and Zinov'ev being arrested in 1935 and shot in 1936. The uncertainties of policies continued, but the Stalin leadership seemed to Bukharin to have the potential for self-reform. In 1934 he also became editor of *Izvestiya* and, in a necessarily-coded fashion, he warned against the dangers of untrammelled despotism in modern industrial states (just as he had in the First World War in relation to Germany). The subsequent invitation to him to work on the draft for a new Soviet Constitution gave him further hope.

A man of courage and a revolutionary who could not conceive of a life divorced from the party and the Revolution, he stayed on at his post despite the risks. His letters to Stalin, or 'Koba' as he still affectionately called him, begged for mutual understanding. But he was arrested in 1937 and dictated a moving testament to his wife repudiating the grotesque charges against him in his forthcoming trial. Although he admitted in court to counter-revolutionary activity, after psychological pressure had been applied (particularly with regard to the fate to be meted out to his second wife Anna and their son if he should refuse to comply), he yet managed to undermine the import of the accusations by qualifying the wording of his 'confessions'.

He was executed by firing squad in 1938. In death he became a symbol of an alternative face of Soviet communism. His ideas were certainly more humane than Stalin's. But his commitment to democratic procedures was weak and even his belief in the need to reconcile the party with the peasantry was less than unshakeable. As a politician he was capable of skulduggery while remaining also a highly cultured and amiable human being. His ability to alter the course of Bolshevism in the 1920s was always slim in the extreme; but reformers in the USSR since the 1960s and especially in the late 1980s found him to be a useful medium through which to suggest that an alternative strategy to Stalinism had been conceivable in the 1920s and 1930s and that the CPSU need not lose all its legitimacy if it were to abandon pride in the achievements of the Stalin period. Bukharin, even in death, continues to influence Soviet life. He acquired posthumous civil rehabilitation in January 1988, and was thereafter re-admitted posthumously to the party. RJS

BUKOVSKY, Vladimir Konstantinovich (b. 1942) Human rights activist, democratic anti-communist, and writer. Bukovsky was repeatedly jailed for dissident activity of different sorts. He was forcibly held in Leningrad's psychiatric hospital (1963–

65), with the label criminally insane and a (false) diagnosis of schizophrenia. From 1965 to 1966 he was interned again. After he had organized a protest demonstration in 1967 (see P. Litvinov (ed.), *The Demonstration on Pushkin Square*, 1969), he was imprisoned in a labour camp until 1970. In 1971 he sent a collection of documents on political abuse of psychiatry to Western psychiatrists and asked for their opinion about them. He served part of a twelve-year sentence (1971–76) before being exchanged for a Chilean Communist leader and deported abroad. His best known book is his memoir *To Build a Castle* (1978). PBR

BULGAKOV, Mikhail Afanas'evich (1891–1940) Prose writer and dramatist. Born and brought up in Kiev, where his father was a Professor of Comparative Religion, Bulgakov's first career was medicine (fictionally described in the stories collected as *A Country Doctor's Notebook*). During the Civil War, Bulgakov was prevented by typhus from seeking emigration, and in 1921 he moved to Moscow with his first wife and embarked on a literary career, initially as the author of satirical *feuilletons* about NEP for *The Hooter* and *On the Eve*. His early short stories expose the scientific delusions of Marxism (*The Fateful Eggs*, *The Heart of a Dog*). Bulgakov's first important success was his play *The Days of the Turbins* (1925–26), an adaptation of his 1925 novel *The White Guard*, which attracted controversy in its production at the Moscow Arts Theatre with its sympathetic portrayal of a monarchist family in Kiev during the Civil War. The theme of the collapse of the White cause is further developed in Bulgakov's play *Flight* (1926–28), while the plays

Zoyka's Apartment (1925) and *The Crimson Island* (1927) extend the socio-political satirical vein in his writing. After 1929 Bulgakov's work is characterized by a preoccupation with the role of the artist in society; his works about Molière (*The Cabal of Hypocrites* (1929–31) and *The Life of Monsieur de Molière* (1932–33)), like his play about the death of Pushkin, *The Last Days (Pushkin)* (1934–35), focus on the tense relationship between the artist and the tyrant. Given the peculiar if intermittent interest Stalin took in Bulgakov's career, this theme inevitably assumes some autobiographical significance. Bulgakov's last play *Batum* (1939) tritely depicts the exploits of the young Stalin, and is obviously an attempt to relieve the plight of himself and of his family at a time when all his works had been banned and he was restricted to writing libretti for the Bol'shoy Theatre.

Much of Bulgakov's prose writing has autobiographical dimensions; *The White Guard*, with its Tolstoyan portrayal of a family in a time of war, displays modernist features in its handling of imagery. The unfinished *Theatrical Novel* (1936–37) is a biting satire on Konstantin Stanislavsky and his theatrical 'method', and expresses Bulgakov's bitterness over the reverses he suffered in 1929 and again in 1936 with the banning of his plays. But his reputation as a novelist rests above all on his masterpiece *The Master and Margarita*, written in secrecy from 1928 to 1940 and published only in the late 1960s by his third wife, Yelena Sergeyevna Shilovskaya, the great love of his life and the prototype for the character of Margarita. The novel interweaves a satire on culture in Moscow in the 1920s with a visitation to that city by the devil, and with an extraordinary retelling of the encounter between Christ and Pilate. The brilliance of this novel's structure and writing and its enormous cultural impact justify Bulgakov's claim to be considered one of the great writers of the Soviet period. He died of hereditary nephritis in 1940.

JAEC

BULGANIN, Nikolay Aleksandrovich (1895–1975) Military and party official. Nikolay Bulganin was a pre-eminently 'political soldier' who achieved high rank in both political and military fields. During the formative years of the Civil War (1918–22) Bulganin worked for the Cheka. He gained administrative experience in the 1920s and early 1930s in various posts, most notably as Chairman of the Moscow City Soviet (1931–37). His political career was established with his appointment as chairman of the RSFSR Council of People's Commissars in July 1937, and from 1939 to 1941 he was deputy chairman of the USSR Council of People's Commissars. After surviving the great purges, surviving the war was a lesser feat. The outbreak of war drew Bulganin into executive political work in the Soviet Army; he was a member of the Military Council and was assigned to various fronts as a trouble-shooter. He emerged from the war with high military rank, perhaps to the distaste of Soviet military professionals, and served as USSR Deputy People's Commissar for Defence (1944–46). As his fortunes rose Bulganin became a member of the Politburo; USSR Minister of Armed Forces (1947–49); Deputy Chairman of USSR Council of Ministers (1944–55), and USSR Minister of Defence (1953–55). However, Bulganin made little personal mark on the development of the Soviet armed forces, which largely remained Stalin's fiefdom until his death. As Chairman of the USSR Council of Ministers (1955–58), Bulganin often accompanied Khrushchev on his foreign visits. Bulganin's downfall was his association with the 'anti-party group' of Molotov, Malenkov and Kaganovich, which resulted in his dismissal from the Presidium in September 1958. He became a pensioner in 1960. RA

BUNICH, Pavel Grigor'evich (b. 1929) A reformist economist and a member of the Congress of People's Deputies (elected from the Academy of Sciences in 1989), Bunich is a department head at the Ordzhonikidze Institute of Management in Moscow. He is a member of the Committee of the Supreme Soviet for Questions of Economic Reform and he is on record as favouring more radical measures than those announced by Nikolay Ryzhkov, the Chairman of the Council of Ministers, in May 1990. These were described by Bunich as 'shock but no therapy'. AHB

BURLATSKY, Fedor Mikhaylovich (b. 1927) A notable reformer within the ranks of the Communist Party, Burlatsky first came to the fore as a young journalist and consultant within the Central Committee in Khrushchev's time and achieved significantly greater prominence in the Gorbachev era. He has made a mark in journalism, academic life and politics, although in the Brezhnev years he played a more minor role and was regarded by some of his more orthodox colleagues as a near-dissident.

Burlatsky was born in Kiev (his father was Russian and mother Ukrainian) and took his first degree at the Tashkent Juridical Institute. His first higher degree (candidate of science) was in law – at the Institute of State and Law in Moscow – and his higher doctorate was in philosophy. From 1951 to 1953 he worked in the Presidium of the Academy of Sciences and during the remainder of the 1950s on the journal, *Kommunist*. In the first half of the 1960s he was a consultant (and for a time head of the group of consultants) of Yuriy Andropov in the Socialist Countries Department of the Central Committee. Burlatsky was also involved in revising Soviet ideology, working closely with Politburo member, Otto Kuusinen, and he was for a time a speech-writer for Khrushchev and accompanied him on six of his trips abroad.

After a spell on *Pravda* which he was forced to leave in 1967 after an article attacking censorship in the theatre – which he co-authored with Len Karpinsky – appeared in another newspaper, Burlatsky took refuge in academic life. As early as 1965 he became the first advocate of a separate discipline of political science in the Soviet Union and some of his own writings, even under Brezhnev, broke new ideological ground, while other of his works said between the lines much more than could be proclaimed overtly.

After heading at the end of the 1960s and beginning of the seventies a group of sociologists which was broken up because of its interest in pursuing critical social research, Burlatsky became in 1972 a sector head at the Institute of State and Law before moving to the Institute of Social Sciences (under the jurisdiction of the International Department of the party Central Committee) where he headed the Department of Philosophy (1975–89).

A prolific writer and shrewd reformist politician, he became more influential after Andropov succeeded Brezhnev and, after losing ground temporarily under Chernenko, came more fully into his own under Gorbachev. In 1983 he was appointed political observer of the Writers' Union weekly newspaper, *Literaturnaya gazeta*, and in March 1990 he became editor-in-chief of that paper. In the meantime his political career had also flourished. In 1989 Burlatsky was elected to the Congress of People's Deputies and, subsequently, to the Supreme Soviet. In 1989 he became a member of the Constitutional Council formed to draw up a new Constitution for the USSR. Since 1987 he has been Chairman of the Public Commission for International Cooperation in Humanitarian Problems and Human Rights, an official body which, however, acquired some of the characteristics of a pressure group promoting better observance of human rights in the Soviet Union. AHB

BUROV, Andrey Konstantinovich (1900–1957) Architect. Born in Moscow, Burov studied under A. Vesnin at Vkhutemas from 1920 to 1925 before becoming a member of OSA. Burov was especially drawn to functional, industrial buildings and, for example, designed pavilions for the 'First All-Russian Agricultural Exhibition' in Moscow in 1923. He also designed Eisenstein's film *Old and New*. JEB

BYALYNITSKY-BIRULYA, Vitol'd Kaetanovich (1897–1957) Painter. Born in Krynki, Byalynitsky-Birulya received his training as a landscapist under Vasiliy Polenov at the MIPSA from 1889 to 1897 before joining the Association of Travelling Exhibitions. After the Revolution he continued to concentrate on the landscape, adjusting it to contemporary themes as in his *Beyond the Arctic Circle* (1935), collective farm themes, and also interpretations of places where Lenin, Tchaikovsky, Tolstoy and other important Russians lived and worked. He is rumoured to have been Khrushchev's favourite artist. JEB

BYCHKOV, Aleksey Mikhaylovich (b. 1928) General Secretary of the All-Union Council of Evangelical Christians-Baptists. An engineer by training, he acquired a good knowledge of English and first became actively involved in church work helping to prepare theological training material. In 1969 Bychkov was elected to the Council's executive as vice-president, becoming general secretary in 1971. During his period of office the Baptists have seen many improvements in their position, including expansion of the Bible correspondence course, the printing or importing of Bibles and other religious literature and the registration of hundreds of new churches. MR

BYKOV, Vasiliy Vladimirovich (born Bykau, Vasil') (b. 1924) The leading Belorussian prose writer of his generation. The principal experience of his life, both for him and his nation, was the Second World War, which he has described in a series of novels, some of them quite critical of the Soviet leadership, others concentrating on the moral issues which faced both soldiers and the civilian population of the occupied territories. In all cases he concentrates on the human experience of war, as it presented itself to individuals and small groups. Particularly important are *The Dead Feel No Pain* (1966), *The Ordeal* (Russian: *Sotnikov*, 1970), and *The Mark of Doom* (1982), the last of which describes the collectivization of agriculture, and shows how the bitterness it caused led some individuals to collaborate with the Germans during the war. From 1987 to 1989 he took a leading role in the establishment of a Belorussian Popular Front. GAH

C

CHABUKIANI, Vakhtang Mikhay-lovich (b. 1910) Outstanding dancer, choreographer, and teacher. Chabukiani's career began in Tbilisi where he studied with Mariya Perini and performed national dances in Georgian operas. He then entered Leningrad Ballet School, graduating in 1929.

A leading soloist at the Kirov Theatre (1929–41), Chabukiani developed a vast repertoire of major roles, including classical and character parts. He received great acclaim for his soaring leaps, dynamic style, and superlative technique, and he excelled in the heroic style of male dance, which he brought to new heights. He danced in numerous modern ballets, including *The Golden Age* (1931), *The Flames of Paris* (1932), and *The Fountain of Bakhchisaray* (1934). In 1934 he was one of the first Soviet dancers to visit the United States.

Chabukiani's career as a choreographer began during the 1930s and grew to include new versions of many classical ballets as well as a host of original works, many of them heroic ballets set to music by Georgian composers. He danced in many of these productions.

Chabukiani's career was vital to the development of the ballet in Georgia. He served as principal choreographer and teacher at the Paliashvili Theatre of Opera and Ballet (1941–73), director and teacher at the Tbilisi Institute of Choreography (1950–73), and director of the choreography department of the Rustveli Theatre (1965–70).

His choreography has included versions of *Giselle* (1942), *Swan Lake* (1945), *Sleeping Beauty* (1959), *The Nutcracker* (1965), and *Cinderella* (1966). His original ballets include *Mzechabuki* (1936), later revised and presented under the title *The Heart of the Mountains* (1938); *Laurencia* (1939); *Sinatle* (1947); *Othello* (1957), for which he received the Lenin Prize; *The Demon* (1961); and *Hamlet* (1971). He has also directed and performed in films, choreographed for the Ukrainian ice ballet, and staged ballets throughout the world. scs

CHAGALL, Marc (Shagal, Mark Zakharovich) (1887–1985) Painter and designer. Born in Vitebsk, Chagall studied with many teachers, including Lev Bakst, before developing his idiosyncratic, decorative style reliant upon both Jewish and Russian traditions. In 1918 Chagall became head of the Vitebsk Popular Art Institute, and worked as a stage designer for Alexander Granovsky's State Jewish Theatre in Moscow (1920–21). After emigrating in 1922, Chagall lived in Germany, France and America. He was soon hailed as one of the most original artists and designers of his time. JEB

CHAKOVSKY, Aleksandr Borisovich (b. 1913) Born in Petersburg, a well-known literary conservative, editor of *The Literary Gazette* (1962–86), and prose writer; he joined the Communist Party in 1941, becoming a candidate member of the Central Committee in 1971 and a full member in 1986. He began his writing career with a war-time trilogy *It Was in Leningrad* (1944–47), followed by the Stalinist novel *Here It's Morning Already* (1949), about Sakhalin fishermen. During the Khrushchev years he was a conservative force with works like *Light of a Distant Star* (1962). In his magnum opus, the neo-Stalinist four-volume *Blockade* (1968–73), he returned to the subject of besieged Leningrad. KC

CHALIAPIN, *see* Shalyapin

CHAYANOV, Aleksandr Vasil'-evich (1888–1939) An original economist and an authority on the peasantry (who was also a creative writer), Chayanov was an advocate in the early Soviet period of genuine agricultural cooperatives. He was arrested in 1930 and accused, with others, of forming an anti-Soviet peasant party, and died in prison camp. In the Gorbachev era Chayanov has been fully rehabilitated and his ideas have attracted favourable attention from Soviet agricultural reformers and critics of compulsory collectivization. AHB

CHAYKOV, Iosif Moiseevich (1888–1979) Sculptor. Born in Kiev, Chaykov studied with Naum Aronson and Bourdelle in Paris before the Revolution and experimented with various Modernist styles. Par-

ticipating in Lenin's Plan of Monumental Propaganda, he designed statues to Liebknecht and Marx in Kiev (1919–22), the first of many statue portraits in the 1920s to 1940s (for example, to Mayakovsky in 1944). Working in both bronze and stone, Chaykov was widely recognized as one of the Soviet Union's leading sculptors. JEB

CHAYKOVSKY, Boris Aleksandrovich (b. 1925) Composer. Boris Chaykovsky was born in Moscow. After studying at the Moscow Conservatory under Shebalin, Shostakovich and Myaskovsky, he graduated in 1949. In 1969 he was awarded a State Prize and was made an Honoured Art Worker of the RSFSR. He is renowned especially for his chamber compositions and is highly regarded in the USSR. GS

CHAZOV, Yevgeniy Ivanovich (b. 1929) Chazov, a prominent cardiologist, was appointed Soviet Minister of Health in February 1987. Formerly the Director of the Moscow Institute of Cardiology and later of the All-Union Cardiology Research Centre, he became a deputy minister of health in 1968. Chazov was Chairman of the Committee of Soviet Physicians for the Prevention of Nuclear War (1981–87) and with the American cardiologist, Lown, established the organization of International Physicians for the Prevention of Nuclear War. For their work in this area, Chazov and Lown jointly received the Nobel Peace Prize in 1985. Chazov has been a member of the Academy of Sciences of the USSR since 1975 and was a full member of the Central Committee of the Communist Party (1982–90). He was replaced by his deputy, I. N. Denisov, in April 1990. AHB

CHEBRIKOV, Viktor Mikhaylovich
(b. 1923) As head of the KGB, Chebrikov supported Mikhail Gorbachev
for the General Secretaryship of the
Central Committee of the Soviet Communist Party in March 1985, but as
Gorbachev's political reforms became
more radical and the political climate
more liberal, he turned against Gorbachev. He was skilfully removed from
office in two stages by Gorbachev in
1988 and 1989 – in the former year
given an apparent promotion to a
Secretaryship of the Central Committee to accompany his full membership of the Politburo, but at the
same time replaced as Chairman of
the KGB and one year later pensioned
off entirely.

Although of Russian nationality,
Chebrikov began his career in the
Communist Party apparatus in Dnepropetrovsk in the Ukraine, a major
political base of Leonid Brezhnev.
Earlier he served in the Soviet army
(1941–46) and from 1946 to 1950
studied at the Dnepropetrovsk Metallurgical Institute. At the time he was
transferred from party work to the
KGB, he was Second Secretary of the
Dnepropetrovsk regional party committee. That move came in 1967 and
coincided with Yuriy Andropov's
appointment as Chairman of the
Committee of State Security. Chebrikov was placed in charge of cadres
within the KGB and was there as
someone Brezhnev could rely on,
given that Andropov was not a Brezhnev client. In 1968 Chebrikov
became a deputy chairman of the
KGB and in 1982 First Deputy Chairman.

In the course of Andropov's fifteen
years as head of the KGB, Chebrikov
proceeded to develop closer ties to
Andropov than with the Brezhnev

group and one of Andropov's earliest
actions when he became General Secretary of the Central Committee in
late 1982 was to push through Chebrikov's appointment as KGB Chairman. In 1983, with Andropov still at
the helm, Chebrikov became a candidate member of the Politburo. As a
reward for supporting Gorbachev for
the leadership following the death of
Chernenko in March 1985, Chebrikov
secured full membership of the Politburo the following month.

In the course of the next few years
Chebrikov's enthusiasm for Gorbachev and his policies markedly
diminished as those policies became
more overtly radical. Chebrikov's political pronouncements showed his own
views to be much closer to those of
Yegor Ligachev. The institutional
interest he represented was a
sufficiently important one for Gorbachev to have to handle his removal
with care, but his promotion to a
senior secretaryship of the Central
Committee and to the chairmanship
of the newly created Commission
on Legal Policy in the autumn of
1988 was a short-lived one. Chebrikov
was removed from these political offices at the September plenary session
of the Central Committee in 1989.
AHB

CHELOMEY, Vladimir Nikolaevich
(1914–1984) Starting as an aircraft
designer, Chelomey became one of the
USSR's leading missile and space-
launcher designers. He is best known
as the designer of the 'Proton'
launcher, since 1965 frequently used
in the space programme, but was also
responsible for a series of ICBMs,
including, it is believed, the SS-11 and
SS-19 missiles. Born into the family of
a teacher, he graduated from the Kiev
Aviation Institute in 1937 and in 1941

started work at the Central Aero-engine Institute. Here Chelomey developed an original pulse-jet motor which was used in the 10X flying bomb, a Soviet equivalent to the V-1, not used in combat. In the post-war years he developed a series of naval and land-based missiles, and space vehicles. A member of the Academy of Sciences from 1962, he was twice made a Hero of Socialist Labour (1959, 1963). He joined the party in 1941. JMC

CHEREMNYKH, Mikhail Mikhaylovich (1890–1962) Graphic artist. Born in Tomsk, Cheremnykh, after studying under Konstantin Korovin and Sergey Malyutin at MIPSA (1911–17), became with Mayakovsky a major contributor of posters to the Okna ROSTA (Windows of the Russian Telegraph Agency) in Moscow. In the 1920s he worked as a caricaturist for various journals, including *Krasniy perets*, while – during the Second World War – continuing to produce political posters. He also worked occasionally for the theatre. JEB

CHERKASOV, Nikolay Konstantinovich (1903–1966) Actor. Originally a stage actor, Cherkasov is best known outside the Soviet Union for the title roles in Eisenstein's films *Aleksander Nevsky* (1938) and *Ivan the Terrible* (1943–48). His first major film role was that of Professor Polezhayev in Ermler's *The Baltic Deputy* (1937) and his other films included: *Peter the First* (1937–39), *Lenin in 1918* (1939), *They Knew Mayakovsky* (1955) and *Don Quixote* (1957). His autobiographical *Notes of a Film Director* has been published in English. RT

CHERNAVIN, Vladimir Nikolaevich (b. 1928) Admiral of the Fleet. Chernavin joined the Soviet

Navy in 1947. A graduate of the Naval Academy (1965) and the Military Academy of the General Staff (1969), he held various command posts and staff positions in the Northern Fleet. He served as commander of the Northern Fleet (1977–81) and Chief of the Main Staff Navy (1981–85). He gained the rank of Admiral of the Fleet in 1982. A candidate member of the CPSU Central Committee since 1981, and a full member since 1986, he became a Deputy to the USSR Supreme Soviet in 1979. Chernavin replaced the aged Admiral Gorshkov as Commander-in-Chief of the Soviet Navy in November 1985 and gained the rank of Deputy Minister of Defence. As Gorshkov had dominated the development of the post-war Soviet Navy since 1956, his replacement by Chernavin may signal a period of reduced influence of the Navy among the Soviet forces. RA

CHERNENKO, Konstantin Ustinovich (1911–1985) Although a politician of far from outstanding ability, Konstantin Chernenko held for thirteen months what was at the time the most powerful post of all within the Soviet political system – the General Secretaryship of the Central Committee of the Communist Party. His rise in the Communist Party hierarchy had been facilitated largely by his patron, Leonid Brezhnev, and his brief period in the top post became something of a conservative interregnum between the bolder leadership of Yuriy Andropov and the still more radically reformist era of Mikhail Gorbachev.

Chernenko, who was born into a Siberian peasant family in Krasnoyarsk region, had only a limited formal education. Such higher education as he picked up was mainly at the Higher Party School in Moscow,

although he also received a quali-
fication following part-time study at
Kishinev Pedagogical Institute in
Moldavia when he was already a
powerful official within that republic.
Apart from the years which he spent
as a member of the Border Guards
(1930–33), most of his career was
devoted to Communist Party organizational work. His duties were those
of a propagandist rather than economic administrator and he worked in
the propaganda and agitation departments of district party committees and
the regional party committee in his
native area before becoming a Secretary of the Krasnoyarsk *kraykom*
(regional party committee) in 1941.
From 1945 to 1948 he was a Secretary
of the Penza regional committee, but
his luckiest transfer came in 1948 when
he moved to Moldavia to become head
of the propaganda and agitation
department of that republic's Central
Committee. His eight years there
included the brief period at the beginning of the 1950s when Leonid Brezhnev was First Secretary of the
Moldavian party and it was the excellent relationship he established with
Brezhnev which was to be the vehicle
of his subsequent upward climb
through the party ranks.

Brezhnev brought him to Moscow
in 1956 as a sector head in the Department of Propaganda and Agitation of
the Central Committee of the Soviet
Communist Party and when Brezhnev
was moved in 1960 from a Secretaryship of the Central Committee
to the Chairmanship of the Presidium
of the Supreme Soviet, he brought
Chernenko with him as his chief of
staff. When Brezhnev became party
leader in 1964 he lost little time in
bringing Chernenko into an important position in the Central Committee

apparatus. He became in 1965 head
of its General Department, the department which works most closely of all
with the General Secretary. In 1966
Chernenko became a candidate
member and in 1971 a full member of
the Central Committee.

It was, however, the second half of
the 1970s before Brezhnev was strong
enough to bring such a faithful client
into the highest echelons of the party
leadership. In successive years Chernenko became a Secretary of the
Central Committee (1976), a candidate member of the Politburo (1977)
and a full member of the Politburo
(1978). With Brezhnev's health
declining, his influence grew, for he
was the Politburo member and Secretary of the Central Committee personally and politically closest to the
party leader. Beginning with the Helsinki conference in 1975, he had
started to accompany Brezhnev on
trips abroad and he took part in Brezhnev's last summit meeting – with
President Carter in Vienna in 1979.

Chernenko was clearly Brezhnev's
own choice to succeed him, but
although Brezhnev's health had been
poor for some years, his eventual death
in November 1982 came quite suddenly and Chernenko was left to fend
for himself. Although he had considerable support within the Politburo, Chernenko found himself
defeated by Andropov and it looked
as if the position of *de facto* 'second
secretary' which he then acquired
would be the highest point of his
career.

As, however, Andropov's health
weakened, Chernenko's political position became stronger and when
Andropov died in February 1984, it
was Chernenko who won the succession struggle against his younger

and much abler opponent, Mikhail Gorbachev. A majority of Soviet leaders, who had been fearful of being swept aside by Andropov's new broom, were concerned that the broom might be wielded with still greater vigour by Gorbachev. They were ready to settle for a quieter life once again, looking, essentially, for Brezhnevism-without-Brezhnev.

In fact Chernenko's short tenure as General Secretary was a time of stalemate. Gorbachev had enough support in leadership circles to be able to carve out for himself extended supervisory functions within the Secretariat of the Central Committee and he was now the informal 'second secretary'. Chernenko was not strong enough either politically or physically to impose his will and Gorbachev, for his part, could do little to implement his policy preferences. It was characteristic of the Chernenko General Secretaryship that no-one in that period was promoted to the Politburo and the only change in the top leadership team was caused by the death of Marshal Dmitriy Ustinov in December 1984.

Under Chernenko there was a slackening of the discipline campaign which had begun under Andropov and the campaign against corruption was soft-pedalled. It was only as Chernenko's health weakened and Gorbachev's influence within the leadership grew that the themes of discipline and reform, which had been broached by Andropov, began to get another limited airing.

Chernenko was seventy-two when he became General Secretary of the Soviet Communist Party (and within two months head of state as well) and it is, thus, not altogether surprising that his leadership was one which merely postponed decisions on the difficult choices facing the Soviet leadership. Although Chernenko was quoted as the ultimate authority in Soviet publications during his period at the top of the party hierarchy, his actual power was not fully commensurate with his formal standing. In foreign policy, Chernenko deferred to Andrey Gromyko, the Soviet Union's long-standing Foreign Minister, and for lengthy periods his ill-health kept him out of the public eye. Chernenko's death on March 10, 1985, just thirteen months after he had succeeded Andropov as Soviet leader, came as no surprise and it was only then – following the demise of three Soviet General Secretaries in as many years – that the leadership passed to a new generation. AHB

CHERNIKHOV, Yakov Georgievich (1889–1951) Architect. Born in Pavlograd, Chernikhov, after graduating from the Academy of Arts in 1917, gave his attention to issues of engineering, transport and factories. A keen supporter of Constructivism in the 1920s and early 1930s, he is now remembered for his architectural textbooks, especially *Architectural Fantasies* (1933). JEB

CHERNOV, Mikhail Aleksandrovich (1891–1938) Responsible for state grain collections under Mikoyan from 1929 onwards, Chernov, who had been a student at Moscow University, was first a Menshevik, but joined the Bolsheviks in 1920. He was People's Commissar for Trade in the Ukraine in 1927, moving at the end of the 1920s to Moscow where he was responsible for grain collections; he was appointed Deputy People's Commissar for Supplies (internal trade) in December 1930. Chernov then became Chairman of the Committee for Agricultural Deliveries in 1933, followed by the post of People's Commissar for Agriculture (April 1934 – October 1937). He was a member of the Party Central Committee from 1934 until he was among those arrested and sentenced to death in the Bukharin trial of March 1938. RWD

CHERNYAEV, Anatoliy Sergeevich (b. 1921) An aide to Mikhail Gorbachev – advising on foreign policy – since 1986, Chernayaev is a representative of the 'New Political Thinking', notwithstanding many years of work in the Central Committee apparatus, including sixteen years as a deputy head of its International Department (1970–86) at a time when it was headed by Boris Ponomarev.

A party member since 1942, he fought in the Second World War. After graduating in history from Moscow University, he taught there for a time, but following Stalin's death he joined the Central Committee apparatus. He served first in the Department of Science and later in the International Department, but spent the years 1958 to 1961 on the staff of *World Marxist Review* in Prague. He maintained links with people of critical views outside the party apparatus and belonged to a reformist political grouping. During the *perestroika* period he has clearly enjoyed the confidence of Gorbachev. AHB

CHERNYAKHOVSKY, Ivan Danilovich (1906–1945) Wartime commander. Chernyakhovsky, a Ukrainian, commanded the Eighteenth Tank Corps, then the Sixtieth Army (July 1942–April 1944). He took part in the battle for Kursk in 1943 and in offensive operations in the Ukraine. His exceptional skill led to his appointment as commander of the Third Belorussian Army Group on the recommendation of Marshal Vasilevsky, Chief of the General Staff. At thirty-eight years of age he became the youngest Soviet general to attain such a high position. Chernyakhovsky was killed by an enemy shell in 1945 during the final assault on East Prussia. RA

CHERNYSHEV, Nikolay Mikhaylovich (1886–1973) Painter. Born in Nikol'skoe, Chernyshev trained in Moscow, St Petersburg and Paris before the Revolution, evolving a lyrical, Symbolist style of painting. A connoisseur of Russian icons and frescoes, Chernyshev tried to adapt some of their principles to Soviet reality, teaching monumental art at Vkhutemas-Vkhutein in the 1920s. He is now remembered for his romantic, if ambiguous, paintings of teenage girls. JEB

CHERVONENKO, Stepan Vasil'evich (b. 1915) Ukrainian by nationality and a graduate of the Taras Shevchenko State University, Kiev, Chervonenko played an important part in feeding alarmist information to Moscow from Czechoslovakia in 1968 (he was Soviet Ambassador to Prague from 1965 to 1973) and in coordinating on the spot the suppression of the Prague Spring.

His early career was spent in the apparatus of the Ukrainian Communist Party, and his ambassadorial career began when he was sent to China in 1959. Then came Prague and after that Paris where Chervonenko was Soviet Ambassador (1973–83). He was a full member of the Central Committee from 1961 until 1989 and head of the Department of the Central Committee for Cadres Abroad until its abolition in 1988. AHB

CHETVERIKOV (Tschetwerikoff), Sergey Sergeevich (1880–1959) A founder of population genetics, evolutionary theorist. The son of a Moscow industrial entrepreneur, Chetverikov graduated from Moscow University in 1906 and taught in the Beztuzhev Higher Courses for Women (1909–19), becoming Russia's leading butterfly systematist. Thereafter he taught as a *dotsent* at Moscow University until 1929. Working at Kol'tsov's Institute of Experimental Biology from 1921 to 1929, he headed a group investigating the genetics of drosophila. In 1926 he published a classic paper, 'On Certain Aspects of Evolution From the Viewpoint of Modern Genetics', that argued for the compatibility of genetics and Darwinism several years before the comparable works of Sewall Wright, R. A. Fisher, and J. B. S. Haldane. In 1925 and 1926 the group undertook studies of natural populations of various drosophila species that confirmed Chetverikov's prediction that wild populations contain large amounts of hidden genetic variation on which natural selection acts to produce evolution, thereby initiating the field of 'experimental' or 'ecological' population genetics. In 1929 Chetverikov was arrested and, after six years in exile, he was invited to Gor'ky University where he taught genetics, conducted research on silkworms, and later became dean of the biological faculty. In 1948 he suffered a stroke and, following official party endorsement of Lysenko's biology, lost his post and pension. He died in 1959 just as his important role in the history of population genetics and evolutionary biology was becoming internationally recognized. MBA

CHIAURELI, Mikhail Edisherovich (1894–1974) Georgian director and scriptwriter. Chiaureli's films included: *The Last Masquerade* (1934), *The Vow* (1946), *The Fall of Berlin* (1950) and *The Unforgettable Year 1919* (1952). The last three films contributed significantly to the Stalin 'personality cult'. RT

CHIBURDANIDZE, Maya (b. 1961) Chess player. She dominated women's chess after her victory over Nona Gaprindashvili in 1978, and was the first Soviet woman to have a chess school of twenty-five boys and girls in Tbilisi named after her in 1985. Born in Kutaisi into the family of an agronomist and schoolteacher, she took up chess at the age of five, became Candidate Master of Chess at twelve, won the Soviet title at sixteen and the world title at seventeen. In 1977, the same year as she won the world women's chess title, she became an international grandmaster. She has continued the Soviet tradition of dominating women's world chess since 1950, following such world champions as Rudenko, Bykova, Rubtsova and Gaprindashvili. JWR

CHICHERIN, Georgiy Vasil'evich (1872–1936) A somewhat unlikely revolutionary with his noble origins, squeaky voice and pince-nez, Chicherin was nonetheless a convinced socialist who served as Soviet foreign minister for most of the inter-war period and played a key part in normalizing relations between the USSR and other states after the revolution. He was born at Karaul on the estate of his uncle Boris Nikolaevich, the distinguished legal philosopher. The family itself was of ancient noble origin, cultivated, cosmopolitan and moderately liberal. His father, a Tsarist diplomat, died when Chicherin was just ten years old and he grew up in an isolated, bookish, religious and relatively impoverished atmosphere. He studied at the Tambov Gymnasium and later, after the family had moved to the imperial capital, in St Petersburg, Chicherin developed a passionate interest in history, literature and philosophy, and became a talented musician (in later life he composed a biography of Mozart). After studies at St Petersburg University he secured employment in the records department of the Tsarist Foreign Ministry, but becoming progressively more politically involved he decided to emigrate in 1904 and lived for the remainder of the pre-war period in Germany, France and Britain. Chicherin associated himself with the Menshevik wing of the Social Democratic Party at this time, and adopted a 'patriotic' position when the First World War broke out in 1914.

Chicherin returned to Russia in January 1918 and immediately joined the Bolshevik party. He became Commissar for Foreign Affairs in May 1918, succeeding Trotsky, and directed Soviet foreign relations from this time forward until the late 1920s. He signed the Brest-Litovsk treaty and led the Soviet delegations at the Genoa Conference of 1922 – which marked Soviet Russia's re-entry into European diplomacy – and at the Lausanne Conference the following year. Chicherin was a diplomat of outstanding talents, as his Western opponents ruefully acknowledged: he had a remarkable facility for languages, an excellent memory and a capacity for hard work, particularly at night. He was nevertheless not a figure of high standing in party terms: he became a member of the Central Committee as late as 1925 (to 1930), and was never a member of the policy-making Politburo. Chicherin suffered from increasingly poor health throughout this period; he spent the years 1928 to 1929 receiving treatment in Germany, and resigned his position 'at his own request' in 1930. He died six years later. SLW

CHICHIBABIN, Aleksey Yevgen'evich (1871–1945) Organic chemist. An 1892 graduate of Moscow University, where he studied with V. V. Markovnikov, Chichibabin worked in a manufacturing laboratory (from 1896), at the Moscow Agricultural Institute (1899–1909), as a *dotsent* at the University of Warsaw (1905–6), and as a professor at the Moscow Higher Technical School (1909–30) and Moscow University (1918–23). His principal research was on pyridines. During the First World War he organized the Russian pharmaceutical industry and was responsible for the first Russian plant for alkaloid manufacture and the production of opium, morphine, codeine, atropine, cocaine, caffeine, aspirin, and other chemicals. In 1924 he published *Foundations of Organic Chemistry*, an influential textbook that went through many editions and was translated into seven languages. For his continuing work on pharmaceuticals after the revolution, he was elected to the USSR Academy of Sciences in 1926 and became the first chemist to win a Lenin Prize. In 1930 he emigrated to France, where he worked in a chemical laboratory at the Collège de France until his death. In 1936 he lost his membership of the USSR Academy of Sciences and his name was expunged from its official records. MBA

CHIRKOV, Boris Petrovich (1901–1982) Film actor. Chirkov is best remembered for playing the heroic

leading role in the Kozintsev and Trauberg Maxim trilogy (1935–39).
RT

CHITANAVA, Nodari Amrosievich (b. 1935) A Georgian agricultural specialist, Chitanava turned to Komsomol and party work in 1959. He was Second Secretary of the Adzhar *obkom* (1973–74), Minister of Agriculture (1974–79), First Deputy Chairman of the Council of Ministers (1979–85), and Party Secretary for Agriculture (1985–89) – all in his native Georgia. In the wake of the Tbilisi riots in April 1989 he was appointed Chairman of the Georgian Council of Ministers.
JHM

CHORNOVIL, Vyacheslav Maksymovych (b. 1937) Ukrainian nationalist and journalist. Chornovil was repeatedly jailed for documenting discrimination against the Ukraine and its culture, and persecution of Ukrainian nationalists. From 1967 to 1969 he was imprisoned for his book *The Chornovil Papers* (1968), and from 1972 to 1985 on charges which included editing the samizdat journal *The Ukrainian Herald*, modelled on the Moscow *Chronicle of Current Events*.
PBR

CHUBAR', Vlas Yakovlevich (1891–1939) Vlas Chubar', a party and state official during the early post-revolutionary period, was born to illiterate parents in a village in Yekaterinoslav province. As he later recalled, he became involved in reading and explaining political publications to the peasants in his village during the 1905 revolution; in his own case it was his reading of Darwin's *Origin of Species* which had destroyed his belief in God and led him to search for the meaning of life in other quarters. In 1907 Chubar' joined the Bolshevik wing of the Social Demo-

cratic Party; he left school four years afterwards and became involved in political work in factories in southern Russia and in Moscow. During 1917 he took an active part in the factory committee movement in Petrograd, where he had secured work in an ordnance factory. After the October revolution he served on the Council of Workers' Control and then (1918–23) the Supreme Council of the National Economy. In 1922 Chubar' was appointed head of the Donbass steel industry; in 1923 he became head of the Supreme Council of the National Economy, in effect the Soviet Union's chief planner, becoming a candidate member of the party Politburo three years later and a full member in 1935. In 1934 he became deputy chairman of the Council of People's Commissars, in effect deputy prime minister, and in 1937 he was named to head the Commissariat of Finances. A model economic organizer and close supporter of Stalin, Chubar' was nonetheless dismissed from his posts in 1938 and was sentenced to death and executed the following year. SLW

CHUKARIN, Viktor Ivanovich (b. 1921) Gymnast. Born in the village of Krasnoarmeyskoe in the Ukraine, he took up gymnastics at the end of the war for health reasons; he became Soviet absolute champion in 1949 and, at the relatively late age of thirty-one, he took the absolute gymnast title at the 1952 Olympics in Helsinki and repeated his success four years later in Melbourne, when he was thirty-five. Altogether he won seven gold, three silver and one bronze Olympic medals, was three times world champion and several times Soviet individual and all-round champion between 1948 and 1956. He retired undefeated after the 1956 Olympics, becoming head of gymnastics at the Lvov Physical Culture Institute. JWR

CHUKHONTSEV, Oleg Grigor'-evich (b. 1938) Born near Moscow in 1938, Chukhontsev made his début in print in the late 1950s, but subsequently found it difficult to publish original poetry and survived as a translator; his first collection appeared only in 1976. Since 1985 he has been recognized as one of the most important lyric poets of his generation. GSS

CHUKOVSKAYA, Lidiya Korneevna (b. 1907) Memoirist and novelist. A literary activist, she criticized Mikhail Sholokhov openly for his persecution of Sinyavsky and Daniel in 1966. Her two-volume *Notes on Anna Akhmatova* is an excellent record of Leningrad life just before the war. She was expelled from the Writers' Union in 1974. Her novels *The Deserted House* (1939–40) and *Going Under* (1971) both involve gradual realizations on the part of their heroines of the realities of Stalinist society. Despite their restrained style of narration, they could not be published in the Soviet Union of those times. BH

CHUKOVSKY, Korney Ivanovich (1882–1969) Born in Odessa, a literary critic and historian, translator, and the best-known Soviet children's author. A translator and interpreter of Walt Whitman and many others who wrote in English, Chukovsky also made influential studies of the theory of translation, including *The Principles of Artistic Translation* (written with Gumilev in 1919 but revised in 1930 and reissued as *The Lofty Art*), which argues that a translator reproduces the original not literally but creatively. Starting with 'The Crocodile' (1917), he began writing for children, typically incorporating riddles, jokes,

puns and other forms of word play in verse form, and also to research the language of children. His extremely popular *From Two to Five* (1928) establishes connections between children's word formation and folk poetry, and contains a wealth of children's speech culled from thousands of letters from parents. His achievements in literary scholarship include some major research on Nekrasov, first replacing thousands of lines expurgated by the tsarist censors for a critical edition of the complete works in 1927, and then *Nekrasov's Literary Mastery* (1952), which won a Lenin Prize in 1962. After 1954 he directed his attention to the creeping bureaucratese in the contemporary language, resulting in *As Alive as Life Itself* (1962). KC

CHUYKOV, Semen Afanas'evich (b. 1902) Painter. Born in Pishpek, Chuykov, after graduating from Vkhutein in 1930, rapidly established himself as a landscapist concerned especially with the steppes, the nomadic peoples, and the social changes introduced by modernization. His colourful, romantic evocations of land and sky are exemplified by *Morning in a Mountain Settlement* (1967). JEB

CHUYKOV, Vasiliy Ivanovich (1900–1982) Wartime and peacetime military commander. Chuykov, of peasant origin, became a regimental commander during the Civil War. After grduation from the Military Academy of Motorization and Mechanization he gained command of a mechanized brigade, a rifle corps, then the Fourth Army (1938–40). He took part in the occupation of Poland and the Soviet-Finnish Winter War before he was assigned as a military adviser to Chiang Kai-shek (1941–42). He commanded the Sixty-Second Army

(1942–45) and participated in the battle of Stalingrad and the final assault on Berlin. After the war he was appointed Deputy Commander, then Commander-in-Chief of the Soviet occupation forces in Germany. Chuykov took charge of the Kiev Military District (1953–60) and was made Deputy Minister of Defence and Commander-in-Chief of Soviet Ground Forces (1960–65). He was simultaneously (from 1961) Chief of Soviet Civil Defence, a post he retained until 1972. RA

CIEPLAK, Archbishop Jan (?–1926) Archbishop of Mohilev and primate of the Roman Catholic Church in the USSR (1920–24). He was tried in Petrograd in 1923, with other leading Catholic clergymen, for 'conspiracy against the Soviet government', because of his opposition to state confiscation of church property and his refusal to end religious instruction of children. He was sentenced to death but the sentence was commuted to ten years imprisonment and in 1924 he was released and expelled from the USSR, probably in exchange for a Polish Communist. MR

COSTAKIS, George (1912–1990) Born into a wealthy family of Greek merchants in Moscow, Costakis became one of the greatest collectors of Russian twentieth-century art and the person who saved many important abstract works which had been condemned by Soviet officialdom. Denied by the Bolshevik Revolution an extended education, Costakis became fascinated by Russian avant-garde art of the first two decades of the century at a time – the worst of the Stalin years – when it was under severe attack. He was able to build up a remarkable collection (purchased at extremely low prices) which he kept at his apartment in Moscow. By the 1970s interest in his collection was intense and he negotiated a deal with the Soviet authorities whereby he was able to emigrate with twenty per cent of his collection, while the remainder went to the Tret'yakov Gallery in Moscow. After his departure from the Soviet Union he lived in Greece where his daughter is now in charge of the Costakis Art Gallery in Athens. AHB

D

DANDARON, Bidiya (1914–1974) Leading Buryat scholar on Tibetan language and customs. Imprisoned from 1937 to 1955, Dandaron was rehabilitated under Khrushchev and allowed to resume work in the Buryat Academy of Social Sciences. He published numerous scientific articles and books, notably a two-volume *Description of Tibetan Manuscripts* (1960 and 1963). In August 1972 he was arrested and later sentenced to five years in a labour camp for his alleged attempts to form a 'Buddhist sect'. He died in imprisonment on 26 October 1974. MR

DANIEL', Yuliy Markovich (pseudonym Arzhak, Nikolay) (1925–1988) Along with Sinyavsky, Yuliy Daniel' was sentenced in 1966 to five years' imprisonment for 'anti-Soviet propaganda'. This was a unique example (at least till the case of Ratushinskaya in 1982) of a Soviet writer being given a criminal sentence on the basis of literary texts. These were satirical short stories, published in the west under his pseudonym, of which the best-known, *Moscow Speaks* (1962) posits the official declaration of a 'day of unpublished murders', a concept with an obvious reference to Stalin's purges. GAH

DAVIDENKOV, Sergey Nikolaevich (1880–1961) Neurologist. After his graduation from Moscow University in 1904, Davidenkov specialized in psychiatry and neuropathology and worked in various medical institutes, hospitals, and clinics in Moscow, Khar'kov, and Baku, settling in Leningrad in 1932. His expertise on degenerative diseases of the nervous system (the subject of his 1911 doctoral dissertation) and on recovery from trauma (gained in the two world wars) led to his recognition as one of the Soviet Union's leading neurologists and his selection as one of the élite doctors to treat Kremlin officials. A pioneer in medical genetics, Davidenkov organized some of the earliest centres for genetic counselling of patients and was one of the first physicians to use wide-scale clinical studies of twins to assess the role of heredity in various nervous diseases. In a highly innovative 1947 book he analysed neuropathology from the viewpoint of genetics, mutations, natural selection, and human evolution. MBA

DAVIDOVICH, Bella Mikhaylovna (b. 1928) Pianist. Bella Davidovich was born in Baku. At the Moscow Conservatory she studied with Konstantin Igumnov and Yakov Flier. After graduating in 1951, she stayed on for a further three years' post-graduate study, and in 1962 was appointed a member of staff. She was awarded first prize in the Fourth International Pianists' Competition in Warsaw in 1949. In 1972 she was made an Honoured Artist of the RSFSR. In 1977 she elected to leave the Soviet Union and live in the West. Her concert performances in the United States have been highly acclaimed. GS

DAVITASHVILI, Leo Shiovich (1895–1977) Paleontologist. A 1925 graduate of Moscow University, Davitashvili worked at the Moscow Petroleum Institute, was elected to the Georgian Academy of Sciences in 1944 and organized and directed its Paleobiology Institute (from 1950). The author of several standard Soviet works on the history of paleontology published in the 1940s, he became a strong supporter of Lysenko and was made a professor at Moscow University in connection with the party's endorsement of Lysenko in 1948. In the succeeding decades he became one of the world's most prolific paleontologists, publishing a dozen books on evolutionary theory, extinction, fossil variability, and sexual selection. Although he was infamous in the Soviet Union for his Lysenkoist views, several of his highly original paleontological works were well received in the West and his textbooks of paleontology are used in most Soviet educational institutions. MBA

DEGTYAREV, Vasiliy Alekseevich (1880 (1879 o.s.)–1949) Perhaps the most eminent of all the Soviet designers of infantry weapons, Vasiliy Degtyarev was born in Tula of a family with a gun-making tradition. At the age of eleven he started work at the local arms factory and from 1906

began his career as a designer. For many years he headed the design department of the Kovrov arms factory. Systems developed by him include a series of machine guns (the DP (1927), DK (1933) and DS (1939)), the PPD (1940) submachine gun, and the famous PTRD 14.5 m. m. anti-tank gun of the war years. A party member from 1941, he was awarded four Stalin Prizes and in 1940 became a Hero of Socialist Labour. JMC

DEMENTEVA, Raisa Fedorovna (b. 1925) A party official at the local level, Dementeva worked first for the Komsomol and since 1952 has had a variety of positions in the CPSU. She joined the CPSU in 1948 and graduated from the Moscow Institute of Economic Statistics in 1957. Most of her work has been in the Moscow party. Her most recent position was that of Second Secretary of the Moscow City Committee. She was a candidate member of the Central Committee (1966–76) and a full member from 1976 to 1986. She has also been a member of the Supreme Soviet. NN

DEMICHEV, Petr Nilovich (b. 1918) A Soviet politician who was Minister of Culture during a period of cultural clampdown and suppression of talent, Demichev was born in Pesochnaya (later Kirov) in the Kaluga region of Russia. He obtained qualifications in mechanical engineering and chemical technology and served in the Soviet army from 1937 to 1944. Immediately after the war he joined the party apparatus and held a series of posts in the Moscow city organization and the Central Committee.

A full member of the Central Committee from 1961, Demichev was First Secretary of the Moscow regional party organization (1959–60), First Secretary of the city of Moscow (1960–

62), a member of the party bureau for the RSFSR (1959–61) and a Secretary of the Central Committee from 1961 until 1974. His responsibilities within the Secretariat were for ideology. A candidate member of the Politburo from 1964, Demichev lost his secretaryship but kept his non-voting membership of the Politburo when he was made Minister of Culture in 1974. In that post he conformed to the norms prevailing in the Soviet leadership at the time and played a significant part in the stifling of talent and creativity in the arts. He was replaced as Minister of Culture in 1986 and went into retirement in September 1988. AHB

DEMUTSKY, Daniil Porfir'evich (1893–1954) Cameraman. Demutsky was the Ukrainian cameraman who shot Dovzhenko's early films from *The Fruits of Love* (1925) to *Ivan* (1932), creating a distinctive visual style imbued with a strong sense of nature and the elements. RT

DENI (Denisov), Viktor Nikolaevich (1893–1946) Graphic artist, born in Moscow. Although he received no extended professional training, Deni became one of the Soviet Union's most distinguished caricaturists and poster artists. Just before the Revolution, he worked as an illustrator for several Petrograd journals, including *Budil'nik* and *Solntse Rossii*, an experience that prepared him for his major contribution to the Okna ROSTA (Windows of the Russian Telegraph Agency) after 1917. Deni is now remembered for his Civil War posters such as *Entente* (1919) and *Denikin's Band* (1919) as well as for his caricatures of contemporaries such as Gor'ky and Lunacharsky. During the years 1919 to 1937 he worked closely with the writer Dem'yan Bedniy, illustrating a number of his works. JEB

DENISOV, Edison Vasil'evich (b. 1929) Composer. Edison Denisov was born in Tomsk. After teaching himself several folk instruments as a child, he studied piano at the Tomsk music school (graduating in 1950), and attended classes in mechanics and mathematics at the Tomsk University (graduating in 1951). He studied piano with Vladimir Belov at Moscow Conservatory and composition with Shebalin (1951–56). After a further three years' post-graduate training, he was appointed to the teaching staff in 1960. From 1968 to 1970 he worked at the Electronic Music Research Centre, Moscow. An avant-garde composer, his *Soleil des Incas* for Soprano, Three Readers and Instrumental Ensemble (1964) was a prize-winning work at the Darmstadt Festival. However, although acclaimed in the West, his work has received no official recognition in the Soviet Union in the form of prizes or honours. He has written several articles on contemporary Western music. GS

DEYNEKA, Aleksandr Aleksandrovich (1889–1969) Painter and graphic artist. Born in Kursk, Deyneka – one of the Soviet Union's most distinguished artists – is now remembered for his renderings of industrial and sports scenes. Graduating from Vkhutemas in 1925, Deyneka became a founding-member of OST and then the October group, with whom he exhibited his first industrial paintings such as *Construction of Factory Shops* (1926). Accepting the tenets of Socialist Realism in the early 1930s, Deyneka produced optimistic, if militaristic, interpretations of the new society such as *Future Fliers* (1937) and *Left March* (1941), and his renderings of war-torn Russia during the years 1941 to 1945 are especially poignant. Apart from his painting, Deyneka was also active as a magazine caricaturist and as a monumental-decorative artist (working on the sports mosaics for the Mayakovsky metro station in Moscow in the 1930s). From 1962 to 1966 Deyneka was Vice-President of the Academy of Arts. JEB

DIKIY, Aleksey Denisovich (1889–1955) Stage director and actor associated with the Moscow Art Theatre and the Vakhtangov Theatre. Dikiy's numerous productions included Zamyatin's play *The Flea* (1925) and Prokof'ev's opera *Love for Three Oranges* (1927). He also played the title roles in the films *Kutuzov* (1943) and *Admiral Nakhimov* (1946). RT

DILIGENSKY, German Germanovich (b. 1930) The Chief editor of the journal, *ME i MO* (World Economy and International Relations) – produced at IMEMO – Diligensky was born in Moscow and graduated from the History Faculty of Moscow University in 1952. A sociologist as well as historian, Diligensky has a particular interest in psychology. He is author of more than one hundred scholarly publications, among them *The Psychology of Classes* (1985). After graduate study and further research at the Institute of History of the Academy of Sciences from 1952 to 1963, Diligensky moved to IMEMO in 1969. Very much a proponent of new thinking on both domestic and foreign policy, Diligensky has made *ME i MO* a more innovative journal since he took over its editorship in 1988. AHB

DMITRIEV, Ivan Nikolaevich (b. 1920) A graduate of first a chemical and later an engineering college, Ivan Dmitriev worked in the engineering and power industries before becoming first secretary of Gor'ky regional party committee (1964–69). He was then head of the construction department of the CPSU Central Committee (1969–88), combining this with vice-chairmanship of the RSFSR Council of Ministers. He was elected a candidate member of the CPSU Central Committee in 1981 and 1986. He has been a consultant to the board of the Industrial-Construction Bank of the USSR since 1988. SLW

DMITRIEV, Vladimir Vladimirovich (1900–1948) Designer, born in Moscow. After attending art school in Petrograd, Dmitriev made his début as a stage designer by decorating Meyerkhol'd's proposed production of Khlebnikov's *Death's Mistake* in 1917. Thereafter, Dmitriev was involved in many experimental productions, including *The Love for Three Oranges* in 1926 for which he made colourful Constructivist sets and costumes. During the 1930s and 1940s he worked frequently for the Bol'shoy Theatre in Moscow. JEB

DOBRONRAVOV, Boris Georg'evich (1896–1949) One of the leading stage actors of the twenties and thirties, Dobronravov played a number of major roles including Vaska in Gor'ky's *The Lower Depths* (1924–25). He died on stage while playing his favourite role, Tsar Fedor in Pushkin's *Boris Godunov.* RT

DOBRYNIN, Anatoliy Fedorovich (b. 1919) An exceptionally long-serving Soviet Ambassador in Washington, Dobrynin is now in semi-retirement but remains an adviser to Mikhail Gorbachev in his capacity as Soviet President. Dobrynin, who joined the Soviet diplomatic service in 1946, served in the United Nations Secretariat from 1957 to 1960. From February 1960 until December 1961 he was head of the Soviet Foreign Ministry's American Department. He was then appointed Soviet Ambassador to the United States – just in time to have to deal with the Cuban Missile Crisis. He remained in Washington (where he was regarded as a highly professional and effective diplomat) until 1986 when he became a Secretary of the Central Committee and was appointed head of its International Department. This was a surprise appointment in some ways for a diplomat who had never previously served in the party organization, but it reflected the Gorbachev leadership's concern with improving state-to-state relations with the rest of the world and the much lower priority accorded to encouraging revolutionary movements. A candidate member of the Central Committee from 1966 and a full member from 1971, Dobrynin was retired from the Central Committee apparatus in late 1988 as part of a major restructuring and cutback in the size of that organization. AHB

DOKUCHAEV, Nikolay Vasil'evich (1891–1944) Architect. Born in Moscow, Dokuchaev studied architecture at MIPSA and the Academy of Arts, Petrograd (1916–17) and achieved his status as a Rationalist in the 1920s. Close to Ladovsky, he believed that architecture, as an art form, should depend on harmony and clarity. He was a strong proponent of standardization in the 1930s. JEB

DOLGIKH, Vladimir Ivanovich (b. 1924) A member of the Soviet Union's top leadership team for seventeen years, Dolgikh found his further promotion blocked after Gorbachev became General Secretary; he was forced to retire in September 1988. Born in the Krasnoyarsk region of Russia, Dolgikh studied at the Mining-Metallurgical Institute in Irkutsk (1943–49) and made a career in industry as an engineer and later factory manager (1962–69) before entering the party apparatus in 1969 as First Secretary of the Krasnoyarsk regional party committee. Within three years he was not only a member of the Central Committee (from 1971) but a Secretary of the Central Committee (from 1972) with special responsibility for heavy industry and energy. At the last Central Committee meeting during Brezhnev's General Secretaryship (in May 1982) Dolgikh was promoted to candidate membership of the Politburo while retaining his Secretaryship. This put him in line for further elevation to one of the top two or three places in the party, but he rose no further and seemed to be out of sympathy with the growing demands for radical economic reform under Gorbachev. When he was removed from the leadership in 1988, the Heavy Industry Department of the Central Committee of which he had been head (1976–83), and had later supervised, was abolished. AHB

DOLLER, Mikhail Ivanovich (1889–1952) Theatre actor and director. Doller began work in cinema in 1923, training in the Kuleshov workshop and working as assistant director to Pudovkin on most of the latter's films between *The Mother* (1926) and *The Feast at Zhirmunka* (1941). RT

DOLMATOVSKY, Yevgeny Aronovich (b. 1915) A poet and literary official, born in Moscow. A party member since 1941, he is a prolific and totally loyal author of orthodox Socialist Realist lyrics on topical public themes, including songs. GSS

DOLUKHANOVA, Zara (Zarui Agas'evna) (b. 1918) Mezzo-soprano. Zara Dolukhanova was born in

Moscow. After studying at the Gnesin Music School, she entered the main Gnesin Music Pedogogical Institute, from which she graduated in 1937. In 1939 she made her début at the Spendyarov Theatre of Opera and Ballet, Yerevan, becoming a soloist with the All-Union Radio and Television in 1944. Since 1959 she has appeared regularly as a soloist attached to the Moscow Philharmonic Organization. She was made a People's Artist of the Armenian SSR in 1952 and a People's Artist of the RSFSR in 1956 and is the winner of several State prizes. She has toured overseas on a number of occasions, where her fine musicianship and arresting vocal qualities have won favourable acclaim. GS

DOMOGATSKY, Vladimir Nikolaevich (1876–1939) Sculptor. Born in Odessa, Domogatsky studied law at Moscow University (1897–1902) before taking private lessons in sculpture in Moscow and abroad. He contributed to Lenin's Plan of Monumental Propaganda with a bust of Byron (1919) and during the 1920s he made his name as a Realist portraitist, for example, of Pushkin (1926) and Tolstoy (1928). JEB

DONSKOY, Mark Semenovich (1901–1981) Film director. Donskoy was noted for his Gor'ky trilogy, *The Childhood of Gor'ky* (1938), *Into the World* (1939) and *My Universities* (1940). His other films included: *How the Steel Was Tempered* (1942), *The Rainbow* (1944) and *The Village Teacher* (1947). RT

DORZHIEV, Avgan (1853–1938) As head of the Buddhist religious orders in Buryatiya Dorzhiev was the major proponent of 'Lamaist modernism' before the Revolution. After 1917 he expounded the compatibility of Bud-

dhism and Communism, convincing scholars that Buddhism was an 'atheist religion'. This strategy led to an increase in numbers of monks in the 1920s. In the winter of 1926 to 1927 he called a 'Congress of Soviet Buddhists'. In 1934 he was exiled to Leningrad. He was arrested in 1937 and died in prison in Ulan-Ude in 1938. MR

DOVZHENKO, Aleksandr Petrovich (1894–1956) Leading Ukrainian film director. Dovzhenko's works were permeated by a lyrical evocation of nature in the Ukrainian countryside. After brief careers as a civil servant, diplomat and illustrator, he made his first films, *Vasya the Reformer* and *Love's Berry* in 1926 and *The Diplomatic Bag* in 1927. His first major film, *Zvenigora* (1928), was somewhat complex and confusing in its lyricism. *The Arsenal* (1929), a portrayal of the revolutionary upheaval in the Ukraine, achieved a broader success but it was *The Earth* (1930), his film ostensibly about collectivization and mechanization in the countryside, that brought Dovzhenko world-wide recognition and is generally still regarded as his masterpiece. But the film was also a personal statement about death and was officially criticized for the absence of a clear political line, for formalism and latent bourgeois nationalism and for 'counter-revolutionary defeatism'. Dovzhenko's first sound film *Ivan* (1932) dealt with the problems of industrialization as seen through the experiences of a young peasant working on the construction of the Dnieper Dam. *Aerograd* (1935) confronted the problems of modernization in the Soviet Far East. His last major film, *Shchors* (1939) was made at Stalin's express suggestion as a 'Ukrainian *Chapaev*' (a reference to the Vasil'ev Brothers' film). Dovzhenko's last years were spent as head of the Kiev studios making documentary films. RT

DRACH, Ivan Fedorovych (b. 1936) A respected Ukrainian poet published since 1962, Drach was born near Kiev and educated at Kiev University. He joined the CPSU in 1959, but since 1962 has clashed frequently with ideological authorities in Kiev and Moscow. Increasingly outspoken in defence of Ukrainian language and culture, Drach was elected Chairman of the Popular Movement of the Ukraine for Perestroika (or Rukh) at its inaugural Congress in September 1989. He was elected to the Ukrainian Supreme Soviet in 1990. JHM

DUBININ, Nikolay Petrovich (b. 1907) Geneticist. A 1928 graduate of Moscow University, Dubinin worked for four years with A. S. Serebrovsky on drosophila genetics. Along with D. D. Romashov, he published important papers on what he called 'automatic genetic processes' (known in the West as 'genetic drift') that led to his appointment as head of the genetics division of N. K. Kol'-tsov's Institute of Experimental Biology (1932–48). There he became internationally famous for his studies of drosophila population genetics, which uncovered unexpectedly large concentrations of recessive lethal mutations in wild populations. Elected a corresponding member of the USSR Academy of Sciences in 1946, Dubinin lost his job in 1948 following party endorsement of Lysenko's antigenetic views, finding work in the Urals in the Forestry Institute. In 1956 he organized an influential Moscow laboratory of radiation genetics in the Biophysics Institute. In 1957 he organized the Institute of Cytology and Genetics of the USSR Academy of Sciences's new Siberian division, but he was fired as director in 1959 because of Khrushchev's displeasure at his opposition to Lysenko. After Khrushchev's removal, Dubinin was elected a full member of the academy (1966) and made director of the reorganized Institute of General Genetics in Moscow (1966–81). His strident nurturism, administrative style, and political attacks on other geneticists alienated him from many colleagues and led to his dismissal as director in 1981 and his separation from the institute in 1988. MBA

DUBININ, Yuriy Vladimirovich (b. 1930) Born in the Kabardin-Balkar ASSR, Dubinin is of Russian nationality and a graduate of MGIMO (the Moscow State Institute of International Relations). He has been a career diplomat, most of whose postings have been to Western Europe. It was, therefore, something of a surprise when he was appointed Soviet Ambassador to the United States in 1986, a post he held until 1990 when he returned to Moscow to become a Soviet deputy foreign minister. AHB

DUDAROVA, Veronika Borisovna (b. 1916) Conductor. Veronika Dudarova was born in Baku, she studied piano at the special music school attached to the Leningrad Conservatory under Pavel Serebryakov, after which she undertook courses in conducting with Lev Ginzburg and Nikolay Anosov at the Moscow Conservatory. On graduating in 1947, she was appointed a conductor of the Moscow State Symphony Orchestra. She became a People's Artist of the RSFSR in 1960. GS

DUDINSKAYA, Nataliya Mikhaylovna (b. 1912) Prima ballerina and leading teacher. Born into a theatrical family, Dudinskaya studied at Petrograd Ballet School (1923–31) and graduated under the tutelage of Agrippina Vaganova, who considered Dudinskaya one of her foremost students.

In 1931 Dudinskaya made her début at the Kirov in *Sleeping Beauty*. She danced with the company from 1931 to 1963 and was known for her superlative technique, psychological depth, wonderful extension, and soaring leaps. She had a broad repertoire of both classical and modern roles. Among her classical roles, she appeared in the original St Petersburg version of *Swan Lake*, in the Grand Pas from *Paquita*, the Vision Scene from *Sleeping Beauty*, the Kingdom of the Shades Scene from *La Bayadère*, and in *Don Quixote* and *Giselle*.

Dudinskaya also danced in ballets from the modern repertoire, often partnered by Vakhtang Chabukiani or Konstantin Sergeev. These ballets included Vasiliy Vaynonen's *The Flames of Paris* (1932), Rostislav Zakharov's *Lost Illusions* (1936), and Sergeev's ballets *Cinderella* (1946) and *The Path of Thunder* (1958). She received much acclaim for her performance in *Laurencia*, choreographed for her by Chabukiani in 1939. This ballet incorporated classical ballet and Spanish character dancing, and was a landmark in the development of Soviet choreography.

Dudinskaya began teaching during her dancing career, and became one of the leading proponents of the Vaganova method. She conducted advanced classes at the Kirov Theatre (1951–70) and served as coach of the Kirov troupe (1951–63). In 1963 she began teaching at Leningrad Ballet School where she staged part of George Balanchine's *Symphony in C*. She has toured extensively, and has received numerous awards. SCS

DUDINTSEV, Vladimir Dmitrievich (b. 1918) Born in Kupyansk near Khar'kov, a prose writer best known for the 1956 thaw novel *Not By Bread Alone* about an inventor's eight-year struggle to have approved his plans for a machine for casting sewerage pipes, supplanting the inferior design made by an entrenched authority figure. The novel not only exposes the counter-productive dogma of Soviet science and its corrupt politics (Drozdov, the name of the novel's antagonist, became a by-word among the intelligentsia for self-seeking bureaucrats) but also, as the title suggests, questions the absolute priority which Soviet ideology accords material progress. Under Gorbachev he published *The White Coats* (1987) which is about Lysenko's campaign against the geneticists. KC

DUDKO, Father Dmitriy Sergeevich (né Dudkiny) (b. 1922) Orthodox clergyman. Born near Bryansk, from poor peasant origins (the Dudkiny surname was changed accidentally), Fr Dudko was ordained on 21 November 1960, having already served eight and a half years in a labour camp. He became known in the early seventies for his fearless preaching on taboo subjects such as the timidity of the Russian Orthodox Church. His influence, particularly among the young, spread when he conducted 'after church discussions' on topics relating to the Christian faith and the way a believer should live his life. This led to his transference to two other parishes. Pressure by the authorities and the media culminated in his arrest on 15 January 1980. After five months in prison, Fr Dudko appeared on Soviet television, confessing to the 'spreading abroad of anti-Soviet materials'. His recantation came as a shock to his followers. It has since been admitted by Fr Dudko that pressure from the KGB was used to elicit a statement from him. MR

DUMBADZE, Nina Yakovlevna (b. 1919) Athlete. She had the misfortune to miss world competition in the pre-war and war years when the USSR did not compete in top world events. Born in Odessa, she became Soviet discus champion in 1937 and was one of the few Soviet world-class athletes who, prior to Soviet membership of the Olympic movement in 1951, enjoyed open professional status. After the war she became European discus champion in 1946 and 1950, but was placed second to Nina Ponomareva at the 1952 Helsinki Olympics when she was already thirty-three. Nevertheless, her world discus record of 57 m 4 cm, set in 1952, remained unbroken until 1960. JWR

DUNAEVSKY, Isaak Osipovich (Iosifovich) (1900–1955) Composer. Isaak Dunaevsky was born in Lokhvitsa and died in Moscow. After graduating from Khar'kov Conservatory in 1919, where he studied violin under Iosif Akhron and composition with Semen Bogatyrev, he moved to Moscow in 1924, where he was active as a composer of ballets, operettas and incidental music. From 1929 to 1941 he lived in Leningrad, where he worked with Utesov's jazz orchestra, after which he returned to Moscow. He was made a People's Artist of the RSFSR in 1950. Immensely popular as a composer of cheerful, melodious songs, his music to the films *Circus* and *Volga-Volga* won the first Stalin Prize in 1941. He is remembered as one of the creators of Soviet operetta. The opening notes of his 'Song of the Homeland' from the film *Circus* (1936) are used as the call-sign of Radio Moscow. GS

DURDENEVSKY, Vsevolod Nikolaevich (1889–1963) Jurist. A professor from 1925, a legal adviser to the USSR Ministry of Foreign Affairs from 1944, a comparative constitutional lawyer, Durdenevsky was an eminent authority on public international law. He advised the Soviet delegation at Potsdam, the Paris Peace Conference, the Geneva and Berlin conferences of 1954, the Warsaw Pact conference of 1955, and the 1956 London conference on Suez, among others. WEB

DZERZHINSKY, Feliks Edmundovich (1877–1926) As founding head of the secret police, a post which he retained until his death, Dzerzhinsky had a well-justified reputation for both ruthlessness and sincerity. From a Polish gentry family, Dzerzhinsky became a revolutionary in Lithuanian-Polish Marxist parties from the age of eighteen, and was associated with the RSDLP from 1906. Frequently in prison and exile, he spent part of his sentence in chains. He was appointed head of the Cheka/OGPU (1917–26) a post he combined with that of People's Commissar for Transport (1921–24) and the chairmanship of VSNKh (1924–26). A workaholic, when in charge of VSNKh with responsibility for industry he unexpectedly showed a sensitive understanding of industrial problems and was greatly admired by non-party specialists. He was a passionate supporter of industrialization and of combining rapid industrialization with good market relations with the peasantry. Thus he wanted to squeeze resources from industry itself and to cut administration. Dzerzhinsky was granted honorary party membership from 1895. He served as a member of the Central Committee (1917–26) and of the Politburo (1924–26). He died of a heart attack in July 1926 after making an emotional attack on the United Opposition at a Central Committee meeting. RWD

DZERZHINSKY, Ivan Ivanovich (1909–1978) Composer. Ivan Dzerzhinsky was born in Tambov and died in Moscow. Following three years' study at the Leningrad Conservatory, where he was a pupil in composition of Petr Ryazanov and Boris Asaf'ev (1932–34), he soon established himself as a composer with his monumental opera *Quiet Flows the Don* (1935), based on Sholokhov's novel. A member of the party from 1942, he was made an Honoured Art Worker of the RSFSR in 1957. His music, written in many different genres, followed closely the precepts of Socialist Realism. GS

DZHEMILEV, Mustafa (Abduldzhemil') (b. 1943) A leader of the movement demanding the right for Crimean Tatars to return to their Crimean homeland, from which they were deported in 1944 for alleged collaboration with the German invaders. From 1962, when he tried to form a youth group in Tashkent, official harassment of him began, taking the form of imprisonment or exile (1966–67, 1969–72, 1974–75, 1975–77, 1979–82 and 1983–86). From 1969 to 1972 he was held for joining the Moscow-based Action Group to Defend Civil Rights, but most of his dissident activity has consisted of organizing Crimean Tatar lobbying and protest actions, especially in Central Asia and Moscow. PBR

DZIGAN, Efim L'vovich (1898–1984) Film director. Dzigan was renowned for his Civil War epic *We from Kronstadt* (1936). His other, less well-known, films included: *Jambul* (1953) and *The Prologue* (1956). RT

DZYUBIN, Eduard Georg'evich *see* BAGRITSKY, E. G.

E

EFANOV (Yefanov), Vasiliy Pro-fov'evich (1900–1978) Painter. After studying in his birthplace Samara, Efanov moved to Moscow where he rapidly gained recognition for his political portraits painted according to the canons of Socialist Realism – for example *A Memorable Meeting* (1937). From the 1940s onwards, Efanov taught at the Surikov Institute and the Lenin Pedagogical Institute in Moscow. JEB

EFROIMSON, Vladimir Pavlovich (1908–1988) Medical geneticist. A student of N. K. Kol'tsov in genetics at Moscow University, Efroimson worked on silkworm research and human heredity. He was arrested and sent to prison camps twice, most recently in 1948 for sending a long letter to Stalin detailing the agricultural losses attributable to Lysenko's techniques. Released in 1955, he began to lead the campaign for the reestablishment of medical genetics in the Soviet Union and became its leading expert, culminating in his two books *Introduction to Medical Genetics* (1963, 1964, 1968) and *Immunogenetics* (1971). His controversial 1971 article in *Novyy mir*, 'Innate Altruism', involved him in a new Soviet nature-nurture dispute. MBA

EISENSTEIN, Sergey Mikhaylovich (1898–1948) Film director. Eisenstein was not only the leading director and theorist of Soviet cinema, he was also a theatre and opera director, script-writer, graphic artist, teacher and critic. He trained as a civil engineer but abandoned his courses and joined the Red Army after the Revolution. Assigned to a theatrical troupe, he later joined the *Proletkul't* Theatre, together with his childhood friend, Maksim Shtraukh. His first stage production, a version of Ostrovsky's *Enough Simplicity for Every Wise Man* (1923) included his first venture into cinema, *Glumov's Diary*. His production of Tret'yakov's *Gas Masks* (1924) on location in a gasworks was an attempt to bridge the gap between the artificiality of the stage and the reality of everyday life. It failed and, as Eisenstein himself put it, he 'fell into cinema'. He had already worked with Esfir' Shub on re-editing Fritz Lang's *Dr Mabuse* for Soviet audiences in 1923 but his first full-length film was *The Strike* (1925), set in 1905, in which he applied to cinema his theory of the 'montage of attractions'. Unlike Kuleshov, Eisenstein thought that montage depended on a conflict between different elements from which a new synthesis would arise. This notion developed partly from his study of Japanese ideograms and partly from his understanding of the Marxist dialectic. It followed from the primacy accorded to montage in this theory that the actor's role was diminished while the director's was enhanced. In his silent films Eisenstein used amateur actors who were the right physical types for the part and called this 'typage': hence an unknown worker, Nikandrov, played the role of Lenin in *October* (1927) and all the parts in his second film, *The Battleship Potemkin* (1926), were played by unknowns.

It was *Potemkin* that secured Eisenstein's reputation both at home and abroad, especially in Germany, where it was a spectacular success and attracted far greater audiences than in the USSR itself. After *Potemkin* he started work on a film about collectivization, *The General Line*, but broke off to make *October* for the tenth anniversary of the October Revolution. When he returned to *The General Line* and completed it in 1929, the party's general line on agriculture had changed and Trotsky had fallen from grace: the film therefore had to be re-edited and it was finally released under the title of *The Old and the New*. The problems Eisenstein encountered in this film were to recur in his subsequent work. In 1929 he went abroad, with his assistants Alexandrov and Tisse, to study the new medium of sound film: he visited Western Europe and then travelled to Hollywood to work for Paramount. His projects were rejected and he went on to start filming *Que Viva Mexico!* with funds provided by Upton Sinclair. This project collapsed in acrimonious exchanges and Eisenstein returned to the Soviet Union in 1932. After several abortive projects, including *Moscow*, a history of the capital, *The Black Consul*, which would have starred Paul Robeson, and a film version of Karl Marx's *Das Kapital*, he began making his first sound feature, *Bezhin Meadow* in 1935. This too was dogged with problems and was eventually stopped on the orders of Boris Shumyatsky in March 1937. Eisenstein was forced to confess his alleged errors in public and this submission, together with the dismissal of Shumyatsky in January 1938, enabled him to start filming again. The result was his most popular film, *Alexander Nevsky* (1938).

When not filming, Eisenstein was nonetheless busy teaching at the State Institute of Cinema, where he had been head of the directing department since his return from abroad in 1932. He also devoted an increasing amount of time and energy to his theoretical writings but his magnum opus *Direction*, like his other work, *Mise-en-Scène*, remained unfinished. His last film was also unfinished: filming of the first part of *Ivan the Terrible* was begun in 1943 in Alma-Ata, where the Moscow studios had been evacuated because of the war, and released in 1945, when it was an instant success and earned Eisenstein and others the Stalin Prize. In Part Two, however, the historical parallels between Ivan and Stalin became too obvious and, although completed, the film was not shown until 1958, well after the deaths of both Stalin and Eisenstein.

He died under a cloud in his own country, but has since been universally acknowledged as one of the cinema's greatest creative geniuses and a towering figure in the culture of the twentieth century. RT

EKK (né Ivakin), Nikolay Vladimirovich (1902–1976) Film director. Ekk trained in Meyerhol'd's workshop and was best known for directing the first Soviet sound feature film *A Path to Life* (1931). RT

EKSTER (Exter), Aleksandra Aleksandrovna (1882–1949) Painter and designer. Born in Belestok, Ekster, after studying at the Kiev Art Institute until 1907, travelled widely in Russia and Europe, especially Moscow, St Petersburg and Paris. Influenced by French Cubism and Italian Futurism, she reached her own system of abstract painting and also revolutionized the art of stage design – making her début at Tairov's Chamber Theatre in Moscow with her sets and costumes for *Thamira Khytharedes* (1916). In 1921 she contributed to the exhibition '5 x 5 = 25' in Moscow, thereby forming an allegiance with the Constructivists. After designing the space movie *Aelita* in 1924, she emigrated to Paris where she continued to work as a stage designer and book illustrator. JEB

ENGEL'GARDT (Engelhardt), Vladimir Aleksandrovich (1894–1984) Biochemist and molecular biologist. A 1919 graduate of Moscow University, Engel'gardt subsequently served as professor of animal biochemistry at the universities of Kazan' (1929–33), Leningrad (1934–40), and Moscow (1936–59) while heading laboratories at the Biochemistry Institute of the USSR Academy of Sciences (1935–59), the Pavlov institute (1944–50), and the medical academy's Institute of Experimental Medicine (1945–52). In the late 1930s, together with his wife and collaborator Lyubimova, he discovered that the muscle protein myosin contracts in the presence of adenosine triphosphate (ATP): the work was internationally hailed as a major discovery in structural biochemistry and bioenergetics that

helped explain how muscles work. As academician-secretary of the biology division of the USSR Academy of Sciences (1955–59), Engel'gardt led the campaign against Lysenko for the development of Soviet molecular biology. In 1959 the Institute of Radiation and Physicochemical Biology (later renamed the Institute of Molecular Biology) was created on his initiative and he served as its director until his death. During the last decades of his life, he continued to fight for greater academic freedom within the Academy. MBA

ERDMAN, Nikolay Robertovich (1902–1970) Dramatist and librettist. Erdman was described by Gor'ky as 'our new Gogol'. He wrote sketches for the music-hall and political cabaret. His first play, *The Warrant* (1924), was produced by Meyerkhol'd. His second play *The Suicide* (1928) was banned while in rehearsal at the Vakhtangov Theatre in 1932. Erdman also wrote new words for Soviet productions of operettas like *The Beggar Student* and *Die Fledermaus* and assisted on the scripts for Aleksandrov's musical comedy films *The Happy Guys* (1934) and *Volga-Volga* (1938). RT

ERENBURG, Il'ya Grigor'evich (1891–1967) Born in Kiev, Erenburg is particularly known for his fiction and memoirs, his journalistic pieces on the Spanish Civil War and the Second World War, and for being the Soviet writer who best knew Europe and its avant-garde. In political emigration in Paris (1908–17), Erenburg began his career as a journalist and undistinguished poet. On his return, he initially rejected the Bolshevik Revolution and spent the Civil War with the Whites, but returned to Soviet Russia in 1923 (although he contrived to live abroad quite frequently in the pre-war years). He launched his career as a successful and prolific Soviet novelist with *The Extraordinary Adventures of Julio Juernito and of His Disciples* (Berlin, 1922), a picaresque satire of life in Europe and Russia from the First World War to the Revolution. His fiction of the Stalin era includes a novel in praise of the First Five-Year Plan, *The Second Day* (1934), and some war fiction – *The Fall of Paris* (1941), and *The Storm* (1947). Erenburg was an important figure in the post-Stalin thaws. His *The Thaw* (1954, 1956) argues inter alia for a less suspicious, less anti-foreign climate. His massive memoirs *People, Years and Life* (1960–65) were influential in reopening for the Soviet reader many aspects of Soviet and European cultural life in the twenties which had long been taboo subjects. KC

ERMLER (né Breslav, Vladimir), Fridrikh Markovich (1898–1967) Film director. Ermler was a Leningrad film director in the realist tradition. His films included: *Katka's Reinette Apples* (1926), *The Parisian Cobbler* (1927), *A Fragment of Empire* (1929), *Counterplan* (1932, with Yutkevich), *Peasants* (1935) and *A Great Citizen* (1937–39). Ermler's films confront the problems of everyday Soviet life in a straightforward unheroic manner. RT

ER'ZIYA (Nefedov), Stepan Dmitrievich (1876–1959) Sculptor. Mordavian by birth, Er'ziya studied sculpture at the Stroganov Institute in Moscow and MIPSA, before travelling to Italy in 1906. He produced some monumental sculpture immediately after the Revolution, and in 1926 emigrated to South America, returning to Moscow in 1950. He is remembered for his portraits, especially in wood. JEB

EYKHE, Robert Indrikovich (1890–1940) A second-ranking party and state official during the inter-war period, Robert Eykhe was born into a peasant family in what is now the Latvian republic. He joined the Bolsheviks in 1905 and in 1917 was elected chairman of the Riga Soviet. During the later 1920s he held the post of chairman of the Siberian territorial executive committee and from 1929 he headed the West Siberian territorial committee of the Communist Party, becoming a full member of the Central Committee in 1930 and a candidate member of the Politburo in 1935. Eykhe headed the People's Commissariat of Agriculture from 1937 until 1938 when he was arrested. He died in imprisonment. SLW

EYKHENBAUM, Boris Mikhaylovich (1886–1959) A Formalist literary scholar, Eykhenbaum became a member of OPOYAZ in 1918. During the twenties he wrote extensively on Russian writers, and especially on Tolstoy, Akhmatova, Lermontov and Nekrasov. His early Formalist writings stress the primacy of formal features in literature and deny the importance of extra-literary factors; for instance, 'How Gogol''s "Overcoat" was Made' (1919) argues that the point of the story is Gogol''s verbal play. In the late twenties, however, he acknowledged the role of extrinsic factors in a literary work. His *Leo Tolstoy* (1928) includes biographical material and combines to some degree the Formalist and sociological approaches. KC

F

FADEEV, Aleksandr Aleksandrovich (1901–1956) Born in Kimry near Moscow, he was a leading socialist-realist prose writer, literary politician and functionary. Fadeev spent from 1912 to 1921 in the Vladivostok area where he joined the party in 1918 and fought for the Reds in the Civil War. From 1926 he took up permanent residence in Moscow where he became a leader of the militant proletarian literary organization RAPP. He published several prose works about the Civil War during the twenties of which *The Rout* (1927), officially considered a classic of socialist realism, earned him broad recognition. *The Rout* shows the influence of Tolstoy and the mark of 'proletarian realism', the literary approach which RAPP writers espoused; the heroes, Red partisans in the Far East, were given fairly realistic psychological portraits, including failings and doubts, an approach which became unthinkable during the thirties and forties when the positive hero was idealized. His second, and unfinished novel, *The Last of the Udegs* (1929–40) is noted for its sociological sweep and ethnographic detail about the Udegs (a Siberian tribe), and for its conviction that political and economic progress will alleviate their lot. When the Writers Union was formed in 1932 most of the RAPP leadership suffered a reversal of fortunes, but Fadeev went on to occupy high positions in the Union which he headed during the grim Zhdanov years 1946–54. His *The Young Guard* (1945), based on a real story of Komsomol resistance in the Donbass region to the German occupation, won a Stalin Prize in 1946, but criticism in 1947 forced Fadeev to rewrite it, giving the party a greater guiding role in the resistance. The 1951 edition has become an exemplar of socialist realism. In the early fifties Fadeev worked on *Ferrous Metallurgy*, but after Stalin's death its informing values were discredited and he never completed the novel. He was demoted from head of the Writers Union in 1954 and, troubled by the revelations of de-Stalinization, shot himself in 1956. KC

FAKHREDDINOV, **Rizautdin** (1859–1936) Islamic educationalist, philosopher and theologian noted for his liberal approach to many issues. He wrote a large number of works on a wide variety of subjects including *Remarkable Women* (1903), a study of the contribution of women to Islamic culture and learning. He served as *kazi* of the Muslim Religious Board in Ufa (1891–1905) and as Mufti of the

USSR Central Muslim Religious Board (1922–36). MR

FALIN, Valentin Mikhaylovich (b. 1926) The son of an art historian and archaelogist, Valentin Falin was born in Leningrad. An intelligent and adaptable Soviet official and foreign policy specialist, he has made a successful career under both Brezhnev and Gorbachev. As a teenager during the war, Falin worked as a lathe operator in the Red Proletarian plant in Moscow, but proceeded to a higher education once the war was over. After graduating from the Moscow Institute of International Relations in 1950, he held a variety of posts in the Soviet Ministry of Foreign Affairs and the Central Committee of the Communist Party. He joined the party in 1953.

His primary speciality has been Germany and from 1968 until 1971 he was head of the Third European Department of the Ministry of Foreign Affairs (responsible for German and Austrian affairs). From 1971 to 1978 Falin was Soviet Ambassador to the Federal Republic of Germany and played a significant part in the improvement of Soviet-German relations. He was first deputy head of the International Information Department of the Central Committee (1978–83) and became in 1983 a leading member of the editorial staff of *Izvestiya*, from where he moved in 1986 to the chairmanship of the Soviet news agency, APN. He attained the most important post of his career in October 1988 when he was chosen to succeed Dobrynin as head of the International Department of the Central Committee. The post was no longer, however, accompanied by a Secretaryship of the Central Committee as it had been under his predecessor.

Falin was elected to candidate membership of the Central Committee in 1986 and promoted to full membership in April 1989. He became a member of the Congress of People's Deputies in the same year and was subsequently elected to the Supreme Soviet. He is a member of the International Affairs Committee of the Supreme Soviet and an important voice in foreign policy debates in Moscow. AHB

FAL'K, Robert Rafaylovich (1886–1958) Painter, born in Moscow. Fal'k is remembered for his Cézannist and Cubist portraits, landscapes and still-lives of the 1910s to 1920s. Trained in private studios and at MIPSA, Fal'k was a member of the Jack of Diamonds group in the 1910s and then of AKhRR in the 1920s. In 1928 he moved to Paris for ten years, and then to Central Asia (1938–44). After the War he taught at the Moscow Institute of Applied and Decorative Art. JEB

FAVORSKY, Vladimir Andreevich (1886–1964) One of the Soviet Union's leading graphic artists and illustrators, Favorsky trained in Moscow and then Munich before the Revolution. He taught at Vkhutemas-Vkhutein (1921–29), influencing an entire generation of young graphic artists, including Goncharov. He designed and illustrated books by many authors, including Dickens and Pushkin, and also investigated monumental painting, creating, *inter alia*, the frescoes for the Soviet pavilion at the 'Exposition Universelle' in Paris in 1937. JEB

FAYKO, Aleksey Mikhaylovich (1893–1978) Dramatist. Fayko wrote satirical comedies such as *The Dilemma* (1921), *Peerpoint Black's Career* (1922) and *Bubus the Teacher* (1925), the latter produced by Meyerkhol'd. After this his career went into a decline. RT

FAYNTSIMMER, Aleksandr Mikhaylovich (1906–1982) Film director. Trained in Pudovkin's workshop, Fayntsimmer's films include the highly original satire *Lieutenant Kizhe* (1934), which marked Prokof'ev's début as a composer of film music, and *The Gadfly* (1955) with a score by Shostakovich. RT

FEDIN, Konstantin Aleksandrovich (1892–1977) Born in Saratov, a prose writer, playwright, and literary functionary (First Secretary of the Writers Union (1959–71) and head of the Board (1971–77)). He spent from 1914 to 1918 in Germany where he was interned during the war, and returned to serve in the provincial press and Red Army, joining the party briefly (1919–21). In 1921 he moved to Petrograd where he joined the Serapion Brothers, forming part of its right (less experimentalist) wing. His best-known work, the novel *Cities and Years* (1924), which is set in both war-time Germany and revolutionary Russia and plays with time sequence, is concerned with the role of the intellectual in history. He returned to this theme for *The Brothers* (1928) which is about a musician who stands outside his revolutionary times and is hence condemned to solitude. In the thirties and forties Fedin's fiction became more representative of socialist realism. For instance, *The Rape of Europe* (1933–35) contrasts a Europe in decline with a Soviet Russia in the ascendant; similarly, *The Sanatorium Arktur* (1940), contrasts a healthy Soviet Russia with a morbid capitalist West. In the forties he began a trilogy which depicts a positive hero in three important moments for Soviet history: *Early Joys* (1945) finds him in Saratov in the

period beginning 1910 which leads up to the First World War; *No Ordinary Summer* (1947–48), set in 1919, shows a decisive turning point in the Civil War but distorts facts under the influence of the personality cult in, for instance, ascribing a strategic victory to Stalin rather than to Trotsky; and *The Bonfire* (1961, 1965) which shows the hero rushing to the defence of his country when the Germans invade in 1941. His best known play is *Bakunin in Dresden* (1922). KC

FEDORCHUK, Vitaliy Vasil'evich (b. 1918) A Ukrainian by nationality and a career intelligence officer, Fedorchuk aquired prominence in Moscow politics in the first half of the 1980s. A party member from 1940, he was an officer in *Smersh* from 1943 to 1947 and in military intelligence until 1970 when he became head of the Ukrainian KGB. When Yuriy Andropov left the Chairmanship of the KGB in 1982 to become a Secretary of the Central Committee (half a year before he became General Secretary on Brezhnev's death in November) Fedorchuk succeeded him in May as head of the KGB for the entire country. That he was a compromise choice, rather than Andropov's preferred successor, was indicated, however, when he was moved in December 1982 to the less powerful post of Minister of Internal Affairs in succession to the Brezhnev client, Nikolay Shcholokov, and he remained head of the MVD until his retirement in 1986. AHB

FEDOROV, Svyatoslav Nikolaevich (b. 1927) A highly successful Soviet eye surgeon who takes private as well as Soviet health service patients and who treats both foreigners and Soviet citizens at his own clinic (using the foreign currency earned to purchase better equipment), Fedorov, a

Russian by nationality, was elected to the Congress of People's Deputies of the USSR in 1989 on the Communist Party list. He is a member of the Committee of the Supreme Soviet for Questions of Economic Reform and he himself is a strong advocate of a market economy and of a substantial measure of privatization. Fedorov is a Corresponding Member of the Academy of Medical Sciences. AHB

FEDOROVSKY, Fedor Fedorovich (1883–1955) Designer. Born in Chernigov, Fedorovsky studied at the MIPSA under Konstantin Korovin and Mikhail Vrubel' before entering Zimon's Opera Company as resident artist. Known for his vivid colours and bravura, Fedorovsky designed many important productions before and after the Revolution, including *Carmen* at the Bol'shoy in 1922 and *Prince Igor* in 1934. JEB

FEDOSEEV, Petr Nikolaevich (b. 1908) One of the leading ideologists of the Brezhnev era, Petr Fedoseev began his career in the ideological apparatus under Stalin and although he survived as Vice-President of the Academy of Sciences with special responsibility for the social sciences until 1988, he had by that time become an obvious anachronism. Of Russian nationality, Fedoseev joined the Communist Party in 1939 and was a member of its Central Committee from 1961 until 1989 when he was one of seventy-four full members who simultaneously 'retired'. Fedoseev edited the journal, *Bol'shevik*, in the early post-war years, worked in the Central Committee apparatus (1950–54), and was Director of the Institute of Philosophy of the Academy of Sciences from 1955 to 1967 when he became Director of the Institute of Marxism-Leninism

attached to the Central Committee of the Communist Party. A Vice-President of the Academy of Sciences from 1971 until 1988, Fedoseev remained an adviser to the Academy's Presidium after his retirement. AHB

FEDOSEEV, Vladimir Ivanovich (b. 1932) Conductor. Vladimir Fedoseev was born in Leningrad. After studying accordion and conducting at the Gnesin Music Institute in Moscow, from which he graduated in 1957, he undertook post-graduate studies in operatic and symphonic conducting under Lev Ginzburg at the Moscow Conservatory, which he completed in 1971. In 1974 he was appointed conductor of the Grand Symphony Orchestra of the All-Union Radio and Television, Moscow. He became a party member in 1963 and was made a People's Artist of the RSFSR in 1973. GS

FERDINANDOV, Boris Alekseevich (1889–1959) Actor, director and designer. Ferdinandov was associated with the Moscow Kamernyy Theatre from 1917 to 1925 and worked thereafter in the provinces. He headed his own 'experimental heroic theatre' from 1921 to 1923 and developed the notion of metric rhythm as the basis of the actor's art. RT

FERSMAN, Aleksandr Yevgen'evich (1883–1945) Mineralogist, geochemist, administrator. A student and protégé of V. I. Vernadsky, Fersman graduated from Moscow University in 1907, studied abroad for several years, and worked under his mentor as senior curator in the Geological and Mineralogical Museum of the Petersburg Academy of Sciences (1912–30) and scientific secretary of its Commission on the Study of Natural Productive Forces (KEPS) (1915–30). Following his election to the Academy of Sciences in 1919, he became director of its Mineralogical Museum (1919–30). In the 1920s he directed the Radium Institute while Vernadsky was abroad (1922–26) and became a key Academy administrator, serving as academician-secretary of its science section (1924–27) and Academy vice-president (1926–29). Removed from many of his posts during the first Five-Year Plan, he headed the Academy's Institute of Crystallography, Mineralogy, and Geochemistry (1930–39), became president of the Academy's Ural affiliate (1931–38), and published *Geochemistry* (4 vols, 1933–39). Extending Vernadsky's ideas, he saw human activity as one of the factors reshaping the earth's crust by extracting, altering, and redistributing its constituents in a process he called 'technogenesis'. A specialist in pegmatites, he travelled widely and located rare deposits, notably radioactive ores, in the Urals, the Kola peninsula, Central Asia, and elsewhere within Soviet territory. Perhaps for this reason, during the Second World War he was made director of the Institute of Geological Sciences (1942–45) and head of the Geological Commission of the Red Army charged with locating and securing strategic materials. MBA

FILATCHEV, Oleg Pavlovich (b. 1937) Painter. Born in Moscow and graduating from the Moscow Institute of Industrial Art where he trained under S. Gerasimov, Filatchev then worked in Korzhev's studio (1968–71). He quickly emerged as a vital, new force in Soviet painting, favouring a contemplative, often allegorical approach, divergent from the more sober conventions of Socialist Realism. JEB

FILATOV, Sergey Mironovich (b. 1925) Sportsman. He was the first Soviet rider to win an Olympic equestrian event, the dressage, in 1960, riding Absent. Born in the Tambov Region, he competed in three Olympics and, besides his gold medal in 1960, he won two bronze medals in the 1964 Games; he was also seven times Soviet champion rider. Upon retirement, he became a riding coach at the Moscow Riding School. JWR

FILIPCHENKO (Philiptschenko), Yury Aleksandrovich (1882–1930) Experimental biologist and a founder of Soviet genetics. After graduating from St Petersburg University in 1905, Filipchenko studied in Europe with Richard Hertwig (1911–12) and became converted to the new experimental biology. In 1913 he opened the first Russian university course in genetics at St Petersburg University, began working with I. I. Ivanov at the Veterinary Laboratory on the inheritance of skull characteristics in hybrid cattle, and taught at V. M. Bekhterev's Psychoneurological Institute, where he became scientific secretary. After the revolution he founded the university's Department of Experimental Zoology and Genetics and published five textbooks and a dozen popular books on biology, eugenics, genetics, and the history of science that appeared in large and numerous editions. He founded the Academy of Sciences' Bureau of Eugenics in 1921 and was active in the Russian eugenics movement until 1925, when he took up agricultural genetics, concentrating on wheat and cattle. In Leningrad he trained a large proportion of Russia's geneticists, including Theodosius Dobzhansky, and his bureau subsequently became the Institute of Genetics, Russia's premier research centre in the field. Relieved of his teaching responsibilities in January 1930, Filipchenko died suddenly in May of cerebral meningitis. MBA

FILONOV, Pavel Nikolaevich (1883–1941) Painter, born in Moscow. Filonov received an irregular art education in St Petersburg, although, with his fierce individualism, he emerged as a key member of the avantgarde before the Revolution. He developed his own theory of painting called Analytical Art or Universal Flowering and supported this highly expressionistic, nervous style throughout the 1920s and 1930s. He was long branded for his 'formalism', although he continued to have many devoted students. JEB

FIL'SHIN, Gennadiy Innokent'evich (b. 1931) A member of Soviet of the Union of the USSR Supreme Soviet, Fil'shin is an active economic reformer and a member of its Planning and Budgetary-Finance Commission. He was elected to the Congress of People's Deputies from the Irkutsk territorial district in 1989 and is a member of the Inter-Regional Group of (radically reformist) Deputies within the legislature. He is a department head at the Institute of Economics of Industrial Production of the Siberian division of the Academy of Sciences. Fil'shin was a critic of the proposals on economic reform of the Council of Ministers of the USSR in May 1990 and proposed a vote of no confidence in the Soviet government. AHB

FLIER (Flière), Yakov Vladimirovich (1912–1977) Pianist and teacher. Yakov Flier was born in Orekhovo-Zueva and died in Moscow. A pupil at the Moscow Conservatory, he studied for a long period with Konstantin Igumnov, finally completing his post-graduate work with him in 1937. Whilst still a student he gained first prize at the Second All-Union Competition of Performing Musicians in Leningrad in 1935, as well as undertaking an extensive international concert tour. He won first prize at the International Pianists' Contest in Vienna the following year. In 1937 he became a teacher at the Moscow Conservatory. A member of the party since 1943, he was made a People's Artist of the USSR in 1966. As a teacher and performer he was highly regarded. GS

FOGEL', Vladimir Petrovich (1902–1929) Actor. Fogel' was a leading actor in Soviet silent films who had trained in Kuleshov's workshop. His most important role was that of the murderer in Kuleshov's *By the Law* (1926) but he also starred in Otsep's serial *Miss Mend* (1926) and in Barnet's *The Girl with the Hat Box* (1928). He committed suicide in 1929. RT

FOKINE (Fokin, Mikhail Mikhaylovich), Michel (1880–1942) Ballet dancer, teacher, and outstanding choreographer and reformer of ballet. Fokine graduated from the Imperial Ballet School in 1898. Upon graduation he joined the Mariinsky troupe as a soloist, an exception to standard practice, and made his début in *Paquita*. As a dancer, Fokine had great elegance, style, and expressiveness, and he performed in a broad range of classical and character roles. In 1901 he began teaching at the Imperial School. The next year he was put in charge of the intermediate class and in 1904, the senior girls' class. He taught until 1911, and his pupils included Yelizaveta Gerdt, Lydia Lopukhova, Yelena Smirnova, and Yelena Lyukom.

Greatly dissatisfied with the rigid,

classical traditions of ballet at the time, in 1904 Fokine proposed choreography for *Daphnis and Chloe*, a two-act ballet, and he accompanied his proposal with suggestions for ballet reform. In particular, he stressed the need for historical authenticity, the need for a unity of dance, music, scenery, and costumes, and the importance of dramatic expression. Although nothing concrete came of this proposal, these ideas formed the basis for all Fokine's later works and indeed his profound influence on the development of ballet in the twentieth century.

In 1905 Fokine choreographed *Acis and Galatea* for a performance at the Imperial School. This ballet incorporated some of his reforms and included a wonderfully acrobatic solo for Nijinsky.

He went on to choreograph a number of ballets and dances in operas for the Mariinsky Theatre, and personally appeared in many of them. These included: *Le Pavillon d'Armide* (1907), his first major work; *The Dying Swan* (1907), a solo dance for Anna Pavlova; *Egyptian Nights* (1908); the dances in *Tannhäuser* (1910); *Carnaval* (1910); the dances in *Orpheus and Eurydice* (1911); *Islamay* (1912); *Eros* (1915); and *Francesca da Rimini* (1915). He also staged *Stenka Razin* for the Russian State Theatre in 1915.

The most important and creative years of Fokine's career, however, were those associated with Diaghilev's Ballets Russes. From 1909 Fokine lived mostly in France, although he returned to Russia to fulfil his obligations at the Mariinsky Theatre. From 1909 to 1912 and again in 1914 he was Diaghilev's chief choreographer. With this company, Fokine collaborated with a group of highly talented and innovative composers and painters (including Benois, Bakst, and Stravinsky), and had an extraordinary group of dancers (including Nijinsky, Karsavina, Bolm and Doubrovska) to work with. The ballets he produced during these years fully realized his ideas for ballet reform and solidified his reputation as the father of modern ballet. Among Fokine's most important ballets were: *Cleopatra* (1909), *Les Sylphides* (1909), the Polovtsian Dances from the opera *Prince Igor* (1909), *Sheherazade* (1910), *Firebird* (1910), *Le Spectre de la Rose* (1911), *Petrushka* (1911), *Thamar* (1912), and *Midas* (1914).

After the Revolution, Fokine settled in New York where he taught and choreographed until his death in 1942. He worked with the Paris Opéra (1934–35), with the Ballet Russe de Monte Carlo (1936–39), and staged ballets in London, Mexico, South America, and Australia. His memoirs, articles, and letters were collected in *Protiv techeniya* (1962). SCS

FOMIN, Ivan Aleksandrovich (1872–1936) Architect, born in Orel. Along with Shchusev and Zholtovsky, Fomin is often regarded as mainly responsible for the development of Socialist Realism in Soviet architecture, although he began his career before the Revolution as a practitioner of the *style moderne*. He studied at the Academy of Arts and then in Western Europe before becoming an Academician in 1915. Shortly after the Revolution he played a major role in the replanning of parts of Petrograd, specifically the Field of Mars. Supporting a more decorative style in the 1930s, Fomin designed the Lermontov metro station in Moscow and submitted projects for a sanatorium in Sochi. JEB

FONVIZEN, Artur Vladimirovich (1882–1973) Painter. Born in Riga, Fonvizen studied at the MIPSA and in Munich, making his real début as a Symbolist painter with the Moscow Blue Rose group in 1907. He then moved towards a more Primitivist style, joining the Jack of Diamonds in 1910. He exhibited with various groups in the 1920s, including Makovets and AKhRR, concentrating on circus scenes and portraits, for example, of Dar'a Zerkalova (1940). His preferred medium was watercolour, in which he demonstrated great virtuosity. JEB

FOREGGER (né Greifenturn), Nikolay Mikhaylovich (1892–1939) An innovative stage director and choreographer, Foregger founded the Theatre of the Four Masks in 1918, producing 'evenings of French farce' starring Il'insky. In the 1920s he organized his own experimental workshop, Mastfor (*Masterskaya Foreggera*), using dance and acrobatics to depict the processes of industrial production. He worked in Moscow and Leningrad from 1924 to 1926 producing the cycle of *Historical Dances*, *The Constructivist Gopak* and *The Dance of Budenny's Cavalry*. He was the Principal Director of the Khar'kov Opera and Ballet Company from 1929 to 1934, choreographing the Polovtsian dances in Borodin's opera *Prince Igor* (1929), Oransky's ballet *The Footballer* (1930) and Brandt's opera *Hopkins the Engineer* (1931). His subsequent career was spent in lesser positions in Kiev and Kuybyshev. RT

FORSH, Ol'ga Dmitrievna (1873–1961) Born in Gunib (Dagestan), a writer of historical novels. Her first novel, *Stoneclad* (1924–25), is about the revolutionaries of the late nineteenth century. It shows the influence of Symbolism, theosophy, and Gogol' (about whom she later wrote in *The Contemporaries* of 1926). She produced two *romans-à-clef* about the Russian literary scene, *The Crazy Boat* (1931) about the milieu in the Petrograd House of Arts in the early twenties, and *The Raven* (published as *The Symbolists* in 1933), and also the three-volume *Radishchev* (1934–39) and a novel about the Decembrists, *The First-Born Sons of Freedom* (1950–53) KC

FROLOV, Ivan Timofeevich (b. 1929) After a career divided between scholarly and political work, Ivan Frolov has achieved a greater prominence under Gorbachev than ever before. A respected philosopher of science, he graduated from the Moscow University Philosophical Faculty in 1953, became a doctor of philosophical sciences in 1966 and a professor in 1970. He joined the Communist Party in 1960.

Frolov had two separate spells on the Prague-based *World Marxist Review* (1962–65 and 1977–79), the latter after ideological differences with the prevailing orthodoxy forced his departure from the editorship of the Soviet journal, *Voprosy filosofii*, which he held from 1968 to 1977. He had worked in the Central Committee apparatus (1965–68) as an aide to the Secretary of the Central Committee, Petr Demichev.

Frolov became successively Chairman of the Scientific Council on Philosophical and Social Problems of Science and Technology attached to the Presidium of the Academy of Sciences (1980), President of the Philosophy Society (1987), Chairman of a new National Committee for the History and Philosophy of Science and Technology (1988) and in 1989 Chairman of an all-union Centre for the

Study of Mankind (attached to the Presidium of the Academy of Sciences with the aim of producing inter-disciplinary scientific co-operation).

Frolov's political career meanwhile flourished under Gorbachev's leadership. He became a member of the Central Committee at the Twenty-Seventh Party Congress in 1986 and editor-in-chief of the party's theoretical journal, *Kommunist*, in the summer of the same year. He rapidly transformed the journal into a readable one containing a diversity of viewpoints. A year later he acquired still greater influence when he joined Gorbachev's personal staff as his aide with special responsibility for ideology. Further promotion followed in 1989 when Frolov was appointed editor-in-chief of *Pravda* in October and a Secretary of the Central Committee in December of that year. In July 1990 he became a member of the Politburo. AHB

FROLOV, Konstantin Vasil'evich (b. 1932) A Vice-President of the Academy of Sciences of the USSR since 1985, Konstantin Frolov has since 1980 been Director of the Academy's Institute of Machine Science. He became a candidate member of the Central Committee at the Twenty-Seventh Party Congress in 1986 and was a full member from 1989 to 1990. He was elected a member of the Congress of People's Deputies in March 1989 and to the Supreme Soviet in May of the same year where he is a member of its Committee on Science, Public Education, Culture and Upbringing. AHB

FRUNZE, Mikhail Vasil'evich (1885–1925) The archetypal 'Red commander', continually eulogized and partly mythologized, Frunze progressed from 'professional revo-lutionary' to military commissar, military commander, military theoretician and military reformer, imposing shape and order on the Soviet military system, the effects of which endure to this day. An adherent of the Bolsheviks after 1904 and participant in the 1905 revolution, arrested and sentenced to death, Frunze undertook agitational work for the party, organizing worker fighting squads and militias during and after the October revolution. In 1918 his military career proper began with his taking command of the Fourth Army on the Eastern Front, bringing order out of chaos and learning the business of command. In July 1919 he took command of the Eastern Front, sensibly using the professional advice of ex-Imperial officers, followed in August by his assignment to the Turkestan Front which completed the rout of the southern group of Kolchak's forces. In 1920, on Lenin's suggestion, Frunze commanded the Southern Front which finally carried through the defeat of Wrangel. Between 1920 and 1924 Frunze served in the Ukraine as the plenipotentiary of the Republic Revolutionary Military Council (RVSR), engaged in successful diplomatic negotiation between the Soviet Ukraine and Turkey and held command of the Soviet forces in the Ukraine and the Crimea.

At the close of the Civil War, Frunze emerged as the champion, the advocate of the 'Red commanders', experienced in command and dissatisfied with Trotsky's approach to the Red Army and military policy. Debates over military doctrine, though important in themselves, also became a screen for political and personal manoeuvring. At the Tenth Party Congress in 1921 Frunze suffered a rebuff at Trotsky's hands. Returning to the fray in July 1921, Frunze re-organized his arguments, emphasising the wealth of experience now available to the Red Army, the need to train for 'manoeuvre operations on a large scale' and, above all, the need for a regular Red Army rather than a militia system.

Trotsky's deadly ridicule served his cause badly. The 'Red commanders' feared an apparent move to defensivism and enduring military conservatism. The very fact that the 'military specialists' (ex-Imperial officers) chose to applaud Trotsky confirmed the worst fears of the 'Red command', a group steadily gaining ground with Frunze in the van. Frunze produced more detailed planning papers: the Red Army should be trained to a 'unified doctrine' and unity should be reflected in peace and war. Plans to end Trotsky's rule over the Red Army gathered pace. In January 1924 a special commission was set up to investigate the state of the Red Army, with Frunze as one of its members. On 11 March 1924 Frunze replaced Sklyansky as Trotsky's deputy and launched at once into plans to re-organize and reshape the Red Army, the era of 'military reform' designed to set up a unified military structure and implement a unified tactical doctrine. This was closely connected with Frunze's intense preoccupation with the scope of a future war and the capability of the Red Army to meet it. These ideas are still widely quoted today, in particular industrial mobilization, strategic planning and the integration of armed forces with society.

Frunze's tenure as Commissar for War completely displacing Trotsky, lasted only briefly. In the summer of 1925 he fell ill. At the end of October he was dead, the victim of a 'medical murder' according to some accounts, forced to undergo an operation urged on him by Stalin but which he could not stand. Frunze's successor, Voroshilov, was Stalin's compromise candidate and definitely Stalin's own man. Frunze's reforms, however, brought stability and a coherent structure to the Soviet military system, preparing the way for the full-scale modernization which he himself saw to be vital. The test of the soundness of much of his theoretical writing which became increasingly sophisticated lies in the varied applications which it finds today, not least in Colonel-General M. A. Garayev's recent work, *M. V. Frunze Military Theoretician* (Moscow, Voenizdat, 1985). JE

FURMANOV, Dmitriy Andreevich (1891–1926) A 'proletarian' prose writer born in Sereda (Kostroma Province) of peasant origins. Furmanov joined the Bolshevik Party in 1918 and was active in the proletarian literary groups October (1923) and VAPP (secretary of its Moscow branch 1924–25). His socialist-realist classic *Chapaev* (1923, made into a popular film in 1934) is based on Furmanov's experiences as a Red Army political commissar to that legendary Civil War commander. The novel contrasts Chapaev's spontaneity to his commissar's political consciousness and chronicles Chapaev's progressive political maturation. *The Revolt* (1925) concerns a struggle against rebellious units in Central Asia. KC

FURTSEVA, Yekaterina Alekseevna (1910–1974) The first woman member of the Politburo (or Presidium of the Central Committee, as it was known in Khrushchev's time),

Furtseva

Furtseva was born into a working-class family in what is now the Kalinin region of Russia. She received a technical education and made her early career in Komsomol and party work. (She joined the party at the age of nineteen in 1930.) From 1942 until 1950 she was a district party secretary in Moscow and in 1950 she became Second Secretary for the city. In 1952 that post brought her candidate membership of the Central Committee of the party.

Furtseva was a close ally of Khrushchev and once he had become party leader her career flourished. In 1954 she became First Secretary of the Moscow city party organization, a post she held until 1957 – from 1956 in conjunction with a Secretaryship of the party Central Committee, even though she had only become a full member of the Central Committee in that year. It was in 1956 also that she attained candidate membership of the Presidium (Politburo) and in 1957 she was elevated to full membership. At the beginning of the 1960s, however, Furtseva's career suffered a downturn. In 1960 she became Minister of Culture, an important office but less powerful than the Secretaryship of the Central Committee from which she was removed, and in 1961 she ceased to be a member of the Presidium of the Central Committee.

As Minister of Culture, Furtseva pursued a conformist course and had no trouble in keeping her ministerial office for the first ten years of Brezhnev's General Secretaryship – until her death in November 1974. Her cultural knowledge was slender and her main function was to maintain political and ideological control over Soviet artistic life. In that she was largely successful. AHB

G

GABO, Naum (Pevsner, Naum Neemya) (1890–1977) Sculptor, born in Bryansk. Often regarded as the father of Constructivist sculpture, Gabo arrived at his severe style after studying in Munich. Returning to Russia in 1917, Gabo and his brother Antoine Pevsner compiled and published their *Realistic Manifesto* (1920). From 1919 to 1922 he designed a number of utilitarian objects such as a radio station, before emigrating to Germany. Subsequently, he lived and worked in France, England and America. JEB

GABRILOVICH, Yevgeny Osipo-vich (b. 1899) Scriptwriter. Gabrilovich's works have included Raizman's *The Last Night* (1937), *Mashenka* (1943) and *A Communist* (1958). RT

GAGARIN, Yuriy Alekseevich (1934–1968) Yuriy Gagarin made the first ever human flight in space on 12 April 1961 in a *Vostok* spacecraft launched from the Baikonur space centre. He was born in a village in the Smolensk region and joined the air force in 1955. After study at the Chkalov military aviation school in 1957 he served as a fighter pilot, joining the group of pioneer Soviet cosmonauts in 1960. After his historic flight Gagarin was an active participant in the space programme, helping to train future cosmonauts. He also became a roving ambassador, propagating Soviet science and technology in many countries of the world. Gagarin joined the party in 1960, served for a period as a Supreme Soviet deputy, and was made a Hero of Socialist Labour in 1961. He was killed in a flying accident in March 1968. JMC

GAGAROV, Dmitriy Nikolaevich (b. 1938) A member of the CPSU since 1966, Dmitriy Gagarov graduated in 1962 from the Far Eastern Polytechnical Institute and in 1978 as an external student from the Higher Party School in Moscow. He worked as an engineer in industry after graduation, and then as first deputy chairman of the Vladivostok town council (1972–73). He was first secretary of a district party committee in Vladivostok from 1973, becoming chairman of the town council in 1975, and moving back to party work as first secretary of the city committee of the CPSU in 1978. He became second secretary of the Primorskiy *kray* party committee in 1979, working from 1983 in the Central Committee apparatus in Moscow, and then returning in 1984 to the Far East as first secretary of the Primorskiy *kray* CPSU committee. He became a full member of the

Central Committee in 1986 and was awarded the Order of Lenin in 1988. SLW

GAISINOVICH, Abba Yevseevich (1906–1989) Historian of biology. A 1928 graduate of Moscow University, Gaisinovich worked briefly as a geneticist before turning to the history of science in the mid-1930s. The world's leading scholar on K. F. Wolff, Élie Mechnikov, and the history of Soviet genetics, he was internationally recognized as the Soviet Union's most erudite historian of biology. MBA

GALICH, Aleksandr Arkadievich (pseud. of Ginzburg) (1919–1977) Guitar poet. Galich was born in Yekaterinoslav (now Dnepropetrovsk) and moved with his family to Moscow in 1926. After training as an actor under Stanislavsky, Galich entered the theatre, spending the Second World War as a forces entertainer, then prospered as a dramatist and film writer. He turned to writing and performing satirical songs in 1962; they circulated widely in clandestine tape recordings, but were published only abroad. In 1971 Galich was expelled from the Union of Writers. Forced into emigration in 1974, he was active as a broadcaster until his accidental death in Paris. One of the great Russian satirists, Galich presented a wide range of human types dealing with typical Soviet situations in life and work and speaking in authentic colloquial language. He was rehabilitated posthumously in 1988, and his work began to be published widely in leading Soviet journals the same year. GSS

GAMALEYA, Nikolay Fedorovich (1859–1949) Microbiologist and epidemiologist. After graduation from Novorossiysk University (1880) and the Military Surgical Academy (1883), Gamaleya studied in Paris with Louis Pasteur (1886). There he helped to improve the rabies vaccine and demonstrated that cattle plague is caused by a filterable virus. In 1886 he helped organize Russia's first bacteriological station in Odessa, where the first rabies vaccinations were performed. In 1899 the Bacteriological Institute was founded in Odessa on his initiative and he served as its director until 1908. He was in charge of public health measures during the outbreak of plague in Odessa (1901–2). He subsequently served as director of the Vaccination Institute in Petrograd (1912–28) and the Central Institute of Epidemiology and Bacteriology (1930–38), and chairman of the microbiology department of the Second Moscow Medical Institute (1938–49). He was the founding and perpetual honorary president of the All-Union Society of Microbiologists and Epidemiologists (1939). During his final years, he headed a laboratory at the Institute of Epidemiology and Microbiology of the USSR Academy of Medical Sciences. Following his death in 1949, the institute was named after him and the Academy established a prize in his honour. MBA

GAMSAKHURDIA, Zviad Konstantinovich (b. 1939) Georgian nationalist and literary scholar. Gamsakhurdia has also been an advocate since the early 1970s of human rights, environmental protection, greater religious and cultural freedom, and the abolition of torture in Georgian prisons. In 1977 he co-founded a Georgian group to monitor observation of the 1975 Helsinki accords. Arrested in 1977, he partially recanted and was freed in 1979. PBR

GAPONENKO, Taras Gur'evich (b. 1906) Painter. Born in Moscow. Gaponenko studied at Vkhutein under Favorsky and P. Kuznetsov before becoming a member of AKhRR in 1929. He accepted the principles of Socialist Realism, exemplified in pictures such as *To Mummy for Lunch* (1935) and *After the Expulsion of the Fascist Invaders* (1943–46). JEB

GAPRINDASHVILI, Nona Terent'-evna (b. 1941) Chess player. Born in the Georgian town of Zugdidi, she dominated world women's chess for sixteen years between 1962 and 1978, being undefeated world champion in that period until her defeat by Maya Chiburdanidze in 1978. She became international master at the age of twenty. JWR

GARDIN, Vladimir Rostislavovich (1877–1965) Film director, actor and scriptwriter before and after the Revolution. Gardin founded the State Film School in Moscow in 1919 and his numerous films include, as director: *The Kreutzer Sonata* (1914), agitfilms in the Civil War period, *The Locksmith and the Chancellor* (1924), *Cross and Mauser* (1925) and *The Poet and the Tsar* (1927); and as actor: *Counterplan* (1932) and *Peasants* (1935). RT

GARIN, Erast Pavlovich (1902–1980) Character actor of stage, radio and film. Garin was associated with the Meyerkhol'd Theatre and specialized in satire. His stage roles included Ehrenburg's *Give Us Europe!* (1924) and Erdman's *The Warrant* (1925 and 1956). His films included: *Lieutenant Kizhe* (1934), *A Musical Story* (1941) and *Zolushka* (1947). RT

GASPARYAN (née Khachatryan), Goar Mikaelovna (b. 1924) Coloratura soprano. Goar Gasparyan was born in Cairo. Receiving her first musical education in Egypt, she moved to Armenia in 1948, becoming a soloist the following year with the Armenian Theatre of Opera and Ballet. Since 1965 she has taught at the Yerevan Conservatory. She was made a People's Artist of the USSR in 1956 and has been awarded several State Prizes. The possessor of an exceptionally wide range, she has several times toured abroad. GS

GAUK, Aleksandr Vasil'evich (1893–1963) Conductor. Gauk was born in Odessa. After studying at the Petrograd Conservatory from which he graduated in 1917, he became conductor of the Leningrad Theatre of Opera and Ballet (1920–31), and was then appointed conductor of the Leningrad Philarmonic (1930–34). He conducted the State Symphony Orchestra of the USSR (1936–41), and was chief conductor of the Grand Symphony Orchestra of the All-Union Radio (1933–36 and 1953–62). Apart from his work in promoting large-scale Soviet orchestral works, he was also active as a teacher and a composer, one of his accomplishments being the restoration of Rakhmaninov's First Symphony from the surviving instrumental parts. He became a People's Artist of the RSFSR in 1954. GS

GAUZE (Gause), Georgiy Frantsevich (1910–1988) Ecologist, microbiologist. A graduate of Moscow University (1931) where he studied ecology with V. V. Alpatov, Gauze performed a series of classic experiments demonstrating that when two or three different kinds of microorganisms were grown together in a given culture medium, one kind always out-competed (and eventually eliminated) the others but, in slightly different media, different strains triumphed. These results, published in his classic monograph *The Struggle for Existence* (Baltimore, 1934), established what came to be called the 'competitive exclusion principle' (or the 'Gause-Witte law') and constituted one of the first experimental demonstrations of competition and natural selection. In the mid-1930s Soviet ecology became highly politicized and Gauze took up work on antibiotics, first at Moscow University, then in the Health Ministry's Institute of Parasitology and Tropical Medicine (1942), and finally as head of the laboratory of antibiotics of the USSR Academy of Medical Sciences (1948), transformed in 1960 into its Institute for New Antibiotics (1960) which he directed. He is chiefly remembered in the Soviet Union as a pioneer in antibiotics research, but in the West as a founder of modern ecological theory. MBA

GDLYAN, Tel'man Khorenovich (b. 1940) The senior investigator and head of a group responsible for especially serious crimes attached to the office of the Procurator General of the USSR, Gdlyan – an Armenian by nationality – has become a popular orator and member of parliament on the basis of his successful prosecution of corruption in high places and his accusations against members of the Politburo and, in particular, Yegor Ligachev. He first achieved prominence as the person who brought to justice leading members of the political establishment of Uzbekistan (the 'Uzbek affair') who had links to senior figures in Moscow, including Leonid Brezhnev's son-in-law, Churbanov – at the time Deputy Minister of Interior.

Although there have been accusations that improper methods were used in extracting confessions in that case which ended with many jail sentences and although Gdlyan and his colleague, Nikolay Ivanov, have been criticized for making subsequent state-ments concerning corruption in the highest circles of the present Soviet leadership without bringing forward any evidence to support it, Gdlyan has become something of a folk hero and a regular speaker at mass rallies in Moscow. He was elected to the Congress of People's Deputies from the Tushinsky district of Moscow in 1989 and has taken a vigorous part in parliamentary debates.

Although a lot of Soviet intellectuals express doubts about some of Gdlyan's more recent accusations – many even of Yegor Ligachev's political opponents argue that there is neither evidence nor reason for believing Gdlyan's accusations of corruption – and although the Congress of People's Deputies passed in 1990 a vote of censure on Gdlyan and Ivanov for their unsubstantiated assertions, the Soviet legislature stopped short of yielding to demands from the country's leadership that Gdlyan and Ivanov be stripped of their parliamentary immunity. That would have meant that they themselves could have faced court charges relating to their methods of investigation and allegedly slanderous remarks. Gdlyan remains a member of the Congress of People's Deputies, but (along with Ivanov) he was expelled from membership of the Communist Party in 1990. AHB

GELOVANI, Mikhail Georgievich (1893–1956) Actor. Gelovani was the Georgian actor best known for his portrayal of Stalin in the films: *The Great Glow* and *The Man with the Rifle* (both 1938), *The Vyborg Side* and *Lenin in 1918* (both 1939), *Valeriy Chkalov* (1941), *The Defence of Tsaritsyn* (1942), *The Vow* (1946) and *The Fall of Berlin* (1950). RT

GEL'TSER, Yekaterina Vasil'evna
(1876–1962) Prima ballerina of the
Bol'shoy Theatre, where she danced
for more than forty years, and the first
ballerina to be named Honoured
Artist of the RSFSR (1925). Daughter
of the celebrated dancer Vasily
Gel'tser, Yekaterina Gel'tser graduated from the Bol'shoy Ballet School
in 1894 and danced with the Bol'shoy
troupe for two years. She then went to
St Petersburg to perfect her technique
with Christian Johansson at the Mariinsky Theatre.

In 1898 Gel'tser returned to the
Bol'shoy where, in 1901, she received
great acclaim for her performance in
Raymonda and was made prima ballerina. After Aleksandr Gorsky took over
the troupe in 1912 Gel'tser performed
in a wide repertoire of classical ballets,
including *Sleeping Beauty*, *Swan Lake*,
and *Coppélia*, and was a great success in
Gorsky's *Salambo* (1910). Her flawless
technique and expressiveness earned
her the title 'queen of adagio'.

Gel'tser continued to dance with the
Bol'shoy troupe after her husband
Vasily Tikhomirov took over the
company in 1924. She danced in his
revivals of a number of classical ballets
and in his landmark production *The
Red Poppy* (1927). Gel'tser retired from
the Bol'shoy in 1935 and toured the
Soviet Union, performing until 1944.
SCS

GEORGADZE, Mikhail Porfir'evich
(1912–1982) As Secretary of the Presidium of the Supreme Soviet, Georgadze signed most Soviet legislation
between 1957 and the end of 1982.
Born near Chiatura, Georgia, he
became a farm administrator and,
after Stalin's death, Minister of Agriculture and Party Second Secretary in
Georgia, before he transfered to
Moscow. JHM

**GERASIMOV, Aleksandr Mikhay-
lovich** (1881–1963) Painter, born in
Kozlov. Generally identified as one of
Stalin's 'court painters', A. Gerasimov
received his training at the MIPSA
under Abram Arkhipov, Konstantin
Korovin and Valentin Serov. He was
a member of AKhRR in the 1920s,
supporting a heroic, rhetorical style
evident in paintings such as *Lenin on
the Tribune* (1930). From 1947 to 1957
he was president of the Academy of
Arts. JEB

GERASIMOV, Gennadiy Ivanovich
(b. 1930) Gennadiy Gerasimov, who
has gained international fame in
recent years as chief spokesman for the
Soviet Ministry of Foreign Affairs, was
born in Kazan' and spent the greater
part of his career as a journalist. He
worked for the weekly, *New Times*, and
the newspaper, *Trud*, and on the *World
Marxist Review* in Prague before spending three years (1964–67) in the
Central Committee apparatus as one
of the team of consultants of Yuriy
Andropov in the Socialist Countries
Department.

Returning to journalism, he worked
for the Novosti press agency and was
chief of their Washington bureau from
1972 to 1977. He was editor-in-chief
of *Moscow News* (1983–86), although
it was only under his successor, Yegor
Yakovlev, that that weekly newspaper
became one of the flagships of *glasnost'*.

However, Gerasimov has been an
important voice of *perestroika* and the
'new political thinking' in his job as
principal spokeman for the Ministry
of Foreign Affairs which he has held
since July 1986. An adept performer
at his frequent press conferences, he
has skilfully interpreted Soviet internal as well as external policy for the
world press. His fluent English and
dry sense of humour have made him

eminently quotable. One Gerasimov coinage in particular has entered the vocabulary of politics – the phrase, the 'Sinatra doctrine', to indicate in 1989 that the Soviet Union was ready to let the East European countries do it *their* way. The contrast being made was with the 'Brezhnev doctrine' which emphasized that the Soviet Union and other Communist countries had the right and duty to intervene to 'defend socialism' in any country of 'the socialist commonwealth' where socialism, as they defined it, appeared to be threatened. AHB

GERASIMOV, Sergey Apollinar'-evich (1906–1985) Film director, actor and scriptwriter. Gerasimov was a member of the Leningrad FEKS group and acted in many Kozintsev and Trauberg films, usually playing a villain. Among the films he directed were: *Komsomolsk* (1938), *Masquerade* (1941), *The Young Guard* (1948) and *Quiet Flows the Don* (1957–58). RT

GERASIMOV, Sergey Vasil'evich (1885–1964) Painter. Born in Mozhaisk, S. Gerasimov studied at the Stroganov Institute (1901–7) and the MIPSA (1907–12). He was attracted to the painting of Konchalovsky and Mashkov although he was never a radical or experimental artist. He taught at Vkhutemas-Vkhutein (1920–29) and after 1930 at the Moscow Polygraphical Institute. He received wide acclaim in the 1930s for his interpretations of the new Soviet countryside such as *Collective Farm Harvest Festival* (1935). JEB

GERDT, Yelizaveta Pavlovna (1891–1975) Celebrated ballerina and teacher. Daughter of the illustrious classical dancer Pavel Gerdt, Yelizaveta Gerdt studied with Anna Johansson at the Imperial Ballet School and graduated in 1908. In 1907 Michel Fokine had given her the role of Armide in *The Animated Gobelins* and she danced in *Chopiniana* at her graduation performance.

Gerdt joined the Mariinsky troupe in 1908 and was promoted to first soloist in 1913. She danced with the company until 1928, performing leading roles in a wide repertoire of ballets, including *Le Pavillon d'Armide*, *Carnaval*, *Raymonda*, *Chopiniana*, *Giselle*, and *Swan Lake*. Gerdt, who was often partnered by Mikhail Dudko, was known for her impeccable technique, sculptural line, and restrained grace. In addition to her classical roles, Gerdt danced in such experimental ballets as Lopukhov's *The Red Whirlwind* (1924) and *Pulcinella* by Igor' Stravinsky and Leonide Massine (1926).

After retiring from the stage, Gerdt taught at the Leningrad Ballet School (1927–34) and coached soloists and taught at the Bol'shoy Ballet School (1935–42, 1945–60). Her students include Maya Plisetskaya, Alla Shelest, Raisa Struchkova, and Yekaterina Maksimova. SCS

GERMAN, Aleksey Borisovich (b. 1938) Probably the best-known of the younger film-makers whose works were 'delayed' in the Brezhnev era, German's two most important films both tackle central questions of personal responsibility in the Stalin period. *Trial on the Road* was made in 1971 but only released in 1986. *My Friend Ivan Lapshin* was delayed for a shorter period and was first shown on television to launch the campaign for a re-examination of the 1930s. RT

GERSHENZON (Gershenson), Sergey Mikhaylovich (b. 1906) Geneticist. A student of N. K. Kol'tsov at Moscow University in the 1920s, Gershenzon was a member of the group at his Institute of Experimental Biology, headed by Sergey Chetverikov, that founded population genetics and conducted the first studies of the genetics of natural populations of drosophila. In the 1930s he worked at N. I. Vavilov's Institute of Genetics in the laboratory of Nobel prize-winner H.J. Muller. In 1937 he moved to Kiev, where he published one of the first studies suggesting that DNA might be the hereditary material (1939). As head of a division of the Institute of Zoology of the Ukrainian Academy of Sciences to 1963, he helped to keep genetics alive throughout the Lysenko period and pioneered the development of molecular biology in the Ukraine. With the rebirth of Soviet genetics (1963–65), he became chief of the Ukrainian Academy's Sector on Molecular Biology and Genetics (1968–73) and director of the molecular genetics division of its Institute of Molecular Biology and Genetics (1973–). In 1975 he created and became editor of one of the best Soviet genetics journals, *Tsitologiya i genetika*, and since 1976 he has been a full member of the Ukrainian Academy of Sciences. MBA

GESSEN (Hessen), Boris Mikhaylovich (1883–1938) Historian and philosopher of science. A party member and a student of physics in the 1920s, Gessen is principally remembered for his paper 'The Social and Economic Roots of Newton's *Principia*', presented at the first international Congress of the History of Science (London, 1931), which argued that Newton's mathematical science addressed the major technical problems created by the mercantile capitalism of his age, for example, shipbuilding, navigation, ballistics, and mining. The paper exercised a formative influence on the development of the history of science in Britain and America. Elected a corresponding member of the USSR Academy of Sciences in 1933, Gessen was arrested and shot in the 1938 purge. MBA

GIDASPOV, Boris Veniaminovich (b. 1933) An example (like Yevgeniy Primakov) of a CPSU leader who has not risen through the bureaucracy. A respected industrial chemist and corresponding member of the Academy of Sciences, Gidaspov worked in research institutes in Kuybyshev (1955–59) and since 1959 in Leningrad. From 1977 he was director of the State Institute of Applied Chemistry and in the 1980s he developed 'Tekhnokhim', a commercial association of research institutes based in Leningrad. Elected to the Congress of People's Deputies (when almost all the Leningrad leadership was defeated), he replaced Yuriy Solov'ev as Leningrad party leader in July 1989, soon acquiring a reputation for conservative policies and a somewhat Russian nationalist disposition. JHM

GILEL'S, Emil' Grigor'evich (1916–1985) Pianist. Gilel's was born in Odessa. Having first studied with Yakov Tkach and Berta Reyngbal'd at the Odessa Conservatory, where he graduated in 1935, he then undertook a further three-year period of study at the Moscow Conservatory with Genrikh Neugauz (Heinrich Neuhaus), being appointed to the staff in 1938. He gained first prize at the Moscow Competition in 1933, and second prize at the International Vienna Competition in 1936, and he won the Ysaÿe Concourse in Brussels in 1938. Apart from being made a People's Artist of the USSR in 1954, he was awarded several State Prizes and was an honorary member of the

London Royal Academy of Music. A veteran international performer, he left many recordings. GS

GINZBURG, Abram Moiseevich (1878–193?) A leading non-party economist in VSNKh in the 1920s, specializing in industry. Born in Vitebsk *guberniya*, the son of a timber industrialist, Ginzburg went to Khar'kov University, but left after one year. He was an active participant in the workers' movement, which resulted in his arrest and exile. He joined the Mensheviks in 1905, but abandoned underground work and became the leader of the Union of Metalworkers in 1906. He specialized increasingly as an economist from 1912, working in the cooperative movement and local government in Kiev, and being put in charge of rationing there in October 1916. He opposed the October Revolution, and was a prominent official in the anti-Bolshevik Kiev *rada* during the Civil War. He held senior posts in VSNKh (1922–29), and prepared the first full VSNKh draft of a five-year plan in Spring 1927. He was the author of several books on industrial economics. Arrested in 1930, Ginzburg was sentenced to ten years deprivation of freedom in the 'Menshevik' trial of March 1931. RWD

GINZBURG, Aleksandr Il'ich (b. 1936) Human rights activist and *samizdat* editor. He was jailed first (1960–62) after editing one of the early *samizdat* literary journals, *Sintaksis* (1959–60), then from 1967 to 1972 for compiling a 'White Book' on the case of the arrested writers Sinyavsky and Daniel, and from 1977 to 1979 for, among other political offences, organizing an aid fund for the families of political prisoners. He was released early in a Soviet-American prisoner exchange, and emigrated to France. PBR

GINZBURG, Moisey Yakovlevich (1892–1946) Architect. Born in Minsk, Ginzburg – a theoretical and practical supporter of Constructivism in architecture – received his professional training in Milan before returning to Russia in 1917. He clarified the principles of Constructivism in two important books, *Rhythm and Architecture* (1923) and *Style and the Epoch* (1924), arguing that architecture should be the organizer, not the decorator, of life. With A. Vesnin, he edited the journal *SA* (*Sovremenna arkhitektura*) (1926–30), and became a de-urbanist in the 1930s. Among his buildings are the House of Textiles in Moscow (1925) and the Government House in Alma-Ata (1927–31). JEB

GINZBURG, Yevgeniya Semenovna (1904–1977) Writer and memoirist. When she was arrested in 1937 in Kazan', she was a teacher, a Communist, and mother of two boys. Her early publications in *Yunost'* in 1965 and 1966 prefigure her two outstandingly powerful volumes of prison and labour camp memoirs, called in English *Journey into the Whirlwind* (1967) and *Within the Whirlwind* (1979), unpublished in the Soviet Union until 1988. The first volume describes her life from 1934 to 1939 and the second ends with her 1955 return to Moscow. Her son is the writer Vasiliy Aksenov, with whom she was reunited in Magadan in 1947, before being rearrested in 1949. BH

GIRENKO, Andrey Nikolaevich (b. 1936) A Secretary of the Central Committee since September 1989, Girenko is a Ukrainian born in the town of Krivoy Rog, the son of an industrial worker who was killed at the front during the Second World War and a mother who was an engineer. He graduated from the mining institute in Krivoy Rog in 1958 and – by extra-mural studies – from the Higher Party School of the Central Committee in 1971.

Girenko worked as an engineer while at the same time making his way up the ladder of the Komsomol in the Ukraine. In 1963 he became First Secretary of the Komsomol for Krivoy Rog, in 1967 First Secretary in Dnepropetrovsk, in 1970 Second Secretary and from 1972 First Secretary of the Central Committee of the Komsomol for the Ukraine.

Girenko moved into the party apparatus in 1975. He held the rank of inspector in the Ukrainian Central Committee and then moved to the Kherson regional party committee as Second Secretary and from 1980 as First Secretary. In 1987 he became First Secretary of the Crimean regional party committee and it was from that post that he was elevated to a Secretaryship of the Central Committee in 1989. Within the Secretariat he has had special responsibilities for a variety of sensitive inter-ethnic issues, including in 1990 that of the Baltic republics. AHB

GLADILIN, Anatoliy Tikhonovich (b. 1935) A prose writer best known as a pioneer of 'youth prose' with his novellas *Chronicle of the Time of Viktor Podgursky* (1956) and *The Brigantine Raises its Sails* (1959). The heroes of this school come from the young generation and experience existential *angst*. Its fiction breaks away from the univocal tradition of socialist realism; the narrative includes slang, fragments of diaries, radio and television broadcasts, popular songs, letters and newspaper articles. Gladilin published his novel *The Prognosis for Tomorrow* in

Germany in 1972 and emigrated in 1976 where he published *The Making and Unmaking of a Soviet Writer* (1979). KC

GLADKOV, Fedor Vasil'evich (1883–1958) A prose writer, born into an Old Believer background in Chernyavka near Saratov. Gladkov was active in the revolutionary literary and political movement from 1900 to the Civil War. He joined the party in 1920, but became a prominent writer and journalist only after moving to Moscow in 1921 and joining the proletarian literary organization Smithy in 1923. Smithy's writers tended to an industrial romanticism with larger-than-life heroes, and this was especially true of Gladkov's fiction. His novel *Cement* (1925) was hailed by Lunacharsky and others as showing the way of the future for Soviet literature and has proved one of the most influential models for socialist realism and essentially *the* prototype of the Soviet production novel. It tells how Gleb Chumalov, a Civil War hero and party activist, returns to his home town and overcomes overwhelming obstacles in restoring its cement factory. The novel is also known for its love plot whereby Gleb's wife Dasha, the Soviet new woman, refuses to be treated as a mere wife and sex object; she abandons her marriage and child in order to devote herself completely to the cause. Gladkov's next novel, *Energy* (1932–38), which tells of the construction of the Dneproges hydroelectric plant during the First Five-Year Plan, is also considered a classic of socialist realism but has never enjoyed the great popularity of *Cement*. In the forties, somewhat in imitation of his mentor Gor'ky, Gladkov embarked on a trilogy about his own childhood: *A Story about Childhood*

(1949), *The Self-Willed Child* (1950) and *Wild Times* (1954); a fourth volume, *Rebellious Youth* (1956, 1961), was not finished. From 1945 to 1948 he was director of the Gor'ky Literary Institute. KC

GLAZUNOV, Il'ya Sergeevich (b. 1930) Painter, born in Leningrad. Glazunov graduated from the Repin Institute, Leningrad, in 1957 and quickly gained the reputation of an 'angry young man' among Soviet artists for his free style and unorthodox subjects. Over recent years he has turned increasingly to Mediaeval Russia as a source of inspiration, although his major genre remains portraiture which he also teaches at the Surikov Institute in Moscow. JEB

GLIER (Glière), Reyngol'd Moritsevich (1875–1956) Composer, conductor and teacher. Reyngol'd Glier (Reinhold Glière) was born in Kiev and died in Moscow. After graduating brilliantly from the Moscow Conservatory in 1900, where his teachers included Ippolitov-Ivanov (composition), Arensky (harmony), Taneev (polyphony) and Hřimalý (violin), in 1901 he became a teacher at the Gnesin music school in Moscow. After a further two-year period (1906–8) studying conducting in Berlin with Oskar Fried, he returned to Russia, being appointed a professor at the Kiev Conservatory in 1913 and its Director in 1914. From 1920 to 1941 he was a professor at Moscow Conservatory. He was made a People's artist of the USSR in 1938 and a Doctor of Arts in 1941. A prolific composer in many genres, his Third Symphony *Il'ya Muromets* (1909–11) is his outstanding pre-revolutionary work. The ballet *The Red Poppy* (1927) was the first Soviet choreographical composition to be written to a rev-

olutionary theme. He both collected folksongs in different countries and endeavoured to popularize Russian-Soviet music. GS

GLIZER, Yudif' Samoilovna (1904–1968) Stage actress. Yudif' Glizer worked with *Proletkul't* from 1921 to 1928, then in the Theatre of the Revolution. She appeared in a wide variety of plays from Schiller's *Mary Stuart* (1930) to Brecht's *Mother Courage* (1960) via Scribe's *The Art of Conspiracy* (1936). She was married to Maksim Shtraukh. RT

GLUSHCHENKO, Ivan Yevdokimovich (1907–1987) Plant breeder, Lysenkoist. Glushchenko graduated from the Khar'kov Agroeconomic Institute in 1930 and became an early partisan of Lysenko's 'Michurinist' biology. Following Lysenko's takeover of the Institute of Genetics of the USSR Academy of Sciences in 1940, Glushchenko was brought in to head its laboratory of plant genetics (1941–65), during which time he was among the most strident of Lysenko's supporters. With the end of Lysenkoism in 1965, Glushchenko moved his work to the Institute of Soil Science of the Lenin All-Union Academy of Agricultural Sciences (1965–75) and, after 1976, headed the laboratory of plant development at its Institute of Applied Molecular Biology and Genetics. MBA

GLUSHKO, Valentin Pavlovich (1908–1988) Valentin Glushko was one of the last survivors of the group of prominent pioneers of the Soviet rocket programme: almost all the main missile and space-launcher motors used to date were developed under his leadership. A Ukrainian, born in Odessa, Glushko graduated from Leningrad University in 1929 and immediately began work at the

Gas Dynamics Laboratory (GDL) then located in Leningrad. Here he created the first Soviet liquid-fuel rocket motor (1930–31). For most of the 1930s he headed GDL, now a department of the Moscow Rocket-Propulsion Institute (RNII), and developed a series of rocket engines. In 1938 he was arrested and worked for a time under a prison regime. After the war Glushko headed the country's principal liquid-propellant rocket engine design organization and in 1974 was appointed head and general designer of the former Korolev design bureau at Kaliningrad, near Moscow. This leading organization of the Soviet space programme later became the scientific-production association 'Energiya': Glushkov was its general director until his death. In 1958 he was elected a full member of the Academy of Sciences. He joined the party relatively late, in 1956, and from 1976 until his death was a full member of the Central Committee. His many awards included Hero of Socialist Labour (1956, 1961), a Lenin Prize (1957) and two State Prizes (1967, 1984). JMC

GODUNOV, Aleksandr (b. 1949) Ballet dancer. Godunov studied at the Riga Ballet School and at the Bol'shoy Ballet School. He began his dancing career with Igor' Moiseev's Young Classical Ballet, with which he performed for three years. He then joined the Bol'shoy troupe in 1971, and received great acclaim for his début performance as Siegfried in *Swan Lake*.

A frequent partner of Maya Plisetskaya, Godunov was flamboyant by Soviet standards, and had a wonderful stage presence. He was well known for his portrayal of the title role in *Spartacus*.

Godunov received a gold medal at the Moscow International Ballet Competition in 1973, and travelled to New York with the Bol'shoy company in 1973 and 1974. During a 1979 tour to New York, Godunov left the Bol'shoy troupe and decided to remain in the West.

Since his arrival in the West, Godunov has danced with several American and South American companies. He was a member of the American Ballet Theater from 1979 to 1982, and has been a guest artist with numerous companies since then. He has also appeared in a number of films and television productions. SCS

GOLEYZOVSKY, Kas'yan Yaroslavovich (1892–1970) Ballet dancer and leading choreographer. A student of Mikhail Obukhov and Michel Fokine, Goleyzovsky graduated from the Imperial Ballet School in 1909. The next year he joined the Bol'shoy troupe with which he danced until 1918, performing in a number of ballets by Aleksandr Gorsky. During his tenure at the Bol'shoy, Goleyzovsky also staged dances, one-act plays, and operettas for Nikita Baliev's Letuchaya mysh' theatre and for Savva Mamontov's Private Theatre.

After he left the Bol'shoy stage, Goleyzovsky embarked on a career as a choreographer. Greatly influenced by both Fokine and Gorsky, he developed his own form of modernism and became a prominent choreographer of the 1920s and 1930s. Not wanting to emigrate, he refused offers to work with Serge Diaghilev's Ballets Russes. He was a major influence on the *Molodoy Balet* (Young Ballet), established by George Balanchine in 1921, as well as on a host of choreographers and dancers. Much of Goleyzovsky's work was characterized by the use of acrobatics and sculptural

poses, the development of choreographic miniatures, and the incorporation of national dances.

From 1918 to 1920 he directed an
experimental children's ballet. He
then established and directed an
experimental studio and workshop
(1919–25) that became known as the
Moscow Chamber Ballet. This group
performed numerous ballets including
Scriabin's *The White Mass*, Debussy's
The Faun, and Strauss' *Salomé*. He also
experimented with popular dances
and choreographed for the circus.

In 1924 Goleyzovsky rejoined the
Bol'shoy troupe as a choreographer.
The next year he created his most
important ballet *Joseph the Beautiful*,
using music by Sergey Vasilenko and
Constructivist decors by Boris
Erdman. Starring Vasiliy Yefimov
and Galina Ulanova, this ballet was
in the form of a tableau vivant, and
created a striking impression. This was
followed in 1925 by the satirical ballet
Theolinda. Goleyzovsky's *The Red
Whirlwind* (1927), to music by Boris
Ber, was an allegorical ballet about the
Revolution and the contrasts between
capitalists and the proletariat. It met
such a hostile reception that he
resigned his position.

Established in the late 1920s, *Goleyzovsky's Thirty Girls* performed at the
Moscow Music Hall. He also worked
in several of the Soviet republics,
staging *Sleeping Beauty* (Khar'kov,
1935), *The Fountain of Bakhchisarai*
(Minsk, 1939), and *De Gul* (Dushanbe,
1941). His ballet *Charda* (1933) was
based on Slavic folklore and his
Polovtsian Dances from the opera
Prince Igor were staged in 1944 and
1953.

Late in his career, Goleyzovsky
choreographed several concert programmes (many using the music of
contemporary composers) and a series
of Choreographic Compositions for
the graduating classes of the Moscow
Ballet School. His last major work was
Leili and Madjnun (1964). Goleyzovsky
was the author of *Models of Russian
National Choreography* (1964). SCS

GOLOSOV, Il'ya Aleksandrovich
(1883–1945) Architect. Born in
Moscow, I. Golosov graduated from
the MIPSA in 1912 and supported
a mild form of Constructivism in the
1920s, as evidenced by his project for
the Palace of Labour in Moscow. He
was a member of OSA. JEB

**GOLOSOV, Panteleimon Alek-
sandrovich** (1882–1945) Architect.
Born in Moscow, P. Golosov graduated from the MIPSA in 1911. He
often referred to the classical heritage
in his designs, for example, in his pavilions for the 'First All-Russian Agricultural Exhibition' in Moscow (1923)
and in his Pravda Polygraphical
Combine in Moscow (1930–34). He
was a member of OSA. JEB

**GOLOVANOV, Nikolay Semeno-
vich** (1891–1953) Conductor.
Nikolay Golovanov was born in
Moscow and died there on 28 August
1953. After receiving his first instruction at the Moscow Synodal School,
where his mentors in choral conducting were Vasiliy Orlov and Aleksandr Kastal'sky, and from which he
graduated in 1909, he went on to study
composition with Ippolitov-Ivanov
and Vasilenko at the Moscow Conservatory. From 1919 to 1928 and
1930 to 1936 he was conductor at the
Bol'shoy Theatre, and then chief conductor from 1948 to 1953. From the
end of the 1920s he worked closely
with the Moscow Philharmonic
organization and the Moscow Radio
Theatre and from 1937 to 1953 was
chief conductor of the Grand Sym-

phony Orchestra of the All-Union Radio. He was a sympathetic piano accompanist. He became a People's Artist of the USSR in 1948 and was the recipient of many State Prizes. GS

GOLOVNYA, Anatoliy Dmitrievich (1900–1982) Cameraman. Golovnya was the cameraman who shot almost all Pudovkin's films. RT

GOL'TSMAN, Abram Zinov'evich (1894–1933) A senior economic official. The son of a carter, Gol'tsman studied furniture-making at Odessa's artisan school. He joined the RSDLP, worked as a trade-union organizer, was arrested, imprisoned, and exiled. He aligned himself with the Bolsheviks in April 1917, becoming a trade union official (1917–21). He was appointed head of the electricity industry (1922–25) and then a senior member of Rabkrin (the Workers' and Peasants' Inspectorate) (1926–30), in which capacity he was responsible for far-reaching proposals to rationalize the organization of industry. Put in charge of the Civil Air Fleet (1930–33), he was killed in an air crash. Gol'tsman had served as a member of the Party Central Committee (1925–33). RWD

GOLUBKINA, Anna Semenova (1864–1927) Sculptor, born in Zaraisk. In spite of her short life, Golubkina is recognized as a major force in the development of Soviet sculpture, thanks especially to her portraits, for example, of Tolstoy (1927). She received her training in the 1890s – at the MIPSA, the Academy of Arts, and in Paris. JEB

GOLUBNICHNY, Vladimir Ivanovich (b. 1936) Athlete. The greatest race walker of modern times, he competed in an astonishing five Olympics between 1956 and 1972, winning the 20 km walk at the 1960 and 1968 Games, taking the silver medal in 1972

and the bronze in 1964. He set his first world record in 1955 and gained his last major victory nineteen years later at the European Championships when he was thirty-eight. Born in the Ukrainian town of Sumy, he turned to coaching there upon retirement from competition. JWR

GONCHAR, Aleksandr Terent'evich (Oles) (b. 1918) A Ukrainian writer and candidate member of the Central Committee of the Soviet Communist Party, Gonchar was Chairman of the Ukrainian Writers' Union from 1959 until 1971. He has been a member of the Ideological Commission of the CPSU Central Committee since 1988 and a member of the Congress of People's Deputies (elected from the Union of Writers of the USSR) since 1989. Gonchar's best-known novel, *Sobor* (The Cathedral) was published in 1968. AHB

GONCHAROV, Andrey Dmitrievich (1903–1979) Graphic artist and painter. While studying at Vkhutemas in Moscow, Goncharov became a member of OST in 1925 and at first moved closely with Deyneka and Pimenov. A versatile artist active in portraiture, monumental painting, and stage design, Goncharov achieved his most memorable creations in book illustration, working on editions of Byron, Dostoevsky, Goethe, Hemingway, Shakespeare and many other authors. JEB

GORBACHEV, Mikhail Sergeevich (b. 1931) The name of Mikhail Gorbachev is inextricably linked with *perestroika* – the attempted radical reconstruction of the Soviet system – and *glasnost'*, the breakthrough in openness which took place in the Soviet Union in the second half of the 1980s. Gorbachev strengthened his power in each successive year from 1985 to 1989 and in every one of those years the reform programme he espoused became more radical. As long-suppressed problems came to the surface, however, and the political climate allowed grievances to be aired, the challenges facing Gorbachev became increasingly daunting.

Gorbachev was born into a peasant family in the village of Privol'noe in the Stavropol' region of southern Russia. He was only ten years of age when Hitler's armies invaded the Soviet Union. His own native area was for a time under occupation and the war years were ones of great hardship for the civilian population. While Gorbachev's father fought in the war – in which he was wounded – he, in common with other children, had to combine study at school with relentless work in the fields since virtually the entire able-bodied male population was in the armed forces.

In the immediate post-war years the young Gorbachev also combined school with intensive summer work on the land. He received the most unusual award for an eighteen-year-old of the Order of the Red Banner of Labour (in 1949) for his achievements during the harvest as an assistant to his father (who received a still higher award). It was the combination of being an exemplary worker and a successful school pupil (he received a silver medal for his performance at school) which gained him admission to the Law Faculty of Moscow University in 1950.

Although it was a far from liberal education which was available in the Law Faculty during the last years of Stalin's life, there was a minority of erudite scholars on the staff whose own education had been a pre-rev-olutionary one. Gorbachev also came into contact with better-educated city students and he himself was a rapid learner. Moreover, after Stalin's death in March 1953 the atmosphere within the university changed and discussion and debate among the students became more open. During his student years Gorbachev was active in the Komsomol organization within the Law Faculty and he joined the Communist Party in 1952.

After graduating in 1955 with the highest category of marks, Gorbachev returned to the Stavropol' area and proceeded to make his career in the Komsomol and party apparatus. His rise within the regional hierarchy was a rapid one. From 1956 to 1958 he was First Secretary of the Komsomol organisation in the city of Stavropol' and by the early 1960s Komsomol First Secretary for the Stavropol' region.

Gorbachev transferred from the Komsomol to the party apparatus in 1962 and by 1966 he was party First Secretary in the city of Stavropol'. Four years later he was the Stavropol' regional party First Secretary at the early age (by the standards of the Brezhnev era) of thirty-nine, and a year later – in 1971 – he became a member of the Central Committee of the Communist Party.

Gorbachev's first important local patron who spotted his talent was Fedor Kulakov, a former Stavropol' party secretary who by the 1970s was in charge of agriculture within the Central Committee Secretariat. Two other senior figures, both of whom had Stavropol' connections, also thought highly of his abilities – Yuriy Andropov and Mikhail Suslov, particularly the former. Both then and later Gorbachev showed great skill in winning support from people of different political dispositions. When Kulakov died suddenly in 1978 it was to Gorbachev that the party leadership turned to fill the slot of Secretary of the Central Committee in charge of agriculture. Gorbachev, by part-time study at the Stavropol' Agricultural Institute, had added in 1967 a second degree in agriculture to his first degree in law and, coming from one of the most important crop-growing areas of the Soviet Union, he had every reason – quite apart from his early experience as an agricultural worker – to make this a major speciality.

When Gorbachev moved to Moscow in 1978 he received rapid promotion, but he had a far from free hand to promote the reforms which he regarded as necessary. In 1979 he became a candidate member of the Politburo while retaining the Secretaryship of the Central Committee he had been accorded the previous year, and in 1980 he became a full Politburo member. Even so, with the ailing Brezhnev still regarding himself as an expert on agriculture and most of the party establishment opposed to the greater autonomy and incentives for peasants Gorbachev deemed to be necessary, the May 1982 'Food Programme', launched with much bombast by Brezhnev, fell far short of the changes Gorbachev wished to introduce.

When Brezhnev died in November 1982, the main candidates for the succession were Andropov and Chernenko and Gorbachev was firmly on Andropov's side. Although Chernenko, by virtue of seniority was the 'second secretary' within the party leadership during Andropov's fifteen months at the helm, Gorbachev was given extended responsibilites by Andropov and it was only the latter's declining health which enabled Chernenko to maintain his foothold as heir apparent.

Gorbachev's supervisory functions were extended by Andropov to embrace the economy as a whole and not just agriculture and under Chernenko they became still broader. While Gorbachev did not at the time have enough support in the Politburo to succeed to the General Secretaryship on Andropov's death in February 1984, he was sufficiently strong to be able to insist on a widening of his supervisory powers to embrace the party organization, ideology and foreign policy as well as the economy. Throughout Chernenko's thirteen months as General Secretary Gorbachev was the *de facto* second secretary.

That in itself did not guarantee him the succession when Chernenko died in March 1985 and, in fact, his elevation to the top party post was strongly contested by several members of the old guard within the Politburo. They preferred the seventy-year-old Moscow party First Secretary, Viktor Grishin, to Gorbachev who had celebrated his fifty-fourth birthday just one week earlier. Andrey Gromyko, who had been impressed by Gorbachev's ability, was one of those who gave him crucial support in the Politburo and Yegor Ligachev, later a critic on many issues but at that time an ally, helped to mobilize support within the Central Committee. Gromyko, in an enthusiastic speech to the Central Committee, was able to cover up the disagreements in the Politburo, and the Central Committee voted unanimously for Gorbachev as the new party leader.

Making full use of the General

Secretary's possibilities to exercise significant influence over appointments, Gorbachev succeeded in changing the composition of the Politburo and the Secretariat of the Central Committee relatively quickly over the next few years. One of his earliest moves – in the summer of 1985 – was to persuade Gromyko to leave the Foreign Ministry he had headed for twenty-eight years and become Chairman of the Presidium of the Supreme Soviet. That enabled Gorbachev to make the like-minded Eduard Shevardnadze Foreign Minister and thus facilitate a change of direction in Soviet foreign policy.

Diplomatic initiatives from Gorbachev soon followed. Whereas President Reagan had not met any of Gorbachev's three predecessors during his first period of office, by the time he left the White House at the end of 1988 he had been Gorbachev's partner at five summits – Geneva 1985, Reykjavik 1986, Washington 1987, Moscow and New York 1988. Summit meetings with President Bush in Malta (1989) and Washington (1990) confirmed the vast improvement in Soviet-American relations (and Soviet relations with the West generally), to which Gorbachev has made a most notable contribution.

A major turning-point on the international scene came in 1989 when a majority of Eastern European countries took decisive steps to regain their national independence and to abandon Communism. The Soviet Union – in sharp contrast with their actions in Hungary in 1956 and Czechoslovakia in 1968 – allowed these domestic developments in neighbouring countries to take their course. Gorbachev had by this time changed most of the top team responsible for the conduct of Soviet foreign policy. In addition to Shevardnadze, another close and important ally, Aleksandr Yakovlev, was overseeing international affairs within the Central Committee secretariat and Gorbachev had two reform-minded advisers on East European affairs and East-West relations, Georgiy Shakhnazarov and Anatoliy Chernyaev, on his personal staff. The changes in several of the East European countries went well beyond the Soviet reform agenda, but the presence of Gorbachev in the Kremlin was a crucial facilitating condition enabling them to take place at all.

At home Gorbachev introduced important political reforms and attempted also to bring in radical economic reform, but the latter proved much more difficult to implement. The cultural liberalization over which Gorbachev presided went far beyond anything Soviet society had previously seen. Real political debate appeared in the mass media and the concept of *glasnost'* which Gorbachev promoted acquired greater substance from year to year. The publication of long-suppressed books included not only Boris Pasternak's *Doctor Zhivago* but also more politically sensitive works, among them Aleksandr Solzhenitsyn's *The Gulag Archipelago* and George Orwell's *Nineteen Eighty-Four* and *Animal Farm*.

The late 1980s saw the introduction of particularly important political reforms. At the Nineteenth Conference of the Soviet Communist Party, held in the summer of 1988, Gorbachev persuaded a predominantly conservative body of delegates to accept reform of the electoral system and this change was actually implemented in March 1989 when elections, which were competitive in a majority of seats, took place for the newly-constituted Congress of People's Deputies. That body, in turn, proceeded to elect a new-style Supreme Soviet. This reform of the legislature was highly significant, for the old Supreme Soviet rarely met and was virtually useless as a critic of the executive. The new legislature, in spite of the fact that the great majority of deputies were members of the Communist Party, soon showed itself to be a body which could not be taken for granted and was not afraid to criticize its prime begetter, Mikhail Gorbachev.

Gorbachev's formal powers and authority grew in the late 1980s but, while he scored relatively well in opinion surveys, he was not as popular at home as he was abroad or as he had been in the Soviet Union in the earliest years of his leadership when his open and vigorous style made a refreshing contrast with that of his three elderly predecessors and when hopes were high that living standards would soon be raised. Throughout this period Gorbachev was, however, more of a reformer than a majority of his Politburo colleagues, for even in promotions to the Politburo he did not have a completely free hand, but had to persuade a majority of his existing colleagues every time he wished to make a change.

Accordingly, he set about enhancing his power and authority within the state, as distinct from party, structures. In 1988 he succeeded Gromyko as Chairman of the Presidium of the Supreme Soviet and in 1989 that post was strengthened and renamed the Chairmanship of the Supreme Soviet. The disadvantage of this for Gorbachev was that it involved him in frequent and lengthy attendance at meetings of the Supreme Soviet which was now in session for some eight months of the year. He found himself acting, in effect, as both Leader and Speaker of the new legislature as well as being head of state and General Secretary of the Communist Party. A more fundamental change in Gorbachev's powers and in that of state institutions occurred in 1990 when in March the headship of state was renamed the Presidency and Gorbachev became the first President in Soviet history. It was decided that in future this office would be elected by universal suffrage at five-yearly intervals, but on the occasion of its creation Gorbachev was elected to it by a vote of the Congress of People's Deputies.

Gorbachev at the same time secured the creation of two new political institutions – a Presidential Council appointed by him and a Council of the Federation which provided an opportunity for the head of the Supreme Soviet of each union republic to have a voice on inter-ethnic and inter-republican issues as Gorbachev, faced by rising national tensions, strove to create a more fully-fledged federalism than the Soviet Union had known before. He was also moving real political power from party institutions to the presidency with the Presidential Council taking over many of the functions that had devolved in the past to the Politburo. At the same time the presidency was separated from the Chairmanship of the Supreme Soviet.

In the meantime reforms had been undertaken in the party organization. Conservative Communists and Russian nationalists pressed for a separate party organization for the Russian republic which Gorbachev resisted until 1990 since it clearly had the potential to become a second centre within the party. As a first concession to the agitation, however, he consented to the creation in late 1989 of a bureau for the direction of party work in the RSFSR, but he himself became its chairman.

Gorbachev had also undertaken a radical restructuring of the all-union Central Committee apparatus. That bureaucracy was cut by approximately 40 per cent from the autumn of 1988 and the number of its departments reduced from twenty to nine. Those which disappeared included most of the economic departments responsible for particular branches of industry. This was an indication of Gorbachev's seriousness about taking the party out of the detailed administration of the economy.

Gorbachev supported in principle an increasingly radical economic reform, but hesitated to move rapidly towards market prices, given that this would mean in many cases sharp price rises and the real possibility of a growth in social unrest which could be exploited by his opponents on both the right and left of the political spectrum. By 1990, however, he was also aware that to adopt too gradual an approach to far-reaching economic reform could be equally dangerous, for it had become abundantly clear that the Soviet economy was falling between two stools – the administered economy was working even less well than it had before it was undermined by the Gorbachev reforms, but the essential institutions of a market economy, such as commercial banks and wholesale trading organizations, did not yet exist.

Gorbachev had played a crucial part in the creation of a political climate in which these and other fundamental issues could be debated. While social and inter-ethnic tensions were higher by 1990 than they were in 1985, this was partly because until the Gorbachev era most serious problems had been swept under the carpet. A growth of political pluralism brought the accumulated grievances of decades into the open and presented Gorbachev with a series of intractable problems.

From the outset of his General Secretaryship, Gorbachev had a strong disposition towards political as well as economic reform, but it was only from 1987, when his personal position in the leadership was strengthened, that he was able to begin to place increasing emphasis on the need for democratization. His own thinking also developed over time and became in some respects more radical in line with advice from intelligent and open-minded advisers he appointed and in response to public opinion and informed criticism.

Many of the most positive features of Gorbachev's leadership – for example, his espousal of concepts new in the Soviet context such as *glasnost'*, a law-governed state, competitive elections, checks and balances as well as greater political and religious liberty than the Soviet Union had hitherto known – were a threat to entrenched interests within the system and provoked countervailing pressures, although they also had, of course, their strong supporters. Similarly, his subordination of the military to political and economic considerations to a degree greater than ever before led to increasing criticism of Gorbachev's policies from military quarters by the first half of 1990. Moreover, although Gorbachev appeared to enjoy support from Kryuchkov, Chebrikov's successor as head of the KGB, it was in the logic of the political reform process on which Gorbachev had embarked that the KGB should in the long run play a much-reduced role in the society in comparison with its activities hitherto.

Gorbachev's policies demonstrated once again that the most dangerous time for an authoritarian regime is when it begins to reform itself. It was hardly to be expected that after centuries of autocratic or oligarchic rule, Russia and the Soviet Union could be fully democratized within the space of five years. Gorbachev's political reforms stimulated opposition from many different groups, including those who advocated instant multi-party democracy and those who wanted to call a halt to the entire process of democratization, in addition to those whose demands were for greater national sovereignty or, in some cases (notably that of the Baltic nations), for complete independent statehood.

By the beginning of the 1990s it was easier for Western observers than for Soviet citizens to declare that the balance-sheet of the Gorbachev years was a highly impressive one. Gorbachev had played a notable part in creating a much better international climate, in reducing the risk of superpower conflict and in assisting the development of what he called a common 'European house'. At home he had presided over the introduction of more political accountability and political freedom than the Soviet Union had known even in the 1920s, the period of Soviet history which had hitherto been the least oppressive.

Yet the unintended consequences of reform – such as the sharpening of inter-ethnic tensions – and the combination of raised expectations and continuing shortages and economic difficulties bulked large in the minds of many Soviet citizens. Soviet society had become more polarized by 1990 and Gorbachev a much more controversial figure than he was four or five years earlier. There were, however, many intellectuals in the Soviet Union who had come to admire him more in the meantime, for they recognized how great had been his contribution in changing Soviet political life almost beyond recognition.

Gorbachev could have followed a different political path and one which would have been less taxing and dangerous for him. The Soviet Union, though in the long term falling further behind advanced Western countries, could have muddled through for some considerable time with a tightening-up of the old system. But Gorbachev was bold and imaginative enough to take a longer view and to embark on a journey of far-reaching reform which would take the Soviet Union into uncharted waters and an ultimate destination which might make the country and system qualitatively different from what they had been before. Yet, the obstacles were so great and the risks so high that by 1990 a counter-revolution against *perestroika* which would bring down Gorbachev and put into reverse, for a time at least, the reform process could not be totally ruled out.

Although sensitive to the constraints upon his actions at any given time, Gorbachev as party leader has eschewed the kind of cautious course which could have brought him the same meaningless standing ovations as Brezhnev commanded until the end of his life. Instead, Gorbachev has established a place – whatever lies ahead – as one of the great reformers in

Russian history and as one of the most positive influences on European developments in the second half of the twentieth century. AHB

GORBACHEVA, Raisa Maksimovna (b. 1932) Although her international fame is a consequence of her marriage to the Soviet leader, Mikhail Gorbachev, Raisa Maksimovna Gorbacheva (maiden name Titarenko) is – like her husband – formidably intelligent. Of Russian nationality, she was born in Siberia in the town of Rubtsovsk in the Altay region. Her parents were railway employees and Raisa Maksimovna was the youngest of three children. After gaining a gold medal at school (for the maximum of five points in all subjects), Raisa Maksimovna entered the Philosophy Faculty of Moscow University, from which she successfully graduated. It was at the university that she and Mikhail Sergeevich Gorbachev met in 1951; they were married in 1953 and their daughter, Irina, was born in Stavropol' in 1957.

Raisa Gorbacheva did sociological research on the way of life of the kolkhoz peasantry in the Stavropol' region in the 1960s and received a candidate of science degree (Ph.D. equivalent) in philosophy. She published a book based upon her dissertation in 1969. She taught in higher education, including the Stavropol' Agricultural Institute, and had the rank of *dotsent* (associate professor).

After Mikhail Gorbachev became Soviet leader, Raisa Maksimovna came very much into the public eye. To a far greater extent than any previous General Secretary's spouse, she accompanied her husband on his travels around the Soviet Union and to foreign countries. For this – as well as for being well-dressed – she has been widely and unfairly criticized in the Soviet Union. Her partnership with her husband is simply an exceptionally close one. On her foreign travels Raisa Gorbacheva has made a virtually uniformly favourable impression on those she met. (A rare exception was Mrs Nancy Reagan.)

Raisa Gorbacheva has broad cultural interests and her independent activity since her husband became Soviet leader has been concentrated mainly on the Soviet Cultural Foundation, on whose presidium she serves. There she has been a useful ally, in his fight to conserve and promote the Russian cultural heritage, for its president, Academician Dmitriy Likhachev. AHB

GORBANEVSKAYA, Natal'ya Yevgen'evna (b. 1936) Human rights activist, poet, and editor. From the late 1950s Gorbanevskaya's poems circulated in *samizdat*. She was briefly interned in a mental hospital in 1968 for her role in the human rights movement. In April the movement's main journal, *A Chronicle of Current Events* (1968–82), began to appear, with her as the first in a long line of editors, who included most notably A. Yakobson, G. Superfin, I. Yakir, S. Kovalev, T. Velikanova, and Y. Shikhanovich. In August she and seven friends demonstrated against the Warsaw Pact invasion of Czechoslovakia. In 1969 she was psychiatrically interned for compiling the book *Red Square at Noon* (1972) about this protest and the subsequent trial. She was released in 1972 and emigrated in 1975 to Paris. PBR

GORBOVSKY, Gleb Yakovlevich (b. 1931) Poet, born and brought up in Leningrad. A bohemian nonconformist in the 1950s, he settled down to become one of the most prominent and prolific official lyric voices of Leningrad. GSS

GORBUNOV, Anatoliy Valer'-yanovich (Gorbunovs, Anatoliis) (b. 1942) A Latvian, despite his Russian sounding name, Gorbunovs has been a Komsomol and party official in Latvia since 1969. He was promoted rapidly in the 1980s, becoming Secretary of Riga *gorkom*, Head of the Central Committee Department of Administrative Organs (1984–85), Secretary of the Central Committee (1985–88) and, in October 1988, Chairman of the Presidium of the Latvian Supreme Soviet. Gorbunovs was perhaps the most popular communist official at this time and maintained good relations with the Latvian People's Front. JHM

GORCHAKOV, Nikolay Mikhay-lovich (1899–1958) A pupil of Vakhtangov, Gorchakov worked as a stage producer and joined the Moscow Art Theatre as assistant director under Stanislavsky in 1924. He was Principal Director of the Moscow Drama Theatre from 1933 to 1938 and Artistic Director of the Theatre of Satire from 1941 to 1943. RT

GOR'KY, Maksim (Peshkov, Aleksey Maksimovich) (1868–1936) A writer, playwright, poet and critic who is considered the father of Soviet literature. Gor'ky was born into a merchant family of Nizhnyy Novgorod (later renamed Gor'ky in his honour). With little formal education, at an early age he set out on his 'wanderings' around Russia, earning money in a number of jobs ranging from barge hauler to icon painter, and pursuing his own education in his voracious reading; he wrote about this early period later in his autobiographical trilogy *Childhood* (1913), *In the World* (1916) and *My Universities* (1922). Gor'ky began his literary career in the 1890s and his early short stories such as 'Chelkash' (1895) are noted for their romanticization of the hobo or drifter as a free spirit. With the novel *Foma Gordeev* (1899) he began a series of epic interpretations of contemporary social history which chart the rise of the bourgois entrepreneur and the development of a dissident intelligentsia within the ranks of that class; other examples include *The Life of Matvei Kozhemyakin* (1910–11) and *The Artamanov Business* (1925).

Early this century Gor'ky became a prominent public figure of distinctly revolutionary leanings. He published in such journals as *The New Word* and *Life* to which Lenin and Plekhanov also contributed, becoming in 1900 the leading force in the Znanie (knowledge) publishing house, a focus in the pre-revolutionary years for realist writers concerned with social issues, and was involved in underground revolutionary activities. He joined the Bolshevik Party in 1905, and soon thereafter began his long, if frequently fraught, association with Lenin. In 1906 he travelled for the party to America which he described critically in 'My Interviews' (1906) and 'In America' (1906). In late 1906 he moved to Capri to join Bogdanov, Lunacharsky and others in a party school they founded there. During this period, Gor'ky, together with Lunacharsky, espoused the philosophy of 'God-building', which Lenin denounced as a heresy; God-building conflates Marxism with a humanistic religiosity and looks to a time when men will become as Gods. It informs several of Gor'ky's writings of this period, and notably his novella *A Confession* (1908). In this decade he also wrote many plays, most of which show

Chekhov's influence but are distinctly more militant politically. The frequently-produced *The Lower Depths* (1902), for instance, is set in a flophouse and depicts the degradation of those whom society has condemned to a demeaning existence.

His most famous work of this time is the somewhat propagandistic novel *Mother* (1906–07) which, despite Gor'ky's own reservations about its literary merits, has become the official progenitor of socialist realism. *Mother* is based on an actual incident in the worker town of Somov where a May Day demonstration was put down by tsarist troops and its leaders arrested and tried. It draws on the tradition of religious hagiography to provide paradigms for representing the hero's progress from a state of 'spontaneity' to one of political consciousness; these paradigms were later to become conventions of socialist realist literature. This progression is in *Mother* made first by the hero, Pavel Vlasov, a young worker, and then, after his arrest, by his simple and religious mother; at the end, she dies a martryr's death in the climactic May Day demonstration.

Gor'ky returned to Russia with the general amnesty of 1913 and became active as an editor and prose writer. After the February Revolution of 1917 he helped organize Petrograd cultural life, but remained initially sceptical about the subsequent Bolshevik Revolution. His series of articles *Untimely Thoughts* (1917–18), published in *New Life*, criticized the Revolution for excessive bloodshed and a disregard for cultural treasures. After Kaplan's attempt on Lenin's life in 1918, Gor'ky sought reconciliation with Lenin, for which he was rewarded in the sense that he, together with his wife the actress Mariya Andreeva, became one of the most powerful figures in Soviet culture. During the period 1918 to 1921 he initiated a large number of cultural endeavours and new institutions (such as the publishing house World Literature); his efforts saved many intellectuals from starvation and even, on occasion, from repression. He was also an early patron of the Serapion Brothers, with many of whom he corresponded later in the twenties.

In 1921 he left the Soviet Union, partly for reasons of health, and eventually settled in Sorrento but remained on good terms with the Soviet Union (which he visited in 1928 and 1929) and continued to publish in its journals. His *In the Land of the Soviets* (1929) discusses his impressions of the economic achievements he saw on these visits. However, Gor'ky's main work of the twenties is the lengthy novel *The Life of Klim Samgin* (begun in 1925 but never finished) which follows forty years of Russian intellectual history dramatized in the life of its protagonist, the ineffectual bourgeois intellectual Samgin.

Gor'ky returned to the Soviet Union triumphantly in 1931 and became the key literary figure in the formation of the Writers Union in 1932 (which he headed). His speech to the First Writers Congress in 1934, over which he presided, provides one of the canonical formulations of the doctrine of socialist realism, the mandatory literary method of Soviet literature. This speech stresses the need for inspiring heroes in literature and calls for writers to look for models in the great heroes of folklore. Gor'ky's longstanding interest in folklore and his periodic attempts at applying folklore techniques and motifs in his own fiction (for instance, in *Folktales of Italy* (1911–13) and *Russian Folktales* (1912–17)) were influential in the vogue of the thirties for writing (somewhat crude) industrial and political parables based on traditional folklore motifs. In the thirties Gor'ky was very active as a literary functionary and editor and in helping unknown writers. He also wrote several plays, of which the best known is *Yegor Bulychev and Others* (1932). However, his writings of this period comprise primarily essays on literary and political issues; the latter were frequently apologia for the increasing terror and provide a sharp contrast to Gor'ky's statements on this issue in the early twenties. He had been plagued by tuberculosis for many years, and he finally died of it in Moscow in 1936. KC

GORSHKOV, Sergey Georgievich (1910–1988) Every inch a charismatic commander, the darling of Western naval correspondents and variously described as the 'Jackie Fisher' of the modern Soviet Navy, Gorshkov's thirty-year incumbency of senior naval command witnessed a massive expansion of Soviet naval capability and the transformation of a coastal defence force into a blue-water fleet globally deployed, fully capable of carrying through an independent naval mission. Joining the navy in 1927, Gorshkov passed out of the Frunze Naval School in 1931, proceeded first to the Black Sea Fleet, though after one year he was on his way to the Soviet Far East and the newly established 'Far East Naval Force' under Viktorov. In the First Naval Brigade with its minesweepers and minelayers, Gorshkov served as navigating officer on the brigade command ship *Tomsk*, rising to brigade navigation officer. In 1937 he attended a command course

in minelaying, returning to the Far East for two years before moving to command a cruiser brigade in the Black Sea Fleet in June 1940, the prelude to his assignment to the higher command course at the Naval Academy in 1941.

Gorshkov fought his war largely with the Black Sea Fleet and with the Azov and Danube Flotillas, supporting the defensive actions in the Black Sea and using his flotilla forces (light coastal units, but heavily armed) to support the Red Army. In November 1942 Rear-Admiral Gorshkov took temporary command of the Forty-Seventh Army defending the Caucasus, but in February 1943 resumed his naval position with the Azov Flotilla, whose operations brought him an association with a wartime colonel, Leonid Brezhnev. A party member since 1942, Gorshkov went on to command the Danube Flotilla in support of the Red Army operations in Yugoslavia and Hungary, returning to the Black Sea Fleet in January 1945, serving as Fleet Chief of Staff (1948–51) and Fleet Commander-in-Chief from August 1951 to July 1955. Promoted by Khrushchev to First Deputy Commander-in-Chief of the Soviet Navy in the summer of 1955, within a matter of months he was installed in January 1956 as Khrushchev's new 'naval broom' to sweep away an antiquated and over-ambitious naval programme.

Gorshkov quickly responded by forming a 'strap-on' navy, installing missiles and searching for new ship designs, new propulsion plants, new systems. Though according pride of place to the submarine, Gorshkov cleverly used the 'submarine argument' to advance the concept of a 'balanced fleet' with powerful, impressive surface units. To counter the American naval threat, he deployed Soviet naval units forward and began the process of global deployment. His advocacy of the vital role sea-power could and should play in Soviet strategic planning was tireless, taking on the aspect of a crusade. After ten years service as Commander-in-Chief he was made a Hero of the Soviet Union and promoted to the rank of Admiral of the Fleet of the Soviet Union two years later in 1967.

As the Soviet Navy expanded apace and deployed into its first global operational exercises (OKEAN), Gorshkov set out his testimony of sea-power, if it can be called that, in a work *Naval Power of the State* (1976) which attracted world wide attention and not a little admiration. But his efforts to implement the independent naval mission and his stress upon the uniqueness of the naval component in and contribution to the Soviet military effort came increasingly into conflict with revised plans in the mid-1970s for integrated strategic forces and an intensified 'combined arms' approach, leading to an impassioned debate within naval circles in the early 1980s. Gorshkov's particular advocacy of the navy was couched in terms of the requirements of the entire Soviet defence community. Gorshkov's rearguard action seems to have been of little avail. His displacement in favour of Admiral Chernavin, a submarine officer, came with surprising abruptness, even in cursory fashion, at the end of 1985. But the 'Gorshkov legacy' cannot be so easily dismissed and his sermonizing on the vital role of sea-power for the Soviet state so quickly forgotten. JE

GORSKY, Aleksandr Alekseevich (1871–1924) Ballet dancer, choreographer, teacher. Gorsky graduated from the Imperial Ballet School in 1889 and danced with the Mariinsky troupe for the next eleven years. In 1896 he was appointed assistant ballet master at the Imperial School and he was instrumental in incorporating Stepanov notation into the curriculum.

In 1898 Gorsky was commissioned to stage Petipa's ballet *Sleeping Beauty* for the Bol'shoy Theatre, where the ballet company had been in serious decline for some years. The production was a success and he was appointed ballet master of the Bol'shoy troupe a post he held until his death in 1924.

Gorsky's tenure at the Bol'shoy was extremely important for the development of Russian ballet. With his well defined artistic programme, he introduced far-ranging reforms and innovations, bringing the company back to a high level of performance. He introduced many lively character scenes and made greater use of the corps de ballet. These conventions were a radical departure from the conventions of nineteenth-century ballet and created a great deal of controversy in the theatre and in the press.

Gorsky staged his own versions of many classics, including his landmark restaging of Minkus' *Don Quixote* (1900), *Swan Lake* (1901), *The Humpbacked Horse* (1901), *Giselle* (1907), *Raymonda* (1908), *Le Corsaire* (1912), and *The Nutcracker* (1919).

He also staged a number of original productions, such as *Gudule's Daughter* (1902), *Salambô* (1910), *The Dance Dream* (London, 1911), *Stenka Razin* (1918), and *The Grotto of Venus* (1923), his last ballet.

Gorsky taught at the Imperial Ballet School (1896–1900) and at the Bol'shoy Ballet School (1902–24). SCS

GOVOROV, Leonid Aleksandrovich (1897–1955) A White officer who became a Marshal of the Soviet Union (1944) and a candidate member of the Central Committee (1952). Born in the present-day Kirov region, he was commissioned as an artillery officer in 1917, was a lieutenant in Admiral Kolchak's forces (1918–19), and served in the Red Army as an artillery commander from January 1920. He graduated from the Frunze Military Academy (1933) and from the General Staff Academy (1938). He was chief of staff of an artillery army in the Winter War with Finland (1939–40) and, at the outbreak of the Great Fatherland War, head of the Dzerzhinsky Artillery Academy. He commanded the Fifth Army before Moscow (October 1941 to April 1942), and the Leningrad Front (June 1942 to May 1945). He joined the Communist Party sometime in 1942. After the war he held a variety of high command posts, including (three times) that of deputy minister of defence. Govorov was named among the targets of the fabricated 'Doctors' Plot' in January 1953, and in July 1953 among army opponents of L. P. Beria (Beria had tried to have him arrested in early 1941). At the time of his death he was Deputy Minister of Defence and C-in-C, Forces of National Air Defence. Father of V. L. Govorov. JHM

GOVOROV, Vladimir Leonidovich (b. 1924) Chief of the Soviet Civil Defence. Govorov joined the Red Army in 1942 and commanded an artillery battery during the war. He became first deputy Commander-in-Chief of the Soviet Group of Forces in Germany (1969–71), the commander of the Baltic Military District (1971–72), the commander of the Moscow Military District (1972–80) and the Commander-in-Chief of the Far East Theatre Forces (1980–84). He gained the rank of Army General in 1977. He was named Deputy Minister of Defence for the Main Inspectorate of the Ministry of Defence in 1984 and in June 1986 he replaced Army General Altunin as the Chief of Soviet Civil Defence. Under Govorov Soviet civil defence has become involved in a broader range of non-military functions such as dealing with the consequences of the Chernobyl' disaster. RA

GRABAR', Igor' Emmanuilovich (1871–1960) Painter, born in Budapest. While associated with many groups before the Revolution, especially the St Petersburg World of Art, Grabar' also played a major role as painter, teacher, restorer and organizer from the 1920s to the 1950s. A painter of landscapes, still-lives and portraits, for example, of Petr Neradovsky (1931) and Sergey Prokof'ev (1934), Grabar' contributed to the rediscovery of Realism in the 1930s writing a detailed appreciation of Il'ya Repin (1937). He also did much to focus attention on icons and church architecture – between 1918 and 1930, for example, he was director of the State Central Art Restoration Studios in Moscow. JEB

GRABAR', Vladimir Emmanuilovich (1865–1956) Lawyer. One of the pre-eminent international lawyers of the pre- and post-revolutionary periods, Grabar' was born in Vienna of parents active in the Slav renaissance movement in Carpathian Rus'. In 1879 Grabar' was able to join his father who had been obliged to flee Austria-Hungary, in Russia. After secondary schooling in Kiev, he graduated in law from Moscow University and spent some years in Paris before returning to complete his post-graduate studies. In 1893 he accepted the post of *privat-dotsent* at Tartu University and during the next quarter century served successively as professor, dean, and librarian.

Grabar' advised the Soviet delegation at the Lausanne Conference (1922–23) and served as legal adviser to the People's Commissariat for Foreign Trade for seven years, returning in 1929 with a personal commendation from A. I. Mikoyan. In retirement he continued to advise part-time and during the 1920s played a major part in drafting Soviet foreign affairs legislation, notably the 1926 Consular Statute of the USSR.

A non-Marxist of a positivist orientation, Grabar' was attacked for his views in the early 1930s, but his stature was unassailable. In the Gorbachev era those criticisms have been rejected. Grabar' left more than 170 scholarly publications, including a capital history of international law in Russia which has been translated into English (1990). His work on the history of international law in England has never been surpassed. His younger brother Igor' became a distinguished art historian.

During the Second World War Grabar' was recalled to teach at Moscow University and continued thereafter to be attached to the Institute of State and Law of the USSR Academy of Sciences. WEB

GRABIN, Vasiliy Gavrilovich (1900–1980) Vasiliy Grabin was one of the Soviet Union's foremost designers of artillery systems, responsible for anti-tank guns and other weapons, including the 'ZIS-3' 76 mm gun which played a major role during the war. Born in Krasnodar', he joined the army in 1920 and studied at the Dzerzhinsky Military-Technical Academy. From 1930 he was engaged in design work, becoming chief designer of an artillery factory in 1934, and from 1942 to 1946 chief of the Central Artillery Design Bureau. A talented designer, Grabin was known as a tough, independently-minded figure who at times developed new weapons in defiance of instructions from above. He was the recipient of four Stalin Prizes and in 1940 became a Hero of Socialist Labour. Grabin was a party member, joining in 1921. JMC

GRANIN (German), Daniil Aleksandrovich (b. 1919) Born in Volyn', a prose writer and literary functionary. A former electrical engineer, party member since 1942 and head of the Leningrad Writers' Organization (1954–69), Granin is best known for his outspoken critiques of the Soviet scientific world made in the classics of the Khrushchev and Gorbachev thaws – *Those Who Seek* (1954), 'One's Own Opinion' (1956), *I Go Into the Storm* (1962), and *The Aurochs* (1987). His fiction of the Brezhnev era engages general moral problems in an urban setting, and environmental issues; he also published, with A. Adamovich, a massive *Book of the Blockade* (1977–81). KC

GRANOVSKY, Aleksandr Andreevich, Bishop Antonin (1860–1927) Leading figure in the Renovationist movement in the Russian Orthodox Church in the 1920s. He became a bishop in 1903. He was soon known for his remarkably liberal views and his career suffered an eclipse after 1908. Immediately after the Revolution he was in Moscow where he attracted a circle interested in church reform. The Renovationist movement gathered momentum from 1921 and by May 1922 had provoked a schism in the Orthodox Church. At the same time, there was deep disagreement within the ranks of the reformers and by August Antonin had founded a 'Union of Church Renewal', dedicated to moral and spiritual reform, to rival the more obviously political 'Living Church' faction led by V. D. Krasnitsky. From 1923, however, he became increasingly isolated and lost prominence in church affairs. MR

GREBNER, Georgy Eduardovich (1892–1954) Scriptwriter. Grebner wrote film scripts, including: *The Bear's Wedding* (1926) and *The Salamander* (1928) (both with Lunacharsky), Piscator's *The Fishermen's Revolt* (1934) and Pudovkin's *Suvorov* (1941). RT

GRECHKO, Andrey Antonovich (1903–1976) Former Minister of Defence. Grechko fought in the Red Cavalry in the Civil War and graduated from a cavalry officer school. After graduation from the General Staff Academy in 1941, he was appointed to senior cavalry commands. Cavalry armies under his charge were involved in the liberation of the Northern Caucasus and Kiev. He led the First Guards Army in its offensive from the Ukraine to Czechoslovakia (1944–45). After the war he gained command of the Kiev Military District (1945–53) and became Commander-in-Chief of Soviet occupation forces in Germany (1953–57). He assisted in the suppression of the June 1953 uprising in the Soviet zone of Germany. In this period he became a Marshal of the Soviet Union. Grechko was promoted to First Deputy Minister of Defence and Commander-in-Chief of Ground Forces (1957–60), Commander-in-Chief of Warsaw Pact Forces (1960–

67), and became Minister of Defence in April 1967. Grechko acquired full Politburo membership in 1973, and was succeeded as Minister of Defence in 1976 by Marshal Ustinov. Despite the onset of detente and the conclusion of the SALT I Treaty in the early 1970s Grechko was a traditional and rather hardline military professional. The Soviet military build-up continued unabated under Grechko. Some have claimed that he favoured a pre-emptive nuclear strike against China as the relations of the two states deteriorated into border clashes, but was overruled by the Politburo. RA

GREKOV, Mitrofan Borisovich (also Martyshchenko, Mitrofan Pavlovich) (1882–1934) Painter, born in Sharpaevka. Grekov is often considered to be the father of Soviet battle-painting. He studied in Odessa before enrolling in the Academy of Arts in 1903 where he took courses with Frants Rubo. Living mainly in Novocherkassk after the Revolution, Grekov painted military scenes of the Revolution and the Civil War such as *To Budennyi's Detachment* (1923), *Gun Carriage* (1927) and *Buglers of the First Cavalry* (1934). The Grekov Studios of Battle-Painting were founded in Moscow in 1935 in his honour. JEB

GREKOVA, I. (née Ventsel', Yelena Semenovna) (b. 1907) Mathematician and prose writer. She began publishing in 1957 and is one of the exponents of the urban women's prose of the 1960s. Her best works, like *The Ladies' Hairdresser* (1965), *Summer in the City* (1965), and *The Department* (1981) explore personal and professional interactions from an intelligent woman's viewpoint. Her worst works (like *The Hotel Manageress*, 1976) are sentimental hymns to female self-sacrifice. BH

GRIBKOV, Anatoliy Ivanovich (b. 1919) First Deputy Chief of General Staff. Gribkov entered the Soviet Army in 1938 and represented the General Staff in various units (1942–44). After the war he served on the General Staff of the Soviet Armed Forces and on the staff of various military districts. He became commander of the troops of Leningrad Military District in 1973 and in 1976 assumed his current post as First Deputy Chief of the General Staff of the Soviet Army and Navy, Chief of the General Staff of the Troops of the Warsaw Pact. He became a full member of the CPSU Central Committee in 1981. Army General Gribkov has worked closely with Marshals Akhromeev and Ogarkov and retains a key post for any reorientation of the military doctrine and strategy of the Warsaw Pact. RA

GRIGORENKO, Petr Grigor'evich (1907–1986) General, human rights activist, and writer. An outstanding army career made Grigorenko a major-general. In 1960, after he criticized Nikita Khrushchev at a party meeting, his advancement ended. He was interned (1963–65) in a prison psychiatric hospital for founding a neo-Leninist group. From 1966 to 1969 he played a key role in the emerging human rights movement, supporting in particular the cause of the Crimean Tatars (see M. Dzhemilev). From 1969 to 1974 he was again psychiatrically interned. He was not allowed – despite official guarantees – to return to the USSR in 1977, after visiting relatives in America. He became a Christian. His *Memoirs* came out in 1983. PBR

GRIGOROVICH, Yuriy Nikolaevich (b. 1927) Ballet dancer and outstanding choreographer. Grigorovich graduated from the Leningrad Ballet School in 1946 and joined the Kirov troupe, performing as a leading *demi-caractère* soloist until 1964. Early in his career he turned to choreography, serving as the principal choreographer at the Kirov Theatre (1962–64) and as chief choreographer and artistic director of the Bol'shoy Theatre since 1964.

Grigorovich's first major ballet *The Stone Flower* (1957) was an immediate success. It incorporated a series of dance suites and intricate acrobatic movements. Alla Osipenko created the leading role, which was later interpreted by Maya Plisetskaya. This ballet was performed in many Soviet cities as well as in both Stockholm (1962) and Sofia (1965).

Based on a Turkish fairytale, *The Legend of Love* (1961) was his next major work. With music by the Azeri composer Arif Melikov, Grigorovich incorporated movements from Oriental dance and created a unity of dance, music and décor. The ballet's dramatic impact was a landmark in the development of Soviet choreography. In 1968 he created *Spartacus*, using his own libretto and music by Aram Khachaturyan. The ballet's great drama and psychological development earned him the Lenin Prize (1970).

Grigorovich's next major works included *Ivan the Terrible*, staged at the Bol'shoy Theatre in 1975 and at the Paris Opéra in 1976; *Romeo and Juliet*, created as a two-act ballet at the Paris Opéra (1978) and as a three-act ballet at the Bol'shoy Theatre (1979); and *The Golden Age* (1987).

He has also staged major revivals of works from the classical repertoire, including all ballets by Tchaikovsky. In many of these Grigorovich reworked the original choreography to emphasize the *corps de ballet*. His revivals have included *Sleeping Beauty* (1963, 1973), *The Nutcracker* (1966), *Swan Lake* (1969, 1980), *Giselle* (1979), *Don Quixote* (1982), and *Raymonda* (1984).

Grigorovich has taught at the Choreography Department of the Leningrad Conservatory since 1973, has served as a judge in several international ballet competitions, and was editor-in-chief of the *Soviet Ballet Encyclopedia* (1981). SCS

GRIN (Grinevsky), Aleksandr Stepanovich (1880–1932) A prose writer. Born near Vyatka (Kirov) the son of a Polish exile, Grin travelled around Russia extensively in his youth working, like Gor'ky, at various occupations. In 1906 he began to write fantastic fiction influenced by Hoffmann, Poe and Mayne Reid. Most of it was set in a romantic world (Grinland) with a rugged coastline peopled by high-spirited adventurers, sailors, desperadoes and beautiful women. His most successful work, *The Scarlet Sails* (1923) was made into a ballet and a film. In 1950 his works were attacked during the anti-cosmopolitan campaign, but have been published again since 1956. KC

GRINEVETSKY, Vasiliy Ignat'evich (1871–1919) An influential engineer and planner. Grinevetsky has sometimes been described as the father of Soviet planning. He graduated from Moscow Higher Technical School in 1896, was made professor of engineering and, by 1914, was director of the School. He designed engines and locomotives. In Khar'kov, while it was under anti-Bolshevik control, he published *Post-war Perspectives of Russian Industry*, which influenced the thinking of Krasin, Lenin, and other prominent Bolsheviks, and which was republished in Soviet Russia in 1922. RWD

GRIN'KO, Grigoriy Fedorovich (1890–1938) An enthusiastic supporter of industrialization from the mid-1920s, and then of collectivization, Grin'ko was a Socialist-Revolutionary before 1917. He opposed the October Revolution, but by 1920 he had joined the Bolsheviks. He studied at Moscow and Khar'kov Universities (1909–13), then served as a soldier and officer (1913–17). He was put in charge of the Ukrainian Gosplan in the mid-1920s, but in December 1929 he moved to Moscow where he was appointed a deputy commissar in the new People's Commissariat for Agriculture (Narkomzem) for the USSR. He became People's Commissar for Finance (October 1930–August 1937), re-establishing a stable currency and a balanced budget. He was a Candidate member of the Party Central Committee (1934–38). He was arrested, tried in the Bukharin trial of March 1938, and executed. RWD

GRISHIN, Viktor Vasil'evich (b. 1914) A long-serving member of the Politburo (1971–86), Grishin was a conservative Communist by disposition and a challenger for the General Secretaryship at the time when it was attained by Gorbachev in March 1985. Within a year of that struggle for the succession to Chernenko he had been ousted entirely from the leadership.

Grishin, the son of a railwayman, was born in Serpukhov, near Moscow. He studied in the 1930s at technical college and by correspondence course and became in succession a train driver, foreman and deputy manager of the Serpukhov Locomotive Depot. He served in the army from 1938 to 1940, joining the Communist Party during that time. He subsequently embarked on a career in the party apparatus. By 1952 he was already second secretary of the Moscow party organization and a member of the Central Committee.

From 1956 to 1967 Grishin was head of the Soviet trade unions, but in 1967 he was given the more powerful post of First Secretary of the party organization in Moscow which he held until late 1985 when he was ousted at Gorbachev's instigation and replaced by Boris Yel'tsin. His removal from the Politburo – of which he had been a full member since 1971 – followed at the next plenary session of the Central Committee in February 1986. AHB

GRISHIN, Yevgeniy Romanovich (b. 1931) Speed skater. Initially a top Soviet cyclist in the early 1950s, he switched to speed skating to become one of the world's greatest skaters. He took part in no fewer than four winter Olympics from 1956 to 1968, winning four gold medals (in the 500 m and 1500 m in 1956 and 1960), a silver medal in the 500 m in 1964, and coming fourth in 1968 at the age of thirty-seven. Upon retirement from competition he took up coaching and was responsible for the 1976 500 m Olympic champion Valeriy Muratov. JW

GRITSAY, Aleksey Mikhailovich (b. 1914) Painter, born in St Petersburg. After studying at the Academy of Arts under I. Brodsky in the 1930s, Gritsay concentrated on landscape painting, especially of the environs of Leningrad. He has had a distinguished career as a teacher in Moscow and Leningrad. Among his students is Nazarenko. JEB

GROMAN, Vladimir Gustavovich (1874–1937?) A leading non-party economist and planner in the 1920s. The son of a teacher of German nationality and a Russian mother, Groman was arrested while a student at Moscow University, and exiled. He eventually graduated in 1908. He was a member of the RSDLP from 1900, and a Menshevik by 1905. He worked as a statistician in Tver' and Penza, developing new methods of studying economic fluctuations. He was a defencist during the war, a leading statistician, and an organizer of food supplies. Under the Provisional Government he was an enthusiastic planner, becoming a leading figure in Gosplan from 1921, combining support for industrialization and for the NEP market economy. He was arrested in July 1930 and was a key figure in the 'Menshevik' trial of March 1931, being sentenced to ten years' imprisonment. RWD

GROMASHEVSKY, Lev Vasil'evich (1887–1980) Epidemiologist. A graduate of Novorossiysk University in Odessa in 1912, Gromashevsky served as head of the department of epidemiology and rector of the Odessa Medical Institute (1918–27), gaining recognition for his work on typhus, typhoid, and cholera during and after the Civil War. He subsequently directed a number of important research centres in public health. He was a central figure in organizing the medical field of epidemiology in the Soviet Union and in formulating government policy in the handling of infectious diseases. He published many works on public health policy and on insect transmission and seasonal variations in the occurrence of infectious enteric diseases. MBA

GROMYKO, Andrey Andreevich
(1909–1989) One of the best-known
Soviet politicians over many years,
Gromyko was also the longest-serving
Foreign Minister in Soviet history,
holding that office from 1957 until
1985. In his earlier years as Foreign
Minister, he was often regarded as no
more than an obedient functionary,
but even then his knowledge and
experience gave him influence and
after he became a full member of the
Politburo in 1973 Gromyko was one
of the most important men in the Politburo, second only to the General Secretary in terms of authority in the
international arena.

Born into a family of Russian peasants in the village of Old Gromyki
in Belorussia, where the majority of
inhabitants bore the name, Gromyko,
the future Foreign Minister studied
economics and agronomy in the 1930s
and worked on the journal, *Voprosy
ekonomiki* (Problems of Economics)
from 1936 to 1939 before being
recruited into the diplomatic service
which had just been purged by Stalin.

Molotov, who had become Foreign
Minister, was impressed by Gromyko
and the latter's promotion was rapid.
As early as 1943 he was appointed
Ambassador to the United States and
in the course of his diplomatic career
he had meetings with every American
President from Roosevelt to Reagan.
Gromyko headed the Soviet delegation at the Dumbarton Oaks conference on the foundation of the
United Nations and participated in
the 1945 Yalta and Potsdam conferences.

From 1946 to 1948 he was Permanent Soviet Representative at the
UN Security Council and in 1949 he
became First Deputy Minister of
Foreign Affairs. In a demotion, linked

to Molotov's loss of favour with Stalin,
he was sent to London as Soviet
Ambassador in 1952, but within a
month of Stalin's death in 1953 he
was back in Moscow as First Deputy
Minister again.

It was a mark of Gromyko's adap-
tability that when his patron,
Molotov, fell foul of Khrushchev in
1957 (as a leading participant in the
so-called anti-party group which was,
above all, an anti-Khrushchev group),
Gromyko became Foreign Minister.
He proceeded to work closely with
Khrushchev who at times, however,
treated him with scant respect. Under
Brezhnev, Gromyko's influence grew
stronger (especially after his promotion to the Politburo in 1973) and
during the brief General Secretaryships of Andropov and Chernenko – when both of these Soviet
leaders were in poor health – Gromyko
exercised more day-to-day power over
foreign policy than anyone else within
the Soviet Union. Although Gromyko
was older than either of them, he was
still in robust good health when
the Soviet Union was faced by its
third leadership succession in as many
years with the death of Chernenko in
1985.

Gromyko gave decisive support at
that time to Gorbachev who may well
have impressed him with the diplomatic success of his visit to Britain just
three months earlier and who was
quite clearly the ablest of the possible
candidates. Gromyko himself was a
highly competent defender of Soviet
interests as he perceived them, but he
lacked the imagination and capacity
for new thinking which Gorbachev
was looking for when he reached the
top leadership post. Since, however,
Gromyko was a figure of high standing
in the Politburo and one, moreover,

to whom Gorbachev owed a political debt, Gorbachev was prepared to break for a time with the precedent established by Brezhnev and followed by Andropov and Chernenko whereby the General Secretary also became head of state. This honorific post of Chairman of the Presidium of the Supreme Soviet was offered to Gromyko who thereby found himself between June 1985 (when he was succeeded at the Foreign Ministry by Shevardnadze) and his retirement in 1988 dealing with domestic matters for the first time since his days as an economist in the 1930s.

When Gorbachev removed a majority of the 'dead souls' on the Central Committee (those members who had already lost the functions which had gained them Central Committee membership in the first place) in April 1989, Gromyko was one of those to go. In July of that year he died. Shortly before his death he published memoirs which were not only economical with the truth but repeated some straight fictions about Soviet foreign policy that glasnost' had already called into question and that were soon to be repudiated by the Soviet leadership itself. AHB

GROSSMAN, Leonid Petrovich (1888–1965) Literary critic, prose writer, and lecturer on literary history and theory. A largely traditional, socio-biographical approach reveals itself in some thirty studies he wrote on nineteenth-century Russian literature (Pushkin, Leskov, Sukhovo-Kobylin and Turgenev) and on comparative topics. The principal focus of his interest was Dostoevsky. JAEC

GROSSMAN, Vasiliy Semenovich (1905–1964) Jewish journalist and novelist who began his career depict-ing working-class life in the Donbass, and then became one of the best known Soviet war correspondents. In the late forties he and Erenburg drew up a documentation of Nazi crimes against the Jews, which was banned in the Soviet Union, and only appeared in the West decades later (*The Black Book*, 1980). The first part of his huge novel about the battle of Stalingrad, *For the Just Cause* (1952), was attacked for its 'abstract humanism', a feature much intensified in the second part, which openly drew the parallel between Hitlerism and Stalinism. All the copies and drafts of this part were seized by the KGB, and it was only published much later in the West (*Life and Fate*, 1980). His memories and reflections on collectivization and the purges, (*Forever Flowing*, 1970), which offer important historical testimony, were equally unacceptable to the authorities. Only in 1988 to 1989 was it found possible to publish these last two works in the USSR. GAH

GROSSU, Semen Kuz'mich (b. 1934) Agronomist and party official from Moldavia, Grossu was Secretary of the Moldavian Communist Party (1970–76), Chairman of its Council of Ministers (1976–80), and was Party First Secretary there from 1980. The last first secretary in the union republics to have been appointed under Brezhnev, he was replaced by P. K. Luchinsky in late 1989. JHM

GRUM-GRZHIMAYLO, Vladimir Yefimovich (1864–1928) Graduating from St Petersburg Mining Institute in 1885, Grum-Grzhimaylo worked as an engineer and manager in various engineering and iron and steel works. During the First World War he set up the 'Metal Bureau' which designed furnaces; he re-established the bureau in 1924. He influenced Soviet technological thinking. He was elected a Corresponding Member of the Academy of Sciences in 1925. RWD

GRUSHEVOY, Konstantin Stepanovich (1906–1982) A life-long friend and ally of L. I. Brezhnev, with whom he studied in the early 1930s. He became a party official in Dnepropetrovsk, was a political officer in the Great Fatherland War, and returned to the Armed Forces in 1953. From 1965 to his death he headed the Political Administration of Moscow Military District – a key post for a General Secretary. JHM

GUBAYDULINA, Sofiya Asgatovna (b. 1931) Composer. Sofiya Gubaydulina was born in Chistopol'. After first studying at Kazan' Conservatory, she went on to Moscow Conservatory where in composition she was a pupil of Nikolay Peyko. After graduating in 1959, she stayed on for a further three years as a post-graduate student, her supervisor being Shaporin. An avant-garde composer, she has experimented widely in various media. GS

GUBENKO, Nikolay Nikolaevich (b. 1941) Gubenko was trained as an actor and joined the Taganka Theatre in Moscow in 1964, since when he has played a variety of supporting parts in many productions. He made his début as a film director in 1972, pursuing this career in parallel with his acting throughout the 1970s and 1980s. Late in 1989, to the surprise and delight of reform-minded figures in the world of the arts, he was appointed Minister of Culture, the first qualified practitioner to hold this post. GSS

GUDYASHVILI, Lado (Vladimir) Davidovich (1896–1980) Painter and designer. Born in Tiflis where he attended art school before the First World War, Gudyashvili then left for Paris in 1919 (returning to Tiflis in 1926). Influenced by Lev Bakst and Modigliani, Gudyashvili was also deeply interested in the national art of Georgia, particularly miniatures and architecture. Apart from his portraits and allegorical scenes, he also designed a number of opera and ballet productions for Tbilisi. JEB

GUKOVSKY, Grigoriy Aleksandrovich (1902–1950) A literary critic and historian, Gukovsky was brought up in Petrograd and influenced by the Formalists, the youngest of the great Leningrad school of teachers and critics. Gukovsky specialized in Russian literature of the eighteenth century. He was exiled during the Second World War, arrested as a Jew in 1948, and died in the Butyrka prison, but had managed to complete books on Pushkin and Gogol'. GSS

GUMBARIDZE, Givi Grigor'evich b. 1945) A graduate of Tbilisi University, Gumbaridze worked in various branches of internal affairs from 1966 to 1986, rarely leaving the Georgian capital. Since 1986 he has been, in rapid succession, head of the Organizational Department of the Georgian Central Committee, First Secretary of Tbilisi *gorkom*, and Chairman of the Georgian KGB. After the Tbilisi riots of April 1989, Gumbaridze was made First Secretary of the Georgian Communist Party, adding, later that year, the position of Chairman of the Presidium of the Georgian Supreme Soviet. In July 1990 he became a member of the Politburo of the CPSU. JHM

GUMILEV, Nikolay Stepanovich (1886–1921) A poet, dramatist and critic, born in Kronstadt. Gumilev was the founder and driving force behind the post-Symbolist Acmeist group in St Petersburg. His collections of lyric verse include *Quiver* (1916) and *Pillar of Fire* (1921). He led expeditions to Africa, and fought heroically in the First World War. He was engaged in military missions abroad under the Provisional Government, but returned to Petrograd and plunged into educational and publishing activities. He was shot as a counter-revolutionary, and virtually unpublished and unpersoned in the USSR until the Gorbachev thaw. His high-toned romanticism of adventure and personal daring made him a powerful covert influence on the first generation of Soviet poets; his contempt for revolutionary authority has made him a hero among emigrants from the Soviet Union. GSS

GURVICH, Aleksandr Gavrilovich (1874–1954) Histologist. After graduating from the University of Munich in 1897, Gurvich worked for a decade in France and Switzerland and became established as a leading histologist of his generation with the publication of his innovative classic, *Morphologie und Biologie der Zelle* (Jena, 1904; 2nd edn, 1930). He became a professor at the Petersburg Higher Courses for Women (1907–18), Tauride University in Simferopol' (1918–23), and Moscow University (1924–30). In the 1920s, stimulated by recent events in physics, Gurvich proposed his novel theory that the dividing cell emits 'mitogenetic rays', a kind of electromagnetic radiation that stimulates other cells to divide in a manner analogous to radioactive decay, thus producing coordinated organic growth and development. Although his Soviet students claimed to have discovered laboratory evidence of such rays, and even to have calculated their frequencies in angstrom units, contemporary Western attempts to replicate these findings proved unsuccessful. He was nonetheless chosen to head the experimental biology division of the All-Union Institute of Experimental Medicine (1930–45) and the Institute of Experimental Biology of the USSR Academy of Medical Sciences (1945–48), where he and his students continued their mitogenetic researches. Although his results remain unverified, Soviet sources continue to portray Gurvich's 'mitogenetic rays' as a major discovery. MBA

GUSEV, Petr Andreevich (b. 1904) Celebrated dancer, choreographer and teacher. Gusev studied with Aleksandr Shiryaev and Vladimir Ponomarev at the Petrograd Ballet School from which he graduated in 1922. During the early 1920s he was also one of the founders of the experimental Young Ballet (*Molodoy balet*).

He danced with the Kirov troupe from 1922 to 1935 where, with his partners Ol'ga Mungalova and Ol'ga Lepeshinskaya, he developed a semi-classical, semi-acrobatic style of dance that figured prominently in the experimental ballets by Lopukhov, including *Tanzsymphonia* (1923), *The Ice Maiden* (1927), *The Nutcracker* (1929), *Coppélia* (1934), and *Bright Stream* (1935). Gusev also danced at the Malyy Theatre (1934–35) and at the Bol'shoy Theatre (1935–45).

In addition to his dancing career, Gusev was a leading teacher, known particularly for his strong classical background and for his instruction in supported adagio. He taught at the Leningrad Theatre Institute (1922–30), the Bol'shoy Ballet School (1935–41), and the Peking Ballet School (1957–60), where he staged a number of ballets. Gusev also headed the Kirov ballet company (1945–50), choreographed for the Stanislavsky and Nemirovich-Danchenko Theatre (1935–41, 1943–46, 1951–57), and headed the ballet companies of the Malyy Theatre (1960–62) and the Novosibirsk Theatre of Opera and Ballet (1962–66).

Gusev created superlative revivals of numerous ballets from the classical repertoire. He also created several original works, such as *Seven Beauties* (1952, Baku), his first full-length ballet, which had a symphonic score by the Azeri composer Kara Karaev; *The Ice Maiden* (1964, Novosibirsk), done in the style of Lopukhov; and *The Three Musketeers* (1966, Novosibirsk).

A prolific writer, Gusev contributed to the literature on dance theory and history and has been associated with several Soviet dance journals. scs

GVAKHARIYA, G. V. (?–1937?) A party economic leader. Gvakhariya held various posts in internal trade in the early 1920s, becoming a leading figure in Rabkrin, where he advocated plans for reorganizing and expanding industry against the advice of special-ist. He moved to VSNKh with Ordzhonikidze in 1930, acting as 'troubleshooter' in the Donbass coal industry. He was appointed director of the Makeevka iron and steel works in 1933. This was the first factory to refuse a subsidy in the campaign to improve industrial efficiency. RWD

GVISHIANI, Dzhermen Mikhaylovich (b. 1928) Son of a prominent Georgian NKVD official ('Dzhermen' is an acronym from Dzerzhinsky and Menzhinsky) and Beria supporter, purged in 1953. He married the daughter of Aleksey Kosygin, probably in the late 1940s – an alliance of political benefit to both families. Deputy Chairman of the State Committee for Science and Technology 1965–85, he was a major spokesman on scientific and management policy under Brezhnev and popularizer in Soviet terms of Western systems and management theory. Under Gorbachev he spent a year as Deputy Chairman of the State Planning Committee before retiring in 1986. JHM

I

IGNAT'EV, Semen Denisovich
(1904–1983) A typical member of the
group of politicians on the verge of
power at Stalin's death, and who lost
out in the subsequent struggles. A
Ukrainian from near the present Kiro-
vograd, Ignat'ev took part in consolidating the new regime in Central
Asia in the 1920s and was in the
Cheka. Between 1935 and 1949 he was
party First Secretary in Buryatiya,
Bashkiriya and Belorussiya. In the next
two years he returned to Uzbekistan
as a plenipotentiary of the Moscow
party authorities, and seems briefly to
have been head of the Central Committe Department for Party Organs.
Between 1951 and 1953 he was USSR
Minister of State Security, and in
January 1953 'unmasked' the 'Doctors
Plot' against the Soviet leadership; this
was a fabricated conspiracy, and it
seems likely that it was aimed *against*
L. P. Beria. Between October 1952
and March 1953 Ignat'ev was a full
member of the Presidium of the
Central Committee, and perhaps also
a Central Committee Secretary.
Eclipsed in the immediate aftermath
of Stalin's death, he returned to positions of moderate responsibility after
Beria's arrest. He was party First Secretary in the Bashkir and Tatar ASSRs
until his retirement in 1960. JHM

IGNATOV, Nikolay Grigor'evich
(1901–1966) Russian politician.
Though not a Khrushchev protégé,
Ignatov was promoted into the Secretariat and the Presidium of the
Central Committee after the fall of the
'anti-party group' and was one of
Khrushchev's strongest supporters in
attacking them. His earlier career was
as party secretary in a number of
regions and, briefly, USSR Minister
for Procurements (1952–53). In 1960
he lost his post in the Secretariat and
in 1961 his Presidium membership. He
subsequently occupied minor state
posts connected with agriculture. WJT

IGRUNOV, Nikolay Stefanovich
(b. 1932) Graduate of Moscow University and party official. Igrunov
worked in Belgorod province until
1974 and thereafter in the Central
Committee apparatus in Moscow, specializing in the internal management
of the CPSU. From 1985 to 1987 he
was Deputy Head of the Organ-
izational-Party Work Department,
before becoming Second Secretary of
the Belorussian Communist Party in
October 1987. He was elected to the
Congress of People's Deputies in 1989.
JHM

**ILF, Ilya (Fainzilberg, Ilya Arnol-
dovich)** (1897–1937) and **PETROV,
Yevgeniy (Kataev, Yevgeniy**

Petrovich) (1903–1942) Ilf and Petrov (brother of Valentin Kataev), the Soviet Union's best-known team of satirists, were both born in Odessa but met only while writing for the Moscow railwaymen's periodical *The Whistle* in 1925. They began to collaborate on humorous sketches for *Pravda* and *The Literary Gazette* before going on to try longer works. Their *The Twelve Chairs* (1928) and *The Golden Calf* (1931) which chronicle the picaresque adventures during NEP of a 'great operator', Ostap Bender, have endured as favourites with the reading public. During the thirties they travelled extensively; six months travelling around the United States (1934–35) produced *One-Storeyed America*, only partially written jointly because Ilf was already suffering from tuberculosis to which he succumbed in 1937. After Ilf's death, Petrov continued writing; he joined the party in 1939 and had almost completed his *Journey to the Land of the Communists* (1939–42) when he was killed in a plane crash in 1942. KC

IL'ICHEV, Leonid Fedorovich (b. 1906) A Soviet politician who reached the highest position of his career in the later years of Khrushchev's leadership, Il'ichev was born in Krasnodar' (then Yekaterinodar') and joined the Communist Party at the age of eighteen in 1924. A graduate of the Institute of Red Professors (1930), Il'ichev taught in higher educational institutions from 1930 until 1938 and from 1938 to 1958 worked on a number of journals and newspapers, including *Bol'shevik*, *Pravda* and *Izvestiya* (of which he was for a time editor-in-chief). From 1958 to 1961 he was head of the Department of Propaganda and Agitation of the Central Committee of the CPSU and in 1961

he became a Secretary of the Central Committee with special responsibility for ideology, a post he kept until 1965. Il'ichev's position as an ideologist was a conservative one and he gave no encouragement to those party intellectuals in Khrushchev's time who were attempting to introduce some reformist ideas. By academic background a 'philosopher', Il'ichev was elected to membership of the Academy of Sciences in 1962. He lost his post in the Central Committee Secretariat in 1965 and, in a demotion, became one of several deputy ministers at the Ministry of Foreign Affairs. AHB

IL'INSKY, Igor' Vladimirovich (1901–1987) Actor. Il'insky was an enormously popular comic actor of stage and screen. He began his career in Foregger's Theatre of the Four Masks in 1918 appearing in French farces and worked in the Meyerhold Theatre from 1920 to 1935, acting in Meyerhold's productions of Verhaeren's *The Dawn* (1920), Mayakovsky's *Mystery-Bouffe* (1921) and Ostrovsky's *The Forest* (1924). He later worked in the Moscow Malyy Theatre. His first film role was the detective in Protazanov's *Aelita* (1924) and he subsequently played with great success in *The Cigarette Girl from Mosselprom* (1924), *The Tailor from Torzhok* (1925), *The Three Millions Trial* and *Miss Mend* (both 1926), *The Kiss of Mary Pickford* (1927) and *The Feast of St Jürgen* (1930). One of his greatest film roles was his portrayal of the bureaucrat Byvalov in Aleksandrov's *Volga-Volga* (1938). RT

ILTNER, Edgar Karlovich (1925–1983) Painter. Born in Burini, Latvia and graduating from the Academy of Arts, Riga in 1956, Iltner taught at the Rosenthal Art School and then at the Academy. Favouring a lyrical style with restrained colour schemes, Iltner concentrated on landscapes and sea-scapes, for example, *All the Ships Are at Sea* (1967) JEB

IL'YUSHIN, Sergey Vladimirovich (1894–1977) Sergey Il'yushin was one of the foremost Soviet aircraft design-ers, responsible for a series of successful military and passenger planes. Born in the Vologda region of a poor peasant family, he became interested in avi-ation in his youth. He joined the party in 1918, graduated from the Zhu-kovskiy Military Aviation Engin-eering Academy in 1926, and began design work in the early 1930s. Much of his early work was connected with long-range bombers. Possibly his greatest achievement was the Il–2, the wartime armoured assault plane which was built in vast quantity and played a major role in the defeat of the German army. In the post-war years Il'yushin was responsible for a series of bombers and transports, including the first Soviet jet bomber, the Il–28 of 1948, and the successful Il–62 pass-enger plane of 1962. Three times a Hero of Socialist Labour (1941, 1957, 1974), he was elected to the Academy of Sciences in 1968. Since his death leadership of the Il'yushin design bureau has been in the hands of his former deputy, Genrikh Novozhilov. JMC

INBER, Vera Mikhaylovna (1890–1972) Poet. Her first collection of poetry was published in 1914 in Paris, where she was studying. Associated with the Constructivists Selvinsky and Zelinsky in the twenties, she returned to a more conservative style in her long poem *Pulkovo Meridian* (1942–46) for which she received a Stalin Prize. BH

INFANTE-ARANA, Frantsisko (b. 1943) Designer. Born in Moscow of a Spanish father and Russian mother,

Infante attended art school there from 1962 to 1965 while working on kinetic art with the Movement group. In 1968 he began to create land happenings using natural materials such as snow and grass, and in the 1970s developed projects for cosmic architecture as well as many interior designs for exhi-bitions. Since 1976 he has been working on an artistic system – the Artifact – that focuses on the interplay between artificial objects and the natural environment. JEB

IOFAN, Boris Mikhaylovich (1891–1976) Architect. Born in Odessa, Iofan – generally recognized as a primary exponent of Socialist Realism in architecture – achieved instant fame when his project won the competition for the proposed Palace of Soviets in Moscow in 1933. He trained in Odessa, St Petersburg and Rome before the Revolution, even designing the first Soviet embassy abroad in Rome in 1923. While interested in functional architecture, as is dem-onstrated by his housing complex on Serafimovich Street in Moscow (1928–31), Iofan is now remembered for his more decorative, Italianate style, exemplified by his designs for the Soviet pavilions at the 'Exposition Universelle' in Paris in 1937 and the New York World's Fair in 1939, and also by his Bauman metro station in Moscow (1939–44). JEB

IOGANSON, Boris Valdimirovich (1893–1973) Painter. Born in Moscow, Ioganson – a supporter of Realism and Academic art – gradu-ated from the MIPSA in 1912 and was an enthusiastic member of AKhRR in the 1920s. His revolutionary and heroic scenes such as the *Interrogation of the Communists* (1933) and *At an Old Ural Factory* (1937) gained him a solid reputation as a Socialist Realist. From

1958 to 1962 he was president of the Academy of Arts. JEB

IOSELIANI, Otar (b. 1934) Georgian film director. Ioseliani studied in Moscow under Dovzhenko and is best known for his lengthy and complex film *Pastorale* (1976), which won the Press Jury Prize at the 1982 Berlin Film Festival. Ioseliani then made *Les Favoris de la Lune* (1984) in France. RT

IPATIEFF, Vladimir Nikolaevich (1867–1952) A leading Russian chemist before and after the revolution. Educated at the Artillery Academy in St Petersburg, Ipatieff was made a professor in 1900, and elected a full member of the Academy of Sciences in 1916. He cooperated with the Bolsheviks in a senior research-organizing capacity in VSNKh in the 1920s. His memoirs published in America are the best guide to industrial research organization under NEP. He remained abroad from 1929, working in America, becoming a world figure in industrial chemistry. RWD

ISACHENKO, Boris Lavrent'evich (1871–1948) Microbiologist and botanist. After graduating from Petersburg University in 1895, Isachenko taught at the Peterhof Agricultural Institute (1902–35) and became director of the Chief Botanical Garden of the USSR Academy of Sciences during the post-revolutionary decade (1917–30). He also created and chaired the department of microbiology at Petrograd University (1918–29) and directed a laboratory of general microbiology at the All-Union Institute of Experimental Medicine in Leningrad (1929–37). He was appointed director of the Institute of Microbiology of the USSR Academy of Sciences in 1939 and was elected full member of that academy in 1946. Most of Isachenko's research concerned marine biology, particularly the microbiological constitution of polar oceans. An island in the Karsky sea was named in his honour. MBA

ISAKOV, Ivan Stepanovich (1894–1967) Former Chief of Naval Staff. Isakov saw active naval service in the Civil War years. He was Chief of Staff, then Commander of the Baltic Fleet (1933–38), and head of the Voroshilov Naval Academy (1938–39). He held the position of First Deputy People's Commissar of the Navy throughout the war (1938–46), and played a key role in determining Soviet naval operations as Chief of Staff of the Soviet Naval Forces (1941–43 and 1946–47). Isakov was Deputy Commander-in-Chief of the Soviet Navy from 1947 to 1950. He acquired the rank of Admiral of the Fleet in 1955. RA

ISAKOVA, Bayan Seilkhanovna (b. 1957) Deputy Chairman of the Soviet of the Union of the USSR Supreme Soviet, Bayan Isakova was elected to the Congress of People's Deputies of the USSR in 1989 from an electoral district in the Kokchetav region of Kazakhstan. A Kazakh by nationality and a member of the Communist Party, she has a higher education in medicine and is a department head in a district hospital. AHB

ISAKOVSKY, Mikhail Vasil'evich (1900–1973) A poet, born near Smolensk. A party member since 1918, Isakovsky was the bard of Stalinist Socialist Realism, a prolific author of orthodox lyrics, including some classic Soviet songs, and a prominent official of the Union of Writers. GSS

ISKANDER, Fazil' Abdulovich (b. 1929) Abkhazian novelist whose affectionate and amusing portrait of his homeland centres round two cycles of tales, one connected with a boy called Chik, the other with the memories of a village elder, from pre-revolutionary times to the post-Stalin period. The latter cycle was published in the Soviet Union without its Stalin chapters (*Uncle Sandro of Chegem*, 1973) which were added in a later western publication (1979); only in 1988 was the novel finally published in full. *The Goatibex Constellation* (1966) was an influential satire on Khrushchev's agricultural campaigns. GAH

IVANOV, Anatoliy Stepanovich (b. 1928) 'Village prose' writer. Ivanov was born in Eastern Kazakhstan, not far from the Siberian border. In his prose he depicts Siberian village life and nature. After completing his studies in the faculty of journalism at Alma-Ata University and doing his army service he settled in the vicinity of Novosibirsk. He moved to Moscow towards the end of the 1960s. Ivanov, who has been a member of the CPSU since 1952, is deeply committed to communism. He has been the Chief Editor of the reactionary literary monthly *Molodaya gvardiya* since 1972. Ivanov's views are blatantly anti-Semitic and pro-Stalinist and they are vigorously promoted in his journal. He holds the Jews, not Stalin, responsible for the destruction of the Russian peasantry in the 1930s. He regards the cultural liberalization of the Gorbachev era as a 'negative tendency' and the proposed reforms as a gateway to anarchy. In essence, he remains an uncompromising opponent of cultural and political change in the Soviet Union. RHP

IVANOV, Il'ya Ivanovich (1870–1932) Reproductive physiologist, animal breeder. After graduating from Khar'kov University in 1896, Ivanov spent two years at the Pasteur Institute in Paris and returned to Petersburg to work in various laboratories in the capital. In 1908 he organized a new physiology division of the Veterinary Laboratory of the Ministry of Internal Affairs and, in 1920, a zootechnical station at Askania-Nova, where he studied hybridization. During the pre-revolutionary decades, he achieved international fame for his pioneering work on artificial insemination, developing techniques for use in cattle and other domesticated animals. After the revolution the laboratory was transferred to Moscow and transformed into the Experimental Veterinary Institute, and he continued to work there (1917–30) except for three years abroad (1921–24). He spent 1926–27 in Africa attempting unsuccessfully to hybridize humans and anthropoid apes through artificial insemination. He returned to work briefly at the Moscow Zootechnical Institute (1928–30). In the late 1920s his techniques went into widespread Soviet use, but he was arrested in December 1930 in connection with the attack on bourgeois specialists during the collectivization of agriculture. Following his release in June 1931, he was exiled to Alma-Ata where he died of a stroke. MBA

IVANOV, Konstantin Konstantinovich (b. 1907) Conductor. Konstantin Ivanov was born at Yefremov. On the death of his father in 1920, he joined a Soviet cavalry regiment, where he became a trumpeter. He later studied conducting at the Moscow Conservatory, graduating in 1937. He held various conducting posts (1935–41) until he was appointed conductor of the Grand Symphony Orchestra of the All-Union Radio Committee (1941–46) and chief conductor of the State Symphony Orchestra of the USSR (1946–65), with which he made several world tours. He is also a composer, the recipient of various State Prizes, and was made a People's Artist of the USSR in 1958. GS

IVANOV, Modest Vasil'evich (1875–1942) Son of a schoolmaster, Ivanov joined the Imperial Russian Navy, graduated from the Naval Academy in 1900, taking part in the First World War with the rank of Captain First Grade. Commanding the cruiser *Diana* between 1915 and 1917 he was elected in May 1917 to command the second Cruiser Brigade of the Baltic Fleet. Other naval officers suffered a dire fate at the hands of disaffected sailors. In November 1917 Ivanov worked with the Bolsheviks in the naval command, acting as adviser to the Navy Minister and, from the end of November 1917, administering the Naval Ministry, joining the Supreme Naval Collegiate as a full member. In recognition of these services and acknowledging his 'devotion to the people and to the revolution', the All-Russian Conference of Fleets in December 1917 conferred the rank of rear-admiral on him, the first such promotion since the October Revolution.

Preventing 'sabotage' within the Naval Ministry and working on plans for the democratization of the Navy, in February 1918 Ivanov proceeded to work with a number of commissions concerned with ship-repairing, moving to the staff of the Southern Front and the centre of the Civil War in August 1919. His subsequent duties and appointments included the Inspectorate of *VeCheka* troops and the organization of watch and defence systems for Soviet maritime borders.

In 1936 he became a Hero of Labour. JE

IVANOV, Nikolay Veniaminovich (b. 1952) Along with Tel'man Gdlyan, Ivanov (who is of Russian nationality) has become something of a folk hero among Soviet citizens for his investigations of corruption among high-ranking officials. Ivanov is an investigator of specially serious cases attached to the office of the Procurator General of the USSR. In 1989 his widespread popular support was demonstrated when he was elected to represent Leningrad in the national-territorial section of the elections for the Congress of People's Deputies of the USSR. He first came to prominence as a result of his investigation of the 'Uzbek affair', a wide net of corruption which involved not only many senior officials in Uzbekistan but Leonid Brezhnev's son-in-law and other highly placed figures in Moscow. Ivanov and Gdlyan extended their accusations of malpractice to embrace also members of the Politburo and, as a result, have been subjected to fierce counter-attack. They were criticized by the new Soviet parliament for making accusations for which they had produced no evidence, but the Congress of People's Deputies declined in 1990 to remove their parliamentary immunity which would have opened up the possibility of Ivanov and Gdlyan themselves being charged with improper investigatory methods and with slander. In that same year, however, Ivanov was expelled from the Communist Party. AHB

IVANOV, V. I. (1885–?) In charge of the construction of the Stalingrad Tractor Factory, Ivanov was the epitome of a crude and violent, but not unpopular, Bolshevik organizer. He had a break-down as a result of the rushed completion of the factory in 1930. Of working-class parentage, he studied at the Kronstadt Military-Naval School, and later worked as an electrician on the railways. Ivanov had been a militant from 1908, joining the party in 1915. He served in the infantry and the Cheka during the Civil War, but was temporarily expelled from the party for disorderly behaviour in a monastery. He held various party, Soviet, and administrative positions in the 1920s. He was put in charge of Stalingrad construction from September 1928 to October 1930, and then worked in other industrial jobs. RWD

IVANOV, Vsevolod Vyacheslavovich (1895–1963) A prose writer, born near Semipalatinsk in Siberia. After a wandering youth, Ivanov entered literature in 1915 under Gor'ky's tutelage, and came to fame with his Civil War story *Amoured Train 14–69* (1922). He published a steady stream of stories and novels throughout his career, but some major works remained unpublished in the USSR until the Gorbachev period (*Z*, first published abroad in 1983). GSS

IVANOV, Vyacheslav Nikolaevich (b. 1938) Sportsman. Born in Moscow, he was the only man in the history of rowing to have won the Olympic Diamond sculls three times: at the 1956, 1960 and 1964 Games. He dominated Soviet single sculls from 1956 to 1966, remaining undefeated in national championships for those eleven years. He was European champion four times between 1956 and 1964, and world champion in 1962. JWR

IVANOV-RAZUMNIK (Ivanov), Razumnik Vasilievich (1878–1946) A literary historian and critic born in the Semipalatinsk region, he is best known as the chief theoretician of the Scythians (1916–24), editor of their journals and miscellanies, and a founder of the Free Philosophical Association (Volfila) in 1918. He contended that the Scythian, a modern heir to the fierce nomadic tribe in Southern Russia around the eighth to seventh century B.C., is first and foremost a maximalist and revolutionary who instinctively revolts against 'any order' and any form of 'philistinism'. A former socialist revolutionary, he was imprisoned on and off between 1933 and 1941 and finally left for Germany. KC

IVANOVS, Janis (b. 1906) Latvian composer. Janis Ivanovs was born in Preili. After graduating from the Riga Conservatory in 1933, where his composition teacher was Jāzeps Vītols, he worked for many years with the Latvian Radio. He was appointed to the teaching staff of the Conservatory in 1944, becoming a professor in 1955, and was made a People's Artist of the USSR in 1965. A prolific composer, he has written twenty symphonies, some of which employ polytonality. Much of his inspiration is drawn from his native Latvia. GS

IVANOVSKY, Aleksandr Viktorovich (1881–1967) Film director. Ivanovsky was a traditionalist director whose works were heavily criticized by the avant-garde. His films included: *The Palace and the Fortress* (1924), *Stepan Khalturin* (1925), *The Decembrists* (1927), *Yudushka Golovlev* (1934), *A Musical Story* (1940) and a version of Pushkin's *Eugene Onegin* (1959). RT

IVANOVSKY, Yevgeny Filippovich (b. 1918) Commander-in-Chief Ground Forces. Ivanovsky, a Belorussian, joined the Red Army in 1936 and commanded a tank regiment on various fronts during the Second

World War. Graduation from the General Staff Academy in 1958 led directly to appointment as First Deputy Chief of Staff, Far East Military District. He became First Deputy Commander (1965–68), then Commander (1968–72) of the Moscow Military District; Commander-in-Chief of the Soviet Forces in Germany (1972–80); and Commander of the Belorussian Military District (1980–85). In 1972 he gained the rank of Army General, having the previous year become a member of the CPSU Central Committee. Ivanovsky capped this model military career by replacing Marshal Petrov in January 1985 as Commander-in-Chief of the Soviet Ground Forces. RA

IVANS, Daynis (ĪVĀNS, Dainis) (b. 1954) A Latvian school-teacher and journalist, Ivans came to prominence in 1986 when he organized opposition to a hydroelectric scheme near Daugavpils. Since October 1988 he has been President of the Latvian People's Front. JHM

IVASHKO, Vladimir Antonovich (b. 1932) Deputy leader to Gorbachev of the Soviet Communist Party. A mining engineer, lecturer and party official, Ivashko was born in Poltava, but trained and spent most of his career in Khar'kov. From 1978 to 1986 he was Secretary for ideology of Khar'kov *obkom*, and then, in rapid succession, Secretary of the Ukrainian Communist Party (1986–87), First Secretary of Dnepropetrovsk *obkom* (1987–88), and Party Second Secretary for the Ukraine (1988–89). Elected First Secretary of the Ukrainian Communist Party in September and of the CPSU Politburo in December 1989, Ivashko faces the difficult task of succeeding V. V. Shcherbitsky and of working with the *Rukh* movement. He was elected to the Ukrainian Supreme Soviet in 1990 and for a period of less than one month (in June of that year) was its chairman. From July 1990, however, he embarked on a new and important phase of his political career in Moscow. At the Twenty-Eighth Congress of the CPSU he was elected to the post of Deputy General Secretary of the Soviet Communist Party. Ivashko, who was backed by Gorbachev, convincingly defeated his principal rival for the deputy leadership, Yegor Ligachev. AHB, JHM

J

JUZELIŪNAS, Julius (b. 1916) Lithuanian composer and teacher. Julius Juzeliūnas was born in Čepoles. After graduating from the Kaunas Conservatory in 1948, he completed his post-graduate studies at the Leningrad Conservatory, where his composition teacher was Viktor Voloshinov. In 1952 he was appointed to the staff of the Lithuanian Conservatory, Vilnius. He was made a People's Artist of the Latvian SSR in 1966 and a Doctor of Arts in 1973. Though politically orthodox as a composer, many of his works include organ parts and are concerned with contrapuntal problems. He has made occasional use of serialism. GS

K

KABALEVSKY, Dmitriy Borisovich (1904–1987) Composer and teacher. Kabalevsky was born in St Petersburg. After first studying at the Skryabin Music School (1919–25), he entered the Moscow Conservatory, taking composition with Myaskovsky and piano with Aleksandr Gol'denveyzer. After graduating in 1930, he was appointed to the teaching staff of Moscow Conservatory in 1932, becoming a professor in 1939. He was editor of the journal *Sovetskaya muzyka* (Soviet Music) (1940–46). A member of the party since 1940, he was made a People's Artist of the USSR in 1963 and a Doctor of Arts in 1965. In 1969 he was appointed president of the Scientific Council of Educational Aesthetics in the Academy of Pedagogical Sciences of the USSR and in 1972 became honorary president of the International Society of Music Education. Since 1954 he has been a member of the USSR Ministry of Culture collegium. A prolific composer in many genres, his overture to the opera *Colas Brugnon* (1938) and his suite *The Comedians* (1945) are internationally renowned. His piano music and music for children have a universal appeal. GS

KABKOV, Yakov Ivanovich (b. 1908) Kabkov, a member of the CPSU from 1930, graduated from an institute of the tinning industry in Odessa in 1937 and later worked in a variety of positions connected with the food and food processing industries in the Ukraine and latterly in Moscow. He was Minister of the Fishing Industry in the Ukraine (1955–57 and 1958–62) and from 1965 onwards worked in the Central Committee apparatus with responsibility for trade and consumer services. He was elected a candidate member of the CPSU Central Committee in 1971, 1976 and 1981. SLW

KACHALOV (né Shverubovich), Vasiliy Ivanovich (1875–1948) Stage, radio and film actor. Kachalov played fifty-five roles in the course of his career at the Moscow Art Theatre, including the leading roles in Aleksey Tolstoy's *Tsar Fedor Ioannovich* (1922), Ivanov's *Armoured Train 14–69* (1927) and Gor'ky's *Enemies* (1935). RT

KADYROV, Gayrat Khamidullaevich (b. 1939) Uzbek party and state official who moved from the town of Chirchik (Tashkent province) to become a department head (1970–84), then Secretary of the Uzbekistan Communist Party. From 1984 to 1989 he was Chairman of the Uzbekistan

Council of Ministers, and then Deputy Minister of Electrotechnical Industry and Instrument Making in Moscow. JHM

KAFENGAUZ, Lev Borisovich (?–1930?) A former Menshevik, a professor at Moscow University, who was in charge of the Central Department of Statistics of VSNKh in the 1920s. During this period Soviet industrial statistics and statistical surveys were among the best in the world. He was presumably exiled in 1930. RWD

KAGANOVICH, Lazar Moisevich (b. 1893) The long-lived Lazar Kaganovich was an old Bolshevik of working-class Jewish origin who became one of the most efficient and ruthless members of Stalin's Politburo. He helped Nikita Khrushchev in his pre-war political career but their relations soured in the post-war era and Kaganovich was a prominent member of the 'anti-party group' which tried unsuccessfully to remove Khrushchev from office in 1957.

Kaganovich, who was born in the village of Kabana in the Kiev region, began work at the age of fourteen in a tannery and when only eighteen joined the Bolshevik Party and became an energetic organiser. An active participant in the Bolshevik Revolution, he made rapid progress in his political career once it had triumphed. He headed the Ukrainian Communist Party from 1925 to 1928, became a candidate member of the Politburo in 1926 and a full member in 1930, while in 1928 he moved from Kiev to the Secretariat of the Central Committee. Kaganovich was First Secretary of the Moscow Party Committee from 1930 to 1935 and responsible, on the one hand, for the construction of the Moscow metro and, on the other, for the destruction of many historical monuments and churches.

Kaganovich was also head of the agricultural section of the party and thus bore substantial personal responsibility for the brutality involved in the collectivization of agriculture between 1929 and 1934. In a sense Kaganovich embodied the Stalin era; he was someone who got things done whatever the human cost. Industries to which he was asked to turn his attention (including the railway industry) usually worked better by the time he had finished with them.

Kaganovich's relations with Khrushchev deteriorated in the early post-war years when Khrushchev (who had worked under Kaganovich earlier both in the Ukraine and Moscow) was himself in charge of the Ukraine. Kaganovich was sent by Stalin to relieve him temporarily of his First Secretaryship of the Ukrainian party organization (although Khrushchev remained Chairman of the Ukrainian Council of Ministers).

Khrushchev's relations with Kaganovich never fully recovered from that episode and Kaganovich's standing even in Stalin's eyes declined during the last years of Stalin's life when many of his most loyal followers became the object of his increasingly irrational suspicion. Kaganovich was, however, a member of the Bureau of nine people within the larger Presidium of the Central Committee which Stalin created in 1952 and after Stalin's death he was one of the most important members of the new collective leadership. When his challenge to Khrushchev in 1957 failed, he was sent first to be manager of a cement works in Sverdlovsk before commencing his long retirement. AHB

KALASHNIKOV, Anatoliy Ivanovich (b. 1930) Wood engraver. Born in Moscow, Kalashnikov has emerged in recent decades as the pre-eminent Soviet wood-engraver. Trained in the reproductive engraving tradition by Ivan Pavlov, Kalashnikov's early engravings were in the realist tradition and enjoyed the patronage of the music publishing houses and the Ministry of Communications (postal designs). In 1988 he became the first Russian ever to be elected an Honorary Member of the Royal Society of Painter-Etchers and Engravers in London. WEB

KALASHNIKOV, Mikhail Timofeevich (b. 1919) One of the best-known of all Soviet weapons designers, Kalashnikov made his name as the creator of the AK 7.62 mm assault rifle, the most widely used and most successful of post-war small arms. Born in the Altai region of Siberia into a peasant family he joined the army in 1938 and soon showed aptitude as an inventor. After being seriously wounded in the autumn of 1941, he began work on the development of his famous rifle, which was adopted by the army in 1949. In the 1970s a 5.45 mm version was introduced. Since 1979 Kalashnikov has been chief designer of the Izhevsk machine-building plant. A party member since 1953, he served as a Supreme Soviet Deputy from 1966 to 1989. Awards include Hero of Socialist Labour (1958, 1976), Stalin Prize (1949) and Lenin Prize (1964). JMC

KALATOZOV, Mikhail Konstantinovich (1903–1973) Georgian film director. Kalatozov's films included: *Salt for Svanetia* (1930), *A Nail in the Boot* (1932), *Valeriy Chkalov* (1941) and *The Cranes Are Flying* (1957), which won the Palme d'Or at the 1958 Cannes Film Festival. RT

KALIN, Ivan Petrovich (b. 1935) Agronomist and party official from Moldavia, Kalin was Secretary of its Communist Party (1976–80), Chairman of the Presidium of its Supreme Soviet (1980–85) and from 1985 to January 1990 Chairman of the Moldavian Council of Ministers. He was not re-elected to the Moldavian Supreme Soviet in 1990. JHM

KALININ, Mikhail Ivanovich (1875–1946) A revolutionary who, like Stalin, spent the years prior to 1917 in the Russian underground (perhaps meeting the general secretary-to-be as early as 1900 when he was deported to Tiflis), Kalinin was one of the few 'Old Bolsheviks' to experience the luxury of a natural death. Although more an ally of Stalin than a devotee, he proved colourless enough to survive his last twenty years as a member of the Politburo.

After the October Revolution and a brief stint as mayor of Petrograd, Kalinin stepped in (at Lenin's suggestion) to head the Central Executive Committee following Yakov Sverdlov's death in 1919. He held that post until 1938 when he assumed the chairmanship of the Presidium of the Supreme Soviet. Kalinin was a candidate member of the first functioning Politburo and was promoted to full membership in 1926, along with Molotov and Voroshilov. Unlike those two, however, he is thought to have sided with Kirov during the 'Riyutin affair' and is said to have opposed the extremes of bloodshed during the Great Purges. (Stalin reportedly commented, 'You always were a liberal', but does not seem to have judged it a serious offence in Kalinin's case.) Kalinin proved flexible enough in 1928 to drop his pro-peasant beliefs and abandon the Rightists, and in general was a high-ranking but never crucial figure in the formative years of Bolshevik rule. His name, out of proportion to his legacy, is still commemorated in the Soviet Union by fourteen cities, most notably Kaliningrad (formerly Königsberg), oblasts, universities, theatres, and Kalinin Prospect in Moscow. MM

KALISTRATOVA, Sofiya Vasil'evna (b. 1907) Barrister, human rights advocate. A member of the Moscow bar, Kalistratova defended the dissidents Gorbanevskaya and Grigorenko in 1970 with skill and determination, and, as a result, was later barred from such activity. She also acted as a legal consultant to dissidents, and in 1977 she joined the Moscow group to monitor observation of the 1975 Helsinki accords. A case was mounted against her (1981–82), but dropped when this monitoring group disbanded. PBR

KALMANOVICH, Moisey Iosifich (1888–1937) Leading Bolshevik economic organizer. Born in a Siberian village, Kalmanovich joined the Bolsheviks in the summer of 1917. He held posts in food supplies and the food industry during the Civil War and in the early 1920s. He became chairman of the Industrial Bank in 1926, chairman of the new state-farm trust *Zernotrest* in 1928, and then deputy chairman of the new People's Commissariat for Agriculture of the USSR in December 1929. He replaced Pyatakov as chairman of the State Bank in October 1930, and was appointed People's Commissar for State Farms (1934–37). He was a candidate member of the Party Central Committee from 1930 to 1937. RWD

KALNBERZIN, Yan Eduardovich (Kalnbērnziņš, Jānis) (1893–1986) A dockworker from outside Riga,

Kalnberzin joined the revolutionaries in 1917 and fought for them in the Civil War. He was then active both in the USSR (where he atended the Institute of Red Professors) and illegally in his native Latvia, where he was imprisoned in 1939. Under the Soviet regime in 1940 he immediately became First Secretary of the Communist Party of Latvia, holding this post until 1959. After the crisis of the 'anti-party group', he was a candidate member of the Politburo (1957–61). He retired in 1970 as President of the Presidium of the Latvian Supreme Soviet. JHM

KAMENEV (Rozenfel'd), Lev Borisovich (1883–1936) Kamenev, one of the most prominent of the early Bolshevik leaders who later fell foul of Stalin, was born in Moscow where his father was an engine driver on the Moscow-Kursk railway. Both parents had completed some post-school education and had belonged to the radical student movement in the 1870s. His father, who had in fact been a fellow student of Ignatiy Grinevitsky, one of the assassins of Alexander II, was promoted to the position of chief engineer at a small nail factory in Vilna while Kamenev was still a schoolboy. He thus spent his childhood years in the company of workers and their children. In 1896 his father moved again, this time to Tiflis to work on the Transcaucasian railways, and all the family went with him. Kamenev completed his secondary education in Tiflis, and before he left school was already in touch with Marxist circles and beginning to read illegal Marxist literature. According to his authorized biography, the first pamphlet the young Kamenev read was Lassalle's 'Programme of the Workers', which encouraged his already developing interest in the labour movement and socialist politics.

Despite a poor assessment of his political reliability Kamenev was able to proceed from school to Moscow University, where he studied in the Law Faculty. Immediately active in student politics, he wrote a series of revolutionary leaflets and helped to organize strikes and demonstrations, as a result of which he was arrested and escorted back to Tiflis to live under police supervision. Kamenev resumed his political activity among local railway workers and shoemakers, and in 1902 went to Paris with the aim of studying revolutionary literature. There he met the leaders of the Social Democratic paper *Iskra* (The Spark), including Lenin, and became associated with the Bolshevik section of the party after the split the following year. He also met and married Trotsky's sister Ol'ga. Kamenev returned to Russia in 1903, continuing to be involved in political activism in Moscow, Tiflis and elsewhere, and participating in successive party congresses. He went abroad again at the end of 1908, becoming joint editor of the Bolshevik paper *Proletariy* (The Proletarian), which was published in Switzerland, and representing the Russian Social Democrats at international socialist congresses. At this time, together with Zinov'ev, he was among Lenin's closest and most trusted collaborators. In 1914 he returned to St Petersburg to take charge of *Pravda* and of the Bolshevik faction in the Fourth Duma. Arrested in 1915 and deported, despite his denunciation of Lenin's policy of 'revolutionary defeatism', he returned to Petrograd soon after the February Revolution and resumed his political work.

Kamenev was elected to the party Central Committee in April 1917 and became editor of the party paper *Pravda*. Initially, like some others including Stalin, he offered conditional support to the Provisional Government and opposed Lenin's 'April Theses', which called for the seizure of power in the relatively short term. Kamenev was also a member of the Petrograd Soviet and of its executive committee, representing the Bolsheviks. He was arrested briefly following the July Days. Kamenev, together with Zinov'ev, resisted Lenin's insistence that the Bolsheviks should themselves take power, and made his opposition public in a joint letter to Gor'ky's newspaper *Novaya zhizn'* (New Life). After the revolution he diverged again from Lenin, arguing that a coalition goverment of all the socialist parties should be formed, and resigned from the Central Committee. Kamenev was however nominated by Lenin as chairman of the Second Congress of Soviets which formally instituted the new socialist order, and he also became briefly the chairman of the new Central Executive Committee (or quasi-parliament). In late 1917 and early 1918 Kamenev was a member of the Soviet delegation at the Brest-Litovsk peace negotiations with Germany, and he went to Britain and Finland as a Bolshevik emissary in the following period. On his return to Russia he became chairman of the Moscow Soviet (1918–26); in 1922 he became deputy chairman of the Council of People's Commissars (in effect vice-premier) and in 1924 he was made chairman of the Labour and Defence Council. He was the first director of the new Lenin Institute (now the Institute of Marxism-Leninism), where he began the publication of scholarly editions of Lenin's works; in 1926 he became People's Commissar of Trade, and then in 1927 Soviet ambassador to Italy.

Kamenev, initially a supporter of Stalin against Trotsky in intra-party disputes, came to support the Left Opposition by the late 1920s and in December 1927 he was expelled from the party by a decision of the Fifteenth Congress. In 1928 he was readmitted after denouncing the Trotskyists in a letter to *Pravda*, and later became head of the Supreme Council of the National Economy and (from 1929) chairman of the Main Concessions Committee. In 1932, however, he was again expelled from the party; he was again re-admitted, but re-expelled in 1934 for what proved to be the final time. In 1935, after Kirov's murder, he was arrested and sentenced to five, later ten years' imprisonment; the following year he was a defendant in the trial of the 'Trotskyite-Zinov'evite terrorist centre' and, as a result of the court's decision, was excuted on 15 August. Hoping to save his wife and children, he begged them publicly to spend the rest of their lives 'defending the great Stalin'. The charges on which he was convicted are nowadays acknowledged to be without foundation, and Kamenev was rehabilitated in 1988.

Kamenev and Zinov'ev were closely associated not only in their political activity before and after the revolution but also in the minds of their contemporaries. They were very different animals, however, in political terms: as Trotsky put it, Zinov'ev was an 'agitator ... led mostly by his political flair'; Kamenev, by contrast, was a 'propagandist' who pondered carefully before acting, and who had also wide interests outside politics and was easy-going by nature, unlike the vindictive Zinov'ev. A diffident, scholarly figure with his red goatee beard and spectacles, clever but politically less effective than his major opponents, Kamenev inclined naturally towards moderation and compromise and lacked the independence of character or conviction to oppose the majority position when it diverged from his own. In the end his willingness to adapt was not enough to save him. SLW

KAMENTSEV, Vladimir Mikhaylovich (b. 1928) A fisheries expert who became the USSR's senior foreign trade official under Gorbachev. Trained in Moscow, he worked in Murmansk (1950–62), and soon after became First Deputy Minister, then in 1979, Minister of the Fish Industry. He was Deputy Chairman of the USSR Council of Ministers and Chairman of its Foreign Economic Commission from 1986 to 1989, but his nomination to retain that office was rejected by the Congress of People's Deputies; Kamentsev then retired. JHM

KAMINSKY, Grigoriy Naumovich (1895–1938) Son of a smith, Kaminsky attended a factory school and then Moscow University Medical Faculty. He joined the party in 1913 and served in Soviet posts in Tula during the Civil War. From 1920 he worked in the People's Commissariat for Agriculture, and was responsible for collective farms from 1925, becoming an enthusiastic supporter of the collectivization drive (1929–30), but was dismissed in January 1930. He held minor posts until February 1934 when he became People's Commissar for Health, first of the RSFSR, then, from July 1936, of both the RSFSR and USSR. A candidate member of the Central Committee (1925–27 and 1930–37), he was one of the rare people at the June 1937 plenum who protested at the repressions. He was arrested immediately. RWD

KANDINSKY, Vasiliy Vasil'evich (1866–1944) Painter, born in Moscow. Although Kandinsky, a pioneer in the devlopment of abstract painting, achieved his reputation in Germany and Russia well before the Revolution, he played a brief but important role in the organization of Soviet artistic affairs (1917–21). He was the first chairman of the Institute of Artistic Culture in Moscow in 1920 and then a co-founder of the Russian Academy of Artistic Sciences in Moscow in 1921. He emigrated to Germany the same year and then in 1933 to France. He died at Neuilly-sur-Seine. JEB

KANTOROVICH, Leonid Vital'-evich (1912–1986) The sole Soviet laureate of the Nobel Prize for Economics. Born in St Petersburg, he graduated from Leningrad University in 1930 and taught there from 1932 until 1960, doubling in the last two years with Novosibirsk at the Siberian branch of the USSR Academy of Sciences; from 1971 he was in Moscow at the Institute of Economic Management at the State Committee for Science and Technology. The work for which he received a Nobel Prize in 1975 (he had earlier been awarded the Stalin Prize of 1949 and a Lenin Prize in 1965) first appeared as a modest brochure of 1939, *Mathematical Methods of Organization and Planning of the Production Process*, formulating for the first time a scientific basis for optimality in economics. His discovery of linear programming laid the foundation of an entire branch of economics, but an English version was not available until 1960 and his *magnum opus, The Best Use of Economic Resources*, written in 1942, was not published in Russian until 1959 and in English until 1965. Voznesensky read both booklet and book in typescript, for they were Leningrad colleagues, and urged Stalin to authorize publication: unfortunately Stalin turned to the other economists of his day, compliant with his simplistic interpretation of Marx's law of value. They recommended suppression of the book, probably because they could not understand it. Kantorovich turned to pure mathematics, but later returned with notable renown to issues of economic dynamics. MCK

KAPITONOV, Ivan Vasil'evich (b. 1915) A Secretary of the Central Committee of the Soviet Communist Party for over twenty years, Kapitonov – a career party official – was born into a peasant family in Serovskoe in what is now the Ryazan' region of Russia. A member of the CPSU from 1939, he held a series of posts in the Moscow party organization and Moscow city soviet from 1940 to 1959, culminating in his First Secretaryships of the Moscow city party from 1952 to 1954 and the Moscow regional party organization from 1954 to 1959, the latter a less powerful post than the former. Kapitonov suffered a further demotion in 1963 when he was sent to the Ivanovo *obkom* as First Secretary, but once Brezhnev had succeeded Khrushchev he received promotion.

From 1965 to 1986 Kapitonov was a Secretary of the Central Committee and for all but the last three of those years he headed the Department of Organizational Party Work. As the supervisor of party cadres he wielded considerable power, but with Andropov as General Secretary his supervisory responsibilities were transferred to light industry (1983–86). In 1986 he was accorded the more honorific post of Chairman of the Central Auditing Commission and he was dropped from the Central Committee of which he had been a full member since 1952. AHB

KAPISTA, Mikhail Sergeevich (b. 1921) A diplomat for most of his career, Kapista – a Ukranian by nationality – is Director of the Institute of Oriental Studies of the Academy of Sciences of the USSR in Moscow. A specialist on the Far East, and on China in particular, Kapista entered the diplomatic service in 1943 and was head of the First Far East Department from 1970 to 1982. A deputy foreign minister from 1982 to 1987, he moved to his present academic post at the beginning of 1987. AHB

KAPITSA, Petr Leonidovich (1894–1984) Kapitsa won the Nobel Prize in 1978 for work in low-temperature physics. He was born in Kronstadt, where his father was a military engineer. He spent the years 1921 to 1934 at Cambridge University, but was refused permission to return there after a visit to the Soviet Union in 1934. A new institute (the Institute of Physical Problems) was built for him in Moscow. He became a Fellow of the Royal Society in 1929, and a full member of the Academy of Sciences in 1939.

Kapitsa showed great courage in his dealings with the authorities. He protested to Stalin and Beria about the arrest of a number of leading physicists, and was successful in saving some of them from almost certain death. In 1945 he refused to work on the atomic bomb because he disagreed with the way in which Beria was running the project. Lucky not to be shot, Kapitsa was under virtual house arrest until after Stalin's death. He continued to use his influence in later years to protect Soviet scientists from repression, and to improve the organization of Soviet science. DH

KAPLAN, Anatoliy L'vovich (1902–1980) Graphic artist. Born in Rogachev, Kaplan, one of the few Soviet artists who has treated the Jewish theme openly in his work, studied at the Academy of Arts under Petrov-Vodkin and Nikolay Radlov (1922–27). Influenced by Vereisky, he concentrated on lithography from the 1930s onwards, often choosing subjects from Sholom-Aleichem. In the late 1960s to 1970s he also produced a number of ceramic works. JEB

KAPP, Artur Iosepovich (1878–1952) Estonian composer and teacher. Artur Kapp was born in Surre-Jaani and died there on 14 January 1952. After graduating from the St Petersburg Conservatory in 1900, where he was a student of Rimsky-Korsakov, he became Director of the Russian Musical Society Music School in Astrakhan (1904–20). From 1920 to 1924 he served as conductor of the 'Estonia' Theatre in Tallinn, and from 1920 to 1943 was on the staff of the Tallinn Conservatory. He was made an Honoured Art Worker of the Estonian SSR in 1945. He did much to develop Estonian musical life and was active as a symphonic and choral composer. His son, Eugen Kapp, is also a notable Estonian composer. GS

KAPP, Villem Khansovich (1913–1964) Estonian composer. Villem Kapp was born in Surre-Jaani and died in Tallinn. Nephew of Artur Kapp, he graduated from the Tallinn Conservatory in 1944, being appointed a member of the teaching staff in 1945. He was made a People's Artist of the Estonian SSR in 1963. He is remembered for his choral music and the national opera *Lembitu* (première 1961). GS

KAPTO, Aleksandr Semenovich (b. 1933) A Ukrainian official in the fields of ideology and culture. Kapto worked for the Komsomol in Dnepropetrovsk and Kiev and was First Secretary of the Ukrainian Komsomol from 1968 to 1972. After six years in the Kiev party organization he became Head of the Department of Culture (1978–79) and Secretary for Ideology (1979–86) of the Ukrainian Communist Party. From 1986 to 1988 he was Soviet ambassador to Cuba and, since 1988, Head of the Ideological Department of the CPSU Central Committee in Moscow. JHM

KARIMOV, Islam Abduganievich (b. 1938) An obscure Uzbek engineer and economist, Karimov benefited from the near total purge of the Uzbekistan leadership in the 1980s. He worked in the Tashkent Aviation Factory (1960–66) and in the Uzbekistan *Gosplan* (1966–83), before becoming Minister of Finances (1983–86) in his home republic. From 1986 to June 1989 he was First Secretary of Kashkadar'ya *obkom* and then succeeded R. N. Nishanov as First Secretary of the Uzbekistan Communist Party. In 1990 Karimov became the President of the Uzbek republic and at the Twenty-eighth Party Congress in July 1990 he was elected to the Central Committee of the CPSU and the Politburo. JHM, AHB

KARLOV, Vladimir Alekseevich (b. 1914) A member of the CPSU from 1940, Vladimir Karlov graduated from Voronezh Zootechnical Institute and from the Higher Party School in Moscow. In 1959 he became First Sec-

retary of Kalinin regional party committee; from 1962 to 1965 he was second party secretary in Uzbekistan; and from 1966 onwards he worked in the agricultural department of the CPSU Central Committee. He was elected a full member of the Central Committee in 1981 and 1986. SLW

KARPECHENKO, Georgiy Dmitrievich (1899–1942) World-renowned botanist, plant breeder. One of the Soviet Union's leading plant cytogeneticists, and one of N. I. Vavilov's closest associates, Karpechenko won international fame in the late 1920s for producing *Raphanobrassica*, a fertile polyploid intergeneric hybrid of the radish and the cabbage. As director of the Laboratory of Genetics of Vavilov's Institute of Applied Plant Breeding (1925–41) and chairman of the department of plant genetics at Leningrad University (1932–41), Karpechenko was one of the most outstanding geneticists to be repressed for his opposition to Lysenko. He was arrested in early 1941 and died shortly thereafter in prison. MBA

KARPINSKY, Len Vyacheslavovich (b. 1929) The son of the prominent old Bolshevik, Vyacheslav Karpinsky, Len Karpinsky (who was named after Lenin), was expelled from the Communist Party in 1975 for reformist activity, including the writing of *samizdat*, and readmitted as recently as 1988. He rose rapidly in the Soviet hierarchy in Khrushchev's time and in the late nineteen-fifties and early nineteen-sixties was successively editor of *Molodoy kommunist*, a secretary of the Central Committee of the Komsomol and a member of the editorial board of *Pravda* and head of that newspaper's department of Marxism-Leninism. He was, however, dismissed from *Pravda*, along with Fedor Burlatsky, in 1967.

Karpinsky moved to *Izvestiya*, but his independent political views led to his being fired from there as well, whereupon he joined the Institute of Sociological Studies and became part of an entire team which was disbanded in the early nineteen-seventies for showing signs of wishing to engage in serious social research.

Karpinsky subsequently worked for Progress Publishing House and, after his expulsion from the party, in more humble employment. As Soviet developments in the later nineteen-eighties caught up with Karpinsky's views, he began to be published again, starting with an article in *Moscow News* in March 1987. AHB

KARPINSKY, Vyacheslav Alekseevich (1880–1965) An old Bolshevik who joined (what was later to become) the Communist Party in 1898 and a friend of Lenin, Vyacheslav Karpinsky was expelled from Khar'kov University for his revolutionary activity. He emigrated in 1904 and worked alongside Lenin in Geneva. He became a prominent editor and journalist of Communist publications both before and after the revolution; on his return to Russia in 1917, he edited first *Krasnaya zvezda* (Red Star) and from 1918 to 1927 was on the editorial board of *Pravda*. From 1936 to 1937 he worked briefly in the apparatus of the party Central Committee as a consultant to the Department of Propaganda. At a time when many old Bolsheviks were being arrested, including members of Karpinsky's own family, he miraculously survived, and worked from 1937 until his retirement for the Academy of Pedagogical Sciences. He was awarded the Order of Lenin three times in the course of his life. AHB

KARPOV, Anatoliy (b. 1951) Chess player. Born in Zlatoust, he became a chess master at fourteen and international grandmaster at nineteen, winning the world chess title in 1975 when the American Bobby Fischer failed to appear for the final; he then beat the Soviet defector Victor Korchnoy by one point in a tense match in 1978, and again in 1981, this time by a clear four points. He lost his ten-year title to the Soviet challenger Gary Kasparov in a replayed world match in the autumn of 1985, postponed from late 1984; he also narrowly lost a further replay in October 1986 and 1988. Acclaimed the greatest universal chess player of all time, Karpov devoted his versatile talents to a variety of academic and social activities, being Chairman of the USSR Peace Fund, member of the Soviet UNESCO Affairs Commission, member of the board of the International Chess Federation and editor-in-chief of the magazine *Chess Review-64*. One of the most popular of all Soviet sports personalities, he featured in the annual top ten Soviet sports personalities as many as ten times from 1973. JWR

KARPOV, Vladimir Vasil'evich (b. 1922) Little is known of Vladimir Karpov's origins; in 1940 he was arrested for anti-Soviet agitation, and served in a penal battalion after being in the camps. He joined the party in 1943, and in 1944 was awarded the USSR's highest decoration for gallantry, Hero of the Soviet Union. After the war he published a series of novels and stories on military themes. He became Chief Editor of the journal *Novyy mir* in 1981, and resigned in September 1986, when he became First Secretary of the Union of Writers and a candidate member of the Central

Committee. He has tried to hold the middle ground in the factional fights that have developed in the Union of Writers since 1986. GSS

KARPOVA, Yevdokiya Fedorovna (b. 1923) A member of the Central Committee of the CPSU since 1976 and a Deputy Chairman of the RSFSR Council of Ministers since 1966, Karpova has served in a variety of state and party positions in the past three decades. After graduating from the Moscow Textile Institute in 1949, she worked as a forewoman in a Yegorovsk weaving mill until 1956 when she was appointed First Secretary of the Yegorovsk City Committee of the CPSU. Shortly thereafter she became USSR Deputy Minister for Light Industry, serving in that capacity for a decade before her appointment to the RSFSR Council of Ministers. Karpova lost her positions only in the 1980s, finally leaving the Central Committee with those who 'requested' retirement in April 1989. NN

KASATKINA, Natal'ya Dmitrievna (b. 1934) Dancer, choreographer, scenarist. Kasatkina graduated from the Bol'shoy Ballet School in 1953 and was a leading character dancer with the Bol'shoy troupe from 1954 to 1976. A talented, versatile dancer, her roles included: Phrygia in *Spartacus*, Mercedes in *Don Quixote*, and ethnic dances in *The Stone Flower*, *Cinderella*, *Raymonda*, and *Swan Lake*.

From the early 1960s Kasatkina and Vladimir Vasilev collaborated as choreographers, creating a large repertoire of ballets that have been staged throughout the Soviet Union and abroad. Their works combine classical and modern styles, often treat contemporary themes, and frequently use the music of contemporary Soviet composers.

Their major works have included: *Vanina Vanini* (1962); *Heroic Poem* (*Geologists*), with music by Nikolay Karetnikov (1964); a new version of *The Rite of Spring* with Kasatkina in the lead role (1965); and *Tristan and Isolde* (1967). Their highly engaging ballet *The Creation of the World* (1971) featured Valeriy Panov as the Devil, Mikhail Baryshnikov as Adam, Irina Kolpakova as Eve, and Yuriy Solov'ev as God. Their film *Choreographic Novellas* (1973) was awarded a State Prize.

In 1977 Kasatkina and Vasilev became artistic directors of the group Moscow Classical Ballet, which has produced numerous works. SCS

KASPAROV, Gary (b. 1963) Chess player. Born in Baku, he was ten when he was chosen to attend the famous Botvinnik chess school. At the age of fifteen he gained the chess Master ranking and became an international master at sixteen. Before his successful world championship match with Karpov (1984–85), he had won the Soviet chess title in 1981 and 1982. An extremely versatile exponent of complex combination play, and psychologically tough, Kasparov became world champion in November 1985 at the age of twenty-two, retaining the title through the 1980s. JWR

KATAEV, Valentin Petrovich (1897–1986) Born in Odessa, and best known as a prose writer, dramatist and screenwriter. Kataev's first success was the satirical novel *The Embezzlers* (1927), decribing the adventures of two bureaucrats. In a similar vein, the play *Squaring the Circle* (1928) takes a comic look at the housing shortage, Kataev's first major socialist-realist work, the fast-moving *Time, Forward!* (1932) tells how workers beat a concrete-pouring record. *A Lonely White*

Sail Gleams (1936), his adventure novel about children in Odessa during the 1905 revolution, was made into a play and a film, but its patriotic sequel about Odessa partisans during the war, *For the Power of the Soviets* (1949) was attacked for minimizing the role of the Communists and rewritten in 1951. After Stalin's death in 1953, Kataev became a founding editor of the journal *Youth* where he remained until 1962 and fostered the rise of the new 'youth prose' movement; he also joined the party in 1958. In the sixties Kataev's fiction such as *The Holy Well* (1965) and *The Grass of Oblivion* (1967), became more experimental, departing from traditional chronology and weaving fantastic and fairy-tale elements into the narrative in a way which was to prove influential in helping Soviet fiction overcome the Stalinist literary heritage. KC

KATSMAN, Yevgeniy Aleksandrovich (1890–1976) Painter and co-founder of AKhRR in 1922. Born in Saratov, Katsman, received his education there and then (1906–16) at the Academy of Arts and MIPSA. A convinced Realist, he used his art to illustrate scenes from the Red Army, the peasantry and the workers as in his famous *Kalyazinsk Lacemakers* (1928). JEB

KATUSHEV, Konstantin Fedorovich (b. 1927) At one time a powerful Secretary of the Central Committee, Katushev is – as of 1990 – Minister of Internal Economic Affairs of the USSR. A party member since 1952, he graduated from the Gor'ky Polytechnical Institute and worked in a car factory before joining the party apparatus. By 1965 he was First Secretary of the Gor'ky regional party committee and in 1968 he was promoted at a very early age by the stan-

dards of Brezhnev's Soviet Union to a Secretaryship of the Central Committee. He was given responsibility for the Socialist Countries Department in a year in which events in Czechoslovakia preoccupied the Soviet leadership.

Katushev remained in the Central Committee Secretariat until 1977 when he became the Soviet Union's permanent representative to Comecon and a deputy chairman of the Council of Ministers. In a further demotion he was sent to Cuba in 1982 as Soviet Ambassador, but was recalled to Moscow during Gorbachev's leadership. From 1985 to 1988 Katushev was Chairman of the State Committee for Foreign Economic Affairs and from 1988 Minister of Internal Economic Affairs. AHB

KAUFMAN, Mikhail Abramovich (1897–1980) Documentary filmmaker and the younger brother of Vertov. He worked as a cameraman on Cine-Eye films of the 1920s. His own films as director included: *Moscow* and *A Day in a Crèche* (both 1927), *Springtime* (1929) and *Our Moscow* (1939). RT

KAULS, Al'bert Ernestovich (b. 1938) A Latvian of working-class origin, Kauls became one of the members of the Presidential Council of the USSR when it was formed in March 1990. He began his career as a manual worker, but after army service studied at the Party School in Riga and specialized in agricultural questions. After a spell as a local Komsomol leader, he became chairman of a collective farm in 1964, from 1974 chairman of the very successful farm, 'Adazhi', and from 1986 head of the agricultural company (*agrofirm*) of that name. Kauls has been a member of the Communist Party since 1960 and of the Congress of People's Deputies since 1989. AHB

KAVERIN (Zilber), Venyamin Aleksandrovich (1902–1989) Born in Pskov, a prose writer and literary scholar, Kaverin began his career along with Lunts as part of the 'Westerner' trend in the Serapion Brotherhood which emphasized plot and experimenting with sub-literary genres. He was also a disciple of the Formalists and close to Tynyanov. His first collection, *Masters and Journeymen* (1923), with its carefully plotted fantastic stories, shows the influence of Hoffmann, Poe and Formalist literary theories. During the twenties he also wrote detective stories, sketches, a literary history of Baron Brambeus and two *romans-à-clef* about his own milieu, *The Troublemaker* (1928) a critical portrait of the Formalist Shklovsky, and *Artist Unknown* (1931) which idealises an avant-garde artist who is largely a composite of Khlebnikov, Filonov and Tynyanov. In the thirties and forties he wrote successful socialist realist works of which the best known is *The Two Captains* (1939) with an adventure-detective approach to Arctic exploration. During the late forties and fifties he published a trilogy about Soviet immunologists, of which the last book, *Searches and Hopes* (1956), treats the theme of intellectual freedom which marked the thaw. After that and until his death he was a prolific writer, publishing primarily autobiographical fiction and memoirs. KC

KAZAKEVICH, Emmanuil Genrikhovich (1913–1962) Prose writer, journalist, dramatist and poet. After some early writing in Yiddish, he made his reputation with romantically heroic Russian-language novels about the Second World War. An admirer of Lenin, Kazakevich became a Party member in 1944; in 1956 he was an editor of the liberal almanac *Literary Moscow*. JAEC

KAZAKOV, Yuriy Pavlovich (1927–1982) Short-story writer whose carefully crafted works, published between 1957 and 1973, did much to revive the tradition of Chekhov and Bunin. His stories were often concerned with lonely individuals searching for a meaning to life, and implied that art had its own value, independent of its contribution to society. He fell silent in his later years, probably because of illness. GAH

KAZAKOVA, Rimma Fedorovna (b. 1932) A poet, born in Sevastopol', educated in Leningrad, settled in Moscow since 1960. Kazakova is a talented author of short personal lyrics which avoid grand themes and public affairs. GSS

KAZANKINA, Tatyana (b. 1951) Athlete. She was the first Soviet middle-distance runner to win two gold medals at one Olympics – at Montreal in 1976, winning the 800 m and the 1500 m. Despite having a child in 1978, she won her third gold medal at the Moscow Olympics in 1980 in the 1500 m in a new Olympic record time. Two weeks later she bettered this and beat Paavo Nurmi's men's record of the 1920s. Born in Petrovsk, she took up running at the age of fourteen, overcame heart problems in her teens to become one of the most outstanding women athletes of all time. She continued to compete in international races well into the 1980s. JWR

KEBIN, Ivan Gustavovich (Käbin, Johannes) (b. 1905) Typical of the Russianized diaspora which ran the Baltic Republics after 1945, Kebin, an Estonian from St Petersburg, joined the Communist Party in 1927, worked in Leningrad, Omsk and Moscow, and was for a short time at the Institute of Red Professors. First Secretary of the Estonian Communist Party (1950–78), and President of the Presidium of the Estonian Supreme Soviet 1978–83. JHM

KEDROV, Mikhail Nikolaevich (1893–1972) Kedrov was a stage actor and director and pupil of Stanislavsky. He joined the Moscow Art Theatre in 1924. RT

KELLER, Boris Aleksandrovich (1874–1945) Botanist, ecologist, agronomist, administrator. Expelled from Moscow University in 1895 for political activities, Keller graduated from Kazan' University in 1902 and was professor at the Voronezh Agricultural Institute (1913–31) and, after 1919, at Voronezh University. Known as a specialist on the botany of the steppes, he joined the party in 1930, reversed himself on several scientific issues, and became active in subordinating botany to state ideology and policy. As part of the Bolshevization of the USSR Academy of Sciences, he was elected a full member in botany in early 1931 and was appointed director of its Botanical Institute (1931–36), its Soil Institute (1935–36), its Botanical Garden (1937–45), and its Turkmen affiliate (1941–45). From 1930 he wrote many articles full of Marxist philosophical rhetoric, that linked Darwinism with the Stalinist campaign for the transformation of nature, supported Lysenko, and attacked genetics. He was elected to the Lenin Academy of Agricultural Sciences in 1935. During the purges, he wrote inflammatory articles attacking fellow academicians as Trotskyites, fascists, and traitors. MBA

KERBEL', Lev Yefimovich (b. 1917) Sculptor. Born in Semenovka. Known for his monuments such as Gor'ky (1959), Marx (1961) and Gagarin (1973) in Moscow, Kerbel' favours a heroic, severe style. After studying under Domogatsky and Matveev at the Repin Institute, Leningrad, and the Surikov Institute, Moscow, he has worked with many media, but especially bronze. JEB

KHACHATUROV, Tigran Sergeevich (1906–1989) Economist. Working as a transport economist between 1930 and 1959 he found a technique for rational investment decisions while official political economy precluded use of time-discounting. After Stalin's death he helped revive theoretical economics in the USSR. Born in Moscow, he graduated from Moscow State University in 1926 and was a teacher and researcher in various transport institutes until appointed head of a department of the Institute of Economics of the USSR Academy of Sciences in 1959; he had served on the Editorial Board of its journal, *Voprosy ekonomiki*, since 1957 and became its Chief Editor in 1966, vacating the post in 1988 for the radical reformer Gavriil Popov. His reputation in the theory of investment and chairmanship of numerous Academy of Sciences Committees (including that of the Association of Institutes of Economics from 1969) brought him into the counsels of the International Economic Association between 1968 and 1989, where, despite his reputation as a conservative among his Soviet peers in latter years, his views on topics of enquiry were dispassionate. MCK

KHADZHINOV, Mikhail Ivanovich (1899–1980) Plant breeder. A graduate of the Khar'kov Agricultural Institute in 1926, Khadzhinov soon became one of the leading Ukrainian plant breeders, specializing in hybrid corn. After 1930 he was one of the principal geneticists of the Ukrainian branch of the All-Union Institute of Plant Breeding (VIR) and published widely on heterosis and hybridization. Following Lysenko's takeover of the VIR in 1940, Khadzhinov transferred to the Krasnodar Agricultural Research Institute, where he headed the section on maize from 1941. In the 1960s he became a Hero of Socialist Labour. MBA

KHARMS (real name Yuvachev), Daniil Ivanovich (1905–1942) Prose miniaturist, poet and dramatist. A leading exponent of the absurd, Kharms contributed to the 1928 manifesto of Oberiu (The Association for Real Art); he figured conspicuously on the avant-garde scene throughout the 1920s with his poetry and eccentric behaviour. In 1927 he wrote a play, *Yelizaveta Bam*. After his arrest in 1931 Kharms concentrated on writing for children's magazines, but was rearrested in 1941 and died in prison in 1942. His black and fantastical humour has earned him a considerable reputation in the West; in the Soviet Union Kharms is still really known only through his writings for children. JAEC

KHAYKIN, Boris Emmanuelovich (1904–1978) Conductor. Boris Khaykin was born in Minsk and died in Moscow. A student at the Moscow Conservatory, he studied piano with Aleksandr Gedike and conducting with Konstantin Saradzhev. On graduating in 1928 he took up a post as a conductor of the Stanislavsky Opera Theatre in Moscow, in 1936 becoming principal conductor of the Leningrad Malyy Theatre. He was chief conductor of the Leningrad Theatre of Opera and Ballet (1944–53) and a conductor with the Moscow Bol'shoy

(1954–78). He also taught at the Moscow and Leningrad Conservatories. A member of the party since 1940, he became a People's Artist of the USSR in 1972, and was awarded many State Prizes and other distinctions. GS

KHEIFITS, Iosif Yefimovich (b. 1905) Film director. Kheifits is a Leningrad director whose career has been closely associated with that of Aleksandr Zarkhi. His films include *The Baltic Deputy* (1937), awarded the Grand Prix at the Paris International Exhibition the same year, *A Member of the Government* (1940), *The Great Family* (1954) and a film version of Chekhov's *The Lady with the Little Dog* (1960). RT

KHLEBNIKOV, Velemir (Viktor Vladimirovich) (1885–1922) Poet. He studied science and mathematics at the universities of Kazan' and St Petersburg, but did not graduate. Khlebnikov was one of the leading Russian Futurists, but never fully involved in professional literary life, he created his own primitivistic, often infantilist style, with many neologisms, to express his vision of a new cosmic order. He experimented with prose and drama; his long poems are particularly innovative (*Ladomir*, 1920). Partly because of his dedicated bohemianism, Khlebnikov has remained the guru of Russian nonconformist poets throughout the Soviet period. GSS

KHODASEVICH, Vladislav Felitsyanovich (1886–1939) Poet and critic, born and brought up in Moscow. Within Symbolism but not of it, Khodasevich achieved maturity after the Revolution (*The Way of the Grain*, 1920; *The Heavy Lyre*, 1923). He emigrated in 1922, dried up as a poet in 1927 (*European Night*) and thereafter worked as journalist and critic.

Practically unpublished in the USSR until the centenary of his birth, Khodasevich is now recognized as one of the key figures in Russian modernism. GSS

KHOKHLOV, Konstantin Pavlovich (1885–1956) Leading stage actor and director. As Principal Director of the Petrograd Bol'shoy Theatre from 1922, Khokhlov was noted for his Expressionist productions, including Kaiser's *Gas* (1922) and Faiko's *Bubus the Teacher* (1925). For the Leningrad Pushkin Theatre he directed Sophocles' *Oedipus Rex* (1924), Lunacharsky's *Poison* (1925) and Trenev's *The Pugachev Rebellion* (1926). From 1931 to 1938 he was Director at the Malyy Theatre where his productions included Tolstoy's *The Fruits of Enlightenment* (1932) and *Enemies* (1933) and Trenev's *On the Banks of the Neva* (1937). He was principal Director of the Lesya Ukrainka Russian Theatre in Kiev from 1938 to 1954: his productions there included Ukrainka's *The Stone Lord* (1939 and 1946), Shaw's *Pygmalion* (1945), Gor'ky's *Enemies* (1951) and Turgenev's *A Month in the Country* (1954). Khokhlov played the role of O. Henry in Kuleshov's film *The Great Consoler* (1934). He was the first husband of Aleksandra Khokhlova, the film actress. RT

KHOKHLOVA, Aleksandra Sergeevna (1897–1985) Film actress. Khokhlova was an extraordinarily powerful and original screen actress. Married first to Khokhlov and then to Kuleshov, she trained in the Kuleshov workshop. Her principal roles included: the Countess in *The Extraordinary Adventures of Mr West in the Land of the Bolsheviks* (1924), Edith in *By the Law* (1926) and Dulcie in *The Great Consoler* (1933). Khokhlova provided

the model for Kuleshov's theories of film acting. RT

KHOLODNY, Nikolay Grigor'evich (1882–1953) Plant physiologist and microbiologist. Kholodny graduated from Kiev University in 1906 and subsequently worked there (1906–41) and at the Institute of Botany of the Academy of Sciences of the Ukrainian SSR (to 1949). His important monograph, *Zhelezobakterii* (1921; 2nd edition in German, 1926), dealt with iron-fixing bacteria. From 1926 to 1928 he did pioneering work on plant hormones and their role in phytotropism. After his death the Institute of Botany of the Academy of Sciences of the Ukrainian SSR was named in his honour. MBA

KHRENNIKOV, Tikhon Nikolaevich (b. 1913) Composer and party worker, Tikhon Khrennikov was born in Yelets. After receiving his first instruction at the Gnesin Music School (1929–32), he entered the Moscow Conservatory, where his teachers were Shebalin (composition) and Neygauz (Neuhaus)(piano). He graduated in 1936. He was head of the Music Section of the Soviet Army Central Theatre (1941–54). In 1961 he was appointed to the Conservatory teaching staff, becoming a professor in 1966. A member of the party since 1947, among his many honours are those of People's Artist of the USSR (1963) and Hero of Socialist Labour (1973). After being appointed Secretary General of the USSR Composers' Union in 1948, he became First Secretary in 1957, which important post he has held ever since. He has served on many national and international committees and is a leading spokesman on matters relating to musical ideology. Of his own compositions, which reflect the doctrine of socialist realism, his operas *In the Storm* (1939) and *Mother* (1957) are frequently performed in the Soviet Union. GS

KHRUNICHEV, Mikhail Vasil'evich (1901–1961) A leading figure in the Soviet armaments industry of the 1940s and 1950s. A Russian from the Donbass, he was a factory director during the 1930s, and between 1938 and 1946 was Deputy People's Commissar successively for Defence Industry, Aviation Industry, and Munitions. From 1946 to 1953 he was Minister for the Aviation Industry, and was then transferred (like many others) to nuclear technology, becoming Malyshev's first deputy at Medium Machine Building until 1955. Thereafter he was Deputy Chairman of the Council of Ministers (1955–56 and in 1961) and Deputy Chairman of Gosplan (1957–61). JHM

KHRUSHCHEV, Nikita Sergeevich (1894–1971) Nikita Sergeevich Khrushchev, who was to become the most colourful of Soviet leaders and one whose name will for ever be associated with de-Stalinization, was born in the village of Kalinovka, in Kursk province, close to the Ukrainian border. His father was a poor peasant who had to leave his family and work in the Ukrainian coalfields each winter in order to eke out a living. In 1909 the whole family moved to Yuzovka (now Donetsk) in the Ukraine.

Khrushchev had only a very few years of formal schooling, but he had a quick mind and great capacity for learning from experience. Among the jobs Khrushchev held as a boy and young man (the memories of which were to remain with him to be used to illustrate and enliven his later speeches and conversations) were those of herdsboy, metal fitter in various factories and mechanic in the Donbass coal mines. As early as 1912 he was sacked from one job for taking part in a strike and in 1917 he was an active member of the Rutchenkovo soviet in the Ukraine, though it was not until 1918 that he became a member of the Bolshevik (later Communist) party.

Khrushchev joined the Red Army early in 1919 and served until the end of the Civil War as a soldier and party worker. By the time he returned to Yuzovka in 1922 – by this time as deputy manager of the Rutchenkovo mines – he had seen much fierce action and had lost his first wife (and mother of two of his children) through death in the Ukrainian famine of 1921. (Khrushchev married again in 1924 and his second wife, Nina Petrovna, survived him by thirteen years, dying in 1984.) Khrushchev was soon offered the job of manager of another mining complex but, conscious of how limited his education had been, sought and received permission to study instead at the Yuzovka Workers' Faculty where he also became a political leader.

From 1924 Khrushchev made his career in the party apparatus. In the intra-party struggles of the 1920s he identified with Stalin's staunch supporter and First Secretary of the Ukrainian party organization, Lazar Kaganovich. Though clever, Khrushchev was no intellectual, and he saw Stalin and his disciple, Kaganovich, as people who got things done. For Kaganovich, Khrushchev's innocence of the finer points of Marxist theory was a positive advantage as was his enormous energy, drive and enthusiasm. Though Kaganovich was later to become a political enemy of Khrushchev, in the 1920s and 1930s he was his most important direct political patron until such time as Khrushchev moved into the orbit of Stalin himself.

Between 1925 and the end of the 1920s Khrushchev made rapid progress in the Ukrainian party apparatus, but when Kaganovich was transferred to Moscow in 1929, Khrushchev also left the Ukraine for the Soviet capital, becoming a student and political worker at the Stalin Industrial Academy. Though formally it was not until 1932 that he cut his ties with the Academy, Khrushchev found political work increasingly crowding out his studies and already in 1931 he had begun his career in the Moscow party apparatus (headed now by Kaganovich) as a district First Secretary. By 1933 he was already second secretary of the party committee for the entire Moscow region and, under Kaganovich's command, he was a driving force behind the reconstruction of Moscow and the building of the city's metro.

Over the next few years, Khrushchev climbed rapidly in the political hierarchy and gained the favour of Stalin. In 1934 he became a member of the party's Central Committee and in 1935 he succeeded Kaganovich as First Secretary of the Moscow city and regional party committee. After three years as Moscow's political boss, he returned to the Ukraine, this time as party First Secretary for that republic. In 1938 he joined the party's top leadership as a candidate member of the Politburo, becoming a full member a year later. Khrushchev survived the worst of the party purges partly because of Stalin's liking for him and partly because he was also in those days a loyal Stalinist who took an active part in purging. But these were times when even loyal Stalinists disappeared, never to appear again, and to survive required an element of luck.

In Khrushchev's own view, his 'lucky lottery ticket' had been Stalin's wife, Nadezhda Allilueva, who had committed suicide in 1932, but earlier had studied alongside Khrushchev at the Industrial Academy and had conveyed to Stalin a very favourable impression of the young Khrushchev.

During the war, Khrushchev, though still a Politburo member, was active on several fronts as a political officer in the army with the rank of Lieutenant-General. Khrushchev was frequently in danger both in battle (including the defence of Stalingrad where he had an important role as the senior political officer) and from Stalin's wrath when reverses occurred and Stalin was seeking a scapegoat. Khrushchev entered Kiev when it was liberated in November 1943 alongside the Soviet soldiers among whom he had lived for more than two years, but from then on he was to devote himself increasingly to his political duties as Ukrainian party leader. In 1944 he was appointed Chairman of the Council of Ministers in the Ukraine in addition to his republican party First Secretaryship and became chiefly concerned with the reconstruction of the Ukrainian economy and political organization.

In 1946 Khrushchev suffered a demotion when, though he kept his Council of Ministers post and his Politburo membership, he was temporarily replaced by Kaganovich as First Secretary of the Ukrainian party organization. By 1948, however, he had been restored to full power in the Ukraine and in 1949 he returned to Moscow to become once again head of the Moscow party organization. Added to that post was a Secretaryship of the Central Committee of the party, so that by the time of Stalin's death in March 1953 Khrushchev had his hands on several important levers of power. Though initially he was ranked behind Malenkov, Molotov, Beria and Kaganovich, within a fortnight of Stalin's death he had become the acting first secretary of the Communist Party of the Soviet Union and in September 1953 he was accorded the title, First Secretary. Within and outside the Soviet Union, Malenkov, however, continued to be regarded as the top leader. Until 1954 his name preceded that of Khrushchev's in lists of Politburo members and there is a sense in which Khrushchev's reign as the supreme Soviet leader, as distinct from party First Secretary, began only in 1954 or 1955. The first two years following Stalin's death were years of collective leadership and struggle for power, a struggle which was to be revived in 1957.

Khrushchev strengthened his position in 1955 when Malenkov was replaced as Chairman of the Council of Ministers by Bulganin. Khrushchev and Malenkov had clashed both on industrial and agricultural policy, but later – when Khrushchev's power was somewhat more secure – he was to take up the cause of the Soviet consumer goods industry which Malenkov had espoused and for which he had come under attack from Khrushchev for the implied reduction in priority accorded heavy industry. Khrushchev's most fateful action, however, was his denuniciation of the Stalin cult and many of the worst excesses of Stalinism at the Twentieth Congress of the Soviet Communist Party in February 1956. There were no doubt several reasons why he decided to do this. One, almost certainly, was to strengthen his position *vis-à-vis* those Politburo colleagues (notably Malenkov,

Molotov and Kaganovich) who had been much more intimately involved in the administration of Stalin's Terror than Khrushchev himself. Another was genuine revulsion against many aspects of Stalin's style of rule and a desire to rehabilitate friends and comrades who had perished in the purges. A third was his wish to enhance the authority of the Communist Party through a process of purification and revitalization.

The speech, however, had unintended consequences. For many Communists in both the East and the West it came as a traumatic shock. Much of the information about Stalin's crimes had already been available but had been ignored or rejected when it came from 'bourgeois' sources. When this same information (with the addition of some new details) came from the lips of the leader of the Soviet Communist Party, it shattered beyond repair the myth of party infallibility. The most serious consequences for the Soviet leadership were in Eastern Europe in the shape of the massive Hungarian uprising and a lesser revolt in Poland. The successful crushing of the Hungarian revolution saved Khrushchev's position but it diminished his and the Soviet Union's standing in the outside world and, taken in conjunction with his Twentieth Congress speech, stimulated a world-wide exodus from Communist parties of many of their leading intellectuals.

It was not, however, Khrushchev's most repressive actions but his more reformist policies, including the measures of de-Stalinization, which alarmed a number of his Politburo colleagues, a majority of whom combined in an attempt to dismiss Khrushchev from office in 1957. Though Malenkov, Molotov, Kaganovich, Bulganin and others succeeded in outvoting Khrushchev in the Politburo, Khrushchev insisted on taking the dispute to the Central Committee as a whole, to which the Politburo was, in principle, responsible. Here he had massive support and completely turned the tables on the 'anti-party group' as he labelled the coalition of those opposed to him. From this time onwards Khrushchev was able to bring an increasing number of his own supporters into the Secretariat of the Central Committee and the Politburo, oust from office his most senior opponents and, in his own words, 'set both internal and foreign policy to a considerable extent'.

Khrushchev's policies, like the man himself, contained many contradictions. He was acutely conscious of the fact that in a nuclear war 'the victor will be barely distinguishable from the vanquished' and he seemed genuinely concerned to improve Soviet relations with the United States. He was the first Soviet supreme leader to visit the USA (in September 1959) and, in many respects, showed a willingness to learn from his numerous trips abroad. Yet, on his own initiative, he wrecked the Paris summit meeting with President Eisenhower, President de Gaulle and British Prime Minister Harold Macmillan in May 1960 in protest against American reconnaissance flights over the USSR, and in 1962 brought the world closer to war by attempting to place Soviet missiles in Cuba. The resolution of the Cuban missile crisis, however, was one of the first steps towards producing 'rules of the game' in the superpower relationship. An important manifestation of improved relations was the signing of the nuclear test ban treaty in August 1963.

Khrushchev took much pride in, and political credit from, the Soviet space programme, especially when in 1961 Yuriy Gagarin became the first man in space. He also earned credit by supporting a massive house-building programme and paying much more attention to the needs of the Soviet consumer, and to agriculture, than had been the case in Stalin's time. His agricultural policies had mixed fortunes, though. The extension of cultivation of crops to the 'Virgin Lands' of Kazakhstan was, on balance, a success, but one which called for massive investment and produced many practical and political problems. The increased investment in agriculture, especially in chemical fertilisers, was beneficial, but his enthusiasm for the growing of maize was carried much too far and interpreted by his critics as maize-mania.

The vigour with which Khrushchev pushed his policies through provoked the hostility of many vested interests. He was greatly given to administrative reorganizations. A major one took place in 1957 with the abolition of many industrial ministries and the creation in their place of regional economic councils. Another was instituted within the Communist Party itself in 1962 when regional party organizations (as well as soviets) were divided into organs for industry and organs for agriculture in such a way that a regional First Secretary was no longer responsible for both of these sectors. In this manner Khrushchev lost the confidence, first, of the state bureaucracy and, second, of the regional party secretaries even though the latter had previously formed his principal power base. His return to the de-Stalinization theme (this time in open session) at the Twenty-Second

Party Congress in 1961 did not endear him to the security police, and his cutting of the size of the army and of officers' pay (together with what the military considered an undue reliance on nuclear at the expense of conventional weapons) lost him support among the senior ranks of the armed services. His use, in his last years of office, of his son-in-law for diplomatic missions lost him the support of the Ministry of Foreign Affairs and of Gromyko personally, while the unpredictability of his policies and his assertive leadership style increasingly worried even those Politburo colleagues who owed their promotion to Khrushchev as well as those, such as Suslov and Kosygin, who had reached the top independently of him.

It was, thus, a coalition of the most important institutional interests within the country which brought about Khrushchev's political downfall in October 1964 when he was removed from both his First Secretaryship of the party and the Chairmanship of the Council of Ministers which he had assumed in 1958 in succession to Bulganin. Khrushchev was rarely mentioned in Soviet books and newspapers during the remaining seven years of his life and such references as there were to him were unfavourable. To alleviate the tedium of his life as a pensioner which weighed heavily upon him and to try to reclaim his place in history, Khrushchev in the last years of his life dictated two volumes of memoirs which were published abroad and which provide important insight on the man and his times. He died on 11 September 1971 at the age of 77.

Though in many respects his immediate successors were more conservative than he was, Khrushchev himself was no liberal. This was exemplified by his attitude towards religion and, to a lesser extent, towards literature and the arts. Thus, for example, in the last five or six years of Khrushchev's period of office more compulsory closures of churches took place than in the rest of the post-Stalin period put together. The inconsistency of his cultural policy was typified by the refusal to publish Pasternak's *Doctor Zhivago* and Khrushchev's personal blessing for the publication of Solzhenitsyn's *One Day in the Life of Ivan Denisovich*.

Khrushchev was, above all, a contradictory political figure – one who was often ruthless and yet possessed human warmth, and a convinced Stalinist who came to abhor many of Stalin's (and some of his own former) actions and who courageously criticized Stalin at a time when a majority of his colleagues were afraid of the consequences of doing so. Khrushchev's historic importance, indeed, lay in his attacks on Stalin, in which he thereby exposed also (perhaps unwittingly) the myth of party infallibility. His claim to a more favourable verdict from history than he received from his immediate successors rests also on his genuine concern with the welfare of ordinary people in the Soviet Union and his ending of the Stalinist practice of sacrificing the present generation for a hypothetical future.

For more than twenty years after his forced removal from political office, Khrushchev was virtually 'unpersoned' by his successors and written out of Soviet history. It was only in the late 1980s, under Gorbachev, that serious assessments of his historic role could begin to appear in Soviet publications. With all his faults (as well as virtues), Khrushchev is now recognized as one of the major figures of the Soviet era. AHB

KHRZHANOVSKY, Andrey Yur'e-vich (b. 1939) Film-maker. Khrzhanovsky is one of the Soviet Union's leading animated film-makers. His major work is his Pushkin trilogy: *I Fly to You in Memory* (1977), *I Am with You Again* (1981) and *Autumn* (1982). RT

KIBAL'NIKOV, Aleksandr Pavlovich (b. 1912) Sculptor. Born in Orekhovo, Kibal'nikov graduated from the Saratov Art Technicum in the 1920s, and soon became known for his bronze and granite portraits of Russian cultural figures such as Chernyshevsky (1948) and Mayakovsky (1954, 1958). He supervised the massive memorial complex *The Brest Fortress* (1972). JEB

KIBRIK, Yevegeniy Adol'fovich (1906–1978) Graphic artist. Born in Voznesensk, Kibrik, after studying in Odessa, enrolled in the Leningrad Vkhutemas and also took lessons from Filonov, although he exchanged Filonov's radical ideas for Socialist Realism in the 1930s. He is remembered for his illustrations of Russian and Western authors such as Gogol' and Nikolay Ostrovsky. JEB

KIPIANI, David (b. 1951) Soccer player. Born in Tbilisi, he was probably Georgia's finest soccer player, playing over 300 games for Dinamo Tbilisi, scoring over 100 goals, and playing twenty games for the Soviet national side. He surprised the soccer authorities by walking out of professional soccer suddenly at the start of the 1982 season, disillusioned by rough play and the apparent leniency of referees. He played thirty-five games in European club competitions, his club winning the Cupwinner's Cup in May 1981. He was voted Soviet footballer of the year in 1977. JWR

KIRICHENKO, Aleksey Illa-rionovich (1908–1975) A Ukrainian ally of Khrushchev, dislodged by rivals in 1960. Graduating from an agricultural institute in 1936 Kirichenko had become a full time official of the Central Committee of the Ukrainian party by 1938, and here he must have come to the attention of Khrushchev. After military service in the south (1941–45), he was secretary for personnel of the Ukrainian Central Committee (1944–45), First Secretary of Odessa *obkom* (1945–49), and Second Secretary, then First Secretary of the Central Committee of the Ukraine (1949–53 and 1953–57). In this last capacity he entered the Presidium of the All-Union Central Committee as a candidate in 1953, and as a full member in 1955. He supported Khrushchev against the 'anti-party group' in June 1957, and in December of that year moved to Moscow as Secretary of the All-Union Central Committee. By 1959 he had charge of Central Committee personnel and seemed to be Khrushchev's informal second-in-command. Kirichenko was demoted to be First Secretary of Rostov *obkom* in January 1960, lost his Secretariat and Presidium positions in May, and was dislodged even from Rostov in June; the rivalry of F. R. Kozlov seems to have been the cause. His death in 1975 was noted only in the military press. JHM

KIRILENKO, Andrey Pavlovich (1906–1990) A Politburo member for twenty-five years, Kirilenko was first brought into the leadership by Khrushchev and remained there throughout almost the entire Brezhnev period, though with declining influence latterly. At first a close ally of Brezhnev's, he was later seen as an obstacle to the promotion of Brezhnev clients to the highest positions.

A Russian of Ukrainian extraction, Kirilenko was a manual worker in his early career – a fitter and electrician in the Voronezh region and a miner in the Ukraine. After joining the Communist Party in 1931 he acquired technical qualifications and in 1938 took his first step on the ladder of the party apparatus as a district party secretary in the Zaporozhe area of the Ukraine; within a year he was the second secretary of the party for the entire Zaporozhe region. Khrushchev was First Secretary for the Ukraine at the time and Kirilenko was to owe much to him for his subsequent promotion.

During the war Kirilenko served in the armed forces from 1941 to 1942 and then became a supervisor of military industry. In 1944 he returned to party work and in 1950 he succeeded Brezhnev as First Secretary of the Dnepropetrovsk regional party organization in the Ukraine. In 1955, by which time Khrushchev was the First Secretary of the Soviet Communist Party, Kirilenko was made party First Secretary for the important industrial region of Sverdlovsk. A year later (at the Twentieth Party Congress) he was elected a member of the Central Committee and in 1957 he became a candidate member of the Presidium of the Central Committee (as the Politburo was then called). Five years later he was elevated to full membership of the Politburo. From May 1962 until April 1966 Kirilenko was First Deputy Chairman of the Bureau of the CC of the CPSU for the RSFSR, and in 1966 he became a Secretary of the Central Committee in conjunction with the full membership of the Politburo he already enjoyed.

Kirilenko, who had joined the coalition against Khrushchev in 1964, was for much of the Brezhnev period supervising both the party organization and Soviet industry within the Central Committee Secretariat. Latterly, however, Chernenko took over as the overseer of party cadres and Kirilenko was dropped *de facto* from the Politburo in October 1982, although this was only formalized in November after Andropov had succeeded Brezhnev who died in that month. Kirilenko's political demise was signalled to Kremlin-watchers when his name was excluded from an obituary published in *Pravda* and signed by all other members of the Politburo, and when Brezhnev died and was lying in state, Kirilenko – who had still not been formally dropped from the Politburo at a plenary session of the Central Committee – went separately from the rest of the Politburo to pay his last respects. AHB

KIRILLOV, Vladimir Timofeevich (1889–1943) Born in the village of Charino (Smolensk region), during War Communism Kirillov became one of the principal poets of the Proletcult and bard of an industrial Prometheanism. He is remembered for such extremist statements as 'in the name of Tomorrow, we will burn our Raphaels ...'. As a revolutionary zealot he was opposed to NEP and left the party in 1921. He was arrested in 1937, but rehabilitated posthumously. KC

KIROV, Sergey Mironovich (1886– 1934) A party and state official whose death by assassination is still controversial, Kirov was born in the small country town of Urzhum in Vyatka province but lost his parents at an early age and was left with two sisters to be cared for by his grandmother. An able pupil, he was awarded a scholarship to Kazan' technical college. According to his autobiographical account he came into contact with revolutionary literature at this time by meeting political exiles, and 'on graduating from the technical school I became a convinced revolutionary, with a leaning towards social democracy'.

After completing college in Kazan' Kirov went to Tomsk where he engaged in further studies and developed contacts with other socialists. In February 1905 he was arrested and held in custody for two or three months; in 1906 he spent nearly a year in Tomsk prison, and later served more lengthy periods. Kirov identified with the Bolshevik wing of social democracy at an early stage and engaged in underground work on their behalf in Tomsk, Irkutsk, and later in the Caucasus.

Kirov was active in party work in the Caucasus during the revolution and Civil War, becoming RSFSR representative with the independent Georgian government in 1920 and a member of the Soviet delegation at the peace negotiations with Poland in the same year and then First Secretary of the Azerbaydzhan party organization the following year. In 1921, at the first party congress he had attended, Kirov was elected a candidate member of the Central Committee. He became a full member two years later. He headed the Leningrad regional party committee from 1926, where he was entrusted with the defeat of the political opposition. Kirov was made a candidate member of the ruling Politburo in the same year, a full member in 1934, and at the same time a member of the Party Secretariat and Orgburo.

On 1 December 1934, in an act which led to mass reprisals but which has still not been satisfactorily explained, Kirov was shot and fatally wounded in the Leningrad party offices by a young communist called Nikolaev. Kirov had been thought of as Stalin's heir-apparent or even as his rival (the party congress in 1934 had greeted him with a massive ovation, although Kirov himself described Stalin as 'the greatest man of all times and all peoples'). His assassination was certainly convenient from Stalin's point of view, and Khrushchev in his 'secret speech' of 1956 did not hesitate to suggest that Stalin had instigated it.

Straightforward and approachable, Kirov appears to have believed in the early 1930s that the battle for industrialization and collectivization had been won and that police terror should therefore be relaxed. One of Kirov's Soviet biographers has certainly claimed that he 'vigorously condemned the repressive measures' that had been taken against the peasantry, and he is also believed to have resisted application of the death sentence to political oppositionists. Kirov, however, had supported Stalin against his earlier rivals and had helped to eliminate those currents of opinion within the party which might have represented a political alternative to what became an increasingly bloodthirsty dictatorship. Buried today in Red Square, his political legacy remains as ambiguous as the circumstances of his death remain obscure. SLW

KIRSANOV, Semen Isaakovich (1906–1972) Poet, born in Odessa. Kirsanov published lyrics and long poems steadily and consistently throughout his lifetime from his début in the mid-1920s, responding loyally to the various social calls made by the party: *Poems in Formation* (1932), *Comrade Marx* (1933), *Poems of War* (1945), *The Time is Ours!* (1950), and many others. GSS

KIRSHON, Vladimir Mikhaylovich (1902–1938) Critic and playwright. One of the founders of Soviet dramaturgy and of RAPP, Kirshon was an influential theatre and film critic in the late 1920s and early 1930s. His plays included: *The Rails are Humming* (1928), *The City of the Winds* (1929), the popular *Bread* (1930), *The Judgement* (1933) and *The Great Day* (1937). He was arrested and executed in 1938. RT

KISILEV, Tikhon Yakovlevich (1917–1983) A candidate member of the Politburo at the time of his death at the age of sixty-five, Kisilev was born into a peasant family in the Belorussian town of Dobrush. A Communist Party member from 1940, he was briefly a schoolteacher before joining the apparatus of the Belorussian Communist Party in 1944. By 1952 he was First Secretary for Brest and in 1955 he became a Secretary of the Central Committee of the Belorussian party.

Kisilev shifted from party to governmental work in 1959 and for a period of almost twenty years (1959–1978) was Chairman of the Council of Ministers of the Belorussian republic. He moved to Moscow in 1978 as a deputy chairman of the Council of Ministers of the USSR. With the death in a car accident of Petr Masherov, the First Secretary of the Belorussian party organization in 1980, Kisilev returned to his native republic as First Secretary and became a candidate member of the Politburo for the last two years of his life. AHB

KITAENKO, Dmitriy Georgievich (b. 1940) Conductor. Kitaenko was born in Leningrad. On completing his course in conducting under Yelizaveta Kudryavtseva at the Leningrad Conservatory in 1963, he went on to postgraduate studies at the Moscow Conservatory, where his teachers were Aleksandr Khazanov (choral conducting) and Lev Ginzburg (operatic and symphonic conducting). He gained further experience spending two years at the Academy of Music in Vienna (1966–67). He was appointed a conductor at the Nemirovich-Danchenko Musical Theatre (1969), becoming principal conductor the following year. He has appeared in Western Europe and in 1975 visited the USA with the Moscow Philharmonic of which he became chief conductor in 1976. He also teaches at the Moscow Conservatory. GS

KLIBANOV, Aleksandr Il'ich Prominent atheist scholar in the field of the study of religious sects. A correspondent of *Bezbozhnik* from the mid-1920s, his first book was published in 1929. He completed a Candidate of Historical Sciences thesis in 1935 on Mennonite colonization and apparently published nothing further until 1955. At the Institute of History of the Academy of Sciences he completed a doctorate in 1960 on reformation movements in Russia in the fourteenth to sixteenth centuries. This major study was published as a book, followed by substantial books on religious sects from the 1860s to 1917 and in the Soviet period. MR

KLIMOV, Elem (b. 1933) Film director. Klimov is one of the most controversial directors of recent years. All his films have been subjected to revision, considerable delay or outright banning. They include: *A Warm*

Welcome or Entry Forbidden to Unauthorized Persons (1964), *The Adventures of a Dentist* (1966), *Sport, Sport, Sport* (1971–76), *Farewell to Matyora* (1982), *Come and See* (1985) and the epic film of the last years of the tsarist regime, the much delayed *Agony* (1973–84). He was elected First Secretary of the Union of Film-makers in 1986 in the vanguard of the radical changes in that organization. RT

KLIMOV, Valeriy Aleksandrovich (b. 1931) Violinist. Valeriy Klimov was born in Kiev. The son of conductor and teacher, Aleksandr Klimov, he studied at the Moscow Conservatory under David Oistrakh, graduating in 1956 and completing postgraduate studies with him in 1960. He has been a soloist with the Moscow Philharmonic since 1957. The winner of the Prague Competition in 1956 and the Tchaikovsky Contest in 1958, he was made a People's Artist of the RSFSR in 1972. GS

KLUTSIS, Gustav Gustavovich (1895–1944) Graphic artist and designer. Born in Ruiena, Latvia, Klutsis, a leading poster artist and supporter of Constructivism in the 1920s, received his education in Riga, Petrograd and Moscow, before assuming a professorship at Vkhutemas (1924–30). Indebted to Lissitzky and Malevich and convinced that art should be 'relevant', Klutsis used photo-montage and collage to produce startling juxtapositions and combinations of social and political images. He died in a prison camp. JEB

KLYCHEV, Izzat (b. 1923) Painter. Born in Kyzyl-Daikhan, one of Turkmenia's primary contemporary artists, Klychev graduated from the Repin Institute, Leningrad in 1953. His main theme is the changing countryside and the collective farm as in his triptych *Day of Joy* (1967). JEB

KLYUEV, Nikolay Alekseevich (1884–1937) Born near Vytegra (Olonetsk region), Klyuev was a prominent peasant poet of the teens and twenties, who was popular in highbrow circles of Moscow and Leningrad. His poetry is marked by peasant dialect and archaisms and is rich in Slavic folklore. He remained a determined rustic, religious sectarian and opponent of the industrial city into the plan years and the thirties when such views were unacceptable. Subject to harsh attacks and unable to publish in the late twenties, he was deported to Siberia in 1933. KC

KNIPPER-CHEKHOVA, Ol'ga Leonardovna (1868–1959) Actress. Ol'ga Knipper was the actress widow of Anton Chekhov, closely associated both with his plays and with the Moscow Art Theatre. After the Revolution she acted in Ivanov's *Armoured Train 14–69* (1927), Dostoevsky's *Uncle's Dream* (1929), Lev Tolstoy's *Resurrection* (1930) and Gor'ky's *Enemies* (1935). She was still playing Mme Ranevskaya, the part she created, in Chekhov's *The Cherry Orchard* at its 300th performance at the Moscow Art Theatre in 1943. RT

KNUNYANTS, Ivan Lyudvigovich (b. 1906) Organic chemist. After graduating in 1928 from the Moscow Higher Technical School, where he studied with A. Chichibabin, Knunyants worked in the USSR Academy of Sciences in its Laboratory for the Study and Synthesis of Plant and Animal Materials (1929–38), the Institute of Organic Chemistry (1938–54), and the Institute of Elementary Organic Compounds (from 1954). Concurrently, from 1932 he worked at the Military Academy of Chemical

Defence, becoming a professor there in 1940, joining the party in 1941, and becoming a Major-General of engineering in 1949. Responsible for the synthesis of many organic compounds and active in war work, he was elected to the USSR Academy of Sciences as a corresponding member in 1946 and a full member in 1953. Over the next two decades he became well known for his central role in the development of plastics and other synthetic polymers, including *kapron*, used in Soviet plastic raincoats. He was also outspoken in his defence of academic freedom, his active opposition to Lysenkoism, and his support for the development of molecular biology. MBA

KOCHETOV, Vsevolod Anisimovich (1912–1973) Born in Novgorod, Kochetov was a conservative prose writer and literary functionary who began publishing in 1938 and joined the party in 1944. During the forties he was a war correspondent and wrote war fiction. His first success was the socialist-realist novel *The Zhurbins* (1952); part family chronicle, part production novel, it is the story of three generations of Leningrad shipwrights who are involved in post-war reconstruction. A staunch right-winger, nationalist and anti-intellectual, in the fifties he was a determined opponent of all liberals associated with the thaws, and in particular of Tvardovsky and his journal *Novyy Mir*. Kochetov's 1958 novel *The Ershov Brothers*, a story about dedicated steelworkers and their struggle with a bureaucrat who attempts to steal an invention, is in part a parody of Dudintsev's *Not by Bread Alone*. It was followed by his increasingly vituperative *The Regional Party Secretary* (1961) and *Just What Do You Want?* (1964); the latter, a spy novel, attacks

a range of targets from cultural exchanges with the West to 'village prose'. Kochetov held a number of literary offices, including that of secretary of the Leningrad Branch of the Writers Union (1953–55) and editor of *The Literary Gazette* (1955–59) and *October* (1961–73). KC

KOGAN, Leonid Borisovich (1924–1982) Violinist. Leonid Kogan was born at Yekaterinoslav (now Dnepropetrovsk) and died at Mytishcha. Receiving his first instruction on the violin as a child, in 1936 he entered the Central Music *desyatiletka* (specialist preparatory music school) attached to the Moscow Conservatory, where he studied under Abram Yampol'sky. He continued his work with Yampol'sky at the main Conservatory, from which he graduated in 1948, after which he undertook postgraduate training until 1953. In 1953 he gained first place in the Queen Elizabeth International Violinists' Competition in Brussels. In 1944 he was appointed a soloist with the Moscow Philharmonic, joining the teaching staff of the Moscow Conservatory in 1952. A member of the party since 1954, he was made a People's Artist of the USSR in 1966. He toured extensively overseas and was well-known for his recordings. GS

KOLBIN, Gennadiy Vasil'evich (b. 1927) A Russian from the Urals city of Nizhnyy Tagil who gained a reputation as an efficient and incorruptible administrator, especially of non-Russian territories (where he is reputed to have learnt Georgian and Kazakh). Kolbin graduated from the Urals Polytechnical Institute (like Ryzhkov, Yel'tsin and others) in 1955 and became an engineer and party official in Nizhnyy Tagil. He was Second Secretary of Sverdlovsk *obkom*

(1971–75), second secretary in Georgia (1975–83) and First Secretary of Ul'yanovsk *obkom*(1983–86). His selection as First Secretary for Kazakhstan in December 1986 provoked riots in Alma-Ata, but he won local approval with his subsequent policies. In 1989 he was elected to the Congress of People's Deputies and Supreme Soviet, and chosen as Chairman of the Committee of Popular Control. JHM

KOLCHINA, Ol'ga Pavlovna (b. 1918) A Soviet political official, active at the provincial and Republic level, Kolchina graduated from the Voronezh Economic Planning Institute in 1939, after which she pursued a variety of positions as an economic planner, a teacher and party worker. Among other positions, Kolchina served as secretary and the second secretary of the Moscow Provincial Committee of the CPSU and as Deputy Chairman of the Presidium of the Supreme Soviet of the RSFSR. She was a candidate member of the Central Committee 1961–86. NN

KOLDUNOV, Aleksandr Ivanovich (b. 1923) Former Commander-in-Chief of USSR Air Defence Forces. Koldunov was a graduate of the Air Force Academy and the General Staff Academy. He served at the front (1943–45) and earned renown as an ace pilot who shot down forty-six German planes. After the war he commanded a fighter aviation regiment, then a division. He was appointed Commander of Moscow Air Defence District (PVO) (1970–75); First Deputy Commander-in-Chief of the Soviet Air Defence Forces (PVO) (1975–78); then from 1978 Commander-in-Chief. He was a full CPSU Central Committee member from 1981 and gained the rank of Marshal

of Aviation. Koldunov and Defence Minister Sokolov were made the scapegoats for the failure of the Soviet Air Defence Forces in May 1987 to intercept the intrusion of the light plane piloted by the West German Matthias Rust which landed on Red Square on Border Guards Day. The Soviet Air Defences were heavily criticized and a number of air defence officials were disgraced. Koldunov was dismissed from active service and demoted. RA

KOLLONTAI, Aleksandra Mikhaylovna (1872–1952) A Soviet political leader and activist on behalf of women, Kollontai is regarded abroad as the single most important Russian feminist. In the USSR, in contrast, she is remembered primarily as a revolutionary figure and diplomat.

Born into the aristocratic Domontovich family, Aleksandra had a traditional upper-class upbringing. She married Vladimir Mikhaylovich Kollontai in 1893, despite parental opposition and had one son, Mikhail, by him. During her marriage, she studied Marxism and did volunteer educational work among the poor. In 1898 she left her husband and travelled to Switzerland to study Marxism.

On her return to Petersburg in 1899 Kollontai began her career as a Marxist writer. She published articles and gave lectures. During the revolution of 1905, she participated in the women's movement, but much of her activity was directed against feminist groups who, from her perspective, were interested only in middle-class women. Like other Marxists, Kollontai opposed feminism as a concept although her own views were often regarded by outsiders as feminist. Kollontai organized a club for working women and in 1908 was one of the few

Social Democrats who attended the First All-Russian Congress of Women. Hers was a strong, radical voice as she informed middle-class Russian feminists of the problems faced by working and peasant women.

Shortly after the Women's Congress, Kollontai fled into exile abroad where she lived for almost a decade, dedicating herself to writing and lecturing about women. During the First World War, Kollontai was active in the anti-war movement and through her efforts became closely associated with Lenin and the Bolsheviks. In 1915 she joined the Bolsheviks. She returned to Russia in March 1917 and worked actively in the Bolshevik cause.

After the Revolution, Kollontai served briefly as Commissar for Social Welfare on the first Council of People's Commissars, helping to draft the new marriage laws and protective legislation for women workers. She married her lover, Pavel Dybenko, a sailor and the new Commissar of the Navy, who was seventeen years younger than she. Their life together occasioned much gossip among Soviet officialdom, both before and after their marriage. The marriage itself lasted only five years.

Kollontai's opposition to the Treaty of Brest-Litovsk led to her resignation from the Council of People's Commissars and ended her friendship with Lenin. After some months in retirement, Kollontai helped to organize the first Congress of Russian Women and Peasants in 1918. The Congress paved the way for the formation, a year later, of Zhenotdel, the women's department of the Communist Party. Inessa Armand, a close ally of Lenin's, was selected to head the new department. Kollontai suffered a heart attack in

late 1919 and, after a long rest, was given a relatively minor position in Zhenotdel. When Armand died suddenly in 1920, Kollontai was chosen as her successor, serving, at the same time, as a secretary of the International Women's Secretariat of the Comintern. She assumed an activist stance in Zhenotdel as an advocate for women, thereby putting considerable pressure on the party. The combination of her strong advocacy on women's issues, her involvement in the Workers' Opposition and persistent gossip surrounding her personal life resulted in her removal as head of Zhenotdel in 1922. Although her radicalism has been exaggerated, her views on women, marriage and male-female relationships were radical departures from those of the Bolshevik leadership.

Kollontai was given a minor diplomatic post in Norway, thus effectively ending her participation in Soviet political life. During her years in Norway, she wrote several political novels about women and their struggles. Kollontai eventually became an Ambassador to Norway and later to Mexico and Sweden, thus achieving prominence as the first woman Soviet diplomat. During the Second World War, she participated in negotiations between Finland and the USSR.

After the war she served briefly as an adviser to the Ministry of Foreign Affairs in Moscow before retiring due to ill health. Although estranged from the Stalinist regime, she received numerous awards from the Soviet government as well as honours from foreign governments. She died of a heart attack in 1952 and was interred in Novodevichy Cemetery.

Kollontai was one of the few prominent Bolsheviks to survive the Purges.

Her exile and her silence about domestic affairs under Stalin no doubt accounted for her survival. A prolific essayist, as well as a novelist, she wrote on women's problems, sexual issues, the workers' situation after the revolution and numerous other questions. Her written legacy is an important one although seldom noted in the USSR. Nonetheless, her contribution to Soviet policies on women after the Bolshevik revolution remains as an enduring and tangible legacy. Some of the early policies have been altered, but others remain. Her contribution to the feminist movement is better recognized abroad than in the USSR where feminism remains an alien, 'bourgeois' concept. NN

KOLMOGOROV, Andrey Niko-laevich (1903–1987) Mathematician. A student of N. N. Luzin, Kolmogorov graduated from Moscow University in 1925. In the mid- and late-1920s, he completed path-breaking work in probability theory that established his early reputation as one of this century's leading mathematicians. He became a full professor of mathematics at Moscow University in 1931 at the age of twenty-eight and, in the early 1930s, established the logical axiomatic foundations of probability theory. In 1939 he was elected a full member of the USSR Academy of Sciences at the age of thirty-six, one of the youngest ever so elected. He did major work in most areas of mathematics, including topology and the theory of functions, as well as such applied fields as biological statistics, mathematical linguistics, econometrics, and mechanics. MBA

KOLODKIN, Anatoliy Lazarevich (b. 1928) One of the foremost Soviet specialists on the law of the sea, Kolodkin was born in Leningrad and has spent the greater part of his career holding various legal posts in the USSR Ministry of the Maritime Fleet and collateral diplomatic assignments in international maritime organizations. His principal monograph *The World Ocean* (1973) – amongst hundreds of articles and books – has been translated into German and English. Kolodkin has represented the Soviet government in several international institutions, including the International Maritime Organization (IMO) and the International Maritime Satellite Organization (INMARSAT), and played an influential part in creating the Soviet maritime satellite organization (*Morsvyazsputnik*).

Holding the rank of professor, he has lectured for years in an adjunct capacity at the Law Faculty of Moscow State University on the law of the sea. Under his leadership the Soviet Association of Maritime Law (founded in 1968) has become the most active legal body of its kind in the USSR, having forged contacts in particular with the United Kingdom (with whom six bilateral symposia were held between 1983 and 1989) and the United States, with whom the first symposium was arranged in 1988. He serves on the Editorial Board of *Marine Policy* (UK) and numerous Soviet professional publications. WEB

KOLPAKOVA, Irina Aleksand-rovna (b. 1933) Soviet ballerina. Kolpakova graduated from the Leningrad Ballet School in 1951 and was the last ballerina to be trained by the celebrated Agrippina Vaganova. She joined the Kirov troupe upon graduation and developed a broad repertoire of classical and modern roles. A lyrical dancer, she became known for her crystal-pure technique and great musicality.

Her classical repertoire includes leading roles in such ballets as *Sleeping Beauty, Giselle, Don Quixote, The Nutcracker, Raymonda,* and *La Bayadère.* She created roles in a number of Soviet ballets, including Katerina in *The Stone Flower* (1957), the Beloved One in *The Coast of Hope* (1959), Desdemona in *Othello* (1960), Shirin in *Legend of Love* (1961), Ala in *The Scythian Suite* (1969), Juliet in Igor' Chernyshev's *Romeo and Juliet* (1969), Eve in *The Creation of the World* (1971), Dream Bird in *Icarus* (1974), and the Spanish Infanta in *Infanta* (1976). Until his departure in 1974 Kolpakova was a frequent partner of Mikhail Baryshnikov.

Kolpakova has toured abroad, receiving particular acclaim for her performance in *Raymonda* and *Sleeping Beauty* (1964, New York) and *Le Papillon* (1982, Paris). She received the State Prize of the USSR (1980), awards at international competitions (1959 Vienna, 1965 Paris), and the Anna Pavlova Prize (1982). She has appeared in a number of documentary films including *Irina Kolpakova, Stars of the Leningrad Ballet* and *Irina Kolpakova Dances.* scs

KOL'TSOV (Koltzoff), Nikolay Konstantinovich (1872–1940) Founder of the Soviet experimental biology. Kol'tsov graduated from Moscow University in 1894 and continued there as a *dotsent* until 1911. Working periodically in Europe (1897–1903), he became converted to the new experimental biology and undertook important studies on cellular morphology. From around 1910, he developed laboratories at the Moscow Higher Courses for Women and at Shanyavsky University where his students specialized in such new experimental fields as limnology,

embryology, physicochemical biology, endocrinology, and cytology. A year after being elected a corresponding member of the Academy of Sciences, he was able to bring these together in his new Institute of Experimental Biology (IEB), established in 1916 with philanthropic funding. After the revolution he was briefly under arrest but was freed with the help of such friends as Maksim Gor'ky and Nikolay Semashko, head of the Commissariat of Public Health (Narkomzdrav), and in 1920 the IEB became part of Narkomzdrav's network of research institutes. A scientific entrepreneur, Kol'tsov founded the Russian Eugenics Society in 1920 and created or edited numerous journals. He strongly supported the development of genetics in the IEB, and while there his protégés Aleksandr Serebrovsky (1918–27), Sergey Chetverikov (1922–29), and Nikolay Dubinin (1932–48) made it the leading Soviet research institute in animal genetics and a world centre of population genetics. Kol'tsov's own special interest was the physicochemical character of the gene, and he published two suggestive monographs, *The Physicochemical Basis of Morphology* (1928, 1929) and *Hereditary Molecules* (1935, 1939), which suggested a structure based on nucleoproteins. In 1938 he was castigated in the press for his earlier views on eugenics and was removed as director of the IEB. He died of natural causes in December 1940. mba

KOMAROV, Sergey Petrovich (1891–1957) Film actor and director. Komarov trained in Kuleshov's workshop. His films as an actor included: *The Extraordinary Adventures of Mr West in the Land of the Bolsheviks* (1924), *The Death Ray* (1925), *Miss Mend* and *By the Law* (both 1926), Pudovkin's *The*

End of St Petersburg (1927), *The House on Trubnaya* and *The Salamander* (both 1928), Kuleshov's *The Happy Canary* (1929) and *The Two Buldis* (1930), Barnet's *Outskirts* (1933) and Pudovkin's *Minin and Pozharsky* (1939). Among the films he directed were the immortal comedy *The Kiss of Mary Pickford* (1927) and *The Doll with the Millions* (1928). RT

KOMAROV, Vladimir Leont'evich (1869–1945) Botanist, plant geographer, scientific administrator. After graduating from St Petersburg University in 1894, Komarov taught botany there from 1898, becoming a professor in 1918. Working concurrently at the Botanical Garden from 1899, he was involved in numerous collecting expeditions (1892–1913) to Central Asia, Manchuria, Korea, and the Sian mountains, where he discovered some seven dozen new species. He was elected to the USSR Academy of Sciences in 1920 and, with the coming of Stalinism, rose rapidly in administration, becoming vice-president of the Academy in 1930, director of its Botanical Institute in 1931, the president of the Academy in 1936, and a deputy of the Supreme Soviet in 1937. Politically compliant, Komarov implemented a major reorganization of the Academy (1938–39), which served political interests while at the same time strengthening the role of scientists in policy-making. In the Lysenko affair, too, Komarov played an equivocal role, supporting some of Lysenko's positions while reinforcing traditional biological disciplines. He launched two major collective projects for which he is remembered, *Russian Botanists* (which ceased publication after only four volumes) and *Flora of the USSR* (30 volumes, 1934–64). MBA

KOMOV, Oleg Konstantinovich (b. 1922) Sculptor. Born in Moscow, Komov studied under Tomsky at the Surikov Institute, Moscow, before embarking on his career as a portrait sculptor. Known for his lyrical style, he has produced many renderings of Russian writers and artists such as Pushkin (1965, 1974) and Soifertis (1967). JEB

KONASHEVICH, Vladimir Mikhaylovich (1888–1963) Graphic artist. Konashevich was born in Novocherkassk. Influenced by the World of Art artists, especially Mstislav Dobuzhinsky, he studied under Konstantin Korovin, Sergey Malyutin and Leonid Pasternak at the MIPSA. While curator at the Pavlovsk Palace Museum (1918–26), he produced a series of landscapes, although he attracted particular attention by his illustrations to children's stories by Chukovsky, Marshak and other Soviet writers. From the 1930s onwards he continued to illustrate creative literature, working in lithography, xylography and other media. JEB

KONCHALOVSKY, Petr Petrovich (1876–1956) Painter and designer, born in Slavyansk. Konchalovsky was already a mature painter before the Revolution, having studied in Paris and at the Academy of Arts. A cofounder of the Jack of Diamonds in 1910, he favoured a Cézannist style, sometimes with Cubist elements, as his many still-lives and portraits of the 1910s and 1920s demonstrate. Accepting the return to Realism and then Socialist Realism in the late 1920s to 1930s, he still retained his individual, informal style as can be seen in his portrait of Meyerkhol'd of 1938. JEB

KONDRASHIN, Kirill Petrovich (1914–1981) Conductor. Kondrashin was born in Moscow and died in

Amsterdam. Having first studied piano at the Stasov Musical Technical College in Moscow, in 1932 he went on to study conducting under Boris Khaykin at the Moscow Conservatory, graduating in 1936. From 1937 to 1941 he worked at the Leningrad Malyy Theatre, after which followed a long spell at the Moscow Bol'shoy (1943–56). In 1960 he became chief conductor of the Moscow Philharmonic, with which he undertook several tours abroad. He was the first Soviet conductor to perform in the United States, which he visited in 1958. In 1978 he emigrated and a year later became conductor of the Amsterdam Concertgebouw. A party member since 1941, he was made a People's Artist of the USSR in 1972. GS

KONDRATIEFF (Kondrat'ev), Nikolay Dmitrievich (1892–1938) Internationally-renowned economist, who discovered 'long-cycles'. A pupil of Tugan-Baranovsky at St Petersburg University, Kondratieff was a sympathizer with the Socialist Revolutionaries. He worked under Chayanov during the war, and for the duration of the Provisional Government he was deputy Minister for Food. From 1920 he organized the Conjuncture Institute and published the famous *Economic Bulletin* (1922–27). An adviser to the People's Commissariats for Agriculture and Finance, Kondratieff supported agricultural development and financial stability against Groman and Gosplan. He was attacked as a 'neonarodnik' and arrested in 1930 as a key witness in the 'Menshevik' trial of March 1931. He was accused of organizing the counter-revolutionary 'Working-Peasant Party' (TKP), but was never brought to public trial. He

was rehabilitated in July 1987, when the Supreme Court declared that the TKP had never existed. RWD

KONENKOV, Sergey Timofeevich (1874–1971) Sculptor. Born in Karakovich, Konenkov, often regarded as the most original of Soviet sculptors, trained at the MIPSA (1892–96) and then St Petersburg and Italy. Known for his wooden evocations of primitive folklore such as Yeruslan Lazarevich (1913), Konenkov also maintained a deep interest in Greek and Roman sculpture. From 1918 to 1922 he participated in Lenin's Plan of Monumental Propaganda and in 1924 departed for America where he lived until 1945. During his American period, Konenkov created many portraits, both of American luminaries and of Russians such as Dostoevsky, Pavlov and Rakhmaninov. In the 1950s Konenkov made a number of large monuments in stone and wood, some of them repeating his favourite theme of Paganini. JEB

KONEV, Ivan Stepanovich (1897–1973) Soviet military commander. Ivan Konev rose from peasant origins to become one of the most senior figures in the Soviet military command during and after the Second World War. After draft service in the tsarist army he entered the Red Army and party in 1918. During and after the Civil War he held various posts as a political commissar before assuming regimental and divisional commands (1927–32). After graduation from the Frunze Military Academy in 1934 he held senior commands, including command of the Second Red Banner Far Eastern Army (1938–40). A range of command posts followed in the critical years (1940–45): Trans-Baikal, then Transcaucasian Military Districts (1940–41); the Nineteenth Army and Western Army Group in the battle for Moscow (1941); the Kalinin Army Group (1941–43); the Steppe, the Second Ukrainian, and the First Ukrainian Army Groups in Soviet offensives in the Ukraine, Poland and the battle for Berlin (1943–45). Thus the troops under Konev's command took part in the battles of Moscow and Kursk, in the liberation of the Ukraine, and in the East Carpathian, Vistula-Oder, Berlin and Prague operations.

After the war Konev became Commander-in-Chief of the Soviet occupation forces in Austria and Hungary (1945–46), Commander-in-Chief of the Soviet Ground Forces and Deputy Minister of War (1946–50), and Chief Inspector of the Soviet Army (1950–51). In the late Stalin years his military career was stalled, but it revived in 1955 when he was appointed First Deputy Minister of Defence and Commander-in-Chief of Warsaw Pact Forces. For five years he presided over the nascent Warsaw Pact structure until he was relieved of these posts for health reasons. After commanding Soviet occupation forces in Germany briefly (1961–62) he worked as Inspector General of the Ministry of Defence. Konev held CPSU Central Committee membership after 1952. RA

KONOTOP, Vasiliy Ivanovich (b. 1916) A Ukrainian worker's son, Vasiliy Konotop became a full-time party official after graduating in 1940 from a Khar'kov engineering institute and working for some years in industry as a chemical technologist and design engineer. In 1956 he was named second secretary of the Moscow regional party organization, becoming in 1959 head of the Moscow regional Soviet executive. He returned to party work in 1963 as head of the Moscow regional party organization, a post he held until 1985; he was also a member of the USSR Supreme Soviet Presidium (1966–85). SLW

KOONEN, Alisa Georg'evna (1889–1974) One of the leading actresses in the twentieth-century Russian and Soviet theatre, Koonen was one of Stanislavsky's favourite pupils. She joined the Moscow Art Theatre in 1906 and left in 1913 for Mardzhanov's Free Theatre where she met her future husband, Tairov. In 1914 they formed the Moscow Kamernyy Theatre. Koonen played all the major classical heroines after 1917. Her principal roles at the Kamernyy Theatre in the Soviet period included: the leading roles in Scribe's *Adrienne Lecouvreur* (1919), *Romeo and Juliet* (1921), Racine's *Phèdre* (1922), Shaw's *St Joan* (1924), the commissar in Vishnevsky's *An Optimistic Tragedy* (1933), Emma in Tairov's stage version of Flaubert's *Madame Bovary* (1940), Paustovsky's *Until the Heart Stops* (1943), Nina in Chekhov's *The Seagull* (1944) and Jakobson's *Life in the Citadel* (1947). RT

KOPELEV, Lev Zinov'evich (b. 1912) Germanic scholar and translator who was a party activist in the collectivization campaign and, during the war, a propaganda officer responsible for work with German prisoners. Arrested in 1945, he spent ten years in labour camps, where he met Solzhenitsyn, and became the prototype for the character of Rubin in the latter's *First Circle*. Expelled from the CPSU in 1968 for publishing in the West an article warning of Stalin's possible rehabilitation, he subsequently published (also in the West) a series of memoirs offering valuable historical testimony on the collectivization, the war and the labour camps. Expelled from the Writers' Union in 1977, he visited West Germany in 1980, and was deprived of his citizenship by the Soviet authorities. GAH

KORBUT, Olga Valentinovna (b. 1955) Gymnast. Athough she won fewer titles than several of her contempories (two individual gold and two silver medals at the 1972 Olympics, and one Soviet and world title in 1970), she probably had more impact on women's gymnastics throughout the world than any other gymnast in history. It was the tiny gymnast's daring innovations – the back flip on the beam and the 'Korbut loop' on the asymmetrical bars – that helped to make women's gymnastics more technically complex and exciting to watch. Born in the Belorussian border town of Grodno, she spurned a career, upon retirement, in coaching or sports administration, becoming instead a housewife and marrying a Soviet pop singer. JWR

KOREN', Sergey Gavrilovich (1907–1969) Celebrated character soloist and choreographer. Koren' graduated from Leningrad Ballet School in 1927. He joined the Malyy Theatre upon graduation, and went on to dance with the Kirov troupe (1930–42) and the Bol'shoy Ballet (1942–60).

Among his most acclaimed roles were Karim in *Partisan Days*, Espada the matador in *Don Quixote*, and his outstanding performance of Mercutio in *Romeo and Juliet*.

As a choreographer, Koren' staged *Swan Lake* in Kishinev (1968) as well as numerous dances in operas and plays. SCS

KORETSKY, Vladimir Mikhaylovich (1890–1983) Legal historian, international lawyer, member and Vice-President of the International Court of Justice (1961–70). Koretsky was a legal adviser at many of the post-war peace conferences, and a member of the International Law Commission (1949–51), a titular member of the Institut de droit international, and an Academician of the Ukrainian Academy of Sciences. He pioneered the development of international economic law (1929) and wrote widely in most areas of public international and comparative law. He dominated Ukrainian involvement in international legal matters until his death. WEB

KORIN, Pavel Dmitrievich (1892–1967) Painter. Korin was born in Palekh. Influenced by Nesterov, he graduated from the MIPSA in 1918 after studying with Konstantin Korovin and Sergey Malyutin. Although he really began his career as a painter after the Revolution, Korin expressed a nostalgia for Ancient Russia, especially icons and church architecture, an interest reflected in patriotic works such as *Aleksander Nevsky* (1942–43). He was also a competent portraitist (for example, his portrait of Renato Guttuso, 1961). JEB

KORNILOV, Boris Petrovich (1907–1938) A poet, born near Nizhniy Novgorod, based in Leningrad from 1925, Kornilov was a talented and productive lyric voice whose work was strongly associated with Leningrad and its history, but whose career was cut short by arrest and execution. GSS

KOROLEV, Boris Danilovich (1884–1963) Sculptor. Korolev was born in Moscow. A primary exponent of Realist sculpture in the 1930s onwards, he received his training in private studios in Moscow in the 1900s before enrolling in the MIPSA in 1910 and then travelling to Western Europe in 1913. He experimented with avant-garde ideas just after the Revolution, for example, his Cubo-Futurist statue to Mikhail Bakunin (1919), but quickly reverted to a simpler style, as can be seen in his subsequent portraits of Lenin (1926), Bauman (1931), etc. JEB

KOROLEV, Sergey Pavlovich (1907 (1906 o. s.)–1966) Sergey Korolev was the outstanding pioneer of the Soviet missile and space programmes. A talented engineer of exceptional organizational ability, he headed the rocket development effort from its inception in 1946 until his death. Born in Zhitomir he graduated from the Moscow Higher Technical School in 1930. Initially interested in aviation, from the beginning of the 1930s he turned to rocketry. In 1933 he became deputy director of the newly established rocket-propulsion research institute (RNII), one of the world's first rocket R&D organizations, founded with the backing of Tukhachevsky. Here Korolev worked on liquid-propellant rockets. In June 1938 Korolev was arrested and for a while imprisoned in the same NKVD design office as Tupolev and many other leading aircraft designers. He then served a period of solidary confinement, spent time in a camp at Kolyma, and worked in another prison design organization, eventually gaining release in July 1944. In 1945 together with a group of Soviet specialists he visited Germany to examine captured V-2 rocket facilities. On his return in 1946 he was appointed chief designer of long-range missiles, at first taking the V-2 as a basis; later developing original designs. In August 1957 the first Soviet ICBM ('R-7') was successfully launched; on 4 October 1957 the first 'Sputnik'. Korolev also

headed the development work for the Gagarin flight in 1961 and also for the first lunar and interplanetary flights. During his lifetime Korolev was not identified by name as leader of the rocket programme. He was extremely tough and demanding, not always easy to work with. Even after Stalin's death he encountered political difficulties, the authorities sometimes favouring more pliant figures like Chelomei and Yangel. In 1953 he joined the party; in 1958 he was elected to the Academy of Sciences. Twice a Hero of Socialist Labour (1956, 1961), he was also awarded a Lenin Prize (1957). JMC

KOROLEV, Yuriy Konstantinovich (b. 1929) Designer and painter. Born in Moscow, a representative of the so called 'severe style' in the 1960s, Korolev, in his mosaics, frescoes, and paintings, favours themes from the early Soviet state such as *The Year 1918 Civil War* (1979). He graduated from the Mukhina Institute in Leningrad and then taught monumental art at the Moscow Art Institute. Since 1980 he has been director of the Tret'yakov Gallery, Moscow. JEB

KOROTCHENKO, Demyan Sergeevich (1894–1969) Ukrainian politician. One of Khrushchev's many Ukrainian clients in the leadership, Korotchenko served as a political commissar in the Red Army during the Civil War before making his career as a local party secretary in the Ukraine and Moscow. Having worked under Khrushchev in the capital, he followed the latter to the Ukraine in 1938 where he eventually became chairman of the Council of People's Commissars (later the Council of Ministers) of the republic. He was a full member of Stalin's large Presidium (1952–53) and a candidate member of the Central Committee Presidium from 1957 to 1961. WJT

KOROTICH, Vitaliy Alekseevich (b. 1936) Ukrainian poet, prose writer and journalist. Korotich studied medicine and after receiving his diploma he worked as a doctor for six years, specializing in cardiology. He began to write poetry in his native Ukrainian and his first collection was published when he was in his mid-twenties. Korotich continued writing; his diverse works include a number of film scripts. In 1979 he became Chief Editor of the Ukrainian monthly *Vsesvit* and remained in this post until 1986. He has travelled widely, particularly in the USA, and his novel *Litso nenavisti* (The Countenance of Hatred), written in 1982, delves into the problem of American hostility towards the Russians which Korotich observed at that time. In summer 1986 he was appointed Chief Editor of the Moscow-based journal *Ogonek* which has been radically transformed under his directorship. This journal now serves as a lively forum for debate on many controversial issues and it has played a vital role in promoting re-examination of the Stalinist past, as well as in pioneering the publication of previously banned works and implementing the rehabilitation of suppressed authors. Korotich has been a member of the CPSU since 1967. He has been a deputy to the Ukrainian Supreme Soviet, a member of the presidium of the Soviet Peace Committee, and the vice-chairman of the Peace Committee of the Ukrainian Republic. He is a secretary both of the Ukrainian and of the USSR Writers' Unions. In the course of his creative and journalistic career he has received a number of public honours and literary prizes. During the Gorbachev era Korotich has emerged as an ardent advocate of the reformist cause and his voice is frequently heard in the media both in his own country and abroad. In 1989 he was elected a member of the Congress of Peoples' Deputies of the USSR from the Khar'kov region of the Ukraine. RHP

KOROVIN, Yevgeniy Aleksandrovich (1892–1964) Lawyer. A leading figure in shaping the early Soviet theories of international law, Korovin's first monograph (1923) on international law of the transition period and his basic textbook (1926) explained how a revolutionary Marxist-Leninist Soviet state could be part of and subject to the international legal system. Although subjected to severe criticism and ultimately retracted, the theory remained influential as an original effort to resolve a difficult dilemma for Marxist theoreticians. In the 1930s Korovin published studies on Japan and international law (1936), on disarmament (1930), on the legal status of military attachés (1941), and several on the law of war and the history of international law. In the later years of the Second World War he published four monographs on international security in the post-war era and on the United Nations.

A corresponding member of the USSR Academy of Sciences and director for a brief period of the Institute of State and Law of the Academy, Korovin held the chair of International Law at Moscow University from the late 1950s to the early 1960s. He lectured at the Hague Academy of International Law and the University of Paris, was elected to the International Council for the Social Sciences of UNESCO, to the International Association of Legal

Sciences, to the International Institute of Space Law, to the Presidium of the International Hugo Grotius Fund, and to the committee of experts of the International Labour Organization. From 1957 he was a member of the Permanent Court of Arbitration at the Hague. He frequently advised Soviet delegations at diplomatic conferences, including the Preparatory Commission of the United Nations and the meetings of the Ministers of Foreign Affairs. Korovin played a leading role in the Soviet Red Cross (1918–39) and in aeronautical societies, the Soviet United Nations Association, the Soviet Association of International Law, and the legal section of the Society for Cultural Relations. WEB

KORYAGIN, Anatoliy Ivanovich (b. 1938) Psychiatrist and human rights advocate. Koryagin obtained a higher degree in psychiatry and was making a good career in Khar'kov when, in 1979, he began to work with a Moscow group which was investigating and combating political abuse of psychiatry. He examined dissidents who had reason to fear psychiatric internment, or re-internment, and analyzed his findings in an article published in *The Lancet* (1981). He was given a twelve-year sentence in 1981 and subjected to extensive mental and physical torture in prison. In 1987 he was one of some 200 political prisoners to be released early. He emigrated to Switzerland. PBR

KORZHAVIN, Naum Moiseevich (Mandel) (b. 1925) A poet, Korzhavin was born in Kiev and educated in Moscow. He was arrested in 1947 and returned to Moscow in 1954. He began publishing in the early 1960s, but dissident activity eventually led to his emigration in 1973, after which he played an important part in literary

affairs. In 1989 he revisited Moscow to great acclaim. GSS

KORZHEV (Korzhev-Chuvelev), Geliy Mikhaylovich (b. 1925) Painter. Korzhev was born in Moscow and attended the Surikov Institute there from 1944 to 1950 where he studied under S. Gerasimov. During his subsequent tenure as a teacher at the Moscow Industrial Art Institute and then at the Academy of Arts, Korzhev taught many important young Soviet artists, among them Nazarenko. Representing the so-called 'severe style' of the 1960s, Korzhev favours heroic, revolutionary scenes, for example, *The Communists* (1957–60). JEB

KOSHKIN, Mikhail Il'ich (1898–1940) Mikhail Koshkin died before seeing the the success of his greatest achievement – design of the T-34, generally acknowledged as the finest tank of the Second World War. He was born in the Yaroslavl' district and in 1918 joined the Red Army. After graduating from the Leningrad Polytechnic Institute in 1934 he began tank design work at a local factory. In 1937 he became chief designer of a tank-building factory at Khar'kov and here led work on a series of prototypes, culminating in 1940 in the T-34 medium tank, many thousands of which were built during the war. For his achievement he was posthumously awarded a Stalin Prize in 1942. JMC

KOSIOR, Stanislav Vikent'evich (1889–1939) An 'Old Bolshevik' – party member from 1907 – who perished in Stalin's purges in 1939, Kosior was head of the Ukrainian Communist Party (1928–38) and a member of the Politburo from 1930 to 1938. Born into a working-class family, he began his own pre-revolutionary career as a worker and became active in the revolutionary movement in Moscow as well as in different parts of the Ukraine. He was one of the earliest organizers of the Ukrainian Communist Party but in 1922 became head of the Siberian bureau of the Central Committee of the party, a post he held until 1925 when he became a Secretary of the Central Committee in Moscow. He was promoted to candidate membership of the Politburo in 1927, the year before he moved back to his native Ukraine as First Secretary. AHB

KOSTANDOV, Leonid Arkad'evich (1915–1984) A technocratic politician, Leonid Kostandov was Minister for the Chemical Industry (1965–80), a member of the Central Committee of the Communist Party from 1971 until his death and a deputy chairman of the Council of Ministers (1980–84). He was born into a professional family in what is now the Soviet republic of Turkmenia and after graduating from the Moscow Institute of Chemical Machine-Construction in 1940 he spent almost his entire career as a technologist or official within the chemical industry. AHB

KOSTELNYK, Father Gavryl (1866–1948) Ukrainian Greek-Catholic priest who headed the Initiative Group for the Unification with the Russian Orthodox Church. Born in Ruski Krstur, Yugoslavia, he studied in Zagreb and Freiburg, receiving a doctorate in philosophy. He was ordained into the Greek-rite Catholic priesthood in 1913 to serve in the L'vov diocese, then in the Austro-Hungarian Empire. In May 1945 he was active in the move to merge the Greek Catholics (Uniates) with the Russian Orthodox Church and presided over the L'vov Council which

brought about this forced union. He was assassinated on 20 September 1948 in L'vov. MR

KOSTRICHKIN, Andrey Aleksandrovich (1901–1973) Actor. Kostrichkin was trained as an actor in the FEKS workshop and appeared in most of the early Kozintsev and Trauberg films. RT

KOSYGIN, Aleksey Nikolaevich (1904–1980) A prominent Soviet politician who was for sixteen years Chairman of the Council of Ministers, Aleksey Kosygin made one of the earliest attempts to reform the economic system inherited from Stalin and modified by Khrushchev, but his 1965 reform ran into domestic opposition and was never fully implemented.

Kosygin, the son of a lathe operator, was born in St Petersburg (later Leningrad). At the age of fifteen he volunteered for the Red Army and served in it during the last two years of the Civil War from 1919 to 1921. After demobilization, he received a technical education in Leningrad and from 1924 to 1930 worked in consumer cooperatives in Siberia. He resumed his studies in Leningrad in 1930 when he entered the Leningrad Textile Institute. Finishing there in 1935, he became one of the beneficiaries of Stalin's purges as the number of those who lost their jobs and in many cases their lives became so great that there was very fast promotion for younger men. Between 1935 and 1937 Kosygin moved from being a skilled worker to shop foreman to factory manager within the textile industry in Leningrad. In 1938 he became head of the industrial transport department of the Leningrad regional party committee and later in the same year chairman of the executive committee of the Leningrad City Soviet. Within months he was a minister – in January 1939 (still a month short of his thirty-fifth birthday) he was appointed People's Commissar for the Textile Industry of the USSR.

Between 1940 and 1946 Kosygin was a deputy chairman of Sovnarkom and from 1943 to 1946 simultaneously Chairman of Sovnarkom of the RSFSR. He played an important part in the organization of the Soviet war economy and was in Leningrad during the period of its blockade from January to July 1942.

When Sovnarkom was renamed the Council of Ministers in 1946, Kosygin was named as one of its deputy chairman, a post he held simultaneously with that of Minister of Finance in 1948. After the death of Zhdanov in 1948, however, Malenkov and Beria instigated a case against the leaders of the Leningrad party organization, many of whose prominent members were arrested and executed. Since Kosygin had been their close associate and various accusations were made against him by condemned prisoners under duress, his life at that time, as Khrushchev observed in his memoirs, 'was hanging by a thread'. He had not, however, been involved in any party infighting but had concentrated on economic administration and partly for that reason and partly perhaps because (as Khrushchev also put it) he had 'drawn a lucky lottery ticket', Kosygin survived. He lost his position as Minister of Finance in the same year he was appointed to it, but he soon rejoined the leadership as a Politburo member (1948–52), candidate member of the enlarged Presidium of the Central Committee (1952–53) and as Minister for Light Industry (1949–53).

Kosygin continued to hold important governmental posts dealing with the economy under Khrushchev but it took him until 1957 to regain a position he had held under Stalin, that of deputy chairman of the Council of Ministers. He was a strong candidate for the chairmanship in succession to Bulganin, but relations between Kosygin and Khrushchev were not warm and Khrushchev took that post himself (in addition to the party leadership) in 1958. It was only when Khrushchev was removed from all his offices that in October 1964 Kosygin finally became Chairman of the Council of Ministers and was seen as one of the top two Soviet leaders, along with Brezhnev who became party chief.

Throughout the remainder of the 1960s Kosygin acted like a Prime Minister in the full sense of the term and it was he who engaged in highest-level talks on behalf of the Soviet Union with President Lyndon Johnson, with President Charles de Gaulle and with the British Prime Minister, Harold Wilson. It was only from the beginning of the 1970s that Brezhnev took over these functions and made increasingly clear that he was the senior partner in the party-government duo.

Kosygin was better aware than Brezhnev of how badly in need of reform was the Soviet economy. The 'Kosygin reform' of 1965 represented the first faltering attempt since NEP to introduce some of the principles of the market into the Soviet economy and terms such as 'profit' were no longer taboo. Kosygin continued to emphasize the need for material stimuli, whereas Brezhnev preferred to talk of 'moral stimuli'. Although it was significantly less radical than the economic reform being proposed by

Gorbachev in 1990, Kosygin's reform of a quarter of a century earlier was perceived as a threat by many party functionaries who were glad of any excuse to emasculate it. When the Czechoslovak 'Prague Spring' combined economic reform with political change which was deemed intolerable by the Soviet leadership, this weakened Kosygin's position and the Soviet military intervention in Czechoslovakia strengthened the position of conservative Communists within the Soviet system.

Kosygin was a technocratic reformer rather than a liberal, but he was highly competent and more far-seeing than most of the Brezhnev group. He accommodated himself, however, to the constraints which they imposed and survived as Chairman of the Council of Ministers until October 1980 when, already mortally ill, he resigned and was replaced by Brezhnev's friend of long standing, Nikolay Tikhonov. In December of the same year Koysgin died, aged seventy-six. AHB

KOTIN, Zhozef Yakovlevich (1908–1979) Kotin is known above all for his leadership of the design work on the KV heavy tank, which played a major role during the war. He was born in Pavlograd in the Ukraine and in 1932 graduated from the Dzerzhinsky Military-technical Academy. From then on he was engaged in design work, most of his career being associated with the famous Leningrad Kirov factory. During the war he was chief designer of a factory in the Urals and simultaneously deputy commissar of the tank industry. He led work on the KV, IS-1 and IS-2 heavy tanks and a series of self-propelled artillery units. In the post-war years his work included design of the 'Kirovets'

heavy-wheeled tractor widely used in Soviet agriculture. Between 1968 and 1972 he was a Deputy Minister of the Defence Industry. He joined the party in 1931. Awards included Hero of Socialist Labour (1941) and four Stalin Prizes. JMC

KOVAL'-SAMBORSKY, Ivan Ivanovich (1893–1962) Film actor. Koval'-Samborsky was one of the most popular actors in Soviet silent films. His roles included: Andrey in *His Appeal* (1925), Arthur Storn in *Miss Mend* (1926), parts in *The Forty-First*, *The Man from the Restaurant* and *The Girl with the Hatbox* (all 1927), and Belyaev in Raizman's *Pilots* (1935). RT

KOVRIGINA, Mariya (b. 1910) A Soviet physician and political official, Kovrigina served as Minister of Health from 1954 to 1959 and was, thereby, on the Council of Ministers of the USSR.

Kovrigina was born into a peasant family in Kurgan *oblast*. She joined the CPSU in 1931 and graduated from Sverdlovsk Medical Institute in 1936. Most of her career was devoted to medical administration at the local and national level. Her early career was spent as an inspector in the Chelyabinsk Provincial Public Health Department, and later as head of the Public Health Department of the Chelyabinsk Provincial Committee of the CPSU. At the age of thirty-two she was made a deputy Minister of Health of the USSR, a position she occupied for eight years. In 1950 Kovrigina was made Minister of Health for the RSFSR and in 1953 First Deputy Minister of Health and a year later Minister of Health of the USSR, a position she held for five years. In 1959 she became the Director of the Postgraduate Medical Institute under the Ministry of Health. She was a member of the Central Committee of the CPSU from 1952 to 1961. During her time at the Ministry of Health the public health system was reorganized and health resorts were brought under the supervision of the Ministry of Health.

During her long career, she published a number of works on the public health system in general and on maternity and children's health care issues in particular. While Minister of Health, Kovrigina travelled widely, representing the USSR at numerous medical congresses and conferences, especially in other socialist states. NN

KOZINTSEV, Grigoriy Mikhaylovich (1905–1973) Film director. Kozintsev was one of the leading Leningrad film directors. With Leonid Trauberg and Sergey Yutkevich he co-founded the Factory of the Eccentric Actor (FEKS) in 1922, and with Trauberg he co-directed: *The Adventures of Oktyabrina* and *Mishka versus Yudenich* (both 1925), *The Devil's Wheel* and *The Overcoat* (both 1926), *Little Brother* and *S.V.D.* (both 1927), *The New Babylon* (1929) and the Maxim trilogy, *The Youth of Maxim*, *The Return of Maxim* and *The Vyborg Side* (1934–38). He then directed a number of films alone, including: *Don Quixote* (1957), *Hamlet* (1964) and *King Lear* (1972). RT

KOZLOV, Frol Romanovich (1908–1965) A major rival of Khrushchev who might well have succeeded him if he had not been incapacitated by a stroke in 1963. Kozlov came from the Ryazan' area, but his name is more associated with Leningrad where he moved in 1928. After graduating from what is now the Leningrad Polytechnical Institute in 1926, he was assigned to the Urals engineering city of Izhevsk, where he was party organ-

izer in a metallurgical factory, and secretary of the city party committee. Between 1944 and 1947 he did unspecified work in the Central Committee apparatus in Moscow, and was then Second Secretary of the Kuybyshev provincial party until 1949. This year saw his return to Leningrad, as a party organizer in the important Kirov works, and it was followed by his rapid rise through the Leningrad party hierarchy; he became First Secretary of Leningrad *obkom* at the end of 1953. Significantly this office did not lead to entry into the Presidium (Politburo) of the Central Committee until early 1957; he was a candidate member of the Presidium from February to June 1957; and a full member thereafter. From December 1957 to March 1958 he was Chairman of the RSFSR Council of Ministers, and from then until May 1960, First Deputy Chairman of the USSR Council of Ministers.

Kozlov must have been behind the fall of Kirichenko, Aristov and Belyaev in May 1960, and he replaced Kirichenko as *de facto* second secretary with responsibility for personnel. The climate of Khrushchev's administration changed after this. Kozlov saw his role as one of restraining Khrushchev's initiatives in the interests of the party bureaucracy, which often coincided with conservative and with Russian interests. He was rumoured to be behind an attempt to depose Khrushchev in February 1963. But his serious stroke in April of that year removed him from politics, and L.I. Brezhnev took over the leadership of the forces opposed to Khrushchev. Kozlov was released from his position of Secretary in November 1964 and died in January 1965. JHM

KOZLOV, Petr Kuz'mich (1863–1935) Naturalist, geographer, and explorer. Prominent in pre-revolutionary Russian explorations of Siberia and Central Asia, Kozlov led the first Soviet expedition to Central Mongolia (1923–26) and planned the expedition to the Tien-Shan range (1931–33). His work in the northern Gobi desert resulted in important finds of Tertiary fossils. MBA

KOZLOVSKY, Ivan Semenovich (b. 1900) Tenor. Ivan Kozlovsky was born in the village of Mar'yanovka. Of humble origins, he studied under Yelena Murav'eva at the Kiev Institute of Music and Drama (1917–19), after which he served in the Red Army for the following five years. In 1924 he became a soloist with the Khar'kov Opera Theatre, joining the Sverdlovsk Theatre in 1925. From 1926 to 1954 he was attached to the Moscow Bol'shoy, where his lyrical tenor voice with its appealing timbre was highly esteemed. He was also a sympathetic performer of Romantic song. He was made a People's Artist in 1940 and is the recipient of several State Prizes. GS

KOZLOVSKY, Sergey Vasil'evich (1885–1962) Designer. Kozlovsky was a set designer who worked in cinema from 1913. His principal designs included: *Polikushka* (1919), Protazanov's *Aelita* (1924), Pudovkin's films from *The Mother* (1926) to *The Deserter* (1933) and various films by Barnet and Kuleshov. RT

KRASIN, Leonid Borisovich (1870–1926) An engineer who later became a prominent diplomat and economic administrator, Leonid Krasin was born in the small provincial town of Kurgan. His father was an official of broadly democratic sentiment, his mother a well-educated woman of wide interests. Krasin received his secondary education in Tyumen and in 1887 entered St Petersburg Technological Institute. About this time he became seriously involved in student radicalism and marxist study, and was eventually expelled from the Institute with no right of readmission, but he continued to engage in political activity and was several times arrested and incarcerated. He later entered Khar'kov Technological Institute, graduated there in 1900 as an engineer, then worked for four years on the construction of large electrical power stations in Baku. Krasin continued to engage in political work and established an underground press on which the Social Democratic paper *Iskra* (The Spark) was printed. He moved closer to Moscow in 1904 and later became chief engineer of the St Petersburg lighting system. Arrested but released in 1908, he left Russia for Germany and went to work for Siemens in Berlin.

Following the October revolution Krasin sided with the Bolsheviks, taking an active part in the Brest-Litovsk negotiations (1917–18); he then became engaged in the supplying of the Red Army and assumed the post of People's Commissar for Trade and Industry. From April 1919 he was also Commissar for Transport and from 1920 to 1926 Commissar for Foreign Trade. Most of Krasin's later career was spent in the diplomatic field: he negotiated with the Baltic states in 1919 and 1920, and signed the Anglo-Russian Trade Agreement in London in 1921. He was a member of the Soviet delegation at the Genoa and Hague Conferences of 1922, and was Soviet ambassador to France from 1924 to 1926, but died in London that year, having just been appointed Soviet ambassador to Britain. Krasin was often regarded abroad as a practical man, 'not really a Bolshevik', who would be flexible on communist principles, and at the Twelfth Party Congress in 1923 he did indeeed propose several modifications of foreign and domestic policies which were later described as 'right-wing opportunistic' in character. Perhaps for this reason he was a somewhat marginal figure in the party and state leadership in the years before his death. SLW

KRASIN, Yuriy Andreevich (b. 1929) An influential Communist Party theorist, Yuriy Krasin was a cautious reformer in Brezhnev's time and he has received promotion under Gorbachev. A Russian born in Penza, Krasin – who joined the Communist Party in 1957 – studied at Leningrad University, but since 1960 has worked in Moscow. From 1963 he was an official of the International Department of the Central Committee of the Communist Party, and in 1975 he moved to the Institute of Social Sciences attached to the Central Committee. In 1987 he was appointed Rector of that institution. AHB

KRASOVSKAYA, Vera Mikhaylovna (b. 1915) Dance critic and historian. A graduate of the Leningrad Ballet School, where she studied with Agrippina Vagonova, Krasovskaya danced with the Kirov Ballet from 1933 to 1941 when she published her first critical reviews. She began to study with Yuriy Slonimsky at the Leningrad Institute of the History of the Arts in 1946, and has been on its staff since 1951. She received a doctor's degree in art criticism in 1955 and a professorship in 1975.

Among the more than 200 articles she has written for Soviet and foreign periodicals, are analytical studies of the work of Soviet dancers and cho-

reographers, as well as surveys of Leningrad ballet seasons. In the later 1950s Krasovskaya was one of the advocates of new ideas, criticizing the overly dramatic approach of some choreographers and urging a new respect for the primacy of dance itself. Her first books dealt with leading trends and personalities in Russian ballet. Continued research culminated in her four-volume history *The Russian Ballet Theatre* (1958–72), marking the first time that any country had produced so extensive a study of the evolution of its theatrical dance. A one-volume condensation appeared as a textbook in 1978. Among Krasovsksaya's fifteen books are important biographies, including *Anna Pavlova* (1964), *Nizhinsky* (1974), and *Nikita Dolgushin* (1985). Another major accomplishment is the first comprehensive history of Western ballet to appear in Russian since 1917: *West-European Ballet Theatre* (1979–1983). She is also a contributor to the American *International Encyclopedia of Dance*.

Krasovskaya's writing is especially notable for its keen perception of historical trends and sensitive analysis of the choreography of such masters as Marius Petipa and Lev Ivanov. SJC

KRAVAL', Ivan Adamovich (1897–1938) Energetic and ruthless economic organizer. A party member from 1919, Kraval' graduated from the Institute of Red Professors in 1924. He was put in charge of labour problems in VSNKh during the 1920s, and later appointed deputy People's Commissar of Labour in 1930. He became first deputy head of TsUNKhU (the Central Administration of National Economic Records, responsible for state statistics) (1933–35), then head of TsUNKhU in 1935. He organized the January 1937 population census, the results of which were suppressed. RWD

KRAVTSOV, Boris Vasil'evich (b. 1922) A member of the CPSU since 1943, Boris Kravtsov graduated in 1952 from the All-Union Juridical Institute as an external student after service in the armed forces during the Second World War, and in the court system thereafter. He was secretary of the party committee of the Ministry of Justice of the USSR (1955–56), and worked in the legal apparatus of the CPSU Central Committee. In 1960 he became first deputy Procurator of the USSR, and in 1971 Procurator of the RSFSR. He has been Minister of Justice of the USSR from 1984, and a candidate member of the CPSU Central Committee since 1986. SLW

KREMER, Gidon Markovich (b. 1947) Violinist. Gidon Kremer was born in Riga, Latvia. Raised in a musical environment, he received his first instruction from his father. In 1954 he entered the *desyatiletka* (specialist preparatory music school) attached to the Latvian Conservatory, after which he studied at the main Conservatory (1957–65). He furthered his studies at the Moscow Conservatory under David Oistrakh, graduating in 1971, and undertook postgraduate training with him until 1973. After gaining prizes in a number of international competitions, he won the Paganini Contest in Genoa in 1969 and the Tchaikovsky Competition in 1970. Since 1974 he has been a soloist with the Moscow Philharmonic Organization. GS

KRESTINSKY, Nikolay Nikolaevich (1883–1938) Krestinsky, a party and state official and later oppositionist, was born in Mogilev to Ukrainian parents. Both his father, a secondary school teacher, and his mother had sympathized with the Populists. Krestinsky graduated from Vilna Gymnasium in 1901 and then entered the Law Faculty of St Petersburg University, obtaining his degree in 1907. He worked as a barrister's assistant and as a barrister until 1917. Already by his late school years, Krestinsky recalled later in his autobiography, he had been influenced by radical ideas; he became a member of the Social Democratic Party in 1903, later siding with the Bolshevik wing. Before the war Krestinsky was engaged in trade union, newspaper and political work on behalf of the Bolsheviks, for which he was several times arrested. For the first year of the revolution Krestinsky headed the Urals party committee. Notwithstanding his support for the 'left communists', who opposed the Brest-Litovsk peace treaty, Krestinsky remained a member of the party Central Committee (1917–21) and from 1919 until 1921 was a member of the central Secretariat and of the Politburo. Krestinsky became People's Commissar for Finance in 1918, holding the post formally until the end of 1922. In October 1921 he was nominated as Soviet representative in Germany. He supported Trotsky in the trade union debates (1920–21) and was a member of the anti-Stalinist opposition in the late 1920s. He later recanted and was appointed deputy People's Commissar for International Affairs in 1930, but he was replaced and expelled from the party in 1937 and the following year was sentenced to death in the trial of the 'anti-Soviet Rightist-Trotskyite Bloc'. He was rehabilitated in the 1960s. SLW

KROVOPUSKOV, Viktor Leonidovich (b. 1948) Sportsman. Greatest of all Soviet fencers, he was four times Olympic sabre champion, winning the individual and team championships at the 1976 and 1980 Olympic Games. He was also six times world champion and voted sabre fencer of the year by the International Fencing Federation in 1976, 1978, 1979 and 1980. Born in Moscow, he studied coaching at the Moscow Physical Culture Institute and held a commission in the armed forces. JWR

KRUCHENYKH, Aleksey Eliseevich (1886–1968) Poet and pamphleteer, born near Kherson, educated in Odessa, then moved to Moscow. One of the founders of Russian futurism, a proponent of 'trans-sense language' (*zaum*), Kruchenykh was a dedicated self-publisher of self-designed books; after 1930 he led a shadowy life in Moscow. GSS

KRUCHINA, Nikolay Yefimovich (b. 1928) Administrator of Affairs within the apparatus of the Central Committee of the Soviet Communist Party since 1983, Kruchina has strong career associations with Gorbachev, having worked as his First Deputy in the Department of Agriculture of the Central Committee from 1978 until 1983. Kruchina, a Russian by nationality who was born in Novaya Pokrovka in the Altay region, joined the Communist Party in 1949 and graduated from the Azov-Black Sea Agricultural Institute in Zernograd in 1952. He worked his way up the hierarchy of the Komsomol between 1952 and 1962 before switching to the party apparatus. He was First Secretary of the Tselinograd *obkom* in Kazakhstan from 1965 to 1978 and he became a member of the Central Committee in 1976. AHB

KRUGLOVA, Zinaida Mikhaylovna (b. 1923) The Chairman of the Presidium of the Union of Soviet Societies for Friendship and Cultural Relations with Foreign Countries since 1975 and a member of the Central Committee of the CPSU since 1976, Kruglova has had a varied career. A veteran of the Second World War and a graduate of the Leningrad Institute of Aviation Equipment Construction in 1951, Kruglova worked in the aviation industry for a time before moving into full-time work for the party in 1960. From 1960 to 1974 she served as First Secretary of the Leningrad-Frunze Raion Committee, the Secretary of the Leningrad City Committee and then Secretary of the Leningrad Provincial Committee. In 1974 she served briefly as Deputy Minister of Culture of the USSR, before assuming her present position. As head of the Union of Friendship Societies, Kruglova has visibility and prestige within Soviet society, although it is not an important policy making organ. NN

KRUPSKAYA, Nadezhda Konstantinova (1869–1939) A noted revolutionary and educator, Nadezhda Krupskaya was the wife of Vladimir Il'ich Lenin. She was born in St Petersburg, the daughter of an army officer, Konstantin Krupsky. Her father's career suffered when he was demoted during an assignment in Poland. Even though he was later cleared, the family did not recover from these reverses, and Konstantin died at an early age. Krupskaya graduated from a gymnasium where she later taught as an assistant. She began a university course, but dropped out after a year. Her involvement with Marxist circles began at an early age, and she considered herself a Marxist by the age of twenty-one. In 1891 Krupskaya became a teacher in the weekend and evening schools for workers.

In 1894 she met the Marxist revolutionary, Vladimir Ulyanov

(Lenin). They were friends for several years before she joined him in his Siberian exile in 1898. Krupskaya herself had been arrested and sentenced to exile in Ufa, Bashkiria. Lenin asked her to join him in Shushenskoe. She was allowed to go to Siberia only if she promised they would be married. And thus they were married in Siberia, and their fates were intertwined for the rest of their respective lives. Her movements and activities from 1898 to 1924 closely paralleled his. Prior to the Revolution, Krupskaya was at times Lenin's aide and secretary, although she also pursued her own work. Her special areas of interest were education, women and children. Childless herself, she was fond of children and emphasized the importance of motherhood in handling the 'women's question' in Russia. Ultimately, it was her concept of woman as mother and worker that prevailed in the Soviet Union. Lenin closely agreed with her views although it would be difficult to discern who influenced whom.

After their respective periods of exile were concluded, Lenin and Krupskaya lived in Western Europe for almost fifteen years, returning to Russia only after the 1905 Revolution and departing again in 1907 when the regime became more conservative. Krupskaya performed numerous functions in the revolutionary movement, spending a good deal of her time as an assistant on the Marxist publications, *Iskra* and *Vpered*. During these years Krupskaya's mother lived with the couple as their housekeeper until her death in 1915. Krupskaya's health deteriorated about 1910, and some of their destinations were chosen with her health in mind. Although aware that her husband was an extraordinary figure, she did not, as far as is known, keep a journal on his life during this period. Both shared the Marxist disdain for exaggerating the role of personality in history. Later, after his death, she wrote *Reminiscences of Lenin*, but these were not a systematic account of his life and works.

In November 1917 their lives changed dramatically when the Bolsheviks came to power. Krupskaya preferred a quiet life out of the limelight and did not particularly enjoy the years in which Lenin was the Chairman of the Council of People's Commissars (Premier) of the Soviet government. They lived in a modest apartment within the Kremlin and ate in the cafeteria provided for government officials. Although referred to as 'the first lady' by foreign visitors, Krupskaya never thought of herself in that light. She perhaps saw less of Lenin during these years than when they lived in exile abroad. Krupskaya herself worked for the Commissariat of Education after the Revolution and was involved in the work of Zhenotdel. Adult education and education for women were among her chief concerns. She was also very active in the Soviet campaign to establish libraries for the working people.

After Lenin's stroke, they resided in Gor'ky where Krupskaya was both nurse and secretary. Her altercation with Stalin, the emissary of the Politburo, was a contributing factor to the comments in Lenin's 'Testament'. After Lenin's death, she took issue with the Central Committee's decision not to publish the 'Testament', and relations between Krupskaya and Stalin were irreparably strained although she later supported him on specific policies. In 1927 she was elected to the Central Committee after supporting Stalin against Zinov'ev and Kamenev.

In the fifteen years after Lenin's death, Krupskaya enjoyed considerable prestige as his widow, but little power. Allowed to retain her apartment in the Kremlin, Krupskaya continued to work in the RSFSR Commissariat of Education until her death. She frequently received visitors, conducted extensive correspondence, and made public speeches on national holidays such as March 8, International Women's Day. Some of her educational and social views coincided with those of Stalin, and he used her ideas when it suited him.

In the post-Stalin period, Krupskaya's work and contributions have received considerable attention in the USSR. Although Kollontai was the better known 'feminist', Krupskaya's image of women is the one promoted in the USSR. Outside the Soviet Union, Krupskaya is little known, except by specialists, and there is a tendency to view her only as Lenin's spouse and not as a revolutionary and political official in her own right. NN

KRYLENKO, Nikolay Vasil'evich (1885–1938) Prior to 1917 Krylenko was extensively involved in party work, closely associated with Lenin and, on several occasions, arrested, imprisoned, or exiled. While in confinement at Khar'kov in 1914 he succeeded in passing the state examination for the Law Faculty at Petersburg University. From March 1918 Krylenko was closely involved with the revolutionary tribunals, becoming chairman of the Military-Revolutionary Tribunal attached to the All-Russian Central Executive Committee (*VTsIK*). He is credited with a considerable role in creating the Soviet Procuracy and succeeded –

against much opposition – in defeating those who sought to structure it as an agency under dual subordination. He helped draft the 1922 RSFSR codes of criminal law and procedure, becoming Deputy People's Commissar of Justice and senior aide to the Procurator of the RSFSR in August 1922, and Procurator in 1929. In 1931 he was appointed People's Commissar of Justice for the Russian Republic and in July 1936 People's Commissar of Justice for the USSR.

Krylenko served on the major codification commissions in the 1920s and wrote standard monographs on RSFSR court organization. In 1927 he supported those close to Pashukanis, who advocated simplification and abbreviations of the criminal code, a position which he later retracted. He was involved in the work of the committees which created the USSR Supreme Court in 1923 and served on the 1936 constitutional drafting commission. He published more than 100 works, mostly relating to the court system, but also of consequence for legal theory of the day. For years he lectured at the Institute of Red Professors and the Institute of Soviet Construction and Law.

Krylenko, who was a keen climber, published four volumes on the geography of the Pamirs. He was also head of the All-Union Chess Federation and the All-Union Society for Proletarian Tourism for many years. Twice he was elected a member of the Central Committee of the Communist Party and a member of the Central Executive Committee, and to the Presidium of the All-Union Central Executive Committee (*VTsIK*) in 1935.

On 31 January 1938 he was arrested on Yezhov's instructions, tried for anti-Soviet activities, and sentenced to death on 29 July 1938. The Military Division of the USSR Supreme Court reversed the guilty verdict on 10 August 1955. Fully rehabilitated, Krylenko's speeches have been republished in posthumous editions, a statue erected in Smolensk, a street named in his honour in Moscow, and commemorative plaques installed at his residences. WEB

KRYLOV, Sergey Borisovich (1888–1958) Distinguished international lawyer, diplomat, and professor. Krylov advised the USSR Ministry of Foreign Affairs (1942–58), was head of the Department of International Law at Moscow State Institute of International Relations (MGIMO) (1948–58), was elected a judge to the International Court of Justice (1946–52), a member of the International Law Commission (1953–56), and to the Permanent Court of Arbitration at the Hague (1956–58). He published more than 200 works, including several studies on the history of the formation of the United Nations, which have been translated into English. WEB

KRYUCHKOV, Vladimir Aleksandrovich (b. 1924) Head of the KGB since 1988, Kryuchkov was born into a worker's family in Volgograd. A member of the Communist Party from 1944, he graduated from the All-Union Juridical Institute by correspondence course in 1949 and from the Higher Diplomatic School in 1954.

His earliest work was in the defence industry (1941–43), but in 1943 he moved into the apparatus of the Komsomol and from 1946 to 1951 worked in the organs of the Procuracy in the Volgograd region. In 1954 he entered the diplomatic service and became Third Secretary in the Hungarian Embassy. This was the beginning of a long association with Yuriy Andropov who was Soviet Ambassador there. When Kryuchkov returned to Moscow it was to work in the Socialist Countries Department of the Central Committee which was headed by Andropov and where Kryuchkov in due course became head of the sector responsible for Hungary. From 1965 to 1967 Kryuchkov was one of Andropov's aides and when in 1967 Andropov was transferred from the Central Committee Secretariat to the chairmanship of the KGB, Kryuchkov followed him there. Krychkov was head of the First Main Administration of the KGB and a member of the collegium of the KGB from 1974 to 1988 and was a deputy chairman of the KGB for the last ten of those years. He was elected to full membership of the Central Committee of the Communist Party at the Twenty-Seventh Party Congress in 1986.

Within the KGB, prior to his becoming its Chairman in 1988, Kryuchkov had responsibility for intelligence gathering abroad rather than domestic surveillance. After Chebrikov, his predecessor as head of the KGB, had become increasingly disenchanted with the policies Gorbachev was pursuing, the support of Kryuchkov for Gorbachev both before and after his appointment to the KGB chairmanship assumed considerable importance.

Kryuchkov soon received further important promotions. He became a full member of the Politburo in September 1989 without having passed through the stage of candidate membership, and in March 1990 Gorbachev made him a member of his Presidential Council. He ceased to be a member of the Politburo following the Twenty-Eighth Party Congress in July 1990. AHB

KRZHIZHANOVSKY, Gleb Maksimilyanovich (1872–1959) An old Bolshevik and engineer, Krzhizhanovsky, a friend of Lenin, inspirer of the GOELRO long-term plan for the electrification of Russia, was, with Strumilin, an influential advocate of comprehensive planning for industrialization throughout the 1920s. He proposed 'energy planning' as the basis for all planning. Educated as an electrical engineer at St Petersburg Technical University, he supported Lenin while a student – his party membership was officially dated from 1893. Before the revolution he worked as a professional power-station engineer. He was one of Lenin's advisers during the Civil War, and was put in charge of the GOELRO Commission in 1920. Krzhizhanovsky became the first head of Gosplan in 1921, a post which he retained until November 1930, apart from a short break (1924–25). Elected Vice-President of the Academy of Sciences in 1929, he held various less important economic and academic posts in the 1930s. He was a member of the Central Committee from 1903–5 and 1924–39. RWD

KUBYAK, Nikolay Afanas'evich (1881–1937) Kubyak, a party and state official in the inter-war period, was born in Meshchovsk into a worker's family. A party member from 1898, he was a participant in the 1905 and 1917 revolutions and from 1918 to 1920 acted as chairman of the Petrograd regional party committee. He briefly supported the Workers' Opposition during this time. In 1922 Kubyak was appointed secretary of the Far Eastern Bureau of the Central Committee, and in 1927 he became a member of the central party Secretariat. He was People's Commissar for Agriculture of the Russian republic (1928–31), but he was arrested during the purges and died in imprisonment. SLW

KUDRYAVTSEV, Vladimir Nikolaevich (b. 1923) Director of the Institute of State and Law of the USSR Academy of Sciences (1976–89), after previously heading a Procuracy research institute, a member of the presidium of the Academy, and the first jurist to be elected an Academy Vice-President (1988). Kudryavtsev is a leading criminologist and specialist in the theory and sociology of law. His more than 200 scholarly publications include a *Theoretical Model Criminal Code* (1987) and major studies of causality in criminology and of social deviations (1984). He has had an important role in shaping *perestroika* legislation, including reforms in mental health care, and is vice-president of the Association of Soviet Jurists and the International Association of Democratic Lawyers. WEB

KUKRYNIKSY. Composite name for **KUPRIYANOV, Mikhail Vasil'evich** (b. 1903), **KRYLOV, Porfiriy Nikitich** (b. 1902), and **SOKOLOV, Nikolay Aleksandrovich** (b. 1903) The greatest of Soviet caricaturists, the Kukryniksy trio has produced memorable posters, satirical leaflets and paintings dealing with many themes – from the problems of NEP to modern art, from the Cold War to women's fashions. But perhaps their most enduring satirical images are of Hitler and his generals during the Second World War. The three artists came together in Moscow in the late 1920s when they were students at Vkhutein and began to work as caricaturists for journals and newspapers such as *Pravda* and *Krokodil*. In addition to their graphics and paintings such as *The Flight of the Fascists from Novgorod* (1944–46), they have also illustrated editions of Chekhov, Gor'ky, Cervantes, Sholokhov and other authors. JEB

KULAKOV, Fedor Davydovich (1918–1978) Kulakov, who was born into a peasant family in the Kursk region of Russia, at one time looked like a future Soviet top leader. His death at the comparatively early age of sixty meant that he is more likely to be remembered as the party official who helped to foster the early career in Stavropol' of Mikhail Gorbachev.

Educated as an agricultural specialist, Kulakov joined the Communist Party in 1940 and spent the war years in Komsomol and party work. From 1944 to 1947 he was head of the agricultural department of the Penza regional party committee where he overlapped with Konstantin Chernenko which may have helped him later to establish relations with Brezhnev. From 1950 Kulakov was chairman of the executive committee of the Penza regional soviet and between 1955 and 1960 Minister of Agriculture and then Minister of Grain Production for the RSFSR.

From 1960 to 1964 Kulakov was First Secretary of the Stavropol' regional party committee and in November 1964 he moved to Moscow to become head of the Department of Agriculture of the Central Committee of the CPSU. (Gorbachev moved from the same post to the same job on Kulakov's death fourteen years later.) In September 1965 Kulakov was promoted to a Secretaryship of the Central Committee and in April 1971 he became a full member of the Politburo and thus one of the senior secretaries within the leadership.

Agriculture remained his principal speciality until his death. AHB

KULAKOVA, Galina Alekseevna (b. 1942) Sportswoman. The greatest of all Soviet women skiers, she was born in the village of Logachi in the Udmurt Autonomous Republic. She took part in no fewer than four winter Olympics (1964–76), winning four gold, two silver and two bronze medals in individual and relay races. She was also five times world champion and many times champion of the USSR. For her services to Olympic sport, she gained the IOC Olympic Order in October 1984. Upon retirement from competitive skiing, she became a coach with the Udmurt Sports Committee. JWR

KULESHOV, Lev Vladimirovich (1899–1970) Film director. Kuleshov began his career in cinema before the Revolution and became one of Soviet cinema's leading film directors and theorists. In 1919 he set up an experimental workshop within the State Film School in Moscow and worked with Pudovkin, Barnet, Khokhlova, Fogel' and others. He was also the founding father of Soviet film theory, developing the notion of montage as the essence of cinema specificity and demonstrating the so-called 'Kuleshov effect' in his experiments with the Workshop. His first feature film was the highly original satirical comedy *The Extraordinary Adventures of Mr West in the Land of the Bolsheviks* (1924). His next film was *The Death Ray* (1925), a thriller that was popular with audiences but not with officialdom. *By the Law* (1926), set in the Yukon during the Gold Rush and based on a story by Jack London, was a great critical success. But his following three films were variously regarded as failures: *Your Acquaintance* (1927), *The Happy*

Canary (1929) and *The Two Buldis* (1930). After this Kuleshov came under increasingly frequent attack, not always officially inspired, for his alleged formalism and his apparent inability to produce a film on a contemporary theme. His subsequent films include at least one further masterpiece, *The Great Consoler* (1934) and *Gorizont* (1933), *Siberians* (1940), *Timur's Oath* (1942) and *We from the Urals* (1944).

Throughout his career Kuleshov was an eminent teacher and Pudovkin wrote of him in 1929: 'We make films but Kuleshov made cinema'. In 1939 he was made a professor at the State Institute of Cinema. His theories of cinema are expounded in Russian in his *The Art of Cinema* (1929), *The Rehearsal Method in Cinema* and *The Practice of Film Direction* (both 1935) and *The Foundations of Film Direction* (1941). RT

KULIDZHANOV, Lev Aleksandrovich (b. 1924) Film director. Kulidzhanov's works include: *The Ladies* (1954), *The House in Which I Live* (1957) and *The Blue Notebook* (1963). He was First Secretary of the Union of Filmmakers from 1965 to 1986. RT

KULIK, Grigoriy Ivanovich (1890–1950?) Conscripted into the Imperial Russian Army in 1912, Kulik served in the First World War, joined the Bolsheviks in 1917 and was arrested for political agitation among the troops. Once in the Red Army, he served with the artillery at Tsaritsyn, where Stalin and Voroshilov controlled the defence. Moving into the First Cavalry Army Kulik commanded its artillery in 1920, continuing to serve with Red Army artillery, taking over the Artillery Administration in November 1926. After attending the Frunze Military Academy in 1932, he took up divisional and corps commands, followed by promotion to Chief of the Artillery Administration in May 1937, rising even further to head the Main Artillery Administration (GAU), the 'brain' of the Red Army in January 1939, an appointment fraught with disastrous consequences. Appointed a Marshal in 1940, as well as a Hero of the Soviet Union, Kulik hopelessly mismanaged the re-equipment of the Red Army with artillery and automatic weapons, dismissing the latter as fit only for 'policemen'.

When war came, Kulik took command of the Fifty-Fourth Army (Leningrad Front) and led it to disaster, for which he was demoted in March 1942 to the rank of majorgeneral. Given command of the Fourth Guards Army at Kursk in 1943, Marshal Zhukov speedily removed him for incompetence, leaving Kulik to serve out the war with the administration raising reserves. Officially, Kulik 'retired' in June 1946, but recent testimony suggests that he was arrested that year, Stalin's patronage having lapsed, lodged in the Kuybyshev Military Prison until 1950 and then shot. Yet in 1957 his rank of Marshal of the Soviet Union was posthumously restored, no doubt as a form of 'rehabilitation'. That Marshal's star, however, had cost the Red Army unaccountably dear. JE

KULIKOV, Viktor Georg'evich (b. 1921) Former Commander-in-Chief Joint Warsaw Pact Forces. Viktor Kulikov, the son of a poor peasant entered the Soviet Army in 1939. He graduated from the Higher Officer's Tank School in 1947, from the Frunze Military Academy in 1953, and from the Military Academy of the General Staff in 1959. During the Second World War he served on various fronts and became Chief of Staff of a tank brigade. After the war he held a succession of commands leading to his appointment in 1967 as commander of Kiev Military District. This was followed in 1969 by the senior post of Commander-in-Chief of the Soviet Group of Forces in Germany. Political honours ensued; Kulikov became a Deputy to the USSR Supreme Soviet in 1970 and member of the CPSU Central Committee in 1971. In September 1971 he became Chief of the General Staff of the Soviet armed forces and First Deputy Minister of Defence of the USSR.

Kulikov gained the position of Commander-in-Chief of the Warsaw Pact forces in January 1977 and earned the rank of Marshal of the Soviet Union. He presided over a period of considerable internal strain in the Warsaw Pact. By the mid-1980s the combination of new budgetary constraints and the prospects of conventional arms control had also created a different politico-military environment for the Warsaw Pact. However, Kulikov remained rather conventional in his outlook. After a meeting of the Warsaw Pact defence ministers in July 1988 he admitted that the efforts of military personnel had turned to safeguarding the world 'not just by force of arms but also through the efforts of the new political thinking', espoused by Gorbachev. Yet at the same time he stressed the traditional need 'to strengthen our defence capability, to boost our operational and combat training'. This conservatism contributed to his replacement as Commander-in-Chief of the Warsaw Pact by Army General Petr Lushev in February 1989. RA

KUNAEV, Dinmukhamed Akhmedovich (b. 1912) Kunaev, a Kazakh by nationality, was born in what is now Alma-Ata. He spent fifteen years as a full member of the Politburo thanks to his close association with Leonid Brezhnev. A metallurgist by occupation, he joined the Communist Party in 1939 and became a full member of the Central Committee of Kazakhstan in 1949. Kunaev established good relations with Brezhnev when the latter was First Secretary of the Kazakhstan party organization in the mid-fifties and he was Chairman of the Kazakh Council of Ministers from 1955 to 1960 (and a full member of the Central Committee of the CPSU from 1956). From 1960 to 1962 he was First Secretary of the Kazakh party, but in 1962 was demoted to the chairmanship of the republican Council of Ministers once again. However, with Brezhnev's election as leader of the CPSU in 1964, Kunaev became republican First Secretary once more and held that post until his dismissal during the Gorbachev era. From 1966 until 1971 Kunaev was a candidate member of the Politburo and in 1971, as part of Brezhnev's strengthening of his position at the top of the party hierarchy, he was promoted to full Politburo membership. Kunaev was a one hundred per cent Brezhnev loyalist and it was no surprise when he was replaced as Kazakh leader in December 1986 (which entailed the loss of his Politburo seat at the next plenary session of the Central Committee in January 1987). However, he had a uniquely long spell in the party's highest policy-making body for a Kazakh and his replacement as First Secretary in Kazakhstan by a Russian,

Kolbin, led to rioting in Alma-Alta. AHB

KUNYAEV, Stanislav Yur'evich (b. 1932) Poet. Kunyaev was born in Kaluga in the Russian Republic. He began to write early and his first poems were published in a school magazine. In 1957 he completed his studies in the Faculty of Philology at Moscow University and left the capital in order to work for a small regional Siberian journal. By 1960 he had returned to Moscow where his conformist literary career has been characterized by a prolific creative productivity and an active participation in the city's literary life. Kunyaev has welcomed *glasnost'* which he regards as an opportunity to correct the 'cosmopolitan' view of history, to show that Stalin cannot be blamed for everything and, more specifically, that it was Trotsky and his like-minded comrades who must be held responsible for the evils of collectivization. Kunyaev has been a member of the CPSU since 1960. He was appointed the Chief Editor of the reactionary literary monthly *Nash sovremennik* in the early autumn of 1989. RHP

KUPREYANOV, Nikolay Nikolaevich (1894–1933) Graphic artist. Studying at the Tenisheva School in St Petersburg (1912–16), Kupreyanov at first looked to Petrov-Vodkin and Ostroumova-Lebedeva as his models. In 1922 he moved to Moscow where, until 1929, he taught at Vkhutemas-Vkhutein and joined OST in 1926. He is one of the most distinguished of Soviet book illustrators, for example, of works by Gor'ky and Nikolay Nekrasov, and has also done many political interpretations such as the woodcut *The Cruiser 'Aurora'* (1923). JEB

KURASHVILI, Boris Pavlovich (b. 1925) Of Georgian nationality, Kurashvili has spent most of his life in Moscow. In the late Brezhnev period he emerged as one of the boldest reformers within the ranks of the Soviet Communist Party and his radicalism – as both a political and economic reformer – became even clearer after Brezhnev's death. In the Gorbachev era he was the first person to succeed in advocating in the pages of a Soviet newspaper the creation of a competitive party system. Although a lawyer by education, his most important academic contributions have been in the realm of political theory and public administration. Having worked at the Institute of State and Law in Moscow since the second half of the 1970s, he became a member of the Centre for Political Science Research when it was founded in that Institute in 1988. His articles – both pre-Gorbachev and in the Gorbachev era – and books have been among the most important and radical contributions to the debates on the nature and future of *perestroika*. AHB

KURCHATOV, Igor' Vasil'evich (1903–1960) The first scientific director of the Soviet nuclear programme, Kurchatov was born into the family of a surveyor and school-teacher in the town of Sim, now in Chelyabinsk *oblast'*. After studying physics at the Tauride University in Simferopol', Kurchatov joined the Physicotechnical Institute in Leningrad in 1925 and remained there until 1942.

Kurchatov helped to set up a strong nuclear group, which made important discoveries in the 1930s. Nuclear research was stopped by the war, but Stalin decided at the end of 1942 to start a small Soviet atomic bomb project. Kurchatov was appointed scientific director, and became a full member of the Academy in 1943. He organised a new laboratory (now the Kurchatov Institute of Atomic Energy) in Moscow. When the nuclear project was expanded in 1945 Kurchatov worked closely with L. P. Beria, who was in overall charge of the project.

Kurchatov had responsibility for all areas of the nuclear programme. He was a superb organizer, able to work with Stalin and Beria, while keeping the respect of the scientists who worked under him. He was in charge of the first atomic bomb test (1949) and the first hydrogen bomb test (1953). In the 1950s he turned his attention to controlled fusion, and tried to arrange collaboration with Western scientists in this area. After Stalin's death he tried to save Soviet biology by warning Khrushchev about Lysenko and protecting geneticists in nuclear institutes. He received many state honours and died in 1960 of a stroke, a result of the extreme tension under which he had worked for many years. D H

KURKOTKIN, Semen Konstantinovich (b. 1917) Chief, Rear Services. Kurkotkin entered the Soviet army in 1937 and gained command of a tank brigade by 1944. He graduated from the Academy of Tank Troops (1951) and the General Staff Academy (1958). He was appointed First Deputy Commander-in-Chief of the Soviet Group of Forces in Germany, the Commander of the Transcaucasus Military District, and then Commander-in-Chief of the forces in Germany. He was named USSR Deputy Minister of Defence, Chief of Rear Services in July 1972, and he retained this post despite the heavy turnover in the Soviet military

command in the early years of Gorbachev's rule. He became a Marshal of the Soviet Union in 1983. R A

KUROEDOV, Vladimir Alekseevich (b. 1906) Chairman of the Council for Religious Affairs attached to the USSR Council of Ministers (1965–1984). Trained as a teacher Kuroedov served in various party posts in Gor'ky *oblast'* before the war, then in the Lithuanian Central Committee (1940–41), in the CPSU Central Committee Agitprop (1946–49), and as a secretary of the Sverdlovsk *obkom* (1949–59). In 1959 he was appointed head of the Council for the Affairs of the Russian Orthodox Church which played a key role in the Khrushchev anti-religious campaign (1959–64). When the Council merged with the Council for the Affairs of Religious Cults in 1965 Kuroedov became chairman of the new body. M R

KUTAKHOV, Pavel Stepanovich (1914–1984) Former Commander-in-Chief of the Air Force. Kutakhov took part in the union of Western Ukraine and Belorussia with the Soviet Union in 1939 and served in the 1939–40 Winter War. During the period 1941 to 1944 he held air force commands on the Leningrad and Karelian fronts, including command of an elite airborne regiment. He graduated from the General Staff Academy in 1957. After a period as First Deputy Commander-in-Chief of the Soviet Air Force (1967–69), in 1969 he was appointed Commander-in-Chief of the Air Force and Deputy Minister of Defence. He became a member of the CPSU Central Committee in 1971 and gained the rank of Chief Marshal of Aviation in 1972. He remained in charge of the Soviet Air Force until his death in December 1984. Kutakhov was responsible not only for the development of new aviation technology and operations but also played a role in the development of Soviet cosmonautics. RA

KUTS, Vladimir Petrovich (1927–1975) Athlete. The most famous Soviet runner of the 1950s, he was the first Soviet male athlete to win an Olympic gold medal. In his relatively short and late-starting career (1953–58), he beat some of the world's best runners, including Zatopek, Pirie, Chattaway and Ibbotson. He first came to world prominence at the age of twenty-seven when he beat the famous Czechoslovak Emil Zatopek at 5000 m in the 1954 European Championships in a new world record. His greatest success came at his one and only Olympics in Melbourne in 1956: he first won the 10,000 m, knocking as much as 31.4 sec off the old Olympic record, then he won the 5000 m. Although he lacked a fast finish, he would exhaust his rivals by his front running, surging ahead and then slowing down. Born in the village of Aleksino in the Suma Region of the Ukraine, he was forced to retire through ill health in 1958 at the age of thirty-one; he died of a heart attack at the early age of forty-eight. JWR

KUUSINEN, Otto Vil'gel'movich (1881–1964) An internationalist old Bolshevik who was a member of Stalin's enlarged Presidium of the Central Committee (1952–53) and also of Khrushchev's Presidium (1957–64), Kuusinen was an adaptable Communist who played a significant part in the revision of Marxist-Leninist doctrine under Khrushchev.

A Finn by nationality, Kuusinen joined the (then Social-Democratic) Party in 1905 and took part in the Russian and Finnish revolutionary movements. He founded and headed the Finnish Communist Party in 1918, attending every Comintern Congress except the second. He emigrated to Moscow in 1930 after the prohibition of the CPF and continued to work as a secretary for the Comintern Executive Committee (IKKI) until 1939. While Chairman of the Presidium of the so-called Karelo-Finnish republic (where he met Yuriy Andropov and helped promote his career), Kuusinen was elected a member of the CPSU Central Committee. When he was appointed to the Presidium in 1957, he was also made a member of the Central Committee Secretariat. He retained both posts until his death. Kuusinen was one of the best-educated Bolsheviks and wrote many works on the Comintern movement and Finnish history. His daughter Kherta was a member of the Politburo of the Finnish Communist Party from 1944 to 1970. MM

KUYBYSHEV, Valeryan Vladimirovich (1888–1935) A prominent economic administrator in the early post-revolutionary period, Kuybyshev was born in Omsk into an officer's family (his brother Nikolay later became a prominent Soviet military commander). Kuybyshev graduated from the Law Faculty of Tomsk University in 1910, already (from the age of sixteen) a member of the Bolshevik party. A political activist before the revolution, he became a political officer attached to various sections of the front during the Civil War and was then appointed to a succession of positions in trade union and economic affairs. In 1921 he became head of the main board of the electrical industry and of the State Commission for the Electrification of Russia (GOELRO). The following year he joined the party

Secretariat and from 1923 was chairman of the Central Control Commission and of Rabkrin (responsible respectively for party discipline and bureaucratic maladministration). In 1926 Kuybyshev succeeded Dzerzhinsky as chairman of the Supreme Council of the National Economy, and in 1929 he joined the Politburo. From 1930 he headed Gosplan and helped to draft the first and second Five-Year Plans. A consistent supporter of Stalin, Kuybyshev's only lapse from orthodoxy appears to have been his support for the Left Communists in 1918. He died of sclerosis of the heart; the city of Samara was given his name later the same year. SLW

KUZ'MIN, Mikhail Alekseevich (1872–1936) Poet, prose writer, dramatist and literary theorist. He was associated firstly with the Symbolist movement and subsequently with the Acmeists, for whom he formulated the concept of 'beautiful clarity'. The homosexual themes of much of his work and his associations with the bohemian cabaret world of St Petersburg attracted scandal and accusations of decadence. His reputation rests particularly on his poetry, which is significantly preoccupied with West European culture, ancient and modern, and with themes of love. Kuz'min is bold in his handling of rhythm and sound within a rigid formal framework. JAEC

KUZ'MIN, Nikolay Vasil'evich (b. 1890) Graphic artist. Born in Serdolbsk. Predominantly an illustrator of editions of the Russian classics (Gogol', Lermontov, Pushkin), Kuz'min has also contributed drawings to many newspapers and journals. Having studied under Ivan Bilibin, Yelizaveta Kruglikova *et al*, he serves as one of the last direct connections with the pre-Revolutionary graphic traditions of the World of Art. JEB

KUZ'MINA, Yelena Aleksandrovna (1909–1979) Film actress. Kuz'mina trained in the FEKS workshop with Kozintsev and Trauberg. Her major film roles were: Louise in Kozintsev and Trauberg's *The New Babylon* (1929), the teacher in their *Alone* (1931), Manka in Barnet's *The Outskirts* (1933), Masha in his *By the Deep Blue Sea* (1936) and Maria/Marta in *Secret Mission* (1950). RT

KUZNETSOV, Nikolay Gerasimovich (1902–1974) Former Commander-in-Chief of the Navy. Kuznetsov entered the Red Navy in 1919, studied in a Naval Officer School after the Civil War, and then graduated from the Naval Academy in 1932. After commanding a cruiser he became Soviet Naval Attaché and Chief Naval Adviser in the Republican Fleet during the Civil War in Spain (1936–37). He directed the reception of Soviet arms transfers into republican ports. This mission was followed by his appointment as First Deputy Commander then Commander of the Pacific Fleet (1937–39). He was People's Commissar of the Navy and Commander-in-Chief of Naval Forces throughout the war (1939–46). Kuznetsov took part in the Yalta and Potsdam conferences in 1945. After the war he was demoted to First Deputy Minister of Navy and Commander-in-Chief of the Navy, and then to Commander of the Pacific Fleet. He was reappointed as Minister of the Navy and Commander-in-Chief of the Naval Forces for the period 1951 to 1953, and then demoted once again to First Deputy Minister of the Navy 1953. Despite these career fluctuations he acquired the rank of Vice-Admiral in 1956. RA

KUZNETSOV, Pavel Varfolomeevich (1878–1968) Painter. Born in Saratov, Kuznetsov was a primary supporter of Moscow Symbolism in the 1900s leading the Blue Rose group and sharing the philosophical ideals of Andrey Bely, Aleksandr Blok and other poets. He received his main art education at the MIPSA, before embarking on his career as a landscapist and still-life painter. He was a member of the Four Arts group in 1924 and that year also visited Paris with his wife, the painter Yelena Bebutova. In the 1930s, accepting the principles of Socialist Realism, he adjusted his lyrical style to the demands of industry and the collective farm. Even so, during the 1930s and 1940s his works were strongly criticized for their alleged formalism. JEB

KUZNETSOV, Vasiliy Vasil′evich (b. 1901) In the course of a remarkably long political career, Kuznetsov was still a candidate member of the Politburo at the age of eighty-five when he was finally retired by Gorbachev at the Twenty-Seventh Party Congress in 1986. Kuznetsov, who was born into a peasant family, joined the Communist Party in 1927. A deputy Soviet foreign minister for many years and from 1977 to 1986 First Deputy Chairman of the Presidium of the Supreme Soviet, he was a member of the Central Committee from 1952 to 1956 and also a member of Stalin's enlarged Presidium of the Central Committee (1952–53). At the time of his elevation to First Deputy Chairmanship of the Supreme Soviet, Kuznetsov was promoted to candidate membership of the Politburo in October 1977 when he was already seventy-six and he remained a nonvoting Politburo member for a further nine years. AHB

KVIRING, Emmanuil Ionovich (1888–1937) An old Bolshevik, leading economic organizer and publicist in the 1920s and 1930s, Kviring was born in a village near Samara, the son of a German colonist who was employed as a rural scribe. A revolutionary from 1905, he worked in a chemist's shop. Kviring joined the Bolsheviks in 1912 and became secretary to the Bolshevik group in the Duma in 1913. During the war he worked in factories in exile. He then held various local posts as a party and economic official mainly in the Ukraine (1917–26). He became the first deputy chairman of VSNKh in 1926, and deputy chairman, then first deputy chairman of Gosplan (1926–31). He was appointed Director of the Economic Institute of the Communist Academy, and held several senior posts in transport, trade, light industry, agriculture, and planning in the 1930s. He was a member of the party Central Committee (1923–34). He was arrested in 1937. RWD

KVITSINSKY, Yuliy Aleksandrovich (b. 1936) A prominent Soviet diplomat who has led important arms control negotiations and since 1986 has been Soviet Ambassador to the Federal Republic of Germany, Kvitsinsky was born in Rzhev in the Kalinin region. He graduated from MGIMO in 1959, joined the Communist Party in 1962 and took a candidate of sciences degree (in law) in 1968. Within the diplomatic service, which he joined in 1959, his specialities have been German affairs and arms control. Among his major appointments before his present ambassadorship were the post of Minister-Counsellor at the Soviet Union's Bonn embassy (1978–81) and Ambassador-at-Large of the

Ministry of Foreign Affairs (1981–86), during which time he led the Soviet delegation taking part in nuclear and space weapons talks in Geneva (1985–86). A candidate member of the party Central Committee from 1986 to 1989, he was promoted to full membership in 1989 but not re-elected at the Twenty-Eighth Party Congress in 1990. AHB

L

LABAS, Aleksandr Arkad'evich (1901–1983) Painter. Born in Smolensk, Labas received his main art education at the Stroganov Institute and then Svomas in Moscow (1912–19). Influenced by Shterenberg, he joined OST in 1925 and became one of its most active members, using an expressionistic style to render aerial views and sensations such as *Airship and a Kindergarten* (1930). JEB

LADOVSKY, Nikolay Aleksandrovich (1881–1941) Architect. Enrolling at the MIPSA in 1914, Ladovsky experienced many aesthetic influences, including those of Romanticism and Futurism. In 1919 he was a member of Zhivskul'ptarkh (a group that believed in the synthesis of painting, sculpture and architecture) and joined the Institute of Artistic Sciences the following year. Ladovsky is remembered for his contribution to the Rationalist school of architecture, a theory and practice that he evolved in the 1920s while teaching at Vkhutemas in Moscow. Close to Dokuchaev and Vladimir Krinsky, he was also a co-founder of ASNOVA in 1923 and of ARU (Architects-Urbanists) in 1928 when he became especially interested in the concept of the Garden City. JEB

LAGUTIN, Boris Nikolaevich (b. 1938) Boxer. He boxed at light middleweight at three Olympic Games, becoming bronze medallist in 1960, and champion in 1964 and 1968. He was also twice European and six times national champion between 1959 and 1968. Born in Moscow, he was unusual for a boxer in that he gained both a coaching diploma and a degree in biology from Moscow State University. Upon retirement, he wrote several research papers, coached and became Chairman of the USSR Boxing Federation. JWR

LAKSHIN, Vladimir Yakovlevich (b. 1933) Literary critic, who during his spell as an editor of *Novyy mir* (1962–70), staunchly supported Tvardovsky's policy of publishing works critical of the current situation and revelatory of the Stalinist past. An heir to the tradition of Belinsky and Dobrolyubov, he believed that the writer has a civic duty to expose social evil from an independent position of moral humanism, and in this conviction he consistently defended, among others, Solzhenitsyn. After a long period of obscurity and occasional publication, he became an editor of *Znamya* in 1986. GAH

LAKTIONOV, Aleksandr Ivanovich (1910–1972) Painter. Born in Rostov-on-Don, Laktionov became a prominent Socialist Realist painter and pedagogue thanks to his study at the Academy of Arts under I. Brodsky (1932–38). Possessing technical virtuosity, he produced a number of 'Photo-Realist' paintings in the 1940s, the most famous of which is *Letter from the Front* (1947). JEB

LANCERAY (Lansere), Yevgeniy Yevgen'evich (1878–1946) Graphic artist and painter. Born in Pavlovsk into an artistic family (his uncle was Alexandre Benois), Lanceray studied in St Petersburg and Paris in the 1890s before becoming a member of the World of Art group. In this way, he served as a direct bridge between the graphic traditions of the *fin de siècle* and the new artistic demands of the Soviet state. He illustrated a number of Soviet editions, including Tolstoy, and was a successful teacher at the Tbilisi Academy of Arts (1922–32). JEB

LANDSBERGIS, Vitautas Vitautovich (Landsbergis, Vytautas) (b. 1932) Born in Kaunas into a family of intellectuals and Lithuanian patriots, Landsbergis studied at the Vilnius Conservatorium and became Professor of Musicology there. He was a founder member of the Sajudis national movement in 1988, and elected to the Soviet Congress of People's Deputies in 1989. Elected President of the Supreme Soviet of the Lithuanian Republic in March 1990, he led the Republic in the period after its declaration of independence from the Soviet Union. JHM

LAPIN, Sergey Georgievich (1912–1988) A state official. Active for most of his life in diplomacy and communications, Sergey Lapin studied in Leningrad and at the Higher Party School in Moscow in 1942. A member of the boards of various Leningrad newspapers in the 1930s, he worked for the USSR Television and Radio Committee (1944–53), as chairman (1970–85), and also directed the TASS news agency from 1967 to 1970. Lapin's other career was a diplomatic one: he worked in the USSR Ministry of Foreign Affairs, serving as Ambassador to Austria (1956–60) and as Ambassador to China (1965–67). He was a full member of the CPSU Central Committee from 1966 to 1986. SLW

LAPTEV, Ivan Dmitrievich (b. 1934) Born near Omsk, Laptev worked as a journalist and in the Central Committee apparatus, before becoming Deputy Chief Editor of *Pravda* from 1978 to 1984. From 1984 he was Chief Editor of *Izvestiya* and succeeded E. M. Primakov as Chairman of the Soviet of the Union in April 1990. JHM

LAPTEV, Vladimir Viktorovich (b. 1924) Pre-eminent Soviet theorist of economic law and intellectual father of at least two draft USSR economic codes, Laptev has published more than 300 monographs and articles, including an English translation of *Khozyaistvennoe pravo* (*Economic Law*). His ideas have played a major part in shaping the 1987 USSR Law on the State Enterprise. He was elected an Academician in 1987. WEB

LARIN, Yuriy (Lur'e, Mikhail Aleksandrovich or Zal'manovich) (1882–1932) Born into a middle-class family in Simferopol', Larin joined the RSDLP in 1900, supporting the Mensheviks. He was exiled for revolutionary activities and, in 1917 as a Left Internationalist, he joined the Bolsheviks. He was a founding member of VSNKh at the end of 1917, and he initiated the nationalization decree of July 1918. A man of out-spoken views, he was an economist and enthusiast for planning, and one of the strongest critics of the capitalist tendencies of NEP. His writings on German war-time planning influenced Lenin during the period of War Communism, and his writings on the dangers of private capital in the mid-1920s influenced Stalin. His daughter married Bukharin. RWD

LATSIS, Otto Rudol'fovich (b. 1934) Economist and journalist. A member of the Communist Party since 1959, he has belonged to its reform wing and has become particularly prominent in the era of *perestroika*. Born in Moscow, Latsis graduated from the Faculty of Journalism of Moscow University in 1956; in 1980 he became a doctor of economic sciences. Between 1956 and 1971 he worked on Soviet newspapers – starting on the provincial *Sovetskiy Sakhalin* and moving on to *Ekonomicheskaya gazeta* and *Izvestiya*. In 1971 he joined the staff of the journal, *Problems of Peace and Socialism*, in Prague and in 1975 entered academic life at the Institute of Economics of the World Socialist System in Moscow. In 1986 he moved from that institute to the editorial staff of the theoretical journal of the Communist Party, *Kommunist*, and in 1987 became its first deputy editor. The author of numerous articles and books, Latsis has adopted a firmly anti-Stalinist approach to Soviet history and has been a vigorous advocate of reform of the Soviet economy. He was elected to the Central Committee of the party at the Twenty-eighth Congress in July 1990. AHB

LATYNINA, Larisa Semenovna (b. 1934) Gymnast. She was arguably the most outstanding woman gymnast in history, winning a total of eighteen Olympic medals: nine gold, five silver and four bronze – a record for men and women. She set a further record in winning one event – the free exercises – three times at the Olympics (1956–64). Altogether she was eight times world champion, seven times European and twelve times Soviet champion. Born Larisa Dirya in the Crimean city of Kherson, she initially took up ballet, but switched to gymnastics at the age of thirteen. Upon retirement, in 1966, she was made Senior Coach to the USSR women's gymnastics team and was an international judge for several years. JWR

LAURISTIN, Mar'yu Iokhannes-ovna (Lauristin, Marju) (b. 1942) Daughter of the first communist Prime Minister of Estonia (who was killed in 1941), she became a sociologist and head of the Department of Journalism of Tartu University. Until 1990 a CPSU member, she was also a dissident and played a leading role in the organization during 1988 of the Popular Front of Estonia, becoming in October a member of its governing council. In 1989 she was elected to the Congress of People's Deputies and to the USSR Supreme Soviet, and in 1990 Deputy Speaker of the Estonian Supreme Soviet. A rare example of a woman in Soviet political leadership. JHM

LAVOCHKIN, Semen Alekseevich (1900–1960) One of the most original of Soviet aircraft designers, Semen Lavochkin was not very successful in getting his designs accepted for serial production. He was born at Smolensk and in 1927 graduated from the Moscow Higher Technical School. After a period of work with A. N. Tupolev and other designers, he headed his own bureau from 1939, designing the LaGG-3, La-5 and La-7 fighters, which saw service during the war. In the post-war years Lavochkin was one of the pioneers of jet aviation, producing a series of original designs. He was made a Hero of Socialist Labour (1943, 1956), was elected a corresponding member of the Academy of Sciences in 1958, and received four Stalin Prizes, Lavochkin joined the party in 1953. JMC

LAVRENT'EV, Mikhail Alekseevich (1900–1980) Mathematician and administrator. A 1922 graduate of Moscow University, where he studied with N. N. Luzin, Lavrent'ev worked in applied mathematics and especially in mechanics, aerodynamics, and hydrodynamics, teaching at Moscow University (from 1927) and the Moscow Chemicotechnical Institute (from 1929) while based at the Steklov Mathematics Institute (1935–60). In 1939 he was elected to the Ukrainian Academy of Sciences and became director of its Institute of Mathematics and a professor at Kiev University (1939–41, 1945–48). While involved in war-time research, and later as vice-president of the Ukrainian Academy of Sciences (1945–48), he became acquainted with Nikita Khrushchev. Elected a full member of the USSR Academy of Sciences in 1946, he returned to Moscow in 1949 and became involved in computer work. He joined the party in 1952 and soon became a close scientific adviser to Khrushchev. This contact allowed him to gain unprecedented support for his brain-child, the creation of the science city at Novosibirsk. As its organizer, he served as vice-president of the USSR Academy of Sciences, the president of its Siberian division, and director of the science city's Institute

of Hydrodynamics (1958–76), as well as a deputy of the Supreme Soviet (1958–79) and a candidate member of the Central Committee of the party (1961–79). MBA

LAVROVSKY, Leonid Mikhaylovich (real name: Ivanov) (1905–1967) Leading dancer, choreographer, and ballet teacher. Lavrovsky studied with Vladimir Ponomarev and graduated from the Leningrad Ballet School in 1922. He joined the Kirov troupe upon graduation and danced with the company for the next thirteen years, performing in a broad range of classical and modern ballets. These included leading parts in *Swan Lake, Raymonda, Egyptian Nights, The Red Poppy, The Age of Gold,* and *The Flames of Paris.* He was associated with the experimental Young Ballet (*Molodoy balet*), founded in 1921 by George Balanchine.

While still a dancer Lavrovsky turned to choreography, receiving great acclaim for his innovative choreography to Schumann's *Etudes Symphoniques* (1930), performed at a Leningrad Ballet School graduation. His first full-length ballet, *Fadette* (1934), to music by Delibes, revealed Lavrovsky's interest in stage production and his use of classical dance as a means of characterization. These qualities were reflected in much of his later choreography as well, and formed the basis for his artistic principles concerning dramatic ballet. His next major works were *Katerina* (1935), a ballet about the serf theatre that had a ballet within the ballet and incorporated Russian folk dance, and *The Prisoner of the Caucasus* (1938), his highly successful staging of Pushkin's narrative poem.

In 1935 Lavrovsky left the stage to become artistic director of the Malyy

Opera Theatre (1935–38), artistic director of the Kirov ballet (1938–42), artistic director of the Armenian ballet (1942–43), and chief choreographer of the Bol'shoy Ballet (1944–56, 1960–64). From 1958 to 1962 he was also artistic director of the Moscow Ice Ballet.

Lavrovsky's most important ballet was his landmark production of *Romeo and Juliet* (1940), a choreographic drama that used Prokof'ev's score and starred Galina Ulanova. This was the first stage adaptation of Prokof'ev in the Soviet Union and one of the earliest adaptations of Shakespeare to ballet. His other major works include: a revival of *Giselle* (1944), considered the definitive version; a revival of *Raymonda* (1945), Prokof'ev's *The Tale of the Stone Flower* (1954); a new version of *Paganini* (1960), a one-act ballet using Rakhmaninov's score and an original scenario; and his very dramatic *Night City* (1961), using Bartók's *The Miraculous Mandarin*.

Lavrovsky collaborated on a film version of *Romeo and Juliet* (1955) and staged a number of ballets abroad. He taught at the Moscow State Theatre Institute and in 1964 was appointed director of the Bol'shoy Ballet School. scs

LAZAREV, Petr Petrovich (1878–1942) Biophysicist, geophysicist. After graduating from Moscow University in 1901, Lazarev worked in its physical laboratory, directed by P. N. Lebedev, and became well known for elaborating the ionic theory of the excitation of nerves, muscles, and sensory receptors, which led to his election as a full member of the Petersburg Academy of Sciences in 1917. He also became interested in geophysical magnetic anomalies during and after the First World War, hoping to use them to locate mineral deposits, but he is remembered principally as the founder of Russian biophysics. Stimulated by the new developments in physics and the rapidly developing experimentalist trends in biology, he obtained philanthropic funds in 1915 through the Moscow Scientific Institute Society to create a Physical Institute, which in 1919 became the Biophysics Institute of the Commissariat of Public Health (renamed the Institute of Physics and Biophysics in 1929). By creating and directing one of the world's first biophysics institutes and teaching biophysics at Moscow University (from 1922), he pioneered the creation of this discipline and trained the first large school of Russian investigators in the field. In 1931 Lazarev was arrested and the following year his innovative institute was liquidated. Released in 1933, he began working in the All-Union Institute of Experimental Medicine, and in 1938 the USSR Academy of Sciences opened a laboratory of biophysics under Lazarev's direction. During the war, the laboratory was evacuated to Alma-Ata, where Lazarev died on 23 April 1942. MBA

LEBEDEV, Vladimir Vasil'evich (1891–1967) Graphic artist. Born in St Petersburg, of the same generation as Bruni, Miturich and Tyrsa, Lebedev belonged to the second wave of the Russian avant-garde. Although he trained at the Academy of Arts and in the private studios of academic artists (1909–16), he was also drawn to the ideas of Malevich and Tatlin. He achieved his reputation as a caricaturist and poster artist, contributing many pieces to the Petrograd Okna ROSTA (Windows of the Russian Telegraph Agency) (1920–21) and to the Okna TASS (Tass Windows) during the Second World War. During the 1920s and 1930s he illustrated many children's books, often by Marshak. JEB

LEBEDEVA, Sarra Dmitrievna (1892–1967) Sculptor. Born in St Petersburg, Lebedeva trained at private studios there (1910–14) and then taught at Svomas, Petrograd (1919–20). Supportive of the classical tradition in sculpture, she adjusted to the demands of Socialist Realism, producing a number of bronze and stone works that became very popular such as *Girl with a Butterfly* (1936) and the portrait of Valeriy Chkalov (1936). JEB

LEGOSHIN, Vladimir Grigor'evich (1904–1954) Film director. Legoshin trained with Kuleshov and Yutkevich and worked with the Blue Blouse theatre group. His major films were: *A Song of Happiness* (1934) and *The Lone White Sail* (1937), generally regarded as one of the best Soviet children's films. RT

LEMESHEV, Sergey Yakovlevich (1902–1977) Tenor. Sergey Lemeshev was born in the village of Staroe Knyazevo and died in Moscow. Of humble origin, he studied at the Moscow Conservatory as a pupil of Nazary Raysky, graduating in 1925. After making his début at the Sverdlovsk Opera and Ballet Theatre in 1926, the years 1927 to 1929 were spent with the Kharbin Opera Company, followed by a further two-year period with the Tbilisi Opera and Ballet. From 1931 to 1965 he was a soloist at the Moscow Bol'shoy, at the same time serving as artistic director of the Moscow Conservatory Opera Studio (1959–61). A member of the party from 1948, he was made a People's Artist of the USSR in 1950. Lemeshev was highly regarded as an opera and chamber singer and is remembered particularly for his performance in 1939 of the complete songs of Tchaikovsky, which were given in five concerts. GS

LENIN, Vladimir Il'ich (1870–1924) Lenin, whose real surname was Ul'yanov, was born in Simbirsk. His family held gentry rank. His father Il'ya was a province-level schools' inspector, having risen from humble social origins. On his father's side, Lenin had a Russian grandfather and a Kalmyk grandmother. Lenin's mother Mariya was born into a middle-class family, which derived partly from German immigrant stock (and which quite possibly included a Jewish ingredient). Il'ya and Mariya had six children, all of whom were academically impressive. The family's material circumstances were comfortable without being luxurious.

Lenin's father died in 1886. The oldest of Lenin's siblings, Aleksandr, was then studying at St Petersburg University and had become involved in a populist terrorist organization. Aleksandr was arrested and hanged in 1887 for his involvement in a plot to kill the emperor Aleksandr III. Lenin, however, passed his final school exams brilliantly and entered Kazan' University as a law student in the same autumn. He, too, joined an underground populist circle and was rusticated for participation in a student demonstration in December 1887. Compelled by the authorities to live in the Kazan' countryside, he studied his executed brother's political books. In 1888 he was permitted to return to Kazan' itself, but not to the university; and again he attended an illegal populist circle. His mother bought an estate in Samara province, and he moved with her. There, too, he joined a revolutionary organization.

Lenin

Lenin and his fellow members started with the agrarian-socialist beliefs of Russian populism, but they inclined increasingly towards Marxism. They studied *Capital* as well as works by the founder of Russian Marxism, G. V. Plekhanov. Lenin also resumed his undergraduate course as an external student at St Petersburg University. In 1891 he was awarded the equivalent of a first-class degree, and in 1892 he was employed as an assistant barrister in Samara.

In 1893 he moved to St Petersburg, ostensibly to pursue his lawyer's career but mainly to join the Marxists in the capital. He was a redoubtable polemicist on economic questions, and was writing prolifically. He not only worked with the Marxist underground but also forged links with so-called 'legal Marxists' such as P. B. Struve. In April 1895 he was sent to Switzerland to make contact with Plekhanov and the Emancipation of Labour Group in Geneva. Returning to St Petersburg, he helped to unify the various illegal groups of Marxists. But in December 1895 he was arrested. He remained in prison until 1897, when he was sentenced to Siberian exile. His political and economic investigations did not cease; and his three years in Yeniseisk province allowed him to complete *The Development of Capitalism in Russia* (1899), which was notable for its attacks on populist thinking and its optimism about Russia's existing level of industrial and agricultural achievement. In Siberia he married N. K. Krupskaya.

After his release in 1900, he tried to operate as an underground organizer but he was a marked man: he therefore opted to emigrate. In Switzerland he contacted Plekhanov. They shared many fundamental conceptions and a deep intolerance of anything they regarded as deviating from Marxist orthodoxy. It was their intention, too, to grasp the leadership of the nascent Russian Social Democratic Labour Party. The chief instrument of their campaign was their newspaper, *Iskra* ('The Spark'), which commenced publication in December 1900.

Plekhanov and Lenin kept the overthrow of the Russian absolute monarchy by the working class at the forefront of the party's objectives; and they referred to their own critics as the 'Economists'. Lenin published his vision of the kind of party needed in contemporary Russia in *What Is To Be Done?* (1902). It caused controversy because of its ultra-centralist and hyper-disciplinary themes. An even greater cause of dispute was the proposed party programme of Lenin and Plekhanov, which enraged many social-democrats who discerned in it an excess of authoritarianism. Plekhanov and Lenin controlled the arrangements for the Second Party Congress in 1903. The supporters of *Iskra* won every major debate. Yet Lenin's plans for a strictly centralized party worried even close comrades like Yu. O. Martov. The *Iskra* team fell into dispute. Martov won the battle over the party rules; but, because of a walk-out by several delegates, Lenin achieved victory in the elections to the central party apparatus.

Factional conflict continued. Plekhanov became disenchanted with Lenin and sided with Martov. Lenin, pleased to have won the Party Congress elections, called his group the *bol'sheviki* (which is the Russian word for 'majoritarians'). Martov's group became known as the *mensheviki* – or 'minoritarians'. The strife between then was intense, especially in emigration. In Russia there was reluctance to take the foreign-based Marxists too seriously.

In 1905 a revolutionary crisis gripped Russia. Lenin urged his party to be less exclusive and less introverted than it had been; his organizational practices were shown to be flexible. And in *Two Tactics of Social-Democracy in the Democratic Revolution* (1905) he argued that the middle class would do a deal with the monarchy; and that, if a 'bourgeois revolution' was ever to be consolidated, it would have to be led by the workers themselves. Lenin demanded a 'provisional revolutionary dictatorship' of socialists. In November 1905 he returned to Russia. Despite being the leading Bolshevik, he could not impose all his opinions with success. In general he judged his comrades to be impetuous in the preparations for insurrection. By the end of the year, moreover, the monarchical repression was intensifying. Lenin's effort to get Bolsheviks to take advantage of the government's offer to hold elections for a state assembly (or *Duma*) was initially ineffective; and he moved towards a conditional rapprochement with the Mensheviks.

These tensions persisted into 1907, when Lenin and other prominent revolutionaries had to emigrate once more. Bolsheviks who disliked the use of the State Duma were headed by A. A. Bogdanov. Lenin in 1909 published a crude attack on Bogdanov's philosophical views in *Materialism and Empiriocriticism*. Bogdanov was expelled from the Bolshevik Centre.

The appearance of being unchallenged among Bolsheviks was illusory. Many of the faction's émigrés were happy to see the back of Bogdanov while yet being appalled by Lenin's resumed endeavour to split the Russian Social-Democratic Labour Party as a whole. The abhorrence of a party-wide split was still fiercer in Russia. Practical organizers in the provincial underground recognized Lenin's intellectual skills and contributions yet despised his schismatic behaviour. A Central Committee plenum in January 1910 drove this message home. Yet he persisted with his chosen policies. And, in fact, dissatisfaction with the Mensheviks intensified among all Bolsheviks in 1911, not least because they failed to pursue aggressively anti-establishment policies in the labour movement. In January 1912 Lenin and his associates called an essentially factional meeting in Prague. A 'Central Committee' was elected which purported to act in the name of the party as a whole.

In 1912 Lenin and G. E. Zinov'ev moved to Galicia, on the Romanov imperial border, in order to direct Bolshevik activity in Russia. But they lacked real power for such direction. Relations between the Galicia-based Central Committee and the legal Bolshevik newspapers (such as *Pravda*) and the illegal Bolshevik committees in Russia continued to be tense and irregular. Lenin also had trouble with other socialist parties in the Socialist International on account of his overt divisiveness. In 1914 he was embarrassed by the exposure of his colleague R. V. Malinovsky as a long-standing police spy.

Russian industrial strikes and demonstrations were interrupted in the same summer by the outbreak of the Great War. Lenin was arrested by Austrian police as an alleged Russian spy. But he quickly secured his passage to Switzerland. There he reformulated many basic ideas. Disgusted by the failure of most German social-democrats to oppose Wilhelm II's war effort, he wrote *The Collapse of the Second International* (1915); and he attributed the outbreak and continuation of the war to the economic rivalries of the Great Powers in his *Imperialism* (which was published only in 1917). He called for a more dynamic and less contemplative Marxism in his private *Notebooks on Philosophy*. By January 1917, under the influence of the Dutch socialist Anton Pannekoek and the Russian Bolshevik N. I. Bukharin, he had concluded that a successful socialist revolution would require the smashing of the old bourgeois state. He attended far-left European socialist conferences at Zimmerwald in 1915 and Kienthal in 1916 in order to attain these ends. His influence upon the European extreme left was growing; but his contacts with his own country's Bolsheviks were very frail.

Like everyone else, Lenin was surprised by the February Revolution's occurrence in Petrograd – as St Petersburg was called from 1914. Nikolay II abdicated and a liberal-led Provisional Government took over. Although its ministers promulgated basic civic freedoms, they refused to pull Russia out of the war, to transfer land to the peasants or to sympathize with workers' grievances against industrialists.

From Switzerland, Lenin organized his return to Russia in a train which took him across Germany with Berlin's official sanction. In Petrograd he expounded his *April Theses*, demanding a transfer of power to socialists as the sole means of avoiding national catastrophe. He envisaged the soviets as the instrument of the new class authority to be established. At their April Conference, the rest of the Bol-

sheviks adopted this strategy. For several months the Mensheviks and the Socialist Revolutionaries controlled the soviets. But recurrent political crises, which pushed these more moderate socialists into accepting ministerial posts in successive government coalitions, dogged the Provisional Government. In addition, the economic and social dislocations of wartime were aggravated. Lenin's alleged role in the holding of an armed anti-government demonstration in July 1917 induced the government to order his arrest. He spent months in hiding in Finland, where he completed his theoretical rationale for the dictatorship of the proletariat, *The State and Revolution*. But on 10 October he returned incognito to a Bolshevik Central Committee meeting and convinced a majority that, with Bolshevik gains in the soviets in Russia and with the apparently improving prospects of international socialist revolution, power should be seized in Petrograd.

The Provisional Government was overthrown on 25–26 October 1917 (or 7–8 November, according to the Gregorian calendar). A Council of People's Commissars was set up after the Second Congress of Soviets. Lenin was the new premier. Decrees on peace, land and other vital matters were issued. 'Soviet power' spread swiftly to the other cities of central, northern and south-eastern Russia. Lenin wrote *Proletarian Revolution and the Renegade Karl Kautsky* (1918) to justify the dictatorship he was establishing.

Domestic discontent increased. Lenin created a new political police, the *Cheka*, and dispersed the Constituent Assembly (which had been elected on the basis of universal suffrage) by force. The international socialist revolution did not take place, and only with the utmost difficulty did Lenin convince the Bolshevik Central Committee of the need to sign a separate peace at Brest-Litovsk with Germany and Austria-Hungary. Vast territories and economic resources were thereby abandoned. The British and French sent forces to intervene in Russian politics. Civil war broke out. White armies under Kolchak, Denikin and Yudenich stormed toward Moscow and Petrograd. Lenin was the main Soviet leader who stayed in the capital for the duration of the fighting whilst his colleagues such as Trotsky, Zinov'ev and Stalin travelled around the country organizing the Red Army and the political and economic arrangements in the rear. Lenin was the linchpin of a system of command which became highly authoritarian and hierarchical. By the end of 1919 the Civil War was mostly won, and the foreign interventionist forces also were withdrawing.

By then much had changed in Russia. Industry and agriculture were in a ruinous condition. Vast numbers of workers and peasants resented Bolshevik authority. The party itself, which had encouraged debate in 1917, had become a tightly-disciplined organization with adjuncts of the Central Committee (especially the Politburo) settling most aspects of grand policy. But social discontent was taking a dangerously political form. The war between Soviet Russia and Poland as well as the peasant revolts and industrial strikes in 1920 threatened an end to the Bolshevik monopoly of state power.

A retreat in economic and social policy was required, as Lenin and the Politburo recognized in February 1921. The Tenth Party Congress in March ratified changes which included the replacement of foodstuffs requisitioning by a graduated tax-in-kind fixed at a lower amount of grain. Lenin's New Economic Policy (NEP) was a retreat accompanied by an intensification of political control. Competing socialist parties and even factions inside the Bolshevik party were banned. But Lenin's chance to preside over this programme was limited by his health. Already weakened by an assassination attempt in August 1918, he was succumbing to the cerebral arteriosclerosis that had killed his father. He had a stroke in 1921 and was poorly for most of 1922. He did not live long enough to say definitively whether he regarded the NEP, with its concessions to private enterprise, as a positive strategy for the long-term attainment of socialism. Moreover, struggles had begun for the succession to him.

Lenin had a low opinion of the potential successors, as he specified in notes that became known as his 'testament'. But in 1922 and 1923 he was particularly annoyed with Stalin who had behaved brusquely in his dealings with the Georgian Communist Party and had amassed great personal power in the central party apparatus in Moscow.

But Lenin's illness worsened. For most of 1923 he was scarcely able to speak or move, and he died at the age of fifty-three on 21 January 1924. His funeral was an occasion of grief for many sections of the population which had little sympathy for Bolshevism. Lenin had been an outstanding Marxist theorist of his generation. He was also influenced by the pre-Marxist Russian revolutionary thinkers; but he remained disinclined to acknowledge his full debt to them. His interests ranged through economics (where his accomplishments were at their peak), political theory and philosophy (where he was a keen but over-confident amateur). He was also a journalist and editor of great competence. He was an imposing party boss and, to the astonishment of most observers, a businesslike statesman. He was cantankerous, but approachable; he had no 'side'. Yet his lack of vanity did not save him from immodesty. He continually implied that, unless he was in charge, the task of making revolution would remain unsatisfactorily discharged.

After his death his writings were canonized as Marxism-Leninism; he would have discouraged this development since he never claimed more for himself than to be applying the ideas of Marx and Engels to the conditions of the early twentieth century. In many respects his regime differed from that of the Romanov monarchy; in others, it was remarkably similar. The same is true of the differences and similarities between the Soviet political system under Lenin and Stalin respectively. The fact that so many arguments about continuity and rupture in the modern Russian past revolve around the historical personality of Lenin is an indication of the man's enormous impact. RS

LENTULOV, Aristarkh Vasil'evich (1882–1943) Painter. After studying in Penza, Kiev, St Petersburg and Paris (1898–1911), Lentulov emerged as a strong supporter of Cézannism and Cubism in the early 1910s, contributing to the Jack of Diamonds exhibitions. Deeply interested in Russian church architecture, icons and folk art, Lentulov gained a reputation for his landscapes in the 1920s

and 1930s such as *Sunset on the Volga* (1928). JEB

LEONIDOV, Ivan Il'ich (1902–1959) Architect. Born in Babino, Leonidov studied under A. Vesnin at Vkhutemas-Vkhutein (1921–27), rapidly emerging as a strong supporter of Constructivism. A member of OSA and co-editor of *SA (Sovremenna arkhitektura)*, he projected a number of distinctive, sometimes visionary buildings in the late 1920s and 1930s, including a planetarium and a Lenin institute. JEB

LEONIDOV (né Vol'fenzon), Leonid Mironovich (1873–1943) Stage actor and director. Leonidov was hailed by Stanislavsky as a great tragic actor. His roles at the Moscow Art Theatre included: Pugachev in Trenev's *The Pugachev Rebellion* (1925), *Othello* (1930), Borodin in Afinogenov's *Fear* (1931) and the title role in Gor'ky's *Yegor Bulychov and the Others* (1934). RT

LEONOV, Pavel Artemovich (b. 1918) Born to a peasant family in the Tula region, Pavel Leonov graduated from the Bauman Technical College in Moscow in 1942, later working in industry. He joined the CPSU in 1944, becoming a local party secretary in the immediate post-war period. He was made first secretary of the Sakhalin regional party committee in 1960 and first secretary of the Kalinin regional party organization from 1978 to 1985. He was elected a full Central Committee member in 1971, 1976 and 1981. SLW

LEPESHINSKAYA (née Potapova), Ol'ga Borisovna (1871–1963) Cytologist, histologist, revolutionary. The wife of revolutionary P. N. Lepeshinsky and a party member since 1898, Lepeshinskaya was active in the Bolshevik take-over in Moscow. In the 1930s she worked in the Institute of Experimental Medicine and advanced the controversial view that both embryonic and specialized cells could spontaneously form from non-cellular organic material, defending her position on the basis of both Marxist philosophical reasoning and purported laboratory evidence. This view was dismissed by most Soviet biologists as contrary to the doctrine of Virchow, well established since the mid-nineteenth century, that all cells are the offspring of other cells. Following official party and government endorsement of Lysenko in 1948, however, her work was incorporated into his 'Michurinist biology', her position was officially endorsed in 1950, and she was elected a full member of the USSR Academy of Medical Sciences. In the mid-1950s, during de-Stalinization, her views lost all support, even among Lysenkoists, and were quietly abandoned. MBA

LESECHKO, Mikhail Avksent'evich (1909–1984) An aviation engineer from Zaporozh'e in the Ukraine who moved into cybernetics at the end of the 1940s. In 1956 and 1957 he was USSR Minister of Instrument-Making and Automotion Equipment, from 1958 First Deputy Chairman of Gosplan, and from 1962 until his retirement in 1980, Deputy Chairman of the USSR Council of Ministers. The latter post was combined until 1977 with that of permanent representative of the USSR to Comecon. JHM

LEVIT, Solomon Grigor'evich (1894–1938) A founder of medical genetics. A Baltic Jew, physician, and Communist Party member from 1920, Levit was active in Marxist circles and became an administrator of the Communist Academy (1926–30). He converted from Lamarckism to genetics in 1928 and, together with A. S. Serebrovsky, formed the Office of Human Heredity and Constitution within the Biomedical Institute of the Commissariat of Public Health. After studying with H. J. Muller in Texas in 1931, he returned as director of the Biomedical Institute and transformed it into the Maksim Gor'ky Institute of Medical Genetics, where he organized an ambitious research and clinical programme, including pioneering studies of twins. This was the world's first institute of medical genetics, and its four volumes of research (1929–36) are classics in the field. He was arrested in January 1938 and was probably shot in May. MBA

LEVITIN, Anatoliy Emmanuilovich (pen-name – A. Krasnov) (b. 1915) Orthodox Christian writer and human rights activist. Imprisoned under Stalin (1949–56), Levitin at first wrote for the *Journal of the Moscow Patriarchate* (1956–58), then wrote commentaries on Church-State themes and church history for *samizdat* circulation from a Christian socialist position. As a result, he lost his job as a schoolteacher. In 1969 he was a founder-member of the Action Group to Defend Civil Rights. For this he was again imprisoned (1971–73), and in 1974 he emigrated to Switzerland. PBR

LEVITSKY, Aleksandr Andreevich (1885–1965) Regarded as the 'father' of Russian film cameramen, Levitsky was involved in cinema from 1910 and taught at the State Film School from 1924. His principal films were: Meyerkhold's *The Picture of Dorian Grey* (1915), Kuleshov's *The Extraordinary Adventures of Mr West in the Land of the Bolsheviks* (1924) and *The Death Ray* (1925). RT

LEVITSKY (Lewitsky), Grigoriy Andreevich (1878–1942) Botanist, cytologist, cytogeneticist. The son of a priest and a student of S. G. Navashin at the University of St Vladimir in Kiev, where he graduated in 1902, Levitsky was one of the world's leading plant cytogeneticists and gave the cytological terms 'karyotype' and 'idiogram' their modern meanings. Prior to 1925 he worked in Kiev as director of a research institute of the Sugar Trust, where he trained a number of students, notably Theodosius Dobzhansky, and wrote one of the first textbooks of cytogenetics, *The Material Basis of Heredity* (1924). He directed the Laboratory of Cytology at N. I. Vavilov's All-Union Institute of Plant Breeding in Leningrad (1925–40). In 1932 he became corresponding member of the USSR Academy of Sciences and a professor in the department of plant genetics at Leningrad University. From 1935 he came into conflict with the followers of T. D. Lysenko. He was arrested in early 1941 and died in prison. MBA

LIBEDINSKY, Yuriy Nikolaevich (1898–1959) Born in Odessa, Libedinsky is best known for his fiction of the twenties and his role as an activist in the proletarian literary groups October and RAPP (of which he was the chief theoretician). Libedinsky joined the party in 1920. His first novella, *The Week* (1922), a classic of socialist realism, tells of provincial Communist organizers during the Civil War who perish in a counter-revolutionary uprising. His novel *The Birth of a Hero* (1930), in which Libedinsky attempted to illustrate RAPP's 'living man' concept by presenting a realistic portrait of the hero, was widely attacked for its failure to depict the larger-than-life hero. KC

LIBERMAN, Yevsey Grigorievich (1897–1983) Economist. His 1962 article in *Pravda* presaged the economic reform of 1965, but proved irrelevant to the more fundamental changes of *perestroika*. Born in Khar'kov, he graduated from that city's Institute of Engineering Economics in 1933 and spent all his career there. When he wrote the article that made him world-famous (to the point of appearance on the cover of *Time* magazine as the prophet of capitalism in the USSR), 'Plan, Profit, Bonuses', he had been since 1946 Head of the Department of Economics and Organisation of the Machine-Building Industry at the Khar'kov Institute where he had graduated. He retired the following year and worked on his sole significant book, published in 1970 and in English in 1971 as *Economic Methods and the Effectiveness of Production*. MCK

LIDIN (real name Gomberg), Vladimir Germanovich (1894–1979) The author of some seventeen novels, several hundred short stories, memoirs, and literary essays, Lidin also taught for twenty-five years at the Gor'ky Literary Institute. His stories are psychologically acute vignettes of everyday life, and his vast acquaintance with the literary world of his day lend his memoirs particular interest. JAEC

LIGACHEV, Yegor Kuz'mich (b. 1920) A conditional ally of Gorbachev in the period before he became party General Secretary, Ligachev has been on the conservative wing of the Politburo since then, coming out against the more radical reforms and reflecting many of the misgivings of the average party official. A strong personality and forceful speaker, he has not, however, acquired wide popularity in the Soviet Union as a whole because he is seen as a man of the apparatus and as a brake on reform.

Ligachev was born in the village of Dubinkino in the Novosibirsk region of Siberia. He graduated from the Ordzhonikidze Aviational Institute in Moscow with an engineering degree in 1943; he did not serve in the armed forces, but worked for a year as a chief engineer in a production group before becoming secretary of a district committee of the Komsomol in his native Novosibirsk region in 1944, the same year in which he joined the Communist Party. In 1949, by which time he had become First Secretary of the Komsomol for the Novosibirsk region, Ligachev switched to the party apparatus, in which he remained apart from the years when he was deputy chairman of the executive committee of the Novosibirsk soviet (1955–58).

Ligachev's second spell in Moscow (his student days being the first) was from 1961 – when he moved from being a secretary of the Novosibirsk *obkom* to work as a deputy department head in the Bureau for party work in the Russian republic – to 1965. He was comparatively out of favour in the Brezhnev years, being sent back to Siberia in 1965 as First Secretary of the Tomsk regional party committee; he remained there until 1983, although he did become a candidate member of the Central Committee (1966–76) and a full member from 1976.

It was Yuriy Andropov who brought Ligachev in from the cold, appointing him head of the Department of Party Organizational Work of the Central Committee in 1983. Later in the same year he became a Sec-

retary of the Central Committee; in April 1985, a month after Gorbachev became General Secretary, full membership of the Politburo was added to this. Ligachev was for a time the *de facto* second secretary to Gorbachev, supervising ideology as well as the party organization. However, Gorbachev's response to a series of Ligachev efforts to slow the pace of change and to criticize implicitly Gorbachev's policies was to clip his wings in September 1988. His duties were confined to agriculture, as its supervisor within the Secretariat and as Chairman of a new Central Committee Commission for Agricultural Questions.

Ligachev has been a critic of what he perceives as excesses of *glasnost'* and has defended the achievements, as he sees them, of the Soviet period against those who wish to criticize much that has happened since 1917. One policy promoted strongly by Ligachev – a non-drinker himself – was the anti-alcohol measures (including a severe cutback in its production and in the number of retail outlets) launched in 1985. Although alcoholism and drunkeness are, indeed, serious Soviet problems, the blunt instruments used against them did not have the desired effect, but led to a sharp increase in illicit distilling and great damage to Soviet finances (through lost revenue) without much improvement in public health. Ligachev's political career effectively ended in July 1990 when at the Twenty-eighth Party Congress he lost all his party positions including Central Committee membership. AHB

LIKHACHEV, Dmitriy Sergeevich (b. 1906) Academician, expert on early Russian literature and culture, President of the Soviet Cultural Foundation which was established in 1986.

Born in St Petersburg and educated at Leningrad University, Likhachev was arrested for his participation in a student discussion group and sent to the Solovki prison complex (1928–32), where he published his first article, a study of thieves' slang. After his release he became a scholar of early Russian literature. He has written prolifically on all aspects of the period, and is probably best known for his attempts to establish the artistic principles of early Russian literature in, for example, *The Poetics of Early Russian Literature* (1967), *Laughter in Old Russia* (with A. M. Panchenko and N. V. Ponyrko, 1984), and *Textology* (1962).

Likhachev has been a staunch defender against official hostility or indifference to Russia's cultural traditions, whether icons, eighteenth-century gardens, or the historic buildings in Leningrad. As a consequence, his nomination as a corresponding member of the Academy of Sciences was blocked three times by politically orthodox colleagues at the Institute of Russian Literature in Leningrad. He finally became a corresponding member in 1953 and a full member in 1970. Under Gorbachev attitudes to the Russian past have changed; hence it was possible for Likhachev to be appointed President of the Culture Foundation in 1987 and to develop his role at the head of the drive to preserve the Russian cultural heritage. He was elected from the Culture Foundation to membership of the Congress of People's Deputies of the USSR in 1989. FCMW

LIKHACHEV, Ivan Alekseevich (1896–1956) A leading industrial manager of the Stalin period, famous even at that time for being able to get round the regulations to further the interests of his factory. Born near Tula, where his father was a printer, Likhachev started as a worker in St Petersburg at the age of twelve, serving in the army during the First World War. He joined the Bolshevik party in June 1917. He was stationed with the Red Guard in Helsingfors during the Civil War and became one of the original members of the Cheka. After recovering from a serious illness in 1921, he worked in the Moscow trade unions (1921–26). Appointed director of the Moscow vehicle works (AMO, later known as the 'Stalin' works – ZIS – and eventually as the 'Likhachev' works – ZIL) (1926–39 and 1940–50), his other appointments were: People's Commissar of Medium Engineering (1939–40); director of an aircraft factory (1950–53); and Minister of Vehicle Transport and Roads (1953–56). He was a member of the party Central Committee from 1939 to 1956. RWD

LIPKIN, Semen Izrailevich (b. 1911) Poet and translator, born in Odessa, resident in Moscow from 1929. One of the most eminent Soviet translators of verse, specializing in the Central Asian epic, Lipkin emerged only in the 1960s as an important original poet. He resigned from the Union of Writers as a result of the *Metropol'* scandal in 1980 and published extensively abroad; he was reinstated under Gorbachev. GSS

LIPSKY, Vladimir Ippolitovich (1863–1937) Botanist. After the revolution Lipsky played an active role in organizing the Academy of Sciences of the Ukrainian SSR and served as its president (1921–28). Thereafter he moved to Odessa to head its botanical garden, where he worked for the remainder of his life. Lipsky made many collecting expeditions to Central Asia, the Far East, Africa, and the Americas (1887–1936) and was the first to describe four plant genera and more than 220 species. He also helped locate sources of oil in the Black Sea area and radioactive minerals in Zhitomir province. MBA

LISITSYAN, Pavel Gerasimovich (b. 1911) Baritone. Lisitsyan was born in Vladikavkaz. He studied at the Leningrad Conservatory (1930–32), completing his training in Yerevan. He was a soloist with the Leningrad Malyy Opera Theatre (1935–37) and with the Armenian Theatre of Opera and Ballet (1937–40). He sang with the Bol'shoy (1940–66), and taught at the Yerevan Conservatory (1967–73). A member of the party since 1949, he was made a People's Artist of the USSR in 1956. He has made several tours abroad and is reputedly the first Soviet artist to have sung in the New York Metropolitan Theatre in 1960. GS

LISSITZKY EL (Lisitsky, Lazar' Markovich) (1890–1941) Designer. Born in Polshchinok. Lissitzky is widely recognized as one of the primary exponents of Constructivist design in the 1920s. After studying as a draftsman and architect in Darmstadt and Moscow (1909–14), he met Malevich in 1918 and became immediately fascinated with the possibilities of Suprematism. In Vitebsk and then in Moscow and Germany, Lissitzky applied the principles of geometric abstraction to book, exhibition, interior and photographic design arguing for an international style that would reflect the aspirations of Socialism and Communism. JEB

LISTOV, Vladimir Vladimirovich (b. 1931) Chemical engineer from West Siberia. After factory and party posts in Kemerovo, Listov became Deputy Minister of the Chemical Industry (1971–77) and then Minister

(1980–86). From 1977 to 1980 he was head of the Central Committee's Department of Chemical Industry. Since 1988 he has been Deputy Chairman of the Council of Ministers Bureau for the Chemical and Forestry Complex. JHM

LIVANOV, Boris Nikolaevich (1904–1972) Actor. Livanov was one of the leading actors of the Moscow Art Theatre and made films from 1924. His numerous stage roles included: Shakhovskoy in Aleksey Tolstoy's *Tsar Fedor Ioannovich* (1924–25) and Rybakov in Pogodin's *The Kremlin Chimes* (1943) and his film roles included: a minor part in Eisenstein's *October* (1927), Karl Renn in Pudovkin's *The Deserter* (1933), the title role in *Dubrovsky* (1936), Bocharov in the Zarkhi and Kheifits *The Baltic Deputy* (1937), Pozharsky in Pudovkin's *Minin and Pozharsky* (1939) and Prince Potemkin in *Admiral Ushakov* (1953). RT

LIZICHEV, Aleksey Dmitrievich (b. 1928) Chief of Main Political Directorate of the Armed Forces. Lizichev joined the Soviet Army in 1946 and therefore had no active service. He did Komsomol work in Leningrad Military District (1949–53) and in 1957 he graduated from the Lenin Military-Political Academy. His career progressed smoothly up the political hierarchy of the army. He was Deputy Chief, then First Deputy Chief of Moscow Military District (1967–72); First Deputy Chief of the Political Directorate of the Soviet Forces in Germany (1973–75); Chief of the Political Directorate of the Transbaikal Military District (1975–80); Deputy Chief of the Main Political Directorate (1980–82); and Chief of the Political Directorate of the Soviet Forces in Germany (1982–85). In July 1985

Lizichev replaced the venerable Army General Yepishev as Chief of the Main Political Directorate of the Armed Forces (Yepishev, the incumbent since 1962, died a couple of months later). The following year Lizichev became an Army General and member of the CPSU Central Committee. RA

LOBANOV, Andrey Mikhaylovich (1900–1959) Stage director. Lobanov's best known productions included Arbuzov's *Tanya* (1939) and Gor'ky's *Summer Folk* (1949). Lobanov was Chief Director at the Yermolova Theatre (1944–58). RT

LOBOV, Oleg Ivanovich (b. 1937) A construction engineer from the Urals, Lobov was Second Secretary of Sverdlovsk *obkom* from 1938 to 1985 (when Boris Yel'tsin was First Secretary), Chairman of Sverdlovsk Oblast' Executive Committee (1985–87) and Deputy Chairman of the RSFSR Council of Ministers (1987–89). His familiarity to senior politicians from the Urals must have assisted his appointment in January 1989 to the tough position of Second Secretary of the Armenian Communist Party. His colleague V. S. Markar'yants was appointed in a similar manner. JHM

LOBOV, Semen Semenovich (1888–1937) An old Bolshevik and leading economic organizer. Born in Smolensk province into a worker's family, Lobov worked in a St Petersburg metal factory (1912–17). He joined the RSDLP in 1913 and served in the Cheka (1917–20). He then held posts in Petrograd fuel organizations (1921–23), was appointed chairman of the North-West Industrial Bureau (1923–26), and chairman of VSNKh of the RSFSR (1926–30). He became first deputy at the People's Commissariat for Supplies (Internal Trade) (1930–32), People's Commissar for the Timber Industry (1932–36) and People's Commissar for the Food Industry of the RSFSR. He was a candidate member of the party Central Committee from 1922 to 1923, and a full member from 1924 until 1937. RWD

LOMAKO, Petr Fadeevich (b. 1904) From 1940 to 1986 the Soviet Union's principal organizer of non-ferrous metallurgy – a field which covers not only lead, tin, zinc and copper but also the precious and rare metals. Between 1957 and 1961 he was head of the Regional Economic Council of Krasnoyarsk province, and between 1962 and 1965 Chairman of Gosplan and Deputy Chairman of the Council of Ministers; but such offices were merely interruptions to his work as Minister (or the equivalent) of Non-Ferrous Metallurgy, a post which he held four times (1940–48, 1950–53, 1954–57, 1965–86). Lomako retired in 1986. JHM

LOMINADZE, Vissarion Vissarionovich ('Besso') (1897–1935) A flamboyant party leader and vigorous supporter of Stalin who showed Leftist inclinations in the 1920s. Born in Kutaisi, the son of a teacher, Lominadze joined the party in March 1917, and held leading party posts in the Transcaucasus (1918–24). In the middle and later 1920s he became a prominent figure in the Comintern, the Komsomol, and the Communist Youth International. He helped to bring about the 'left turn' in the Chinese party in 1927 on mandate from Stalin, but he was apparently not directly responsible for the Canton débâcle usually attributed to him. Together with Shatskin, Lominadze pressed for Left policies (1928–29). He was expelled from the party Central Committee on 1 December 1930, accused of forming a Leftist 'anti-party group', which cooperated with the Rightist group of Syrtsov to form a '"Left"-Right bloc'. He was an energetic party organizer in the Magnitogorsk plant (1933–35), but he committed suicide in his car when called to Chelyabinsk. He was a candidate member of the party Central Committee (1925–30) and then a full member (1930). RWD

LOMOV (Oppokov), Georgiy Ippolitovich (1888–1938) An old Bolshevik, leading politician, and economic organizer. Educated as a lawyer, Lomov joined the RSDLP in 1903, working as a clandestine revolutionary within Russia, for which he was frequently arrested. Occupying party posts in Moscow during the time of the Provisional Government, he was appointed People's Commissar for Justice after the October Revolution. In the spring of 1918 he sided with the Left Communists. He then held various posts in VSNKh (1918–22), headed the Oil Syndicate in 1923, and other important posts in the fuel industry and VSNKh (1924–30). He moved as first deputy chairman to Gosplan with Kuybyshev in 1931. Lomov was a candidate member of the party Central Committee (1925–27), then a full member (1927–34). He was arrested in 1937 and executed without a public trial. RWD

LOONE, Eero (b. 1935) Estonian philosopher. Born in Tartu, Estonia, Loone studied first history at Moscow University and then philosophy at the Institute of Philosophy of the Academy of Sciences in Moscow before returning to Estonia where he was later to establish an international reputation as a leading and innovative interpreter of Marxism and philosophy of history. A member of the Communist Party from 1965, he has taught at the University of Tartu since 1963, with the title of professor since 1985. From 1986 to 1989 he was head of the department of philosophy and since 1989 has been head of the department of philosophy and political science of the University of Tartu. Loone was a founding member of the independent Estonian Union of Scientists established in 1989. His major work, *Contemporary Philosophy of History* was published in Tallin in 1980 and in English as *Soviet Marxism and Analytical Philosopies of History* in 1990. AHB

LOPUKHOV, Fedor Vasil'evich (1886–1973) Ballet dancer, teacher, and leading choreographer. A student of Nikolay Legat, Lopukhov graduated from the Imperial Ballet School in 1905. He appeared as a soloist at the Maryinsky Theatre (1905–9, 1911–22), the Bol'shoy Theatre (1909–10), and on an American tour (1910–11).

In 1922 Lopukhov, who had been experimenting with choreography since 1910, left the stage to serve as artistic director of the Kirov troupe, a post he held three times (1922–30, 1944–45, and 1951–56). He also founded and directed the ballet troupe at the Malyy Theatre (1930–35), served as artistic director of the Leningrad Ballet School (1936–41), and served as artistic director of the choreography department of the Leningrad Conservatory (1962–73).

Lopukhov's role in the development of Soviet ballet can scarcely be underestimated. His career as a major choreographer began after the Revolution, when he restaged a number of classical ballets, thus preserving the traditions of the Imperial School. These included *Sleeping Beauty*,

Swan Lake, The Humpbacked Horse, Raymonda and *Don Quixote*.

More importantly, however, Lopukhov's strikingly unconventional choreography was at the forefront of the modernist movement of the 1920s. Among the elements he introduced into his ballets were acrobatics, speech and song, athletic movements, and folk dances. He utilized Constructivist decor and staged all Shostakovich's ballets. Lopukhov greatly influenced the Young Ballet (*Molodoy balet*), the experimental group founded by George Balanchine in 1921, and indeed an entire generation of dancers and choreographers, among them Yuriy Grigorovich.

One of Lopukhov's first major works was the once-performed *Tanzsymphonia* (1922), based on the life-cycle of the Universe and using Beethoven's Fourth Symphony. Balanchine and Leonid Lavrovsky numbered among the dancers.

This was followed in 1924 by *The Red Whirlwind*, an allegorical ballet in two 'processes' based on the Revolution, and *Night on Bald Mountain*. Lopukhov choreographed Stravinsky's *Pulcinella* (1926) and *Le Renard* (1927) as well as a 1927 'choreodrama' entitled *The Serf Ballerina*, which starred Ol'ga Mungalova and became a landmark in choreography for its combination of classical dance and acrobatics.

Lopukhov created new versions of such works as *The Nutcracker* (1929), *Harlequinade* (1933), and *Coppélia* (1934). He choreographed *Christmas Eve* (1938) and *Pictures at an Exhibition* (1953) for the Moscow Art Theatre, and was influential in founding ballet companies in a number of Soviet republics. He was the author of *Life of a Ballet Master* (1925), *Sixty Years in Ballet* (1966), and *Candid Choreographic Revelations* (1972). SCS

LOSABERIDZE, Ketevan (b. 1949) Sportswoman. She was the first Soviet woman to win the Olympic archery competition in 1980. Born in Georgia, she was several times world, European and national champion. Outside sport, she graduated in mathematics from the Kutaisi Pedagogical Institute and taught mathematics at Tbilisi University upon retiring from sport. JWR

LOTMAN, Yuriy Mikhaylovich (b. 1922) Literary critic, semiotician and cultural historian. A man with an encyclopedic knowledge of Russian literary life in the late eighteenth and early nineteenth century, Lotman's considerable international reputation nonetheless rests upon his position as founder of the Soviet school of structural poetics with major theoretical works (1964, 1970 and 1972), and a book on the semiotics of cinema (1973). In recent years, together with B. A. Uspensky, he has become involved in the semiotics of culture as applied to Russian history. Under his aegis the University of Tartu has become the centre of Soviet structuralism. In 1987 he was unsuccessfully nominated as a corresponding member of the Academy of Sciences. FCMW

LOZINSKY, Mikhail Leonidovich (1886–1955) Poet and translator, born and educated in St Petersburg. A minor figure in his own right, but a major poet through his translation of the *Divine Comedy* (1939–45), one of the greatest achievements of Soviet literature. GSS

LUCHINSKY, Petr Kirillovich (b. 1940) One of the few Moldavians to be active in All-Union politics, Luchinsky was First Secretary of the Moldavian Komsomol (1967–71), Secretary for Ideology of the Moldavian Communist Party (1971–76), and First Secretary of Kishinev *gorkom* (1976–78). He then moved to the CPSU apparatus in Moscow as deputy head of the Department of Propaganda (1978–86) and in January 1986 was appointed Second Secretary of the Tadzhikistan Communist Party. In late 1989 he returned to his native Moldavia as First Secretary of the republic's party organization. In July 1990 he was elected to the Politburo. JHM

LUCHISHKIN, Sergey Alekseevich (b. 1902) Painter. Born in Moscow, Luchishkin trained at Svomas and Vkhutemas (1918–24), assimilating the ideas of abstract painting formulated by Exter, Popova, *et al*. From 1923 to 1932 he was associated with the so-called Projection Theatre in Moscow, although his forte remained studio painting. A member of OST, he depicted sports parades and everyday urban scenes such as *The Balloon Has Flown Away* (1926). JEB

LUGOVSKOY, Vladimir Aleksandrovich (1901–1957) Poet, born in Moscow. He served in the Red Army during the Civil War; new work appeared steadily from 1925 to 1937, when his work was publicly condemned. Lugovskoy then kept a very low profile until the Khrushchev thaw. He was posthumously recognized as one of the most important Soviet lyric poets. GSS

LUKA (Voino-Yasnetsky, Valentin Feliksovich), Archbishop (1877–1961) Leading surgeon who became an Orthodox bishop. Ordained in 1921, he continued to work as a doctor, but ten days after his appointment as Bishop of Tashkent and Turkestan in 1923 he was sent into exile

for two years. From this time until 1941 he served a number of terms of internal exile, though between the first and the second he was able to publish his *Essays on Septic Surgery*. Returning to surgery during the war years, Archbishop Luka was able to publish a second volume of his essays in 1946 for which he was awarded a Stalin prize. In later years his book *The Spirit, the Soul and the Body* appeared in *samizdat* form. At the time of his death he was Archbishop of Crimea and Simferopol'. MR

LUKASHUK, Igor' Ivanovich (b. 1926) For many years Professor and head of the Department of International Law and Relations at Kiev University. A specialist on the law of treaties, adviser to Ukrainian delegations at international conferences, Lukashuk is especially known for methodological innovations in developing a systems approach to international law. In 1986 he moved to the Institute of State and Law of the Soviet Academy of Sciences, where he occupies a senior research position. WEB

LUKIANENKO, Lev Hryhorovych (b. 1927) Born near Chernigov and educated as a lawyer at Moscow University, Lukianenko became a full-time party worker in L'vov *oblast'*. He was sentenced to death in 1961 for the formation of a Ukrainian Workers' and Peasants' League, but the sentence was commuted. Upon his release from prison, he helped found, in 1976, the Ukrainian Helsinki Group, of which he was Chairman in the late 1980s. He was elected to the Ukrainian Supreme Soviet in 1990. JHM

LUKONIN, Mihail Kuz'mich (1918–1976) Poet, born in Astrakhan'. A party member since 1942, he saw active service in Finland and the

Second World War, after which he settled in Moscow. His range of subject matter is broad, from intimate lyrics to topical and historical subjects.

GSS

LUK'YANOV, Anatoliy Ivanovich (b. 1930) Chairman of the Supreme Soviet of the USSR and a close ally of Mikhail Gorbachev within the Soviet leadership, Luk'yanov was born in Smolensk and during the Second World War began work at the age of thirteen in military industry. The war over, he was able to resume studies and he graduated from the Law Faculty of Moscow University in 1953. Though two years ahead of Gorbachev in that Faculty, he was acquainted with him and they worked together in the Faculty Komsomol organization, although Luk'yanov became a member of the Communist Party only in 1955.

Luk'yanov had a series of appointments involving legal expertise. He was a consultant of the legal commission attached to the Council of Ministers of the USSR (1956–61) and from 1961 to 1976 a senior official in, and then deputy head of, the department of the Presidium of the Supreme Soviet concerned with the activities of soviets. He moved briefly to the apparatus of the Central Committee of the party (1976–77) as a consultant in the Department of Party Organizational Work before returning to the Presidium of the Supreme Soviet as head of its Secretariat.

Luk'yanov held that post until 1983 when, with Yuriy Andropov in the General Secretaryship, he became First Deputy Head of the General Department of the Central Committee which works especially closely with the party leader. When Gorbachev succeeded Chernenko in the top party post in March 1985 Luk'yanov became head of the General Department. In January 1987 he was elevated to a Secretaryship of the Central Committee and from November of the same year he was simultaneously head of the Administrative Organs Department of the Central Committee, responsible for overseeing, among other bodies, the military and the KGB. Luk'yanov moved out of the party Secretariat in the autumn of 1988, becoming a candidate member of the Politburo in September of that year and First Deputy Chairman of the Presidium of the Supreme Soviet in October when Gorbachev was elected Chairman. With the headship of state strengthened as an institution in 1989 and renamed Chairmanship of the Supreme Soviet, Luk'yanov was again First Deputy Chairman to Gorbachev.

A more radical restructuring of the Soviet political system in March 1990 and the creation of a new executive Presidency of the USSR, to which Gorbachev was elected by the Congress of People's Deputies, led to a separation between the Presidency and the Chairmanship of the Supreme Soviet. Luk'yanov succeeded Gorbachev in the latter post.

As power has moved increasingly to the new state institutions, Luk'yanov has become one of the most important politicians in the contemporary Soviet Union. He has maintained close links with the legal profession (not least, with academic lawyers in the Institute of State and Law) and has responsibility for seeing through a large body of new and fundamental legislation.

AHB

LUNACHARSKY, Anatoliy Vasil'-evich (1875–1933) A somewhat unlikely revolutionary with his professorial manner and pince-nez, Lunacharsky was the first Soviet Commissar for Enlightenment (or Education) and was also a literary theorist, playwright and cultural commentator of genuine distinction. He was born in Poltava, the son of a radically-minded official. At the age of fifteen, he later recalled, he had begun to study Marxism in the Kiev Gymnasium he attended and already considered himself a socialist. He undertook propaganda work among students and workers, and then went to Zurich University where he studied natural sciences and philosophy and also extended his knowledge of Marxism. After a stay in France he returned to Russia in 1899 and became involved in socialist propaganda in Moscow where, after a betrayal, he was arrested. Released and allowed to return to Kiev, he resumed his political activities and was again arrested. Further periods of arrest and incarceration followed. Lunacharsky was already an active contributor to journals on philosophy and psychology and a close friend of the philosopher A. A. Bogdanov, whose sister he married. Before the revolution Lunacharsky lived for the most part abroad, associating with émigré circles and with figures such as Gor'ky, who shared Lunacharsky's and Bogdanov's somewhat unorthodox 'God-building' views at this time. During the war he joined the 'internationalist' group of which Trotsky was also a member, but after the February Revolution he gravitated towards Lenin and Zinov'ev, offering, as he later put it, to 'put myself at the disposal of the Bolshevik Central Committee'. His offer was accepted.

When the first Soviet government was formed after the October Revolution Lunacharsky was given the post of Commissar for Enlightenment (or Education), which he held until 1929. He also played a modest part in cultural work at the various fronts during the Civil War. From 1929 until 1933 he headed the Learned Council of the USSR Central Executive Committee, and was then appointed Soviet ambassador to Spain. He died on his outward journey, at Menton in southern France. Lenin, who had a somewhat cool relationship with him, described Lunacharsky as an 'exceptionally gifted man'; Gor'ky called him 'brilliant and resourceful', although 'too much of a bookworm' and careless in his personal relationships. Trotsky regarded him as brilliant and very talented, but ultimately a dilettante. Lunacharsky's considerable reputation rests ultimately upon his literary and cultural writings, particularly his contributions to aesthetics; he was an ineffective politician and an incompetent administrator, although he was able to use his influence to spare the creative intelligentsia and objects of cultural or historical significance from some of the worst of the rigours of the Civil War. SLW

LUNTS, Lazar Adolf'ovich (1892–1980) The pre-eminent Soviet specialist in private international law. Lunts worked until 1941 advising the USSR Ministry of Finance and took part in the nationalization cases (arising out of Soviet nationalization of foreign property (1917–18)) by looking after Soviet interests in New York. For years he represented the USSR in the International Labour Organization and also acted as a commercial arbitrator. He wrote more than 100 monographs and articles, his three-volume *Course in International Private Law* (1959–66) gaining him an international reputation and a State Prize. WEB

LUNTS, Lev Natanovich (1901–1924)
A literary scholar and playwright,
Lunts was the chief theoretician of the
Serapion Brothers. In 1922 he wrote
the group's manifesto, which criticizes
Russian literature as boring, unplotted
and poorly crafted; he shared this
emphasis on plot with his mentor
Shklovsky. In Lunts's 'To the West'
(1923) he advises as a remedy drawing
on popular literary genres from the
West such as adventure fiction. His
four plays include *The City of Truth*
(1924) which has dystopian elements
reminiscent of Zamyatin's *We*. He
died in Hamburg of an embolism in
the brain. KC

LUSHEV, Petr Georg'evich (b. 1923)
Army General. During the Second
World War Petr Lushev, like Dmitriy
Yazov, fought on the Leningrad and
Volkhov fronts. Among other battles,
he took part in the siege of Leningrad.
He graduated from the Malinovsky
Military Academy for Armoured
Forces (1954) and the Voroshilov
General Staff Academy (1966). After
commanding a tank division he was
appointed in succession: commander
of the First Guards Tank Army in East
Germany, first deputy commander of
the Group of Soviet Forces in
Germany, commander of the Volga
Military District, and commander of
the Central Asian Military District.
The latter command from 1977 to
1980 must have given Lushev an
important role in the initial Soviet
involvement in Afghanistan.

In 1981 he became an Army
General, a member of the CPSU
Central Committee, and commander
of the Moscow Military District, a key
post for political control during the
Andropov, Chernenko, and Gorbachev successions that followed. He
had been a Deputy to the Supreme

Soviet since 1980. In July 1985 Lushev
was named Commander-in-Chief of
the Soviet Forces in Germany and in
August 1986 he replaced Marshal
Petrov as First Deputy Minister of
Defence. Even before Gorbachev
assumed power Lushev had strongly
supported individual initiative in
command and control and the need
for criticism from below. Lushev's
views on important issues, therefore,
appear similar to Gorbachev's and this
similarity is reinforced by his support
for Gorbachev's arms control
proposals. He was rewarded in February 1989 when he replaced Viktor
Kulikov as Commander-in-Chief of
Warsaw Pact forces. (Three months
later Lushev became the first Soviet
officer holding this position to visit
Britain.) He is likely to play a key
role in the military restructuring of
Warsaw Pact forces and in the transformation of the Warsaw Pact into a
looser, more political organization to
accommodate the national views of
member states. RA

LUSIS, Janis Voldmarovich (b. 1939)
Athlete. Born in Elgava, Latvia, he
was the greatest of all Soviet javelin
throwers, competing in four Olympics,
becoming Olympic champion in 1968
with a new world record that lasted
four years, and taking silver in 1972
and bronze in 1984. He was also
twelve times Soviet javelin champion
and four times European champion
between 1962 and 1971. He retired
from competitive sport in 1972, and
concentrated on coaching at the
Alksnis Air Force College in Riga.
JWR

LYAPUNOV, Aleksey Andreevich
(1911–1973) Mathematician, a
founder of Soviet cybernetics. After his
graduation from Moscow University
in 1933, Lyapunov worked at the

Steklov Mathematics Institute of the USSR Academy of Sciences on number theory and the theory of functions. He joined the party in 1944 and became a second lieutenant in charge of directing artillery fire. After the war he became involved in information theory, programming, and cybernetics and worked at the Artillery Academy and, after winning his doctorate in 1949, at the Geophysics Institute. This new expertise led to a professorship at Moscow University in computational mathematics (1952–62) and a research appointment in the Steklov Institute's department of applied mathematics under future Academy president M. V. Keldysh. In the 1950s he was a key figure in the development of Soviet cybernetics and an outspoken defender of its ideological legitimacy. Intrigued by DNA as an informational molecule, he helped mobilize Soviet mathematicians in support of genetics. In 1962 he moved to the science city at Novosibirsk, was elected a corresponding member of the Academy in 1964, and spent his final decade in the science city, at the institutes of mathematics and theoretical cybernetics, teaching and investigating programming and computation, and their relation to such fields as evolutionary theory and mathematical linguistics. MBA

LYATOSHINS′KY, Boris Mykolayovich (1895–1968) Ukrainian composer and teacher. Boris Lyatoshins′ky (Lyatoshinsky) was born in Zhitomir and died in Kiev. He studied law and music simultaneously, graduating from the Kiev University Faculty of Jurisprudence in 1918 and the Kiev Conservatory, where he was a pupil of Glier, in 1919. The rest of his life was spent as a teacher at the same Conservatory, where he was appointed a Professor in 1935. He also taught at the Moscow Conservatory (1935–38 and 1941–44). He was made a People's Artist of the Ukrainian SSR in 1968. A prolific composer, he did much to develop Ukrainian musical life. GS

LYKOVA, Lidiya Pavlovna (b. 1913) A party and state official at the Republic level, Lykova completed her education as a teacher in 1940. She later completed a candidate's degree in economics in the Academy of Social Sciences of the Central Committee. Lykova joined the CPSU in 1938 and spent most of her career in party and state work. She served as second secretary of the Ivanova Provincial Party Committee and the Smolensk Provincial Party Committee in the 1960s. She later served as Minister for Social Security of the RSFSR and most recently as Deputy Chairman of the Council of Ministers of the RSFSR. Lykova was one of the officials involved in the long-term campaign against alcoholism in the RSFSR. A member of the Supreme Soviet, she served as Chairman of the Commission for Women's Labour and Living Conditions, for the Protection of the Mother and the Child. She was a candidate member of the Central Committee from 1961 to 1976 and a full member from 1976 1986. NN

LYPKIVSKY, Metropolitan Vasyl′ (1864–1938?) Metropolitan of the Ukrainian Autocephalous Orthodox Church. Lypkivsky studied at the Kiev Theological Seminary, then at the Academy, from which he graduated as candidate in theology in 1889, and he was ordained in 1891. He was a founder of the 'Brotherhood of the Resurrection' which became the All-Ukrainian Orthodox Church Council.

He was elected by this Council as the Metropolitan of Kiev and All Ukraine on 23 October 1923. Government pressure brought about his removal from this post in 1927. He was arrested and exiled in 1938 to the Solovki islands where he died. He wrote some reminiscences, *History of the Ukrainian Church.* MR

LYSENKO, Trofim Denisovich (1898–1976) Agronomist, agrobiologist, founder of 'Lysenkoism' and 'Michurinist biology'. Born into the family of a Ukrainian peasant, Lysenko studied agronomy at various schools and breeding stations in Poltava, Uman, and Kiev and served as head of legume selection at an experimental station in Gandzha (Kirovabad), Azerbaydzhan. In 1929 he became famous for 'vernalization' (making winter wheat sowable in the spring by burying germinating seeds in snow before planting) and was given a laboratory in the All-Union Institute of Genetics and Selection in Odessa. N. I. Vavilov and other prominent agronomists gave Lysenko credibility and support, but his meteoric rise to prominence during the first five-year plan depended principally on the backing of agricultural and political authorities, who saw in him a cooperative peasant whose inexpensive techniques fitted collectivization. In 1931 the government created a journal to popularize his work, *Yarovizatsiya*, later renamed *Agrobiologiya*.

In the early 1930s 'vernalization' came to include almost anything done to a crop before planting in order to alter its development. Lysenko devised such techniques for a wide range of vegetables, fruits, and grains and, although none were properly tested, they were applied to many millions of hectares of crops. In 1934 Lysenko became the scientific director of the Odessa institute and a full member of the Ukrainian Academy of Sciences for this work. He subsequently devised analogous techniques for the summer planting of potatoes (1935); grafting or 'vegetative hybridization' (late 1930s); the 'cluster method' of forestation (1948–50); and the maize (1956) and butterfat (1958–62) campaigns. Designed to over-fulfil government quotas, his untested, inexpensive nostrums were widely introduced, only to be quietly phased out when they proved unsuccessful.

In 1935 Lysenko was joined by Leningrad philosopher I. I. Prezent, who began to elaborate his agronomic practices into theory and handled his public relations. Two pamphlets propounded the view that every plant goes through distinct developmental stages or phases and that by altering conditions at the end of a developmental stage, the heredity of the plant could be destabilized or 'cracked', making it plastic and malleable. Following the death of Ivan Michurin, Lysenko claimed that his approach was 'Michurinist biology' and portrayed himself as an agricultural Stakhanovite. He was appointed to the government's Central Executive Committee (1935–37) and became assistant to the president of the council of the Supreme Soviet (1937–50). During the purges of the late 1930s he claimed that geneticists had fascist ties and had sabotaged Soviet agriculture. In 1938 after two presidents of the Lenin All-Union Academy of Agricultural Sciences (VASKhNIL) were arrested and shot in rapid succession, Lysenko assumed the post himself and held it for almost two decades. With the help of the NKVD, he used his new position to harass and undermine Vavilov's supporters. In 1939 Lysenko was elected to the USSR Academy of Sciences and appointed to its presidium. In late 1940 Vavilov was arrested, his closest associates disappeared, and Lysenko left Odessa to replace him as director of the Academy's Institute of Genetics in Moscow, a post he held until 1965.

After the Second World War genetics was resurgent, but in mid-1948 Stalin filled VASKhNIL with Lysenkoists and, at its surprise August session, Lysenko announced that 'the Central Committee has read my report and approved it'. Castigating genetics as a capitalist, idealist, bourgeois enterprise linked to fascism, the report asserted that heredity was a malleable property of the whole organism and that one species could be transformed into another in one generation; it categorically denied the reality of intraspecific competition, genes, and any special hereditary material. In the edicts that followed the session, genetics was banned, most Soviet geneticists were fired from their jobs, laboratories were disbanded, institutions reorganized, and degree certification and curricula in biology fell under Lysenkoist control.

The massive Soviet reforestation programme (1948–52) employed Lysenko's cluster method of planting, and the extensive losses of seedlings led to open criticisms of his views, spearheaded by botanist V. N. Sukachev, beginning in 1952. With de-Stalinization, Lysenko was forced to resign as president of VASKhNIL in 1956 and it appeared for a time that his hegemony over Soviet biology was ending. In late 1958, however, he gained Nikita Khrushchev's strong support and Lysenko again briefly became president of VASKhNIL from 1961 to 1962. Brilliant Western work on DNA aroused the interest of powerful chemists, physicists, and mathematicians, and by 1963 Khrushchev was in open conflict with the USSR Academy of Sciences over Lysenkoism. After Khrushchev's removal in October 1964 the Ministry of Agriculture and the two Academies established a joint investigative commission which concluded in late 1965 that Lysenko's work was improperly carried out and that all of his agricultural techniques were useless. In 1965 Lysenko was removed as director of the Institute of Genetics, but he continued as a full academician and kept control of his Lenin Hills farm, where he worked until his death in November 1976. MBA

LYUBIMENKO, Vladimir Nikolaevich (1873–1937) Botanist, plant physiologist. A graduate of the Forestry Institute in Petersburg in 1898, Lyubimenko was one of the leading plant physiologists of his generation. As concurrent professor at Petrograd University (1915–24) and the Chemical Pharmaceutical Institute (1922–30), he wrote the influential botanical text *Kurs obshchei botaniki* (1923) and organized laboratories of plant physiology in Leningrad, Khar'kov, and Kiev. In 1929 he transferred to the Ukraine to become head of the division of chemical plant physiology at the Institute of Botany of the Academy of Sciences of the Ukrainian SSR (1929–37). Most of his research dealt with the chemical aspects of plastids and pigments, photosynthesis, and photoperiodism. Lyubimenko was highly critical of Lysenko's 'stage theory' of plant development, and may have been repressed. MBA

Lyubimov

LYUBIMOV, Yuriy Petrovich (b. 1917) Stage director. Lyubimov has been one of the most innovative stage directors and actors in the post-war period. He was Chief Director of the Moscow Taganka Theatre from 1964 until his emigration in 1983. His best known productions include Brecht's *The Good Person of Szechuan* (1963) and an adaptation of Dostoevsky's *Crime and Punishment* (1982), re-staged at the Lyric Theatre, Hammersmith, London in 1984. RT

M

MACHAVARIANI, Aleksey Davidovich (b. 1913) Georgian composer, teacher and conductor. Aleksey Machavariani was born in Gori. On graduating from the Tbilisi Conservatory in 1936, he remained for a further period of postgraduate study, after which he joined the teaching staff, becoming a Professor in 1963. He was artistic director of the Georgian State Symphony Orchestra (1956–58). He was made a People's Artist of the USSR in 1958. A prolific national composer, his ballet *Otello* (première 1957) achieved great success and was made into a film. GS

MACHERET, Aleksandr Venyaminovich (1896–1979) Film director and theorist. Macheret trained with Foregger and worked in the Blue Blouse theatre group. His films include: *Men and Jobs* (1932) and *Swamp Soldiers* (1938). He also played a major part in restoring and cataloguing the Gosfil'mofond film archive after the Second World War. RT

MAIOROV, Boris Aleksandrovich (b. 1938) Sportsman. Boris and his twin Yevgeny were born in Moscow, graduated together from the Moscow Aviation Institute in 1961, and played as strikers in the Moscow Spartak ice-hockey team with Vyacheslav Starshinov – comprising the best attacking trio in ice-hockey history. The same trio played for the Soviet ice-hockey team in the 1960s during which time Boris was captain (1962–68), and the team were undisputed European and world (amateur) champions (1963–68), and Olympic champions in 1964 and 1968. JWR

MAKARENKO, Anton Semyonovich (1888–1939) Born in Bespol'e (near Khar'kov), a writer and educator, Makarenko based his pedagogical writings on his experiences directing two reform schools, the Gor'ky Colony near Poltava (1920–28) and the Dzerzhinsky Commune (1927–35). His methodology outlined in the semi-fictional *Pedagogical Poem* (often translated as *The Road to Life*, (1925–35)) and in its sequel *A Book For Parents* (1938), contrasts with the liberal, permissive pedagogical theories prevalent among Soviet educators of the twenties. He ran his colonies on para-military lines and stressed discipline, conformity to rules and compulsory labour. KC

MAKAROV, Valeriy Leonidovich (b. 1937) Prominent Soviet economist and Director of the Central Institute of Economics and Mathematics (TsEMI) in Moscow. A native of Novosibirsk, Makarov graduated from the Moscow State Economic

Institute in 1960. He took the higher degree of Candidate of Sciences (in Economics) at Leningrad University in 1965 and his Doctorate of Sciences (in Mathematics) at the Institute of Mathematics of the Siberian branch of the USSR Academy of Sciences in 1968. From 1960 to 1983 Makarov (who became a corresponding member of the Academy of Sciences in 1979) worked in the Institute of Mathematics of the Siberian branch of the Academy of Sciences. He was Director of the Institute of Industrial Organization (1983–85) and in 1985 moved to the directorship of one of the Soviet Union's major social scientific institutes, TsEMI. His major book, *Mathematical Theory of Economic Dynamics and Equilibrium* was published in 1973. In his younger days, Makarov was a tennis player of national ranking. AHB

MAKAROVA, Nataliya (b. 1940) An outstanding ballerina, Makarova entered Leningrad Ballet School in 1953 and joined the Kirov troupe upon graduation. She received great acclaim for her début in *Giselle* and soon became a leading soloist. She developed a broad repertoire of major roles in both classical and modern ballets, including *Romeo and Juliet*, *The Fountain of Bakchisarai*, *The Kiss*, and *La Valse*. She received a gold medal at the Varna International Ballet Competition (1965) and was named Honoured Artist of the RSFSR (1969).

Makarova defected to the West in 1970 and has performed extensively with the American Ballet Theater. She has also danced as a guest artist with numerous other companies. She has staged several ballets, including a full-length version of *La Bayadère* (1979), and has appeared in the Broadway musical comedy *On Your Toes*. She has appeared with the Kirov company in both London (1988) and the Soviet Union (1989), the first dancer who emigrated to the West to return to dance with the Soviet troupe. SCS

MAKAROVA, Tamara Fedorovna (b. 1907) Film actress. Makarova's films have included: *The Deserter*, *The Conveyor Belt of Death* (both 1933), *Komsomolsk* (1938), *The Vow* (1946) and *The Young Guard* (1948). RT

MAKEEV, Valentin Nikolaevich (b. 1930) An engineer who was second secretary of the Moscow City party organization (1976–80) and Deputy Chairman of the USSR Council of Ministers (1980–83). Apparently a loser in the power struggles of the early 1980s, he was moved to Secretary of the Central Trade Union Council. JHM

MAKHKAMOV, Kakhar Makhkamovich (b. 1932) A Tadzhik mining engineer trained in Leningrad, Makhkamov moved from mining administration in 1961 to head the Executive Committee of Leninabad province, Tadzhikistan. From 1963 to 1982 he was Chairman of Gosplan in his home republic, and then Chairman of its Council of Ministers (1982–85). Makhkamov became First Secretary of the Tadzhikistan Communist Party in December 1985, resigning briefly during unrest in Tadzhikistan in February 1990. He was elected in July 1990 to the Politburo. JHM

MAKSIMOV, Vladimir Emelyanovich (b. 1932) Novelist whose youth was spent in orphanages and approved schools, on collective farms and building sites, experiences which he described in frank and dramatic form in his earliest stories, one of which appeared in *Pages from Tarusa* (1961). His *Seven Days of Creation* (1972) gave a merciless picture of the life of a working-class family in Stalin's Russia in a framework now openly Christian: it could be published only in the West. As a result, he was excluded from the Writers' Union in 1973 and emigrated in 1974. *Quarantine* (1973) put Stalinism in the context of the history of the Russian state, seen as constantly betraying its people for foreign innovations, but argued that the Russian people were worthy of salvation. Since 1974 Maksimov has been principal editor of the journal *Kontinent*, which pursues a neo-Slavophile editorial line, but is broad-minded in its literary policy. GAH

MAKSIMOV, Yuriy Pavlovich (b. 1924) Commander-in-Chief Strategic Rocket Forces. Yuriy Maksimov joined the Red Army in 1942, graduating from the Frunze Military Academy (1950) and the General Staff Academy (1965). After service at the front (1943–45) he held command and staff posts. He was named First Deputy Commander (1978–79) and Commander of the Turkestan Military District (1979–84). He gained the rank of Army General in 1982 and was Commander-in-Chief of the Southern Theatre of War (1984–85). This theatre, which is believed to encompass South-West Asia, had grown in significance on account of tensions in the Persian Gulf and the continuing military operations in Afghanistan. In July 1985 Maksimov replaced Marshal Tolubko and became Deputy Minister of Defence and Commander-in-Chief of the Strategic Rocket Forces. He has been a member of the CPSU Central Committee since 1986 (a candidate member since 1981). RA

MAKSIMOVA, Yekaterina Sergeevna (b. 1939) Leading Soviet ballerina. A student of Yelizaveta Gerdt,

Maksimova graduated from the Bol'shoy Ballet School in 1958, though she made her début in 1957 when she danced Masha in The *Nutcracker*. Maksimova joined the troupe of the Bol'shoy Ballet in 1958, and is the frequent partner of her husband, Vladimir Vasil'ev. A versatile dancer, she has developed a broad and varied repertoire, including leading roles in both classical and modern ballets. She is known for her dramatic qualities, comic nuances, and the impressive purity of her technique.

Her first major role was Katerina in Yuriy Grigorovich's *The Stone Flower* (1959). Coached by the celebrated Galina Ulanova, Maksimova's *Cinderella* (1964) received great acclaim. This was followed by Kitri in *Don Quixote* (1965), Masha in Yuriy Grigorovich's *The Nutcracker* (1966), Phrygia in Grigorovich's *Spartacus* (1968), the Girl in Vasil'ev's *Icarus* (1971), and Shura Azarova in Oleg Vinogradov and Dmitriy Bryantsev's *The Hussar's Ballad* (1980). Maksimova has also appeared in films, including films of two one-act ballets by Dmitriy Bryantsev: *Galatea* (1978), after Shaw's *Pygamalion*, and *The Old Tango* (1979).

Maksimova has toured widely, including appearances as Juliet in Maurice Béjart's *Romeo and Juliet* (Brussels and Moscow, 1978) and as a guest artist with the Kirov Ballet during a 1988 tour to Paris. She has also received many awards and prizes at international ballet competitions. SCS

MALENKOV, Georgiy Maksimilyanovich (1902–1988) Malenkov was for a short time after Stalin's death the most powerful political leader in the Soviet Union, but he was soon overtaken in the power struggle by

Nikita Khrushchev. Earlier Malenkov had made an unsavoury career as a ruthless ally of Stalin and Beria who bore direct responsibility for the deaths of many former colleagues and subordinates. Yet, as Chairman of the Council of Ministers in the immediate post-Stalin period he adopted a more conciliatory attitude towards both Soviet society and the West than did many of his colleagues.

Malenkov was born into a middle-class family in Orenburg in the Urals. He joined the Red Army in 1919 and fought in the Civil War. Having joined the Communist Party in 1920, he was a political commissar of the Bolshevik forces in Turkestan before the war ended. Following further studies and graduation from the Moscow Higher Technical Institute in 1925 Malenkov entered the apparatus of the Central Committee of the CPSU.

During the 1930s Malenkov held positions of greater personal responsibility for the purges than did Khrushchev (although Khrushchev was by no means guiltless) and he had more to lose from Khrushchev's de-Stalinization campaign twenty years later. During the last twelve years of Stalin's life Malenkov was one of the most powerful of those close to him. A Central Committee member from 1939, a candidate member of the Politburo from 1941 and a full Politburo member from 1946, he was also during the Second World War a member of the State Defence Committee. After the war he was a deputy chairman of the Council of Ministers.

When Stalin died in March 1953 there was a brief period when Malenkov not only succeeded to the Chairmanship of the Council of Ministers but was running the Secretariat of the party Central Committee as well.

Within less than two weeks, however, he had to relinquish his party Secretaryship, but even so, Malenkov's name headed the list of Soviet leaders until well into 1954.

Malenkov, who was described by Khrushchev as 'a typical office clerk and pen-pusher' who would 'freeze and kill anything that's alive' if given any power, was forced to resign as Chairman of the Council of Ministers in February 1955. He remained in the Presidium of the Council of Ministers (Politburo), but when he joined the coalition against Khrushchev which the latter dubbed the 'anti-party group', his political career was finally brought to an end by Khrushchev's successful counter-attack. He was expelled from both the Presidium and the Central Committee and dispatched to Eastern Kazakhstan as manager of a hydro-electric power station. When Malenkov returned to Moscow it was as a pensioner and during his long retirement he was only rarely seen in public. AHB

MALEVICH, Kazimir Serverinovich (1878–1935) Painter. Malevich was born near Kiev. Although he achieved his reputation as a stellar member of the avant-garde before the Revolution, his influence on the first generation of Soviet artists and architects such as Klutsis and Luchishkin was considerable. Assimilating Cubism and Futurism while living in Moscow, Malevich arrived at his abstract style of painting known as Suprematism in 1915. After the Revolution, especially while teaching in Vitebsk (1919–22), he proceeded to apply his methods to architecture and design, while compiling intricate theoretical statements. He had a one-man show in Warsaw in 1927, and thereafter returned to a more figurative style, for example *Girl with a Comb* (1932). JEB

MALINOVSKY, Rodion Yakovlevich (1898–1967) Former Minister of Defence. Malinovsky, a Ukrainian, was a non-commissioned officer in the tsarist army before entering the Red Army in 1919. He had a varied military career in the inter-war period, acting as a military adviser in the Spanish Civil War and as an instructor at the Frunze Military Academy before assuming senior command posts. Among the armies he commanded were the Southern Army Group, the Don Operational Group (1942), and the Second Guards Army in the Stalingrad counter-offensive (1942–43). He also commanded army groups in offensive operations in the Ukraine, Romania, Hungary, Austria and Czechoslovakia (1943–45). The Transbaykal Army Group was placed under his charge in the war with Japan in 1945. This last role made him a natural choice as Commander-in-Chief of Soviet Forces in the Far East (1947–53) and commander of the Far Eastern Military District (1953–56). The Korean War and the emergence of China as a communist power enhanced the importance of these posts. Malinovsky was appointed First Deputy Minister of Defence and Commander-in-Chief of Soviet Ground Forces (1956–57) and then Minister of Defence until the end of his life (1957–67). In this period he presided over the rapid build-up of Soviet strategic power. RA

MALYSHEV, Vyacheslav Aleksandrovich (1902–1957) Leading Soviet industrialist of the Stalin period, who organized the tank industry during the Second World War. A workaholic, Malyshev was described as a 'human rocket', and was said to have taken only one week's holiday in ten years. Born in the Komi region, the son of a teacher, he worked as a railway mechanic and engine driver, attending the Railway Technical School (1920–24). He became a party member in 1926 and did his military service in 1927. He was sent as a party 'thousander' to Moscow Higher Technical Institute (the Bauman Institute) (1930–34), where he was the scourge of the old specialists. He organized work on diesel locomotives, in which he had been interested for many years. He then worked in, and was later head of, the diesel sector of the Central Locomotive Project Bureau, becoming the People's Commissar of Heavy Engineering in 1939. This was combined with the deputy chairmanship of the Council of People's Commissars (1940–44), People's Commissar of Medium Engineering (1940), and People's Commissar for the Tank Industry (1941). People's Commissar for Transport Engineering was his next job, then the chairmanship of Gostekhnika (1947) and (1955–57), and Minister for Shipbuilding (1950–53). He was a member of the party Central Committee 1939–57. RWD

MANAENKOV, Yuriy Alekseevich (b. 1936) A Secretary of the Central Committee of the CPSU since September 1989, Manaenkov was born in a village in the Tambov region of Russia into the family of a collective farm worker. A Communist Party member from 1960, he worked both as an agronomist and as a journalist before joining the party apparatus in 1968 where he was employed mainly in his native region From 1984 to his election as a Secretary of the Central Committee in 1989 he was First Secretary of the Lipetsk regional party organization. AHB

MANDEL'SHTAM, Nadezhda Yakovlevna (1899–1980) Memoirist. Born in Khazina, trained as an artist in the studio of Aleksandra Ekster, she became a major writer after the arrest and death of her husband, the poet Osip Mandel'shtam. Her memoirs, called in English *Hope Against Hope* and *Hope Abandoned*, chronicle with increasing power her life with her husband and in isolation, and her friendship with Anna Akhmatova. She memorized and hid Mandel'shtam's poetry, survived and witnessed both the courage and, more often, the cravenness of others and became a heroine in the West, to which she never travelled. Her memoirs have now been published in the Soviet Union. BH

MANDEL'SHTAM, Osip Emil'evich (1891–1938) A poet and prose writer, born in Warsaw and brought up in St Petersburg. He established himself as one of the leading post-Symbolists with the collection *Stone* (1913), and his major stature confirmed with *Tristia* (1922). Mandel'shtam's work consists mainly of short lyric poems using figurative language whose referents derive from a highly personal model of cultural and historical reality. Stylistically and ideologically out of tune with post-Revolutionary literary and intellectual life, he was allowed to publish poetry until 1928, and produced two books of experimental prose, *The Noise of Time* (1925) and *The Egyptian Stamp* (1928). He ·then struggled to remain within literature as an essayist (*Journey to Armenia*, 1933). In 1934 he was arrested and sentenced to three years' administrative exile. He attempted suicide, but then, in Voronezh, created some of his greatest lyric poetry; this work was committed to memory by his wife and first published abroad more than twenty years after the poet's death. Mandel'shtam was allowed to return to Moscow in 1937; he was re-arrested in 1938, and died in a camp near Vladivostok. He was rehabilitated in 1956, but substantially republished in the USSR only in the 1970s. One of the most original and influential poets of the twentieth century, whose early dense complexity of style gives way to a simpler but still difficult manner in the lyrics of the exile period. A proud and courageous man, aware of his stature, Mandel'shtam was irreconcilably opposed to utilitarian or political demands on art. He is immortalized in his widow's two volumes of memoirs. GSS

MANIZER, Matvey Genrikhovich (1891–1966) Sculptor. Born in St Petersburg, Manizer adapted his lessons in academic sculpture received before the Revolution at the Academy of Arts to the demands of the new Realism in the 1920s, contributing to Lenin's Plan of Monumental Propaganda and becoming a member of AKhRR. He was responsible for several important statues and complexes in the 1920s and thirties, for example *To the Victims of 9 January, 1905* (1931) in Leningrad, and also worked on the Revolution Square metro station in Moscow (1936–39). JEB

MANKIN, Valentin Borisovich (b. 1938) Sportsman. One of the world's finest yachtsmen in the 1960s and 1970s, he competed in four Olympics (1968–80), becoming Olympic champion three times in different classes: the Finn in 1968, the Tempest in 1972 and the Star in 1980. In between he took a silver medal in the Tempest class in 1976. Born near Kiev, he did most of his sailing out of Sevastopol'

from the Black Sea Naval Yacht Club.
JWR

MANTSEV, Vasiliy Nikolaevich
(1888–1939) An old Bolshevik, a
leading member of the Cheka/OGPU,
and an industrial organizer. Mantsev
joined the party in 1906 and was one
of those who sided with the Left Communists in spring 1918. He studied at
the Juridical Faculty of Moscow University, becoming the head of, first the
Moscow, then the Ukrainian Cheka
during the Civil War. He was a
member of the collegia of both OGPU
and Rabkrin in 1923. Dzerzhinsky
took him to VSNKh with other Chek-
ists in 1924, and he remained there
after Dzerzhinsky's death in 1926,
having made a good impression on the
non-party specialists in VSNKh. In
1928 he was simultaneously head of
the planning department, Rector of
the Industrial Academy, chairman of
the Arbitration Commission, chairman of the Council on Local Trade
Affairs, and chairman of the Council
of Textile Syndicates. After leaving
VSNKh in 1930, he became Deputy
People's Commissar for Finance and
chairman of the Committee on State
Orders (1930–34). He was a witness
at the Bukharin trial in March 1938,
but was executed in 1939. RWD

**MARCHENKO, Anatoliy Tikhono-
vich** (1938–1986) Worker, human
rights activist, and author. He was
imprisoned five times for social or political deviance: for trying to leave the
USSR without permission (1960–66);
after writing the first detailed account
of the post-Stalin labour camp system
(1968–69) published as *My Testimony*
in 1969; for views expressed in camp
(1969–71); for violating his surveillance regime (1975–79); and for
writing and circulating his own works
on socio-political topics (1981–86). In

1986 he died in prison on hunger-
strike, in circumstances which led
his widow Larissa Bogoraz, a long-
standing dissident, to suspect foul
play. PBR

**MARDZHANOV, Konstantin Alek-
sandrovich (Mardzhanishvili,
Kote)** (1872–1933) Georgian stage
director. Mardzhanov worked at the
Moscow Art Theatre and left in 1913
to found his own Free (*Svobodnyy*)
Theatre. After 1917 he staged mass
revolutionary theatrical spectacles in
Petrograd, striving to reflect the
'tempo of the contemporary epoch'.
He returned to Georgia in 1923 and
became one of the founding fathers of
Georgian Soviet theatre. RT

MARETSKAYA, Vera Petrovna
(1906–1973) Eminent stage and film
actress. Maretskaya was a pupil of
Vakhtangov, worked with Zavadsky
and played leading roles at Mossoviet
Theatre from 1940 including the title
role in Afinogenov's *Mashenka* (1941).
She began her film career in comedies
such as Protazanov's *The Tailor from
Torzhok* (1925) and Barnet's *The House
on Trubnaya* (1928) and went on to
more serious and heroic roles in the
Zarkhi and Kheifits *A Member of the
Government* (1940) and *The Village
Teacher* (1947). RT

**MARKAR'YANTS, Vladimir
Surenovich** (b. 1934) An Armenian
who has spent most of his life in the
Stavropol' region. He was Chairman
of the Executive Committee of Stavropol' City from 1974 to 1976, in
which capacity he must have been well
known to M. S. Gorbachev. Later he
became First Secretary of Stavropol'
gorkom (1982–85) and Secretary of the
kraikom (1985–88). This background
must lie behind his appointment in
January 1989 to the difficult job of
Chairman of the Armenian Council of

Ministers; compare the career of O. I. Lobov. JHM

MARSHAK, Samuil Yakovlevich (1887–1964) A poet and translator, born in Voronezh, who showed precocious early promise. He spent the years 1912 to 1914 in England. Marshak moved to Petrograd in 1922 and became involved in children's literature. He published his satirical masterpiece *Mister-Twister* in 1933. In 1938 he moved to Moscow. He is a highly regarded translator of English poetry, especially of Burns and the Shakespeare sonnets. GSS

MARTINSON, Sergey Aleksandrovich (b. 1899) Actor. Martinson worked with Meyerkhol'd, specialising in grotesque caricature roles, including the productions of Erdman's *The Warrant* (1925), Tret'yakov's *Roar, China!* (1926) and Vishnevsky's *The Final and Decisive Battle* (1931). He also acted in numerous film comedies, playing roles ranging from Coolidge Curzonovich Poincaré in the experimental FEKS satire *The Adventures of Oktyabrina* (1924) to Hitler in *The New Adventures of Schweik* (1943) and *The Third Stroke* (1948). RT

MARTYNOV, Leonid Nikolaevich (1905–1980) A poet, born in Omsk. Martynov was active as poet and journalist in Siberia before the Second World War, but was silenced from 1947 to 1955. Thereafter he was recognized as an important and original philosophical poet. GSS

MARTYNOV, Vladen Arkad'evich (b. 1929) The Director of the Institute of World Economy and International Relations (IMEMO) of the Academy of Sciences of the USSR since 1989, Martynov was born in Saratov and graduated from Leningrad University in 1952 before pursuing graduate studies there (1952–55) and going on to teach political economy in the Leningrad Engineering-Economic Institute (1955–57). Since 1957 he has been at IMEMO – from 1961 to 1971 as head of the sector of agrarian problems and from 1971 as deputy director until he succeeded Primakov as director in 1989. A member of the state commission of the Council of Ministers on economic reform, Martynov is a Corresponding Member of the Academy of Sciences. Among his books as editor and co-author are *Contemporary Imperialism: Tendencies and Contradictions* (1988) and *Contemporary Monopoly Capitalism* (8 volumes, 1981–85). AHB

MASALIEV, Absamat Masalievich (b. 1933) A Kirghiz, trained as a mining engineer, Masaliev transferred to party work in Osh *oblast'* in 1961. He was Chairman of the Executive Committee of the Kirghiz capital Frunze (1972–74), Secretary for Industry of its Central Committee (1974–79), and First Secretary of Issyk-Kul' *obkom* (1979–85). Since November 1985 Masaliev has been First Secretary of the Kirghiz Communist Party. In 1986 he became a member of the Central Committee of the CPSU and in July 1990 was elected to the new, expanded Politburo. JHM

MASHEROV, Petr Mironovich (1918–1980) A teacher from the Vitebsk region who fought with the partisans in Belorussia (1941–44), and became a politician there. He was First Secretary of the Komsomol of Belorussia from 1947 to 1954, after which he was promoted to party work and held office in Minsk and Brest provinces. From 1962 to 1965 he was Second Secretary of the Belorussian Central Committee of the party, and, for most of the Brezhnev period, First Secretary (1965–80). This brought with it candidate membership of the All-Union Politburo (1966–80). He was killed in a car accident in 1980. JHM

MASHKOV, Il'ya Ivanovich (1881–1944) Painter. Like Fal'k, Konchalovsky, and Lentulov, Mashkov was a member of the Jack of Diamonds group before the Revolution when he had studied at the MIPSA under Konstantin Korovin and Valentin Serov. Known for his still-lives and portraits, for example, *Lady with Pheasants* (1911) and *Moscow Victuals. Loaves* (1924), often with local motifs, Mashkov taught at Vkhutemas until 1930. Among his pupils were Deineka and Goncharov. JEB

MASLENNIKOV, Arkadiy Afrikanovich (b. 1931) A leading Soviet journalist, Maslennikov became in April 1990 press secretary to President Mikhail Gorbachev – a new post attached to the new-style presidency. Maslennikov, an economics graduate of Moscow University where he studied in the first half of the 1950s (overlapping with the Gorbachev and Anatoliy Luk'yanov) worked for a time at the Institute of World Economy. From there he moved to *Pravda* as a special correspondent from 1965, working successively in India, Pakistan and Great Britain. When he returned to Moscow in the late 1980s he became the editor responsible for capitalist countries on *Pravda* and a member of the editorial board of the newspaper. In August 1989 he became the founding head of the press centre attached to the Supreme Soviet of the USSR and in April 1990 the head of the press service – and press secretary – of the President of the USSR. AHB

MASLYUKOV, Yuriy Dmitrievich (b. 1937) A leading Soviet politician with a technocratic background in military industry, Maslyukov has been Chairman of the State Planning Commission (Gosplan) and the First Deputy Chairman of the Council of Ministers since 1988, a full member of the Politburo from September 1989 to July 1990 and a member of the Presidential Council since March 1990.

Born in Leninabad in the Tadzhik republic, Maslyukov is Russian by nationality and an engineer by education and training. He graduated from the Leningrad Institute of Mechanics in 1962 and joined the Communist Party in 1966. Between 1962 and 1974 he worked in a series of ever more senior engineering posts before moving into an administrative post in the Ministry of Defence Industry. From 1979 to 1982 he was First Deputy Minister of the Defence Industry and in that latter year moved to Gosplan as First Deputy Chairman with special responsibility for the armaments industry. He became a full member of the Central Committee in 1986, a candidate member of the Politburo in February 1988 and a full Politburo member in September 1989.

With his present responsibilities as head of Gosplan, together with Presidential Council and Politburo membership, and his extensive knowledge of military industry, Maslyukov has as one of his more important responsibilities the overseeing of the conversion of a considerable part of Soviet defence industry to civilian production. AHB

MASOL, Vitaliy Andreevich (b. 1928) Ukrainian by nationality and Chairman of the Council of Ministers of the Ukraine since 1987, Masol has been a member of the Communist

Party since 1956. In 1986 he became a member of the Central Committee of the CPSU and in 1989 was promoted to full membership. His background has been in industry, where he rose through the ranks to become a factory manager, and in the economic planning organs of the Ukraine where he was deputy head of the Ukrainian Gosplan from 1972 to 1979 and its head from 1979 to 1987 when he took over as head of government in the Ukraine. Masol, who has a higher technical education, was elected to the Congress of People's Deputies of the USSR in 1989 from the Lenin territorial district of the Donetsk region. He was critical of Ryzhkov's May 1990 economic reform package from a conservative rather than more radically reformist standpoint.
AHB

MASSALITINOVA, Varvara Osipovna (1878–1945) Character actress. Massalitinova was associated with the Malyy Theatre from 1922. Her stage appearances included Tolstoy's *The Fruits of Enlightenment* (1932), *The Death of Tarelkin* (1936) and Leonov's *The Wolf* (1939). She is however more widely known for her portrayal of the old woman in Donskoy's Gor'ky film trilogy (1938–39).
RT

MATVEEV, Aleksandr Terent'evich (1878–1960) Sculptor. Born in Saratov, after a varied education there, in Moscow, St Petersburg and Western Europe (assimilating the influences of Bourdelle and Rodin), Matveev became a professor at the reformed Academy of Arts in 1918. For Lenin's Plan of Monumental Propaganda he produced one of the first statues to Marx (outside the Smony Institute, Petrograd, in 1918), and later he did many portraits of Russian luminaries such as Chekhov and Gor'ky. JEB

MATVEEVA, Novella Nikolaevna (b. 1934) Poet, born near Leningrad, resident in Moscow since the early 1960s. Matveeva is the only prominent female guitar poet of the first generation; her songs and poems have an element of winsome escapist fantasy.
GSS

MAVRINA, Tat'yana Alekseevna (b. 1902) Graphic artist. Born in Nizhniy Novgorod, a pupil of Fal'k at Vkhutemas in the 1920s, and much influenced by Russian icons and *lubki*, Mavrina is remembered for her book illustrations and graphic renderings of old Russian towns, as in her album *Ancient Russian Towns* (1942–48). JEB

MAYAKOVSKY, Vladimir Vladimirovich (1893–1930) A poet, who came to Moscow from Georgia in 1906, involved himself in underground revolutionary activity, and studied art from 1911. A leading light in the Futurist movement, he made his name with swaggering dramatizations of his own outsize personality (first collection, *I*, 1913; long poems include *A Cloud in Trousers* (1915) and coarse declarations of opposition to the art of the past (*A Slap in the Face of Public Taste*, with Khlebnikov and others, 1912). Wholeheartedly committed to the revolutionary cause, he cast himself as its 'drummer-boy' ('Left March', 1918), worked as slogan writer in the early 1920s, and versified its myths in the long poems *150,000,000* (1920), *Vladimir Il'ich Lenin* (1924), *Good!* (1927), and *At the Top of my Voice* (1930). The intimate strain in his work, often seen as fatally self-suppressed, culminates in the great tragic love poem *About This* (1923). In the early 1920s he led 'The Left Front of Art' (LEF), promoting politically committed, stylistically experimental art closely linked with contemporary advances in technology. Mayakovsky frequently travelled abroad after 1922, most notably to the USA in 1925. He found himself increasingly out of tune with Soviet literary developments in the late 1920s; his satirical plays *The Bed-Bug* (1928) and *The Bath-House* (1929) are directed against the new philistinism. He committed suicide. Posthumously canonized as the leading poet of Soviet communism and heavily promoted as the official bard of Stalin's Russia, Mayakovsky in fact called mightily, with unfailing inventiveness, for the liberation of the individual spirit from the restrictions that accrue from physical and ideological inertia. GSS

MAZUROV, Kirill Trofimovich (1914–1989) The most prominent of a group of Belorussian politicians who were active in All-Union affairs in the 1970s. Like others in it he made his mark in the partisan movement in Belorussia during the Second World War, and he became First Secretary of the Belorussian Komsomol immediately after it. After a number of party posts in Minsk he became Chairman of the Council of Ministers of Belorussia in 1953, and party First Secretary there from 1956 to 1965. The latter position earned him candidate membership of the CPSU Presidium (Politburo). When Brezhnev came to power he was promoted to First Deputy Chairman of the Council of Ministers and full member of the Politburo. But in November 1978, he was retired from both these positions, allegedly on health grounds. He reappeared in public life in the mid 1980s as head of the Council of Veterans of War and Labour, and wrote disparagingly of Brezhnev. JHM

MEDVED, Aleksander Vasil'evich (b. 1937) Sportsman. One of the most outstanding men in the history of free-style wrestling, he was the only wrestler to win the Olympic title at three Games (1964–72). He was seven times world superheavyweight champion, three times European and eight times national champion. Born in the village of Belaya Tserkov, near Kiev, he settled in Minsk where he became Candidate of Pedagogical Science and, upon retirement from competitive wrestling, head of the Physical Education Department of the Minsk Radio Engineering Institute, continuing to work in wrestling as an international referee. JWR

MEDVEDEV, Nikolay Nikolaevich (b. 1933) Although a Russian by nationality, Medvedev is a member of Sajudis and the Sejm in Lithuania and has defended the Lithuanian cause in Moscow where he is a member of the Soviet of Nationalities of the USSR Supreme Soviet, having won a substantial majority in Kaunas in the elections to the Congress of People's Deputies of the USSR in 1989. Medvedev belongs to the Inter-Regional Group of Deputies within the Soviet parliament and he is a member of the Commission of the Soviet of Nationalities on Nationality, National Policy and Inter-Ethnic Relations. He has a higher technical education and is a sector head in a scientific institute in Kaunas. AHB

MEDVEDEV, Roy Aleksandrovich (b. 1925) One of the most prolific and objective of Soviet historians, Roy Medvedev wrote many of his most important works while being treated as a dissident by the Soviet authorities from the nineteen-sixties to the late nineteen-eighties. Expelled from the Communist Party under Brezhnev in 1969 and denied a position in an academic institution, Medvedev continued to do a prodigious amount of research as a private scholar; in the Gorbachev era his contribution has been recognized within his own country as it already had been for many years by foreign scholars.

Even during his lengthy period as a dissident, Medvedev was an untypical one, inasmuch as he took a much more favourable view of Marx and Lenin than did the majority of dissidents and placed most, although not all, of the culpability for the gulf between revolutionary ideals and what actually happened in the Soviet Union on Stalin and his collaborators. Medvedev's views were shared by many reformers within the Communist Party, although they either expressed them less boldly or only in private during the Brezhnev years. His outlook is fully in tune with the political reform and *glasnost'* of the Gorbachev era and it was a logical development that Medvedev should be readmitted to the Communist Party (in 1989) and be widely published in the Soviet Union itself. He was elected to the Central Committee of the party in 1990.

Among Roy Medvedev's numerous writings, *Let History Judge*, his history of Stalinism published in English in 1971, and in a new and extensively revised edition in 1989, stands out as his major work. His other books include *On Socialist Democracy* (1975), *Political Essays* (1977), *The End of Silence* (1981), *Khrushchev* (1982) and *All Stalin's Men* (1983).

Medvedev's political comeback within his own country has been a spectacular one and he was able to demonstrate public support as well as support from party reformers now in influential positions. He topped the poll in the competitive election in the Voroshilov district of Moscow in 1989 and became a member not only of the Congress of People's Deputies but subsequently of the Supreme Soviet as well. He has already shown himself to be a skilful parliamentarian, one generally supportive of Gorbachev but attentive to the rights of minorities. He is a member of the Committee of the Supreme Soviet for Questions of Legislation, Legality and Law and Order and was elected Chairman of a Commission of the Congress of People's Deputies set up to investigate the activities of the group in the USSR Procuracy headed by Tel'man Gdlyan and Nikolay Ivanov. AHB

MEDVEDEV, Vadim Andreevich (b. 1929) The member of the Politburo and Secretariat of the Central Committee overseeing ideology from September 1988 until July 1990, Medvedev made his early career in Leningrad. He studied and later taught economics at Leningrad University and from 1956 to 1968 lectured at the Leningrad Institute of Railway Transport and at the Leningrad Technological Institute. He entered the party apparatus of the Leningrad city organization in 1968 as secretary responsible for ideology, and in 1970 moved to the Central Committee in Moscow as a deputy head of the Department of Propaganda where until 1973 his immediate superior was Aleksandr Yakovlev.

From 1978 to 1983 Medvedev was Rector of the Academy of Social Sciences of the Central Committee of the CPSU, but he re-entered the Central Committee apparatus as head of the Department of Science and Educational Institutions (1983–86). His promotion has been quite rapid during Gorbachev's General Secretaryship. He became a Secretary of the Central Committee with responsibility for the Department of Socialist Countries in 1986 and in 1988 became a full member of the Politburo while retaining his Secretaryship.

Medvedev has been a less radical reformer than Yakovlev but generally supportive of Gorbachev within the Soviet leadership. He was not re-elected in July 1990 to the Politburo, Secretariat or even the Central Committee; he was, however, brought into the Presidential Council. He has been a Corresponding Member of the Academy of Sciences since 1984 and a member of the Congress of People's Deputies since 1989. AHB

MEDVEDEV, Zhores Aleksandrovich (b. 1925) The identical twin brother of Roy, Zhores Medvedev was born in Tbilisi and is a graduate of Leningrad University. He was a prominent geneticist and biochemist within the Soviet Union who incurred the wrath of the authorities in Brezhnev's time with his *samizdat* works which, among other things, showed the damage which had been done to Soviet science by T. D. Lysenko and which analysed censorship of the mail in the Soviet Union. He was incarcerated in a psychiatric hospital in 1970 but released following strong protests from sections of the scientific community within the Soviet Union and abroad. When on a visit to Britain he was deprived of his Soviet citizenship and he has lived in London since 1973. He was able to visit the Soviet Union again for the first time in the late 1980s. In Britain Medvedev has combined scientific work as a gerontologist at the National Institute for Medical Research with a remarkable number of books and articles of a Sovietological nature. His books include *The Rise and Fall of T. D. Lysenko*, *The Medvedev Papers*, *Ten Years after Ivan Denisovich* and *Soviet Science*. AHB

MEDVEDKIN, Aleksandr Ivanovich (1900–1989) Film director. Medvedkin is best known for his work on the film train in the Donbass region in the early 1930s and for his biting satires *Happiness* (1934) and *The Miracle Worker* (1937). RT

MEKHLIS, Lev Zakharovich (1889–1953) Former Chief of the Main Political Administration of the Red Army. Mekhlis, who was Jewish, was born the son of a clerk. During the Civil War he worked as a political commissar and became a senior official in the People's Commissariat of Workers and Peasants Inspectorate (1921–22). For the next five years he worked as an official in the party Central Committee apparatus and in Stalin's personal secretariat. Mekhlis was editor of *Pravda* (1930–37). After this varied background he was appointed Deputy People's Commissar of Defence and Chief of the Main Political Administration of the Red Army for the period 1937 to 1940. This gave Mekhlis a key role in enforcing the party political line and fostering patriotism in the armed forces in advance of the Nazi attack. He also held the posts of People's Commissar of State Control (1940–41) and Minister of State Control (1945–49). During the Nazi-Soviet war he was a member of the military councils of several Armies and Army Groups. RA

MEKK (von Meck), Nikolay Karlovich (1863–1929) Chairman of the board and largest shareholder on the Moscow-Kazan' railway before the revolution, Mekk remained in Soviet

Russia as a senior adviser and planner in the People's Commissariat for Transport in the 1920s. He was arrested and executed in 1929. RWD

MELIKOV, Arif Dzhangirovich (b. 1933) Composer. Arif Melikov was born in Baku. Having studied at the Azerbaydzhan Conservatory as a pupil of Kara-Karaev, he graduated in 1958, becoming a member of the teaching staff in 1965. He was made an Honoured Art Worker of the Azerbaydzhan SSR in the same year (1965). Often utilizing national material in his compositions, his colourful ballet *The Legend of Love* (1961) has been widely performed in the Soviet Union. GS

MELIK-PASHAEV, Aleksandr Shamil'evich (1905–1964) Conductor. Aleksandr Melik-Pashaev was born in Tbilisi and died in Moscow. His major performances included Borodin's *Prince Igor* and Prokofiev's *War and Peace*, and an American Academy of Arts Prize for his recording of Musorgsky's *Boris Godunov*. GS

MEL'NIKOV, Konstantin Stepanovich (1890–1974) Architect. Mel'nikov was born in Moscow. One of the primary forces of early Soviet architecture with a highly individual interpretation of Constructivism, he was harshly criticized during the Stalin regime for his 'formalism'. Trained firstly as a painter at the MIPSA and then in private architectural studios in Moscow, Mel'nikov attracted attention after the Revolution with his Makhorka Tobacco pavilion at the All-Russian Agricultural Exhibition in Moscow (1923) and then with his audacious design for the Soviet pavilion at the 'Exposition des Arts Décoratifs' in Paris (1925). A member of ASNOVA and OSA, Mel'-nikov was involved in many projects for garages, houses (including his own), a Garden City, etc., although after 1930 few of his designs were implemented. JEB

MEL'NIKOV, Leonid Grigor'evich (b. 1906) Russian politician. A client of G. M. Malenkov, Mel'nikov spent almost his entire career in the Ukraine. Beginning as a Komsomol secretary in Donetsk, he rose to become second secretary of the republic in 1945. In 1949 Mel'nikov succeeded Khrushchev as First Secretary of the Ukrainian party. After Stalin's death, he was removed from his post in the Ukraine and dropped from candidate membership in the Presidium; Mel'-nikov was the most prominent casualty of Beria's drive to promote national cadres. Although he openly supported Malenkov in the Spring of 1953, the latter was unable to restore his fortunes after Beria's fall. Mel'-nikov subsequently served in a number of minor state posts. WJT

MEL'NIKOV, Yakov Fedorovich (1896–1960) Sportsman. Born in Moscow, he became a top speed skater before the 1917 Revolution and was instrumental in developing the sport after 1917. He was Russian champion in 1915, and dominated Soviet speed skating for twenty years, until the age of forty-one in 1935, setting over twenty national records at various distances. He was the only Soviet athlete to hold any pre-war European title. Since 1960 an annual Mel'nikov Memorial Speed Skating Championship has been held in the USSR. JWR

MENDYBAEV, Marat Samievich (b. 1936) A Kazakh engineer, Mendybaev worked in coal-processing factories in Karaganda until 1970 and then moved to the local party organization, becoming Second Secretary of Karaganda *gorkom* in 1979. He was then two years in the Kazakhstan Central Committee apparatus, three years as an official in Kustanai province and became First Secretary of Alma-Ata *obkom* in 1985. From 1988 to 1989 Mendybaev was Second Secretary of the Kazakhstan Communist Party and then became Deputy Chairman of the Council of Ministers of Kazakhstan. JHM

MENZBIR (Menzbier), Mikhail Aleksandrovich (1855–1935) Zoologist, ornithologist, biogeographer, comparative anatomist. A student of N. A. Severtsov, Menzbir graduated from Moscow University and became its professor of zoology in 1886. His classic work *Birds of Russia* (1883–85) established his international reputation as one of the world's leading ornithologists, but he was also a zoologist in the broad natural history tradition, publishing important works on systematics, comparative anatomy, biogeography, and ecology. The leading zoological supporter of Darwinism in Russia, he was also receptive to morphology, embryology, and other new trends of his day and trained several generations of leading Russian zoologists, including morphologist A. N. Severtsov and experimentalist N. K. Kol'tsov. He was elected a corresponding member of the Petersburg Academy of Sciences in 1896. A liberal democrat, he left Moscow University in 1911 in protest at its political take-over by tsarist education minister Kasso and taught at the Bestuzhev Higher Courses for Women (1911–17). After the revolution, he briefly returned to Moscow University as rector (1917–19) but once again found political control of the university unacceptable. In the

1920s he edited an eight-volume edition of Darwin's works (1925–29) and was elected an honorary member of the USSR Academy of Sciences (1926) and subsequently a full member (1929). As president of the prestigious Moscow Society of Naturalists (1915–35), he managed to maintain its quality and relative autonomy through the First World War, two revolutions, the Civil War, and the imposition of Stalinism. MBA

MENZHINSKY, Vyacheslav Rudol'fovich (1874–1934) An old Bolshevik who became head of the Soviet security police, Menzhinsky was born in St Petersburg, the son of a schoolteacher. A party member from 1902, he returned to Russia from West European and American exile in the summer of 1917 and was briefly the first People's Commissar for Finance after the Bolshevik Revolution before becoming Consul-General in Berlin from 1918 to 1919. From late 1919 he was one of the leaders of the Cheka and from 1926 to 1934 the Chairman of OPGU (as the security forces were known by that time). Unlike the next three secret police chiefs – Yagoda, Yezhov and Beria – Menzhinsky died a natural death. AHB

MERETSKOV, Kirill Afanas'evich (1897–1968) Former Chief of General Staff. Meretskov was the wartime commander with greatest responsibility for the campaign against Finland (1941–44). He served as Chief-of-Staff of Moscow, of the Belorussian Military Districts, and of the Special Red Banner Far Eastern Army (1931–36), He survived the purges to command the Volga then Leningrad Military Districts (1938–39), and gained his first experience of combat against the Finns as Commander of the Seventh Army during the Winter War (1939–40). He was briefly Chief of the General Staff in autumn 1940, and Deputy People's Commissar of Defence in 1941. Meretskov's primary wartime role was as Commander of the Volkhov, then Karelian Army Groups (1941–45), which earned him the rank of Marshal of the Soviet Union. He was an independent-minded commander and Stalin had to warn him twice towards the close of the campaign against Finland that, if he exceeded his brief in pressing the Soviet offensive against Finland, he would promptly be dismissed. He also commanded the First Far Eastern Army Group in the war with Japan, and various military districts in the post-war years. RA

MERKUROV, Sergey Dmitrievich (1881–1952) Sculptor. Merkurov was born in Aleksandropol'. After studying in Zurich and Munich, he emerged as a leading Realist sculptor with his famous statue to Dostoevsky in Moscow (1913; erected 1918). Working in granite and marble, he produced a number of other statues after the Revolution, including the Timiryazev in Moscow (1923) and several portraits of Kalinin, Lenin and Tolstoy. JEB

MESSERER, Asaf Mikhaylovich (b. 1903) Dancer, choreographer, teacher. Messerer took private ballet lessons with Mikhail Mordkin and danced with the ballet company of Moscow's Theatre of Working Youth before entering the Bol'shoy Ballet School, from which he graduated in 1921.

He was a leading soloist at the Bol'shoy Theatre from 1921 to 1954. Excelling in a wide range of styles – from heroic to romantic to comic – Messerer displayed impeccable technique and breathtaking jumps. In classical roles he often used expressive gestures in place of pantomime, sometimes provoking an uproar on the part of the audience and the administration. In addition to his extensive classical repertoire, Messerer was a master of grotesque and athletic roles, such as the Acrobat in *The Red Poppy* and the Fanatic in *Salambô*. His frequent partners included his sister Sulamith and, later, his wife, Irina Tikhomirnova.

Messerer taught at the Bol'shoy Ballet School from 1921 to 1960 and began teaching advanced classes at the Bol'shoy Theatre in 1942. Among his pupils are Galina Ulanova, Maya Plisetskaya (his niece), and Yekaterina Maksimova. He served as ballet master for the Bol'shoy foreign tours of 1956, 1958, and 1962, and assisted with founding a ballet school at Théâtre de la Monnaie, Brussels.

As a choreographer, Messerer has staged versions of numerous classical ballets, including *Sleeping Beauty* (1936), *Swan Lake* (1937), and *Coppélia* (1974). He has also staged original works, such as *Schumaniana* (1924), *Battle of the Toys* (1924), *Class Concert* (1960), and *Ballet School* (1962). He has appeared in films, received the State Prize of the USSR (1941), and is the author of *Lessons of Classical Dance* (1967) and *Dance, Thought, Time* (1979), his memoirs. SCS

MESYATS, Valentin Karpovich (b. 1928) A Soviet politician with a specialization in agriculture, Mesyats was born in the Kemerovo region of Russia and graduated from the Timiryazev Agricultural Academy in Moscow in 1953. He worked as an agronomist, as a Secretary of the Moscow *obkom* and as First Deputy Minister of Agriculture for the Russian republic before being sent in 1971 to work with Bre-

zhnev's ally, D. A. Kunaev, as second secretary of the Communist Party of Kazakhstan. In 1976 he was brought back to Moscow as Minister of Agriculture for the USSR, a post he held until November 1985 when he became First Secretary of the Moscow regional party committee. He was still in that office in the early summer of 1990, although his relations with Gorbachev have been cool and he has been critical of aspects of the post-1985 reform programme. Mesyats was elected to the Congress of People's Deputies in 1989.
AHB

METREVELI, Aleksander Irakl'-evich (b. 1944) Sportsman. Unlike some other East European countries, the USSR has never produced a top world tennis player. The nearest any Soviet player has come to top world rankings was Metreveli. Born in Tbilisi, he dominated Soviet tennis from 1966 to 1973, and won nine European titles (1967–73), often with his doubles partner, the Estonian Toomas Leius. His best international performance was winning the Australian Open tennis title. Upon retirement from competition he turned to sports journalism and, with the encouragement of cooperatives in the late 1980s, opened a string of private tennis clubs along the Black Sea coast.
JWR

MEYERKHOL'D, Vsevolod Emil'e-vich (1874–1940) Meyerkhol'd was undoubtedly the leading figure in twentieth-century Russian, if not world, theatre. He joined the Moscow Art Theatre at its inception in 1898 as an actor and director and created the roles of Treplev in Chekhov's *The Seagull* and Tusenbach in *Three Sisters*. He toured with his own Theatre of New Drama between 1902 and 1905, initially with a repertoire of Chekhov

and Gor'ky in the naturalistic style of the Moscow Art Theatre but gradually moving towards a more modernistic theatre of conventions in plays such as Maeterlinck's *Monna Vanna* and Przybyszewski's *The Golden Fleece* and *Snow*.

Meyerkhol'd returned to the Moscow Art Theatre in 1905 at Stanislavsky's invitation to run that theatre's experimental studio. 'In a nutshell,' wrote Stanislavsky, 'the credo of the new studio led to a point where realism had outlived its time.' The studio closed in 1906 and Meyerkhol'd again toured with what he now called the Society of New Drama, playing in works by Gor'ky, Hauptmann, Ibsen, Maeterlinck and Strindberg. In the same year Meyerkhol'd became Principal Director for Komissarzhevskaya's theatre in St Petersburg and his productions included Ibsen's *Hedda Gabler*, Maeterlinck's *Sister Beatrice* and Blok's *The Fairground Booth*. Here he developed the theory and practice of his notion of the actor as a kind of marionette manipulated by the director. In its extreme form this idea led to a break with Komissarzhevskaya in 1907. In 1908 Meyerkhol'd moved to the Imperial theatres and his productions at the Aleksandrinsky Theatre included Molière's *Don Juan* (1910), Shaw's *Pygmalion* (1915), Ostrovsky's *The Storm* (1916) and Lermontov's *Masquerade* (1917). At the Marinsky he produced several operas, notably Wagner's *Tristan and Isolde* (1909), Gluck's *Orpheus and Eurydice* (1911) and Richard Strauss's *Elektra* (1913). Under the pseudonym of Doctor Dapertutto he also ran an experimental drama studio where his productions were heavily influenced by the stylized methods of the *commedia dell'arte* and edited the journal *Love for Three Oranges*. At this period in his career he made two films, one of Wilde's *The Picture of Dorian Gray* (1915) and the other of Przybyszewski's *The Strong Man* (1916).

After the Revolution Meyerkhol'd proclaimed the virtues of a revolutionary upheaval in theatre in his *Theatrical October* (1920) but was restrained from realizing this programme when put in charge of the theatre section of the People's Commissariat of Enlightenment by Lunacharsky. He was the first director to stage a Soviet play, Mayakovsky's *Mystery-Bouffe* (1918) and the repertoire of his theatre in the early twenties reflected his demand for 'tendentious plays, plays that have only one end in view – to serve the cause of the Revolution'.

His most brilliant productions from this era have changed the face of theatre and the most notable of these are Verhaeren's *The Dawn* (1920), Crommelynck's *The Magnanimous Cuckold* and Sukhovo-Kobylin's *The Death of Tarelkin* (both 1922), Tret'-yakov's version of Martinet's *Earth Rampant* (1923), Ehrenburg's *Give Us Europe!* (1924), Faiko's *Bubus the Teacher* and Erdman's *The Warrant* (both 1925). He also produced revised versions of classics such as Ostrovsky's *The Forest* (1924), Gogol''s *The Government Inspector* (1926) and Griboedov's *Woe from Wit* (1928). In these productions Meyerkhol'd developed his theory of bio-mechanics which subjugated the actor's mind and body to the discipline of gymnastic control and the actor more completely to the dictates of the director. He continued his association with Mayakovsky, producing both *The Bed-Bug* (1929) and *The Bath House*, premiered in March

1930 less than a month before Mayakovsky's suicide. He also produced Vishnevsky's *The Final and Decisive Battle* (1931) for the first time. At the end of his career he returned again to the classics and his production of Dumas' *The Lady with the Camellias* (1934) marked a certain rapprochement with the naturalistic style of Stanislavsky.

Nevertheless in the increasingly conservative artistic climate of the 1930s Meyerkhol'd was subjected to accusations of Formalism and 'systematic deviation from Soviet reality' and to a campaign of character assassination. On 8 January 1938 his theatre was closed and in March Stanislavsky invited Meyerkhol'd to work as his assistant at his Opera Theatre. When Stanislavsky died in August 1938, he told his assistant Bakhrushin, 'Take care of Meyerkhol'd; he is my sole heir in the theatre – here or anywhere else.' Meyerkhol'd became the theatre's Artistic Director and his last production of Verdi's *Rigoletto*, had its première on 10 March 1939.

He was arrested on 20 June and his wife's body was found shortly afterwards, mutilated like that of Rigoletto's Gilda. Meyerkhol'd was shot in prison on 2 February 1940. He was officially rehabilitated on 22 November 1955. RT

MEZHLAUK, Ivan Ivanovich (1891–1938) A teacher by profession, Mezhlauk graduated from Khar'kov University in 1916. A party member from 1918, he was chief of supplies for the Red Army during the Civil War, and a leading industrial manager and party official in the 1920s. He occupied important positions in the apparatus of Sovnarkom (1930–33), including the secretaryship of STO. He then held posts in education administration

(1936–37). He and V. I. Mezhlauk were brothers. RWD

MEZHLAUK, Valeriy Ivanovich (1893–1938) An old Bolshevik engineer, leading economic organizer and planner held in high regard by both Soviet citizens and foreigners working in the USSR. Born in Khar'kov, the son of a teacher, Mezhlauk graduated from Khar'kov University in 1917, and joined the party. He held economic posts in the Ukraine during the Civil War. During the NEP period he was a prominent figure first in transport, then in VSNKh (1924–31), where he was in charge of metal industries for several years. He was first deputy chairman of Gosplan (1931–34), chairman (1934–37), People's Commissar for Heavy Industry after Ordzhonikidze's death in 1937, and People's Commissar for the Engineering Industry (1937). He was also deputy chairman of Sovnarkom and the STO (1934–37). A candidate member of the party Central Committee (1927–34), he was a full member from 1934 until he was arrested and executed in 1938. RWD

MICHURIN, Ivan Vladimirovich (1855–1935) Practical agronomist. A self-styled Russian Luther Burbank without formal education, Michurin established an experimental plot in the town of Kozlov in 1875 where he sought to create new fruit varieties using stock-scion grafting ('vegetative hybridization') and other practical techniques. His work was largely ignored until 1920 when Lenin, impressed by popular works on American agriculture, decreed that his work be studied. During the collectivization of Soviet agriculture, Michurin was heroically portrayed in the press as a model of practical achievement. The town of Kozlov was renamed Michu-

rinsk in 1932, and in 1935 he was named a member of the Lenin All-Union Academy of Agricultural Sciences and an honorary member of the USSR Academy of Sciences. Throughout his life Michurin had disdained all theory, but after his death T. D. Lysenko assumed his mantle, characterizing his own increasingly elaborate theories as 'Michurinist biology'. From 1930 Michurin was depicted in the Soviet Union as a major scientist of great achievement, and this trend has continued even after the official repudiation of Lysenkoism in 1965. MBA

MICHURINA-SAMOILOVA, Vera Arkad'evna (1866–1948) Actress. Michurina-Samoilova was a popular actress whose post-Revolutionary stage appearances included Wilde's *An Ideal Husband* (1923), Tolstoy's *The Fruits of Enlightenment* (1928), *Woe from Wit* (1928 and 1941) and *Enemies* (1933). She also played a leading part in entertaining the population during the siege of Leningrad in the Second World War. RT

MIKHALKOV, Nikita Sergeevich (b. 1945) Film director and actor. Mikhalkov's works include: *Slave of Love* (1975), *Unfinished Piece for Mechanical Piano* (1976), *Five Nights* (1978) and *Oblomov* (1979). He is the younger brother of Mikhalkov-Konchalovsky. He has recently become known as one of the least enthusiastic supporters of *perestroika* RT

MIKHALKOV-KONCHALOVSKY, Andrey Sergeevich (b. 1937) Film director. Mikhalkov-Konchalovsky's first film *The First Teacher*, set in Kirghizia after the Revolution and confronting the political and educational problems facing the new regime, marked the beginning of a 'new wave' in Soviet cinema. His subsequent films have included: *Asya's Happiness* (1966), adaptations of Turgenev's *A Nest of Gentlefolk* (1969) and Chekhov's *Uncle Vanya* (1971) and *Siberiade* (1980). RT

MIKHAYLOV, Nikolay Aleksandrovich (b. 1906) Russian political figure. Despite his lack of secondary education, N. A. Mikhaylov used a career in journalism as a springboard into the party leadership. While serving as party secretary in a metallurgical plant, he became involved in the local party press and soon landed a position on the staff of *Pravda*. A year later, in 1938, he became editor of *Komsomol'skaya Pravda* and, in the same year, the First Secretary of the Komsomol. From 1952 to 1953 he was a Central Committee Secretary and head of the *agitprop* department. Mikhaylov succeeded Khrushchev as Moscow party boss in 1953 but soon suffered a sharp decline, being appointed Ambassador to Poland in 1954, Minister of Culture in 1955, and Ambassador to Indonesia in 1960. He retired in 1963. WJT

MIKHAYLOV, Vasiliy Mikhaylovich (1894–1937) A party and government official during the interwar period, Mikhaylov was a worker's son who joined the Bolsheviks in 1915 and became an activist in the printers' trade union and on the Moscow soviet after the revolution. Mikhaylov was a member of the central party Secretariat (1921–22) and was subsequently engaged in party and trade union work in Moscow. In the late 1920s he favoured reconciliation with the Right Opposition and was later arrested. He died in imprisonment. SLW

MIKHOELS (né Vovsi), Solomon Mikhaylovich (1890–1948) A leading Soviet Jewish actor and director, Mikhoels was particularly associated with the works of Sholom Aleikhem. He was the artistic head of the Moscow Jewish Theatre from 1929 and appeared in Roshal's film *The Oppenheim Family* (1939). RT

MIKOYAN, Anastas Ivanovich (1895–1978) Anastas Mikoyan was a survivor in Soviet politics of legendary skill. He worked with every Soviet leader from Lenin to Brezhnev, during which time he made an apparently effortless transition from Bolshevik revolutionary to Stalinist to anti-Stalinist ally of Khrushchev. Though this can be seen as opportunism so finely honed as to become an art form – putting the Vicar of Bray's performance into appropriate village hall perspective – there is more to be credited to Mikoyan's account than his virtuoso (and morally dubious) talent for staying alive – and in high office – under a succession of very different leaders, including Stalin at his worst. He was a politician of real ability who at times played a skilful and important part in international diplomacy and at others a key role in domestic economic policy and administration.

Mikoyan was born, the son of a carpenter, in the Armenian village of Sanain. He attended a theological seminary in Tbilisi, following which he completed his first year of study at the Echmiadzin Theological Academy, back in his native Armenia, before devoting himself to full-time revolutionary activity. He joined the Bolshevik party in 1915 and following the February 1917 Revolution he organized the Echmiadzin soviet. Party work over the next few years took him to various parts of the Caucasus but, in particular, to Baku. It was here that Mikoyan's luck, or talent for survival, was first in evidence. The story of how the 'Twenty-six Baku Commissars' were shot in September 1918 by the British occupying forces has entered Soviet history, but there were a few Bolshevik leaders in Baku who escaped arrest at that time, and one of them was Mikoyan. Before long he was arrested in Krasnovodsk and 'only by chance', as the *Great Soviet Encyclopedia* puts it, 'escaped execution'.

In the earliest years of Soviet rule Mikoyan spent most of his time in the Caucasus, soon gaining the rank of regional party secretary. He met Lenin on a number of occasions, but was an early beneficiary of the patronage of his fellow-Caucasian, Stalin. In 1922 he was elected to candidate membership and in 1923 to full membership of the Central Committee of the party and in 1926 to candidate membership of the Politburo. He thus attended Politburo meetings for forty years (as a full member from 1935) until his retirement in 1966.

During much of that time he held a series of ministerial or quasi-ministerial posts in the spheres of trade and industry. He was appointed People's Commissar for External and Internal Trade at the age of thirty, a post he held from 1926 until 1930 when he became People's Commissar for Supplies. During the rest of his political life he was at various times the Commissar or Minister responsible for trade as a whole, for a particular branch of industry or an overlord of trade and industry. Thus, from 1937 until 1955 he was a deputy chairman of the Council of People's Commissars (renamed Council of Ministers in 1946) and from 1955 to 1964 he was First Deputy Chairman of the Council of Ministers. For more than a year (1964–65), he was the formal head of

the Soviet state as Chairman of the Presidium of the Supreme Soviet.

During the Great Purge of 1936 to 1938, when all Soviet party and state officials were at high risk, Mikoyan survived, though with far from clean hands. Even under Stalin, however, he attempted at times to exercise a moderating influence, as on the occasion when he was the only member of the Politburo to argue during a meeting in 1943 against the deportation of all Chechen and Ingush nations from the Northern Caucasus. While agreeing in principle (and even then, perhaps, from tactical necessity) that the Chechens and Ingushes deserved to be deported, Mikoyan voiced concern that the deportations would damage the reputation of the Soviet Union abroad. In the last years before Stalin's death in 1953, Mikoyan, though still formally a member of the leadership, fell out of Stalin's favour, as did Molotov. Khrushchev was later to observe that 'if Stalin had lived much longer, Molotov and Mikoyan would have met a disastrous end'.

But Mikoyan survived – as always – to become one of Khrushchev's strongest supporters during the first post-Stalin decade. An apocryphal story told in the Soviet Union was of Mikoyan and Khrushchev coming out of a Politburo meeting and into a torrential rainstorm. Mikoyan, who had the only umbrella among Politburo members, said to Khrushchev: 'You take it. I'll just dodge between the raindrops'. Mikoyan was on Khrushchev's side against the latter's conservative opponents within the leadership during the 'anti-party group' crisis of 1957. The formidable diplomatic skills of Mikoyan, of whom it was said he could make a billiard ball out of a hedgehog, were also drawn upon by Khrushchev and put to the service of easing international tension through conciliation and compromise. It was he, for example, who was given the task in 1962 of persuading Fidel Castro of the necessity of removing the Soviet missiles which had been placed in Cuba a few weeks earlier.

After surviving Khrushchev's political downfall and continuing as a Politburo member for the first eighteen months of Brezhnev's General Secretaryship, Mikoyan was to become one of the first high-level Soviet leaders to be allowed to go into honourable retirement. Though in all probability he had no choice in the matter of ending his long political career, a rule (later abandoned) that Politburo members should not continue beyond the age of seventy was applied and no disgrace was attached to Mikoyan's name. AHB

MIKOYAN, Artem Ivanovich (1905–1970) Like his better-known brother, the political leader Anastas Mikoyan, Artem was born in Armenia. In 1936 he graduated from the Zhukovsky Military Aviation Engineering Academy and then worked for a period at the Douglas factory in the United States. From 1938 he served as deputy chief of the Polikarpov aircraft design bureau. In 1940, as head of a design bureau, he began his long association with M. I. Gurevich (who retired in 1964), creating the MiG-1, the first of a highly successful series of fighters. In the spring of 1946 he created the MiG-9, the first Soviet jet fighter, going on to create the MiG-15, used with great success in the Korean War. The MiG-19 of 1954 was one of the world's first supersonic fighters; its successor, the MiG-21, proved to be

the most widely deployed military plane of the postwar years. Mikoyan was elected to the Academy of Sciences as a full member in 1966. Twice made a Hero of Socialist Labour (1956, 1957), he received six Stalin and state prizes, and one Lenin Prize. He served for many years as a Supreme Soviet deputy and joined the party in 1925. JMC

MILYUTIN, Vladimir Petrovich (1884–1937) A senior economic organizer and publicist. Milyutin, who joined the RSDLP in 1903, enduring frequent arrest, was at first a Menshevik, but in 1910 moved over to the Bolsheviks. He was an internationalist during the war. He was appointed first People's Commissar for Agriculture during the Civil War then deputy chairman of VSNKh. He held numerous posts in economic administration in the 1920s, of which the most important was that of head of the Central Statistical Administration at the time when it was being wrested from the hands of the specialist statisticians (1928–30). He served as vice-chairman of Gosplan from 1929, and was a leading figure in the Communist Academy. A member of the party Central Committee from April 1917 to 1918, he resigned temporarily after the October Revolution, as he had been an advocate of coalition government. He became a candidate member from 1920 to 1922. RWD

MINDADZE, Aleksandr Anatol'-evich (b. 1949) Scriptwriter. Mindadze is a leading Soviet scriptwriter known for his collaboration with Vadim Abdrashitov. The structure of Mindadze's plots owes much to the model of Alfred Hitchcock. RT

MINTS, Isaak Izrailovich (b. 1896) A party member since 1917, Mints has written widely on the history of the

CPSU, the Revolution and the Civil War, and the history of Soviet society. Chairman of the scientific council for the study of the October Revolution since 1962, he has had a major influence on Soviet historical analysis of the 1917 Revolution. JB

MIRSKY, D. S. (Svyatopolk-Mirsky, Prince Dmitriy Petrovich) (1890–1939) Literary critic, born near Khar'kov, brought up and educated in St Petersburg; his father was Minister of the Interior (1904–5). Mirsky fought in the White Army during the Civil War, emigrated, and taught at London University (1922–31). He moved to Moscow in 1932; his career as a pugnacious and prolific critic was cut short by arrest in 1937. He died in the camps. He began to be republished in the USSR during the 1970s. GSS

MITROKHIN, Dmitriy Isidorovich (1883–1973) Born in Eysk, Mitrokhin – one of the leading graphic artists of the Soviet Union – trained at the MIPSA, at the Stroganov Institute and then in Paris (1902–05). Close to the World of Art and Union of Russian Artists, he began to illustrate books in 1904. From 1919 to 1923 he was curator of graphics at the Russian Museum, Leningrad, and from 1924 to 1930 taught at the Vkhutemas-Vkhutein there. Working with lithography, linocuts and woodcuts, he illustrated many authors, including Hugo, Poe and Viktor Shklovsky. JEB

MITURICH, Petr Vasil'evich (1887–1956) Graphic artist. Miturich was born in St Petersburg. Known for his illustrations, portraits and landscapes, he received his art education in Kiev and then at the Academy of Arts (1909–16). Serving with the army (1916–21), he became interested in military engineering, especially forms of transport, and designed a so-called

undulator and other fantastic machines. His experimental spatial graphics of *circa* 1918 to 1921 paralleled the phonic searchings of his friend the poet Velemir Khlebnikov, and he taught graphic arts at Vkhutemas from 1923 to 1930. JEB

MOISEENKO, Yevsey Yevseevich (b. 1916) Painter. Training in Kalinin and then at the Repin Institute in Leningrad under Osmerkin, Moiseenko achieved his reputation as a dramatic interpreter of war scenes in the 1960s, when he painted a series of personal memories of the Second World War, for example, *Cherries* (1967). His expressive brushwork and ability to evoke intimate mood distinguish his art from the more histrionic style of the 1930s to 1940s. JEB

MOISEEV, Igor' Aleksandrovich (b. 1906) Leading choreographer and artistic director of the State Folk Dance Ensemble. Moiseev graduated from the Bol'shoy Ballet School in 1924, joined the Bol'shoy troupe, and performed as a soloist until 1939. His repertoire included such roles as the lead in *Joseph the Beautiful*, the Slave in *La Bayadère*, and the lead in his own ballet, *The Football Player* (1930), which marked his début as a choreographer. His early choreography also included dances for Prokof'ev's opera *Love for Three Oranges* (1930), *Salambô* (1932), and *Three Fat Men* (1935).

In 1936 he was appointed director of the choreography department of the Moscow Theatre of Folk Art and organized a national folk-dance festival featuring amateur dancers from all the Soviet republics. This group became the State Folk-dance Ensemble in 1937 and was the first Soviet company to bring folk dancing to the professional stage. Originally a group of thirty-five dancers, the Ensemble has grown to become one of the Soviet Union's largest companies, numbering more than a hundred performers and with a repertoire of more than 200 dances. Accompanied by its own orchestra, which includes a number of folk instruments, the Ensemble has toured throughout the USSR and more than forty countries with enormous success. Recent tours have included performances in the United States in 1986 and 1989.

Moiseev's choreography is based on authentic folk dances, often characterized by complex geometric patterns and virtuoso leaps and kicks. Among the Ensemble's well known dances are *Dance of the Cossack Tatars*, *The Partisans*, *Bulba*, *The Ukrainian Suite*, and *The Road to Dance*, for which Moiseev received the Lenin Prize. In addition, Moiseev choreographed *Spartacus* for the Bol'shoy Ballet (1958), founded the State Concert Ensemble (1966), and choreographed a number of one-act ballets including *The Polovtsian Dances* (1971) and *Night on Bald Mountain* (1938). scs

MOISEEV, Mikhail Alekseevich (b. 1939) Army General. The appointment of the relatively junior and unknown Moiseev as Chief of General Staff of the Armed Forces and First Deputy Minister of Defence in December 1988 as successor to Marshal Akhromeev came as a surprise, but a surprise in keeping with the Gorbachev approach to the rejuvenation of the military high command. Born in 1939, Moiseev is the first Chief of General Staff not to have seen active service during the war and he was elevated to the post after only brief experience as commander of a military district. His early years were spent in the Far East and it was there that he joined the Army in 1958 and attended the local tank school. Later, Moiseev graduated from the Frunze Military Academy (1972) and the Military Academy of the General Staff (1982). A series of junior command and staff posts led to his appointment as chief of staff of a military district. In January 1987 he succeeded Yazov, the present Minister of Defence, as Commander-in-Chief of the Far Eastern military district. Moiseev, a Russian, joined the Communist Party in 1962. In 1989 he was elected to the Congress of People's Deputies as one of the party's candidates. As a young and vigorous Chief of Staff, Moiseev is now a key figure in the restructuring of the Armed Forces at a time of force reductions and a potentially far-reaching reassessment of Soviet military doctrine. jmc

MOKANU, Aleksandr Aleksandrovich (Mocanu, Alexandru) (b. 1934) One of the two deputy chairmen of the Soviet of the Union of the USSR Supreme Soviet, Mokanu is Moldavian by nationality and was elected to the Congress of People's Deputies of the USSR from a Moldavian electoral district in 1989. Mokanu, who is a graduate of the Kishinev Agricultural Institute and has a higher degree in economics, was formerly Chairman of the Supreme Soviet in the Moldavian republic. ahb

MOLOTOV (Skryabin), Vyacheslav Mikhaylovich (1890–1986) An old Bolshevik and for many years Stalin's right-hand man, Molotov, whose real name was Skryabin and who was related to the Russian composer, Aleksandr Nikolaevich Skryabin, was born into a middle-class family in the Vyatka province of Russia. He studied at the *gymnasium* in Kazan' and later at Kazan' University and joined the Bolshevik faction of the Social Democratic Revolutionary (later Communist) Party in 1906 when he was only sixteen. He was exiled to remote parts of the Russian empire on several occasions before 1917 because of his revolutionary activities. It was in 1912 that he adopted the pseudonym, Molotov, meaning 'the hammer', although that did not save him from further periods of exile. He was editor of *Pravda* at the time of the February Revolution of 1917 and he worked closely with both Lenin and Stalin and in opposition to the Provisional Government.

After the Bolsheviks seized power Molotov was put in charge of the economy of the northern region and he was responsible for the compulsory nationalization of factories and workshops in seven northern provinces. He subsequently became head of the Ukrainian party organization, a sign of Stalin's trust in him, for Stalin was responsible for Nationality Affairs. Molotov became a candidate member of the Politburo as early as 1921 and a full member in 1926 and from 1921 to 1930 he was, in effect, 'second secretary' to Stalin within the Secretariat of the Central Committee.

Both in the 1920s and subsequently Molotov was a loyal Stalinist and he took a leading part in the liquidation of the Mensheviks and in purging the followers of Zinov'ev in Leningrad. He preceded Kaganovich as First Secretary of the Moscow party organization before becoming Chairman of the Council of People's Commissars in 1930. He was thus head of the Soviet government in name, although in reality Stalin wielded far more power. It was while he was still Chairman of the Council of People's Commissars in

1939 (Stalin took over the post in 1940) that Molotov became in addition Commissar (from 1946 Minister) of Foreign Affairs. He held that post throughout the Second World War and during the early years of the Cold War. Molotov was Foreign Minister until 1949 and again from 1953 to 1956. During the war he was also deputy chairman (to Stalin) of the State Defence Committee. He was very close to Stalin during the Yalta and Potsdam Conferences in 1945 and although he offered advice to Stalin, he never deviated from Stalin's line, even though Stalin sometimes invented differences between them in order to gain further concessions from the Western leaders with whom he was negotiating.

While Molotov remained in high office in the last years of Stalin's life (he was deputy chairman of the Council of Ministers) he had become distrusted by the increasingly paranoiac Stalin and although he was a member of the enlarged Presidium of the Central Committee which replaced the Politburo in 1952 (of which Molotov had been a full member continuously for twenty-six years), he was not invited to meetings of its inner body, the 'bureau'. Molotov's Jewish wife Polina Zhemchuzhina was in exile when Stalin died and Molotov's own life, along with that of other long-term Stalinists, was under serious threat of another purge on the eve of the dictator's death.

Molotov, however, opposed Khrushchev's de-Stalinization and was critical of many of his other policies, including the attempt to repair relations with Tito's Yugoslavia. He was a principal member of the anti-party group which attempted to remove Khrushchev from office in

1957 but which had the tables turned on them by Khrushchev who received the backing of the Central Committee. Molotov, who had already been replaced by Shepilov as Foreign Minister in 1956, lost his posts of deputy chairman of the Council of Ministers and Minister of State Control. He was dropped from the Presidium of the Central Committee and expelled from the Central Committee itself, but was given two subsequent minor jobs – in comparison with those to which he had been accustomed – as Soviet ambassador to Mongolia (1957–60) and chief Soviet delegate to the International Atomic Energy Agency in Vienna (1960–62).

Molotov began a long retirement in 1962 and in April 1964, during the last months of Khrushchev's leadership, it was announced that he had been excluded from the Communist Party. He was readmitted twenty years later – in the summer of 1984 – when his former subordinate Andrey Gromyko was exercising great influence during Chernenko's General Secretaryship. He wrote memoirs during his retirement which by the end of the 1980s had still not been published.

Molotov, who looked the part of the middle-class professional as befitted both his family origins and governmental career, had a great deal of blood on his hands, having signed – along with Stalin – the death warrants of many of his innocent colleagues. As Foreign Minister, he was a formidable but unconstructive opponent for his Western counterparts and his negativism earned him the nickname, 'Mr Nyet', from sections of the Western mass media. AHB

MOOR (Orlov), Dmitriy Stakhievich (1883–1946) Graphic artist. Born in Novocherkassk, Moor – one of the Soviet Union's greatest caricaturists – studied with Petr Kelin and worked as a journal illustrator in Moscow before the Revolution. During the 1920s he contributed caricatures to *Pravda*, *Krokodil* and many other newspapers/journals, and also designed posters, some of which have become internationally famous such as *Have You Volunteered?* (1920) and *Help!* (1921–22). His satirical attitude towards the Russian church and the Western bourgeoisie was especially vitriolic, and he influenced an entire generation of Soviet artists, including the Kukryniksy and Reshetnikov. JEB

MOSKALENKO, Kirill Semenovich (1902–1985) Marshal of the Soviet Union. Moskalenko, a Ukrainian, served in the Red Army and attended a course for Red Commanders in the 1920s. By 1938 he had risen to chief of an artillery brigade and in 1939 he graduated from the Dzerzhinsky Artillery Academy. He fought with distinction in the Soviet-Finnish War. He commanded the First Guards Army on the Stalingrad Front (1942); the Fortieth Army, Voronezh Front (1942–43); and the Thirty-Eighth Army, the First then the Fourth Ukraine Front. He took an active part in the liberation of Kiev. He headed Moscow Military District's anti-aircraft defence system from 1948 to 1953. The advent of Khrushchev boosted Moskalenko's career: he became commander of the Moscow Military District in 1953 and was promoted to Marshal of the Soviet Union. From 1956 he was a CPSU Central Committee member. In 1960 Khrushchev placed him in command of his brain-child – the Strategic Rocket Forces, a post which carried the brief of Deputy Minister of Defence. But this command was transferred to

Marshal Biryuzov in 1962, and from 1964 to 1966 Moskalenko was also temporarily stripped of his deputy minister's post. From 1962 he was Chief Inspector of the Ministry of Defence. RA

MOSKVIN, Andrey Nikolaevich (1901–1961) Cameraman. Moskvin was a leading cameraman best known for his work on the films of Kozintsev and Trauberg from *The Devil's Wheel* (1926) to *The Vyborg Side* (1939). He also worked with Eisenstein on *Ivan the Terrible* (1945–48) and with Kozintsev on *Don Quixote* (1957). RT

MOSKVIN, Ivan Mikhaylovich (1874–1946) Actor. One of Russia's leading stage actors, closely associated with the Moscow Art Theatre from its first production in 1898, Nemirovich-Danchenko's staging of Aleksey Tolstoy's *Tsar Fedor Ioannovich*. Moskvin was Director of the Theatre from 1943 until his death. He also appeared in films, including *Polikushka* (1919) and *The Station Master* (1925). RT

MOSKVIN, Ivan Mikhaylovich (1890–1939) Moskvin, a party official who had joined the Bolsheviks in 1911, and the son of an office worker, became active in student politics and then, after the revolution, in the Petrograd railway industry. He subsequently worked in the Petrograd party organization itself and served as a candidate member of the Central Committee Secretariat in Moscow from 1927, later (from 1930) working as a department head in the Supreme Council of the National Economy. He was arrested during the purges and died in imprisonment. SLW

MOVSISYAN, Vladimir Migrano-vich (b. 1933) Born near Spitak in Armenia, Movsisyan worked as an agricultural scientist and administrator until 1967, when he switched to party work. He was head of the Agricultural Department of the Armenian Central Committee (1975–78), and then Deputy Chairman (1978–84) and First Deputy Chairman of the Armenian Council of Ministers with responsibility for agriculture. In February 1988 he was given the additional charge of refugee affairs. In April 1990, Movsisyan was elected First Secretary of the Armenian Communist Party. He became a member of the Politburo in July 1990. JHM

MRAVINSKY, Yevgeniy Aleks-androvich (1903–1988) Conductor. Yevgeniy Mravinsky was born in St Petersburg. After studying at the Petrograd Institute, he then worked as a mime artist at the Imperial Mariinsky Theatre. In 1924 he entered the Leningrad Conservatory, where he studied conducting with Aleksandr Gauk and Nikolay Mal'ko, graduating in 1931. He conducted at the Leningrad Opera and Ballet Theatre (the present-day Kirov Theatre) (1932–38) until his appointment as principal conductor of the Leningrad Philharmonic in 1938. He has also taught as a professor at the Leningrad Conservatory. Under has baton the Leningrad Symphony has risen to a remarkably high standard and he has been responsible for numerous premières of Soviet works, including many by Shostakovich and Prokof'ev. Among his honours are People's Artist of the USSR (1954) and Hero of Socialist Labour (1973). GS

MUKHINA, Vera Ignat'evna (1889–1953) Perhaps the Soviet Union's greatest sculptor, Mukhina achieved lasting fame for her colossal statue of the *Worker and the Collective Farm Girl* erected on top of the Soviet pavilion at the Exposition Internationale in

Paris in 1937. Although she interpreted the principles of Socialist Realism here, Mukhina assimilated many artistic concepts, including Cubism and Futurism, before accepting the Stalin style: before the Revolution, for example, she worked in Mashkov's studio, was close to Ekster at the Chamber Theatre and travelled to Paris with Popova in 1914. In the early 1920s, while designing a number of 'relevant' works such as *Flame of the Revolution* (1919), Mukhina also worked as a fashion designer. In the 1930s and 1940s, she turned to porcelain and glassware, but sculpture remained her preferred medium. JEB

MUKHITDINOV, Nuritdin Akramovich (b. 1917) The first person of Central Asian origins to achieve any prominence in the Soviet leadership. A soldier from 1939 to 1946, Mukhitdinov was party First Secretary in Namangan and Tashkent provinces (1948–51), Chairman of the Council of Ministers of Uzbekistan (1951–55), and became First Secretary of the Uzbekistani Central Committee in December 1955. At the Twentieth Party Congress the opportunity was taken to introduce him as a candidate member into the CPSU Presidium (Politburo) – a gesture, perhaps, to non-Slavs now that the Transcaucasian hold on the leadership had been broken. After the crisis of the 'anti-party group' Mukhitdinov was promoted to Central Committee Secretary and full member of the Presidium. But he never left any mark on Kremlin politics and was dismissed from his posts at the Twenty-second Congress in October 1961. He was Soviet ambassador to Syria from 1968 to 1977. JHM

MURADELI, Vano Il'ich (1908–1970) Composer. Vano Muradeli was born in Gori (Georgia) and died in Tomsk. He received his initial musical training in composition and conducting at the Tbilisi Conservatory, and after graduating in 1931, he spent three years playing in various Georgian theatres as composer, actor and conductor. The years 1934 to 1938 were spent at the Moscow Conservatory, working with Myaskovsky. From 1942 to 1944 he was principal and artistic director of the Central Ensemble of the Soviet Navy. A member of the party since 1942, he was made a People's Artist of the USSR in 1968. In 1948 his opera *The Great Friendship*, along with works by Prokof'ev, Shostakovich and others, was censured in a resolution of the Central Committee, though he was later restored to favour. His opera *October* (première 1964) has been highly acclaimed in the Soviet Union. GS

MURADYAN, Sarkis Mambreevich (b. 1927) Painter. Born in Yerevan, Muradyan graduated from the Yerevan Art Institute in 1951 and soon became known as one of Armenia's leading painters of colourful portraits and landscapes. His favourite theme is the contrast between the old and the new as demonstrated by *In My Town* (1967). JEB

MURAKHOVSKY, Vsevolod Serafimovich (b. 1926) A Soviet politician with close ties to Mikhail Gorbachev, Murakhovsky is Ukrainian by nationality and a member of the Communist Party from 1946. Between 1944 and 1950 he served in the Soviet army, taking part in the Second World War. Between 1954 and 1975 Murakhovsky worked in a series of Komsomol and party posts in the Stavropol' region where Gorbachev was also rising through the Komsomol and party apparatus. From 1975 to 1978 he was First Secretary of the Karachaevo-Cherkessk *obkom*, but when Gorbachev went to Moscow in 1978 as a Secretary of the Central Committee, Murakhovsky returned to Stavropol' to succeed him as First Secretary of the regional party committee. A full member of the Central Committee from 1981, Murakhovsky became a First Deputy Chairman of the Council of Ministers and Chairman of a newly-created State Committee for the Agro-Industrial Complex (*Gosagroprom*) in 1985, posts he held until 1989 when *Gosagroprom* was abolished. AHB

MUSAKHANOV, Mirzakhamud Mirzarakhmanovich (b. 1912) Uzbek by nationality and son of a famous Turkestan revolutionary, Musakhanov graduated from the Moscow Textile Institute in 1937 and worked in industry before entering party and state service in Uzbekistan and at national level. A member of the CPSU from 1943, he worked as a secretary of the All-Union Council of Trade Unions (1959–61) and as a secretary of the Uzbek party Central Committee (1961–65), later becoming first deputy prime minister of the Uzbek republic. From 1970 to 1985 he was First Secretary of the Tashkent regional party committee, and he was elected a full Central Committee member in 1976 and 1981. SLW

MUTALIBOV, Ayaz Niyazi Ogly (b. 1938) An Azeri engineer from Baku, Mutalibov worked on the design of kitchen equipment and in factory management until the late 1970s. He was Chairman of Gosplan in Azerbaydzhan (1982–89), and then became for a few months Chairman of the Azerbaydzhan Council of Minis-

ters. During the brief revolt in Azerbaydzhan in January 1990 he replaced A-R.Kh. Vezirov as First Secretary of the Azerbaydzhan Communist Party. In July 1990 he was elected to the Politburo as well as to the Central Committee of the CPSU. JHM

MYASKOVSKY, Nikolay Yakovlevich (1881–1950) Composer and teacher. Nikolay Myaskovsky was born in Novogeorgievsk and died in Moscow. The son of an army officer, he first studied military engineering, though an interest in music led him to take lessons with Glier in Moscow (1903) and with Kryzhanovsky in St Petersburg (1903–6). He entered the St Petersburg Conservatory in 1906, where he studied with Rimsky-Korsakov and Lyadov, graduating in 1911. With the advent of the First World War, the years 1914 to 1916 were spent in active service at the front. On being demobilized in 1921 he became a Professor at Moscow Conservatory, where his pupils included many notable Russian composers. He was made a Doctor of Arts in 1940 and a People's Artist of the USSR in 1946. In 1948, together with Prokof'ev, Shostakovich and others, he was accused of 'formalism'. A prolific composer in many genres, he left twenty-seven symphonies. GS

MYL'NIKOV, Andrey Andreevich (b. 1919) Painter and designer. After studying under Grabar' and Oreshnikov at the Repin Institute in Leningrad (1946), Myl'nikov began to experiment with many media, including monumental painting and mosaics (for example, for the Vladimirskaya metro station in Leningrad in 1955). Political recognition came when he was chosen to design the Lenin image for the drop curtain at the Palace of Congresses in the Kremlin in 1961.

However, Myl'nikov also produces more intimate, lyrical paintings such as *Verochka at the Dacha* (1957). JEB

MZHAVANADZE, Vasiliy Pavlovich (b. 1902) A Georgian, and career soldier from 1924, he was Deputy Commander for Political Affairs of the Kiev and the Carpathian Military Districts from 1946 to 1953, and had the rank of Lieutenant-General. He was brought in to head the Georgian party in 1953, apparently as a nominee without links to any of Georgia's warring factions. After the crisis of the 'anti-party group' he became a candidate member of the CPSU Presidium (Politburo). He retired from both positions in 1972. Under his administration the symbols of Stalinism were retained in Georgia (and only there); but Georgian morale and access to All-Union politics declined markedly, and corruption increased. JHM

N

NADIRADZE, Aleksandr David-ovich (1914–1987) Aleksandr Nadir-adze is best known as head of the design bureau responsible for the SS-20 missile and shorter-range, solid-propellant systems now being destroyed under the INF agreement. He was born at Gori in Georgia, the son of a teacher. In 1940 he graduated from the Moscow Aviation Institute and during the war participated in the development of the 'Katyusha' rocket artillery system. From 1958 he headed the Soviet Union's leading solid-propellant missile research and design centre. In 1981 Nadiradze was elected to the Academy of Sciences. Twice made a Hero of Socialist Labour, he did not join the party. JMC

NAGIBIN, Yuriy Markovich (b. 1920) Short story and cinematic script writer, whose participation in the collection *Literary Moscow* (1956) helped to argue the case for the autonomy of art. He has since bolstered this case in a series of stories about musicians, artists and writers of the past. He has also written about religious figures, notably Avvakum and Metropolitan Philip (who condemned the terror of Ivan the Terrible), implying concern for freedom of belief and conscience. GAH

NALBANDYAN, Dmitriy Arkad'-evich (b. 1906) Painter. Born in Tiflis, Nalbandyan is one of the last surviving representatives of the original phase of Socialist Realism, and he continues to uphold its principles in his political portraits (for example, of Andrey Gromyko, 1979). He studied under Lancéray at the Tbilisi Academy of Arts before working for Mosfil'm as a designer (1931–34). He emerged as a committed artist during the Second World War when he worked for the Okna TASS (TASS Window) in Yerevan and then in the late 1940s and 1950s when he produced many portraits of Stalin, Lenin, Gor'ky, etc., as in *Lenin Visiting Gor'ky in 1920 (the Appassionata)* (1954–56). Travelling frequently in India, Italy and France, Nalbandyan is rumoured to have created more than 3,000 works. JEB

NARIMANBEKOV, Togrul Far-manovich (b. 1930) Painter. Born in Baku, Narimanbekov is among the primary artists of Azerbaydzhan, known for his bright landscapes, seascapes and allegories such as *Morning on the Caspian* (1957) and *Fertility* (1970). He studied at the Azimzade Art Institute of Azerbaydzhan and then in Riga (1955). JEB

NAROVCHATOV, Sergey Serge-evich (1919–1981) Poet and literary official, born near Sratov, studied in Moscow. He saw army service in Finland and the Second World War; he became a party member in 1943. Narovchatov's early concentration on patriotic soldier's verse later broadens into intimate and narrative themes. He edited the journal *Novyy mir* from 1974 until his death. GSS

NASRIDDINOVA, Yadgar Sady-kovna (b. 1920) An Uzbek party and state official who became internationally prominent when she chaired the Soviet of Nationalities of the Supreme Soviet (1970–74) and, in a less favourable light, when she was finally expelled from the Communist Party in 1988 after recurrent charges of corruption, Nasriddinova was none the less the single most important woman of minority background in the early post-Stalin period.

Nasriddinova, an engineer, graduated from the Tashkent Institute of Railway Engineering in 1941. Although she worked briefly in railway construction, after she joined the Communist Party in 1942 her career was focused on Komsomol, party and state work in Uzbekistan. After serving as a Komsomol official for several years, she became First Secretary of a district committee. This was followed in 1952 by positions as Minister of Construction Materials and in 1955 as Vice-President of the Uzbek Council of Ministers. In 1954 she was elected to the Central Committee of the Uzbek Party and two years later to the Central Committee of the CPSU on which she remained for twenty years. Nasriddinova became Chairman of the Presidium of the Supreme Soviet of Uzbekistan in 1959, a position which entitled her to service as a Vice-Chairman of the Presidium of the Supreme Soviet of the USSR.

Nasriddinova's political career was based in Uzbekistan until 1970 when she became Chairman of the Soviet of Nationalities of the Supreme Soviet of the USSR, a position she held for four years. As Chairman of one of the two chambers of the Supreme Soviet, Nasriddinova received considerable publicity both as a woman and as a member of a national minority. By this time, however, the rumours regarding her extravagance with state funds (especially for her son's costly wedding in 1969) could not be ignored by Brezhnev, who is reported to have chastised her with a mild 'You were stupid to hold a wedding like that'.

In 1974 she became a deputy minister of the USSR Building Materials Industry, a demotion. By 1976 the Party Control Committee had decided to expel Nasriddinova, but the decision was rescinded after her supporters sent a flurry of telegrams in protest. She had over a decade of reprieve until renewed attention to corruption in Uzbekistan revealed her illegal pardons for cronies accused of large-scale theft and bribe-taking. NN,MM

NAVASHIN (Nawaschin), Sergey Gavrilovich (1857–1930) Plant cytologist and embryologist. After studying at the Petersburg Medico-surgical Academy (1874–78), Navashin transferred to Moscow University, graduated in 1881, and subsequently worked there and at the Petrov Academy (1884–89). Specializing in the morphology and taxonomy of mosses, he earned his master's degree at Petersburg University (1894) for his study of a parasitic fungus of birches. He was professor and chairman of the botany department at Kiev University (1894–1915) where he won international fame for his confirmation and discussion of double fertilization in angiosperms (1898), work which led to his election to the Petersburg Academy of Sciences (1901). An excellent microscopist, he undertook comparative studies of the chromosomal complement in various species and developed karyology as a taxonomic tool, training a Kiev school of cytology that included Kushakevich, Delone, S. Levitsky, and Th. Dobzhansky. In 1915 he moved to Tbilisi and, with his election to full academy membership in 1918, became head of botany at Tbilisi University. In 1923 he was invited to Moscow to organize the new Timiryazev Biological Institute and directed it until 1929, when it came under the Communist Academy. MBA

NAZARBAEV, Nursultan Abishevich (b. 1940) A Kazakh and, apparently, an ordinary worker at the Karaganda Metallurgical Combine (Temirtau), Nazarbaev moved to local Komsomol and party work in 1969, and rose to be Second Secretary of Karaganda *obkom* (1977–79). From 1979 to 1984 he was Central Committee Secretary for Industry, and from 1984 to 1989 Chairman of the Kazakhstan Council of Ministers. Nazarbaev succeeded G. V. Kolbin as First Secretary of the Communist Party of Kazakhstan in June 1989, bringing to the job a reputation for outspokenness on issues such as ecology and ethnic relations; he combined the post with that of President of the Supreme Soviet of Kazakhstan in early 1990. A member of the Central Committee from 1986, he

joined the Politburo in July 1990. JHM

NAZARENKO, Tat'yana Grigor'evna (b. 1944) Painter. Born in Moscow, Nazarenko is widely regarded as one of the most talented of the Soviet Union's younger artists. She graduated from the Surikov Institute, Moscow in 1968 where she studied under Gritsay and Zhilinsky, before working with Korzhev at the Academy of Arts, Moscow. Nazarenko's romantic interpretation of historic events is clearly demonstrated by her masterpiece *The Decembrists* (1978). JEB

NECHITAYLO, Vasiliy Kirillovich (1915–1980) Painter. Nechitaylo studied at the Repin Institute, Leningrad and then under S. Gerasimov at the Surikov Institute in the 1940s before achieving his reputation as an interpreter of historic and revolutionary events. Much of his painting is devoted to the image of Lenin such as *On Red Square* (1961–64). JEB

NECHKINA, Militsa Vasil'evna (b. 1901) Historian of the Russian revolutionary movement, social thought and historiography. A prolific author, her main books include *The Society of United Slavs* (1927), *A. S. Griboedov and the Decembrists* (1947), *The Decembrist Movement* (1955) and *V. O. Klyuchevsky* (1974). JB

NEIZVESTNY, Ernst Iosifovich (b. 1926) Sculptor, painter, writer, and advocate of human rights. Severely wounded in the war, he was expelled from the Artists' Union in 1954 for his rejection of Socialist Realism in favour of an expressionist style and humanistic, sometimes religious themes (see E. Egeland, *Ernst Neizvestny: Life and Work*, 1984). Readmitted in 1956, he was expelled again in 1963 after publicly polemicizing with N. S. Khrushchev, who made philistine attacks on his works. Later he was readmitted once more, and in 1971 Khrushchev's widow commissioned him to sculpt a tombstone for her husband's grave. In 1975 the Artists' Union expelled him a third time, after his requests to travel abroad were rejected. He began to speak out for human rights, and in 1976 he emigrated. His main studio is in New York, but he has also worked in Zürich and Sweden. PBR

NEKRASOV, Viktor Platonovich (1911–1987) Kiev novelist, journalist, writer of plays and film-scripts, and advocate of human rights. He achieved fame for a novel about his war experiences, *In the Trenches of Stalingrad* (1946). In 1963 he was severely criticized by Khrushchev for writing too favourably about America in *On Both Sides of the Ocean* (1962). From 1966 onwards he spoke out against the rehabilitation of Stalin, anti-semitism, the death penalty, the imprisonment of Ukrainian nationalists and other dissidents, and the exiling abroad of outstanding cultural figures. For this he was punished by searches of his home, confiscation of his manuscripts, and expulsion from the Communist Party and the Writers' Union. In 1974 he was forced to emigrate to Paris, where he became an editor of *Kontinent* and a broadcaster for Radio Liberty. In the USSR his books were outlawed. In 1987 rehabilitation of his reputation began. PBR

NEMCHINOV, Vasiliy Sergeevich (1894–1964) An economist and statistician. A scholar of great integrity, highly respected in the Soviet Union and abroad, Nemchinov graduated from the Moscow Commercial Institute in 1920. He joined the Party in 1940. One of the few Marxist statisticians in the 1920s, he designed a new method for measuring economic differentiation among the peasantry, and provided Stalin with crucial data on the grain problem in early 1928. In the 1930s he worked in the Agricultural Academy, then occupied the post of director from 1940 to 1948. He upheld the honour of statistics in the Lysenko discussion, and had to resign his post. He was appointed chairman of the Council for the Study of Productive Forces in 1949. In the years after Stalin's death he pioneered the use of mathematics and statistics in planning and economics, and founded the Central Economics-Mathematics Institute. He was made a member of the Academy of Sciences in 1946, and a member of its presidium (1953–62). He was awarded an honorary Doctorate of Social Science by the University of Birmingham in 1964. RWD

NEMIROVICH-DANCHENKO, Vladimir Ivanovich (1858–1943) One of Russia's leading stage directors. He was already a successful novelist and playwright when he became director of the Moscow Philharmonic Society's drama course in 1891 and he used this opportunity to develop in practice his ideas on increased naturalism in acting. He founded the Moscow Art Theatre with Stanislavsky in 1898 and took charge of the literary side of the theatre, working closely with Chekhov. After the Revolution he also organized the Music Studio which from 1926 became the Nemirovich-Danchenko Music Theatre, producing light operas and operettas. His most famous stage productions in the Soviet period include Trenev's *The Pugachev Rebellion* (1925), Ivanov's *The Blockade* (1929), Gor'ky's *Yegor Bulychov and the Others* (1934) and *Enemies* (1935), Trenev's *Lyubov' Yarovaya* (1936) and

Pogodin's *Kremlin Chimes* (1942). His musical productions include Offenbach's *La Périchole* (1922), Bizet's *Carmen* (1924), Krenek's *Johnny* (1929), Verdi's *La Traviata* and Shostakovich's *Katerina Izmaylova* (both 1934). After Stanislavsky's death in 1938 Nemirovich-Danchenko became sole head of Moscow Art Theatre until his own death. RT

NEPRINTSEV, Yuriy Mikhaylovich (b. 1909) Painter. Neprintsev was born in Tiflis. He studied at the Repin Institute, Leningrad and then worked at the front as a war artist during the Second World War. The battle theme is Neprintsev's preferred subject as is demonstrated by his large oils such as *Rest after Battle* (1955). He is also known as an illustrator of works such as those by Victor Hugo and Vladimir Korolenko. JEB

NERODA, Georgiy Vasil'evich (1895–1983) Sculptor. Born in Chernigov, Neroda was one of the primary exponents of Socialist Realist sculpture. He scored his first success with his busts of Lenin and Anatoliy Lunacharsky in the mid-1920s after studying at the MIPSA (1913–17). He is remembered for his monumental groups and statues such as *For the Power of the Soviets* (1932) and the portrait of Ordzhonikidze in Kislovodsk (1952). JEB

NESMEYANOV, Aleksandr Nikolaevich (1899–1980) Organic chemist, scientific administrator. After his graduation from Moscow University in 1922, Nesmeyanov remained there, becoming professor in 1935. Specializing in elementary and metallic organic compounds, he worked at the Institute of Fertilizers and Insecticides (1930–34) and became director of the Institute of Organic Chemistry of the USSR Academy of Sciences (1939–54) and of its newly formed Institute of Elementary Organic Compounds (1954–80). Elected a full member of the Academy in 1943, he joined the party in 1944 and rapidly rose in administration, serving as head of the Academy's chemistry division (1946–48), rector of Moscow University (1948–51), president of the USSR Academy of Sciences (1951–61), and a deputy of the Supreme Soviet (1950–62). Nesmeyanov's presidency saw great triumphs in Soviet science in nuclear physics and space, but it is also remembered for his leadership in the de-Stalinization and liberalization of the Academy, his attempts to free science from political and ideological intrusion, his opposition to Lysenkoism, and his policy emphasis on the development of interdisciplinary research, which led in 1957 to the creation of the Academy's Siberian division and its science city at Novosibirsk. The opposition to some of these moves led to his early retirement from the presidency in 1961, and he subsequently ran one of the chemistry divisions. In his later years, he became well known for developing synthetic caviar. MBA

NESTERENKO, Yevgeny Yevgen'evich (b. 1938) Bass. Yevgeny Nesterenko was born in Moscow. After first training at the Leningrad Structural Engineering Institute, he entered the Leningrad Conservatory, where he studied under Vasiliy Lukanin, graduating in 1965. In quick succession he was a soloist with the Leningrad Malyy Theatre (1963–67), the Leningrad Kirov Theatre (1967–71) and then with the Moscow Bol'shoy. From 1967 to 1971 he taught solo singing at the Leningrad Conservatory and from 1972 to 1974 was a teacher at the Gnesin Music Institute, Moscow. Since 1975 he has been in charge of the Faculty of Singing at Moscow Conservatory. He was awarded first place in the 1970 International Tchaikovsky Competiton. A member of the Party since 1974, he was made a People's Artist of the USSR in 1976, winning a Lenin Prize in 1982. GS

NESTEROV, Mikhail Vasil'evich (1862–1942) Painter. Nesterov was born in Ufa. Although his career was formed before the Revolution, he worked well into the Soviet period and contributed directly to the return to Realism in the 1920s. Graduating from the MIPSA in 1886, Nesterov joined the Society of Travelling Exhibitions in 1898, thereby demonstrating his support of the Realist movement. He was especially concerned with religious and historical themes, although after the Revolution he achieved recognition as a portraitist, for example, of Viktor Vasnetsov (1925) and Ivan Pavlov (1935). He died in Moscow in 1942. JEB

NESTEROVA, Natal'ya Igon'eva (b. 1944) Painter. Born in Moscow and one of its most promising younger artists, Nesterova trained at the Surikov Institute (1955–1966) under Gritsay and Zhilinsky. She is known for her lyrical landscapes, especially of the Crimea and the Caucasus, and for her interpretations of everyday life, such as *The Park* (1978). JEB

NETTO, Igor Alexandrovich (b. 1930) Soccer player. One of the most popular of all Soviet soccer players, he was captain of the USSR team for ten years between 1955 and 1965, during which time the team became Olympic champions in Melbourne (1956) and European Champions in 1960. Altogether he gained more than fifty caps

playing at left half between 1952 and 1960, finally handing over the captaincy to Valentin Ivanov on 16 May 1965. Born in Moscow, he joined Moscow Spartak in 1949 and played over 360 league games for them during which time they won five league championships. JWR

NEYGAUZ (Neuhaus), Genrikh Gustavovich (1888–1964) Pianist and teacher. Genrikh Neygauz (Heinrich Neuhaus) was born in Yelizavetgrad and died in Moscow. Springing from a gifted musical family, he received his first piano lessons from his father. Making his first concert tour at the age of nine, he played in Germany (1904–06) and in Italy (1909). In 1906 he studied composition with Paul Juon in Berlin and took further piano study (1912–14) with Leopold Godowsky in Vienna. From 1918 to 1922 he taught at the Kiev Conservatory. From 1922 to 1964 he was a professor at the Moscow Conservatory (from 1935 to 1937, its Director). He was made a People's Artist of the RSFSR in 1956. Neygauz was not only a brilliant pianist, but a gifted teacher, among his pupils being Gilel's and Rikhter. He left several works on piano performance, including *The Art of Piano Playing* (London, 1983). GS

NIKICH (Nikich-Krilichevsky), Anatoliy Yur'evich (b. 1918) Painter. Born in Petrograd, Nikich, who studied under Ioganson and Osmerkin at the Surikov Institute in Moscow – graduating in 1942 – is known for his portraits and still-lives. His deeply philosophical interpretations of historical and contemporary events, such as *War Correspondents* (1965), have received wide acclaim. JEB

NIKITIN, Aleksey Vasil'evich (1937–1984) Miner and organizer of free trade union activity. In 1969 he warned the management of his mine in Donetsk in the Don Basin that safety measures were being dangerously neglected. When a disaster later occurred, he organized protests and was consequently interned in mental hospitals (1972–76). Later he was interned again (1977–80) for enquiring about emigration at a Moscow embassy. In 1980 he was examined and found normal by a dissident psychiatrist, A. Koryagin. He tried to form a free trade union, and also showed workers' living conditions to two foreign journalists (see K. Klose, *Russia and the Russians*, 1984). For this he was interned a third time (1980–84). He was released just before dying of cancer. PBR

NIKLUS, Mart-Olav (b. 1934) Teacher, zoologist, translator, Estonian nationalist, and human rights activist. He was first imprisoned (1958–66) on charges of subversion. In 1980 he received a fifteen-year sentence for his Estonian *samizdat* activity and his role in the coordination of joint protests by Lithuanians, Latvians, and Estonians. PBR

NIKODIM (Rotov, Boris Georgievich), Metropolitan (1929–1978) Born near Ryazan', the son of a Communist Party member, Nikodim secretly enrolled for the correspondence course of the Leningrad Theological Seminary and Academy at the age of sixteen. He joined the Church openly after being expelled from the Ryazan' Pedagogical Institute in 1947, and became a tonsured monk in the same year at the age of eighteen. Thus began his meteoric career in the Church: parish priest at twenty-one, dean of Yaroslavl'

Cathedral at twenty-five, bishop and head of the Foreign Department of the Moscow Patriarchate at thirty-one, Metropolitan of Leningrad by the age of thirty-four. A highly-trained and educated theologian, he led his church into the World Council of Churches in 1961 and brought about links with the Roman Catholic Church. He died of a heart attack in the arms of the newly-elected Pope John Paul I, while at the Vatican attending the funeral of the previous Pope. MR

NIKOLAEVA (Volyanskaya), Galina Yevgen'evna (1911–1963) Born near Tomsk, Nikolaeva, a trained physician, wrote poetry and scenarios but is best known for her fiction. Two years after her father and husband were arrested in the purges of 1937, she began publishing poetry influenced by Tikhonov. The Central Committee's discussion of post-war difficulties on kolkhozes inspired her to visit a collective farm. Two of the resulting sketches, 'The Kolhkoz "Tractor"' (1947) and 'Traits of the Future' (1949) were published in *Pravda*. These sketches became the basis for her 1950 novel *Harvest*, which won a Stalin Prize and charts the remarkable progress of a backward kolkhoz under the party's guidance. Her 1957 novel *Battle en Route*, which became an official model of socialist realism, shows how Stalinist managers in a tractor factory were retrograde and had to be replaced by more forward-looking representatives of the new age. The popularity of both works is partially accounted for by their (for their times) daring love plots. KC

NIKOLAEVA, Klavdiya Ivanovna (1893–1944) A Soviet political figure, active in the Communist Party and government until her death in 1944, Nikolaeva is little known outside the

USSR. Of working-class background, she was born in St Petersburg and began her career as a bookbinder. As a twelve-year-old child, she began revolutionary work and was jailed at fifteen. She joined the RSDLP in 1909 and suffered frequent arrest and exile before the revolution. A contributor the party's journal *Rabotnitsa* (The Woman Worker), she became one of its editors in 1917 after her release from exile. After the Bolshevik Revolution Nikolaeva worked among women in Petrograd and helped to organize the 1917 Conference of Women Workers in that city. In 1920 she became head of the Petrograd section of Zhenotdel, working closely with working-class women whose humble origin she shared. From 1924 to 1926 she was the head of Zhenotdel. She fell briefly into disfavour in the mid-1920s because of her support of Zinov'ev in the succession struggle. In 1928 she returned to favour and became a party official in the Caucasus. From 1930 to 1933 she headed the party's Agitation and Propaganda Department, the organ which assumed some of the former responsibilities of Zhenotdel. She was a full member of the Central Committee (1924–25 and 1934–44), and a candidate member (1925–34). She was one of only a few old Bolsheviks reelected to the Central Committee in 1939.

From 1936 until 1944, she served as a secretary of the Central Trade Union Council and as a member of the Presidium of the Supreme Soviet. She was buried in Red Square. NN

NIKONOV, Aleksandr Aleksandrovich (b. 1918) A Russian who, almost certainly, was born, lived, and perhaps trained in independent Latvia before 1940, in which year he became both a member and an official of the Soviet Communist Party. He was Minister of Agriculture in Latvia (1951–61), and for two periods in the 1950s was a member of the Latvian Party Politburo. Eclipsed, he became director (1963–78) of the Stavropol' Agricultural Research Institute, where in 1967 M.S. Gorbachev gained agricultural qualifications. In 1978 Nikonov moved to a position in the Lenin All-Union Academy of Agricultural Sciences in Moscow. From 1984 he was President of this Academy, and from 1986 to 1989 Deputy Chairman of the State Committee for the Agro-Industrial Complex. He has been influential in the rehabilitation (1987) of A.V. Chayanov, N.D. Kondratieff and other economists of the 1920s (whose work he may have known in 'bourgeois' Latvia) and in other agricultural policies under Gorbachev. JHM

NIKONOV, Viktor Petrovich (b. 1929) Nikonov, who briefly held the powerful combination of offices of Secretaryship of the Central Committee of the CPSU and full membership of the Politburo (1987–89), was born in the Rostov region of Russia and received an agricultural higher education. A member of the Communist Party from 1954 he worked as an agronomist throughout most of the nineteen-fifties but joined the party apparatus in 1958. Between 1958 and 1960 he was in the agricultural department of the Krasnoyarsk regional party committee and in 1961 he spent some time as an instructor in the Party Organs Department of the Central Committee of the CPSU for the Russian republic. From 1961 to 1967 he was second secretary of the Tatar regional party committee and from

1967 to 1979 First Secretary of the Mariysky *obkom*.

Between 1979 and 1983 he headed an agro-chemical combine, work which would bring him into contact with Gorbachev who was overseeing agriculture within the Central Committee Secretariat at that time. From 1983 to 1985 Nikonov was Minister of Agriculture for the RSFSR and in April 1985 – clearly at Gorbachev's instigation – he became Secretary of the Central Committee responsible for agriculture. In June 1987 he was elevated to full membership of the Politburo, but was a less radical reformer than the times required and he was dropped from the leadership and went into retirement in September 1989. AHB

NILIN, Pavel Filippovich (1908–1981) A prose writer, who was born in Irkutsk and joined the party in 1944. Nilin's first novel, *Man Climbs Higher* (1936), about Donbass workers, won a Stalin prize and Nilin turned it into a film scenario *The Great Life*. Part Two of the film was attacked by government decree in 1946 and not released until 1958. Nilin returned to prominence under Khrushchev; his thaw novellas about the security organs, *The Trial Period* and *Cruelty* of 1956, question the old ideal of the unflinching revolutionary who never hesitates to kill. KC

NILSEN, Vladimir Semenovich (1905–1938) Cameraman. Nilsen was the cameraman who worked with Aleksandrov on his musical comedies *The Happy Guys* (1934) and *The Circus* (1936) and with Eisenstein. RT

NISHANOV, Rafik Nishanovich (b. 1926) One of the few Uzbek leaders to escape charges of corruption in the 1980s, Nishanov was born near Tashkent and spent most of his career until 1963 in Tashkent city and province administration. He was Secretary for Ideology of the Uzbekistan Communist Party (1963–70) but seems to have quarrelled with the Rashidov leadership, for he spent the next fifteen years as Soviet ambassador to Sri-Lanka and Jordan. Surviving this ill wind he rapidly became Chairman of the Presidium of the Supreme Soviet (1986–88) and First Secretary of the Communist Party of Uzbekistan (1988–89). In June 1989 he was elected Chairman of the USSR Soviet of Nationalities, a full-time and demanding post under the new regime. JHM

NISSKY, Georgiy Grigor'evich (b. 1903) Painter. Born in Novobelitsa, Nissky studied under Aleksandr Drevin and Fal'k at Vkhutein in the late 1920s, and was one of the first Soviet artists to produce original artistic interpretations of the new industrial landscape, of transport scenes and the expanding urban peripheries – as in *Polustanok* (1951) and *February* (1957). JEB

NIVINSKY, Ignatiy Ignat'evich (1881–1933) Graphic artist and designer. Born in Moscow, Nivinsky attended the Stroganov Institute of Industrial Art in Moscow (1893–99) before entering Zholtovsky's studio. In 1911 he turned to etching as his preferred medium and thereafter produced several graphic cycles of landscapes. In 1921 he designed Yevgeniy Vakhtangov's production of *Princess Turandot* and, until 1930, taught etching at Vkhutemas-Vkhutein. JEB

NIYAZOV, Saparmurad Ataevich (b. 1940) A Turkmen trained in Leningrad, Niyazov was ten years in the party apparatus in Ashkhabad, rising to the post of Head of the Department of Industry (1979–80). He was First Secretary of Ashkhabad *gorkom* (1980–84), and, for nine months, Chairman of the Turkmenistan Council of Ministers. In December 1985 Niyazov became First Secretary of the Communist Party of Turkmenistan, combining the post in 1990 with that of President of its Supreme Soviet. A member of the Central Committee of the CPSU from 1986, he joined the Politburo in July 1990. JHM

NORSTEIN, Yuriy Borisovich (b. 1941) Animator. Norstein is one of the leading animators in Soviet cinema. He has made more than forty films, including *The Tale of the Invisible City of Kitezh* (1971). RT

NOVIKOV, Aleksandr Aleksandrovich (1900–1976) Former Commander-in-Chief of the Air Force. Novikov was Chief of Staff then Commander of the Air Forces of Leningrad Military District (1940–41). During the Winter War against Finland he held the position of Chief of Staff of the air forces on the North-Western Front, and was appointed Commander of the Air Force on the Leningrad Front for the 1941 to 1942 period. His primary role was the restoration of the Air Force after the destruction it suffered at the opening of the war with Germany. Novikov held the post of Commander-in-Chief of the Soviet Air Force, and Deputy People's Commissar for Defence (1942–46). He was in charge of coordinating air force operations for various fronts, for the battles of Stalingrad and Kursk, and for the campaign against the Japanese Kwantung Army. In 1944 he gained the rank of Air Chief Marshal. He was placed in command of long-range aviation in 1953, and was also Deputy Commander-in-Chief of the Air Force (1954–56). RA

NOVIKOV, Ignatiy Trofimovich (b. 1906) A Ukrainian who graduated from the Dneprodzerzhinsk Metallurgical Institute in 1932, and moved into the field of power station construction and management. He headed the building of the Kremenchug Hydroelectric Station on the Dnieper between 1954 and 1958, and became Minister for Power Station Construction (1958–62). Then for more than twenty years he was Chairman of the State Committee for Construction (Gosstroi) and Deputy Chairman of the USSR Council of Ministers, retiring in 1983. JHM

NOVIKOV, Igor' Aleksandrovich (b. 1929) Athlete. Although he was born in Drezna in the Moscow Region, he grew up in the Armenian capital Yerevan. It was there that he became an all-round athlete and took up the modern pentathlon as a young man. He went on to become the most eminent of all Soviet pentathletes, competing in four Olympics (1952–64), and leading his team to victory in the 1956 and 1964 Games, and to second place in 1960, winning the individual title himself in 1964. He was also four times world pentathlon champion (1957–62), and nine times Soviet champion (1953–64). JWR

NOVIKOV, Vladimir Nikolaevich (b. 1907) Novikov trained as an army engineer and worked in the armaments industry until the late-1950s. He was deputy to D. F. Ustinov (1941–48 and 1954–55), and from 1955 to 1957 was First Deputy Minister of General Machine Building. After a year as head of Leningrad Regional Economic Council, he moved to Gosplan, first of the RSFSR and then of the USSR which he chaired (1960–62). From 1965 until his retirement in December 1980, Novikov was Deputy Chairman of the USSR Council of Ministers with responsibilities in the engineering area. JHM

NOVOZHILOV, Viktor Valentinovich (1892–1970) Mathematical economist. His innovative concepts of the efficient allocation of capital investment first published in 1939 were ignored at the time but he and his work were instrumental in reviving economic theory in the USSR after Stalin's death. Born in Khar'kov, he graduated from Kiev University in 1915 and taught statistics in various Ukrainian institutions until moving to Leningrad in 1922, where he continued in teaching and research, with appointments at the Leningrad Polytechnical Institute (1935) and the Petrograd Engineering Economics Institute (1944). His 1939 paper on 'methods of the comparative measurement of the economic effectiveness of plan variants' was the fruit of a flourishing school of Leningrad economists and his colleague there, L. V. Kantorovich became, with V. S. Nemchinov, the trainers of a new wave of economic theorists as soon as Stalin's death allowed public exposition of rigorous ideas. All three received Lenin Prizes in 1965 and his 1967 book, translated into English as *Problems of Cost-Benefit Analysis in Optimal Planning* (1970), achieved international recognition. MCK

NUREYEV, Rudolf (b. 1938) Leading ballet dancer and choreographer. Nureyev grew up in Ufa, began his training with private teachers, and first performed with the Ufa Opera Ballet. He later entered Leningrad Ballet School from which he graduated in 1958. He made his début with the Kirov troupe the same year, and won instant recognition for his great energy, breathtaking footwork and leaps, and vivid stage presence. As a soloist he partnered many leading ballerinas.

Nureyev defected to the West in 1961, was an immediate success in Europe, and soon became one of the world's leading male dancers. He has performed with many major companies, including the Paris Opéra Ballet, the Royal Ballet, American Ballet Theater, and the Martha Graham Dance Company, and the Boston Ballet. He was Margot Fonteyn's partner for many years, and received great acclaim for his performances in ballets including *Giselle* and *Swan Lake*. He created the company Nureyev and Friends (1974), a Nureyev festival in London (1977), and a tribute to Nijinsky with the Joffrey Ballet (1981).

Nureyev has choreographed many ballets including *Swan Lake*, *Don Quixote*, *Sleeping Beauty*, *Romeo and Juliet* and *The Nutcracker*. In 1982 he was named director of the Paris Opéra Ballet, for which he has staged several works. He has also appeared on television, in films, and on Broadway. SCS

O

OBORIN, Lev Nikolaevich (1907–1974) Pianist and teacher. Lev Oborin was born in Moscow. After first studying at the Gnesin Music School, he went on to the Moscow Conservatory, where he was a pupil of Konstantin Igumnov (piano) and Nikolay Myaskovsky (composition). He graduated in 1926, and in 1927 he won the First Chopin International Pianists' Competition in Warsaw, being the first Soviet performer to take part in any international contest. In 1928 he joined the staff of the Moscow Conservatory. He was made a People's Artist of the USSR in 1964. He was the first performer of Khachaturyan's Piano Concerto, and the work is dedicated to him. GS

OBRAZTSOV, Sergey Vladimir-ovich (b. 1901) Obraztsov began his career as a theatre director and actor. He played various roles at the Moscow Art Theatre between 1922 and 1936. He first used puppets in his stage performances in 1920 and became head of the State Central Puppet Theatre in 1931. He produces shows for both adults and children. Since 1956 he has also worked in films. RT

OBRAZTSOVA, Yelena Vasil'evna (b. 1937) Mezzo-soprano. Yelena Obraztsova was born in Leningrad. She graduated from the Leningrad Conservatory, where she was a pupil of Antonina Grigor'eva, in 1964. In 1962 she won first prize at the All-Union Vocalists' Contest named after Glinka and in 1970 was awarded first place in the Fourth International Tchaikovsky Competition. Whilst still a student she was invited to sing the part of Marina Mnishek in Musorgsky's *Boris Godunov* at the Moscow Bol'shoy, of which company she became a permanent member in 1964. She was made a People's Artist of the USSR in 1976 and is the recipient of several State Prizes. She has frequently travelled abroad, where the musical-dramatic qualities of her singing have been much praised. GS

OBROSOV, Igor' Pavlovich (b. 1930) A Moscow-born painter, influenced by Petrov-Vodkin, Obrosov paints restrained, romantic landscapes and portraits, such as that of the writer Vasiliy Shukshin (1980). He graduated from the Moscow Higher Industrial Art Institute in 1954. JEB

OBUKHOVA, Nadezhda Andreevna (1886–1961) Mezzo-soprano. Nadezhda Obukhova was born in Moscow and died at Feodisya. A student of the Moscow Conservatory, from which she graduated in 1912, she was a pupil of Umberto Masetti. From 1916 to

1943 she was a soloist at the Moscow Bol'shoy. An excellent linguist, she excelled in many different areas of vocal performance, ranging from opera to simple folk-songs, all of which she performed with great artistry. She was made a People's Artist of the USSR in 1937 and was awarded a State Prize in 1943. She was also active as a writer, leaving a number of articles and autobiographical reminiscences. GS

OGARKOV, Nikolay Vasil'evich (b. 1917) Former Chief of General Staff. Ogarkov became renowned in the late Brezhnev period as an independent-minded military intellectual who sought resources to meet new military-technical priorities. Born the son of a peasant, he graduated from the Military Engineering Academy (1941) to pursue a career as a military engineer. He entered the Red Army in 1938, and in the period 1941 to 1945 was a regiment, brigade and division engineer. He held important positions in the engineering branch of Soviet forces after the war, which were used to build his career as a staff officer in the Carpathian, Primor'e and especially Far Eastern Military Districts. He graduated from the General Staff Academy in 1959. Senior command posts followed. For example, he was First Deputy Commander of the Belorussian Military District (1963–65), and Commander of the Volga Military District (1965–68). He gained candidate (1966) then full membership (1971) of the CPSU Central Committee, and in 1968 was elevated to First Deputy Chief of General Staff of the USSR Armed Forces. His influence on military planning in the Brezhnev period was assured when he became Chief of Staff and First Deputy Minister of Defence in January 1977.

Soviet sources note that Ogarkov had an influential role in the build-up of the Soviet forces, in raising their combat readiness and in elaborating issues of Soviet military science. However, Ogarkov's military thinking and priorities frequently conflicted with those expressed by party leaders. He was reluctant to concede that there could be no victors in a nuclear war as Brezhnev finally stated in 1981. In the early 1980s he also stressed the theme of improved theatre-wide command and control, called for heightened military vigilance and argued in favour of investment in new conventional military technologies. The party leadership opposed large new military expenditures and in September 1984 Ogarkov lost his position as Chief of General Staff and thereby his voice in these central military debates. Ogarkov was appointed commander of the Western Theatre of Military Operations. He held this non-operational but influential command post until his replacement in November 1988 by Army General Stanislav Postnikov. RA

OISTRAKH, David Fedorovich (1908–1974) Violinist, teacher and conductor. David Oistrakh was born in Odessa and died in Amsterdam. He commenced his musical training at the age of five under Petr Stolyarsky, with whom he continued his studies at the Odessa Institute of Music and Drama, graduating in 1926. In 1928 he moved to Moscow, becoming a soloist with the Moscow Philharmonic in the period 1932 to 1934 and 1941 onwards, and joined the teaching staff of the Moscow Conservatory in 1934. He won first prize at the All-Union Violinists Competition in Leningrad in 1935, and at the Ysaÿe Contest in Brussels in 1937. A member of the party from 1942, he was made a People's Artist of the USSR in 1953 and was awarded an honorary doctorate by Cambridge University in 1969. One of the best known performers and a notable teacher (his concert tours abroad commenced in the 1950s), he was highly esteemed as an international performer and recording virtuoso. Some autobiographical notes were published in the journal *Sovetskaya Muzyka* (Soviet Music), No.9, 1958. GS

OISTRAKH, Igor' Davidovich (b. 1931) Violinist and conductor. Igor' Oistrakh, son of David Oistrakh, was born in Odessa. He received his musical training from his father, under whom he studied as a child, then as a student at the Moscow Conservatory, graduating in 1955. Following a further three years' postgraduate study at the Conservatory, in 1958 he became a soloist with the Moscow Philharmonic. He was awarded first place in the International Wieniawski Competition for Violinists held in Poznań in 1952. Made an Honoured Artist of the RSFSR in 1968, he travels extensively. He is remembered especially for his fine duo performances and recordings with his father. GS

OKHLOPKOV, Nikolay Pavlovich (1900–1967) Actor and director. Okhlopkov was an accomplished stage and film actor and director. He worked with Meyerkhol'd from 1923 to 1930 and was head of the Moscow Realist Theatre from 1930 to 1937. His major film roles included: *Men and Jobs* (1932) and *Aleksander Nevsky* (1938). RT

OKUDZHAVA, Bulat Shalvovich (b. 1924) Poet and historical novelist, born in Moscow, the son of a Georgian father and an Armenian mother, both

party officials, both arrested in 1937. After active service in the Second World War, Okudzhava studied at Tbilisi University and became a provincial schoolteacher. He joined the party on the rehabilitation of his parents in 1955 (his father posthumously) and moved to Moscow. With his guitar-accompanied songs he became one of the most characteristic poets of the Khrushchev thaw, achieving immense popularity through clandestine tape recordings. He turned to writing historical novels in the 1960s. Okudzhava's songs have pure, gentle lyricism and occasional satirical bite. Since the Gorbachev thaw he has become an acknowledged classic, and has frequently spoken out on political issues. GSS

OL', Andrey Andreevich (1883–1958) An architect. Born in St Petersburg, Ol' studied at the Institute of Civil Engineers there from 1901 to 1910 and also taught there in the 1920s. Although interested in the *style moderne*, as seen in his design for Leonid Andreev's dacha (1907), Ol' was more concerned with practical, functional construction as demonstrated by his House Commune in Leningrad (1927–29) and his House of Soviets in Ulan-Ude (1928). JEB

OLESHA, Yuriy Karlovich (1899–1960) Prose writer, dramatist and poet. Olesha grew up in Odessa. In 1919 he volunteered for the Red Army, breaking with his parents, who fled to Poland. In 1922 he started working in Moscow for the railwaymen's newspaper *The Hooter*, writing satirical verses under the pseudonym of 'The Chisel'. He wrote a fantastical novel for children, *The Three Fat Men* (1924, published 1928, staged 1930). His masterpiece, the short novel *Envy* (1927), brought him fame, although acclaim was soon to give way to confusion about the political implications of a story where the representatives of the new world are soulless and spiritual values seem to remain with the bankrupt characters of the past. The work's strikingly tangible visual imagery and metaphors lend themselves fruitfully to Freudian interpretations. It was later staged as *A Conspiracy of Feelings* (1929). The wistful, occasionally sentimental mood of *Envy* is more prominent in Olesha's short stories, where youth and innocent love are idealized. After pleading for the cause of humanism in his speech at the 1934 Writers' Congress, Olesha was to write no major new works. A fragmentary work, *Not a Day Without a Line*, consisting of autobiographical and other reflections, was published posthumously in 1961. JAEC

OLEYNIK, Boris Il'ich (b. 1935) One of the two deputy chairmen of the Soviet of Nationalities of the USSR Supreme Soviet, Oleynik is a Ukrainian poet and a Secretary of the Ukrainian Writers' Union organization. A member of the Communist Party, he was elected to the Congress of People's Deputies in 1989 on the party's reserved list. Oleynik, who has been active in the ecological movement in the Ukraine, was appointed Chairman of the Commission of the Supreme Soviet to study the situation in Nagorno-Karabakh. AHB

OPARIN, Aleksandr Ivanovich (1894–1980) Biochemist. A student and protégé of biochemist A. N. Bakh, Oparin worked on plant enzymes and the technical biochemistry of food production, but he became internationally known in the late 1930s for his theory of the biochemical origin of life on earth, first published in 1924 but better known in its more soph-

isticated 1936 variant, *The Origin of Life on Earth*. The theory posits that in the early oceans, the natural occurrence of colloidal coacervate droplets created chemical pools separated by a membrane from the surrounding medium, and that life emerged from a natural selection of such droplets that favoured those with the fastest rates of reaction, the most stable internal configurations, and the ability to grow and divide most rapidly. Oparin worked at the Institute of Biochemistry of the USSR Academy of Sciences from 1935 and served as its director 1946–80. Immediately after the party's public endorsement of Lysenko in 1948, Oparin was appointed academician-secretary of the biology division of the USSR Academy of Sciences (1948–55) and presided over the dismantling of Soviet genetics. He also resisted the development of Soviet molecular biology. MBA

ORBELI, Leon (Levon) Abgarovich (1882–1958) Physiologist, administrator. A 1904 graduate of the Petersburg Military Medical Academy, Orbeli studied with Pavlov and worked at the Institute of Experimental Medicine (1907–20), visiting laboratories abroad (1909–11). After the revolution, he remained in Leningrad to head departments of physiology at the Institute of Physical Education (1918–57), the First Leningrad Medical Institute (1920–31), and the Military Medical Academy (1925–50). Groomed as Pavlov's heir apparent, he became a member of the USSR Academy of Sciences (AN) in 1935, director of its Pavlov Institute of Physiology (1936–50), and director of the Institute of Evolutionary Physiology and Higher Nervous Activity of the USSR Academy of Medical Sciences (AMN) (1939–50). Following the AN reorganization of 1939, he became academician-secretary of the division of biological sciences and, during the war, vice-president of the AN (1942–46), a general in the army medical service, and director of the Military Medical Academy (1943–50). Orbeli's research emphasized the evolution of the human nervous system and, as a strong partisan of genetics, he lost most of his posts following the party's endorsement of Lysenko (1948) and the infamous 'Pavlov session' that followed it (1950). Nonetheless, he remained director of the Pavlov Institute facility at Koltushi, where he protected several geneticists, and the AN created an Institute of Evolutionary Physiology for him, which he directed until his death in December 1958. MBA

ORDZHONIKIDZE, Grigoriy Konstantinovich (1886–1937) Georgian revolutionary who later became a leading economic official in the inter-war period. Ordzhonikidze was the son of a minor nobleman in the village of Goresha in Kutaisi province. He was educated locally and then at a medical school in Tiflis, where he graduated in 1905. He had become a member of the Social Democratic Party two years earlier, identifying with the Bolshevik wing and, during the 1905 revolution, had been arrested while smuggling arms. He went afterwards to Germany but returned to Baku and to political activism in 1907. He was again arrested and deported. At the end of 1910 Ordzhonikidze went to Paris, where he made contact with Lenin's supporters. He later carried out political missions on their behalf in Russia and abroad. He was arrested again in St Petersburg in 1912 and was sentenced to three years' hard labour, followed by exile. He was involved in the establishment of soviets in Yakutsk after the February Revolution and in June 1917 returned to Petrograd.

Ordzhonikidze became a member of the Petrograd party committee and of the Petrograd soviet at this time, and after the revolution was appointed to a succession of posts supervising military activity on the western and southern fronts. He was among those who entered Baku in May 1920 and in that and the following year was actively involved in the establishment of Soviet rule in Armenia and Georgia. After holding several leadership posts in the party organization in the Caucasus, Ordzhonikidze became chairman of the Central Control Commission and of Rabkrin (responsible for party discipline and the state bureaucracy respectively) between 1926 and 1930 and was then appointed chairman of the Supreme Council of the National Economy and from January 1932 Commissar for Heavy Industry. Ordzhonikidze was a candidate member of the Politburo 1926–30 and a full member from 1930 onwards. A mustachioed, devil-may-care activist rather than a bureaucrat by nature, 'comrade Sergo' became increasingly disillusioned by the progress of the purges during the 1930s: his deputy, Pyatakov, was arrested and executed, his eldest brother was shot after torture, and his own flat was searched. After two no doubt directly-expressed telephone conversations with Stalin, Ordzhonikidze took his own life. SLW

ORESHNIKOV, Viktor Mikhaylovich (b. 1904) Painter. Born in Perm', Oreshnikov studied there and then at the Leningrad Vkhutein before emerging as an important practitioner of Socialist Realism from the late

1930s onwards. He is remembered for his interpretations of Lenin, such as *Lenin Taking the Examination at St. Petersburg University* (1947), and also for his portaits of contemporaries. JEB

ORGANOV, Nikolay Nikolaevich (1901–1982) A powerful provincial official whose political advance was halted under Khrushchev. Born in Zaraysk, south-east of Moscow, he fought for the Bolsheviks in the Civil War, and became a party official in the Ivanovo and Yaroslavl' areas. From 1939 to 1958, with the exception of military service (1941–42), he was in the Far East and Siberia, becoming party First Secretary of the Maritime Province (1947–52) and of Krasnoyarsk *krai* (1952–58). His next posts – Deputy Chairman of the RSFSR Council of Ministers (1958–59), Chairman of Presidium of the RSFSR Supreme Soviet (1959–62) and Ambassador to Bulgaria (1963–67) – must be seen as demotion. Like some other prominent figures of the early 1950s, he was brought back to Moscow under Brezhnev, becoming head of a Central Committee Department from 1967 to his retirement in 1973. The name and functions of this department have never been divulged. JHM

ORLOV, Yuriy Fedorovich (b. 1924) Physicist and human rights activist. He first expressed public dissent in 1956, after which he had to leave Moscow for Yerevan, where he became a corresponding member of the Armenian Academy of Sciences. Returning later to Moscow, in 1976 he was the founding head of the Moscow group to monitor observation of the 1975 Helsinki accords. For this he was arrested in 1977 and given a twelve-year sentence. In 1986 he was released early and emigrated to the USA. PBR

ORLOVA, Lyubov' Petrovna (1902–1975) Actress. Orlova was an extremely popular screen actress renowned for her roles in the musicals *The Happy Guys* (1934), *The Circus* (1936) and *Volga-Volga* (1938), directed by her husband Grigoriy Aleksandrov. RT

OSHANIN, Lev Ivanovich (b. 1912) Poet and literary official, born in Rybinsk and educated in Moscow. A party member since 1944, he is a prolific writer of loyal lyrics, including some classic Soviet songs. GSS

OSINSKY (also Ossinsky), N. (Obolensky, Valeryan Valeryanovich) (1887–1938) An old Bolshevik, a leading organizer and politician with independent and original ideas. A princely title is often wrongly attributed to Osinsky. His father was the son of a small landowner, a veterinary surgeon in charge of stables. Osinsky was an enthusiastic advocate of such diverse causes as democracy in the party, the mass use of the motor-car in the Soviet Union, and honest statistics. He was responsible for a substantial and unexpected improvement in some Soviet statistics (1932–35). He was a member of the RSDLP from 1907, and was frequently arrested. He studied economics in Munich and Berlin. After the revolution he supported the Left Communists in spring 1918, and organized the Democratic Centralists (1920–21). He was an advocate in 1920 of centralized agricultural planning, one of Trotsky's sympathizers in 1923, and gave some support to Bukharin in 1928. He held many leading posts in the economy of which the most important were the position of head of the Central Statistical Administration (1926–28), and of its successor the Central Administration for National-

Economic Records (1932–35). He was a candidate member of the party Central Committee (1921–22, and 1925–38). He was a witness at the Bukharin trial in March 1938, and executed later in the year. RWD

OSIPOV, Vladimir Nikolaevich (b. 1938) Russian nationalist, *samizdat* writer and editor. He was first imprisoned (1961–68) for organizing poetry readings by young people on Moscow's Mayakovsky Square. He then edited the Russian nationalist *samizdat* journal *Veche* (1971–74), which focused on environmental, social, religious, and historical themes. He supported Solzhenitsyn in his debate with Sakharov. For editing *Veche* he served a second term in captivity (1974–82). PBR

OSIP'YAN, Yuriy Andreevich (b. 1931) A member of the Presidential Council of the USSR since its creation in March 1990, Osip'yan is Armenian by nationality but was born in Moscow. A leading Soviet physicist and a Vice-President of the Academy of Sciences of the USSR, he joined the Communist Party in 1959.

The author of more than one hundred and fifty scientific publications, Osip'yan is Director of the Institute of Physics of Rigid Bodies and has carried out important research in the physics of material science. He is a holder of the P.N. Lebedev gold medal for distinguished scientific work and an honorary member of a number of foreign academic and scientific associations. Osip'yan was elected to membership of the Congress of People's Deputies in 1989. AHB

OSMERKIN, Aleksandr Aleksandrovich (1892–1953) Painter. Osmerkin was born in Yelizavetograd. After studying in Kiev (1911–13), he enrolled in Mashkov's studio in Moscow and became associated with the Jack of Diamonds group. He taught at Vkutemas-Vkhutein in the 1920s and then at the Repin Institute, Leningrad (1932–47). Known for his still-lives and landscapes such as *Moika. White Nights* (1927), Osmerkin, like his mentors, used Cézanne as a constant point of reference. JEB

OSSOVSKY, Petr Pavlovich (b. 1925) Painter. Born in Malaya Viska, Ossovsky graduated from the Surikov Institute in Moscow in 1950 after studying under S. Gerasimov. Known for his colourful, if severe, style, Ossovsky prefers the monumental genre, as in his triptych *Mexico* (1962–64). JEB

OSTROVSKY, Nikolay Alekseevich (1904–1936) Ostrovsky was born in Volynia and is best known as author of *How the Steel Was Tempered* (1932–34), a socialist-realist classic. He joined the Komsomol at fifteen and fought in the First Cavalry during the Civil War. Throughout the twenties he was active in the Komsomol, and joined the party in 1924. Ostrovsky began writing in the late twenties, but the first chapters of his 1927 to 1928 Civil War novella were lost. He became blind and progressively weaker from bone disease, but nevertheless wrote his semi-autobiographical *How the Steel Was Tempered* which tells of Pavel Korchagin, a young rowdy who is progressively transformed through the example and guidance of others into a selfless Communist, triumphing over terrible odds and only finally succumbing to a terminal illness. Now on every Soviet high-school reading list, it became immensely popular when the author's own fate was publicized; its hero is held up as a prime example of the positive hero. From his sickbed, Ostrovsky worked on its film version and began a novel on the Civil War,

Those Born of Storms (1934–36), but only the first volume of the latter was finished. KC

OTSEP, Fedor Aleksandrovich (1895–1949) Scriptwriter and film director, Otsep's most important and popular films included: the serial *Miss Mend* (1926), *Earth in Captivity* (1928) and *The Living Corpse* (1929). He emigrated in 1929. RT

OVCHINNIKOV, Yuriy Anatol'-evich (1934–1988) Molecular biologist, administrator. A 1957 graduate of Moscow University, Ovchinnikov was a student and protégé of M. M. Shemyakin and worked at his Institute of the Chemistry of Natural Compounds of the USSR Academy of Sciences throughout his career (1960–88). His principal areas of research were the physicochemical structure and function of various proteins and polypeptides, and the molecular biology of membranes and membrane transport. As Shemyakin's heir apparent, Ovchinnikov was elected a corresponding member of the USSR Academy of Sciences in 1968 and, shortly after Shemyakin's death in 1970, a full member and the director of his institute. He also assumed his mentor's role in orchestrating the technical infrastructure of Soviet mol-

ecular biology and managed to rebuild the institute (renamed the Institute of Bio-organic Chemistry in 1974) into one of the most beautiful, modern, technologically sophisticated, and well-equipped research centres in the Soviet Union. He joined the party in 1962 and was a member of its Central Auditing Committee (TsRK) (1976–88) and a candidate member of the Central Committee (1981–88). MBA

OVECHKIN, Valentin Vladimirovich (1904–1968) After spending his youth as a teacher and Komsomol official in the countryside, and then as political officer in the Red Army, Ovechkin became the first Soviet writer to describe openly the atrocious conditions on the collective farms and the maladministration which caused them (*District Routine*, 1952). A supporter of Khrushchev's agricultural reforms even *before* Stalin's death, he became disillusioned and depressed by their incompleteness in practice. After submitting a memorandum recommending a radical decentralization of the collective farms, he was admitted to a mental hospital, apparently because he had suffered a nervous breakdown. GAH

P

PAKHMUTOVA, Aleksandra Niko-laevna (b. 1929) Composer. Aleksandra Pakhmutova was born in Beketovka. After graduating from the Moscow Conservatory in 1953, where she studied with Shebalin, she stayed on for further postgraduate training, finishing in 1956. Winner of many prizes, she was made a People's Artist of the USSR in 1977. She is renowned within the Soviet Union for her popular songs, her Trumpet Concerto (1955) and the Concerto for Orchestra (1972). GS

PAKHOMOV, Aleksandr Fedorovich (1900–1973) Graphic artist and painter. Born in Varlamovo. A pupil of Sergey Chekhonin and Mstislav Dobuzhinsky at the Stieglitz Institute in Petrograd (1915–17); 1920–22), Pakhomov developed the fine graphic traditions of the World of Art group. From the late 1920s onwards, he was close to Lebedev and Samuil Marshak, he illustrated many children's books, and also turned to the Russian classics. JEB

PANFEROV, Fedor Ivanovich (1896–1960) Prose writer, journalist and dramatist. A party member since 1926, Panferov is best known for his epic works set in the countryside, which promote collectivization as a necessary and desirable development. His four-part *The Bruski Estate* (1926–36) describes peasant life after 1917, while the trilogy *Mother Volga* (1953–60), portrays the difficulties of reconstructing agriculture after the war and after the Twentieth Party Congress. Another trilogy, *The Struggle for Peace* (1945–54), is set in war-time. He was criticized by Gor'ky for the poor craftsmanship of his writing. From 1931 until the end of his life he edited the journal *October*. JAEC

PANFILOV, Gleb (b. 1934) Film director. Panfilov's innovative and controversial films include *The Beginning* (1970), *Tema* (1980, not released), *Valentina* (1981) and *Vassa Zheleznova* (1983), based on Gork'y's play. RT

PANKRATOVA, Anna Milhaylovna (1897–1957) A leading Soviet historian of the 1930s to 1950s, Pankratova wrote about the history of the Russian working class and revolutionary movement, and edited many collective works. A member of the Party Central Committee from 1952 to 1957, she was chief editor of *Voprosy Istorii* from 1953 to 1957. JB

PANOV, Valery (b. 1940) Ballet dancer and choreographer. Panov graduated from the Leningrad Ballet School in 1957 and danced with the Malyy Ballet (1957–64) and the Kirov Ballet (1963–72). He excelled in dramatic roles and received particular notice for his portrayal of the title role in *Hamlet* (1970) and the Devil in *The Creation of the World* (1971). He received the Lenin Prize in 1969.

Panov emigrated to Israel in 1974 and has since appeared with numerous companies, including the London Festival Ballet and the Berlin Opera Ballet. He has choreographed several works for the Berlin Opera Ballet, including *Cinderella, Le Sacré du printemps, The Idiot,* and *War and Peace,* and has appeared in many of them with his wife, Galina Panova. scs

PANOVA, Vera Fyodorovna (1905–1973) Prose writer. She flourished in the forties with three Stalin Prize novels: *Travellers* (1947), *The Factory* (1947), and *The Bright Shore* (1949). After 1940 she lived in Leningrad. In 1953 her *Seasons* showed corruption among highly-placed bureaucrats. She wrote a cycle of works from a child's viewpoint in the fifties and historical novels in the sixties. BH

PANTELEEV, Aleksandr Petrovich (1874–1948) Actor. Panteleev was a pre-revolutionary actor who directed several early Soviet films including one of the first agit-films *Congestion* (1918), based on a script by Lunacharsky. RT

PANYUSHKIN, Aleksandr Semenovich (1905–1974) Born in the Volga city of Samara (now Kuybyshev), Panyushkin fought in the Civil War and became a career officer (1924–38), including service in the frontier forces. He was Deputy Head of a Central Committee Department (1944–47), twice ambassador to China (1939–44, 1952–53), and ambassador to the USA in the crucial 1947 to 1952 period. From 1959 – perhaps from 1953 – to his retirement in 1973 he was head of an unnamed

department of the Central Committee, most probably concerned with Soviet personnel working abroad. JHM

PARADZHANOV, Sergey Iosifovich (1924–1990) Film director. Paradzhanov was probably the most famous of the older generation of Soviet filmmakers. His films are marked by a distinctive expressive romanticism and a stunning use of colour and folkloristic imagery. For these very reasons his films have often been officially criticized for obscurantism. His major films are *Shadows of Our Forgotten Ancestors* (1965), *The Colour of Pomegranates,* also known as *Sayat-Nova,* (1969) and *The Legend of Suram Fortress* (1984). He has also worked in theatre and television. RT

PARFENOVICH, Vladimir Ivanovich (b. 1958) Sportsman. The first Soviet canoeist to win three gold medals at one Olympics, he took the 500m singles and 500 and 1000m double kayak races (both with Sergey Chukhray)) in the space of two days at the 1980 Moscow Olympics. Born in Minsk, he took up kayak racing at fifteen and quickly established himself as a powerful canoeist capable of sudden sustained spurts. JWR

PARNOK, Sofiya Yakovlevna (1885–1933) Poet and critic. Her collections of poetry began in 1916 and continued throughout the twenties. She wrote love poetry addressed to other women, one cycle about her relationship with Tsvetaeva, whom she met in 1914. Her lyrics are in a pure classical, allusory style. BH

PÄRT, Arvo (b. 1935) Estonian composer. Arvo Pärt was born in Paide. A composition student of Heino Eller at the Tallinn Conservatory from which he graduated in 1963, Pärt worked in the music department of the Estonian Radio (1958–67). He emigrated in

1980. Though he can write with charming simplicity as in the children's cantata *Meie Aed* (Our Garden) (1959), other works can be extremely complex. His St John Passion (*Passio Domini nostri Jesu Christi Secundum Joannem*), completed in 1982, was first performed in Munich. GS

PASHUKANIS, Yevgeniy Bronislavovich (1891–1937) One of the very few original Marxist-Leninist legal philosophers of international stature, Pashukanis has been closely identified with the legal and philosophical implications of the rapid withering away of state and law after a socialist revolution. Of Baltic origin, he read law at Petersburg University but was obliged, because of his revolutionary activities, to complete his studies at the University of Munich, where he studied law and political economy. He joined the Bolshevik Party in 1918, served briefly as a people's judge in the Moscow region, and then worked for several years as a legal adviser in the People's Commissariat for Foreign Affairs of the Russian Republic.

The publication of his principal work *General Theory of Law and Marxism* (1924) brought him immediate acclaim; the book, published in several editions and translated into several languages, supressed after the mid-1930s, was republished in the Soviet Union in 1982. In the late 1920s Pashukanis and the school of young jurists around him came to dominate legal research and teaching in the Soviet Union. The transition to economic planning and concomitant reliance upon law caused Pashukanis to revise his views publicly on three occasions (1930, 1934, 1936).

Pashukanis was on the editorial boards of the major law periodicals and encyclopedias (1924–30). He taught law at Moscow University and the Institute of Red Professors of the Communist Academy, helped draft civil legislation, and held several senior positions in the Communist Academy. The syllabi and textbooks in the law schools were revised to reflect his approach, and he was the author of influential works on public international law. After several mergers of journals and institutes to strengthen the position of Marxist jurists, Pashukanis became director of the Institute of State, Law, and Soviet Construction (later renamed several times), the editor-in-chief of its new law journal, and co-editor of another journal published by the USSR Central Executive Committee (1929–30).

Despite revisions and retractions Pashukanis' commodity-exchange theory of law dominated the early 1930s and materially influenced Soviet legal policy. Although the theory in the end was incompatible with the Stalin-Vyshinsky emphasis from 1936 on the restoration of stability of laws, it is still unclear why in January 1937 Pashukanis was summarily arrested, tried, and executed. Western contemporaries recall him as authoritarian and domineering, one brought up in the revolutionary school of hard knocks 'where courtesies are unknown and one attacks to survive'. He was legally rehabilitated in March 1956 by the RSFSR Supreme Court. WEB

PASKAR', Petr Andreevich (b. 1929) A Moldavian who worked in Moscow for fourteen years as First Deputy Chairman of the USSR Gosplan, Paskar' was an agronomist until 1959, and then in party and state posts in Moldavia. He was Secretary of the

Central Committee of the Moldavian Communist Party (1962–70) and Chairman of the Moldavian Council of Ministers (1970–76) before being promoted to Gosplan to supervise agricultural planning. After civil disturbances in Moldavia he was brought back in January 1990 to his former position there of Chairman of the Council of Ministers. JHM

PASTERNAK, Boris Leonidovich (1890–1960) Poet and prose writer, and translator; born in Moscow, the son of an eminent painter. Pasternak originally intended to become a musician, but he studied philosophy in Marburg and Moscow. He made his début as a poet in 1913, when he took part in the Moscow Futurist group 'Centrifuge', and produced four dazzling books of lyrics: *Twin in the Clouds* (1914), *Above the Barriers* (1917), *My Sister Life* (1922), and *Themes and Variations* (1923), especially notable for their nature imagery and impassioned individual vision.

The 1920s saw a turn to subjects from revolutionary history in the long poems *The Year 1905* (1925–26), *Lieutenant Schmidt* (1926–27), and *Spektorsky* (1931); at the same time, Pasternak began publishing imaginative (*Tales*, 1925) and autobiographical (*Safe Conduct*, 1931) prose. The collection *Second Birth* (1932) is the last new work reflecting the early lyric manner; after it until the Second World War came selections from previous collections (1933, 1935, 1937). Meanwhile, partly as a response to political pressures, Pasternak turned to translation: his Shakespeare was collected in 1949, his *Faust* appeared in 1953, and his many translations from the Georgian were collected in 1958. The war brought renewed lyric inspiration and a plainer

style (*On Early Trains*, 1943; *Earth's Expanse*, 1945), and after it Pasternak returned to translation, while working in private on what he regarded as his most important literary work, the novel *Doctor Zhivago*. This was finished in 1956 and published abroad the following year, letting loose one of the great literary scandals of modern times. Pasternak was reviled by Soviet politicians and writers, and compelled to refuse the Nobel Prize, which was awarded in 1958.

Rehabilitation began the year after his death, and has continued steadily, culminating in the Soviet publication of *Dr Zhivago* (1988). Pasternak is recognized as one of the great poets of the twentieth century, and revered for his steadfast dedication to literature and the creative life. GSS

PATOLICHEV, Nikolay Semenovich (1908–1989) An important provincial and industrial administrator of the 1940s and 1950s who never quite made it to the highest echelons of power. Son of a Civil War hero, he was party First Secretary in Yaroslavl' (1939–41), briefly Central Committee Secretary (1946–47) and candidate member of the Central Committee Presidium (1952–53). After two years as Deputy Foreign Minister, he became USSR Minister of Foreign Trade in 1958, a post he retained until his retirement in 1985. He wrote interesting memoirs in which he claimed a close association with Stalin. JHM

PAULS, Raymond Voldemarovich (Pauls, Raimonds) (b. 1936) Pauls, a Latvian, born and educated in Riga, is a professional composer and jazz pianist, and not a member of the CPSU. In the late 1980s he was artistic director and chief conductor for Latvian State Radio and Television. When he was appointed Chairman of the Latvian State Committee for Culture in November 1988, this seems to have been the first case of a non-communist minister in the USSR since the 1920s. JHM

PAULYUK, Yanis Antonovich (b. 1906) Painter. Born in Riga, Paulyuk studied at the Academy of Arts there (1939–46), but was never satisfied with the strictures of conventional academic or Realist art. One of the leading Baltic painters, Paulyuk is known for the virtuosity of his colourful improvisations, as in *Let There Always Be Sunshine* (1967). JEB

PAUSTOVSKY, Konstantin Georg'evich (1892–1968) A prose writer, born in Moscow. Noted for its classic limpid style and sensitive portrayal of nature, Paustovsky's most celebrated work is the autobiographical *Tale of My Life* (1945–63). In the Khrushchev period he played an important part in rehabilitating and publishing purged writers, notably through editorship of the important almanacs *Literary Moscow* (1956) and *Pages from Tarussa* (1961). GSS

PAVLOV, Georgiy Sergeevich (b. 1910) An old associate of Brezhnev from his studies in Dneprodzerzhinsk, he became a party official in a number of provinces and in 1965 'Administrator of Affairs' (i.e. business manager) of the Central Committee headquarters. Keeping this position throughout the Brezhnev period, he retired in 1983. JHM

PAVLOV, Ivan Petrovich (1849–1936) Physiologist, psychologist. The son of a priest, Pavlov began his training in a seminary but soon transferred to Petersburg University, where he studied with the brilliant right-wing physiologist and surgeon I. F. Tsion (E. Cyon), graduating in 1875. He then studied circulatory physiology in

K. N. Ustimovich's laboratory at the Medico-Surgical Academy, graduating in 1879, and spent the next decade heading the physiological laboratory at the clinic of S. P. Botkin, taking two years off (1884–86) to study in the German laboratories of Rudolf Heidenhain and Karl Ludwig. A *privat-dotsent* at the Medico-Surgical Academy from 1883, Pavlov became chairman of its pharmacology department in 1890 and then of its physiology department (1896–1924).

Concurrently, he headed the physiology laboratory of the Institute of Experimental Medicine, where he undertook a series of studies of the physiology of digestion, summarized in an 1897 publication, that involved aseptic surgical intervention throughout the digestive tract in an effort to study normal functions in the healthy animal. He found that the properties of salivary secretions differed with the food consumed and located 'the enzyme of enzymes' (enterokinase) in intestinal secretions (1894). His work on digestive physiology was awarded the Nobel prize for physiology or medicine in 1904, making Pavlov the first Russian to win a Nobel prize. In 1907 he was elected a full member of the Academy of Sciences.

During the remainder of his career (1902–36), Pavlov focused on the physiology of the nervous system and higher nervous activity. He began with studies of salivation, a quantifiable process with which he was already familiar from his studies of digestion. He had already observed dogs salivating in anticipation of meat, even in its absence. In opposition to the common view of subjective psychologists that this was the result of a dog wishing for food, Pavlov saw salivation as an automatic reflex of a new sort, one that had been created or conditioned by experience and was triggered by a signal. He tested this view with his famous experiments in which a dog was conditioned to associate bell-ringing with feeding, with the result that the bell soon triggered the salivation conditioned reflex. In Pavlov's view, such conditioned reflexes served an evolutionary role throughout the animal kingdom by allowing the development of individuated adaptive behaviour. During the remainder of his career, Pavlov used analogous controlled experimental settings to explore how conditioned reflexes were created, modified, and attenuated by stimuli of varying kind, intensity, timing, and pattern.

Pavlov had never been especially political, and he greeted the Bolshevik revolution and its aftermath without enthusiasm. His international fame protected him from the turbulence of the times, however, and for ideological and political reasons Bolshevik leaders were anxious to keep Pavlov working in Russia. When he complained that the exigencies of the famine and the Civil War were making it difficult to feed his experimental dogs, maintain his staff and students, and procure materials, Lenin authorized the sale of gold abroad to provide money to support his laboratory. In the 1920s Pavlov occasionally spoke out in strong terms against Bolshevik policies, including the attacks on religion, the growing political control over academic and cultural life, and the arrests and brutalities, but the government continued to treat him well. In 1925 he became director of the Institute of Physiology of the USSR Academy of Sciences. Working there and at the Institute of Experimental Medicine, he created a large school of physiological researchers.

Pavlov's experiments had located the cerebral hemispheres as the site of conditioned reflex activity and, after the revolution, his researches turned increasingly to the study of higher nervous activity. After 1918 he made regular visits to study patients at a nearby psychiatric clinic. Workers in Pavlov's laboratory began to investigate experimentally induced neuroses by setting conditioned reflexes in opposition. In subsequent decades a number of investigators attempted, with limited success, to extend Pavlov's analysis to all forms of human mental activity and psychiatric dysfunction.

In the West Pavlov is sometimes seen as a 'behaviourist' who treated the psyche as a black box and believed that behaviour is shaped entirely by conditioning. This view is largely mistaken. In 1926 reports from Pavlov's laboratory did suggest that conditioned reflexes could be inherited, but N. K. Kol'tsov and his wife Maria Sadovnikova, who did experimental work on animal behaviour, went over the data with Pavlov and convinced him that the results did not confirm an inheritance of acquired characteristics and were compatible with a genetic interpretation. As a result, Pavlov publicly withdrew his endorsement of Lamarckian inheritance and organized in 1926 an experimental station at Koltushi, near Leningrad, devoted to the study of 'the genetics of higher nervous activity'. This institution provided a centre for the Pavlovian study of animal behaviour and, during Lysenkoism, a haven for unemployed geneticists.

In the early 1930s Soviet propaganda portrayed Pavlov as a model 'materialist' psychologist and in the mid-1930s he publicly accommodated himself to the Soviet regime in a widely published statement to young students. After his death, Pavlov was canonized in the press, and his protégé, L. A. Orbeli, replaced him as director of the Pavlov Institute, the physiological division of the Institute of Experimental Medicine, and the Koltushi station. The party's endorsement of Lysenko in 1948 led to the infamous 'Pavlov session' of the Academy of Medical Sciences in 1950 where Orbeli and his catholic biological interpretation of the Pavlov legacy was officially replaced by a dogmatic ideological 'Pavlov cult' advocated by other Pavlov students that resisted neurophysiological and physicochemical approaches to brain function. This group dominated Soviet physiology, psychology, and psychiatry until the 1960s. Since that time new experimental approaches to brain study have developed and the important contributions of other trends and schools in Soviet psychology have begun to be recognized and studied. MBA

PAVLYCHKO, Dmytro Vasyl'ovych (b. 1929) A Ukrainian poet, born near Ivano-Frankovsk and educated at L'vov University, Pavlychko has published since the early 1950s. Though a CPSU member since 1954, he was one of the Ukrainian writers who sought to press on with de-Stalinization in 1962; since then he has frequently been in bad favour with party officials. Increasingly anxious over the future of Ukrainian language and culture, he founded, in 1988, the Taras Shevchenko Ukrainian Language Society. In September 1989 Pavlychko chaired the inaugural Congress of the Popular Movement of the Ukraine for Perestroika (or *Rukh*). JHM

PEL'SHE, Arvid Yanovich (1899–1983) An old Bolshevik of Latvian origin, Pel'she was the last Politburo member to have actively participated in the revolution of 1917 in Petrograd. He was a full member of the Politburo from 1966 until his death, aged eighty-three, in 1983.

Born into a peasant family in the Bauska region of Latvia, ' joined the Bolsheviks in 1915 as a sixteen-year-old manual worker. Between the February and Bolshevik Revolutions he was a member of the Petrograd soviet. He joined the Cheka in Moscow in 1918 and took part in the unsuccessful attempt to establish Soviet power in Latvia in 1919. After a spell in the armed forces, he studied at the Institute of Red Professors in Moscow. In the 1930s he was involved in the administration of new state farms and taught in a variety of educational institutions, including the Central School of the NKVD.

With the incorporation of Latvia into the Soviet Union, Pel'she's importance within the Soviet system increased. He was the secretary of the Latvian Communist Party responsible for propaganda and agitation from 1941 to 1959 when he became First Secretary of the Latvian Central Committee. In 1966 he was elected not only to full membership of the Politburo, but moved at that time to Moscow to the Chairmanship of the Committee for Party Control. As such, he was highly illiberal in his attitudes to party members accused of ideological deviation but relatively tolerant of the corruption which became increasingly widespread during the Brezhnev era. AHB

PERESTIANI, Ivan Nikolaevich (1870–1959) Georgian film director and actor. Perestiani's films included:

Father and Son (1919), *In Days of Struggle* (1920), *Arsen Dzhordzhiashvili* (1921) and the pioneering Civil War film *The Little Red Devils* (1923). RT

PEREVERZEV, Valeryan Fedorovich (1882–1968) A Marxist literary theorist and critic. After an education in the sciences, Pereverzev was exiled for revolutionary activity. In exile he wrote *Dostoevsky's Craft* (1912), which attributes Dostoevsky's literary output to the unhappy state of the lower middle class and the rise of the *raznochintsy*. He is best known for *Gogol''s Craft* (1928), which most fully develops his argument that every aspect of an author's style is determined by his class origins and the position of his class in the course of historical change. Influenced by Plekhanov, and opposed to both the biographical and Formalist approaches to literature, he insisted that literary production was directly connected to the prevailing mode of economic production. This ultra-orthodox interpretation of the base/superstructure relation came to be known in the late twenties as 'Pereverzevism' and 'vulgar sociologism'. Criticism of his theories was fierce in the thirties; he was arrested and imprisoned in 1938, but rehabilitated in 1956. In the fifties he wrote on Old Russian literature and in the sixties on the history of Russian Realism. KC

PERVUKHIN, Mikhail Georg'evich (b. 1904) A technocratic minister who made his name in industry and then advanced extremely rapidly up the hierarchy thanks to Stalin's purges, Pervukhin is most notable for his political (and physical) longevity. He was only thirty-five when he received his first major post as Commissar of Electric Power Plants and Electrical Industry, and a relatively young forty-eight when elected to the Presidium after the Nineteenth Party Congress in 1952.

He stayed on in Khrushchev's Presidium and probably did not actively participate in the 'anti-party group's' effort to oust the First Secretary in 1957. Even so, he lost his post as head of the short-lived *Gosekonomkomissiya* and was made Minister of Medium Machine Construction before suffering a long series of demotions. His career included a spell as head of the State Committee for Foreign Economic Liaison, as Ambassador to the GDR, as a deputy to the Supreme Soviet, and, until the late 1970s, as a member of the Council of Ministers State Planning Commission. MM

PETRAKOV, Nikolay Yakovlevich (b. 1937) A leading Soviet economic reformer, Petrakov became one of Mikhail Gorbachev's personal assistants at the beginning of 1990 and at the same time was invited to found, as first Director, a new Institute of the Market. He thus became one of the Soviet Union's most influential social scientists and the first economist to be appointed a *pomoshchnik* (assistant) of the party General Secretary.

Petrakov, of Russian nationality and a Muscovite by birth, graduated from Moscow University in 1959 and from as early as 1965 (the year in which he joined the Communist Party) he became deputy director of the Central Economic-Mathematical Institute (TsEMI), a post he held until the end of 1989. A corresponding member of the Academy of Sciences, Petrakov is a member of the editorial board of the journal, *Voprosy ekonomiki* (Problems of Economics). He is the author of numerous significant publications, including *Democratization of the Economic Mechanism* (1988). AHB

PETRITSKY, Anatoliy Galaktion-ovich (1895–1964) Designer and painter. Born in Kiev, Petritsky was a leader of the Ukrainian avant-garde, who achieved renown as a stage designer, especially in the 1920s. While studying at the Kiev Art Institute (1910–18), he experienced the influence of Ekster, but quickly reached his own interpretation of Constructivism – as in his costumes and sets for the ballet *Nur and Anitra* (1923). Living in Khar'kov and Kiev from the late 1920s onwards, he continued to work as a landscapist, caricaturist and stage designer, although his later style lacked the dynamism of the early phase. JEB

PETROSYAN, Tigran Vartanovich (1929–1984) Chess player. An Armenian born in the Georgian capital of Tbilisi, he took the world chess title from Botvinnik in 1963 and retained it for six years before losing to Boris Spassky. He had become an international grandmaster in 1952 at the age of twenty-three and soon established himself as an original chess tactician, winning the Soviet title in 1959, 1961 and 1969 and, to the surprise of many, made a comeback in 1975, winning the national title for the fourth time. Besides his interest in chess, he studied philosophy, becoming a candidate of Philosophical Sciences in 1968 and publishing *Chess and Philosophy* in the same year. He had his own chess school in Moscow and edited the weekly *Chess-64.* JWR

PETROV, Andrey Pavlovich (b. 1930) Composer. Andrey Petrov was born in Leningrad. A student in composition of O. Yevlakhov at the Leningrad Conservatory, he graduated in 1954. A member of the party since 1957, he was made a People's Artist of the RSFSR in 1976. Twice a winner

of State Prizes, his ballet *The Shore of Hope* (1959) has won official esteem in the Soviet Union, while the suite from another ballet *The Creation of the World* (1971) is available on a European disc. GS

PETROV, Ivan Ivanovich (real name Krauze) (b. 1920) Bass. Ivan Petrov was born in Irkutsk. He received his education at the Glazunov Music School, Moscow, where his tutor was Anatoliy Mineev, graduating in 1941. He also took part in performances of the Opera Ensemble conducted by Ivan Kozlovsky. In 1943 he made his début at the Bol'shoy Theatre, where he sang until 1970. The winner of several State Prizes and the Order of Lenin, he was made a People's Artist of the USSR in 1959. He has toured abroad, made numerous recordings and has appeared in several films. He was made an honorary member of the Paris Opéra in 1954. GS

PETROV, Vasiliy Ivanovich (b. 1917) Military commander. Petrov was a teacher at a secondary school before he entered the Soviet Army in 1939. He held command and staff posts during the war and graduated from the Frunze Military Academy in 1948. Further command and staff posts after the war led to command of the Far Eastern Military District (1972–76). He became a Deputy to the Supreme Soviet in 1974 and a member of the CPSU Central Committee in 1976. From 1976 he was First Deputy Commander-in-Chief of the USSR Ground Forces and was placed in command of the newly created Far East Forces Command (1979–80). This established Petrov as the most prominent 'Far Easterner' in the Soviet High Command. Petrov, by now a Marshal of the Soviet Union, was Commander-in-Chief of Soviet Ground Forces from 1980 until he was replaced in January 1985 by Army General Ivanovsky. He gained the post of First Deputy Minister of Defence but lost this also in July 1986, perhaps on account of opposition to initiatives by Gorbachev. RA

PETROV, Vladimir Mikhaylovich (1896–1966) Film director. Petrov's most important films included: *Fritz Bauer* (1930), *The Storm* (1934), *Peter the First* (1937–39), *Kutuzov* (1944) and *The Battle of Stalingrad* (1949). RT

PETROV-BYTOV (né Petrov), Pavel Petrovich (1895–1960) Film director. Petrov-Bytov was most active in the campaign for 'proletarianization' of cinema (1929–32). His somewhat mediocre films included: *The Whirlpool* (1927) and *Cain and Artem* (1929), based on a story by Gor'ky. RT

PETROV-VODKIN, Kuz'ma Sergeevich (1878–1939) Painter. Born in Khvalynsk, Petrov-Vodkin studied at the MIPSA (1897–1904) before travelling to France (1908–10). Responding to the Symbolist aesthetic and cultivating a deep interest in Russian icons, he favoured a religious, contemplative style of painting as in *The Bathing of the Red Horse* (1912). Adjusting his philosophical canons to the new Realism, he painted portraits and scenes from the Revolution and the Civil War and, as a professor at the Leningrad Vkhutemas-Vkhutein in the 1920s, he taught and influenced a number of young painters, including Samokhvalov. JEB

PETRUSHEVSKAYA, Lyudmila (b. 1938) Short-story, play, and film writer. She began publishing in 1972, but little has appeared until recently. Notable works are the story *Observation Point* (1982) and the play *Three Girls*

in Blue (1983), staged in Moscow in 1986), which describe cynical men and distraught women in ironic, realistically contemporary language. BH

PETUSHKOVA, Yelena Vladimirovna (b. 1940) Sportswoman. She was the most successful horsewoman in the USSR, winning the gold medal in team competition and silver in an individual event at the 1972 Olympics on the black stallion Pepel, following a silver medal at the 1968 Olympics. She was also three times world and five times national champion in equestrian events between 1966 and 1974. Born in Moscow, she gained her candidate degree in Biological Sciences at Moscow University three years before her Merited Master of Sport title. Upon retirement from competition she devoted herself to biological research and a number of public offices, such as Vice-President of the Soviet Olympic Committee and a member of the Dressage Commission of the International Equestrian Federation. JWR

PIKSANOV, Nikolay Kiryakovich (1878–1969) A bibliographer, textologist and historian of Russian literature, Piksanov graduated from Dorpat (Tartu) University in 1902 and became a professor of Russian literature at Moscow and Leningrad Universities, and in 1931 a corresponding member of the Academy of Sciences. He published on Russian Freemasonry, Griboedov, Pushkin, Lermontov and Gor'ky. KC

PILNYAK, Boris (Vogau, Boris Andreevich) (1894–1937) Born in Mozhaisk, Pilnyak was the most popular prose writer of the early twenties. Influenced by Bely, Remizov and Scythianism, he welcomed the Revolution as a visceral force that would destroy Petrine (European) Russia. His major novel, *The Naked Year* (1921), attempts to convey the effect of the Revolution and its chaotic aftermath on people representing different social strata and political positions. Composed of a series of episodes, the novel eschews linear plot, relying instead on 'musical' repetition for unity. Like most of Pilnyak's fiction, it contains repetitions of phrases and entire pages, quotations from Old Russian literature (actual and invented), *skaz* language, archaic and obscure vocabulary together with parodied sovietese, documents and philosophizing. Pilnyak's success began to decline in 1926 when 'The Story of an Unextinguished Moon' was taken as depicting Frunze's death as a murder. All copies of the journal containing it were confiscated, and Pilnyak denounced the work. Then, after he published *Mahogany* (1929) abroad, he was expelled from the Federation of Soviet Writers. His attempt at regaining favour, the production novel *The Volga Flows Down to the Caspian Sea* (1930), was also met with criticism, and Pilnyak recanted. He was arrested in 1937 and rehabilitated posthumously. KC

PIMEN, Patriarch (Izvekov, Sergey Mikhaylovich) (1910–1990) Patriarch of the Russian Orthodox Church from June 1971 until his death at the beginning of May 1990, Pimen (family name: Izvekov) was ordained a priest in 1932 but was a choir-master until 1935. He spent part of the later Stalin years in prison, but in 1957 he was consecrated as a bishop, created Archbishop in 1960 and Metropolitan of Leningrad and Ladoga just a year later. He became Metropolitan of Krutitsy and Kolomonskoe in 1963 which put him in line for the succession

to the Patriarchate. In June 1971 Pimen succeeded Aleksi (Alexis) as Patriarch, although he appears to have had no theological education. He was a product of Russia's long monastic tradition rather than of special 'job-orientated' episcopal training. He promoted the official Soviet foreign policy line over the years and travelled widely as a member of the World Peace Committee. He met Gorbachev in 1988 and gained official approval for the celebration of the millenium of Christianity in Russia. He was elected a member of the Congress of People's Deputies in 1989 and although already seriously ill accepted his place there since it was a sign of the new official tolerance of religion. MR

PIMENOV, Yuriy Ivanovich (1903–1977) Painter. Born in Moscow, Pimenov graduated from Vkhutemas in 1925 and was a founder member of OST. Pimenov, like Deyneka, Vyalov, and Vil'yams, used an Expressionist style to depict Soviet industrialization and urbanization, as, for example, in *Give to Heavy Industry* (1927). In the 1930s Pimenov accepted Socialist Realism, producing documentary, but still romanticized pieces such as *New Moscow* (1937). From 1945 to 1972 he taught at the State All-Union Institute for Cinematography. JEB

PINAEVA, Ludmila Iosifovna (b. 1936) Sportswoman. Born in Krasnoe Selo near Leningrad, she won more awards in the Olympics, world and European championships than any other Soviet canoeist. She won the kayak singles event at the 1964 and 1968 Olympic Games, and the pairs at the 1972 Games, taking the bronze medal in that event in 1968. In addition she was five times world (1966–71), nine times European

(1961–71) and twenty-one times national champion between 1960 and 1972. JWR

PISKOTIN, Mikhail Ivanovich (b. 1924) An academic lawyer, political scientist and journal editor of distinction, Mikhail Piskotin was born in the Udmurtskaya ASSR in the Urals and is of Russian nationality. He fought in the Second World War from 1942 to 1945 in battles on the Voronezh, Steppe, First Ukrainian, First Belorussian, and the First and Third Ukrainian fronts and was seriously wounded. After the war he studied at the Kazan' Juridical Institute (1945–49), worked in the Ministry of Justice of the Baskhir ASSR (1949–50) and in 1950 began his postgraduate studies at the Institute of Law (later Institute of State and Law) of the Academy of Sciences in Moscow. There he spent most of his academic career, being editor-in-chief of the journal, *Soviet State and Law* from 1978 to 1987.

When a new Centre of Political Science Research under the joint auspices of the Institute of State and Law and the Soviet Association of Political Sciences was established in 1987, Piskotin became its first head. He remained in that post until 1989 when he was appointed editor of the journal of the new Soviet legislature, *Narodnyy deputat*.

In his own writings Piskotin has been a strong advocate of far-reaching economic and legal reform and his book, *Socialism and State Administration* (first published in Russian in 1984, in a second Russian edition in 1988 and in an English translation in 1989) was one of the most systematic critiques of the case for economic reform (from the standpoint of a specialist on public administration) to be published in the Soviet Union prior

to Gorbachev becoming General Secretary. AHB

PLASTOV, Arkadiy Aleksandrovich (1893–1972) Painter. Born in Prislonikha, Plastov studied at the Stroganov Industrial Art Institute and the MIPSA (1912–17). Acknowledging the mastery of Valentin Serov, Plastov regarded the Russian countryside as his major theme, putting this to didactic use in the 1930s and 1940s as in *Collective Farm Festival* (1937) and *A Fascist Flew Past* (1942). He also painted portraits of contemporaries and illustrated books. JEB

PLISETSKAYA, Maya Mikhaylovna (b. 1925) Outstanding prima ballerina and choreographer. Plisetskaya studied with Yelizaveta Gerdt and Mariya Leont'eva at the Bol'shoy Ballet School and also took courses with the celebrated teacher Agrippina Vaganova. Plisetskaya's extraordinary technical ability and wonderfully expressive stage presence began to receive notice during her school years, particularly in her graduation peformance of the 'Grand Pas' in *Paquita*.

She joined the Bol'shoy troupe in 1943 and developed an exceptionally broad repertoire of leading roles in classical and modern ballets. She was noted for impeccable technique, soaring jumps, musicality, and ability to portray dramatic tragedy.

Her early roles included the lead in Leonid Lavrovsky's *Raymonda* (1945) and the dual character Odette-Odile in *Swan Lake* (1947), a role which became the greatest in her repertoire. Her other classical roles included leads in *Sleeping Beauty, Giselle, Don Quixote,* and *Romeo and Juliet*. She also excelled in the modern repertoire, including Rostislav Zakharov's *The Fountain of Bakhchisaray*, versions of *The Stone*

Flower by both Leonid Lavrovsky and Yuriy Grigorovich, Vakhtang Chabukiani's *Laurencia,* and Igor' Moiseev's *Spartacus.* In 1967 she danced the lead in Alberto Alonso's *Carmen Suite,* a role for which she received great acclaim.

Plisetskaya's choreography has included *Anna Karenina* (1972) and *The Seagull* (1980), both using music by her husband Rodion Shchedrin. She appeared in the films *Stars of the Russian Ballet* (1953), *Swan Lake* (1957), and *Plisetskaya Dances* (1966). She has been a guest artist with numerous companies and has toured extensively. In 1987 she was named artistic director of the Spanish National Ballet and in 1988 she performed at the Soviet-American festival 'Making Music Together' and was honoured by a special tribute from the Martha Graham Company. SCS

PLYUSHCH, Leonid Ivanovich (b. 1939) Mathematician, human rights activist and literary critic. In 1969, as a Kiev correspondent of the journal *A Chronicle of Current Events,* he became a founder-member of the Moscow-based Action Group to Defend Civil Rights. He also wrote pseudonymous *samizdat* articles on literary-political themes, using a liberal Marxist approach and a combination of linguistic, psychological and political analysis. He was interned in a prison psychiatric hospital (1972–76), before an unusually strong campaign organized by his wife and foreign groups, including eventually the French Communist Party, gained his release. He was deported to France. His torture with psychotropic drugs is documented in his memoirs, *History's Carnival* (1979), and in T. Khodorovich (ed.), *The Case of Leonid Plyushch* (1976). PBR

PODGORNY, Nikolay Viktorovich (1903–1983) Soviet head of state from 1965 to 1977 and in the later Khrushchev years and earlier Brezhnev years an important member of the Politburo, Podgorny – a Ukrainian by nationality – was born in Karlovka in the Poltava province of the Ukraine. He was the son of a foundry worker whose own early career was as a manual worker in industry. From 1931 to 1939 Podgorny was employed in the Ukrainian sugar industry, latterly as chief engineer for a group of sugar refineries.

Podgorny embarked on his political career in 1939, becoming a deputy people's commissar of the food industry in the Ukraine; only a year later he was accorded the same title in the food industry commissariat of the USSR as a whole. Podgorny was director of the Moscow Technological Institute for the Food Industry (1942–44), once again deputy commissar for the food industry in the Ukraine (1944–46) and the Ukrainian government's representative in Moscow (1946–50).

Podgorny's career in the Communist Party apparatus took off in 1950 when he became first secretary of the Khar'kov regional party committee, a post he held until 1953 when he became second secretary of the party for the Ukraine as a whole. He was a strong and somewhat sycophantic supporter of Khrushchev, never stinting in his fulsome praise, and his career flourished as Khrushchev's grip on the levers of power became tighter. In 1956 Podgorny became a member of the Central Committee, in 1958 a candidate member of its Presidium and in 1960 a full member. He left Kiev for Moscow in 1963 to become a Secretary of the Central Committee of the CPSU while retaining his full Presidium (Politburo) membership.

After the fall of Khrushchev, Podgorny continued to be a prominent member of the top leadership team, although never a particularly impressive one. He lost his Secretaryship of the Central Committee in 1965 but became instead Chairman of the Presidium of the Supreme Soviet, the titular head of state. His position within the leadership weakened in the early nineteen-seventies when his supporter, Shelest, was replaced as Ukrainian First Secretary by Brezhnev's supporter, Shcherbitsky, and he was finally removed from all of his offices in 1977. Brezhnev himself wished to take over as head of state and Podgorny resisted this move. As a result he was brusquely removed from the Politburo in May and from the Chairmanship of the Presidium of the Supreme Soviet in June without any face-saving formulas such as the fiction that he had retired 'at his own request' or for health reasons. A H B

PODRABINEK, Aleksandr Pinkhosovich (b. 1953) Auxiliary doctor (*feldsher*) and human rights activist. For his dissent, he was barred from completing his training as a doctor. In 1977 he co-founded the Working Commission to Investigate the Use of Psychiatry for Political Purposes (1977–81), and wrote a book on psychiatric abuse, *Punitive Medicine* (1979). For this activity he served terms in labour camps and exile (1978–81 and 1981–83). In 1987 he became chief editor of the weekly human rights bulletin *Express-Khronika*. P B R

POGODIN, Nikolay Fedorovich (1900–1962) Dramatist, born near Rostov-on-Don. He began as a

journalist, and turned to playwriting in 1929, becoming the foremost Soviet dramatist of his time, most notably through his trilogy on the life of Lenin, *The Man with the Gun* (1937), *Kremlin Chimes* (1941), *No.3, Pathétique* (1958). G S S

POKROVSKY, Mikhail Nikolaevich (1868–1932) The founder of Soviet Marxist historical scholarship, Pokrovsky was a prolific historian and an energetic administrator. A Bolshevik from 1905, he pioneered the historical materialist analysis of Russian history, arguing that it had been determined by economic processes and class struggle, not by great rulers. After the October Revolution he was elected chairman of the Moscow soviet, and in 1918 was appointed deputy people's commissar of education. He played a leading part in establishing and heading the Communist Academy, the Institute of Red Professors, and the Central Archival Administration, in setting up the Workers' Faculties (*rabfaki*), and in founding historical journals such as *Marxist Historian* and *Class Struggle*. His publications, including *A Brief History of Russia* (1920–23) were extremely influential, and the Society of Marxist Historians (which he had also founded) was dominated by the 'school of Pokrovsky'. He died in 1932 an honoured figure. Before long, however, Stalin's intervention in historical debates changed orthodox interpretation of Russian history, and by 1936 Pokrovsky's ideas were condemned as schematic, mechanistic and anti-Marxist. Intellectually rehabilitated after 1956, though still seen as guilty of a simplified Marxist approach to history, his main works were republished in the 1960s. J B

POLEVOY, Boris (Kampov, Boris Nikolaevich) (1908–1981) Born in Moscow, Polevoy was a prose writer, journalist and war correspondent, who joined the party in 1940 and served as editor of *Youth* from 1962 to 1981. His socialist-realist classic, *The Story of a Real Man* (1946), concerns a pilot who lost his legs in a war-time crash but went on to fly again. KC

POLONSKAYA, Yelizaveta Grigore'vna (1890–1969) Born in Warsaw, she studied medicine at the Sorbonne before beginning her writing career. In the twenties she was associated with the Serapion Brothers and known as a poet. During the thirties she wrote sketches for *Pravda* and in later years she translated and wrote memoirs. KC

POLONSKY (real name Gusin), Vyacheslav Pavlovich (1886–1932) Literary critic and journalist. Polonsky began writing about modern literature while studying psychoneurology. In 1905 he became involved in Menshevik activity. His first monograph was a study of poster art in the Revolution; later he had a distinguished career as editor of *Press and Revolution* (1921–29) and of *Novyy Mir* (1926–31). An independent-minded critic, he wrote several volumes of articles in which émigré writers, fellow-travellers, Futurists or Proletarians were all objectively assessed. Bakunin was a lifelong interest. Latterly he renounced his preoccupation with Freud's concepts of the unconscious. He died of typhus soon after falling into political disfavour. JAEC

POLOZ'KOV, Ivan Kuz'mich (b. 1935) The First Secretary of the Communist Party of the Russian republic since June 1990 and a Politburo member since July of that year, Poloz'-kov is a Communist traditionalist of Russian nationality whose views are close to those of Yegor Ligachev. He was fairly narrowly defeated in the first round of voting for the Chairmanship of the Supreme Soviet of the Russian republic in May 1990 (458 votes to Yeltsin's 503). Poloz'kov, who has been a conservative Communist critic of radical political and economic reform, served in the Soviet army (1954–57), joined the Communist Party in 1958, and from 1958 to 1975 was engaged in Komsomol and party and soviet work in the Kursk region. From 1975 to 1978, 1980 to 1983 and 1984 to 1985 he worked in the apparatus of the Central Committee of the CPSU, in the last period as a sector head in the Department of Party Organizational Work at a time when it was led by Ligachev. Poloz'kov was First Secretary in Krasnodar' from 1985 to 1990. He became a member of the Central Committee of the CPSU in 1986, a member of the Congress of People's Deputies of the USSR in 1989 and a deputy in the Supreme Soviet of the RSFSR in 1990. AHB

POLYANSKY, Dmitriy Stepanovich (b. 1917) A prominent Soviet politician under Khrushchev and Brezhnev, Polyansky, a Communist Party member from 1939, was born into a peasant family in the Ukraine. After working on a state farm he studied at the Khar'kov Agricultural Institute from which he graduated in 1939 and thereafter made his career in the party and state apparatus. After holding a series of party secretaryships at the regional level, he became Chairman of the Council of Ministers for the RSFSR in 1958, a post he held until 1962. In 1958 Khrushchev brought him into the Presidium of the Central Committee as a candidate member and he was promoted to full membership in 1960. He remained in the Presidium (from 1966 named Politburo) until 1976, by which time, however, his relations with Khrushchev's successor, Brezhnev, were strained and he was dropped from the Soviet top leadership team. From 1965 to 1973 Polyansky was First Deputy Chairman of the Council of Ministers of the USSR (to Kosygin) and from 1973 to 1976 Minister of Agriculture. Thereafter he served abroad as a Soviet ambassador until his retirement. AHB

POMERANTSEVA, Erna Vasil'evna (1899–1980) Folklorist. Pomerantseva's main interest was in folk narrative, especially the development of the Russian folk-tale tradition in the nineteenth and twentieth centuries. She also wrote on folk poetry, and collected large numbers of tales in the field. FCMW

PONOMARENKO, Pantaleimon Kondrat'evich (1902–1984) Politician. While working for Malenkov in the Central Committee apparatus, Ponomarenko was elected First Secretary of the Belorussian Communist Party in 1938. He held this post throughout the war, directing the partisan movements in Belorussia and overseeing the subsequent re-Stalinization of the republic. From 1948 to 1952 he worked in the All-Union Secretariat and was a candidate member of the Presidium from 1953 to 1956. In 1954 he became second secretary of Kazakhstan. As his patron Malenkov's fortunes declined after 1954, Ponomarenko's did likewise. From 1956 to 1964 he held a number of diplomatic posts. WJT

PONOMAREV, Boris Nikolaevich (b. 1905) An influential Soviet politician – especially in the sphere of foreign policy and ideology – over many years, Ponomarev joined the Communist Party as early as 1919 and served in the Red Army during the Civil War. He studied at Moscow University and at the Institute of Red Professors and entered the party apparatus as a propagandist in 1926. In 1936 he joined the Comintern as a senior official and after further work in the sphere of propaganda and agitation, including the deputy directorship of the Institute of Marx-Engels-Lenin, Ponomarev began an exceptionally long stint as head of the International Department of the Central Committee which began in 1955 and ended only in 1985 shortly after Gorbachev became party General Secretary. He was a candidate member of the Politburo from 1972 to 1986 and his membership of the Central Committee itself, which began at the Twentieth Party Congress in 1956, ended as recently as April 1989 when he was included in a long list of party 'elder statesmen' who 'resigned' simultaneously in that month.

Although in Brezhnev's time, the International Department of the Central Committee under Ponomarev's headship contained some people of ability, Ponomarev himself was a conservative Communist who adapted slowly to change. At times there was tension between his department and the Ministry of Foreign Affairs which Gorbachev attempted, with some success, to overcome by appointing a career diplomat from the Ministry of Foreign Affairs, Anatoliy Dobrynin, as Ponomarev's successor. AHB

PONOMAREV, Nikolay Afanas'evich (b. 1918) Painter and graphic artist. Born in Aleksandrovsk-Grushevsky, Ponomarev studied in Rostov-on-Don and then, under Lentulov and Osmerkin, at the Surikov Institute, Moscow. His central subject is manual labour, and he received particular acclaim for his series *Miners of the Donbas* (1949–50). He is the current President of the Academy of Arts, Moscow. JEB

PONOMAREVA, Nina Ivanovna (b. 1929) Athlete. Ponomareva became the first-ever Soviet Olympic champion, winning the discus on 20 July 1952 in Helsinki. She went on to compete in three more Olympics, taking the bronze in 1956 and winning a gold medal in 1960. Born in Sverdlovsk, she retired from competition to Kiev where, as Nina Romaskova, she worked as coach with the Ukrainian Sports Committee. JWR

POPENCHENKO, Valeriy Vladimirovich (1937–1975) Boxer. He was one of the most exciting middleweight boxers in modern amateur boxing. A fiercely aggressive, hard-hitting yet technically superb boxer, he scored most of his wins on knock-outs. Besides being Olympic middleweight champion in 1964, he was awarded the Barker Cup as best boxer at the 1964 Olympic Games. He was twice European (1963 and 1965) champion and six times Soviet champion (1959–1965). Born at Kuntsevo, Moscow, he learned his boxing while a student at the Lengrad Naval Engineering College, eventually becoming a candidate of Technical Sciences in 1968. On retiring from boxing he became head of the Physical Education Department of the Bauman Technical Institute in Moscow. He died in a fall at work at the early age of thirty-eight. JWR

POPKOV, Viktor Yefimovich (1932–1974) Painter. Born in Moscow, a pupil of Kibrik at the Surikov Institute, Moscow (1952–58), Popkov at first concentrated on graphics, but he built his real reputation on his paintings of urban life such as *Plasterers* (1959) and *Builders of Bryatsk* (1961). JEB

POPOV, Aleksandr Dmitrievich (1892–1961) Stage director and theorist of drama. An actor at the Moscow Art Theatre before the Revolution, Popov worked in the Vakhtangov Theatre until 1930 when he became Artistic Director of the Theatre of the Revolution. From 1935 to 1960 he was head of the Red Army Theatre. His major productions included: *The Turning Point* (1927), Pogodin's *After the Ball* (1934) and his *The Silver Span* (1939) and an adaptation of Sholokhov's *Virgin Soil Upturned* (1957). RT

POPOV, Gavriil Kharitonovich (b. 1936) Prominent economist and politician. Popov, who is of Greek ethnic origin, is a radical economic and political reformer who in the Brezhnev era introduced management studies into Moscow University. He became a member of the Communist Party in 1959, the year of his graduation from the Economics Faculty of Moscow University where he stayed on as a teacher, becoming Dean of the Economics Faculty in 1977. With support from the State Committee of Science and Technology and particularly of its then deputy chairman, Zhermen Gvishiani, Popov campaigned for the introduction of business studies in his own university and elsewhere in the Soviet Union. A professor from 1971, he published ten books on management techniques in the 1970s alone.

During the period of *perestroika* he has become ever more prominent as a public figure. In 1988 he was appointed Editor-in-Chief of the journal *Voprosy ekonomiki* in succession to the conservative Tigran Khachaturov. A year later he was elected to membership of the Congress of People's Deputies where he quickly became one of the leaders of the Inter-Regional Group of Deputies who constituted a pressure group within the legislature for more radical change. Popov attained still greater political significance in 1990 when he was elected Chairman of the Moscow city soviet following his success and that of the 'democratic platform' in the Moscow local election in March of that year. His own standpoint and that of a majority on the soviet was so much more radical than that of the First Secretary of the Moscow party organization and of the party committee that clashes soon occurred. Popov resigned from the Communist Party in July 1990. AHB, MCK

POPOV, Pavel Il'ich (1872–1950) The founder of Soviet state statistics, Popov was greatly respected by Lenin, whom he first met in the late 1890s. The son of a rural scribe in Irkutsk, he was first arrested for revolutionary activities in 1896, but he did not join the party until 1924. He worked in local and national statistical offices in various capacities before the revolution. In 1918 Popov proposed the formation of the Central Statistical Administration (TsSU) to Lenin, and was appointed its first head (1918–26). He was dismissed after a dispute with Stalin about the work of TsSU, and from that time he held minor posts. RWD

POPOV, Vladimir Dmitrievich (b. 1941) The chief editor of a new party journal, *Dialog* (Dialogue) which began publication in January 1990, Popov was born in the village of Plotnikovo in the Kuransk region of the Russian republic. He started out as a metal worker, but after graduating from the Chelyabinsk Polytechnical Institute, he became a member of its staff and secretary of the Komsomol organization there. He worked in the Central Committee of the Komsomol (1971–74) and between 1974 and 1979 at the Academy of Social Sciences attached to the Central Committee of the Communist Party. His first experience of journalism was as editor of the student journal, *Studencheskiy meridian* (1979–87), following which he worked in the apparatus of the party Central Committee, first in the Department of Science and Educational Institutions and (following its abolition) in the Ideological Department. It was from there that he was appointed in November 1989 to take charge of the editorial direction of the new monthly journal, *Dialog*. AHB

POPOVA, Lyubov' Sergeevna (1889–1924) Painter and designer. Born near Moscow, Popova started her education as a pupil of Yuon and Stanislav Zhukovsky (1907–8), developing her distinctive artistic world-view after studying Cubism in Paris (1912–13 and 1914) and after her encounters with Malevich and Tatlin in Moscow. In 1916 she reached her own method of abstract painting which, after the Revolution, she applied to many areas of design, especially scenography and textiles, becoming a primary exponent of Constructivism. In 1918 she joined the faculty at Svomas, in 1920 was a member of the Institute of Artistic Culture and in 1921 contributed to the '5 × 5 = 25' exhibition in Moscow. JEB

POSOKHIN, Mikhail Vasil'evich (b. 1910) Architect. Born in Tomsk, Posokhin, one of the Soviet Union's most distinguished architects, received his training as an engineer, geodesist and designer in Kuznetsk until he moved to Moscow in 1935. Indebted to I. Golosov, he worked on many buildings in the 1940s onwards such as the large administrative office block on Frunze Street and the high rise building on Vostaniya Square (1948–54), both of which incorporate the eclecticism of the Stalin style. However, he is best remembered for his Palace of Congresses in the Kremlin (1959–61), his CMEA headquarters (1963–70) and his supervision of the New Arbat complex on Kalinin Prospect, all of which dispense with the decorativism of traditional Socialist Realism and emphasize functionality and clarity of form.

JEB

POSPELOV, Petr Nikolaevich (1898–1979) Russian historian and ideologist. Rather like a liberal Suslov (with whom he occasionally sparred), P. N. Pospelov spent much of his career elucidating and defending Khrushchev's doctrinal positions. During the 1940s he wrote many historical works and held leading positions in the Higher Party School, the Academy of Social Sciences and similar bodies. He also spent considerable time in *agitprop* activities, including two stints as editor of *Pravda*. Pospelov entered the Central Committee Secretariat in 1953 and was a candidate member of the Presidium from July 1957 until the Twenty-Second Congress in 1961. Pospelov's close links to Khrushchev were underscored by his appointment as the latter's deputy in the newly created RSFSR Party Bureau in 1956. He was dropped from the Secretariat in 1960.

WJT

POSTYSHEV, Pavel Petrovich (1887–1939) A relatively minor party official during the inter-war period, Postyshev was born in Ivanovo-Voznesensk into a weaver's family. He qualified as an electrician and soon became a political activist, engaging in political work from 1901 onwards and joining the Bolsheviks in 1904. An active participant in the 1905 and 1917 revolutions, Postyshev became involved in the establishment of Soviet rule in Eastern Siberia. In 1926 he became a party secretary in the Ukraine, and served as a member of the party Secretariat in Kiev or Moscow from this date onwards. In 1934 he became a candidate member of the Politburo, but in 1937 he was relieved of his posts and in 1938 he was arrested. He died in imprisonment.

SLW

PREOBRAZHENSKA, Ol'ga Iosifovna (1871–1962) Prima ballerina and teacher. Preobrazhenska studied at the Imperial Ballet School with such illustrious teachers as Enrico Cecchetti, Christian Johansson, Marius Petipa, and Lev Ivanov. She joined the Maryinsky troupe upon graduation in 1889 and danced on the Imperial stage for more than twenty-five years. Renowned for her superb technique, elegance, musicality and lyricism, Preobrazhenska had a wide and varied repertoire. She danced leading parts in all major classical ballets, including *Coppélia*, *Sleeping Beauty*, *Swan Lake*, *Giselle*, and *La fille mal gardée*. She created leading roles in Marius Petipa's *Harlequinade* and in Michel Fokine's *Egyptian Nights*. Preobrazhenska made a number of foreign tours, appearing at La Scala, the Paris Opéra, Covent Garden, and with Serge Diaghilev's Ballets Russes. She taught at the Imperial (later Petrograd) Ballet School (1901–2, 1914–21) and at Akim Volynsky's School of Russian Ballet (1917–21). Following the Revolution, Preobrazhenska settled in Paris, where she taught at the Studio Wacker from 1924 to 1960. scs

PREOBRAZHENSKAYA, Ol'ga Ivanovna (1881–1971) Film director. Preobrazhenskaya was one of the first women film directors in Soviet cinema. Her most famous work, *Women of Ryazan'* (1927), depicted the lot of downtrodden peasant women before the Revolution. RT

PREOBRAZHENSKY, Yevgeniy Aleksandrovich (1886–1937) An economist and party activist of radical inclination, Preobrazhensky was born into a priest's family in the town of Bolkhoz in central Russia. According to his later autobiography, he was very religious as a child but became a convinced atheist by the age of fourteen and identified with the revolutionary cause by his later school years. He became involved in underground political work in Orel' and later in Moscow and elsewhere. After the February revolution Preobrazhensky returned to the Urals, where he was elected to the regional party committee and was involved in the establishment of Soviet rule. He took part in the struggle against Kolchak on the eastern front, and was slightly wounded; he was subsequently recalled to Moscow to work on *Pravda* and took part in the drafting of the 1919 Party Programme. After further party and state work in the Urals, Preobrazhensky became a Central Committee Secretary responsible for financial matters within both party and state institutions. A firmly left-

wing Communist who had crossed swords with Stalin as early as 1917, Preobrazhensky was a member of the Trotskyist opposition and repeatedly deplored the erosion of the party's internal democracy (as he conceived of it). He was expelled from the party several times, finally in 1935, and was then arrested and imprisoned. He appeared as a prosecution witness at the trial of Zinov'ev but perished himself in imprisonment the following year. His *ABC of Communism*, written jointly with Bukharin, remains an influential exposition of socialist theory, and his economic writings enjoy a considerable reputation. SLW

PREZENT, Isaak Izrailovich (1902–1970?) Agronomist, philosopher. A Party member since 1921, Prezent became an ideological activist in biology around 1930. In 1935 he joined with Lysenko and became his chief ideologist, leading the attack on genetics. He probably played a central role in creating the theories at the core of 'Michurinist biology'. Teaching at Leningrad University (1931–48) he formulated so-called 'creative Darwinism' which, contrary to Darwin's view, denied that intra-specific competition played any role in evolution. Appointed a member of the Lenin All-Union Academy of Agricultural Sciences (VASKhNIL) in mid-1948, he helped orchestrate its infamous August session, which confirmed the party's support for Lysenko, and worked in the VASKhNIL apparatus (1951–56) to enforce compliance. In 1956 he went to work at the Institute of Genetics of the USSR Academy of Sciences but, after a falling out with Lysenko, he faded from public view even before the repudiation of Lysenkoism in 1965. MBA

PRIMAKOV, Yevgeniy Maksimovich (b. 1929) Primakov is highly unusual among Soviet party leaders in that a large part of his career has been in academic life. His childhood and youth were spent in the Georgian capital of Tbilisi but he is of Russian nationality. Primakov, who joined the Communist Party in 1959, became a full member of the Academy of Sciences in 1979.

A graduate of the Moscow Institute of Oriental Studies and of Moscow University, he worked from 1953 to 1962 in the State Committee of the USSR Council of Ministers for Television and Radio Broadcasting. From 1962 to 1970 he was a journalist on *Pravda* (Middle East correspondent, 1966–70) before moving to be Deputy Director of IMEMO (1970–77).

Primakov became Director of the Institute of Oriental Studies of the Academy of Sciences in 1977 and remained in that office until 1985 when he returned to IMEMO, this time as Director. In 1986 he was elected to candidate membership of the Central Committee of the Communist Party and in 1988 became the head of a new Department for World Economy and International Relations within the USSR Academy of Sciences charged with the coordination of the activities of the various internationally-oriented institutes.

From the late 1980s Primakov's promotion has been especially rapid. He was elevated from candidate to full membership of the Central Committee in April 1989 and in September of the same year became a candidate member of the Politburo. He was elected to the Congress of People's Deputies and the Supreme Soviet in 1989 and from June 1989 until March of the following year he was Chairman of the Soviet of the Union. He gave up that latter post upon being appointed to Gorbachev's Presidential Council when it was formed in March 1989. He also ceased to be a candidate member of the Politburo when that rank was abolished in July 1990.

Primakov has travelled widely and has a broad range of academic and political contacts in the Soviet Union and abroad as a result of the high offices in policy-oriented international institutes which he held. He has been an influential adviser to the Soviet leadership on foreign policy and on Middle Eastern affairs, in particular.
AHB

PRISTAVKIN, Anatoliy Ignat'evich (b. 1931) Pristavkin was born near Moscow and was brought up in various orphanages. He graduated from the Gor'ky Institute of Literature in 1959, and during the 1960s and 1970s published a series of autobiographical and documentary novels and stories about construction work in Siberia. He joined the Communist Party in 1965. In 1987 his novel *The Golden Cloud* was one of the first literary sensations of *glasnost'*. Pristavkin was the leading figure behind the formation of the pro-*glasnost'* group 'April' within the Union of Writers in March 1989. GSS

PROKHANOV, Ivan Stepanovich (1869–1935) Founder of the Evangelical Christian Union in 1909. Prokhanov was brought up in a Molokane family which became Baptist. He studied engineering in St Petersburg, becoming involved with the evangelical groups founded by Lord Radstock. From 1895 to 1898 he studied theology abroad. After his return to St

Petersburg, he was employed by the Westinghouse company until 1921, working in his spare time for the church, and as a religious publisher. From 1921 to 1928 he worked full time for the church and despite some difficulties with the Soviet authorities led it through a period of unprecedented growth. He drew up plans for an evangelical city in Siberia, for which a site was even allocated. In 1928, during a visit abroad, he learnt of the worsening situation of the churches and decided not to return to the Soviet Union. He died in exile in Berlin in 1935. MR

PROKOF'EV, Aleksandr Andreevich (1900–1971) Poet and literary official, born near Leningrad and based in that city throughout his career. A party member from 1919, he served in the Civil War. He is noted for patriotic, old-fashioned lyrics in folksy style. GSS

PROKOF'EV, Sergey Sergeevich (1891–1953) Composer, pianist and conductor. Sergey Prokof'ev (Prokofiev) was born in Sontsovka and died in Moscow. Showing outstanding musical gifts at an early age, he received his first piano lessons from his mother. After some tuition with Glier in Moscow, he entered the St Petersburg Conservatory in 1904 (aged thirteen), where he studied composition with Lyadov, orchestration with Rimsky-Korsakov, and formal analysis with Wihtol (Vītols). He graduated in composition in 1909 and in piano (under Anna Esipova) in 1914, winning at the same time the Anton Rubinstein prize for his First Piano Concerto. A ballet was commissioned by Diaghilev in 1914. After a period of extensive concert tours, Prokof'ev left for the United States in 1918,

returning to Europe in 1920. The following years were spent in incessant activity as composer and performer, both in Europe, the USA and USSR. In 1932 he returned to Russia, which remained his home for the rest of his life. He was made a People's Artist of the RSFSR in 1947. A prolific composer in varied genres, many of his compositions are in the standard international concert repertoire. In his own country, however, his relations with the State were uneasy and he was accused of 'formalism' in 1948 together with Shostakovich, Myaskovsky and others. GS

PROKOF'EV, Yuriy Anatol'evich (b. 1939) Born in the Karakalpak ASSR, Prokof'ev has worked all his life in Komsomol and party jobs in Moscow. He was First Secretary of Kuybyshev *raikom* (1983–85), head of a department of Moscow *gorkom* (1985–86), Secretary to the *gorispolkom* (1986–88) and second secretary of the *gorkom*, before becoming First Secretary of the Moscow City organization of the CPSU in November 1989. He joined the Politburo in July 1990. JHM

PROKOF'EVA-BEL'GOVSKAYA, Aleksandra Alekseevna (1903–1984) Cytogeneticist. A 1930 graduate of Leningrad University, Prokof'eva worked in the laboratory of genetics of the USSR Academy of Sciences (transformed into the Institute of Genetics in 1933) headed by N. I. Vavilov, where she collaborated with the American Nobel prize-winner H. J. Muller (1933–37), on studies of drosophila cytogenetics. After marrying co-worker Mark Bel'govsky, she changed her last name to the hyphenated form. She subsequently worked in the Institute of Cytology, Histology, and Embryology (1945–48), the Antibiotics Institute (1948–56), the Biophysics Institute (1956–62), and (after 1962) Engel′gardt's Institute of Radiation and Physiocochemical Biology (renamed the Institute of Molecular Biology). With the official renunciation of Lysenko in 1965, she was elected a corresponding member of the USSR Academy of Medical Sciences. Trained as a drosophila cytogeneticist, and one of the world's leading experts on heterochromatic chromosomal regions, Prokof′eva became the leading Soviet expert in human cytogenetics. MBA

PROPP, Vladimir Yakovlevich (1895–1970) A folklorist influenced by the Formalists. The publication of his *Morphology of the Folktale* in 1928 (reprinted 1968) received little notice, but its translation into English in 1958 created a powerful response among Western anthropologists, especially in Levi-Strauss; it is still a classic of folklore and Structuralism. Propp used structural analysis to demonstrate that folktales are categorized by the characters' functions in the plot; folktale structure, he argued, is invariable and not related to the social order which produced the tale, an unusual position at the time. His *Historical Roots of the Magic Folktale* (1946) was attacked as 'cosmopolitan'. In *The Russian Heroic Epic* (1955–58), he reversed his position, relating epics to specific time periods and social groups. In *Russian Agrarian Holidays* (1983), he discussed the economic basis of each holiday. He was a professor of folklore at Leningrad University from 1938 to his death. KC

PROROKOV, Boris Ivanovich (1911–1972) Graphic artist and painter. Born in Ivanovo-Voznesenk, Prorokov received his training at Vkhutein, studying under Konstantin Istomin and Moor, before beginning his career as an illustrator, for example, for *Krokodil*. He is remembered for his graphic albums and posters such as *Here's Your America* (1948) and *This Must Never Be Repeated* (1958–59). JEB

PROTAZANOV, Yakov Aleksandrovich (1881–1945) Film director. Protazanov was the leading director of popular films in the twenties and thirties. He began making films before the Revolution and his early career included the first screen adaptation of Tolstoy's *War and Peace* (1915). His next major film was *Father Sergius* (1918), the first feature produced after the Revolution. Protazanov emigrated to France in 1920 but returned to the Soviet Union in 1923. His next film was the extraordinary *Aelita* (1924), which involved a fantasy about a revolution on Mars, with sets by Constructivist designers. His subsequent films were notable for the wide variety of genres that they encompassed from *The Three Millions Trial* (1926), a satire on contemporary capitalist values, through *The Forty First* (1927), a tale of Civil War heroism, and *Don Diego and Pelagia* (1928), which satirized the effects of bureaucracy on country life, to the brilliant anti-religious satire, *The Feast of St Jürgen* (1929). Protazanov's last films were *Tommy* (1931), whose hero was a British soldier drafted in to fight against the Bolsheviks in the Civil War but who changes sides, and *Nasreddin in Bukhara* (1943). Of all the Soviet film directors who, in the shadow of Eisenstein and the other acknowledged masters, have been undervalued, Protazanov is by far the most underrated and, in the West at least, remains the least known. RT

PROTOPOPOV, Oleg Alekseevich, *see* BELOUSOVA, Ludmila Yevgen'evna

PROZUMENSHCHIKOVA, Galina Nikolaevna (b. 1948) Swimmer. She had the unique merit of being the first Soviet swimmer to win an Olympic event – the 200 m breast stroke at the 1964 Tokyo Olympics at the age of fifteen. Strangely enough, she had only learned to swim four years previously, joining a Sevastopol' swimming school at thirteen and progressing from novice to Olympic champion in two years. Born in Sevastopol', she continued her success after the 1964 Olympics, winning two silver and two bronze medals at the 1968 and 1972 Olympics in the 100 and 200 m breast stroke; she also became European champion three times (1966–70), and Soviet champion fifteen times (1963–73). JWR

PRUNSKENE, Kazimera-Danute Prano (Prunskiene, Kazimera-Danute) (b. 1943) A Lithuanian economist, Prunskene was a member both of the CPSU and, from 1988, of the Council of Sajudis. She was rector of an economics institute in Vilnius before becoming Deputy Chairman of the Lithuanian Council of Ministers, and a deputy to the Soviet Congress of People's Deputies in 1989. Prunskene was elected Premier-Minister of the Lithuanian Republic in March 1990. JHM

PRYANISHNIKOV, Dmitriy Nikolaevich (1865–1948) Agricultural chemist. A student of K. A. Timiryazev, Pryanishnikov graduated from Moscow University (1887) and the Petrov Academy (1889) and did postgraduate studies abroad (1892–94) on albumin metabolism in plants that led to his master's (1896) and doctoral (1900) dissertations. In 1895 he joined the staff of the Moscow Agricultural Institute (renamed the Timiryazev Agricultural Academy in 1923) where he worked for the rest of his life, including two years as rector (1916–17). He pioneered research in Russia on plant chemistry and nutrition, nitrogen fixation, and fertilizers and published important research on the metabolism of ammonia, asparagine, phosphorus, and potassium salts in plants and soil chemistry that led to his election to the Academy of Sciences as a corresponding member (1913) and full member (1929). An influential pedagogue, he was active in the development of scientific agriculture in Russia, teaching courses at Moscow University (1891–1931), directing the Golitsyn Agricultural Courses for Women (1900–17), and writing a series of influential and pioneering textbooks notably *Agriculture for the Specialist* (1898; 10th ed., 1938), *Fertilizer Science* (1900; 5th edn, 1922), *Plant Chemistry* (1907), and *Agrochemistry* (1934). During the Soviet period, he organized research in various new fertilizer institutes, worked in Gosplan on the chemicalization of agriculture, helped his student N. I. Vavilov to create the Lenin All-Union Academy of Agricultural Sciences (VASKhNIL), and was elected a member (1935). During the late 1930s Stalinist support for Vil'yams undermined Pryanishnikov's influence, but he was never repressed, perhaps due to the fact that one of his devoted students was the wife of Beria. MBA

PUDOVKIN, Vsevolod Illarionovich (1893–1953) Film director. Pudovkin was one of the leading Soviet film directors and was also an important actor and theorist. He originally studied chemistry and physics

303

and was imprisoned by the Germans in the First World War. After the Revolution he became a founder member of Kuleshov's Workshop at the Moscow State Film School and acted in his *The Extraordinary Adventures of Mr West in the Land of the Bolsheviks* (1924), *The Death Ray* (1925) and *The Happy Canary* (1929). Pudovkin's own first film as director was a comedy, *Chess Fever* (1925) and this was followed by a scientific short, *The Mechanics of the Brain* (1926). His three major films were *The Mother* (1926), based loosely on Gor'ky's account of the 1905 Revolution; *The End of St Petersburg* (1927), dealing with the events of 1917; and *Storm over Asia* (1929), a treatment of the British occupation of Mongolia. Pudovkin's first sound film was *A Simple Chance* (1932) but, apart perhaps from *The Deserter* (1933), his later work deteriorated for reasons not entirely within his control. His subsequent films include *Victory* (1938), *Admiral Nakhimov* (1946) and *The Return of Vasiliy Bortnikov* (1953). His theoretical writings, influenced by Kuleshov, elaborated the role of montage in cinema specificity, although he accorded a higher importance to the role of the actor than did his fellow film-maker, Eisenstein. Pudovkin's essays, 'The Film Scenario' and 'The Film Director and Film Material' are essential texts in the analysis of film technique. RT

PUGO, Boris Karlovich (Pugo, Boriss) (b. 1937) Born in Kalinin, the son of a Latvian communist émigré, Pugo has been an official since 1961. He was First Secretary of the Latvian Komsomol (1969–70), Secretary of the All-Union Komsomol (1970–74) and First Secretary of Riga *gorkom* (1975–76). Then he moved to the KGB of Latvia, of which he was First Deputy Chairman (1977–80) and Chairman (1980–84). From 1984 to 1988 he was First Secretary of the Latvian Communist Party, and then became Chairman of the All-Union Committee of Party Control, the body which handles (*inter alia*) the rehabilitation of Stalin's victims. Pugo has been a candidate member of the Politburo since September 1989. Careers, like Pugo's, which combine youth and nationality affairs with security have been common in Soviet politics. JHM

PUKHOVA, Zoya Pavlovna (b. 1936) Chairperson of the Soviet Women's Committee since 1987 and successor to Valentina Nikolaevna Tereshkova. Pukhova, Russian by nationality and a member of the CPSU since 1962, was a weaver in the Balashov textile factory in the town of Ivanov from 1952 to 1973, where she was awarded the title of Hero of Socialist Labour. First elected as a People's Deputy to the Supreme Soviet in 1966, she later became chair of the Supreme Soviet's commission concerned with women's work, daily life and the welfare of mother and child. Appointed director in 1973 of the Eighth March weaving factory in Ivanov, she was named chairperson of the Ivanov oblast' Soviet executive committee in 1985, and elected to the reformed Congress of People's Deputies in 1989. Known for her pointed speech to the Ninteenth Party Conference in 1988 in which she criticized the appalling working conditions for women in the textile industry, she has also argued against the suggestion that women should come out of the labour force at a time of *perestroika*. MB

PUSHKIN, Aleksandr Ivanovich (1907–1970) Ballet dancer and leading teacher. Pushkin studied at Nikolay Legat's private school and with Aleksandr Shirayev and Vladimir Ponomarev at the Leningrad Ballet School, from which he graduated in 1925. Thereupon he joined the Kirov troupe and was a principal dancer with the company from 1925 to 1953. He particularly excelled in classical variations, such as the Blue-Bird pas de deux from *Sleeping Beauty*. In addition to his classical roles, Pushkin created the parts of Philippe in Vasiliy Vaynonen's *The Flames of Paris* (1932) and the Poet in Rostislav Zakharov's *Lost Illusions* (1936).

Pushkin began teaching at Leningrad Ballet School in 1932 and from 1953 also taught advanced classes at the Kirov Theatre. With his comprehensive mastery of the male repertoire and his extraordinary ability to break down and analyze movements, Pushkin was considered the foremost teacher of classical ballet in Leningrad and the veritable standard of perfection. Hundreds of the combinations he developed are still being used.

Pushkin's outstanding students include Nikita Dolgushin, Oleg Vinogradov, Yuriy Grigorovich, Rudolf Nureyev, Mikhail Baryshnikov, and Valeriy Panov. He also taught some westerners who studied at the Kirov, and assisted in training dancers in various Soviet republics. scs

PYATAKOV, Georgiy (Yuriy) Leonidovich (1890–1937) A prominent Communist politician and administrator, described by Lenin in 1922 as 'a person of undoubtedly outstanding will and outstanding talents, but too much attracted by administering and the administrative side of affairs to be relied upon in a serious political question'. The son of a well-to-do sugar industrialist, Pyatakov, originally an anarchist, joined the Bolsheviks in 1910. He sided with the Left Communists in Spring 1918, and the Military Opposition in 1919. He was a supporter of Trotsky (1920–27), and was expelled from the party, but his membership was restored when he decided to support Stalin's industrialization policy in 1928. He headed the Ukrainian Bolshevik government in 1918, and held leading posts in VSNKh (1921–26). He was bitterly attacked by Dzerzhinsky at the July 1926 Central Committee plenum for supporting the United Opposition. Pyatakov was appointed first vice-chairman, then chairman of the State Bank (1928–30); he organized credit reform, but was dismissed for encouraging inflation. Under Ordzhonikidze he was a very senior official of VSNKh (1930–32), and then of the People's Commissariat for Heavy Industry of which he was deputy head with wide responsibilities (1932–36). He was the principal defendant in the January 1937 trial and was executed. He had been a candidate member of the party Central Committee (1921–23), and then a full member (1923–27, 1930–37). RWD

P'YAVKO, Vladislav Ivanovich (b. 1941) Tenor. Vladislav P'yavko was born at Krasnoyarsk. On graduating from the Lunacharsky Theatrical Institute in 1965, he became a soloist with the Moscow Bol'shoy. He spent 1968 to 1969 in further training at La Scala, Milan. He obtained second prize at the Fourth International Tchaikovsky Competition in Moscow in 1970. He was made an Honoured Artist of the RSFSR in 1978. He has toured extensively abroad and has made a number of recordings. GS

PYR'EV, Ivan Aleksandrovich
(1901–1968) Actor and director.
Pyr'ev was originally a *Proletkul't* actor
but later became a film director.
His numerous films include the satire,
The Government Official (1931), the
anti-fascist work *The Conveyor Belt of
Death* (1933), the drama *The Party
Card* (1936) and the musical
comedy *Tractor Drivers* (1939). His last
films were adaptations of Dostoevsky.
RT

R

RÄÄTS, Jaan (b. 1932) Estonian composer. Jaan Rääts was born in Tartu. A pupil of Heino Eller at the Tallinn Conservatory, he graduated in 1957. From 1956 to 1966 he was music director firstly of the Estonian Radio, then of Estonian Television. A member of the party since 1964, he was made a People's Artist of the Estonian SSR in 1977. Composer of seven symphonies, his work reflects current ideological trends. GS

RABINOVICH, Isaak Moyseevich (1894–1961) Designer. Born in Kiev, Rabinovich – one of the Ukraine's most talented stage designers – attended the Kiev Art Institute (1906–12) and Ekster's private studio (1917–18), supporting her lyrical interpretation of Cubism and then Constructivism. From the 1920s to the 1950s he lived primarily in Moscow, designing many productions at MKhAT, the Bol'shoy and the Malyy Theatres, including *Lysistrata* (1923) and *Sleeping Beauty* (1936). JEB

RADEK (Sobel'zon), Karl Berngardovich (1885–1939) A party publicist during the inter-war period, internationalist in his outlook, witty and eloquent but opportunistic and politically lightweight, Radek was born in L'vov in a Jewish family strongly influenced by German culture. From

the age of fourteen he was active in the workers' movement in Galicia and began to contribute to socialist periodicals. Radek attended Cracow University, nominally to study law, but soon left for Switzerland where he became active in radical émigré politics. There followed periods of socialist journalism in Warsaw and in various parts of Germany, where he developed contacts with left-wing Social Democrats. After the start of the First World War Radek returned to Switzerland where he took part in the Zimmerwald and Kienthal conferences of anti-war socialists.

Radek arrived in Petrograd shortly after the Bolsheviks had seized power and threw himself into diplomatic and journalistic work. He was a member of the Soviet delegation at the Brest-Litovsk peace conference and directed the Central European section of the Commissariat of International Affairs; he was also a fraternal delegate to German and Norwegian communist congresses and from 1920 served as one of the secretaries of the Communist International, delivering reports at most of its early meetings. Radek sided with the Trotskyist opposition in the mid-1920s and lost his positions on the party Central Committee and the Communist International executive committee, securing the very modest consolation of the rectorship of the Sun Yat-Sen University in Moscow. In 1927 he was expelled from the party and exiled, but in 1929 he recanted and was re-admitted. In 1936 he demanded the death penalty for Zinov'ev and Kamenev, but by the end of the year he too had been arrested and the following year he was sentenced to ten years' imprisonment. (He was cleared of charges and rehabilitated in 1988.) He is believed to have been murdered by fellow prisoners in 1939 or shortly afterwards. 'A little man, with a huge head, protruding ears ..., spectacles and a large mouth with yellow, tobacco-stained teeth', as the British diplomat Bruce Lockhart described him, Radek was a talented satirical journalist and a valued adviser on foreign, particularly German, affairs, but he was widely disliked and was never a member of the highest leadership circles. SLW

RADLOV, Sergey Ernestovich (1892–1958) Stage director whose career began with theatrical work on the Civil War fronts, Radlov organized mass revolutionary festivities in Petrograd and ran the Popular Comedy Theatre there from 1920 until 1922. Between 1923 and 1927 he directed a series of Expressionist productions of the classics such as *Lysistrata* (1924) and *Othello* (1927). He also worked as an opera and ballet director: his productions included Prokof'ev's *Love for Three Oranges* (1926) and Berg's *Wozzeck* (1927). He was Artistic Director of the Leningrad Opera and Ballet Company from 1931 to 1934, producing Rossini's *William Tell* (1932) and *The Fountain of Bakhchisaray* (1934). From 1936 to 1938 he was Artistic Director of the Leningrad

Pushkin Theatre, where he directed the première of Afinogenov's *Salute to Spain* (1936). He was simultaneously head of the Youth (Molodoy) Theatre (1929–42). RT

RAIKH, Zinaida Nikolaevna (1894–1939) A stage actress who trained under Meyerkhol'd and became his wife and the leading actress in his theatre. Her roles included: Ostrovsky's *The Forest* and Ehrenburg's *Give Us Europe!* (both 1924), Faiko's *Bubus the Teacher* and Erdman's *The Warrant* (both 1925), Gogol''s *The Inspector General* (1926), *The Magnanimous Cuckold* (1928), Mayakovsky's *The Bath House* (1930), Vishnevsky's *The Final and Decisive Battle* (1931) and Meyerkhol'd's version of Dumas' *The Lady of the Camellias* (1934). Three of these productions were still in the repertoire in the week before the Meyerkhol'd Theatre was closed in January 1938. She was brutally murdered after Meyerkhol'd's arrest in June 1939. RT

RAIZMAN, Yuliy Yakovlevich (b. 1903) Film director. Raizman is one of the leading veteran film directors in the realist tradition. His many films, spanning a career lasting almost sixty years of active work, include: *Penal Servitude* (1927), *The Earth is Thirsty* (1930), *Pilots* (1935), *The Last Night* (1937), *A Communist* (1958), *Your Contemporary* (1968), *Private Life* (1983) and *A Time of Wishes* (1984). He is also Artistic Director of the Mosfil'm Studios. RT

RAKHLIN, Natan Grigor'evich (1906–1979) Conductor. Natan Rakhlin was born in Snovsk. After spending the years 1923 to 1927 at the Kiev Conservatory studying violin, he entered the Lysenko Institute of Music and Drama where he was a pupil in conducting of Aleksandr Orlov. On graduating in 1930, he then went on to study theory and composition in Leningrad. He was in charge of the State Symphonic Orchestra of the Ukrainian SSR (1937–41 and 1946–62) and was chief conductor of the State Symphony Orchestra of the USSR (1941–45). In 1966 he founded and headed the State Symphony Orchestra of the Kazan' SSR and since 1967 taught at the Kazan' Conservatory. A member of the party since 1947, and the recipient of many honours, including that of the Order of Lenin, he was made a People's Artist in 1948. GS

RAKOVSKY, Khristian Georgievich (1873–1941) Rakovsky, a cultivated and cosmopolitan diplomat and statesman who later became an influential member of the Trotskyist opposition, was born in the Bulgarian town of Kotel, the son of a prosperous trader with connections on his mother's side with the Bulgarian revolutionary movement. The young Rakovsky conceived a strong sympathy for Russia based partly on his experience of that country's support against the Turks. Rakovsky became politically active while still a school pupil and was compelled to further his studies elsewhere, entering the medical faculty at Geneva University and becoming acquainted with the city's émigré circles. After three years Rakovsky moved to Berlin, and then to Zurich and to Montpellier, where he completed a doctoral dissertation. Rakovsky had married a Russian by this stage, and in 1899 made a visit to St Petersburg. For the most part, however, he was based in Paris, where he practised briefly as a doctor, and in the Balkans, where he helped to organize an internationalist grouping of socialists after the First World War had broken out. Rakovsky was

arrested in Rumania in 1916 but was freed the following year by Russian troops and reached Petrograd by late 1917. During the Civil War he represented the Soviet government on the south-western front, and then became chairman of the provisional revolutionary government of the Ukraine in 1918, combining it with other positions. Rakovsky remained in the Ukraine until 1923 when he was appointed Soviet representative to Great Britain, becoming Soviet ambassador to France two years later.

Rakovsky, an early and firm friend of Trotsky, was an open and effective opponent of Stalin in intra-party disputes; as a result he was expelled from the party in 1927 and banished, first to Saratov and then to Astrakhan'. Rakovsky continued to contribute to discussions within the Trotskyist movement during this time, particularly in a celebrated letter on the degeneration of Soviet power which continues to enjoy some influence. In 1934, believing that the USSR's international position made this necessary, Rakovsky recanted, but he was arrested and was one of the major defendants in the purge trial of 1938. He was sentenced to twenty years' imprisonment and died in detention in 1941. SLW

RASHIDOV, Sharaf Rashidovich (1917–1983) Uzbek political leader. One of a group of Central Asian politicians closely associated with L. I. Brezhnev during the 1970s and early 1980s, Sharaf Rashidov began his party career as a journalist prior to the Second World War. Severely wounded in 1942, he was discharged from the army and returned to journalism, editing the republican party organ *Kzyl Uzbekistan* and occupying posts in the Uzbek Supreme Soviet and the writers' union. A member of the republican party bureau from 1954, Rashidov became Uzbek First Secretary in 1959, a position which he held until his death in late 1983. He was a candidate member of the Central Committee Presidium (renamed the Politburo in 1966) from 1961 until 1983. It was to his close ties to Brezhnev that Rashidov owed both his long tenure in the leadership and his celebrated status as a writer. After his death, the Uzbek party organization was subjected to a purge on account of the stagnation and corruption over which he had presided. WJT

RASPUTIN, Valentin Grigor'evich (b. 1937) Born in Irkutsk, a prose writer of the 'village prose' school and outspoken champion of environmentalist causes, Rasputin sets the majority of his works in his native Siberia. He attracted attention with a series of novellas, beginning with *Money for Maria* (1967), and *The Final Deadline* (1970). Each of them centres around an idealized heroine who exemplifies the countryside and its traditional values, often contrasted with her urbanized children to the detriment of the latter. *Live and Remember* (1975) describes how an army deserter deteriorates after being thus cut off from his community and becomes animal like, destroying his loyal wife in the process. Rasputin's most famous work, *Farewell to Matyora* (1976), a polemic with Soviet industrial Prometheanism, describes some villagers' last months on their island home, Matyora, which is to be submerged in a hydroelectric scheme. Criticized for his negative attitude towards modernization, Rasputin published little until *Fire* (1985). *Fire* is set in a Siberian lumberjack's settlement and rep-

resents a partial reevaluation of Rasputin's earlier critique of modernization, but sounds the alarm at the erosion of moral values in contemporary Soviet society and the widespread drunkenness, indifference and violence.

Rasputin was elected to the Congress of People's Deputies in 1989 and was appointed to the Presidential Council in March 1990, its only member who did not belong to the Communist Party. KC

RATUSHINSKAYA, Irina Borisovna (b. 1954) Political activist and poet. Ratushinskaya was born, brought up, and educated in Odessa. She began writing poetry and plays as a teenager, and was involved in civil rights activism equally early. She qualified and worked as a teacher. In September 1982 she was arrested and condemned to twelve years' penal servitude for 'anti-Soviet agitation'. She was released in 1986 after an international campaign on her behalf, and allowed to leave the USSR. Ratushinskaya has published several books of poems and memoirs, which have been widely translated. In 1989 her work began to appear in the USSR. GSS

RAYKIN (Raikin), Arkadiy Isaakovich (1911–1987) A satirical comedian who succeeded in making fun of officialdom long before Gorbachev's *glasnost'*, Raykin was a talented performer who retained his popularity in the Soviet Union over many years. A Jew born in Riga, he trained as an actor in Leningrad in the early 1930s and established his own theatre there at the end of that decade. He continued to perform in Leningrad even during the wartime blockade. Raykin satirized the Soviet bureaucracy as well as many of the problems of everyday Soviet life and, given his fame as a comedian, the honour of People's Artist was given to him quite late (in 1968). He moved from Leningrad to Moscow in the early 1980s. AHB

RAZGON, Lev Emmanuelivich (b. 1908) A Jewish writer born in Belorussia, the son of a skilled factory worker, Razgon had his promising career suddenly interrupted when he was arrested, aged thirty, in 1938 and spent almost all of the period between then and 1955 in prison or labour camp. He wrote memoirs with little hope that they could be published in his own lifetime. It was not until 1988 that extracts from them appeared in Soviet journals and only in 1989 that they were published in book form in an edition of 100,000 copies. Their impact was such that he was voted one of three most popular authors by readers in Moscow. Razgon became a founding member of the board of the organization, Memorial, founded in 1988 to commemorate the victims of Stalin and to work for their full rehabilitation. AHB

RAZUMOVSKY, Georgiy Petrovich (b. 1936) A Gorbachev ally within the Soviet leadership, Razumovsky supervised party cadres within the Secretariat. A Russian, he was born in the town of Krasnodar and graduated from the Kuban Agricultural Institute in 1958. After working as an agronomist, he entered the party apparatus in 1961, the same year in which he became a party member. From 1961 to 1971 he was employed in the Krasnodar party organization, but moved to Moscow in 1971 to spend two years in the Central Committee apparatus. On his return to Krasnodar, the neighbouring territory to Gorbachev's Stavropol', Razumovsky headed from 1973 to 1981 the executive committee of the regional soviet.

Razumovsky was recalled to Moscow in 1981 and worked in agricultural administration in the Council of Ministers before returning to Krasnodar in 1983 as party First Secretary of the region. Gorbachev's confidence in him was indicated by his appointment in 1985 to head the Department of Party Organizational Work of the Central Committee, an important department to place in the hands of someone loyal to the General Secretary. In March 1986 Razumovsky became a Secretary of the Central Committee and in February 1988 a candidate member of the Politburo. When a reorganization of the party apparatus took place in October of that year Razumovsky emerged as head of the Department of Party Construction and Cadres Policy of the Central Committee and as Chairman of a new Central Committee Commission with the same title. However, his career in the party leadership appeared to end in July 1990 when he was not re-elected even to the Central Committee. AHB

RESHETNIKOV, Fedor Pavlovich (b. 1906) Painter. Born in Sursko-Litovskoe, Reshetnikov (a graduate of Vkhutein) started his career as a caricaturist before moving into genre painting as his central medium. His sentimental pictures such as *Home for the Holidays* (1948) and *Poor Grades Again* (1952) find a curious parallel in Norman Rockwell's interpretations of everyday America. JEB

REVENKO, Grigoriy Ivanovich (b. 1936) The one Ukrainian among the original sixteen members of the Presidential Council of the USSR appointed by Gorbachev in March 1990, Revenko is a graduate of the L'vov Polytechnical Institute and the Academy of Social Sciences attached to the Central Committee of the CPSU.

From 1958 to 1961 he worked as an engineer in an Odessa factory, since when he has been a full-time offical in first the Komsomol and then the party apparatus. Between 1968 and 1972 Revenko was second secretary of the Komsomol for the Ukraine. In 1972 he moved into the apparatus of the Ukrainian party Central Committee, after which he became a secretary and then second secretary of the Kiev regional committee of the party.

Revenko had a spell in Moscow (1984–85) as an inspector within the apparatus of the Central Committee of the CPSU and latterly as a deputy head of the Department of Party Organizational Work. He returned to the Ukraine as First Secretary of the Kiev party in 1985. He was elected to membership of the Central Committee of the CPSU in 1986 and to the Congress of People's Deputies and the Supreme Soviet of the USSR in 1989. He is a member of the Commission for International Policy of the Central Committee of the CPSU and a candidate member of the Politburo of the Ukrainian party. AHB

REYZEN, Mark Osipovich (1895–1970?) Bass. Mark Reyzen was born in the village of Zaitsevo. After entering the Khar'kov Conservatory in 1917, he made his début in 1921 at the Khar'kov Operatic Theatre, becoming a soloist at the Leningrad Theatre of Opera and Ballet (1925–30) and then at the Moscow Bol'shoy (1930–54). From 1965 to 1970 he was on the staff of the Moscow Conservatory. Made a People's Artist of the USSR in 1937, he was awarded State Prizes in 1941, 1949 and 1951. Possessing a voice of unusual richness and mel-

odiousness, he recorded extensively and has toured abroad. GS

RIGERT, David (b. 1951) Weightlifter. He was second only to Alekseev in international weightlifting distinction. In the middle-heavyweight (up to 100 kg) category, he won a gold medal at the 1976 Montreal Olympics, was six times world and nine time European champion, breaking as many as sixty-three world records, the last in 1981. He retired to coaching in 1983, being responsible for Soviet champion Aleksander Gunyashev. JWR

RIKHTER (Richter), Svyatoslav Teofilovich (b. 1915) Pianist. Svyatoslav Rikhter was born in Zhitomir. He received his first music lessons from his father, who was a pianist and organist. From 1933 to 1937 he was an accompanist at the Odessa Opera and Ballet Theatre, after which he studied intermittently at the Moscow Conservatory (1937–46) under Genrikh Neygauz (Heinrich Neuhaus), graduating in 1947. He won first prize in the All-Union Competition of Musical Performers in 1945. Since 1950 he has toured incessantly and is one of the best-known Soviet pianists. Among his many honours are those of People's Artist of the USSR (1961), Hero of Socialist Labour (1975) and several State Prizes. GS

RODCHENKO, Aleksandr Mikhaylovich (1891–1956) Painter and designer. Rodchenko was born in St Petersburg. After studying at the Kazan' Art School (1910–14), he enrolled in the Stroganov Industrial Art Institute in Moscow. He quickly made contact with the avant-garde artists such as Malevich and Tatlin and, by 1915, was developing his own system of abstract art. Like his wife

Stepanova, Rodchenko was a member of the Institute of Artistic Culture in 1920 and the following year contributed to the '5 × 5 = 25' exhibition in Moscow, implying that studio painting was dead and that creative energies should be directed into functional design. During the 1920s he was active in many areas of design – typography, scenography, interior design (such as his famous project for a Workers' Club in 1925) and was a primary supporter of the *Lef* group. From 1923 onwards he gave increasing attention to photography as a central medium, although he continued with painting (figurative and non-figurative) in the 1930s and 1940s. JEB

RODNINA, Irina Konstantinovna (b. 1949) Figure skater. She was the most celebrated of all Soviet figure skaters, winning the Olympic pairs title three times and the world pairs title a record ten times. Born in Moscow, initially she teamed up with Aleksey Ulyanov from 1968 to 1972, under her coach Stanislav Zhuk; in this period she won the Soviet championships twice, the European and world titles three times and the Olympic gold medal in 1972. From 1973 she changed partners to the stronger and younger Aleksander Zaytsev (b. 1952), soon to become her husband. At the same time, she changed coaches to Tatyana Tarasova. Within nine months the new pair had won the 1973 world championships and all the season's top awards. They went on to become undisputed world, Olympic and European champions until their retirement after the 1980 Olympics – even with Irina having taken time off to have a baby in 1979. JWR

RODOV, Semen Abramovich (1893–1968) A proletarian poet, literary theoretician and critic who joined the party in 1918. During the twenties Rodov joined Smithy, then was an office bearer in MAPP and VAPP, edited and was the theoretician for their *On Guard* (1923–25) and published three volumes of poetry. In 1936 he was accused of being a Trotskyite. After the war he was a translator. KC

ROKOSSOVSKY, Konstantin Konstantinovich (1896–1968) Military commander, former Defence Minister (Poland). Rokossovsky, the son of a Polish father and Russian mother, began work as a construction worker before entering the tsarist army in 1914. As a Red Army cavalry commander in the Civil War he fought in Siberia, the Far East and Mongolia. He took cavalry officer training in the 1920s, then commanded a brigade, division, and corps before he was arrested in 1937 and imprisoned for almost three years. He was very fortunate to survive the purges of the military and when Hitler attacked in June 1941 he was reinstated as a cavalry corps commander in the Ukraine. Senior command positions followed: Commander of Bryansk Army Group (July-September 1942); Commander of the Don Army Group in the battle for Stalingrad (1942–43); Commander of the Central Army Group in the Kursk battle (1943); Commander of the First, then the Second Belorussian Army Groups (1943–45). His operational command in these battles was significant in the Soviet repulse of the Nazi forces. After the war Rokossovsky was made Commander-in-Chief of Soviet Forces in Poland (1945–49). In 1949 he was sent to Poland, where until 1956 he was Deputy Chairman of the Polish

Council of Ministers and a Politburo member of the Central Committee of the Polish Workers Party. He also became Polish Minister of Defence with the title Marshal of Poland. Stalin used him in this capacity to maintain control over Poland. He was expelled from Poland when Gomulka came to power and returned to the USSR to become Soviet Deputy Minister of Defence (1956–62), apart from a short interlude as Commander of the Transcaucasian Military District. From 1962 he was Inspector-General of the Soviet Ministry of Defence. RA

ROMADIN, Nikolay Mikhaylovich (b. 1903) Painter. Born in Samara, Romadin studied at Vkhutemas-Vkhutein from 1923 to 1930. Romadin was especially impressed by the painting of Fal'k, Konchalovsky, Mashkov and Shterenberg. Avoiding overt political references, he treats the Russian landscape as his main vehicle of expression, as in *Princess River* (1954) and *Pink Spring* (1967). JEB

ROMANOV, Grigoriy Vasil'evich (b. 1923) For a time in the first half of the 1980s, one of the Soviet Union's most powerful politicians, Romanov clearly aspired to the party leadership but he was unable to compete successfully with Mikhail Gorbachev. Romanov appealed to a harder-line constituency but he was clearly Gorbachev's inferior both in terms of intelligence and political agility and Gorbachev's success in March 1985 resulted in Romanov collecting an early pension.

Romanov was born into a peasant family in the Novgorod region of Russia. He became a shipbuilding engineer after qualifying through study at evening class and by correspondence course. He joined the Communist Party in 1944 and worked as a designer and engineer until 1955 when he entered the party apparatus. He made his career in Leningrad and by 1961 was a Secretary of the city party committee. In 1970 Romanov became First Secretary for Leningrad, a post he held until 1973. His career advanced slowly under Brezhnev, but in 1973 he became a candidate member and in 1976 a full member of the Politburo. It was when Yuriy Andropov became General Secretary and was looking for new recruits to the top leadership team who did not belong to the Brezhnev group that Romanov got his major promotion – to a Secretaryship of the Central Committee of the CPSU while retaining his Politburo membership. With this move to Moscow in 1983 Romanov became one of a handful of especially influential figures within the leadership and a potential candidate for the top post in the future.

Romanov's Leningrad background had given him extensive experience of military industry and within the Secretariat he supervised the armed forces and defence industry. With an eye to his own future chances he supported Chernenko for the General Secretaryship in 1984 and Grishin in 1985. The seventy-year-old Grishin would have been expected to make way in due course for Romanov. However, Gorbachev surmounted this challenge and Romanov was unceremoniously dismissed from the leadership in July 1985 (when he was still below the Politburo average age) to be followed by Grishin later in the the year. AHB

ROMASHOV, Boris Sergeevich (1896–1958) Dramatist. Romashov's plays included the satire *Meringue Pie* (produced by Meyerkhol'd in 1925),

Fighters (1934) and *A Great Force* (1947). RT

ROMM, Mikhail Il'ich (1901–1971) Director and scriptwriter. Romm originally trained as a sculptor but later became an important film director and scriptwriter. He directed the last major Soviet silent film *Boule de Suif* (1934), based on the Maupassant short story and is also famous for his films *Lenin in October* (1937) and *Lenin in 1918* (1939). Other films include: *Secret Mission* (1950), *Nine Days of One Year* (1962) and *Ordinary Fascism* (1966). RT

ROOM, Abram Matveevich (1894–1976) Film director. Room was an original and talented film director and scriptwriter. He joined Meyerkhol'd's theatre in 1923 and moved into films the following year. His major works included: *The Bay of Death* (1926), *Third Meshchanskaya* (also known as *Bed and Sofa* (1927), *The Ghost That Never Returns* (1929), *The Plan for Great Works* (1931), *A Strict Young Man* (1934, from a script by Yuriy Olesha, never released), and *The Offensive* (1945). RT

ROSHAL', Grigoriy L'vovich (1899–1983) Film director. Roshal' studied with Meyerkhol'd and then became a film director. His works included: *The Salamander* (1928, from a script by Lunacharsky), *A Petersburg Night* (1934), *Dawns of Paris* (1936), *The Oppenheim Family* (1938, from the novel by Leon Feuchtwanger) and the biographical films *Academician Ivan Pavlov* (1949), *Musorgsky* (1950) and *Rimsky-Korsakov* (1952). RT

ROSLAVETS, Nikolay Andreevich (1881–1944) Composer. Nikolay Roslavets was born in Dushatin and died in Moscow. He graduated in 1912 from Moscow Conservatory, where he studied violin under Hrimaly and

composition with Aleksandr Il'insky and Vasilenko. He was an active member of the Association for Contemporary Music and was editor of the music journal *Muzykal'naya kul'tura* (Musical Culture) (1924). The years 1931 to 1933 were spent in Tashkent, after which he taught at the Moscow Musical Polytechnic. The composer of some of the first Russian atonal music (a Violin Sonata of 1913), his enthusiasm for serial music and the avant-garde led him into ideological conflict. His work has attracted attention in the Western world. GS

ROSTROPOVICH, Mstislav Leopol'dovich (b. 1927) Cellist, conductor, and pianist. Mstislav Rostropovich was born in Baku. Raised in a musical environment, he was educated at the Moscow Conservatory, where he studied performance with Semen Kozolupov and composition with Vissarion Shebalin, graduating in 1948. Appointed to the staff of the Moscow Conservatory, he taught also in Leningrad. On winning the International Cellists' Competition in Prague in 1950, he became a celebrated performer, being awarded a Lenin Prize in 1963. He began a second career as a conductor in the 1960s, whilst in recent times he has shown great skill as a pianist. In 1974, in increasing conflict with the authorities, he went abroad with his wife, Galina Vishnevskaya. He was appointed conductor of the National Symphony Orchestra, Washington, D. C. in 1975, becoming music director in 1977. The Rostropoviches were deprived of their Soviet citizenship in 1978, but in the new political climate of the Soviet Union, they were given an emotional welcome on their first return visit. In 1981 an international cello competition was organized in Paris in his name. Prokof'ev, Shostakovich, Britten and Lukas Foss are some of the composers who have dedicated works to him. He was awarded an honorary doctorate in 1975 by Cambridge University. GS

ROTMISTROV, Pavel Alekseevich (1901–1982) Former Chief Marshal of Armoured Forces. Rotmistrov had a formative influence on the development of the armoured and mechanized forces of the Soviet Army. As a commander and as a military theoretician he played a crucial role in developing the modern offensive capability of the Soviet ground forces. He had experienced service in armoured units of the Soviet Army already in the 1930s, and commanded an armoured brigade in the Winter War. During the war with Germany he commanded a tank corps in the Battle of Stalingrad and was Commander of the Fifth Guards Tank Army in the fighting on the Kursk-Orel line and in the rout of the German forces at Belograd and Khar'kov. By 1944 he had been appointed Deputy Commander of Armoured and Mechanized Forces of the Soviet Army. After the war he commanded the Soviet armoured occupation troops in Germany, then the armoured and mechanized forces in the Far East. This experience made him a natural appointee as Commander of the Armoured Forces of the Soviet Army and Head of the Main Administration of the Armoured Forces (1955–58). From 1958 to 1964 he headed the Armoured Forces Military Academy. From 1964 to 1968 he was Deputy Minister of Defence. Rotmistrov wrote extensively on contemporary warfare and military science, especially tank warfare and the nature of the armoured offensive. RA

ROZENEL', Natal'ya Aleksandrovna (1902–1965) Actress. Rozenel' (also known as Lunacharskaya-Rozenel'), was a leading stage and screen actress in the 1920s. She was married to Lunacharsky, who wrote most of her film scripts for her. She acted with the Malyy Theatre and played the Soviet equivalent of a 'vamp' in silent films such as *The Bear's Wedding* (1925), *Miss Mend* (1926) and *The Salamander* (1928). RT

ROZHDESTVENSKY, Gennadiy Nikolaevich (b. 1931) Conductor. Gennadiy Rozhdestvensky was born in Moscow. At the Moscow Conservatory, from which he graduated in 1954, he studied conducting with Nikolay Anosov (his father) and piano with Lev Orborin. From 1951 to 1960 he was an assistant conductor and from 1965 to 1970 principal conductor of the Moscow Bol'shoy. During the period 1961 to 1974 he was also conductor and artistic director of the Grand Symphony Orchestra of the All-Union Radio and Television. He held the post of conductor of the Stockholm Philharmonic (1974–77), was guest conductor for three years of the BBC Symphony from 1978, and then chief conductor of the Vienna Symphony Orchestra (1981). Apart from being made a People's Artist of the USSR in 1976, he has been the recipient of various international honours and several recordings made under his baton have won universal acclaim. He is also active as a teacher and has written works on conducting and aspects of music. GS

ROZHDESTVENSKY, Robert Ivanovich (b. 1932) Poet and literary official, born in the Altay, educated in Moscow. He made his literary début in 1950. He is the most orthodox-minded among the eminent poets of his generation; too talented to be crass, he is especially noted as the poet of high civic ideals. A prestigious three-volume collected works was published in 1985. GSS

RUBTSOV, Nikolay Mikhaylovich (1936–1971) Poet. Of northern peasant origin, he did various menial jobs before coming to Leningrad in 1959; he moved to Moscow in 1962. Rubtsov is the only significant poet among the 'village school' of writers who appeared in the early 1960s. GSS

RUDAKOV, Konstantin Ivanovich (1891–1949) Graphic artist. Rudakov was born in St Petersburg. While studying at the Academy of Arts (1913–22), he followed the World of Art artists such as Mstislav Dobuzhinsky and Lancéray in concentrating on book illustration and design. From 1923 onwards he worked for various publishing-houses and in the 1930s achieved particular recognition for his illustrations of Gogol', Lermontov, Maupassant, Pushkin and other writers. JEB

RUDNEV, Konstantin Nikolaevich (1911–1980) An armaments designer and manufacturer from Tula. Chairman of the State Committee for Defence Technology (1958–61), and Deputy Chairman, USSR Council of Ministers (1961–65). From 1965 until his death in office he was Minister of Instrument Making, Automation Equipment and Control Systems, and praised for his contribution to Soviet rocket technology. JHM

RUDZUTAK, Yan Ernestovich (1887–1938) Born in Latvia, the son of a farmhand, Rudzutak became a party and state official in the inter-war period. A party member from 1905, he took part in the revolutionary events of that year and was also a participant in the October Revolution in Moscow.

From 1920 he headed the railway workers' union and was general secretary of the Trade Union Council; he subsequently held regional party posts, becoming a member of the central party Secretariat in 1923 and from 1924 to 1930 People's Commissar for Transport. From 1931 Rudzutak served as chairman of the Central Control Commission (responsible for party discipline) and headed Rabkrin (responsible for the working of the state bureaucracy). A full member of the Politburo from 1926 to 1932, Rudzutak was nonetheless arrested in 1937 and died in prison the following year. SLW

RUSAKOV, Konstantin Viktorovich (1909–1986) A Soviet politician who developed close ties with both Andropov and Brezhnev, Rusakov was born in Toropets in what became the Kalinin region of Russia. By education a civil engineer, and a party member from 1943, he made a career in the ministerial system before entering the party apparatus. He had several spells as a deputy minister for the fish industry before and also after being USSR Minister for the Fish Industry (1950–52) towards the end of Stalin's life. Following diplomatic work involving other Communist countries (he held the rank of Counsellor in the Soviet Embassy in Warsaw from 1958 to 1960 and was Ambassador to Mongolia, 1962–64), Rusakov joined the Department for Liaison with Communist and Workers' Parties of Socialist Countries of the Central Committee of the CPSU in 1964. The Socialist Countries Department was headed at that time by Andropov and Rusakov became first a deputy head (1964–65) and then First Deputy Head (1965–68). Andropov had moved to the Chairmanship of the KGB in 1967 and Rusakov was promoted to the headship of the Socialist Countries Department in 1968 and to full membership of the Central Committee in 1971.

Rusakov left the department for a five-year period in the 1970s to work as one of the full-time aides of the General Secretary, Leonid Brezhnev (1972–77), an interlude which helped to advance his career, for when he returned as chief of the Socialist Countries Department in 1977 he was accorded the rank of Secretary of the Central Committee. He retained that post and departmental headship for a further nine years – through the General Secretaryships of Andropov and Chernenko as well as Brezhnev's remaining years – but with Gorbachev at the helm he was replaced by Vadim Medvedev in early 1986. By that time Rusakov, a more conservative Communist than his successor, was already in failing health. AHB

RYANGINA, Serafima Vasil'evna (1891–1955) Painter. Born in St Petersburg, Ryangina used her appreciation of academic art (she trained at the Academy of Arts) (1912–18) to develop the principles of Socialist Realism in her industrial scenes and portraits of the 1930s and 1940s. Her large oil *Higher, Ever Higher* (1934) was hailed as a prime example of the new Soviet style. JEB

RYAZANOV, David Borisovich (1870–1938) The first and most distinguished Soviet historian of Marxism, Ryazanov was a controversial figure in (and out of) the early Bolshevik Party, as well as one of its leading scholars. Withdrawing from active politics after the Civil War, as founding director of the Marx-Engels Institute from 1921 he produced the first Soviet editions of

the collected works of Marx, Engels and Plekhanov. Notoriously outspoken, he protested against the arrest of some of those implicated in the 'Menshevik affair' in late 1930, for which he was dismissed and expelled from the party. Sent into internal exile, he died in obscurity. JB

RYAZANOV, El'dar Aleksandrovich (b. 1927) Popular film director. Ryazanov is best known for comedies such as *Railway Station for Two* (1983), a satire on the inefficiencies and petty corruptions of Soviet life. RT

RYAZHSKY, Georgiy Georgievich (1895–1952) Painter. Born in Ignat'evo, Ryazhsky studied in private studios in Moscow before 1917 and then at Svomas. In spite of a momentary interest in abstract art, he emerged as a supporter of Heroic Realism and AKhRR, depicting the new Soviet state, especially the position of Soviet woman – evident, for example, in *The Delegate* (1927). JEB

RYBAKOV, Anatoliy Naumovich (b. 1911) A writer born in Chernigov. His father, Naum Aronov, was an engineer of Jewish origin. In 1919 his family moved to Moscow where on completing his secondary education Rybakov worked for two years in factory labour as a stevedore and driver. He entered the Moscow Transport Institute in 1929. In his final year he was arrested on a trumped-up charge and sentenced to three years internal exile in Siberia. Released on 5 November 1935, he was prohibited from living in any large city and spent from 1936 to 1941 working as an auto mechanic and driver in places such as Ufa, Kalinin, and Ryazan'. Mobilized as a private in June 1941, he was among the first Red Army units to enter Berlin as a major in charge of transport in the IV Guards Rifle Corps.

He began writing (under his mother's name of Rybakov) while still serving in the occupying forces at Reichenbach, Germany. His first novel *Kortik* (The Dirk) was published in 1948, establishing him at once as a writer of children's adventure stories. In 1950 he published *Voditeli* (The Drivers), for which he won the Stalin Prize. His further writing includes: *Yekaterina Voronina* (1955); *Bronzovaya ptitsa* (The Bronze Bird, 1956), the sequel to *Kortik*; *Priklyuchenie Krosha* (The Adventures of Krosh, 1960); *Leto v Sosnyakakh* (Summer in Sosniaki, 1964), an anti-Stalinist novel; *Kanikuly Krosha* (Krosh on Holiday, 1966); *Neizvestnyy soldat* (The Unknown Soldier, 1970, the final part of the *Krosh* trilogy); *Vystrel* (The Shot, 1975, ending the *Kortik* trilogy); *Tyazhelyy pesok* (Heavy Sand, 1978); *Deti Arbata* (Children of the Arbat, written 1966, published 1987). Most of his books have been adapted for either television or cinema, and translated into twenty-two Soviet and twenty-three foreign languages. HS

RYKOV, Aleksey Ivanovich (1881–1938) Rykov, Lenin's successor as Soviet premier, was born in Saratov. His father, a peasant, died when he was just eight years old leaving the family in great poverty. The young Rykov, a capable student, soon abandoned his religious beliefs and turned to radical politics. He entered the Law Faculty of Kazan' University in 1900 and soon became active in Social Democratic circles. After several encounters with the police and the courts Rykov became an underground revolutionary, travelling both at home and abroad under a variety of false identities. He was arrested several times, imprisoned and exiled. After the February Revolution Rykov returned to Moscow, where he was elected to the Presidium of the Moscow soviet and helped to organize the seizure of power in October. Although he favoured a broad coalition of socialist parties Rykov became a member of the new Soviet government as Commissar for Internal Affairs, where he concerned hmself particularly with the food supply to the capital. He moved in 1918 to head the Supreme Council of the National Economy, helping to organize food supplies for the Red Army, and became a Politburo member in 1919. In 1924, following Lenin's death, Rykov became the new Chairman of the Council of People's Commissars (or premier). A believer in party unity and opponent of oppositional movements, Rykov nonetheless became associated with the Right Opposition in the late 1920s and was compelled to give up all his posts in 1930. He served until 1936 as Commissar for Transport, but was arrested in 1937 and executed following the show trial which took place the following year. Rykov was rehabilitated in 1988. SLW

RYLOV, Arkadiy Aleksandrovich (1870–1939) Painter. Rylov was born in Istobenskoe. A student of the Stieglitz Institute of St Petersburg and then of the Academy of Arts where he took courses with Arkhip Kuindzhi (1888–97) he established himself as an important landscapist before the Revolution. From 1918 to 1929 Rylov taught at the Leningrad Vkhutemas-Vkhutein. While continuing with his lyrical interpretations of woods and water, he also gave attention to the Lenin theme as in *V. I. Lenin on the Gulf of Finland* (1934). JEB

RYNDIN, Vadim Fedorovich (1902–1974) Designer. Born in Moscow, Ryndin – a leading Soviet stage designer – studied in Voronezh (1917–22) before moving back to Moscow. He favoured a mild form of Constructivism, as can be seen in his sets for Vsevolod Vishnevsky's *Optimistic Tragedy* (1933). In 1953 he became artist-in-chief at the Bol'shoy. JEB

RYUTIN, Martem'yan Nikitich (1890–1937) The only Communist leader within the USSR to organize an opposition to Stalin after 1930. Ryutin, the son of a peasant from a village near Irkutsk, was a primary school teacher and an army officer during the war, who joined the Bolsheviks in 1914. He held military and party posts during the Civil War, his guerrilla activity in Siberia was legendary. His party posts were in Irkutsk, Dagestan, and Moscow in the 1920s. He was a supporter of Uglanov and the 'Rightists' in 1928, and became deputy editor of the army newspaper *Krasnaya Zvezda* (Red Star) (1929–30). He was expelled from the party and arrested in the autumn of 1930 after criticizing Stalin's policies. He was released in January 1931. In March 1932, however, he wrote an Appeal and a 160-page document – known as the 'Ryutin platform' – criticizing party policies and calling for 'an end to Stalin's leadership'. He was sentenced to ten years' imprisonment after the majority of the Politburo refused Stalin's proposal to sentence him to death. He was eventually executed after a new trial, held in his absence, in January 1937. He was rehabilitated in June 1988. He had been a candidate member of the party Central Committee from 1927 to 1930. RWD

RYUYTEL', Arnol'd Feodorovich (Rüütel, Arnold) (b. 1928) An Estonian agronomist who came late to politics, Ryuytel' had been a sailor, teacher, deputy director of an agricultural research station, director of a state farm, and Rector of the Estonian Agricultural Academy (1969–77), before becoming Secretary for Agriculture of the Estonian Communist Party (1977–79). He was First Deputy Chairman of the Estonian Council of Ministers from 1979 to 1983, Chairman of the Presidium of the Estonian Supreme Soviet from 1983 to 1990, and President of that body from March 1990. JHM

RYZHKOV, Nikolay Ivanovich (b. 1929) The Chairman of the Council of Ministers of the USSR since 1985, Ryzhkov has been one of the leading political figures of the era of *perestroika*. A Russian by nationality, although born in a village in the Donetsk region of the Ukraine, Ryzhkov is an engineer and technocrat by professional background.

He worked his way through the ranks of the large engineering plant, Uralmash, in Sverdlovsk from skilled worker in the 1950s to factory manager (1970–71). He joined the Communist Party in 1956. From 1971 to 1975 Ryzhkov was general manager of a large complex of factories, the Uralmash industrial association.

In 1975 he moved to Moscow to embark on a new ministerial career. His initial appointment was as First Deputy Minister of Heavy and Transport Machine-Building (1975–79) and in 1979 he became First Deputy Chairman of Gosplan. He was given his first senior party appointment by Andropov in late 1982 when he became a Secretary of the Central

Committee of the CPSU and head of its Economic Department.

His earlier political connections were with A. P. Kirilenko rather than Brezhnev and this, together with his relative pragmatism, made him in Gorbachev's eyes an attractive alternative Chairman of the Council of Ministers to the aged Brezhnevite, Nikolay Tikhonov, whom Ryzhkov in fact replaced as head of the Soviet government in September 1985, just half a year after Gorbachev succeeded Chernenko as party leader. At the very first meeting of the Central Committee after Gorbachev's election to the General Secretaryship in March 1985 – the April plenum – Ryzhkov had been elevated to full membership of the Politburo. It was only four years earlier that he had become a member of the Central Committee.

Ryzhkov has been an industrious and generally respected Chairman of the Council of Ministers during a time when that post has presented quite exceptional difficulties. The ministerial network which Ryzhkov has headed has still been the only set of institutions capable of organizing the Soviet economy but it has worked even less well than hitherto as various measures of reform have been undertaken and economic management has fallen between the two stools of a partially abandoned command economy and very partially introduced market relations.

Ryzhkov himself has been a cautious reformer and has been viewed by the more enthusiastic Soviet marketeers as an impediment to progress. His own pronouncements have tended to accord more reluctant and qualified approval to radical economic reform than have those of Gorbachev. Nevertheless, his caution has certainly been shared by a large number of Soviet officials as well as by many ordinary citizens, although by 1990 pressures were growing from such leading economic advisers as Abalkin, Petrakov and Shatalin – and from a larger section of the public than hitherto – for more daring measures of reform than Ryzhkov had previously been prepared to countenance.

A personable and approachable politician in comparison with many of his predecessors, Ryzhkov has had quite a favourable public image in the Soviet Union, notwithstanding some occasionally severe attacks on him in the new Soviet legislature. He became a member of the Congress of People's Deputies in 1989 and is a member *ex officio*, as Chairman of the Council of Ministers, of the Presidential Council of the USSR established in March 1990. AHB

RZHESHEVSKY, Aleksandr Georgievich (1903–1967) Actor and scriptwriter. Rzheshevsky's scripts included: Pudovkin's *A Simple Chance* (1930), Shengelaya's *The 26 Commissars* (1932) and Eisenstein's ill-fated *Bezhin Meadow* (1935–37). His association with this last project blighted his future career. RT

S

SABSAI, Pinkhos Vladimirovich (1893–1980) Sculptor. Sabsai was born in Odessa and later, after graduating from the Leningrad Vkhutemas in 1926, moved to Azerbaydzhan where he achieved recognition for his monumental marble portraits of political leaders, including Kirov (1939) and Lenin (1955–56). JEB

SABUROV, Maksim Zakharovich (b. 1900) Politician. After working in industrial administration for a decade, Saburov joined the USSR Gosplan in 1938 and became its chairman in 1941. For most of the subsequent sixteen years, Saburov was, under various titles, the USSR's chief economic planner. He was a member of the party Presidium from 1952. Though generally reckoned a Malenkov client, he appears not to have supported his patron during the struggle for the Premiership (1954–55). Saburov's career suffered a severe blow in December 1956, when he received much of the blame for a capital investments crisis created by the Sixth Five-Year Plan and it was ended in mid-1957 when he was removed from his posts after supporting the 'anti-party group's' attempted coup against Khrushchev. WJT

SAGDEEV, Roal'd Zinnurovich (b. 1932) Outstanding Soviet physicist and former director of the Institute of Space Research in the Soviet Union. A supporter of Sakharov and campaigner for his release from exile in Gor'ky, Sagdeev was elected as one of the representatives of the Academy of Sciences to the Congress of People's Deputies of the USSR in 1989. By nationality a Tatar, Sagdeev is a Muscovite by birth and a graduate of Moscow University. He worked successively at the Institute of Atomic Energy of the Academy of Sciences of the USSR, the Institute of Nuclear Physics of the Siberian section of the Academy of Sciences, as a professor at Novosibirsk University and as a leading researcher at the Institute of High Temperature Physics before becoming head of Soviet space research in 1973. Elected to corresponding membership of the Academy of Sciences in 1964, he has been a full Academician since 1968. In recent years he has devoted much attention to the issue of global warming. AHB

SAKALAUSKAS, Vitautas Vladovich (Sakalauskas, Vytautas) (b. 1933) Sakalauskas was an engineer and factory director in Kaunas before moving to party work in 1965. He was Chairman of Vilnius City Executive Committee (1969–74), First Secretary of Vilnius *gorkom* (1974–83), and First Deputy Chairman of the Lithuanian Council of Ministers (1983–84). After a year in the All-Union Central Committee apparatus in Moscow, Sakalauskas was appointed Chairman of the Lithuanian Council of Ministers in November 1985. He was defeated at elections for the Lithuanian Supreme Soviet in early 1990. JHM

SAKHAROV, Andrey Dmitrievich (1921–1989) A nuclear physicist, popularly known as 'the father of the Soviet H-bomb', Sakharov became a dissident in the Brezhnev years and a public figure under Gorbachev. The son of a Moscow physics teacher, he studied physics at Moscow State University. After graduating in 1942 he worked as an engineer in an arms plant on the Volga. In 1945 he began graduate work in theoretical physics at the Lebedev Physics Institute of the Academy of Sciences in Moscow.

In 1948 Sakharov became involved in the nuclear weapons programme and played a crucial role in the development of the first Soviet hydrogen bomb, which was tested in 1953, and of subsequent thermonuclear weapons. He also did pioneering research on controlled thermonuclear reactions. He was elected a full member of the Academy of Sciences in 1953, and received many state honours.

Sakharov believed that the Soviet Union needed nuclear weapons in order to maintain the balance of power. While never abandoning his belief, he became concerned in the late 1950s about the harmful effects of radioactive fall-out, and began to campaign for an end to nuclear weapons tests. This brought him into conflict with Khrushchev, who wished to continue testing. Sakharov pressed in 1963 for the Partial Test Ban Treaty, which confined nuclear tests to underground sites. In the 1960s he spoke out on an increasing range of issues, including the state of Soviet biology and the pollution of Lake Baykal.

In 1968 Sakharov wrote an essay on 'Progress, Peaceful Coexistence and Intellectual Freedom', which called for genuine Soviet-American cooperation and a convergence of the two social systems. When this was published in the West he was barred from secret work and deprived of many of his privileges. He remained a member of the Academy and a researcher at the Lebedev Institute. His physics research, which now assumed second place to his public activities, focused on gravitation and cosmology.

In the 1970s Sakharov campaigned against the abuse of human rights in the Soviet Union. He wrote letters to the authorities about cases of illegal repression, and publicized those cases abroad when no action was taken to redress the injustice. In 1975 he was awarded the Nobel Peace Prize. In January 1980 he was banished to Gor'ky (a closed city) and allowed to return to Moscow only in early 1987, following a historic telephone call from Mikhail Gorbachev in December 1986. Sakharov continued to campaign against injustice, and became a qualified supporter of Gorbachev's reforms; he himself favoured a more thoroughgoing liberalization and democratization than that proposed by the Gorbachev leadership.

Sakharov enjoyed immense moral authority because of the wisdom and courage with which he had fought for human rights, in spite of intense harassment by the state. He was elected to the Congress of People's Deputies in 1989 as a representative of the

Academy of Sciences, and became at once a very prominent member of the new Soviet legislature. He died suddenly on 14 December 1989 during the Second Congress of People's Deputies, having been politically active to his last day. DH

SALMANOV, Vadim Nikolaevich (1912–1978) Composer and teacher. Vadim Salmanov was born in St Petersburg and died on 27 February 1978 in Leningrad. After studying at the Leningrad Conservatory as a pupil of Mikhail Gnesin, he graduated in 1941, after which he served in the Red Army. He taught at the music school (*uchilishche*) attached to the Leningrad Conservatory (1946–52), and was appointed to the staff of the Conservatory proper in 1951. Awarded the Glinka Prize of the RSFSR in 1970, he was made a People's Artist of the RSFSR in 1972. A composer of high quality, one of his most outstanding works was his secular 'poem-oratorio' *The Twelve* (1957), written to words by Aleksandr Blok. GS

SALYKOV, Kakimbek Salykovich (b. 1932) A Kazakh mining engineer who had worked in non-ferrous metallurgy in Karaganda and Dzhezkazgan provinces, Salykov became Second Secretary of Dzhezkazgan *obkom* in 1973. From 1975 to 1984 he was attached to the Central Committee apparatus in Moscow, and was then made First Secretary of the Karakalpak *obkom* in Uzbekistan; it is rare for a native to be transferred among the union-republics of Central Asia. In June 1989 he was elected to be full-time Chairman of the Supreme Soviet Standing Committee on Questions of Ecology and Rational Use of Natural Resources. JHM

SAMOILOV, David Samuilovich (Kaufman) (b. 1920) Poet, born and educated in Moscow. He served in the Second World War, but has rarely used the experience in his poetry, preferring more remote historical subjects. He is a highly regarded translator, and has also written on the history of Russian rhyme. GSS

SAMOILOVA, Konkordiya Nikolaevna (1876–1921) An early revolutionary and a supporter of Lenin, Samoilova played a variety of roles in the revolutionary movement. Prior to the revolution she worked as an editor and office manager for *Pravda* and as an editor for *Rabotnitsa*, the women's newspaper. She was among the founders of Zhenotdel and an editor of the journal *Kommunistka*. An important figure in the development of Zhenotdel within the Communist Party, Samoilova is not widely known. In 1921 she contracted cholera while on a mission for the Soviet government in the Volga region and died. NN

SAMOKHVALOV, Aleksandr Nikolaevich (1894–1971) Painter. Born in Bezhets, Samokhvalov was, like Deyneka, one of the first Soviet artists to give attention to the theme of sports and the new Soviet woman – as in *Girl with a Shot* (1933). Graduating from the Leningrad Vkhutemas in 1923, he became a member of the October group in 1928 and thereafter spent much time in Central Asia. JEB

SAMOSUD, Samuil Abramovich (1884–1964) Conductor. Samosud was born in Tiflis (present day Tbilisi) and died in Moscow. On graduating from the Tiflis music *uchilishche* (secondary school) in 1906, where he studied cello, he went on to further study in Prague and Paris, where his mentors included Casals, d'Indy and Colonne. On his return to Russia he held various posts, in 1918 being appointed chief conductor of the Leningrad Malyy Theatre. From 1936 to 1943 he was principal conductor of the Moscow Bol'shoy. Following a seven-year period with the Nemirovich-Danchenko (Stanislavsky) Musical Theatre, in 1953 he was appointed chief conductor of the All-Union Radio Symphony Orchestra. From 1957 till the time of his death he was principal conductor of the Opera-Symphony Orchestra of the All-Union Radio and TV. Honoured with several State Prizes, he was made a People's Artist of the USSR in 1937. GS

SANEYEV, Viktor Danilovich (b. 1945) Athlete. He was the greatest triple jumper in Olympic history competing in four Olympics (1968–80), winning three and setting a new world record in each, and taking a silver medal at the age of thirty-five in 1980. It was at the Moscow 1980 Olympics that he was accorded the honour of carrying the Olympic torch round the Lenin Stadium track. He was the first Soviet triple jumper to win in the Olympic Games; in addition, he was seven times Soviet champion (1968–75). Born in Sukhumi, Georgia, he graduated from the Georgian Sub-tropical Plant Institute in 1969 and the Tbilisi Physical Culture Institute in 1975. JWR

SAR'YAN, Martiros Sergeevich (1880–1972) Painter. Sar'yan was born in Novyy Nakhichevan. After attending the MIPSA (1897–1903), he worked as a Symbolist painter, exhibiting with the Blue Rose group in 1907. After 1910, however, he redis-covered the East, bright colours and energetic brushwork distinguishing works such as *Head of Persian Girl* (1913) and earning him the title of the 'Russian Matisse'. From the 1920s onwards he combined this richly primitive style with socio-political themes as demonstrated by landscapes such as *The Mountain March of the Armenian National Units* (1933). After spending 1926 to 1928 in Paris, he divided his time between Yerevan and Moscow, painting and teaching, although during the Stalin period he was often criticized for his 'formalist' tendencies. JEB

SATS, Natal'ya Il'inichna (b. 1903) Stage director, dramatist and critic, and the virtual founder of Soviet children's theatre. Sats was the Artistic Director of the Moscow Children's Theatre from its inception in 1921 until 1937 and head of the Kazakh Children's Theatre in Alma-Ata from 1944 to 1950. Sats also wrote plays for children including *The Little Black Boy and the Monkey* (1927) and *Fritz Bauer* (1928). RT

SAVCHENKO, Igor' Andreevich (1906–1950) Ukrainian film actor and director. Savchenko's career began on the stage. He acted in *The 26 Commissars* (1932) and directed, among other films, *The Accordion* (1934), *Bogdan Khmelnitsky* (1941) and *Taras Shevchenko* (1951). RT

SAVITSKY, Mikhail Andreevich (b. 1922) Painter. A representative of the 'severe style' of the 1960s, Savitsky graduated from the Surikov Institute in 1957. Many of his paintings are connected with his personal experi-ences of the Second World War such as *Partisan Madonna* (1967) and *The Gates of Vitebsk* (1967). JEB

SAVOSTYUK, Oleg Mikhaylovich (b. 1927) Painter and designer. Born in Moscow, Savostyuk graduated from the Surikov Institute, Moscow in 1953 and is now a professor there. He is known for his posters often designed together with B. Uspensky. He is the current Secretary of the Union of Artists of the USSR. JEB

SAYANOV, Vissarion Mikhaylovich (Makhnin) (1903–1959) Poet, novelist, literary official, Sayanov was born in Geneva and brought up in Siberia as the child of political exiles. He settled in Leningrad in 1922. He began as a Komsomol bard, and later turned to writing novels on contemporary history, emphasizing patriotism and socialist construction. GSS

SCHNITTKE (Schnitke, Shnitke), Al'fred Garrievich (b. 1934) Composer. Schnittke was born in Engel's, in the German Volga Republic. He received his first piano lessons in Vienna (1946–48), where his father was posted as correspondent of a Soviet newspaper. After graduating at the Moscow Conservatory in 1958 under Yevgeniy Golubev, he stayed on for a further three years' post-graduate study, being appointed a member of the teaching staff from 1961 to 1972. He also worked at the Experimental Studio of Electronic Music, Moscow. In recent years he has become one of the leading avant-garde Soviet composers, a number of his works, such as the Third Violin Concerto (1978), being performed and highly acclaimed in the West. His Concerto Grosso No. 2 was written for the West Berlin Philharmonic Orchestra to mark its centenary in 1982. Unlike most Soviet composers, he appears to have received no official honours or distinctions. A Fourth Violin Concerto, written in 1982, was given in West Berlin in 1984. GS

SEDYKH, Yuriy (b. 1955) Athlete. Three times Olympic hammer champion, 1976, 1980 and 1988, he dominated world hammer throwing for some twelve years. Born into a Zaporozhe Cossack family in a village near Rostov-on-Don, he took up hammer throwing at seventeen in Kiev, coming under the coaching of former Olympic champion Anatoliy Bondarchuk. At 186 cm tall and with a competitive weight of 110 kg, he was one of the lightest and fastest throwers; he could run the 100 m in under 12 seconds. JWR

SEIFULLINA, Lidiya Yakovlevna (1889–1954) The daughter of a Russian Orthodox priest and a former Socialist Revolutionary, Seifullina found favour as a prose writer of the twenties. Her popular novella *Virineya* (1924), made into a play 1925), a Soviet classic, tells of a peasant woman's struggle for emancipation. KC

SELEZNEV, Gennadiy Nikolaevich (b. 1947) Appointed editor of the weekly newspaper for teachers, *Uchitel'skaya gazeta*, in December 1988, Seleznev – a Russian by nationality – was born in the town of Serov in the Sverdlovsk region. A graduate of Leningrad University by external study, Seleznev was a lathe operator who joined the Communist Party in 1970. He has made his career both in the Komsomol apparatus and in journalism and was chief editor of the newspaper, *Komsomol'skaya pravda* (1980–88). AHB

SEL'VINSKY, Il'ya L'vovich (1899–1968) Poet, born in Simferopol', educated in Moscow. The foremost lyric talent among the Constructivist school in the 1920s, Sel'vinsky then turned to drama in verse. He fought in the Second World War, joining the party in 1941. He continued publishing verse tales and dramas, experimenting ceaselessly in form and style. GSS

SEMASHKO, Nikolay Aleksandrovich (1874–1949) Organizer of public health. A party member since 1893, Semashko participated in revolutionary and party activities including the October Revolution in Moscow. In 1918 he organized the Commissariat of Public Health (Narkomzdrav) and became its first commissar, organizing a network of research institutes (GINZ) that provided support both for new institutes and for others created just before the revolution by the Moscow Scientific Institute Society. Under his leadership the commissariat supported innovative research in such 'progressive' fields as eugenics, social hygiene, epidemiology, and health in the workplace. In the political changes attending the first Five-Year Plan, Semashko lost his post and subsequently adopted a low profile. In 1944 he was elected to the newly-formed USSR Academy of Medical Sciences. MBA

SEMENOV, Nikolay Nikolaevich (b. 1896) Chemical physicist. A graduate of Petrograd University in 1917, Semenov worked during the 1920s in various Leningrad scientific institutions, notably the Yoffe institute, seeking to apply the new developments in quantum physics to chemical problems. In the late 1920s he developed a theory of branching chemical chain reactions that led to the creation of his Institute of Chemical Physics (1931), his election as a corresponding member of the USSR Academy of Sciences at the age of thirty-three (1929) and a full member at thirty-six (1932), and his winning, together with Hinshelwood, the 1956 Nobel prize in chemistry. A party member since 1947 and the first Soviet scientist to win a Nobel prize, Semenov became head of the Academy's Chemical Sciences division (1957–71), a deputy of the Supreme Soviet (1960–70), and a candidate member of the Central Committee

(1961–66). He used this prominence to reshape Soviet science. One of Lysenko's most distinguished and outspoken critics, he fought to establish molecular genetics and to reshape the Academy into a bastion of politically autonomous pure science. Much of his agenda was realized in the Academy reorganizations of 1961, which transferred many technology institutes from the Academy to industrial ministries, and of 1963, which joined chemistry and biology into an Academy sector headed by Semenov and made him vice-president of the Academy (1963–71). MBA

SEMENOVA, Lyudmila Nikolaevna (b. 1899) Actress. Semenova was a lively stage and screen actress, who began in Foregger's theatre and moved into cinema. Her films include: *The Devil's Wheel* (1926) and *The New Babylon* (1929), both directed by Kozintsev and Trauberg, Room's *Third Meshchanskaya* (1927) and Ermler's *A Fragment of Empire* (1929). RT

SEMICHASTNYY, Vladimir Yefimovich (b. 1924) First Secretary of the Ukrainian Komsomol from 1947 to 1950, Semichastnyy moved to the Moscow apparatus of the All-Union Komsomol and became a close adherent of A. N. Shelepin. Between 1958 and 1961 he was Shelepin's immediate successor in three positions – First Secretary of the Komsomol, head of the Central Committee Department of Party Organs, and Chairman of the KGB. He was also party Second Secretary in Azerbaydzhan from 1959 to 1961. As head of the KGB (1961–67), he must have given at least tacit blessing to the deposition of Khrushchev. Nevertheless he was demoted (to Deputy Chairman of the Ukrainian Council of Ministers) in 1967, and further demoted in 1981. He was a

critic of Brezhnev in the late 1980s.
JHM

SERAFIMOVICH (né Popov), Aleksandr Serafimovich (1863–1949)
Writer. Plays by Serafimovich included *Marianna* (1918) and the stage adaptation of his Civil War novel *The Iron Torrent* (1924), which was produced by Okhlopkov at the Realist Theatre (1934) and was the subject of several ideas for filming by Eisenstein. RT

SERBIN, Ivan Dmitrievich (1910–1981) Serbin headed the Defence Industry (or Defence) Department of the CPSU Central Committee for twenty-three years, from 1958 to 1981, but surprisingly little else is known about him. A Russian from Krasnodar, he graduated in mechanics and mathematics from Moscow University in 1935 and took up work in a factory, probably near Podol'sk outside Moscow. He entered the Defence Industry Department (or its equivalent) in 1942 after a brief wartime evacuation to West Siberia, and rose to become its head sixteen years later. His obituary in 1981 praised his contribution to the Soviet space programme. JHM

SEREBROVSKY, Aleksandr Pavlovich (1884–1938) A prominent Soviet industrialist and organizer of the gold industry at Stalin's request in the late 1920s and 1930s. Serebrovsky's book on the subject is a classic of Soviet industrialization, but slides over the use of forced labour. Born in the Urals, the son of a *narodnik*, he joined the RSDLP in 1903, enduring frequent arrest, exile, and torture (1902–8). He was educated as an engineer in Brussels (1908–11), and then held posts in various factories in Russia (1911–17), including the post of chief mechanic at the Nobel works. He served in the Red Army and the armaments industry. During the Civil War Serebrovsky was appointed head of the Azerbaydzhan Oil Trust (1920–26), head of the Oil Syndicate (1926–28), and put in charge of the gold industry from the end of 1927. He became a deputy People's Commissar for Heavy Industry in 1936. He was a candidate member of the party Central Committee from 1925 until 1938. He was arrested in 1937. RWD

SEREBROVSKY, Aleksandr Sergeevich (1892–1948) Leading Soviet biologist, geneticist. After studying with N. K. Kol'tsov at Moscow University, Serebrovsky did pioneering research in the 1920s on poultry genetics, human heredity, biometrics, population genetics, and evolutionary theory. He originated the terms 'genofond' ('gene pool', the genetic composition of a population) and 'genogeografia' ('gene geography', the study of changes in the geographical distribution of alleles) and used them in path-breaking studies of domesticated poultry in the mountainous regions of the Caucasus. Serebrovsky coined the term 'antropogenetika' (human genetics) in 1923 and, with S. G. Levit, helped to found the world's first institute of medical genetics. An active Marxist, he was also a leader of 'Bolshevik eugenics' in the 1920s, and was the first to propose the idea of widespread human artificial insemination for eugenic purposes. Working in the Communist Academy and the Moscow Zootechnical Institute (1927–32), he pioneered the study of gene structure and orginated the theory of 'step-allelism'. In the mid-1930s he emerged as the leading Soviet animal breeder and one of Lysenko's most outspoken critics, but was never arrested. In the late-1930s he pioneered techniques for the biological control of insect pests. As chair of the genetics department of Moscow University (1930–48), he trained two generations of Soviet geneticists. MBA

SEREBRYAKOV, Leonid Petrovich (1890–1937) Party and state official. Serebryakov, who later became one of the principal Trotskyist oppositionists, was born in Samara, the son of an engineering worker. The family was a poor one and had to move frequently in search of employment. The young Serebryakov had a limited schooling and was soon employed as a lathe operator, coming into contact at the same time with illegal political literature. At the age of just fifteen he was already a member of the Social Democratic Party committee in Lugansk. In the following years he continued his political work and was repeatedly arrested, imprisoned and banished. During the First World War Serebryakov served briefly in the army, where he helped to organize a mutiny, and in 1917 he was involved in the establishment of a Soviet in Kostroma. In October 1917 Serebryakov became a member of the Presidium of the Moscow Soviet and a secretary of the regional party committee. From 1919 to 1920 he worked as a secretary in the central party apparatus, and then in late 1921 became People's Commissar for Transport. A quiet man of indifferent health who did not attract the attention of contemporaries, Serebryakov supported Trotsky in the trade union dispute (1920–21) and was later associated with the Left Opposition. He was expelled from the party in 1927, recanted and was readmitted in 1930, but was arrested and executed in the purge trials of the late 1930s. His wife Galina (born in 1905) achieved some modest renown as a writer on political subjects. SLW

SEREBRYANYI, Iosif Aleksandrovich (1907–1979) Painter. Serebryanyi was born in Gorodnya in the Ukraine. A representative of early Socialist Realism, as in his painting *The Second All-Russian Congress of Soviets at the Smolnyi* (1937), he received his art education in Poltava and then at the Leningrad Vkhutein where he studied under Rylov. He was active as a portraitist and historical painter. JEB

SERGEEV, Konstantin Mikhaylovich (b. 1910) Outstanding premier danseur and choreographer. Sergeev entered the evening course of Leningrad Ballet School and later switched to the full-time course from which he graduated in 1930. He was a student of Viktor Semenov and Vladimir Ponomarev. While still a student he toured with Iosif Kshesinsky's troupe, performing a variety of classical roles. He joined the Kirov troupe in 1930 and was a leading dancer until he retired from the stage in 1961.

A superlative dancer, Sergeev excelled in lyrical-romantic roles, becoming a model of the premier danseur noble. He developed a broad repertoire of both classical and modern parts, and was well known as a partner of Galina Ulanova and, later Nataliya Dudinskaya. Sergeev was celebrated for his performance as Siegfried (*Swan Lake*), Prince Desiré (*The Nutcracker*), and Albrecht (*Giselle*). Among his other important roles were: Vatslav in *The Fountain of Bakhchisaray* (1934, with Ulanova), Romeo in Leonid Lavrovsky's *Romeo and Juliet* (1940, with Ulanova), Lenny in *The Path of Thunder* (1958, with Dudinskaya), Ali-Batyr in *Shurale* (1951), and Andrey in *Taras Bulba* (1955).

In addition to his career as a dancer, Sergeev was a leading choreographer, particularly from the 1950s to the

1970s. He was chief choreographer at the Kirov Theatre (1951–55, 1960–70) and artistic director of the Leningrad Ballet School (1938–40, 1973–). He staged major revivals of numerous Petipa ballets, including *Raymonda* (1948), *Swan Lake* (1950), and *Sleeping Beauty* (1952). His own choreography emphasized psychological and dramatic content, and some of his early works reflect the conventions of Socialist Realism. Among his major ballets are: his highly acclaimed *Cinderella* (1946), in which he partnered Dudinskaya: *The Path of Thunder* (1958); *In the Distant Planet* (1962); *Hamlet* (1970); *The Left Hander* (1976); and *The Legend about Jeanne d'Arc* (1980).

Sergeev has toured extensively, and received State Prizes in 1946, 1947, 1949, and 1951. SCS

SERGEEV-TSENSKY (real name Sergeev), Sergey Nikolaevich (1875–1958) Novelist and, briefly, poet. An author of historical novels about Russian writers and about the 1905 Revolution, Sergeev-Tsensky is best known for his vast epic *The Transformation of Russia* (1914–58, far from complete after seventeen separate parts), and for his trilogy about the Crimean War, *The Ordeal of Sevastopol'* (1936–39). JAEC

SERGEY, (Starogorodsky, Ivan Nikolaevich), Patriarch (1867–1944) Patriarch and head of the Russian Orthodox Church under Stalin. He was appointed rector of the St Petersburg Theological Academy in 1901 and in the same year consecrated as bishop. He served in various dioceses until the death of Patriarch Tikhon in 1925. From that time he became the effective head of the Russian Orthodox Church, or at least that part of it which recognized the Soviet regime. On 29 June 1927 he made a controversial declaration of loyalty to the Soviet state, thanking the government for its concern for the needs of religion. In 1943 Stalin permitted the church to hold a Council at which Sergey was formally elected Patriarch. MR

SEROV, Vladimir Aleksandrovich (1910–1968) Painter. Much indebted to his study under I. Brodsky at the Academy of Arts, Leningrad, Serov was a primary representative of Socialist Realism and one of Stalin's 'court painters'. He worked in various areas, including caricature, poster and book illustration, but he is now remembered for the heroic style of his oil paintings. He achieved national prominence after the Second World War with his historical paintings such as *Lenin Proclaims Soviet Power* (1947) and genre scenes such as *Peasant Messengers Visiting Lenin* (1950). He played a crucial role in the organization of art affairs under Stalin and Khrushchev and from 1962 until his death was President of the Academy of Arts, Moscow. JEB

SEVERTSOV, Aleksey Nikolaevich (1866–1936) Zoologist, morphologist, evolutionary theorist. After graduating from Moscow University in 1889, Severtsov studied animal morphology in Europe and subsequently was professor at Dorpat University (1898–1902), Kiev University (1902–11), and Moscow University (1911–30). His international distinction led to his election to the USSR Academy of Sciences (1920) and the Ukrainian Academy of Sciences (1925). In 1910 he elaborated a theory of evolution emphasizing the role of correlated variability. In two subsequent works (1914, 1925) he distinguished four major trends of evolution: aromorphosis (major progressive developments), idioadaptation, coenogenesis, and degeneration. His classic synthetic work on evolutionary morphology, published in German, was *Morphologische Gesetzmässigkeiten der Evolution* (1931). In 1930 he founded the USSR Academy of Sciences' laboratory of evolutionary morphology, which became in 1934 its Institute of Evolutionary Morphology and Paleontology and, in honour of his seventieth birthday in 1936, the Severtsov Institute. He was succeeded by his protégé I. I. Shmal'gauzen (Schmalhausen). Although Severtov opposed Lamarckism and Lysenkoism, his legacy was embraced after his death by both orthodox Darwinians and Lysenkoists. MBA

SHADR, Ivan Dmitrievich (1887–1941) Sculptor. Shadr was born in Shadrinsk. Bourdelle and Rodin were his early mentors in Paris after he attended art school in Yekaterinburg and St Petersburg, and their influence can be traced in his project for a *Monument to World Suffering* (1915). He contributed to Lenin's Plan of Monumental Propaganda with reliefs of Marx and Liebknecht, but achieved real recognition with his famous statue *The Cobblestone is the Proletariat's Weapon* (1927) and his various portraits of Gor'ky and Lenin. He was a member of AKhRR. JEB

SHAFRAN, Daniil Borisovich (b. 1923) Cellist. Shafran was born in Petrograd. After studying with his father, a gifted cellist, he entered the Leningrad Conservatory as a pupil of Aleksandr Shtrimer, graduating in 1950. From 1943 he was a soloist with the Moscow Philharmonic. In 1937 he won the All-Union Competition of Violinists and Cellists in Moscow, gained first prize in the All-World Festival of Youth and Students Contest in Budapest in 1949, as well as the International Cellists' Competition in Prague in 1950. He was President of the Jury of the International Tchaikovsky Contest for Cello in 1974 and 1978. A member of the party since 1945, he was made a People's Artist of the USSR in 1977. GS

SHAGAL, Mark Zakharovich, *see* **Chagall**, Marc

SHAGINYAN, Marietta Sergeevna (1888–1982) Born in Moscow, before the Revolution a Symbolist poet, but after the Revolution Shaginyan wrote fiction, essays and memoirs. Under the pseudonym Jim Dollar she published *Miss Mend or the Yankees in Petrograd* (1924–25), an attempt at a Soviet detective novel. Her experimental novel *K. i K.* (1929) contains four narrators' versions of a commissar's disappearance and his own critique of their versions. She later wrote production fiction, such as *Hydrocental* (1930–31), travelogues and sketches of literary personalities, and two novels about Lenin's life, for which she won the Lenin Prize in 1972. KC

SHAKHLIN, Boris Sergeevich (b. 1932) Gymnast. He competed in three Olympic gymnastics competitions winning six gold medals and being overall champion in Rome in 1960, and an individual champion in 1956 and 1964. Born in Ishim, Tyumen region, he was overall European (1955) and world (1958) champion, and an individual European champion five times (1955–63), and world champion three times. JWR

SHAKHNAZAROV, Georgiy Khosroevich (b. 1924) A leading party intellectual and influential adviser of Mikhail Gorbachev, Shakhnazarov has been an increasingly important political figure as well as a strong advocate of the more objective and systematic study of politics in the Soviet Union. A man of broad talents, he is the author of works of science fiction as well as numerous books and articles on political topics.

An Armenian by nationality, Shakhnazarov was born in Baku. He fought in the Second World War and thereafter studied at the Moscow Institute of Law. He took a candidate of sciences degree and higher doctorate in law and since 1987 he has been a corresponding member of the Academy of Sciences. As an academic he has been, along with Fedor Burlatsky, one of the two main advocates of the institutionalization of political science in the Soviet Union. His book, *Socialist Democracy*, published in 1972, advocated a freer and fuller flow of information to Soviet citizens and was also unusual for that time in recognizing the existence of different interests within Soviet society. Shakhnazarov has been President of the Soviet Association of Political Sciences since 1974 and was a Vice-President of the International Political Science Association from 1974 to 1988. He has made notable contributions to the New Thinking in both Soviet domestic and foreign policy. He has written extensively on the need for self-government and in an article published in 1984 he argued that 'political ends do not exist that would justify the use of means liable to lead to nuclear war'.

While maintaining close links with academic life, Shakhnazarov has spent the greater part of his career working in the Central Committee apparatus. He was first brought into Yuriy Andropov's group of consultants in the Socialist Countries Department of the Central Committee by Fedor Burlatsky in the early 1960s. Shakhnazarov remained in that department after Burlatsky left, apart from a spell in Prague at the beginning of the 1970s on the journal *World Marxist Review*. From 1972 until 1986 he was a deputy head and from 1986 to 1988 First Deputy Head of the Socialist Countries Department. In early 1988 he became one of Gorbachev's full-time aides, but even before that was one of his informal advisers.

Shakhnazarov was elected to the Congress of People's Deputies in 1989 on the Academy of Sciences list and is a member of the Committee of the Supreme Soviet on Questions of Legislation, Legality and Law and Order. He is also a member of the commission set up to draft a new Constitution for the USSR. Shakhnazarov has broad cultural and scholarly interests and has been an important link between the party apparatus and the intelligentsia. It was at his instigation that a sector for the study of political systems was set up at the Institute of State and Law (1979–85) and succeeded by a more independent Centre for Political Science Research established in 1987 with Mikhail Piskotin as its first head. AHB

SHAKIROV, Midkhat Zakirovich (b. 1916) A party member from 1944, Shakirov, a Bashkir, graduated as an engineer in 1942 and later worked in industry before becoming a government and party official in the Bashkir republic. In 1963 he was named first secretary of the Ufa city party committee, becoming first secretary of the Bashkir regional party committee in 1970 until his disgrace and forced retirement in 1987. Shakirov was a member of the USSR Supreme Soviet Presidium from 1970 to 1987 and was elected a full member of the CPSU Central Committee in 1971, 1976, 1981 and 1986. SLW

SHALAEV, Stepan Alekseevich (b. 1929) A Communist Party member from 1954 and a Mordvinian by nationality, Shalaev worked in the timber industry, latterly as a factory manager, before moving into the Soviet trade union movement in 1963. In 1980 he became Minister for the Timber and Paper Industry and it was indicative of the lack of independence of Soviet trade unions that he could go straight from ministerial office to the chairmanship of the trade union organization of the USSR in 1982. A candidate member of the Central Committee from 1981 to 1982, and a full member from 1982, Shalaev remained head of the trade unions until early 1990 when, in response to mounting dissatisfaction on the part of Soviet workers, he was replaced. AHB

SHALAMOV, Varlam Tikhonovich (1907–1982) Purged in 1937 when already an established young writer, he resurfaced under Khrushchev after some twenty horrific years in camps and exile, but could not publish the powerful, laconic *Kolyma Tales* based on those experiences. Together with other unacceptable writings, they earned him a reputation in *samizdat* and in the West which dwarfed his Soviet status as author of five slender volumes of verse (1961–72). Shalamov died in isolation and embitterment. Not until the late 1980s was the gulf between his official and unofficial reputations at last bridged with a torrent of posthumous publications in the Soviet press. MAN

SHALYAPIN, Fedor Ivanovich (1873–1938) Bass. Shalyapin was born in Kazan' and died in Paris. Born of a poor family, he displayed musical talent at an early age, learning both from his mother and from singing in the church choir. After various jobs, at the age of twelve he participated in performances of the Kazan' Opera. In 1890 he joined the chorus of Semenov-Sumarsky's travelling opera troupe, as a result of which he toured extensively. He took free lessons in singing from Dmitriy Usatov in Tbilisi (1892–93), eventually joining the Tbilisi State Theatre in 1893. After ever-increasing success he made his début at the Imperial Mariinsky Theatre on 5 April 1895 in the part of Mephistopheles. In September 1896 he was invited to join Mamontov's Private Opera Company. In 1901 he made his first foreign appearance at La Scala, Milan, and this was the start of his illustrious international concert career, singing in Rome (1904), Monte Carlo (1905), Berlin (1907), besides taking part in Diaghilev's Russian seasons in Paris (1908, 1913) and London (1913, 1914). He performed at the New York Metropolitan (1907–8). He remained in Russia after the Revolution, being made a People's Artist (one of the first ever to be awarded) in 1918, though this was withdrawn when he left Russia in 1922 to live abroad. A legend in his time, his magnificent voice and dramatic powers were universally acclaimed. His memoirs and autobiography are available in English. GS

SHAPORIN, Yuriy (Georgiy) Aleksandrovich (1887–1966) Composer and teacher. Shaporin was born in Glukhov and died in Moscow. Descended from an artistic family, he learnt to play the cello and piano as a child. He spent the period 1906 to 1908 at the Historical-Philological Faculty at Kiev University where he studied composition with G. Lyubomirsky, going on to study law at St Petersburg University until 1912. He then entered the St Petersburg Conservatory as a pupil of Sokolov, Cherepnin and Shteynberg, from which he graduated in 1918. After working as a conductor and composer in various theatres, and acting as chairman of the Leningrad Branch of the Association of Contemporary Music (1925–30), he moved to Moscow, becoming a critic, then a teacher at Moscow Conservatory in 1939. He was made a professor in 1940. He served as Secretary of the Union of Soviet Composers (1952–66), and was made a People's Artist of the USSR in 1954. A prolific composer, he is remembered for his patriotic cantatas and the opera *The Decembrists* (1953). GS

SHAPOSHNIKOV, Boris Mikhaylovich (1882–1945) Former Chief of General Staff. Shaposhnikov, a talented career officer in the tsarist army, graduated from the Academy of the General Staff in 1910. After entering the Red Army as a volunteer he became one of its key staff officials during the Civil War. He was Assistant to the Chief of Staff of the Red Army (1921–24); Assistant to the People's Commissar for Military Affairs, then Commander Leningrad Military District (1925–27); and Commander of Moscow Military District (1927–28). He was appointed Chief of Staff of the Red Army for the period 1928 to 1930. His influence as a military theoretician grew as Commandant of the Frunze Military Academy (1932–37). Shaposhnikov also acted as Chief of the General Staff (1937–40) and from July 1941 (when he replaced Zhukov) until May 1942. He was promoted to Marshal of the Soviet Union in 1940. During the wartime conferences Shaposhnikov was conspicuous amongst his fellow officers as a military intellectual. His

submissiveness to Stalin, however, dissuaded him from propounding original ideas on his own account. RA

SHATALIN, Stanislav Sergeevich (b. 1934) One of the most outspokenly radical economists in the contemporary Soviet Union and an increasingly influential one, Shatalin was appointed to Gorbachev's Presidential Council when it was first formed in March 1990. The previous year he succeeded Abel Aganbegyan as academic secretary responsible for the Economics division of the Academy of Sciences, a post of considerable potential influence over the development of that discipline in Soviet academic institutions.

Shatalin, who is Russian by nationality, was born in the town of Pushkin in the Leningrad region. He attained prominence as an economist within the institutions of the Academy of Sciences, in the State Committee of Science and Technology (GKNT) and at Moscow University. He has been an outspoken advocate of the need to move speedily towards the development of market relations within the Soviet economy. AHB

SHATROV, Mikhail Filippovich (né Marshak) (b. 1932) Playwright. Shatrov is particularly known for his cycle of eight plays about Lenin, beginning with *In the Name of the Revolution* (1958, filmed in 1964) and concluding with *Onward ... Onward ... Onward* (1988). The cycle also includes *The Sixth of July* (1964, filmed in 1968) and *The Peace of Brest*, written in 1962 but not staged until 1987 because of its portrayal of Trotsky and Bukharin and their disputes with Lenin. RT

SHCHARANSKY, Anatoliy Borisovich (b. 1948) Mathematician, Zionist, and human rights activist. In the early 1970s he became active in the Jewish emigration movement, and in 1976, as its informal representative, he joined the Moscow group to monitor observation of the 1975 Helsinki accord. He was imprisoned as an alleged American spy (1977–86), even though the evidence did not support the charge, and released early in a Soviet-American exchange of prisoners. His memoirs appeared in 1988. PBR

SHCHEDRIN, Rodion Konstantinovich (b. 1932) Composer and pianist. Shchedrin was born in Moscow. Stemming from a musical family, he spent the years 1945 to 1950 at the Moscow Choral School, after which he entered the Moscow Conservatory as a student of Shaporin (composition) and Yakov Flier (piano). After a further four years' postgraduate work, he joined the teaching staff, where he remained until 1969. He was appointed Secretary of the Union of Soviet Composers in 1962 and chairman of the administrative board of the Composer's Union of the RSFSR in 1973. Awarded a State Prize in 1972, he was made a People's Artist of the USSR in 1981. One of the most gifted of the post-Shostakovich generation of Soviet composers, his many works, ingeniously combining folk elements with contemporary musical devices, have been highly praised, though only his *Carmen* Suite is well known in the West. The orchestral concerto *Zvony* (Chimes), utilizing bell sounds, was commissioned by the New York Philharmonic in 1968. He is married to the ballerina Maya Plisetskaya. GS

SHCHELOKOV, Nikolay Anisimovich (1910–1984) A Soviet politician who was close to Leonid Brezhnev and Konstantin Chernenko over many years and who acquired notoriety for his corruption, Shchelokov was born into a Ukrainian working class family in Almaznaya. He was a graduate of what was to become the principal school for politicians of the Brezhnev era – the Dnepropetrovsk Metallurgical Institute (1933) – and a party member from 1931. His ties with Brezhnev went back to pre-war Dnepropetrovsk and he was chairman of the city soviet from 1939 to 1941.

During the war Shchelokov was a political officer in the army (as was Brezhnev) and in 1951 – a time when Brezhnev was First Secretary of the Moldavian Central Committee – he was transferred to Moldavia where he became an ally also of Chernenko. Shchelokov remained in Moldavia (and held a number of senior posts in the party and state administration) until 1966 when, with Brezhnev installed as General Secretary, he was brought to Moscow as Minister of Internal Affairs. In the same year he became a candidate member, and in 1968 a full member, of the Central Committee.

Shchelokov remained head of the MVD (or ordinary police, as distinct from the KGB) for the next fourteen years, during which time both that ministry and he personally acquired a well-earned reputation for corruption. So long as Brezhnev was party leader, Shchelokov was, however, immune from overt attack. When Andropov succeeded Brezhnev he lost no time in changing this state of affairs and little over a month after succeeding to the General Secretaryship he forced Shchelokov into retirement. In June 1983 Shchelokov was expelled from the Central Committee and investigations of his activities raised the possibility of his being brought to trial. Andropov's death in February 1984 and Chernenko's succession meant some short-lived relief for Shchelokov, but as Chernenko's health declined and Gorbachev's influence grew Shchelokov came once again under attack. In November 1984 he was accused at a Supreme Soviet meeting of bringing discredit to the rank of army general (which he had been accorded in 1976) and he was stripped of that rank. One month later he committed suicide. AHB

SHCHERBAKOV, Aleksandr Sergeevich (1901–1945) Party official and political head of the Soviet armed forces during the Second World War. Shcherbakov was born in the Moscow region into a worker's family. A party member from 1918, he studied at the Sverdlov Communist University (1921–24) and later at the Institute of Red Professors. After Komsomol and party work in central Russia he became First Secretary of the Moscow city and regional party organization in 1938, becoming a member of the Central Committee the following year and a candidate Politburo and Secretariat member from 1941 until 1945. During the war Shcherbakov served as head of the Main Political Administration of the Red Army. He died shortly before the war had ended of a heart attack after a long illness; he is buried in the Kremlin Wall. SLW

SHCHERBITSKY, Vladimir Vasil'-evich (1918–1990) Very much a client of Leonid Brezhnev, Shcherbitsky was the last Brezhnevite to retain a seat in Gorbachev's Politburo. He remained a member of that body until September 1989 – just half a year before his death in early 1990.

A Ukrainian by nationality, Shcherbitsky was born in the Dnepropetrovsk region of the Ukraine and graduated from the Dnepropetrovsk Chemical Technological Institute. From 1941 (the year in which he joined the Communist Party) until 1945, Shcherbitsky served in the Soviet army. In the post-war period he worked his way up through the ranks of the party organization, mainly in his native region (and Brezhnev's political base) of Dnepropetrovsk. By 1955 he was holding Brezhnev's old job of First Secretary of the Dnepropetrovsk regional party organization and from 1961 to 1963 he was a candidate member of the Presidium of the Central Committee. He was then demoted, but once Brezhnev had succeeded Khrushchev as party leader, Shcherbitsky's career flourished. In 1965 his candidate membership of the Presidium (Politburo) was restored and in 1971 he became a full member of the Politburo. One year later he succeeded Petro Shelest as party First Secretary for the Ukraine. He took a tough line against any manifestations of Ukrainian nationalism and was more highly regarded in Moscow than in the Ukraine (beyond the ranks of his placemen in the party apparatus).

The main reasons why Shcherbitsky succeeded in remaining in the Politburo and in charge of the Ukraine for a further seven years after Brezhnev's death were that he sought to pay lip service to policies which, under Gorbachev, were uncongenial to him, that the Ukraine (unlike the Baltic republics and the Caucasus remained relatively quiet in the later 1980s) and the fact that he had placed so many supporters in key positions in the Ukrainian party that it was difficult to get the Ukrainian party organization to take the initiative in removing him. In fact, the Central

Committee in Moscow dropped him from the Politburo in September 1989 before a plenum of the Central Committee of the Ukrainian party attended by Gorbachev in Kiev replaced him later that month by Vladimir Ivashko. AHB

SHCHIPACHEV, Stepan Petrovich (1899–1980) Poet and literary official, born near Perm'. He became a party member in 1919, and fought in the Civil War, remaining with the army as a political officer and journalist until 1935, becoming a military journalist again in the Second World War. His themes are orthodox, his style and form unadventurous. GSS

SHCHUKIN, Boris Vasil'evich (1894–1939) Stage actor. Shchukin worked in the Vakhtangov Theatre and the Moscow Art Theatre and started making films at the end of his short life. His film roles included: Raizman's *Pilots* (1935) and Romm's *Lenin in October* (1937) and *Lenin in 1918* (1939). RT

SHCHUKO, Vladimir Alekseevich (1878–1939) Architect and designer. Shchuko was born in Berlin, but trained at the Academy of Arts from 1896 to 1904, before travelling extensively in Western Europe and then becoming a designer for the Antique Theatre in St Petersburg (1908–11). In 1911 he designed the Russian pavilion for the 'Universal Exposition' in Turin, a concept that he reinterpreted for the pavilion of the Foreign Section at the 'All-Russian Agricultural Exhibition' in Moscow in 1923. Classical by inclination, Shchuko also designed the architectural part of the Lenin monument at the Finland Station, Leningrad (1926) and helped in the general planning of the Lenin Library, Moscow (1928). JEB

SHCHUSEV, Aleksey Viktorovich (1873–1949) Architect. Born in Kishinev, Shchusev was the designer of more than 150 projects, including the Lenin Mausoleum (1926–30), a theorist of considerable merit, and one of the Soviet Union's most distinguished architects. Well established before the Revolution, he moved easily from Neo-Classicism of the 1910s to Constructivism of the 1920s to Socialist Realism of the 1930s (see his Moscow River Bridge and Institute of Marx-Engels-Lenin for Tbilisi in 1938). His Kazan' Station, Moscow, realized over the period 1912 to 1940, incorporates all these styles. JEB

SHEBALIN, Vissarion Yakovlevich (1902–1963) Composer and teacher. Shebalin was born in Omsk and died in Moscow. On graduating from the Moscow Conservatory in 1928 as a student of Myaskovsky, he was appointed to the teaching staff, being made a professor in 1935 and then its director (1942–48). Awarded State Prizes in 1943 and 1947, in which year he was also made a People's Artist of the RSFSR, in 1948 he was accused of 'formalism', along with Myaskovsky, Prokof'ev, Shostakovich, and others and was temporarily dismissed from his post. He was officially rehabilitated in 1958. Though few of his many compositions are well known in the West, his music, especially the opera *The Taming of the Shrew* (première 1957) was highly regarded in the Soviet Union. He was also active as an editor, completing Musorgsky's unfinished opera *Sorochintsy Fair*, and as a writer on music. GS

SHEBOLDAEV, Boris Petrovich (1895–1937) A leading party organizer and one of the most active if somewhat independent-minded supporters of forced collectivization. Born in

Paris, the son of a doctor, Sheboldaev lived in St Petersburg from 1900. He joined the party in 1914, served in the army (1914–17), and held military and party posts in the Transcaucasus during the Civil War. He was appointed party secretary of the Lower Volga region (1928–30), of the North Caucasus (1930–34), and of the Azov-Black Sea region (1934–37). He was a member of the party Central Committee (1930–37). He was executed in October 1937, and then posthumously sentenced to death in December of the same year. RWD

SHEFNER, Vadim Sergeevich (b. 1915) Poet and prose writer, born in Petrograd. He served in the Second World War, becoming a party member in 1945. Based in Leningrad, he is one of the leading Soviet philosophical poets, dealing with human beings in their relationships with nature and technology. GSS

SHEGAL', Grigoriy Mikhaylovich (1889–1956) Painter. Shegal' was born in Kozel'sk and, after a course of study at the Academy of Arts, he moved to Tula in 1918, then enrolled at Vkhutemas in 1922 under Shevchenko. Supporting a documentary style, he joined AKhRR in 1928 and soon gained recognition for his interpretations of important events from the Revolution, such as *The Flight of Kerensky from Gatchina in 1917* (1936–38). JEB

SHELEPIN, Aleksandr Nikolaevich (b. 1918) Russian politician. One of the many Khrushchev clients who helped remove their patron in 1964, A. N. Shelepin started his career in Komsomol work and from 1952 became head of that body. In December 1958 he replaced Serov as KGB chairman; Shelepin's links to the security services dated back to the late

thirties. He entered the Secretariat at the Twenty-Second Congress and in November 1961 left the KGB. After Khrushchev's removal, in which he played a part, he became a full member of the Central Committee Presidium (renamed the Politburo in 1966). This promotion – combined with his known personal ambition – may have made him too great a threat to Brezhnev, for in 1967 he was removed from the Secretariat to become head of the Soviet trade unions. In 1975 he was removed from the Politburo as well. WJT

SHELEST, Petr (Petro) Yefimovich (b. 1908) A Ukrainian politician who came to the fore under Khrushchev, Shelest was born into a poor peasant family. He entered the Communist Party in 1928 and after an early career as a worker was employed in supervisory positions in industry and in the Komsomol and party apparatus. From 1941 to 1954 he was head of the industrial department of the Chelyabinsk regional party committee and in 1954 he became a secretary of the Kiev party organization; by 1957 he was First Secretary in Kiev.

Shelest clearly enjoyed the patronage of Khrushchev and as Khrushchev's power grew so Shelest's career advanced. In 1962 he was appointed to a Secretaryship of the Central Committee of the Ukrainian Communist Party and in 1963 he became First Secretary for the Ukraine. He was elevated to candidate membership of the Presidium of the Central Committee of the CPSU in December 1963 and, shortly after Khrushchev's fall, this became (in November 1964) full membership.

Shelest's relations with Brezhnev later deteriorated, however. Although Shelest took a very hard line against the Czechoslovak reformers in 1968 – probably out of concern lest the virus of democracy should cross the Czechoslovak border into the Ukraine – he made an attempt to conciliate the Ukrainian intelligentsia who were increasingly unhappy about what they saw as the consequences of Russification of their republic. Brezhnev took the view that Shelest was being too soft on Ukrainian nationalism and he had, in any event, his own protégé, Shcherbitsky, whom he wished to put in charge. In May 1972 Shelest was in fact replaced by Shcherbitsky as Ukrainian First Secretary and less than a year later (in April 1973) he was dropped from the Politburo. AHB

SHELKOV, Vladimir Andreevich (1896–1980) Leader of the unofficial 'True and Free Seventh Day Adventists' (1954–1980), who broke away from the official Adventist Church in the USSR (1924–28), because of their rejection of military service and state registration. Shelkov ran an underground printing press and himself wrote 110 religious works. He spent twenty-three years in Soviet prisons. In the 1970s he was responsible for sending many documents abroad, protesting about lack of religious liberty in the USSR. As a result, in 1979 he was sentenced to five years imprisonment and died in a camp aged eighty-four. MR

SHEMYAKIN, Mikhail Mikhaylovich (1908–1970) Organic chemist, administrator. A 1930 graduate of Moscow University, Shemyakin worked at the Dyestuffs Institute (1930–35) and then, in the USSR Academy of Sciences, at its institutes of experimental chemistry (1935–45), biological and medical chemistry (1945–61), and organic chemistry

(1957–59). He was elected a corresponding member of the Academy in 1953 for his work on the synthesis of various antibiotics, culminating in the full synthesis of tetracycline (1966), but his early work on amino acid metabolism and protein polypeptides led to his most important series of researches (1953–70), many done with his protégés, Yu. A. Ovchinnikov, on protein synthesis. As part of the Academy's attempt to overcome Soviet lags in molecular biology occasioned by Lysenkoism, Shemyakin was elected a full member in 1958. He organized and directed (1959–70) its new Institute of the Chemistry of Natural Compounds (renamed the Institute of Bio-organic Chemistry in 1974) and, following the 1963 Academy reorganization, he became head of the new division of biochemistry, biophysics, and the chemistry of physiologically active compounds (1963–70) and organized the division's new research complex at Pushchino. Shemyakin is credited with creating the scientific and organizational infrastructure of Soviet molecular biology. MBA

SHENGELAYA, Nikolay Mikhaylovich (1903–1943) Film director. Shengelaya was a director and one of the founders of Georgian cinema. His films include: *Eliso* (1928), *The 26 Commissars* (1932) and *The Golden Valley* (1937). RT

SHEPILOV, Dmitriy Trofimovich (b. 1905) Russian political figure. A Khrushchev protégé who turned on his patron unsuccessfully, D. T. Shepilov began his rise to power as a political commissar in the Ukraine during the war. It was there that he met Khrushchev. After the war, he went to work in the Central Committee apparatus until late 1952 when he was appointed chief editor of *Pravda*. His fortunes rose with those of his patron and in July 1955 he left *Pravda* for the Secretariat of the Central Committee. At the Twentieth Congress he became a candidate member of the Central Committee Presidium and in June 1956 he replaced Molotov as Foreign Minister. In 1957, however, he joined with the so-called 'anti-party group' which tried to unseat Khrushchev. This perceived disloyalty made him the target of especially bitter attacks after the group's defeat. WJT

SHEPITKO, Larisa (1938–1979) Film director. Shepitko studied under Dovzhenko and was married to Klimov. She made four feature films before being killed in a car crash: *Heat* (1963), *Wings* (1966), *You and I* (1971) and *The Ascent* (1977). RT

SHEREMET, Konstantin Filippovich (b. 1923) Leading Soviet authority on constitutional law, administrative law, and local government. Professor Sheremet graduated from Moscow University Law Faculty and taught there until 1968, when he moved to the Institute of State and Law of the USSR Academy of Sciences. He served as sector head and from 1976 to 1987 as a deputy director, becoming in 1988 editor of *Sovetskoe gosudarstvo i pravo* (Soviet State and Law). Sheremet has played an important role in drafting Soviet local government legislation. WEB

SHEVARDNADZE, Eduard Amvrosievich (b. 1928) Soviet Foreign Minister since 1985, Eduard Shevardnadze has been one of the outstanding successes in the Soviet leadership. In spite of his previous lack of experience of foreign policy, he was soon to display political flexibility and diplomatic skill and to earn the respect of Western foreign ministers and

leaders with whom he came into contact.

A Georgian and the son of a schoolteacher, Shevardnadze was born in the village of Mamati in Georgia. He graduated from the Party School of the Georgian Communist Party in 1951 and from the History Faculty of the Kutaisi Pedagogical Institute in 1960.

Shevardnadze made the earliest part of his career in the Komsomol apparatus which he joined in 1946. A Communist Party member from 1948, he was promoted quite rapidly within the Komsomol, especially after Stalin's death, and by 1957 he was First Secretary of the Komsomol for the Georgian republic. In 1961 he transferred to the Communist Party apparatus and worked as a district party secretary until 1964 when he moved to the Georgian Ministry of Public Order (from 1968 called the Ministry of Internal Affairs). This was the ministry concerned with the ordinary police – as distinct from the KGB – and with 'ordinary' as distinct from political crime. Yet some of the crime Shevardnadze had to deal with as First Deputy Minister (1964–65) and as Minister (1965–72) was on an extraordinary scale. Moreover, the head of the mafia was none other than the First Secretary of the Georgian party organization, V. P. Mzhavanadze.

When Shevardnadze found his efforts to impose law and order blocked at the top, he risked his life by compiling a dossier on Mzhavanadze and taking it to Moscow. Mzhavanadze was a candidate member of the Politburo at the time and if the Brezhnev leadership had chosen to back him, more than Shevardnadze's career would have been at stake, since Mzhavanadze could have trumped up serious charges against him. The evidence, however, was sufficiently compelling to lead to the removal of Mzhavanadze and it was Shevardnadze (at the relatively early age of forty-four) who took his place as Georgian First Secretary.

During Shevardnadze's years as head of the Georgian party organization there were several attempts on his life. He continued to fight the local mafia and earned their hatred at the same time as he attained the respect of most Georgians. Georgia, under Shevardnadze, became the most reform-minded of all Soviet republics. He introduced as much limited economic reform as was possible in the Brezhnev years and also encouraged experiments designed to increase the power of local soviets.

Shevardnadze became a member of the Central Committee of the Soviet Communist Party in 1976 and a candidate member of the Politburo in 1978. When the struggle for succession to the party leadership took place at the time of Chernenko's death, Shevardnadze was firmly on the side of Gorbachev. Gorbachev's home area of Stavropol' in the North Caucasus is close to Georgia and both Gorbachev and Shevardnadze moved more or less in parallel through offices in their local Komsomol and subsequently party organizations. Their neighbourly contacts date back to the early 1960s.

When Gorbachev became party leader in 1985, he lost little time in promoting Shevardnadze to full membership of the Politburo and in surprising the world by making him Foreign Minister in place of the long-serving Andrey Gromyko. Both promotions were good moves. Shevardnadze was subsequently to be a staunch ally for Gorbachev in debates on domestic reform as well as a willing and highly capable exponent of what became known as the 'New Thinking' in foreign policy.

In the international arena, Shevardnadze's charm has enabled him to establish good relations with people of different political outlooks. But his success has been more than a public relations one. Important shifts in Soviet foreign policy have taken place during Shevardnadze's time as Minister of Foreign Affairs and while he was not their chief architect, he has played a very substantial part in their implementation. Shevardnadze became one of the most forthright critics of the Soviet military intervention in Afghanistan and was an influential advocate of bringing all the Soviet troops home.

Shevardnadze has also refashioned the Soviet Ministry of Foreign Affairs and has promoted well-educated officials and people more enlightened than their predecessors to senior posts. One potential threat to his position in Soviet political life – essentially outside his control – is the growth of nationalist and even pro-independence sentiment in Soviet Georgia. Following the brutal killings of a number of young and peaceful demonstrators in Tbilisi in April 1989 Shevardnadze's Georgian home political base became less secure, although Shevardnadze himself was not involved in the decision to use violence against the demonstrators and he deplored the actions of the military which so outraged Georgian opinion. How far autonomous developments in Georgia will affect Shevardnadze's position in the Soviet leadership remains to be seen. He has by this time many supporters in Moscow and continues to enjoy Gorbachev's confidence. When the new Presidency was created in March 1990, Shevardnadze became a member of the Presidential Council. He was, however, one of a number of prominent Soviet leaders who ceased to be a member of the party Politburo when that body was revamped four months later.

Shevardnadze's wife belongs to a Georgian intelligentsia family which suffered greatly during Stalin's purges and that has also no doubt been a factor contributing to Shevardnadze's firmly held anti-Stalinist and reformist views. So far as foreign policy is concerned, Shevardnadze's own personality has made a distinctive and positive contribution to the improvement in the international climate since 1985. AHB

SHEVCHENKO, Aleksandr Vasil'-evich (1882–1948) Painter. Shevchenko was born in Khar'kov. Between 1899 and 1910 he studied at the Stroganov Institute, Moscow, in Paris and at the MIPSA (where he took courses under Konstantin Korovin and Valentin Serov). In 1910 he became a member of the Jack of Diamonds group, sharing the Neo-Primitivist interests of Natal'ya Goncharova and Mikhail Larionov. During the 1920s Shevchenko taught at Vkhutemas and, in 1926, was co-founder of the Painters' Workshop. In the 1930s he tried to adapt his varied experiences to socio-political themes, indicated, for example, by his *Collective Farm Girls Waiting for the Train* (1933). JEB

SHEVCHENKO, Valentina Semen-ovna (b. 1935) Chairman of the Presidium of the Supreme Soviet of the Ukraine and Vice-Chairman of the Presidium of the Supreme Soviet of the USSR, Valentina Shevchenko

is a Ukrainian, born in Kiev and a graduate of Kiev University. A teacher by original profession, she subsequently made a career in the Komsomol and party apparatus in the Ukraine and in March 1985 became the first woman member of the Bureau of the Central Committee of the Ukrainian party. She has been a member of the Central Committee of the CPSU since 1986, a member of the Soviet Women's Committee since 1987 and an elected member of the Congress of People's Deputies and of the Supreme Soviet (in the Soviet of Nationalities) since 1989. AHB

SHEYNIS, Viktor Leonidovich (b. 1931) A leading research worker at IMEMO, Sheynis has been one of the boldest and most innovative of Soviet social scientists. Born in Kiev, he graduated from the History Faculty of Leningrad University in 1953 and from 1953 until 1958 was a history teacher at a Leningrad middle school. Trouble with the authorities led to his employment as a manual worker in the Kirov factory in Leningrad from 1958 to 1964 when he was able to begin graduate studies in the department of economics of contemporary capitalism of Leningrad University where he went on to teach until 1975. He took his candidate of science degree in 1966 and his higher doctorate in 1982. Since 1975 he has been employed by IMEMO and since 1977 has lived in Moscow. The author of over one hundred and fifty scholarly publications, Sheynis has increasingly turned his attention in recent years to the problems of reform of the Soviet system. Among his works in English are *Developing Nations at the Turn of the Millenium* (1987) and a contribution to S. Hirsch (ed.), *New Soviet Voices on Foreign and Economic Policy* (1989). AHB

SHIFRIN, Nisson Abramovich
(1892–1961) Designer. Born in Kiev,
Shifrin received his art education, like
Rabinovich, at the Kiev Art Institute
in the early 1910s, and in 1918 became
especially interested in the work of
Ekster. In the 1920s he rapidly
emerged as an original stage and book
designer and he continued to
command respect as an uncompromising artist until his death – witnessed, for example, by his
experimental sets and costumes for
Virgin Soil Upturned (1957). JEB

SHIRINSKY, Sergey Petrovich
(1903–1974) Cellist. Shirinsky was
born in Yekaterinodar and died in
Moscow. He graduated from the
Moscow Conservatory in 1923, where
he was a pupil of Anatoly Brandukov,
with whom he undertook post-
graduate work until 1929. He was
made an artist of the Bol'shoy Theatre
Orchestra (1920) and was a member
of the 'Persimfans' ensemble, a notable
Soviet symphony orchestra which performed without a conductor (1923–
32). He was also a permanent member
of the Beethoven Quartet. At various
times he was leader of the Moscow
Philharmonic Orchestra, the State
Symphony Orchestra, and the Radio
Symphony Orchestra. From 1931 he
taught at the Moscow Conservatory.
He was awarded a State Prize in 1946
and was made a People's Artist in
1965. GS

SHIRYAEV, Aleksandr Viktorovich
(1867–1941) A dancer, choreographer
and teacher, Shiryaev is known as the
'father of Russian character dance'
and as one of Marius Petipa's chief
collaborators. He began his dancing
career at the age of ten and graduated
from the St Petersburg Imperial Ballet
School in 1885. For the next twenty
years he danced with the Maryinsky

troupe, particularly excelling in
character roles including his Jester in
both *The Nutcracker* and *Mlada*.

By 1896 Shiryaev was Petipa's chief
assistant and in 1901 he replaced the
late Lev Ivanov as assistant ballet
master. He revived a number of Petipa
ballets but, when not appointed to
succeed Petipa in 1905, resigned from
the troupe and spent the next twelve
years performing with other companies and abroad.

In 1917 he rejoined the Maryinsky
troupe and danced until 1921 when he
retired to teach and develop a method
for teaching character dance. In 1939
he and two of his students published
The Fundamentals of Character Dance,
which remains the classic work on the
subject. In 1941 he published his
memoirs. SCS

**SHKAPSKAYA (born Andreev-
skaya), Mariya Mikhaylovna**
(1891–1952) Poet. All her poems were
printed before 1925; after that she
worked as a travelling correspondent.
Her poetry collections include *Mater
Dolorosa* (1920), *Blood-Ore* (1922), and
a long poem *Reality* (1923). Her poems
in prose are especially noteworthy.
She describes an ominous situation for
modern women, male progress at
female cost. To date, her poems have
not been republished in the Soviet
Union. BH

SHKIRYATOV, Matvey Fedorovich
(1883–1954) A party official closely
allied with Stalin in the conduct of the
purges. His achievements included the
dissolution of the Society of Old Bolsheviks. The son of a peasant, born in a
village near Tula, Shkiryatov worked
first in the village, and then as a tailor.
He joined the Bolsheviks in 1906 and
suffered frequent arrest and exile. He
served in the army in 1915. He later
became a prominent official in the tai-

lors' trade union (1918–21). He joined the staff of the party Central Committee in 1921, becoming a leading figure in the Central Control Commission and Rabkrin (1921–34), a member of the Commission of Party Control (1934–54), Deputy Chairman (1939–52), and Chairman in 1952. He was a member of the party Central Committee (1939–54). RWD

SHKLOVSKY, Viktor Borisovich (1893–1984) Born in Petersburg, Shklovsky was a prominent avant-garde theorist of literature and film, a prose writer, memoirist and screen writer; his 'The Resurrection of the Word' (1914) is regarded as the first text of the Formalist movement. He was a founder of its association OPOYAZ in 1916, and also close to the Serapion Brothers, Futurists and Constructivists. In emigration in Berlin (1922–23), he published his two most successful novels, the semi-autobiographical *A Sentimental Journey, 1917–1922* (1923) and the experimental *Zoo, or Letters Not About Love* (1923). His theoretical works of the early twenties, such as *The Knight's Move* (1923) and *The Theory of Prose* (1925), represent an extreme statement of Formalism. Shklovsky maintained that not merely does literature have no connection with extra-literary reality, but its main point is its formal features: the themes, content and protagonists of a work of literature are not self valuable, but merely 'motivations' for play with devices. He is also known for developing such concepts as 'defamiliarization', 'retardation', and 'defacilitation', and for his studies of Tolstoy. Shklovsky recanted his Formalism under pressure in 1930, and turned to more traditional literary theory and scholarship, semi-historical works, and film scripts. KC

SHKURAT, Stepan Iosifovich (1886–1973) Actor. Shkurat was closely associated with the films of Dovzhenko: *The Earth* (1930), *Ivan* (1932), *Aerograd* (1935) and *Shchors* (1939). RT

SHLIKHTER, Aleksandr Grigorovich (1868–1940) A Ukrainian revolutionary and old Bolshevik, food supply organizer, and publicist. The son of a carpenter, Shlikhter was a revolutionary from 1887, and was first exiled in 1888. He studied at Khar'kov and Berlin Universities (1889–91). He joined the Bolsheviks in 1903 and was exiled to Siberia for life in 1908. He was appointed People's Commissar for Food (1917–18), and then food supply organizer in Siberia, Vyatka, and elsewhere. He was the People's Commissar for Food in the Ukraine in 1919. A member of the party Orgburo (1923–25), and People's Commissar for Agriculture in the Ukraine (1927–29), he was vice-president of the Ukrainian Academy of Sciences during the 1930s. He was a member of the Ukrainian party Central Committee (1924–37), and a candidate and then full member of the Ukrainian Politburo (1926–37). RWD

SHLYAPNIKOV, Aleksandr Gavrilovich (1884–1943) Shlyapnikov, a radically-inclined trade union activist who held minor administrative posts in the early post-revolutionary period, was born in the town of Murom to lower-middle-class parents who were Old Believers. His father died when he was just two years old and the family was left in a position of some hardship. Shlyapnikov had little formal education and was punished in school for his (literally) unorthodox views. After school he turned to a variety of occupations, latterly becoming an apprentice fitter in a shipbuilding yard in St Petersburg. He soon became an industrial and political activist, suffered repeated dismissal, joined the Social Democratic Party (1901) and was arrested and imprisoned. He spent the years 1908 to 1914 abroad in France, Britain, and Germany.

Shlyapnikov initially took a 'patriotic' attitude towards the war but was elected to the Petrograd Soviet in February 1917 and began to organize the Red Guard or workers' militia. He also became president of the metalworkers' union, and was elected Commissar for Labour in the first Soviet government although he had expressed some doubts as to whether the time was quite right for a Bolshevik seizure of power. Proud of his genuinely working-class credentials, Shlyapnikov became a member of the broadly syndicalist Workers' Opposition in 1920 and was effectively exiled to the Paris embassy (1924–25), where he devoted himself to completing his memoirs. In 1926 he signed a joint letter repudiating 'any organized expression of opinion contradicting party decisions', but in 1933 he was expelled from the membership and was subsequently arrested and imprisoned. Shlyapnikov died in detention; his entertaining memoirs in three volumes are perhaps his most enduring legacy. SLW

SHMAL'GAUZEN (Schmalhausen), Ivan Ivanovich (1884–1963) Anatomist, embryologist, and a founder of the modern theory of evolution. The son of a leading Russian botanist, Shmal'gauzen was the protégé of Russia's most distinguished morphologist, A. N. Severtsov. During the period 1921–1935, Shmal'gauzen worked at Kiev University and at a research institute of the Ukrainian Academy of Sciences, where he wrote influential textbooks on comparative anatomy and conducted innovative embryological studies. In 1935 on the eve of his mentor's death, he moved to Moscow, was elected to the USSR Academy of Sciences, and became director of its Severtsov Institute of Animal Morphology. In 1938 he became professor of Darwinism at Moscow University and began a remarkably productive decade that saw the publication of four classics of evolutionary theory: *The Organism as a Whole in Individual and Historical Development* (1938); *Trends and Laws of the Evolutionary Process* (1939); *Factors of Evolution* (1946), published in English in 1949; and *Problems of Darwinism* (1946). From 1946 on, he was an outspoken critic of Lysenko's 'creative Darwinism' and lost his job following Lysenko's triumph in 1948. For the remainder of his career, he worked at the Institute of Zoology on the origin of terrestrial vertebrates and on cybernetic approaches to evolutionary theory. MBA

SHMARINOV, Dementiy Alekseevich (b. 1907) Graphic artist. Shmarinov was born in Kazan'. One of the Soviet Union's foremost graphic artists, his reputation rests on his illustrations to a wide diapason of Russian and Western classics by Dostoevsky (1935–36), Lermontov (1941), Shakespeare (1959–60), etc. Trained under Nikolay Prakhov in Kiev and Dmitriy Kardovsky in Moscow, he began his career as an illustrator in the 1920s. In the Second World War he also produced patriotic posters, including the famous *We Will Not Forget, We Will Not Forgive* (1942). JEB

SHMELEV, Nikolay Petrovich (b. 1936) One of the most outstanding economic reformers in the Soviet Union today and also a talented creative writer, Nikolay Shmelev was

345

born in Moscow and educated at Moscow University. Although it is only in the Gorbachev era that he has achieved widespread renown, his writings on economic questions during the Brezhnev years were also innovative for that time.

Shmelev in his earlier years was related by marriage to Nikita Khrushchev. His first wife, from whom he was divorced in 1962, was Khrushchev's granddaughter (and adopted daughter after the death of her father, Khrushchev's son, and the arrest of her mother during the war).

Shmelev, who has a higher doctorate in economics and the rank of professor, was a researcher at the Institute of Economics of the Academy of Sciences from 1958 to 1961 when he moved to the Institute of Economics of the World Socialist System (IEMSS). In 1968 he entered the Central Committee apparatus for a brief period (he had joined the party in 1962) and worked in the Propaganda Department at a time when its acting head was Aleksandr Yakovlev. Shmelev returned to IEMSS in 1970 and remained there until 1982 when he moved to Arbatov's Institute of the USA and Canada where, as of 1990, he heads the department which studies the role of the United States in the world economy.

Most of Shmelev's creative writing prior to 1987 had been 'for the drawer'. He had been either unable to have it published or unwilling to make the changes Soviet editors wished to impose upon him. In 1987, however, his impressive novella, *Pashkov's House*, appeared in *Znamya* just three months before *Novyy mir* published one of his most influential economic articles – a particularly searing indictment of the unreformed Soviet economy which included the acknowledgement that unemployment already existed within the Soviet Union's administrative-command economy and that some unemployment would also be inevitable in the transition to a market economy. Shmelev's talent as a writer has helped to ensure that his economic articles, as well as his literary works, receive wide attention when they appear in the monthly journals.

In 1989 Shmelev topped the poll in the second round of voting by the Academy of Sciences for the election by 'public organizations' of their share of members of the Congress of People's Deputies. As a parliamentarian, he has advocated an end to the artificial restrictions on the sale of alcohol and has proposed large-scale imports of consumer goods to the Soviet Union and the sale of land to private individuals. AHB

SHMIDT (Schmidt), Otto Yul'evich (1891–1956) Mathematician, explorer, administrator. A 1908 graduate of Kiev University, Shmidt published on abstract algebra and group theory and taught mathematics as a *dotsent* at Kiev University (1916–20) and as a professor at the Moscow Technical Forestry Institute (1920–23) and Moscow University (1923–56). He joined the party in 1918, became director of Gosizdat (1921–24) and chief editor of the *Great Soviet Encyclopedia* (1924–41), and was active in the Communist Academy. He came to public attention by leading ships on polar expeditions in 1929, 1930, 1932 and 1933 to 1934, and was appointed head of Glavsevmorputi (1932–39), an agency charged with finding a northern sea route. Elected a corresponding member of the USSR Academy of Sciences (1933) and a full member (in mathematics and geography in 1935), he organized and directed its Geophysics Institute (1937–49) and served as Academy vice-president (1939–42). In 1937 he organized a drifting arctic research station, 'North Pole', and became world renowned in 1938 for heading the expedition to rescue its staff. MBA

SHOLOKHOV, Mikhail Aleksandrovich (1905–1984) One of the most famous Soviet novelists and winner of the Nobel Prize for Literature in 1965 for *Quiet Flows the Don* (1928–40), Sholokhov has become a national institution, winning many high honours; his works have been published in the Soviet Union in at least eighty million copies and in eighty-four languages. In 1922 he joined the militantly 'proletarian' Komsomol literary group 'The Young Guard' and the Communist Party in 1932. Most of his early fiction, such as the short stories in the anthologies *Tales of the Don* (1926) and *The Tulip Steppe* (1926), is about the Cossacks in the Soviet period (he was not himself a Cossack although born in Kruzhilin in the Don [Cossack] Military Region).

Quiet Flows the Don is set between 1912 and 1922 and treats particularly the role of the Cossacks in the Revolution and Civil War, focusing on the story of the passionate and tragic love of the protagonist, Grigoriy Melekhov, who vacillates between the Reds and the Whites. Sholokhov encountered some difficulties in publishing this saga, but since the late thirties it has been regarded as the great national epic. There have been periodic charges that the novel was plagiarized and based on a work by a member of the White Guard; the issue continues to be controversial.

His next major work, *Virgin Soil Upturned* (1932–60), a saga about collectivization, encountered more publication difficulties and the second part appeared only in 1960. He wrote extensively about the Second World War, including many agitational war sketches, and the novel *They Fought for the Motherland* (1943–69) which concerns fighting in the Don region but includes flashbacks into the protagonists' pre-war lives there. His last major work, 'The Fate of Man' (1957), was considered an answer to the pessimism of Hemingway's *The Old Man and the Sea*, and shows how a veteran who lost his entire family in the war regains his sense of purpose and identity with the Motherland when he adopts a war orphan. KC

SHORIN, Aleksandr Fedorovich (1890–1941) Sound engineer. Shorin invented the Soviet system of mechanical sound recording used for films such as *Counterplan* (1932) and *Chapaev* (1934), and he also developed the telegraph system widely used in the USSR. He was awarded a State Prize in 1941. RT

SHOSTAKOVICH, Dmitriy Dmitrievich (1906–1975) Composer, pianist and teacher. Dmitriy Shostakovich was born in St Petersburg and died in Moscow. After receiving his first musical tuition from his mother, he entered the Leningrad Conservatory, where he graduated in piano under Leonid Nikolaev in 1923 and in composition under Maksimilyan Shteynberg in 1925. He joined the teaching staff of the Leningrad Conservatory in 1937, becoming a professor in 1939, teaching at the Moscow Conservatory from 1943 to 1948. He became a member of the party in 1960. He was made a People's Artist of the USSR in 1954, a Hero of Socialist Labour in 1966, as well as being a recipient of many international honours and awards. Shostakovich's composition is directly related to the development of Soviet music. Twice censured in 1936 and 1948 for ideological failings, his music contains many satirical elements suggesting a strong element of personal protest. As a symphonist, he is one of the major figures of the twentieth century, his Seventh ('Leningrad') Symphony (1942) doing much to foster support for the Russian wartime cause. His opera *The Lady Macbeth of Mtsensk* (1934) (revised under the title of *Katerina Izmaylova*) (1956) is an outstanding work of the Soviet era, while some of the chamber compositions are part of the standard international repertoire. The recently published *Testimony* (1980) by Solomon Volkov, is said to be based on Shostakovich's own utterances, but its validity has been questioned. GS

SHOSTAKOVICH, Maksim Dmitrievich (b. 1938) Conductor. Maksim Shostakovich, son of composer Dmitriy Shostakovich, was born in Leningrad. After studying at the Moscow Conservatory, where his teachers were Yakob Flier (piano) and Aleksandr Gauk and Gennady Rozhdestvensky (conducting), he was appointed assistant conductor of the Moscow Symphony Orchestra in 1963 and of the State Symphony Orchestra of the USSR in 1966. From 1971 to 1981 he was principal conductor of the Grand Orchestra of the All-Union Radio and Television and several times travelled abroad. In 1981 he defected and settled in America, where he appears frequently as a guest conductor. He is an excellent pianist. GS

SHPET, Gustav Gustavovich (1879–1937) A philosopher and literary scholar influenced by Husserl's theory of language, Shpet was one of the early formulators of Soviet semiotics. Much of his early work was on the philosophy of history (for example, *History as a Problem in Logic*, 1916). Shpet's greatest theoretical work was done in the twenties when he attempted to define the functions of universal grammatical categories. Shpet argued against confusing language 'the central system of signs' with psychology, advancing instead language as a social process. He was influenced by Wilhelm von Humboldt in his *Inner Form of the Word* (1927) which emphasizes consciousness' social character; in works such as *An Introduction to Ethnic Psychology* (1927) he posits a collective consciousness as a sort of *langue* to the *parole* of the individual's own sociocultural consciousness. In his three-volume *Aesthetic Fragments* (1922–23), he argues against the prevailing conception of poetry as being distinguished from prose by reason of its visual imagery, instead insisting that its distinctive feature is its verbal characteristics – especially the use of metaphor. He also characterizes the novel as a purely rhetorical form, manifesting a particular ideology. Shpet also wrote on Bely, Blok, and translated Dickens, Thackeray, and Byron. He was a professor at Moscow University from 1918, but was arrested and died in a Siberian labour camp in 1937. KC

SHPINEL', Iosif Aronovich (1892–1980) Designer. Shpinel' graduated from VKhUTEMAS and became a leading film set designer. Among the films for which he designed the sets were: *The Arsenal* (1929), *Ivan* (1932), *Boule de Suif* and *A Petersburg Night* (both 1934) and Eisenstein's *Ivan the Terrible* (1943–48). RT

SHTEMENKO, Sergey Matveevich
(1907–1976) General Staff Chief. A
Don Cossack by origin, Shtemenko
entered the Red Army in 1919. After
graduation from General Staff
Academy he became a Section Chief in
the Office of Operations of the General
Staff (1940–42). He impressed Stalin
and was promoted to Deputy Chief of
Operations of General Staff in 1943,
and Chief of Operations, Deputy Chief
of General Staff for the period 1943 to
1948. Shtemenko was directly
involved in the elaboration and planning of many major operations and
had frequent direct contact with
Stalin. In 1948 he was placed in
charge of the General Staff and
appointed USSR Minister of the
Armed Forces. But his career waned
in 1952 as he was relieved as Chief of
General Staff and demoted to Chief
of Staff of Soviet Forces in Germany.
After Stalin's death he was demoted
in rank and disappeared from public
life for three years until the rout of the
'anti-party group' in 1956. In a career
revival he became Chief of the Main
Staff of Soviet Ground Forces (1962–
65), Deputy Chief of General Staff
(1965–68), and in 1968 First Deputy
Chief of the General Staff with the
rank of army general. In 1968 he published his revealing memoirs. RA

SHTERENBERG, David Petrovich
(1881–1948) Painter and graphic
artist. Shterenberg was born in Zhitomir. Before returning to Russia in
1917, he lived for many years in Paris,
moving closely with the Cubists.
Under Anatoliy Lunacharsky, he
became head of the Visual Arts
Section of the People's Commissariat
for Enlightenment (IZO NKP) and
played a crucial role in the reorganization of artistic affairs (exhibitions, museums, art education).

Shterenberg was a founder member
of OST in 1925 and, after 1930, was
particularly active as an illustrator of
children's literature. JEB

**SHTRAUKH, Maksim Maksimov-
ich** (1900–1974) Actor. Shtraukh
began his career as a stage actor
and worked with *Proletkul't* and
Meyerkhol'd. A childhood friend of
Eisenstein, Shtraukh acted in that
director's first film *Glumov's Diary*, part
of his stage production of *Enough Simplicity for Every Wise Man* (1923). He
also appeared in Eisenstein's films *The
Strike* (1925), *The Battleship Potemkin*
(1926), *October* (1927) and *The Old and
the New* (1929). But Shtraukh was
probably best known for his portrayal
of Lenin in Yutkevich's films *The Man
With A Gun* (1938), *Tales of Lenin*
(1958) and *Lenin in Poland* (1966). He
was married to Yudif' Glizer. RT

SHUB, Esfir' Il'inichna (1894–1959)
Director. Shub was the leading director of compilation documentary films
such as *The Fall of the Romanov Dynasty*
and *The Great Path* (both 1927), *Lev
Tolstoy and the Russia of Nicholas II*
(1928), *Today* (1930), *K. Sh. E.* (1932)
and *Spain* (1939). She also edited
imported films for Soviet distribution
and worked, for instance, with Eisenstein on reducing Fritz Lang's *Dr
Mabuse* to a normal feature-length
film, and on making a compilation
film out of British newsreel footage
during the Second World War. RT

SHUKHAEV, Vasiliy Ivanovich
(1887–1973) Painter. Shukhaev was
born in Moscow. Supporting the traditions of the World of Art group, he
studied at the Stroganov Institute in
Moscow (1897–1905) and the
Academy of Arts (1906–12). During
his temporary emigration in France
(1921–35) he worked as a stage
designer, portraitist, and muralist. In

349

1947 he became a professor at the Academy of Arts, Tbilisi. JEB

SHUKHMIN, Petr Mitrofanovich (1894–1955) Painter and graphic artist. Born in Voronezh, Shukhmin studied in Moscow and then at the Academy of Arts (1912–16). He joined AKhRR in 1922 and attracted attention by his documentary, photographic style as in *The Order to Attack* (1927). He was also active as a graphic artist producing caricatures and portraits. JEB

SHUKSHIN, Vasiliy Makarovich (1929–1974) Film director, actor and writer who had the unique distinction of being valued both by the authorities and by the oppositional intelligentsia. Perhaps this was because both in cinema and literature he portrayed the archetypal mid-twentieth-century Soviet experience: the psychological and spiritual conflicts of people born in the countryside but having to adapt to an urban way of life. His *Snowball Berry Red* (1973) was especially popular, with its portrayal of a criminal trying to go straight by working on a *kolkhoz*. He published a novel about the seventeenth-century rebel Sten'ka Razin, but his ardent aspiration to make a film about him was thwarted by the authorities. This may have been a cause of the heart attack which led to his premature death. GAH

SHUMYATSKY, Boris Zakharovich (1886–1938) Shumyatsky had been a party activist, administrator and diplomat when he was appointed head of the Soviet film industry in 1930. During his period in office he laid the foundations for a cinema that combined the requirements of ideology and mass entertainment. He was dismissed and executed in January 1938. RT

SHVARTS, Yevgeny L'vovich (1896–1958) Playwright and children's writer. His plays, seemingly for children and based on Andersen or Perrault, are allegories of contemporary Soviet reality and of good and evil in the adult world. They include: *The Naked King* (1934, produced in 1960); *The Shadow* (1940), and *The Dragon* (1943–44), the latter two produced consistently only in the early 1960s. Shvarts also worked on the staff of children's literary magazines. His collected plays were first published in 1956. Their dialogue is snappy and humorous, but their overall effect is darkly grim. BH

SHVERNIK, Nikolay Mikhaylovich (1888–1970) Russian politician. A party member from 1905, Shvernik was active in the revolutionary struggle long before 1917. He made his career in a number of party and trade union posts. From 1930 to 1944 he was First Secretary of the trade unions and from 1946 to 1953 Chairman of the Presidium of the USSR Supreme Soviet. A candidate Politburo member (1939–52), he became a full member of Stalin's large Presidium but was returned to candidate status in March 1953. After the 1957 'anti-party group' crisis Shvernik was again raised to full membership and was accordingly a harsh critic of the fallen members of the group. He headed the Party Control Commission from 1956 until his retirement in 1966. WJT

SILLARI, Enn-Arno Augustovich (b. 1944) An Estonian, Sillari headed the Tartu City Party Committee before moving on to Tallinn and assuming the First Secretaryship of the Tallinn party organization. Sillari made his mark in August 1989 by calling for an 'understanding of the Estonian point of view' on the issue of independence. He emerged from the bruising CPE session in March of 1990 as the leader of the majority wing which formed a new pro-independence Communist Party. Moscow acknowledged Sillari as First Secretary of the republic and he was received by Gorbachev in April. At the Twenty-eighth Party Congress in July 1990 Sillari was elected to the Central Committee of the CPSU and to the Politburo. MM

SIMEONOV, Konstantin Arsen'e-vich (b. 1910) Conductor. Simeonov was born in the village of Koznakovo. After first training as a singer, he entered the Leningrad Conservatory where he studied conducting with Aleksandr Gauk. He graduated in 1936 and was appointed conductor of a symphony orchestra in Petrozavodsk, a post he retained for five years. After a period of guest conducting, he became an assistant conductor at the Ukrainian Theatre of Opera and Ballet, Kiev (1961–66), after which he obtained a post with the Leningrad Theatre of Opera and Ballet (the Kirov). He returned to the Ukrainian Theatre in 1975 as chief conductor. The holder of several State Prizes and awards, he was made a People's Artist of the USSR in 1962. Best known in the Western world for his recordings, he has several times toured abroad. GS

SIMONIA, Nodari (b. 1932) Born in Tbilisi, Simonia spent his first eighteen years in his native Georgia, but moved to Moscow in 1950 to enter the Institute of International Relations (IMO) as a student. He pursued both his undergraduate and graduate studies there and subsequently became an innovative social scientist and historian whose work came in for criticism from more orthodox scholars in Brezhnev's time. He made, however, a significant contribution to Soviet new thinking on the Third World. Simonia has written extensively on the theory of historical development, his particular area of speciality being Asian history. His numerous books include *The East: Paths of Development* (1975) and *Evolution of Eastern Societies: Synthesis of the Modern and Traditional* (1984). For many years a researcher at the Institute of Oriental Studies of the Academy of Sciences in Moscow (1958–88) and from 1974 a Professor of the Institute of Social Sciences, Simonia became in 1988 a deputy director of IMEMO and Director of the Centre of Development Studies established there. AHB

SIMONOV, Konstantin Mikhaylovich (1915–1979) Poet, novelist, dramatist, high literary and party official. Born in Petrograd, he made his literary début as a poet in 1934. He joined the party in 1942. He made his name and founded his vast personal wealth as a war correspondent, the author of universally known soldier's lyrics ('Wait for me, and I'll return', 1941), and the Stalingrad novel *Days and Nights* (1943–44). He was also an important dramatist, especially for the anti-American play *The Russian Question* (1946). Simonov edited the journal *Novyy mir* from 1946 to 1950 and again from 1954 to 1958. GSS

SIMONOV, Ruben Nikolaevich (1899–1968) Stage actor and director. Simonov was associated with the Vakhtangov Theatre, of which he was the Principal Director from 1931 to 1968. His major productions were: Sholokhov's *Virgin Soil Upturned* (1931), Pogodin's *Missouri Valse*

(1950) and a revival of Gor'ky's *Foma Gordeev* (1956). RT

SIMONYAN, Rayr Rayrovich (b. 1947) The son of a retired army general (now active in the movement, Generals for Peace), Rayr Simonyan was elected party secretary for IMEMO by colleagues who wanted a reformer in that office. He is one of the influential proponents of far-reaching economic reform in the younger generation of Soviet scholars. Simonyan, who was born in Brest, took his first degree at Moscow University in geography before turning to economics and taking a candidate of sciences degree in 1973 and his higher doctorate in 1987. He has been at IMEMO since 1974, latterly as a sector head. Simonyan is active both as a scholar and as a proponent in the mass media of radical reformist measures, including the institutionalization of private property and of the market. AHB

SINYAVSKY, Andrey Donatovich (pseud. Abram Terts) (b. 1925) Literary scholar and prose writer, who taught at Moscow University and the Institute of World Literature. His initially anonymous *samizdat* essay *What is Socialist Realism* (1956) showed in erudite and witty style that official Stalinist literature resembled the classicism of Catherine II's epoch, and called instead for a 'fantasmagoric art'. Between 1956 and 1962 he practised what he preached by publishing in the West (under his pseudonym) a series of fantastic satirical tales on life in Stalin's Russia. Arrested along with Daniel' in 1965 and accused of 'anti-Soviet propaganda' on the basis of these, he refused to plead guilty at his trial, and argued that it was illegitimate to base such an indictment on literary texts. After seven years in a labour camp, he emigrated to Paris in 1972, where he teaches at the Sorbonne. He was a co-founder with Maksimov of the journal *Kontinent*, but broke away from it because of what he saw as its rigid political line, and founded his own more free-thinking journal, *Syntax*. GAH

SISAKYAN, Norayr Martirosovich (1907–1966) Biochemist, administrator. A 1932 graduate of the Moscow Agricultural Institute, Sisakyan joined the staff of the Biochemical Institute of the USSR Academy of Sciences in 1935 and, after joining the party in 1937, became head of its laboratory of enzymology in 1939. An early advocate of Lysenko's biological theories, he published many articles and books (1948–53) claiming that those theories found support in studies of the metabolism of agricultural plants. He was rewarded in 1953 by his election to the USSR Academy of Sciences as a corresponding member in the biology division. When Lysenko gained Khrushchev's support in 1959, Sisakyan became academician-secretary of the Academy's division of biological sciences and later the chief scientific secretary of the Academy presidium (1963–66). In those posts he sought, with limited success, to develop molecular biology without undermining Lysenko's authority. MBA

SIZOVA, Alla Ivanovna (b. 1939) Leading ballet dancer. Sizova entered Leningrad Ballet School in 1949 and graduated in 1958 under the tutelage of Natal'ya Kamkova. She began receiving acclaim very early in her career, particularly for her 1957 performance in *Don Quixote* and her performance of the *pas de deux* from *Le Corsaire* at a national ballet competition in 1958.

After graduating Sizova joined the Kirov troupe and became a leading soloist. With her brilliant technique and warm stage presence, Sizova excelled in romantic roles and has developed a broad and varied repertoire. She danced leading parts in ballets including *The Nutcracker*, *Giselle*, *Sleeping Beauty*, *Romeo and Juliet*, and *Swan Lake*. In addition, she has appeared in a host of modern ballets, creating such roles as The Girl in *The Leningrad Symphony* (1961), Ophelia in *Hamlet* (1970), and Beautiful Rose in *The Charmed Prince* (1972). She was a frequent partner of Mikhail Baryshnikov before his departure to the West. Sizova has toured abroad with the Kirov troupe and was awarded the Anna Pavlova Prize (1964). scs

SKOBLYKOVA, Lidiya Pavlovna (b. 1939) Speed skater. She won a record six gold medals at the winter Olympics, starting with the 1500 and 3000m at the 1960 Squaw Valley Olympics, and finishing with all four women's races at the 1964 Innsbruck Games; she thereby repeated her world championship success of the previous year and then swept the board once more at the 1965 world skating championships. She won as many as forty gold medals altogether in her long career, including twenty-five at world championships and fifteen at national championships. Born in the Urals industrial town of Zlatoust, she joined the Chelyabinsk skating club at sixteen. From 1974 onwards she was head of the Physical Education Faculty of the Trade Union High School in Moscow. JWR

SKULME, Dzhemma Ottovna (b. 1925) Painter. Born in Riga, daughter of the painter and teacher Otto Skulme (1898–1967) and a graduate of the Academy of Arts in Riga (1949),

Dzhemma Skulme is widely recognized as one of Latvia's most distinguished contemporary painters. While paying homage to Cranach, Rubens and Velazquez, she also draws on local folk motifs and rituals, as in *Festivity* (1965) and *The Dialogue* (1981). JEB

SLIPY, Cardinal Iosyf (1892–1984) Head of the Ukrainian Catholic Church (1944–84). He studied in L'vov, Innsbruck and Rome, gaining a doctorate in theology. From 1926 he was rector of the Greek Catholic Seminary in L'vov, and from 1920 rector of the Academy. In 1939 Slipy was appointed Archbishop of L'vov and in 1944 Metropolitan of L'vov and Galych. Arrested by the Soviet authorities in April 1945, he was sentenced to eight years in a labour camp, but was eventually to serve seventeen years. Released in early 1963, he was expelled from the USSR the same year. In 1965 he became a Cardinal and in 1975 assumed the title of Patriarch of the Ukrainian Catholic Church. MR

SLONIMSKY, Sergey Mikhaylovich (b. 1932) Composer, teacher, and pianist. Slonimsky was born in Leningrad. A student of the Leningrad Conservatory, he was a pupil of Orest Yevlakhov (composition) and Vladimir Nil'sen (piano). After graduating in 1955, he stayed on for a further three years' postgraduate study, joining the teaching staff in 1958. He was made an Honoured Artist of the RSFSR in 1978. Prolific in output and employing contemporary techniques, allied with folk elements, he is one of the most gifted and resourceful composers of his generation, his ballet *Icarus* (première 1971) being especially successful. His opera-ballad *Mary Stuart* (1980), for which he was awarded a Glinka Prize in 1983, was given in Leipzig in 1984. GS

SLONIMSKY, Yuriy Iosifovich (1902–1978) Dance historian and librettist. Recognized as the founder of the Soviet school of analytical ballet criticism. While a student at the school of Russian Drama in Petrograd in 1918, Slonimsky took private lessons in dance from students of the Petrograd Ballet School. While attending law school in 1919, he began to publish dance criticism under a pseudonym. Eventually he wrote more than 400 articles on ballet. Many of them appear in the collection *In Honour of Dance* (1968).

Slonimsky advocated a concept of 'choreographic dramaturgy' in which libretto, music, and dance are fully integrated. In 'Our Point of View' (in *The Bolshoi Ballet*, 1960, he noted that 'classical dancing, more readily than any other kind, blends with the music, comprising a "choreographic melody".... However, content must be given priority if art is to attain the maximum of expression'. This point of view guided his historical writings. Of particular importance among his works are *Tchaikovsky and the Ballet Theatre of His Time* (1956), *Didelot* (1958), *Giselle* (1969), *Pushkin's Ballet Verses* (1974), and *The Dramatic Art of Nineteenth-Century Ballet* (1977).

Also a practical man of the theatre, Slonimsky was one of the founders of The Young Ballet (*Molodoy balet*) with which the young Balanchine began his choreographic career. Slonimsky commemorated that experience in 'Balanchine: The Early Years' (translated by John Andrews, *Ballet Review* (1975)). His ballet librettos included *Youth* (1949), *Path of Thunder* (1958), *Coast of Hope* (1959), and *Leli and Mejnun* (1953).

From 1932 Slonimsky taught dance history at the Leningrad Ballet School. In 1937 he established a department of choreography there with Fedor Lopukhov and lectured on the analysis of ballet productions. In 1922, 1924, and from 1932 to 1961, he was on the staff of the Leningrad Institute of the History of the Arts. Thereafter, he held a professorship in the department of choreography of the Leningrad Conservatory. In 1959 he received an honorary doctorate from the University of Paris. SJC

SLUTSKY, Boris Abramovich (1919–1986) Born in the Donbass, educated in Khar'kov, and in Moscow since 1937. He served in the Second World War, joining the party in 1943. After the war he was based in Moscow. He was one of the foremost exponents of the war theme in Soviet poetry; but his most important work, a series of bitterly satirical lyrics, was hardly published in the Soviet Union until the Gorbachev period. GSS

SLYUN'KOV, Nikolay Nikitovich (b. 1929) Until recently, a full Politburo member and Secretary of the Central Committee, Slyun'kov headed the Economic Department of the Central Committee from 1987 to 1988 and was Chairman of the Commission on Socio-Economic Policy of the Central Committee (1988–90).

A Belorussian by nationality, Slyun'kov was born into a peasant family in Gorodets in the Gomel' region. After a technical education he worked in industry until 1972, from 1965 to 1971 as Director of the Lenin Tractor Plant in Minsk and in 1971 to 1972 as General Manager of the Production association for Tractor Construction in that city. In 1972 he became First Secretary of the Minsk party organization, a post he left in 1974 to become a deputy chairman of Gosplan with special responsibilities for machine-building. In 1983 he returned to Belorussia in the important position of First Secretary of the republican party organization.

During the period in which Gorbachev has been General Secretary and Ryzhkov Chairman of the Council of Ministers, Slyun'kov had further promotion. Ryzhkov, with whom Slyun'kov worked closely in Gosplan, may have been an especially important influence on this. In 1986 Slyun'kov became a candidate member of the Politburo, in 1987 a Secretary of the Central Committee and in the same year a full member of the Politburo while retaining his Secretaryship. In July 1990, however, he lost not only his Politburo position but also his seat on the Central Committee.

A Communist Party member since 1954, Slyun'kov was elected on the party slate to the Congress of People's Deputies in 1989. His attitude to economic reform has been characterized more by caution than by enthusiasm. AHB

SMELYAKOV, Yaroslav Vasil'evich (1913–1972) Born in Volhynia, he began as a Komsomol bard, but spent the years 1934 to 1937 in the camps. Later he was a prisoner of war in Finnish hands, and was rearrested in the late 1940s, eventually being rehabilitated in 1956. There is a strong patriotic note in his poetry; the vicissitudes of his life prevented his great talent finding full expression. GSS

SMIDOVICH, Sof'ya Nikolaevna (1872–1934) A Communist Party official and head of Zhenotdel. Smidovich was born into the intelligentsia, the daughter of a lawyer and a school teacher, in Tula. After high school she taught the peasants on the family estate. In Moscow in the 1890s to continue her education, she met P. V. Lunacharsky, the older brother of A. V. Lunacharsky (later a prominent Bolshevik political official). She married Platon Lunacharsky and worked with him in the revolutionary movement. For a time they resided in France in the 1890s, then returned to Russia in 1898. She joined the RSDLP at that time. In 1901 they were arrested and imprisoned. After Lunacharsky suffered a stroke, they were released and he died in 1904.

Sof'ya worked for the Moscow Party Committee after his death and then married P. G. Smidovich in 1906. They were frequently arrested for their work in the revolutionary movement. Prior to the revolution she was a secretary of the Moscow Party.

After the revolution Smidovich worked in the Commissariat of Education and then, in 1919, became head of the Moscow section of Zhenotdel. When Kollontai was removed as head of the All-Union Zhenotdel in 1922, Smidovich succeeded her. Smidovich was an administrator, rather than a leader, and more traditional in her attitudes towards women than Kollontai. She was very concerned about the problems of homeless children in Russia and about the loose morals of the 1920s. In 1924 she stepped down as head of Zhenotdel but continued to be associated with its projects. She was an editor of *Rabotnitsa* and *Kommunistka* and wrote quite extensively about the problems of women.

In 1931 she was appointed Deputy Chairman of the Committee for Improving the Working and Living Conditions of Women, under the USSR Central Executive Committee.

Smidovich was a member of the Central Control Commission of the party and an officer of the All-Union Society of Old Bolsheviks prior to her death from heart failure in 1934. NN

SMIRNOV, Georgiy Lukich (b. 1922) A leading Soviet ideologist of the Gorbachev era, Smirnov has spent most of his career in party ideological work. He was one of Gorbachev's personal aides from 1985 to 1986 and since January 1987 has been Director of the Institute of Marxism-Leninism of the Central Committee of the Communist Party. That institute, traditionally a bastion of orthodoxy and of defensiveness about party archives and offical dogma, has become much more open to new ideas. Smirnov himself has played an important part in re-examining the past, in releasing new information, and in the rehabilitation (usually posthumous) of the victims of Stalin.

Smirnov was born in the Okt'yabrsky region south of Volgograd into a family of Cossack peasant stock. Bad eyesight kept him out of the army during the war, but he worked in the Komsomol underground in an occupied area. He joined the party after the Battle of Stalingrad and began a career as a party official. He took time out of his career to study on several occasions – most notably at the Philosophy Department of the Academy of Social Sciences of the Central Committee from 1953 to 1957. From 1965 to 1983 Smirnov worked in the Department of Propaganda of the Central Committee and especially closely with Aleksandr Yakovlev between 1969 and 1973 when Yakovlev was First Deputy Head of the department and Smirnov deputy head. Smirnov succeeded to the position Yakovlev had vacated in 1974, a

year after Yakovlev's departure to the Soviet Embassy in Canada.

Smirnov, who has been a corresponding member of the Academy of Sciences since 1981 and a full member from 1987, was elected to candidate membership of the Central Committee of the Communist Party in 1976; he has been a member of the Central Committee's Ideological Commission since its creation in 1988. AHB

SMIRNOV, Ivan Nikitich (1881–1936) A leading supporter of Trotsky and the Left Opposition. Smirnov, a party member (1899–1927 and 1930–33), was a factory worker before the revolution. He became a notable figure in the Siberian Red Army during the Civil War. He was one of the last of Trotsky's supporters to retain contact with him, smuggling out of the Soviet Union a critical document on the economy in autumn 1932, which was then published in Trotsky's *Bulletin of the Opposition*. Expelled from the party in January 1933, Smirnov was one of the accused in the Zinov'ev-Kamenev trial in August 1936, and was executed. He was rehabilitated in June 1988. RWD

SMIRNOV, Vil'yam (William) Viktorovich (b. 1941) One of the Soviet Union's most prominent political scientists and a leading administrator in that field, Smirnov is well known in international scholarly circles through his active participation in the International Political Science Association. His published works include books on *The Political Mechanism of City Administration in the USA* and *Democracy and Political Participation* (1986, co-author).

Smirnov was born in Serpukhov in the Moscow region and graduated from the Law Faculty of Moscow University where he also pursued his graduate studies. His working career has been spent in the Institute of Sociology and the Institute of State and Law where he succeeded Mikhail Piskotin in 1989 as head of the Centre for Political Science Research which had been established two years earlier.

Smirnov was General Secretary of the Soviet Association of Political Sciences from 1977 until 1981 and had the difficult task of organizing the International Political Science Association Congress held in Moscow in 1979, a time when the discipline itself and the arrival of its foreign practitioners were deeply distrusted by the Brezhnev leadership. Smirnov has been a Vice-President of the Soviet Association of Political Sciences since 1981 and a Vice-President of the International Political Science Association since 1988. AHB

SMOKTUNOVSKY, Innokenty **Mikhaylovich** (b. 1925) Stage and screen actor. Smoktunovsky achieved his reputation while working at the Leningrad Gor'ky Theatre from 1957 to 1960 for his performances as Prince Myshkin in Dostoevsky's *The Idiot*, Sergey in Arbuzov's *An Irkutsk Story* and Dzerzhinsky in Pogodin's *The Kremlin Chimes*. He turned to filmmaking in 1960 and played the leading roles in Romm's *Nine Days of One Year* (1962) and Kosintsev's *Hamlet* (1964). RT

SMYSLOV, Vasiliy Vasil'evich (b. 1921) Chess player. The most 'durable' of all top Soviet chess players, he won only one world championship (1957–58) and one national championship (in 1949), yet his top-level chess career spanned forty years – he was a semi-finalist in the 1984 to 1985 world title eliminator at the age of sixty-three. Born in Moscow, he became international grandmaster in

1950; he had lost to Botvinnik in the world title final in 1948, but beat him for the Soviet title the following year. JWR

SNECHKUS, Antanas Yuozovich (Snieckus, Antanas) (1903–1974) A Lithuanian who joined the Communists in 1920 and moved to the USSR in the following year. From 1926 he was an illegal party activist inside Lithuania, and became First Secretary of its Communist Party when Soviet rule was installed in 1940. He retained this post until his death in 1974. He survived several changes of regime and policy in the Kremlin, and his political skills are credited with blunting some of the effects of Sovietization on Lithuania, in particular the immigration of Russians. JHM

SNEZHNEVSKY, Aleksandr Vladimirovich (b. 1904) Psychiatrist. A party member since 1945, Snezhnevsky was elected to the USSR Academy of Medical Sciences in 1962. He is known for his social and ideological analysis of schizophrenia and for his role in the psychiatric treatment of anti-social behaviour, including political and religious dissent. MBA

SOBCHAK, Anatoliy Aleksandrovich (b. 1937) Sobchak is one of the members of the Congress of People's Deputies and of its inner body, the Supreme Soviet, who has become a national figure in the Soviet Union since the new parliament was established in 1989. He has proved to be a skilful and outspoken parliamentarian, an effective speaker who has not been afraid to challenge any member of the Politburo. (He clashed, in particular, with the Chairman of the Council of Ministers, Nikolay Ryzhkov, in a Supreme Soviet debate in early 1990.) Sobchak was appointed chairman of a commission established by the Congress of People's Deputies to investigate the killing of young participants in a peaceful demonstration in Tbilisi in April 1989 and he is a member of the Supreme Soviet Committee for Questions of Legislation, Legality and Law and Order.

Sobchak is an academic lawyer by profession and head of the Law Faculty of Leningrad University. A radical reformer and founding member of the Inter Regional Group of Deputies within the Soviet parliament, he left the Communist Party in July 1990. He represents a Leningrad territorial constituency in the Congress of People's Deputies and enjoys strong support in that city. This was reflected in his election to the important post of Chairman of the city soviet (or Mayor of Leningrad) in May 1990. AHB

SOBINOV, Leonid Vital'evich (1872–1934) Tenor. Sobinov was born in Yaroslavl' and died in Riga. He came from a musical family but he entered the Jurisprudence Faculty of Moscow University in 1890, where he graduated in 1894. During his time as a student, his remarkable voice attracted attention and he took lessons with Aleksandr Dodonov at the School of Drama and Music of the Moscow Philharmonic Society. After a period assisting a Moscow lawyer, in 1897 he joined the Bol'shoy Theatre, where he was to remain almost the rest of his life, though he also sang with the Imperial Mariinsky Theatre in St Petersburg. One of the great Russian tenors of his era, he also performed frequently abroad and made many recordings. He was made a People's Artist of the Republic in 1923. GS

SOBOLEV, Sergey L'vovich (b. 1908) Mathematician. After graduating from Leningrad University in 1929, Sobolev worked in the USSR Academy of Sciences at the Seismological Institute (1929–32) and the Steklov Mathematics Institute (1932–43), serving as a professor of mathematics at Moscow University (1935–57). He was elected a corresponding member of the Academy at the age of twenty-four (1933) and a full member at the age of thirty (1939), joining the party in 1940. During the war he became involved in the bomb project and worked at the Institute of Atomic Energy (1943–57). He became actively involved in the development of computers and helped still ideological criticism of cybernetics. Together with M. A. Lavrent'ev, he helped to create the science city at Novosibirsk, creating its Institute of Mathematics – which he had directed since 1957 – and serving as professor at Novosibirsk University (1960–76). MBA

SOFRONITSKY, Vladimir Vladimirovich (1901–1961) Pianist and teacher. Sofronitsky was born in St Petersburg and died in Moscow. After first studying in Warsaw, he spent the years 1914 to 1921 at the Petrograd Conservatory, where he was a pupil of Leonid Nikolaev. During the period 1921 to 1935 he gave many concerts, including ones in Warsaw and Paris. He was appointed professor at the Leningrad Conservatory (1936–42), followed by a similar appointment at Moscow (1942–61). He was made an Honoured Art Worker of the RSFSR in 1942 and was awarded a State Prize in 1943. GS

SOIFERTIS, Leonid Vladimirovich (b. 1911) Graphic artist. Soifertis was born in Il'intsy. After studying at the Khar'kov Art Institute, he rapidly made his name as an illustrator and caricaturist, working for journals such as *Smena* (Change) and *Krokodil*. His interpretations of the home front in the Second World War such as *No Time* (1941) are particularly engaging. JEB

SOKOL'NIKOV, Grigoriy Yakovlevich (1888–1939) A Jewish lawyer who became a prominent financial administrator during the early post-revolutionary years, Sokol'nikov was born in Romny, a town in the Poltava province, where his father worked as a doctor. The family moved to Moscow when he was in his early school years, and it was here that he first became acquainted with populist and Marxist literature. Sokol'nikov became a Bolshevik in 1905, played a part in the December insurrection in Moscow and thereafter became an active party propagandist, suffering arrest, imprisonment and exile. After escaping from detention he made his way to Paris, where he met Lenin and Krupskaya and completed his legal and economic education. He spent the early war years in Switzerland and then returned to Russia in 1917 in the famous 'sealed train' provided by the German government.

Sokol'nikov became a member of the Moscow party committee and of the Moscow Soviet, and took part in editing the party press. After the October Revolution he served in the Soviet delegation at the Brest-Litovsk peace negotiations and then directed the nationalization of the banks. During the Civil War he served in the military command on the eastern and later on the southern front. Afterwards he was appointed chairman of the Turkestan Commission of the Central Executive Committee, which involved him in the establishment of Soviet rule throughout Central Asia, and then (1922–26) he became Commissar of Finances, concentrating particularly

upon the introduction of balanced budgets and a stable currency. He was a candidate member of the Politburo from 1924 until 1926, but his unorthodox views (including support for the existence of several different political parties) led to a fall from grace in the late 1920s. Sokol'nikov subsequently associated himself with the majority position and in 1929 became Soviet ambassador to Britain and deputy Commissar for Foreign Affairs (until 1934). Two years later, however, he was arrested, and in 1937 he was sentenced together with Radek to ten years' imprisonment. He died in prison in obscure circumstances; Sokol'nikov was rehabilitated in 1989. SLW

SOKOLOV, Aleksandr Vsevolodovich (Sasha) (b. 1943) Sokolov was born in Ottawa, the son of a Soviet military attaché; the family returned to Moscow in 1946. He studied at the Department of Journalism of Moscow University, and published a few stories in the provincial press. He emigrated in 1975 and lived in the USA, Canada, France, and Greece. Three novels brought him a reputation as the most talented prose writer of his generation: *A School for Fools* (1975), *Between Dog and Wolf* (1980), and *Palisandriya* (1985). In 1989 Sokolov's work began to be published in the USSR, and in the autumn of that year he became the first major émigré writer to return on a permanent basis. He lives in Moscow, retaining his Canadian citizenship. GSS

SOKOLOV, Boris Matveevich (1889–1930) and **SOKOLOV, Yuriy Matveevich** (1889–1941) B. M. Sokolov, folklorist, ethnographer and Director of the Museum of the Peoples of the USSR, and Yu. M. Sokolov,

Sokolov

folklorist, member of the Ukrainian Academy of Sciences. The brothers collaborated in collecting folklore, but their books were mainly written independently. In 1936 Yu. M. Sokolov was attacked for his views on the origin of the epic *byliny*. His recantation is reflected in the orthodox Stalinist textbook *Russian Folklore* (1938, English translation 1966). FCMW

SOKOLOV, Sergey Leonidovich (b. 1911) Former Minister of Defence. Sokolov, the son of a clerk, worked as a Komsomol official before entering the Red Army in 1932. By 1941 he was a battalion tank commander and steady promotion followed during the war years until he became the commander of the armoured and mechanized forces of an army on the Karelian Front. In the period 1945 to 1965 Sokolov held a number of staff and command posts. He assumed command of the Leningrad Military District in 1965 and was named First Deputy Minister of Defence in 1967. The aged Marshal Sokolov was chosen as the successor to Marshal Ustinov as Minister of Defence when Ustinov died in December 1984. This lowered the profile of the military in the Soviet leadership since Sokolov was widely regarded as a transitional leader. Once Gorbachev assumed power Sokolov appeared as an obstacle to Gorbachev's modernization programme. He was retired in disgrace alongside Marshal Koldunov in May 1987, and replaced by the more reformist-minded Dmitriy Yazov, after an emergency Politburo meeting criticized the Ministry of Defence for failing to intercept the flight to Red Square by the West German Matthias Rust. RA

SOKOLOV, Yefrem Yevseevich (b. 1926) A Belorussian from near Mogilev, Sokolov worked as an agricultural specialist in Brest province and in the Pavlodar region of Kazakhstan before moving to full-time party jobs in 1967. He was in the Belorussian party apparatus from 1969 to 1977, First Secretary of Brest *obkom* (1977–87), and became First Secretary of the Belorussian Communist Party in 1987. In July 1990 he became a member of the Politburo of the CPSU. JHM

SOKOLOVSKY, Vasiliy Danilovich (1897–1968) Wartime commander and former Chief of the General Staff. Sokolovsky graduated from the Red Army Staff Academy in 1921. After holding high staff and command positions in the inter-war period he became Chief of Staff on the Western Front (1941–43); Commander of the Western Front (1943–44); and Chief of Staff for the First Ukrainian Front, then Deputy Commander of the First Belorussian Front. He helped to prepare and implement the L'vov, Vistula-Oder, Berlin and other wartime operations. After this distinguished war record Sokolovsky became known in the West as the Deputy Commander-in-Chief, then Commander-in-Chief, of the Soviet occupation forces, and Head of the Soviet Military Administration in Germany (1945–49). Having been in charge of the Soviet blockade of West Berlin, Sokolovsky became a Marshal of the Soviet Union. For over a decade he was Soviet First Deputy Minister of Defence (1949–60) and for a further eight years Chief of the General Staff of the Soviet Army and Navy (1952–60). Subsequently he became Inspector-General for the Ministry of Defence. Sokolovsky directed the preparation of a seminal work on

Soviet strategy, *Military Strategy*, published in 1962, which strongly influenced Soviet military thinking and the Western perception of Soviet strategy for many years. RA

SOLNTSEVA, Yul'ya Ippolitovna (b. 1901) Actress. Solntseva began her career as an actress, primarily but not exclusively in films directed by her husband Dovzhenko. She played in *Aelita* and *The Cigarette Girl from Mosselprom* (both 1924), *The Earth* (1930) and *Shchors* (1939). After Dovzhenko's death she directed a number of films based on his scripts: *A Poem of the Sea* (1958), *A Tale of Flaming Years* (1961) and *The Enchanted Desna* (1965). RT

SOLOGUB, Fedor Kuz'mich (Teternikov) (1863–1927) Poet and novelist. The only prominent Russian Symbolist to emerge from the lower classes, Sologub taught school mathematics in the provinces and then in St Petersburg until 1907, meanwhile publishing lyric poetry and eventually the famous novel *The Petty Demon* (1907, reprinted 1933, 1958); he remained in Russia after the revolution but took little part in literary life. GSS

SOLOMENTSEV, Mikhail Sergeevich (b. 1913) A powerful figure in the Soviet political leadership over many years and a conservative Communist of Russian nationality and peasant background, Solomentsev was born in what is now the Lipetsk region of the Russian republic. In the 1930s he was a collective farm worker, but he studied in his spare time and graduated from the Leningrad Polytechnical Institute in 1940.

Solomentsev worked in industry from 1940 until 1954, first as a manual worker and later as a chief engineer and factory manager, before becoming a full-time politician. He held a series of regional party secretaryships and became a full member of the Central Committee in 1961. In 1966, less than two years after Brezhnev succeeded Khrushchev, Solomentsev became a Secretary of the Central Committee, and in 1971 he was made a candidate member of the Politburo while giving up his Secretaryship in order to become Chairman of the Council of Ministers of the Russian republic.

He was not a Brezhnev client and received no further promotion during Brezhnev's general secretaryship, but his views were not greatly dissimilar from Brezhnev's and he held on to the positions he had already attained. When Andropov became General Secretary Solomentsev was moved to the chairmanship of the Committee of Party Control and in December 1983, after a long wait, he was accorded full membership of the Politburo.

A conditional ally of Gorbachev at the time of his succession to Chernenko in March 1985, Solomentsev was never an enthusiast for *perestroika* and in his capacity as Chairman of the Party Control Committee he continued to take a restrictive and unsympathetic view of those who had been expelled from the party for ideological deviations and who sought readmission. Gorbachev finally secured Solomentsev's retirement from the Politburo and active politics in September 1988. AHB

SOLOUKHIN, Vladimir Alekseevich (b. 1924) Lyric poet and prose writer. His *Byways of Vladimir* (1957) was the first work to draw public attention to the problem of the neglect of rural Russia and of the nation's cultural heritage, a theme which he developed, with special attention to churches and icons, in *Letters from the Russian Museum* (1966) and *Dark Ikons* (1969). His public espousal of belief in a 'supreme being' brought him a rebuke in *Kommunist* in 1982. GAH

SOLOV'EV, Yuriy Filippovich (b. 1925) Solov'ev was the first member of the Soviet top leadership team to have his political career ended as the result of a competitive election. A cadidate member of the Politburo from 1986 to 1989 he failed to be elected to the Congress of People's Deputies of the USSR when standing as a candidate in Leningrad which had long been his political base. He was subsequently replaced as First Secretary of the Leningrad regional committee of the party and dropped from his candidate membership of the Politburo.

Solov'ev, who was born in the Kuybyshev region of Russia, received a higher technical education and joined the Communist Party in 1955. Earlier he had fought in the Second World War (1943–44) and was demobilized after being twice wounded. In the post-war period he made his career as an engineer and manager in the construction of the Leningrad metro before becoming a deputy chairman of the executive committee of the Leningrad city soviet (1973–74) and joining the party apparatus in 1974. By 1978 he had become First Secretary of the Leningrad city party organization. He was Minister of Industrial Construction of the USSR (1984–85) and from 1985 to his forced retiral in 1989 First Secretary of the Leningrad regional party committee. AHB

SOLOV'EV-SEDOY, Vasiliy Pavlovich (1907–1979) Composer. Solov'-ev-Sedoy (real name Solov'ev) was born in St Petersburg and died in Leningrad. A student of the Leningrad

Conservatory, where he was a pupil of Petr Ryazanov, he graduated in 1936. From 1925 he was a pianist with the Leningrad Radio, while during the Second World War he was organizer and musical director of a variety show 'Yastrebok' (The Fighter). He held various posts with different branches of the Union of Soviet Composers (1948–74). Made a People's Artist of the USSR in 1967 and a Hero of Socialist Labour in 1975, he was a deputy to the Third, Fourth and Fifth Congresses of the Supreme Soviet of the USSR. Though composing in contrasting genres, he is remembered primarily for his songs, which in their mixture of patriotism, nostalgia and Russian colouring had great popular appeal. His song 'Podmoskovnye vechera' (Evenings in the Moscow Woodlands) achieved international renown. GS

SOLZHENITSYN, Aleksandr Isaevich (b. 1918) One of the great names in Russian literature of the late twentieth century, he was born in Kislovodsk to a tsarist artillery officer who was accidentally killed before his son's birth, leaving Solzhenitsyn's mother to support them both after the Revolution by menial secretarial work. In adolescence Solzhenitsyn came increasingly under the influence of Marxist-Leninist orthodoxy. He was academically gifted, studying mathematics and physics at Rostov University, where he graduated with distinction in 1941, but also pursuing his love of literature by completing an external course at the Moscow Institute of Philosophy, Literature and History. One notable project of the late 1930s was his long essay on the defeat of Samsonov's Russian army at Tannenberg, the germ of his later *August 1914*.

A year before graduation he had married a fellow-student, Natalya Reshetovskaya, but they were parted by the outbreak of war in 1941. Solzhenitsyn was transferred from the ranks to a training school for artillery officers. By 1945, when he was arrested at the front for political indiscretions in his private correspondence, he was a captain, twice decorated for bravery, and exemplary commander of an acoustic range-finding battery. He began his eight-year sentence in camps in and around Moscow. In 1947, morally and ideologically disorientated as well as physically exhausted, he was fortunate to be transferred to the relatively benign regime of Marfino special scientific prison, the setting for his best-known novel, *The First Circle*. His encounters and experiences in captivity were beginning to erode his Marxist-Leninist beliefs and move him closer to the Christianity of his childhood. It was at Marfino too that he composed and committed to memory some of the first of 12,000 lines of labour camp verses.

In 1950, after antagonizing the prison authorities, Solzhenitsyn was transferred to a far harsher special camp for political prisoners at Ekibastuz in Kazakhstan, and three years later he began his exile 'in perpetuity' in a remote village in southern Kazakhstan. It was here, while working as a schoolteacher, and, secretly, as a writer, that he fell gravely ill with cancer. His successful treatment in a Tashkent clinic in 1954–55 forms the background for the novel *Cancer Ward*.

By the time he was released from exile during the Khrushchev liberalization of 1956, he had begun the first version of *The First Circle* as well

as various dramatic works. Now he moved to Miltsevo in central Russia, the setting for one of his most successful short stories, 'Matrena's Home'. By 1957 he was living in Ryazan' near Moscow, reunited with Reshetovskaya, who had divorced him during his captivity, and devoting every free minute to clandestine writing in a wide range of genres.

Among the works of the late 1950s is his masterful, understated re-creation of labour camp life, *One Day in the Life of Ivan Denisovich*, which, emboldened by the anti-Stalinist tone of the Twenty-Second Party Congress in 1961, Solzhenitsyn submitted to the most liberal literary journal of the day, *Novyy mir*. The editor, Aleksandr Tvardovsky, was so affected by it that he contrived, against all the odds, to publish it in 1962 with the blessing of Khrushchev himself.

This event brought Solzhenitsyn overnight fame, a huge influx of letters from ex-prisoners and the suppressed hostility of crypto-Stalinists. In 1963 three more stories appeared, including 'Matrena's Home', but official criticism was mounting, and in 1964 Solzhenitsyn's candidacy for a Lenin Prize was sabotaged by hostile literary functionaries. The overthow of Khrushchev left him further exposed and when, in the following year, the KGB confiscated *The First Circle* and part of his literary archive, his very liberty seemed threatened. After 1966 his literary works ceased to be published in the Soviet Union for more than twenty years.

In 1967, with no hope of publishing even the toned-down version of *The First Circle* or his new novel, *Cancer Ward*, Solzhenitsyn further antagonized literary officialdom by addressing a lengthy and accusatory open letter to the Fourth Congress of the Union of Writers. Meanwhile, his novels circulated widely in *samizdat*, and their eventual triumphant reception in the West earned him a vituperative denunciation from *Literaturnaya gazeta*. Beleaguered, yet protected by his world-wide fame and the very audacity of his tactics, Solzhenitsyn secretly completed *The Gulag Archipelago* in 1968, his vast survey of the labour camp system, based on collective testimony. After smuggling it abroad, he turned his full attention to his epic historical cycle, *The Red Wheel*.

Solzhenitsyn's expulsion from the Writers' Union in 1969, far from consigning him to oblivion, was followed by his award of the 1970 Nobel Prize for Literature. At the same time, his first marriage was ending in acrimony and litigation. (Not until 1973 could he formalize his marriage to Natalya Svetlova, by whom he has had three sons.)

A full-scale press campaign against Solzhenitsyn in the wake of the 1971 Western publication of *August 1914* stopped short of arrest, but the immeasurably more vitriolic official response to the appearance abroad of *The Gulag Archipelago* in 1973 culminated in a charge of treason, deprivation of citizenship, and forcible expulsion from the Soviet Union. His description of these events forms the climax of the autobiographical *The Oak and the Calf* (published 1975).

After first living in Zurich, Solzhenitsyn moved with his family to Cavendish, Vermont in 1976. In a number of public pronouncements in Europe and America during the seventies and early eighties, he continued to warn of the ineffectuality of the West's resistance to communism. His remarks rarely failed to antagonize a substantial portion of his audience, and some held that the writer had declined into didacticism and mystical Russian nationalism. Meanwhile, he devoted his energies to publishing a new authorized collected works, founding a repository for eye-witness accounts of the Revolution, and, above all, continuing work on *The Red Wheel*: an expanded version of *August 1914* appeared in Russian in 1983; *October 1916* followed in 1984 and *March 1917* in 1986–88.

Even as Western interest in Solzhenitsyn was declining, increasing publicity was given in the Soviet Union to the possibility of his political rehabilitation and republication there. In late 1988 gatherings took place to celebrate his seventieth birthday and his essay 'Live Not by Lies' was published. By summer 1989 his expulsion from the Writers' Union had been annulled, 'Matrena's Home' had been republished after twenty-six years, and *Novyy mir* had begun, despite repeated objections and interventions, to serialize *The Gulag Archipelago*, fuelling speculation that Solzhenitsyn would soon return to his homeland in person. MAN

SOROKIN, Mikhail Ivanovich (b. 1922) A career officer who entered the Soviet Army in 1941 and later graduated from the Frunze and the General Staff Military Academies. He was First Deputy Commander, Far Eastern Military District (1974–76), and Commander, Leningrad Military District (1976–81). Promoted to General of the Army in late 1981, his next position is obscure; a command in Afghanistan has been suggested. He became Inspector General and

Deputy Minister of Defence in 1987. JHM

SPASSKY, Boris Vasil'evich (b. 1937) Chess player. His chess exploits are best remembered for his matches with the American Bobby Fischer to whom he lost 12.5 – 8.5 in Reykjavik in 1972. He had taken the world title from Petrosyan three years before, having lost to him in the 1966 final. Born in Leningrad, he became an international grandmaster at the age of nineteen, graduated three years later from Leningrad University and won the Soviet title in 1962 and 1973. But he virtually retired from world chess in 1974, residing abroad with his Icelandic wife. JWR

SPENDYAROV (Spendyaryan), Aleksandr Afanas'evich (1871–1928) Composer, conductor and teacher. Spendyarov was born in Kakhovka in the Crimea and died in Yerevan. Trained initially in the Jurisprudence Faculty of Moscow University, from which he graduated in 1895, he later studied composition under Nikolay Klenovsky in Moscow (1892–94) and with Rimsky-Korsakov in St Petersburg (1896–1900). For a number of years he lived in the Crimea, where he did much to popularize Russian music, in 1924 moving to Yerevan. He was made a People's Artist of the Armenian SSR in 1926. He is remembered for his opera *Almast* (composed 1916–28) and for several picturesque orchestral works such as the *Crimean Sketches* (1907) and *Yerevan Studies* (1925). GS

SPIRIDONOV, Ivan Vasil'evich (b. 1905) Russian politician. A Leningrad politician who became a casualty in Khrushchev's struggle with Frol Kozlov, I. V. Spiridonov did not enter full-time party work until 1950. By 1957, however, he had risen through the Leningrad organization and was First Secretary of both the provincial and urban party committees. At the Twenty-First and Twenty-Second Congresses, Spiridonov was outspoken in his attacks on both Stalin and the 'anti-party group', and was rewarded with election to the Secretariat at the latter Congress in 1961. Barely six months later he lost his positions in both the Secretariat and the Leningrad party organization at Khrushchev's hands. He was transferred to the ceremonial position of Chairman of the USSR Soviet of the Union. WJT

SPIRIN, Aleksandr Sergeevich (b. 1931) Molecular biologist. After graduating from Moscow University in 1954, Spirin worked with his mentor A. N. Belozersky at the Biochemical Institute of the USSR Academy of Sciences where they did internationally significant research comparing base ratios in DNA and RNA that provided the first evidence of the existence of transfer RNA (tRNA). This was the first of a series of path-breaking studies by Spirin on the structure and function of informational RNA, ribosomes, 'informosomes', and protein synthesis that led to his meteoric advancement in Soviet science and his appointment as director of the nucleic acids laboratory of the Academy's Biochemistry Institute (1962–73), professor in Moscow University's department of plant biochemistry (from 1964) and its chairman (from 1973), and organizer and director of the Academy's Protein Institute at Pushchino (from 1967). One of the youngest scientists elected to the USSR Academy of Sciences in recent years, he became a corresponding member at the age of thirty-four (1966) and a full member at thirty-nine (1970). MBA

STALIN, Iosif Vissarionovich (1879–
1953) Stalin arguably was the most
influential person in the history of the
Soviet Union. The impact of Lenin
was vital but comparatively brief,
while Stalin's was protracted and profound. He was already becoming a
major figure in the Soviet system
during Lenin's five years in command
(1918–22), became General Secretary
of the party in 1927 and for about a
generation, 1930 to 1953, was clearly
the dominant figure in the Soviet
Union. This is not to assert that Stalin
was solely responsible for all that happened in the Soviet Union since
Lenin's passing. Stalin faced some
open or covert opposition during
much of his career, delegated substantial authority and was unable
simply to impose his will on large historic trends. Nevertheless, his personal
style left an indelible mark on the
Soviet system and his personal interventions at key junctures in Soviet
history determined, for good or ill, the
direction that the country was to take.
The struggle that his successors have
had with his image and legacy testifies
to his historical importance. Khrushchev in 1956 began a campaign to
denigrate Stalin, blaming him for
many odious features of the Soviet
history and the inadequacies of the
system that he bequeathed. But the attack on 'the cult of personality' threatened to undermine the legitimacy of
the entire system and encouraged dis-
senting criticism to such an extent that
Khrushchev's successors until the Gorbachev era preferred imposed amnesia
to a continuation of the recon-
sideration of Stalin's place in Soviet
history. While Stalin's existence was
admitted, along with the observation
that he was a good Bolshevik and
patriot in some ways, little was said or

written about him in official Soviet
media, and the problem of coming to
terms with his impact on Soviet history
and the Soviet Union today was
strictly suppressed.

Born in the Georgian town of Gori,
the son of an alcoholic cobbler and a
pious peasant woman, Iosif Vissarionovich Dzhugashvili seemed an
unlikely candidate for historic fame or
infamy. His first step out of his
impoverished and culturally peri-
pheral position in life came through
the Orthodox Church. Thanks to the
hard work of his mother, his father
having died when he was about ten,
Iosif attended an Orthodox elementary school in Gori and then a seminary in Tbilisi. In these institutions
he was obliged to learn the Russian
language, which facilitated his
acquaintance with western literature
and social ideas. For a time he was
drawn to the Georgian nationalist
movement but soon embraced
Marxism, which in the late 1890s was
just beginning to be a force in Georgia.
In 1899 he was expelled from the seminary and began his life-long career in
politics.

'Koba', as he was known in the
Social Democratic movement, worked
in the underground political movement in Transcaucasia as an organizer
and agitator until 1911, taking only
brief voluntary trips out of this region
to attend the Tammerfors Conference
of the party in 1905, and the Stockholm and London conferences of 1906
and 1907 respectively. He sided with
the Bolshevik faction soon after it
emerged in 1903 and usually was at
odds with the majority of the Georgian
Social Democrats, who were Mensheviks. In 1912 he moved his activities to St Petersburg and the next year
Lenin, who had previously had but

little contact with Koba, arranged his cooptation to the Bolshevik Central Committee. In this capacity, and as an editor of *Pravda*, Stalin twice visited Lenin in his residence in Austrian Poland. Lenin commissioned him to write a lengthy essay on the nationality question, which was published in 1913 over the pseudonym 'Stalin'. Life in the underground was difficult, involving six arrests and protracted periods in jail or exile in remote parts of the Empire. Although he escaped four times, the February Revolution of 1917 found Stalin deep in Siberia completing a sentence of exile.

Returning on 12/25 March 1917 to the Petrograd of the Dual Power, Stalin with some difficulty asserted his seniority over the local Bolsheviks and once again became an editor of the party organ. His political line at this time was conciliatory toward the majority of Mensheviks and Socialist Revolutionaries in the Soviet, accepting the Provisional Government and a defensive war. When Lenin proposed his April Theses, taking a radical anti-government and anti-war stance, Stalin was slow to concur. But by June he had come around to Lenin's position. When Lenin fled to Finland in the summer of 1917, Stalin emerged as the principal spokesman for the Central Committee at the Sixth Party Congress. In October he was reserved in his support for Lenin's insistence on armed insurrection and did not play a major role in the actual seizure of Petrograd.

In the new Soviet government Stalin's first office, which he retained until 1922, was People's Commissar of Nationality Affairs. This was a major responsibility, owing to the centripetal tendencies of the ethnic minorities of the former Russian Empire and the strategic importance to the Soviet state of retaining these areas. Stalin supported a federative approach to the reintegration of Russia and the borderlands, and he played a major role in drafting the RSFSR constitution of 1918 and the USSR constitution of 1924. But his interpretation of federalism was highly centralist and Russian nationalist, so much so that in his last months of activity in 1922 and early 1923 Lenin sharply disagreed with Stalin's 'Great Russian chauvinism'. He also held the post of People's Commissar of State Control/Workers'-Peasants' Inspectorate (1919–22). When the Politburo and Orgburo were established in 1919, Stalin joined these vital party bodies. From 1918 to 1920 the Civil War obliged Stalin to devote more of his acitivities to military affairs than to either of his people's commissariats. He served as a political supervisor of Red forces fighting the Whites and Poles, and also took an active role in various commissions dealing with the war, including the Revolutionary Military Soviet and the Soviet of Workers' and Peasants' Defence. In his wartime activities he clashed with Trotsky, the People's Commissar of War.

By the time Lenin was incapacitated in late 1922, Stalin had established himself as the most broadly experienced member of the Soviet hierarchy, albeit much less visible than Trotsky. His capacity for effective administration was recognized by his election as General Secretary of the party on 3 April 1922, a position that he made into the main centre of authority in the entire political system. Possession of this position obviated the necessity of having to compete with other leading Bolsheviks to be Lenin's successor. Stalin already had the key office and could use it to organize support within the secretarial apparatus of the party and to identify his leadership with 'the party'. This placed Trotsky, Zinov'ev, Kamenev and their supporters in the position of appearing to undermine party unity when they sought to attack Stalin. And when they tried to attack his assertion that it was possible to build socialism in the USSR alone, they appeared to sow defeatism. Armed with these advantages, Stalin was never seriously endangered by his rivals, and by the end of 1927 had removed Zinov'ev and Kamenev from the Politburo.

Up to this point in his career Stalin had seemed a successful administrator rather than a backer of risky, innovative policies. But from 1928 to 1930 he staked his career on hazardous campaigns to transform agriculture and industry. In December 1929 he proposed the 'liquidation of the *kulaks* [more prosperous peasants] as a class' and the next month approved a party decree that ordered the rapid collectivization of agriculture. The party Secretariat also undertook to raise dramatically the targets for the development of heavy industry that the First Five-Year Plan had set. The institutional and cultural format of the Soviet economy as it has existed for over half a century was shaped by Stalin's policies in the early 1930s, and in the 1980s his heirs were struggling to deal with serious economic shortcomings involved in this system without dismantling the entire structure.

The anti-*kulak* campaign resulted in immense loss of life and the rise of the *Gulag*, the system of labour camps. But in the early 1930s Stalin was not perceived in the party as a killer of comrades or as the object of remarkable adulation. The adulation, as an inescapable feature of Soviet culture, began in mid-1933, and continued for the rest of Stalin's life, embracing all the arts, education, the daily press and toponymy. The killing of comrades may have started as early as the assassination of Kirov in December 1934, though in Stalin's time this was regarded as the work of class-enemies. It definitely started when Zinov'ev and Kamenev were sentenced to death in a show trial in August 1936, and it expanded vastly in 1937 to 1938 when most of the Central Committee and a large part of the entire Soviet elite was destroyed by imprisonment or execution. Not only former opponents of Stalin, including Bukharin, fell victim, but also many of Stalin's clients, including six members of the Politburo. Although the depredations among Communists subsided by 1939, Stalin's arbitrary and massive terror endowed the Soviet state and its police with an intimidating image.

By 1939 Stalin diminished the slaughter within his elite, possibly because of the increasing danger of war with Germany. This apprehension evidently persuaded him to assume the chairmanship of the Council of People's Commissars in May 1941. Having seen the policy of alliance with France fail at the Munich Conference of 1938, Stalin determined to strike a bargain with Hitler. This he achieved in the treaty signed in his presence on 23 August 1939, following hasty negotiations in Moscow. It divided eastern Europe into German and Soviet spheres, thus enabling the USSR to annexe eastern Poland, Estonia, Latvia, Lithuania and parts of Romania and Finland in

1939 to 1940. Only Finland resisted, and the difficulty that the Red Army encountered in subduing this small state might have warned Stalin that his forces were not ready for war with Germany. He appears to have reasoned that in any case Hitler would not risk the splendid situation that he enjoyed in 1941 by attacking the USSR. Thus Stalin at first responded to the invasion of 22 June with stunned disbelief. Soon he regained his poise and assumed the chairmanship of the newly-created State Committee of Defence, the office of People's Commissar of Defence and the new title of Supreme Commander of the Armed Forces. In the first year of the war his leadership was costly, owing to his aversion to strategic retreat and his penchant for ill-prepared offensives. But by the autumn of 1942, when the Battle of Stalingrad was joined, he had formed a cadre of generals in whom he placed confidence, and thenceforth was on balance a highly effective warlord. His ability to comprehend complex military, economic and political variables contributed much to the eventual Soviet victory of 1945, which brought him the honorific title of 'Generalissimus'. This was a promotion from the rank of 'Marshal of the Soviet Union', which he had assumed in 1943.

During the war Stalin negotiated directly with British and American leaders, meeting Churchill and Roosevelt at Tehran (1943) and Yalta (1945) and Truman, Churchill and Attlee at Potsdam (1945). Stalin proved a tenacious and effective advocate of Soviet interests as he perceived them, playing on the theme that his country was doing most of the fighting and needed more assistance and that Soviet postwar security required recognition of her interest in Germany and eastern Europe, especially Poland. After the war he presided over the establishment of the zone of Soviet client-states that remained until 1989 a monument to his policy. The independent status of Yugoslavia within this zone was, however, a reminder of a failure that was uncharacteristic of Stalin: antagonizing a weaker adversary without crushing it. In maintaining Soviet power to the line of the 'iron curtain' Stalin showed a steady determination not to be impressed by American displeasure or atomic weapons. He alone did not invent the Cold War, but he did establish the premise that adversarial relations with the United States were a price worth paying for Soviet status as a superpower, a principle that his successors long respected. In Asia Stalin's postwar foreign policy seemed much less certain of its objectives. At first he seemed more interested in Soviet bases than a Communist victory in China, but from December 1949–February 1950 he received Mao Zedong and grudgingly agreed to a somewhat noncommittal treaty of friendship.

In his last years Stalin seemed to be searching for a dramatic solution to the critical problems of Soviet agriculture. In 1948 he supported a huge scheme of shelterbelts and dams, which, along with Lysenko's biological theories, were supposed to 'transform nature'. He also imposed an extreme degree of cultural isolation on the USSR, a legacy that his successors mitigated only partially. He turned with murderous vehemence against Soviet Jews at this time, but this was only one dimension of an apparent degeneration of his personality. Longtime personal aides and such important Politburo colleagues as Molotov,

Voroshilov and Beria were threatened in the early 1950s. By March 1953 Stalin had given sufficient indications that he was about to embark on another bout of slaughter within his own elite that his lieutenants had ample reason to wish him dead. His demise on 5 March 1953 may have been the result of a cerebral haemorrhage, as the medical bulletins stated, but suspicions remain that it may not have been an entirely natural death. Stalin's body was embalmed and placed beside Lenin's, but in 1961 the party decreed that his misdeeds required that it be removed. It was interred in the row of graves of honoured leaders, adjacent to the Lenin Mausoleum. RHMCN

STANISLAVSKY (né Alekseev), Konstantin Sergeevich (1863–1938) A stage director, actor and teacher and one of the most important theorists of twentieth-century theatre. Stanislavsky co-founded the Society of Literature and Art in 1888 with his former teacher Komissarzhevsky and his first production, of Tolstoy's *The Fruits of Enlightenment* was in 1891, Stanislavsky rejected the style of histrionic acting and declamatory speech then prevalent in the Russian theatre and strove for a more realistic style of acting and more naturalistic sets and costumes. In this he was strongly influenced by the German Meiningen Players whom he saw on their second visit to Moscow in 1890. The actors in Stanislavsky's Society formed the nucleus, together with Nemirovich-Danchenko's students in the Music Drama School of the Moscow Philharmonic Society, of the ensemble of the Moscow Art Theatre when the two men founded it in 1898. On the opening night Stanislavsky set out the aims of the new theatre: 'We are striving to create the first rational, moral and generally accessible theatre and we are dedicating our lives to this aim'.

The first production was of Aleksey Tolstoy's *Tsar Fedor Ioannovich* but Stanislavsky's greatest triumphs were his productions of the plays of Chekhov: *The Seagull* (1898), *Uncle Vanya* (1899), *Three Sisters* (1901), and *The Cherry Orchard* (1904), also playing Astrov, Vershinin and Gayev in the last three. The actors were trained in a new way of acting that brought out the inner psychological state of the character and was, by contemporary standards, very restrained and understated. Stanislavsky aimed to expunge any element of falsehood and to create a unity between acting and staging and a complete illusion of reality in the theatre. He also produced Gor'ky's *Smug Citizens* and *The Lower Depths* in 1902. With Nemirovich-Danchenko he produced innovative versions of the Russian classics, including Griboedov's *Woe from Wit* (1906), Gogol''s *The Government Inspector* (1908), Turgenev's *A Month in the Country* (1911) and Dostoevsky's *Selo Stepanchikov* (1917). He flirted briefly with Symbolism, producing the works of Maeterlinck and Andreev in the years between 1905 and 1917.

From 1912 Stanislavsky headed the Moscow Art Theatre's First Studio which aimed to train the younger generation of actors in the Stanislavsky 'method'. One of the studio's greatest successes was a production of *Twelfth Night* (1917). While Stanislavsky toured with the company in Western Europe and the USA from 1922 to 1924, Nemirovich-Danchenko effected a reorganization that merged the Studio with the general company of veteran actors. Stanislavsky also became involved in opera productions for the Bol'shoy Theatre's Opera Studio, which was later to bear his name. His productions there included Tchaikovsky's *Eugene Onegin* (1922), Rimsky-Korsakov's *The Tsar's Bride* (1926), Puccini's *La Bohème* (1927), Rimsky-Korsakov's *The Golden Cockerel* (1932), Rossini's *The Barber of Seville* (1933) and Bizet's *Carmen* (1935). After suffering a heart attack on stage in October 1928 while playing Vershinin in Chekhov's *Three Sisters*, Stanislavsky was forced to abandon acting and concentrate both on his productions and on his pedagogical work. When Meyerkhol'd's theatre was closed in 1938, Stanislavsky put aside their long-standing rivalry and made him his deputy. His published work in English includes: *An Actor Prepares* (1936), *Stanislavsky Rehearses 'Othello'* (1948) and *Building a Character* (1950).

Almost everyone active in Russian and Soviet theatre this century had at some time some contact with Stanislavsky and was influenced by him or reacted against him or his Moscow Art Theatre. He was the central theatrical figure and his influence has been felt world-wide, but especially in the United States through the 'method' school of acting which is, at least in part, based on a misunderstanding of Stanislavsky's own positions. R T

STANKEVICH, Sergey Borisovich (b. 1954) Stankevich is a Soviet politician of a new type who, although a Communist Party member, owes his growing prominence to electoral success and independent judgement. A Ukrainian by ethnic origin but a Moscow-based scholar (a senior research fellow at the Institute of General History of the Academy of Sciences of the USSR), Stankevich was elected to the Congress of People's Deputies from the Cheremushsky district of Moscow in 1989. He quickly made his mark as a skilled parliamentarian and became an active member of the Inter-Regional Group of Deputies of radically reformist dispostion. Although not a member of the Supreme Soviet of the USSR in its first year of existence as a full-time parliament, Stankevich became a member of its Committee for Questions of Legislation, Legality and Law and Order. In 1990 he was elected to the Moscow city soviet and chosen to be its deputy chairman. A fluent English speaker, Stankevich has been a frequent commentator on Soviet developments since the creation of the Congress of People's Deputies for the Western mass media. He has also been a strong advocate of better support services for Soviet parliamentarians and made a first-hand study of the facilities available at the American Congress. A H B

STARAVOYTOVA, Galina Vasil'-evna (b. 1946) Academic and politician. Galina Staravoytova has rapidly gained political popularity and become one of the most prominent, capable and hard-working women in Soviet public life. A Russian by nationality, Staravoytova was invited to stand for the Congress of People's Deputies of the USSR in 1989 by a Yerevan constituency and was supported by the overwhelmingly Armenian electorate in a competitive election. She joined the Inter-Regional Group of Deputies who favour faster and more radical reform. In 1990 she added a deputyship of the Congress of People's Deputies of the RSFSR to her membership of the all-union parliament, being elected from her native city of Leningrad. An ethnographer by profession, with a higher degree in psychology, Staravoytova has taken a specialist interest in the nationalities question in the Soviet Union. AHB

STAROSTYN, Andrey Petrovich (b. 1906) Soccer player. He was one of four famous footballing brothers who helped to found the Spartak Sports Society and develop Soviet soccer during the 1930s. Nikolay Starostyn was born in 1902 in Moscow, played for Moscow Spartak and the Soviet national team (against foreign workers' teams) in the late 1920s and 1930s, and headed the Moscow Spartak Sports Society between 1955 and 1975. Aleksandr Starostyn (1903–1975) was born in the village of Pogost in what is now the Yaroslavl' Region. He too played soccer for Moscow Spartak and was Soviet team captain during the 1930s; he eventually became Chairman of the Russian Soccer Federation. Andrey Starostyn was born in Moscow; he played for the Moscow Spartak team that won the Soviet league title four times, and the Soviet national team during the 1930s. After the war, in 1959, he became Chairman of the Soviet Soccer Federation and head of team sports on the Spartak Central Council, then Chairman of the USSR Soccer Coaches Council. Petr Starostyn (1909–1982) was born in Pogost, played for Moscow Spartak in the 1930s and worked as an engineer on retirement from soccer.

All four brothers were arrested immediately after the war and sent to labour camps for between eight and ten years because, it was alleged, 'they had all been abroad and told friends about life abroad'. The time abroad had, in fact, been with Soviet soccer teams, playing against foreign workers' and communist opposition. Andrey Starostyn claims that they were persecuted because Beria, who had played for a Georgian Dinamo soccer team in his youth, disliked the idea of Spartak taking over from Dinamo as the number one Soviet team (Spartak had, in fact won the League and Cup in 1939 and 1940). JWR

STASOVA, Yelena (1873–1966) A Soviet political figure and secretary of the Bolshevik party, Stasova was one of Lenin's earliest supporters and one of the oldest surviving old Bolsheviks at the time of her death. Stasova was born into a prominent family. Her father was an attorney, her aunt Nadezhda Stasova an early feminist and founder of the Sunday schools where both Krupskaya and Yelena Stasova worked in the 1890s. A member of the RSDLP since 1898, Stasova worked for the revolutionary cause in Petrograd and abroad. As secretary of the Petrograd party, she was involved in organizational and conspiratorial work for the underground party for several years before being arrested in 1904. Because of her total devotion to the cause, she was given the nickname, 'The Absolute'. Over the next few years she lived both abroad and in Russia.

In 1912 she became a candidate member of the Central Committee shortly before her exile in Siberia. After the March Revolution she was a secretary to the Central Committee, then was pushed aside as Yacov Sverdlov gained more authority. For a time after the Bolshevik Revolution, Stasova withdrew from politics and then returned to work as a secretary to the Central Committee at the time of the Eighth Party Congress when Sverdlov was ill. When the Secretariat was organized in 1919, Stasova continued administrative work there for about a year before resigning in protest over leadership manoeuvres. She was one of very few women on the Central Committee of the Communist Party after the revolution.

Although near the centre of power in the early days of the Bolshevik Revolution, Stasova was principally a staff person rather than a power broker in the Secretariat. She viewed herself as an organizer rather than a theoretician in a revolutionary movement which valued theoreticians over administrators. Some sources claim she was an excellent organizer; others argue that her work was inferior to that of Sverdlov, a human computer whose illness and subsequent death created a vacuum that led to the formal establishment of a Secretariat. Stasova was never seriously considered for a leadership position, and she refused lower staff positions in the 1920s. After 1920 she worked for the Comintern in several different capacities. She was an organizer of the First Congress of the Peoples of the East in Baku (1920). One of the few prominent women who, by her own choice, did not play an active role in Zhenotdel after the Revolution, Stasova remained active in a variety of assignments over the next two decades. In 1938, she moved from political to literary work as editor of *International Literature*, until her retirement after the Second World War.

Stasova received many honours including four Orders of Lenin. She is buried in the Kremlin Wall in recognition of her long service to the party. NN

STEN, Anna (née Stenskaya-Sudakevich, Anna) (b. 1908) Sten was a leading popular actress in silent films. She appeared in: *The Girl with the Hat Box* (1927), *Earth in Captivity*, *The House on Trubnaya* and *Storm Over Asia* (all 1928) before emigrating first to Germany and then to America. She was married briefly to Otsep. RT

STENBERG, Georgiy Avgustovich (1900–1933) and **STENBERG, Vladimir Avgustovich** (1899–1982) Designers. Born in Moscow, the Stenberg brothers are now remembered for their movie posters of the 1920s in which they used daring formal juxtapositions and montage. Students at the Stroganov Institute, Moscow and then Svomas (1912–20), they were influenced particularly by Malevich and Rodchenko and were enthusiastic supporters of Constructivist design. JEB

STEPAKOV, Vladimir Il'ich (1912–1987) Born in Kaluga, Stepakov worked his way up through the Moscow party apparatus, of which he was second secretary at the beginning of 1961. For most of the next ten years he was head of the Central Committee Department of Propaganda or its equivalent. This was interrupted for a short period from 1964 to 1965 when he assumed the chief editorship of *Izvestiya* from the disgraced A. I. Adzhubei. It is not known why he left the Department of Propaganda in 1970; no successor was named for seven years. He was ambassador to Yugoslavia from 1971 to 1978. JHM

STEPANOVA, Varvar Fedorovna (1894–1958) Painter and designer. Stepanova was born in Kovno. After marrying Rodchenko in 1913, she attended the Stroganov Art Institute in Moscow and, after 1917, became a leading member of the avant-garde. Contributing to the '5 × 5 = 25' exhibition in 1921, Stepanova asserted that the functional nature of Constructivist design should replace the aesthetics of studio painting. In this way, she made a valuable contribution to the development of textile, stage and book design, especially in the 1920s. JEB

STEPONAVIČIUS, Archbishop Julijonas (b. 1911) Roman Catholic Archbishop of Vilnius since 1958. In 1961, during Khrushchev's anti-religious campaign, he was exiled from his diocese to a small village, largely because of his refusal to ban catechism classes for children. Petitions to the state authorities from Lithuanian Catholics for his return were for long unsuccessful, but eventually in the new political climate, he was able to take over his diocese in early 1989. MR

STOZHAROV, Vladimir Fedorovich (1926–1973) Painter. Stozharov was born in Moscow. Graduating from the Surikov Institute in 1951, he concentrated on still-lives and landscapes, especially scenes of Old Moscow and local Russian villages, such as *Mount Shotov* (1964). With their heavy impasto, his paintings often bring to mind the style of Konchalovsky, Mashkov, and Lentulov. JEB

STROEV, Yegor Semenovich (b. 1937) A Secretary of the Central Committee of the CPSU since September 1989 and a Politburo member from July 1990, Stroev was born into a Russian peasant family and began his own career as an agricultural worker. From 1973 to 1984 he was Second Secretary and from 1985 to 1989 First Secretary of the Orlovsk *obkom*. Between 1984 and 1985 Stroev worked in the Central Committee apparatus in Moscow with the rank of inspector. AHB

STROGOVICH, Mikhail Solomonovich (1894–1984) One of the leading Soviet specialists on criminal procedure and a staunch proponent of the 'presumption of innocence', Strogovich combined teaching with practical work in justice agencies. A party member from 1943, he taught criminal procedure in several Moscow law faculties and was elected a corresponding member of the USSR Academy of Sciences (1939) and Academician of the Polish Academy of Sciences (1959). His textbooks on criminal procedure nurtured three generations of Soviet lawyers. The 1968 edition was recalled after printing because it advocated introducing the concept of presumption of innocence. WEB

STRUGATSKY, Arkadiy Natanovich (b. 1925) and **STRUGATSKY, Boris Natanovich** (b. 1933) The Strugatsky brothers, writers of science fiction, were born in Batumi. Arkadiy was trained as a specialist in Japanese studies and lives in Moscow; Boris is an astronomer who has worked at the Pulkovo observatory, and lives in Leningrad. The brothers began publishing in 1956; their earliest stories were relatively conventional tales of space adventure that were popular with young people. Gradually, their work became structurally more complex and the themes more pointedly political. In the sixties the Strugatsky brothers began publishing a string of futuristic parables written in the tradition of the eighteenth-century *conte philosophique*, that raised serious questions about fundamental aspects of contemporary Soviet life. *It's Difficult To Be a God* (1964) describes life in a totalitarian society and, although containing a distinctive element of humour, indicates a certain influence from Zamyatin. *Predatory Things of the Age* (1965), examines the problem of goal-lessness in a completely materialist society. *The Second Coming of the Martians* (1967), possibly the Strugatskys' funniest book to date, is a Gogolian satire on mindless officials.

Snail on a Slope (1966–68), which shows the influence of the Polish fantasist Stanislaw Lem, has as its central metaphor a giant forest that is being studied by a group of investigators with patent similarities to the secret police. *The Fairytale of a Troika* (1968) describes a universe in the form of a skyscraper ruled by revolutionary sewer cleaners. *The Inhabited Island* (1969) deals with thought control exercised through a series of government transmitters.

The Strugatskys have been attacked for their stories, and increasingly found it necessary to publish in provincial journals. There was a long hiatus beginning in the seventies when they did not publish at all. They nevertheless have become popular not only in Eastern Europe, but throughout the world, members of a select company of metaphysical explorers of the fantastic that includes Lem and Borges. KC

STRUMILIN, Stanislav Gustavovich (1877–1974) Economist. A pioneer in labour economics and in techniques of central planning, his Menshevik adherence (he joined the Bolsheviks only in 1923) brought marginalization, but never worse, at the peak of Stalin's purges. Born in Dashkovtsy, he studied at the St Petersburg Polytechnical Institute in Russia's first economics faculty under the eminent P. B. Struve and M. I. Tugan-Baranovsky. Adopting their (qualified) Marxism, his political activity earned him two periods of internal exile before the 1917 revolutions – he was a Menshevik delegate to the Party Congresses abroad of 1906 and 1907. Lenin appointed him to the staff of the new State Planning Committee in 1921, in recognition of his early work (1913) on how plan consistency could be achieved by detailed, physical projections of requirements and availabilities, a 'balance method' used not only then in GOELRO but as the fundament of Stalin's Five-Year Plans. Among many studies in the economics of labour was a path-breaking assessment of the value of education and training, measured by wage differentials (1924). His studies of regional development in the Urals, the region to which the ex-Menshevik was banished in 1937, earned him a Stalin Prize in 1942. Reintegrated into the Planning Committee in 1943, he produced another notable study in 1946, a concept of the rate of interest acceptable to Stalin's naive interpretation of the law of value under socialism. MCK

STUCHKA, Petr Ivanovich (1865–1932) Early Bolshevik who twice served (1917–18) as People's Commissar of Justice. Stuchka played a key role in abolishing the Imperial Russian legal system and creating the succeeding Soviet organs. After serving briefly in Soviet Latvia, he returned to the RSFSR as Deputy People's Commissar of Justice and as Chairman of the RSFSR Supreme Court (1923–32). He played a major role in drafting Soviet legislation on the procuracy and courts, the criminal codes, and systematic collections of laws. Elected in 1918 to the Communist Academy, he organized the sector for the general theory of state and law. In the 1920s he published several fundamental works on the RSFSR Constitution and legal theory, and edited a major law journal, encyclopedia, and RSFSR Supreme Court reports. Attacked by Vyshinsky in 1938, his views have been rehabilitated and his principal works reissued in Russian and Latvian language editions. WEB

375

SUDAKOV, Il'ya Yakovlevich (1890–1969) Director and actor. Sudakov was closely associated with the Moscow Art Theatre. He produced Bulgakov's *Days of the Turbins* (1926), Ivanov's *Armoured Train 14–69* (1927) and Kataev's *The Embezzlers* (1928), all under Stanislavsky's direction, and Afinogenov's *Fear* (1931). He took charge of the Moscow *TRAM* (Theatre of Worker Youth) in 1933 and was Artistic Director of the Moscow Malyy Theatre from 1927 to 1944. RT

SUKACHEV (Sukatschew), Vladimir Nikolaevich (1880–1967) Leading botanist, phytogeographer, ecologist, forestry expert. A 1902 graduate of the Petersburg Forestry Institute, Sukachev worked there until transferring to the Botanical Museum (1912–18). In 1915 he was a founding member of the Russian Botanical Society. After the revolution, he was elected a corresponding member of the Academy of Sciences (1920) and became a central figure in Soviet botany, serving as professor at the Forestry Institute (1919–41), the Geography Institute (1919–25), the Botanical Garden (1924–33), and Leningrad University (1925–41).

Sukachev combined expertise in plant systematics with an early interest in experimental and theoretical biology and was a leading advocate of the ecological study of plant communities, which he first termed 'plant sociology' and later 'phytocoenology' and 'phytogeocoenology'. A classic 1928 paper reporting the results of experiments involving six distinct varieties of dandelion (*Taraxacum officiale*) was widely cited in Western literature as one of the earlier experimental demonstrations of the complex action of natural selection in nature.

Sukachev joined the party in 1937 and, with the blockade of Leningrad, was evacuated to Sverdlovsk (1941–43). Elected a full member of the USSR Academy of Sciences in 1943, he founded its Forestry Institute and moved his base to Moscow as professor at the Moscow Forestry Institute (1944–48) and Moscow University (1946–53), and as president of both the Botanical Society (1946–63) and the Moscow Society of Naturalists (from 1955).

From the late 1930s Lysenko and Prezent advocated so-called 'creative Darwinism' which denied the reality of intraspecific competition (for example, that seedlings planted closely together in clusters would compete with each other for food, sunlight, or nourishment). This brought them into direct conflict with Sukachev's expertise. Following the party's endorsement of Lysenko in 1948, Sukachev gave leading geneticists safe haven in his Forestry Institute.

From 1949 to 1951 Lysenko's reforestation programme, which involved 'clustering' seedlings, resulted in great losses and rendered Lysenko vulnerable. As editor of *Botanicheskiy Zhurnal* (1946–58) and the *Bulletin of the Moscow Society of Naturalists* (1948–67), Sukachev authorized the first articles critical of Lysenko's theories (1952) and, following Stalin's death, mounted a campaign against them. Khrushchev came to Lysenko's defence in December 1958, leading to Sukachev's removal as institute director and editor of the botanical journal and his demotion to head of a forestry laboratory. MBA

SUKHAREV, Aleksander Yakovlevich (b. 1923) Elected Procurator General of the USSR in May 1988, Sukharev is the first person to hold that position since Stalin's death without rising through the ranks of the Procuracy. A graduate in law, Sukharev spent his early career in the Komsomol and then in the administrative organs department of the Central Committee of the CPSU. He was First Deputy Minister of Justice (1970–84) and RSFSR Minister of Justice from 1984 to 1988. WEB

SULIMOV, Daniil (Danila) Yegorovich (1890–1937) An old Bolshevik and leading economic administrator. The son of a factory worker in the Urals iron industry, Sulimov worked in the same factory until 1914. He had joined the RSDLP in 1905, organized factory workers, and was arrested. He was called up for army service in 1914. He held senior posts in the economic administration of the Urals and in the party there (1917–27). He was appointed first deputy People's Commissar for Transport (1927–30), chairman of the Council of People's Commissars of the RSFSR, replacing Syrtsov (1930–37), and was himself replaced by Bulganin. He was a candidate member of the party Central Committee (1921–23), a full member (1923–37), and a member of the Orgburo (1927–30). He was executed in 1937 and rehabilitated in 1956. RWD

SULTAN-GALIEV, Mirza Said (1892–1939?) A Kazan' Tatar intellectual of the Revolutionary period who sought a synthesis between Bolshevism and a secularized, modernizing and nationalist Islam. He came to prominence during 1917 in the Kazan' Socialist Committee, a body which owed more to the Socialist Revolutionaries than to the Social Democrats, but which offered the Bolsheviks almost their only access to Volga Muslim opinion. Sultan-Galiev joined the Bolsheviks in November 1917, and became the only Tatar member of the Kazan' Council of People's Commissars. After Kazan' was taken by the Czechs in 1918, he was welcomed by Stalin into the Commissariat of Nationalities, and by 1920 he was the only Muslim in its three-man Collegium. He was arrested in May 1923 in one of the earliest cases of the use of force for purposes of party discipline, and expelled from the party in June 1923. Incredibly (as it now seems to us) he continued to popularize his views until the late 1920s, views which sought to use Leninist organizational principles in the interests of Muslim emancipation from European (including Russian) rule. He was never seen again after his second arrest in 1929, but purges of his supporters in the Tatar ASSR and elsewhere continued until the end of 1932. 'Sultangalievism' continues to be of symbolic importance to radical Muslims inside and outside the USSR. JHM

SURITS, Yelizaveta Yakovlevna (b. 1923) Dance historian. A graduate of the Moscow Lunacharsky State Institute of Theatre Art, Surits received a master's degree in art history in 1970. She worked at the Bakhrushin Museum from 1951 to 1960, and then at the Moscow Theatre Library until 1964. Since then she has headed the dance section of the Moscow Institute of the History of Arts. A contributor of articles to many periodicals, she is the editor of *All about Ballet* (1966) and author of the definitive work on the early years of Soviet ballet, *Choreographic Art of the Twenties* (1979). She was an editor of the Soviet *Ballet Encyclopedia* (1981) and a contributor to the *Great Soviet Encyclopedia* as well as to the American *International Encyclopedia of Dance*. In 1987 she was appointed a charter member of the US/USSR Joint Commission on Theatre and Dance Studies, sponsored by the American Council of Learned Societies and the Soviet Union of Theatre Workers. SJC

SURKOV, Aleksey Aleksandrovich (1899–1983) Poet, literary and party official, born near Yaroslavl'. He fought in the Civil War and joined the party in 1925. He was active as a literary official from 1928. He occupied high posts in the Union of Writers (First Secretary, 1952–59) and the party (candidate member of the Central Committee, 1956–66), and important editorships. He enjoyed great popularity as a soldier's poet during the Second World War. GSS

SUSLOV, Mikhail Andreevich (1902–1982) One of the most powerful men in the Soviet Union over many years, Suslov was born into a poor peasant family in the Saratov region of Russia. After study at the Plekhanov Economic Institute and at the Institute of Red Professors, Suslov (a Communist Party member from 1921) joined the party apparatus in 1931. In the later 1930s he was one of the beneficiaries of Stalin's purges, promotion being fast for those who survived. He was head of a department and then a secretary of the Rostov *obkom* (1937–39) before becoming First Secretary of the Stavropol' regional party committee, a post he held from 1939 to 1944.

From 1944 to 1946 Suslov, who had been elevated to membership of the Central Committee of the CPSU in 1941, was in charge of the reincorporation of Lithuania into the Soviet Union and he conducted there a policy of mass deportations. His postwar career was one in which he carried responsibilities for both ideological affairs and foreign policy. In 1946 he became head of the Propaganda and Agitation Department of the Central Committee and in the following year was made a Secretary of the Central Committee which he combined from 1949 to 1951 with the post of editor-in-chief of *Pravda*.

In the last year of Stalin's life, Suslov was a member of his enlarged Presidium of the party Central Committee, and from 1955 until his death in January 1982 he enjoyed continuous membership of the Politburo (called Presidium of the Central Committee, 1953–66). As a senior secretary with a seat both on the Secretariat and the Politburo he became a key figure in the Soviet leadership. Unostentatious in his political style and personal life, Suslov preferred to wield power behind the scenes. Essentially a conservative Communist, he was often at loggerheads with Khrushchev but his support for him against the 'anti-party group' was important in 1957. Suslov was much more comfortable with the outlook and approach of Leonid Brezhnev and his backing for Brezhnev, given that he had independent standing within the leadership and was in no sense a Brezhnev client, was invaluable for the latter.

Suslov's long period in senior positions in the Central Committee apparatus gave him ample opportunity to exercise patronage and the wide range of his appointees in high places constituted the main source of his political strength. As overseer of ideology and foreign policy within the Central Committee Secretariat he was cautious and unimaginative. Although personally untainted by corruption, he did little or nothing to combat the graft which became increasingly widespread during the

Brezhnev period of Soviet history. His relations with Andropov were cool and it was only after Suslov's death in January 1982 that Andropov was able to return to the Secretariat of the Central Committee and put himself in line for the succession to the General Secretaryship. AHB

SVASHENKO, Semen Andreevich (1904–1969) Ukrainian film actor. Svashenko's career was closely associated with Dovzhenko. His films include: *Zvenigora* (1928), *The Arsenal* (1929) and *The Earth* (1930), Pudovkin's *The Deserter* (1933), *The Gadfly* (1955) and *Quiet Flows the Don* (1957). RT

SVERDLOV, Yakov Mikhaylovich (1885–1919) Sverdlov was effectively the administrative head of the Soviet party and state for the first two years after the revolution. He was born in Nizhniy Novgorod (now Gor'ky), son of an engraver. A lively but restless and independent-minded pupil, the young Sverdlov soon came into contact with socialist literature and became involved in political agitation among the local work-force, making discreet use of his father's printing works for the purpose. Sverdlov became a Social Democrat in 1901 and the following year was arrested for the first time following a student demonstration. He gravitated towards the Bolsheviks after the party split and became an underground political worker on their behalf in Kostroma, Kazan' and elsewhere in central Russia. He was repeatedly arrested, imprisoned and deported. After the February Revolution he made his way to Petrograd, where he became a party secretary and chairman of the Central Executive Committee (a quasi-parliamentary body), presiding over its first six sessions after the revolution.

He was also a member of the commission which prepared the Soviet constitution of 1918. In the spring of 1919 Sverdlov caught a serious illness and died a few days later.

Sverdlov was an organizer of genius and his presence was sorely missed. He reorganized the party's central apparatus, relying on his capacity for hard work and exceptional memory, and became in effect the party's first general secretary. Although installed in leading positions in both party and state Sverdlov had no personal ambitions or indeed particular objectives and he remained completely loyal to Lenin's overall direction. Lunacharsky, in his near-contemporary portrait of Sverdlov, noted that 'whereas Lenin and a few others provided the intellectual guidance for the revolution, between them and the masses – the party, the Soviet government apparatus and ultimately all Russia – like a spindle on which it all resolved, like a wire transmitting it all, stood Sverdlov'. He was a small, bespectacled man of very Jewish-looking appearance, dressed in leather from head to foot in what came to be the traditional manner for commissars. Lenin, in his obituary, declared: 'Such men are indispensable. To replace him we need a whole squad of others.' SLW

SVETLANOV, Yevgeniy Fedorovich (b. 1928) Conductor. Svetlanov was born in Moscow. After studying at the Gnesin Music Institute, he entered the Moscow Conservatory in 1951 where his teachers were Yury Shaporin (composition) and Aleksandr Gauk (conducting). Whilst still a student, he held the post of assistant conductor of the Grand Symphony Orchestra of the All-Union Radio and Television, and shortly after his graduation from the

Conservatory in 1955 was appointed to a post at the Bol'shoy Theatre (1956), of which he was chief conductor (1963–65). In 1965 he was appointed principal conductor of the State Symphony Orchestra of the USSR. A person of diverse tastes, he has received numerous honours and awards. He was made a People's Artist of the USSR in 1968 and was the recipient of a Lenin Prize in 1972. He became Secretary of the Board of Soviet Composers in 1974 and was also a guest conductor of the London Symphony Orchestra. He is also a composer and writer. He was awarded a Paris Grand Prix for his recording of the complete Tchaikovsky symphonies. GS

SVETLOV, Mikhail Arkad'evich (1903–1964) Poet, born in Yekaterinoslav (now Dnepropetrovsk). He fought in the Civil War, then settled in Moscow. He became famous as the author of universally known revolutionary songs 'Granada' (1926) and 'Kakhovka' (1935), but was subsequently in the shadows until the Khrushchev thaw. GSS

SVILOVA, Yelizaveta Ignat'evna (1900–1976) Film editor. Svilova was wife and assistant to Vertov. RT

SVIRIDOV, Georgiy Vasil'evich (b. 1915) Composer and party worker. Georgiy (Yuriy) Sviridov was born in Fatezh. The son of a postal worker, he eventually entered the Leningrad Conservatory in 1936, where he became a pupil of Shostakovich, graduating in 1941. Since 1956 he has lived in Moscow. A member of the party, he was appointed Secretary of the Board of the USSR Composers' Union (1962–74), and First Secretary of the Union of Soviet Composers of the RSFSR (1968–73). He was made a People's Artist of the USSR in 1970 and a Hero of Socialist Labour in 1975. Sviridov's work is held in high esteem in the Soviet Union. Tonal and optimistic in nature, it is politically unexceptionable. Among his most successful works are *Songs to Words of Robert Burns* (1955), *Poem in Memory of Sergey Yesenin* (1956), and *Oratorio Pathétique* (1960), for which he was awarded a Lenin Prize. GS

SYRTSOV, Sergey Ivanovich (1893–1937) Syrtsov, a party and government official during the early post-revolutionary years, was born in Yekaterinoslav province. He studied at Petrograd Polytechnical Institute and became a party member in 1913. He took part in the establishment of Soviet rule in Rostov-on-Don, and in 1920 became secretary of the Odessa regional party committee. From 1921 until 1923 he worked in the central party apparatus in Moscow, latterly as head of the Agitation and Propaganda Department. In 1926 he became secretary of the Siberian territorial party committee and in 1929 Chairman of the Council of Ministers (or premier) of the Russian republic. From that year he was also a member of the Politburo. In 1930, however, Syrtsov was expelled from the Central Committee for oppositional activity and lost his leading positions. He was arrested during the purges and died in imprisonment. SLW

T

TAGER, Pavel Grigor'evich (b. 1903) Sound engineer and inventor. It was Tager who developed the system of optical sound recording used in the first Soviet sound feature film *A Path to Life* (1931). RT

TAHL, Mikhail Nekhem'evich (b. 1936) Chess player. He was born in Riga, Latvia, graduated from the Latvian State University in 1958, having become international grandmaster and won the Soviet chess title the year before. He also took the national chess crown in 1958, 1967, 1972 and 1974, and beat Botvinnik for the world chess title in 1960; he ceded the title to him a year later. Like Botvinnik and Smyslov he remained at the top of Soviet chess for a long period – some thirty years. He devoted much of his time to promoting chess in his native Latvia, editing the Latvian journal *Chess* from 1960 to 1970 and supervising the Riga chess school named after him. JWR

TAIROV, Aleksandr Yakovlevich (1885–1950) A major stage director whose reputation has been somewhat overshadowed by that of Vakhtangov. Tairov worked in Mardzhanov's Free Theatre in 1913, producing two pantomimes and in 1914, with his wife Koonen and others, he founded the Kamernyy (Chamber) Theatre to realize his notion of a 'theatre of emotionally saturated forms', a kind of 'neo-realism' in opposition to Stanislavskian realism. His most important productions in this period included Beaumarchais's *The Marriage of Figaro* (1915), Wilde's *Salome* (1917), Scribe's *Adrienne Lecouvreur* (1919) and Claudel's *Tidings Brought to Mary* (1920), *Romeo and Juliet* (1921) and Racine's *Phèdre* (1922), which Lunacharsky described as Soviet theatre's first great step towards genuine monumentalism. These productions used Cubist sets and a balletic style of acting but his next productions marked a break with what he called 'abstractions' and a move towards 'concrete realism' using Constructivist methods similar to those of Meyerkhol'd. Typical of this period are his versions of Ostrovsky's *The Storm* and Shaw's *St Joan* (both 1924), O'Neill's *Desire under the Elms* and *The Hairy Ape* (both 1926) and *All God's Chillun Got Wings* (1929) and Treadwell's *Machinal* (1933). Tairov was also responsible for the first production of a work by Brecht on the Soviet stage: *The Threepenny Opera* (1930). His productions of Vishnevsky's *An Optimistic Tragedy* (1933) and *Egyptian Nights* (1934), a compilation drawing on the works of Shaw, Pushkin and Shakespeare, brought accusations of 'formalism' and Tairov was forced to run his theatre under the watchful eye of a management committee. He adapted himself to the tenets of Socialist Realism with some success, notably in his production of *Madame Bovary* (1940), Chekhov's *The Seagull* (1944) and Gor'ky's *The Old Man* (1946). But his name is most closely associated with the development of the Kamernyy Theatre in Moscow, with the broadening of the methods of theatre in general and the broadening of the style and repertoire of Soviet theatre in particular. RT

TAKTAKISHVILI, Otar Vasil'evich (b. 1924) Composer and state official. Taktakishvili was born in Tbilisi. After studying at the Tbilisi Conservatory, from which he graduated in 1947, he was appointed to the teaching staff, as well as becoming conductor, then Artistic Director, of the Georgian State Choral Kapella. A member of the party since 1951 and of the Central Committee of the Georgian Communist Party from 1963, he was appointed Minister of Culture of the Georgian SSR in 1965. Three times awarded State Prizes, he was made a People's Artist of the USSR in 1974, and was the recipient of a Lenin Prize in 1982. Prolific as a composer, he is best known outside the USSR for his colourful Piano Concerto (première 1951). GS

TALYZIN, Nikolay Vladimirovich (b. 1929) Talyzin, a Russian politician and economic administrator born in Moscow, received a higher technical education before working as an engineer and as a deputy head of a scientific research institute. Between 1965 and 1975 he was a deputy minister and then First Deputy Minister of Communications of the USSR and from 1975 to 1980 the Minister. In 1980 he was appointed permanent Soviet representative at Comecon and in the same year became a deputy chairman of the Council of Ministers of the USSR.

Talyzin received an important promotion in 1985 when he was made Chairman of Gosplan, becoming at the same time First Deputy Chairman of the Council of Ministers. He was not a great success in that office and in October 1988 he was demoted to his previous post of representing the Soviet Union at Comecon; in September 1989 he was removed from the candidate membership of the Politburo which he had acquired in October 1985 and in the same year he retired from his Comecon duties. AHB

TAMKEVIČIUS, Father Sigitas (b. 1938) Lithuanian Catholic priest. Founding member of the Catholic Committee for the Defence of Believers' Rights in 1978. In 1983 he was tried for 'anti-Soviet slander' and sentenced to six years in prison camps and four in exile. MR

TARASEVICH, Lev Aleksandrovich (1868–1927) Bacteriologist. After graduating from Novorossiysk University in Odessa in 1891, Tarasevich continued his studies at the Medico-Surgical Academy in Petersburg (1891–96), Paris (1897), Kiev University (1898–1900) and the Pasteur Institute (1900–2). He served as professor at Novorossiysk University (1902–7) and Moscow University (1907–11), leaving after the direct take-over of the universities by education minister L. A. Kasso. Devoting himself in the 1910s to organizing private scientific institutions, he taught at the Bestuzhev Higher Courses for Women (1908–18), founded and coedited the influential

Moscow monthly *Priroda* (1912–27), and worked with the Moscow Scientific Institute Society (1913–18). He was also active in introducing new medical and bacteriological trends into Russia. After the revolution he achieved a high position in the Commissariat of Public Health, presiding over its scientific medical council (1918–27), creating and directing the State Pasteur Institute for Public Health (1918–27), and returning to the Moscow University Medical School as professor (1918–24). MBA

TARASOVA, Alla Konstantinovna (1898–1973) Actress. Regarded as one of the great actresses of the Moscow Art Theatre, Tarasova was closely associated with Chekhov roles, from Masha in *Three Sisters* (1941) to Mme Ranevskaya in *The Cherry Orchard* (1958) and Mme Arkadina in *The Seagull* (1960) and with Tolstoy, appearing in the title role in *Anna Karenina* (1937). Her roles in the Soviet repertoire included Yelena in Bulgakov's *The Days of the Turbins* (1926), Masha in Ivanov's *Armoured Train 14–69* (1927) and Gor'ky's *Enemies* (1935). Her films included *The Storm* (1934) and *Peter the First* (1937–39). She was Director of the Moscow Art Theatre from 1951 to 1954. RT

TARASOV-RODIONOV, Aleksandr Ignat'evich (1885–1938) Prose writer and literary activist. Having particpated in the revolutionary movement in 1905 and in 1917, Tarasov-Rodionov later worked as a magistrate and was involved in setting up the proletarian literary organizations *Kuznitsa* (The Smithy) and RAPP. Works such as *Chocolate* (1922), *Grass and Blood* (1924), and his incomplete autobiographical trilogy *Heavy Steps* (1927–) were all considered ideologically incorrect; he was eventually accused of Trotskyism, arrested and executed. JAEC

TARAZEVICH, Georgiy Stanislavovich (b. 1937) A Belorussian geologist, Tarazevich became a party official in 1972 and was First Secretary of Minsk *gorkom* from 1983 to 1985, before being promoted to Chairman of the Presidium of the Belorussian Supreme Soviet. In June 1989 he was elected (against some opposition) to chair the Commission on Nationality Policy and Inter-Nationality Relations of the USSR Soviet of Nationalities. JHM

TARICH, Yuriy Viktorovich (1885–1967) Belorussian film-maker and scriptwriter. Tarich was one of the older generation who worked in the Mongolian film industry in the 1940s. His films included: *The Wings of a Serf* (1926), *Hatred* (1930) and *The Eleventh of July* (1938). RT

TARKOVSKY, Andrey Arsen'evich (1932–1986) Film director. Tarkovsky was a pupil of Romm and emerged as the most talented and intriguing Soviet film director of the post-war period. His earliest films were: *The Steamroller and the Violin* (1961) and *Ivan's Childhood* (1962). He first came to prominence with the epic *Andrey Rublev* (1969) which deals with the problem of the artist's relationship with his environment and with the question of artistic freedom. His next film was a science fiction epic *Solaris* (1973), which was in some ways a Soviet equivalent to Kubrick's *2001: A Space Odyssey*. Then Tarkovsky made two deeply personal and rather inaccessible films, *The Mirror* (1976) and *Stalker* (1980). These were given only limited release in the Soviet Union and he went abroad and made: *Nostalgia* (Italy, 1983) and *The Sacrifice* (Sweden, 1986). During his long fight with cancer he was discussing the possibility of returning from exile. He died in Paris and has subsequently been reinstated in his homeland. RT

TATLIN, Vladimir Yevgrafovich (1885–1953) Designer and painter. Tatlin was born in Moscow. His first career was as a seaman and his art training was erratic, although he twice attended courses at the MIPSA. From his abstract reliefs of 1914 onwards, Tatlin arrived at the concept of his enormous Monument to the Third Communist International (1919–20) in which he proposed using metal and glass for their practical, functional effect. Often regarded as the father of Russian Constructivism, Tatlin continued to design utilitarian objects until the early 1930s, including a one-man glider called Letatlin. From the 1930s to the 1940s he worked on stage productions and also returned to figurative painting. JEB

TCHAIKOVSKY, *see* Chaykovsky

TEDIASHVILI, Levan Kitoevich (b. 1948) Sportsman. He grew up in the Georgian hills where he practised the folk wrestling style of *chidaoba*. Switching to free-style wrestling he became Olympic middleweight champion in 1972 and light-heavyweight champion in 1976. He was also four times world champion between 1971 and 1975, three times European champion and four times national champion. Born in the village of Gegmoubani, he became an extremely versatile wrestler: besides his free-style achievements, he was Georgian *chidaoba* champion for several years and the world *sambo* (unarmed combat – similar to judo) champion in 1973. JWR

TELINGATER, Solomon Benediktovich (1903–1969) Graphic artist and designer. Telingater was born in Tiflis. After studying in Baku and Moscow, he began to work as an illustrator for Baku newspapers, settling permanently in Moscow in 1925. Close to the *Lef* group, especially Klutsis, Lissitzky, and Rodchenko, Telingater supported Constructivism, applying its principles to interior, poster and especially book design. He was a pioneer in the advancement of axonometric layout. JEB

TENDRYAKOV, Vladimir Fedorovich (1923–1984) Became a novelist after early experience as a teacher and Komsomol official in the Vologda region. His best novel, *Death of a Great Man* (1968), relates with considerable frankness the story of a *kolkhoz* from the revolution to the death of its chairman in 1953, drawing parallels between him and Stalin. Most of Tendryakov's novels are lively and polemical, concerned with the moral problems that arise from rural life, education and religion; these are combined in *On Apostolic Business* (1969), about a scientist who abandons profession and family to go and seek God by working as an ordinary *kolkhoznik* (collective farm worker). GAH

TERESHKOVA, Valentina Vladimirovna (also known as Nikolaeva-Tereshkova) (b. 1937) Soviet cosmonaut, Chairman of the Soviet Committee on Women (1977–87) and a member of the Central Committee of the CPSU. Tereshkova was a little-known parachutist when she became the world's first woman astronaut and the tenth astronaut on earth. Her flight into space on Vostok VI in 1963 catapulted her into global celebrity status.

Valentina (Valya) Tereshkova was born into a working-class family in the Yaroslavl' region. Her father died in the Second World War, and the family endured considerable hardship in the next few years. After elementary school she worked in a tyre factory and later in a textile factory in Yaroslavl', continuing her education on a part-time basis at the Yaroslavl' Technical Textile College where she graduated in 1960. Active in the Komsomol, Tereshkova was elected to its Yaroslavl' regional committee. She joined the CPSU in 1962.

Tereshkova pursued parachute jumping as a hobby and was a qualified amateur parachutist. She volunteered for the Soviet cosmonaut programme in 1961 after Yuriy Gagarin's flight, and was accepted. Although she lacked many of the formal qualifications for cosmonauts, she made remarkable progress within the programme and was soon promoted to the rank of lieutenant. Tereshkova's historic three-day space flight in June 1963 was a journey of more than one million miles. She returned to earth an overnight celebrity. Her flight was one of the longest in the early 1960s. Premier Khrushchev bragged that it lasted longer than the flights of all four American astronauts combined. Not long after her historic orbit, Tereshkova became a Captain. During the 1960s she continued her education, graduating from the Zhukovsky Aviation Academy in 1969.

In late 1963 Tereshkova married fellow-cosmonaut Adrian Nikolaev and took the name Nikolaeva-Tereshkova. The couple had one child in 1964.

In 1968 she became the Chairman of the Soviet Committee on Women, an office she held until early 1987 when she became head of the Soviet Society for Friendship and Cultural Relations with Foreign Countries. In that capacity she was a Soviet representative to numerous international conferences. A member of the Central Committee from 1971 to 1990, Tereshkova is one of the best known women in the contemporary Soviet Union.

As the first woman in space, Tereshkova has been lauded at home and abroad. She is a symbol of Soviet achievement. A member of the Presidium of the Supreme Soviet, she has frequently travelled abroad as a representative of the Soviet government. She has been a member of numerous Soviet delegations focused on women's concerns, including the international conferences convened during the United Nations' Decade on Women. Among her many awards are Hero of the Soviet Union, the Order of Lenin, and Hero of Socialist Labour from Czechoslovakia. NN

TEVOSYAN, Ivan Fedorovich (1902–1958) A leading industrialist under Stalin, who was the subject of Aleksandr Bek's fictionalized biography *The New Appointment* ('Novoe naznachenie'). Tevosyan was the epitome of hard work, honesty, rigidity, and unconditional obedience to Stalin. His original patronymic was Tovadrosovich, but Stalin renamed him when appointing him a Hero of Socialist Labour. The son of an artisan tailor in Baku, he joined the party in 1918 in Azerbaydzhan. He graduated from the Mining Academy in 1927, and was sent to Britain to gain experience of modern plant. He then worked in the Elektrostal factory in Moscow, becoming the chief engineer. He was appointed head of Spetstal' (1931–36); deputy People's Commissar of the Defence Industry (1937–39), People's Commissar of the Shipbuilding Industry (1939–40), People's Commissar (later Minister) for the Iron and Steel

Industry (1940–49), and deputy chairman of the Council of Ministers (1949–57). Tevosyan was sent as ambassador to Japan after criticizing Khrushchev's proposals to establish regional economic councils (1957–58). RWD

TIKHOMIROV, Vasiliy Dmitrievich (1876–1956) Premier danseur, choreographer, and teacher. Tikhomirov graduated from the St Petersburg Ballet School in 1893 and joined the Bol'shoy troupe. With his superb technique and vivid scenic presence, Tikhomirov was highly acclaimed for his interpretation of major classical roles.

In addition to dancing with the Bol'shoy, Tikhomirov worked as choreographer (from 1913) and headed the Bol'shoy troupe (1925–30). As a choreographer he recreated a number of classical ballets, including Act Three of *La Bayadère* (1923), *Sleeping Beauty* (1924), and Act Two of *La Sylphide* (1925).

Tikhomirov was perhaps most renowned as an outstanding teacher, having begun teaching in 1896. Many of his techniques became fundamental in the training programmes at the Moscow school. His pupils included numerous leading dancers, such as Asaf Messerer, Mikhail Mordkin, and Victorina Krieger. SCS

TIKHON (Belavin, Vasiliy Ivanovich), Patriarch (1865–1925) Head of the Russian Orthodox Church during the early years of Soviet power. Appointed bishop of Aleutia and Alaska in 1898, Tikhon served in various dioceses until his selection as Patriarch in 1918. Initially he denounced the new communist rulers but later called for political loyalty to the Soviet state. MR

TIKHONOV, Nikolay Aleksandrovich (b. 1905) The chairman of the Soviet Council of Ministers for almost five years, Tikhonov was a politician of a technocratic background who owed much to a long-standing friendship with Leonid Brezhnev. He was born into a middle-class Ukrainian family in Khar'kov twelve years before the revolution and his first job, in 1924, was as an assistant train driver. He later became a technician in a mine before pursuing further studies and qualifying as an engineer from the Dnepropetrovsk Metallurgical Institute.

Between 1930 and 1947 Tikhonov was variously a technical engineer, mine supervisor and chief engineer. During the 1930s he got to know his near contemporary, Brezhnev, in the Ukraine, but he himself was in no hurry to make a political career. He did not join the Communist Party until he was forty. When Tikhonov did enter politics, it was in governmental rather than party administration. He joined the Ministry of Ferrous Metallurgy in 1950 and by 1955 was a deputy minister. Following Khrushchev's abolition of most of the central industrial ministries, Tikhonov returned to the Ukraine to become chairman of the Dnepropetrovsk regional economic council in 1957. From 1960 onwards, however, he spent the remainder of his career in Moscow as deputy chairman of the USSR State Scientific and Economic Council (1960–63), deputy chairman of Gosplan (1963–65), deputy chairman of the Council of Ministers (1965–76) and from 1976 as First Deputy Chairman of the Council of Ministers to Kosygin.

Tikhonov was already in his seventies when his career reached its highest points. In 1978 he became a candidate member of the Politburo and just one year later he was a full member. When Kosygin retired from the Chairmanship of the Council of Ministers in 1980, it was Tikhonov, at the age of seventy-five, who succeeded him. What is even more surprising is that he held that post until he was eighty, including three years after Brezhnev's death. Although he survived both the Andropov and Chernenko general secretaryships, he did not last long under Gorbachev. He was replaced as head of the Soviet government by Nikolay Ryzhkov in September 1985. AHB

TIKHONOV, Nikolay Semenovich (1896–1979) Born in Petersburg, Tikhonov was a poet, prose writer and literary functionary (a secretary of the Writers Union from 1944 until the sixties). A Serapion Brother, in the twenties he wrote poetry influenced by Gumilev and Khlebnikov. His collection of Civil War poetry, *Mead* (1922), contains his best-known work 'The Ballad of the Blue Packet'. In the late twenties and thirties he wrote on socialist construction in Central Asia and exotic travel literature; his short prose of this period is highly plotted and often fantastic, with a distinct dash of revolutionary romanticism. His poem 'Kirov Is With Us' (1941) won a Stalin Prize. KC

TIMOFEEV-RESOVSKY (Timoféeff-Ressovsky), Nikolay Vladimirovich (1900–1981) Radiation geneticist, evolutionary theorist. A graduate of Moscow University (1922), Timofeev-Resovsky worked (1921–25) at N. K. Kol'tsov's Institute of Experimental Biology in the group headed by S. Chetverikov. There, based on his drosophila research, he published several seminal papers dis-

tinguishing the penetrance (frequency of appearance), expressivity (degree of expression), and specificity (localization) of gene expression which became standard in genetics.

In 1925, in exchange for Oscar Vogt's study of Lenin's brain, Timofeev-Resovsky was invited to Vogt's Kaiser Wilhelm Institute of Brain Research at Buch, near Berlin, where he worked for two decades (after 1936 as head of the division of genetics and biophysics). There he became world-renowned in two fields: population genetics and radiation genetics. In 1925 the Chetverikov group began its studies of the genetics of wild populations of drosophila, but the first such study (published in 1927) was undertaken in Berlin by Timofeev-Resovsky together with his wife Helena (née Fiedler, also a member of the Chetverikov group). In the 1930s he continued his work on population genetics and published several key papers on evolutionary theory that established him as the Continent's leading population geneticist. In the early 1930s he began to study the mutagenic effects of radiation and, together with physicists Max Delbruck and K. Zimmer, elaborated the 'target theory' approach to gene structure. These works had a great influence on Erwin Schrödinger and brought the future Nobel Prize winner Delbruck into molecular genetics research.

At the end of the Second World War Timofeev-Resovsky was arrested by the Soviet secret police and was held in a Moscow prison and subsequently in a *sharashka* (a prison camp devoted to research). Released in 1955, he worked in a laboratory of biophysics in the Urals (1955–64), giving lectures and workshops on molecular biology and radiation genetics that helped to train a new Soviet scientific generation.

Following the renunciation of Lysenkoism in 1964, he moved near Moscow to the space research complex at Obninsk where he worked at the Institute of Medical Radiology of the USSR Academy of Medical Sciences (1964–69). In 1966 he won the Kimber prize of the US National Academy of Sciences, but attempts to elect him a full member of the USSR Academy of Sciences in the late 1960s led to a press campaign accusing him, without evidence, of having supported Nazi policies, and he lost his post, spending his final years as a consultant. In 1987 Soviet author Daniil Granin published a heroic popular biography of Timofeev-Resovsky entitled *Zubr* that excited new controversy, leading to moves (1987–88) for his official legal rehabilitation. MBA

TIMOSHENKO, Semen Konstantinovich (1895–1970) Military commander. Semen Timoshenko, who began life as a village labourer, became one of the leading Soviet wartime commanders. After service in the tsarist army he entered the Red Army in 1918 and was a cavalry regiment, brigade, and corps commander during the Civil War. He graduated from a course for commander-commissars in the Military-Political Academy in 1930. He held senior command posts, becoming Commander of the North Caucasian, Khar'kov, then Kiev Military Districts (1937–40). Having escaped the purges of the military, he took part in the occupation of Poland as commander of the Ukraine Front, and he was in charge of the Soviet winter offensive against Finland (1939–40). He was subsequently elevated to People's Commissar for Defence (July

1940–July 1941). From 1941 to 1942 he was Deputy People's Commissar for Defence and Commander-in-Chief of the Western, then South-western Strategic Sectors. He became commander and Supreme Headquarters representative in several operations (1942–45), including the Third and Fourth Ukrainian Fronts in the advance through Romania, Bulgaria, Yugoslavia, Hungary, Austria and Czechoslovakia. His accomplishments did not lead to high office after the war; until 1960 he was given command of the South Ural and Belorussian Military Districts. From 1960 he was Inspector-General of the Ministry of Defence, and from 1961 Chairman of the War Veterans Committee. RA

TISSE, Eduard Kazimirovich (1897–1961) Latvian-born cameraman. Tisse was associated with Eisenstein. His films included: all Eisenstein's works, Gardin's *Hammer and Sickle* (1921) and Dovzhenko's *Aerograd* (1935). RT

TITOV, Vitaliy Nikolaevich (1907–1980) Secretary of the Central Committee of the Soviet Communist Party and political figure. Like so many Soviet leaders of the Khrushchev period, V. N. Titov made his career in the Ukrainian party machine, serving in Khar'kov from 1944 to 1961. In 1953 he replaced Podgorny, under whom he had been second secretary, as Khar'kov's party leader. In 1961 he became chief of the Central Committee Party Organs department and in 1962 he was made a Central Committee Secretary. When Podgorny came under attack in 1965, Titov lost both of these posts, being one of a number of high officials with Khar'kov connections who were demoted. Titov became second secretary in Kazakhstan; in 1970 he was appointed permanent representative to Comecon, a post he held until his death. WJT

TITOV, Yuriy Yevlamp'evich (b. 1935) Gymnast. He won a total of thirty-three medals during his gymnastics career, including thirteen gold at world, Olympic and European championships between 1957 and 1962. His highest achievement was overall world champion in 1962. Born in Omsk, he became, upon retirement from competition, coach, international judge, Chairman of the USSR Gymnastics Federation and, since 1956, President of FIG – the only Soviet official to receive such a distinction. JWR

TKACHEV, Aleksey Petrovich (b. 1925) and **TKACHEV, Sergey Petrovich** (b. 1922) Both painters, born in Chugunovka, and both graduates of the Surikov Institute in Moscow where they studied under S. Gerasimov, the Tkachevs have made an important contribution to the rediscovery of genre painting. Favouring everyday subjects as in *A Windy Day* (1956–57), the brothers often work on the same paintings. JEB

TOLSTOY, Aleksey Nikolaevich (1883 [o.s. 1882]–1945) Prose writer, poet and dramatist. In 1907 he began publishing short stories and poems reflecting Symbolist tendencies. With the story *The Lame Gentleman* (1912), a portrayal of the gentry in decline, he moved towards realism. From 1914 to 1918 Tolstoy visited England and France as a war correspondent. In 1918 he emigrated to Paris, and then moved to Berlin in 1921, where he became involved with the 'Change of Landmarks' group, which promoted compromise with the Soviet regime. Tolstoy worked on their newspaper *On*

the Eve until his return to Moscow in 1923. With him he brought his autobiographical story *Nikita's Childhood*, a science-fiction story, *Aelita*, and the novel *Sisters*, which was to form the first part of his great trilogy of the Revolution, *The Road to Calvary* (1922–41). Tolstoy's return to the Soviet fold was considered a propaganda triumph. His later works on contemporary themes are less interesting than his major historical trilogy *Peter I* (1929–45, incomplete), and his two plays about Ivan the Terrible (1941–43). His novel *Bread* (1935–37) exaggerated Stalin and Lenin's roles in the Civil War at the expense of Trotsky's. Tolstoy is prized in the USSR as a classic of socialist realism, while fully meriting his wider reputation. JAEC

TOLSTYKH, Boris Leont'evich (b. 1936) Characteristic in his youth, his profession, and the rapidity of his promotion, of the new generation of specialists who have reached the top under M S. Gorbachev. An electronics engineer from Voronezh, Tolstykh was director of an electronics enterprise there until 1985. Brought to Moscow as Deputy Chairman of the State Committee for Science and Technology, he became chairman of that body, and Deputy Chairman of the USSR Council of Ministers in April 1987. Tolstykh was transferred to the post of Chairman of the State Committee for Computer Technology and Information Science in 1989. JHM

TOLUBKO, Vladimir Fedorovich (b. 1914) Former Commander-in-Chief of Strategic Rocket Forces. Tolubko, a Ukrainian, was a village teacher before entering the Soviet Army in 1932. He saw active service on several fronts during the war. After the war he held staff and command posts, including that of aide to the

Supreme Commander of Soviet Forces Group in Germany, and commander of an army, before he was appointed first deputy Commander-in-Chief of the Soviet Rocket Forces in 1960. This post made Tolubko a central figure with the Strategic Rocket Forces (so-named from 1963) because of the frequent change in Commanders-in-Chief. He moved to become Commander of the Siberian and Far Eastern Military Districts (1968–72), a move which raised the profile of the Soviet strategic forces in the conflict with China. After this sensitive posting he was named USSR Deputy Minister of Defence and Commander-in-Chief of the Strategic Rocket Forces in 1972. He held this critical post during the Soviet missile build-up under Brezhnev, with the rank of Marshal of Artillery, and only retired in July 1985. His successor was Army General Yuriy Maksimov. Tolubko was a candidate member of the CPSU Central Committee from 1971 and full member from 1976. RA

TOMASHEVSKY, Boris Viktorovich (1890–1957) A renowned Pushkin scholar, literary historian, and analyst of the problems of versification who was close to the Formalists, Tomashevsky compiled and edited numerous scholarly editions of Russian writers, including the collected works of Pushkin. KC

TOMSKY, Mikhail Pavlovich (1880–1937) One of the few workers in the early Soviet leadership and the leading figure in the Soviet trade-union movement in the 1920s, Tomsky grew up in St Petersburg in conditions of poverty. Organizing strikes from the age of fourteen, he joined the RSDWP in 1904, and in the 1905 Revolution was chairman of the Reval (Tallinn) Soviet. Subsequent party and trade-union activity was brought to an end with his arrest in 1909 and his sentence to five years hard labour, followed by exile. Returning to political life in 1917, Tomsky became leader of the Moscow trade unions after the October Revolution, and chairman of the Central Council of the Soviet Trade Unions (VTsSPS) in 1919. Meanwhile he was elected to the Party Central Committee in 1919 and to candidate membership of the Politburo in 1920. Though temporarily demoted from the VTsSPS leadership in 1921 for insufficiently resisting efforts to promote 'proletarian democracy' in the trade unions, he was reinstated in 1922 and made a full member of the Politburo. As such he strengthened both the party's control over the trade unions and the centralism of the trade-union organization. His residual commitment to improving workers' conditions, however, brought him into conflict with the policies of the Stalinist majority in the Politburo (1928–29). In July 1928 he openly backed Bukharin's and Rykov's opposition to the use of 'extraordinary measures' for forcibly extracting grain from the peasants and to excessive goals for industrial growth. Stalin's defeat of the 'Right deviation' effectively ended Tomsky's career. His resignation from the chairmanship of VTsSPS in December 1928 was confirmed in April 1929, and he was removed from the Politburo in July 1930. Thanks to timely recantations, he remained a full member of the Central Committee until the beginning of 1934, when he was demoted to candiate membership. During the first major show trial in August 1936, Zinov'ev and others included Tomsky among supposed participants in terroristic conspiracies against the Soviet leadership. The day after being implicated he committed suicide. He was officially rehabilitated in 1988. JB

TOMSKY, Nikolay Vasil'evich (1900–1984) Sculptor. Now remembered for his enthusiastic support of Socialist Realism and his statues of Lenin in Voronezh (1940), Vologda (1952) and East Berlin (1970), Tomsky also tried to develop the traditions of eighteenth- and nineteenth-century Russian sculpture. After the Second World War he executed a number of monumental complexes such as *Victory* for the Volga-Don Canal (1954), while teaching at the Surikov Institute (1948 onwards). From 1968 until his death he was President of the Academy of Arts, Moscow. JEB

TOPCHIEV, Aleksandr Vasil'evich (1907–1962) Organic chemist, administrator. A 1930 graduate of the Moscow Chemicotechnical Institute, Topchiev joined the party in 1932 and worked at the Moscow Technological Institute of Food Industry (1938–40) and the Moscow Petroleum Institute (1940–49, director 1943–47). In the late 1940s he was suddenly elevated to high administrative posts, first as assistant minister of higher education (1947–49), and then as chief scientific secretary of the presidium of the USSR Academy of Sciences (1949–58), following his unprecedented direct election as a full member of the Academy in 1949, without first being a corresponding member, in a non-election year. In the 1950s as the Academy's chief administrative officer he played a central role in nurturing de-Stalinization in the Academy and empowering the Soviet scientific community while serving political interests. In June 1958 he was eased out

of his post for political reasons and became an Academy vice-president and director of the Moscow Petrochemical Institute. MBA

TOPORNIN, Boris Nikolaevich (b. 1929) A constitutional law specialist at the Institute of State and Law of the USSR Academy of Sciences. Topornin was among the first Soviet scholars to undertake research on the political system, and has been actively involved in drafting the USSR Constitution and collateral legislation. Several of his books have been translated into English. Elected a corresponding member of the USSR Academy of Sciences (1987), he directs the philosophy and law section, and was elected director of the Institute of State and Law in 1989. Topornin has also served as President of the USSR Football Association for several years. WEB

TOVSTONOGOV, Georgiy Aleksandrovich (b. 1915) Tovstonogov has been Principal Director of the Leningrad Gor'ky Theatre since 1956: he was responsible for the production of Dostoevsky's *The Idiot* that brought Smoktunovsky to prominence. RT

TOVSTUKHA, Ivan Pavlovich (1889–1935) The head of Stalin's personal secretariat for most of the 1920s, Tovstukha was the son of an office worker. He was a revolutionary from 1905, was exiled and in 1912 fled abroad. He joined the Paris section of the party in 1913, working as a labourer, a kitchen-hand, and a taxi-driver. During the Civil War he was a leading official under Stalin of the People's Commissariat for Nationalities. He served on the Central Committee staff (1921–24 and 1926–30). He was deputy director of the Lenin Institute (later known as the Marx-Engels-Lenin Institute) until his death. He was elected a candidate member of the party Central Committee in 1934. RWD

TRAININ, Aron Naumovich (1883–1957) A. N. Trainin is best known in the West for his influential writings on criminal responsibility for war crimes and his role in drafting the Statute of the Nuremburg Tribunal. A progressive revolutionary but not a party member, Trainin graduated in 1908 from Moscow University, having been active in the revolutionary student movement during 1905. Two early essays on patterns of criminality in the Moscow Province from 1884 to 1887 and on 'Class Struggle and Punishment in the History of Russian Law' gave evidence of his inclinations towards criminal law. He left his studies at the University in 1911 as a protest against the Kasso reforms, returning only after the Revolution.

In 1921 Trainin became a professor and in 1946 was elected a corresponding member of the USSR Academy of Sciences. His textbooks on the general and special parts of the criminal law nurtured the rising generation of Soviet jurists during the 1920s, and he co-authored the standard commentaries on the RSFSR Criminal Code. His monographs on complicity (1941) and the constituent elements of a crime (1946, 1951, and 1957) were amongst the first on the subject in the Soviet Union. His study on war crimes, published in London in 1944, developed concepts put forward in his works on 'criminal intervention' (1935) and on the defence of peace and the criminal law (1937).

After the Second World War Trainin became active in the International Association of Democratic Jurists and travelled frequently to Western Europe. In 1952 he was caught up in the 'anti-cosmopolitan' campaign and an incipient 'lawyer's plot' against Stalin. His works were criticized and his academic post placed in jeopardy. Stalin's death forestalled the culmination of these accusations, and Trainin was returned to his positions.

Trainin published more than 200 works and is believed to have played a significant role in criminal law reform measures under consideration in the 1930s to 1950s. This dimension of his activities, however, remains obscure. An edition of Trainin's selected works was published in Moscow in 1969. WEB

TRAPEZNIKOV, Sergey Pavlovich (1912–1984) A poor peasant from Astrakhan' who 'took an active part in the collectivization' of agriculture, and rose to become a Central Committee department head, and corresponding member of the Academy of Sciences. A minor party official in Moldavia after the war, he encountered there the future General Secretaries Brezhnev and Chernenko. In 1965 he became head of the Central Committee Department for Science and Educational Establishments, and held it until his retirement in 1983. JHM

TRAUBERG, Il'ya Zakharovich (1905–1948) The younger brother of Leonid, Il'ya Trauberg began his career as a film critic in 1927, worked with Eisenstein and directed his cinematic masterpiece *The Blue Express* in 1929. RT

TRAUBERG, Leonid Zakharovich (b. 1902) Veteran film director and scriptwriter of the Leningrad school. In 1922 Trauberg co-founded FEKS with Grigoriy Kozintsev. His films include: *The Adventures of Oktyabrina*

and *Mishka Versus Yudenich* (1925), *The Devil's Wheel* and *The Overcoat* (1926), *Little Brother* and *S. V. D.* (1927), *New Babylon* (1929), *Alone* (1931), *The Youth of Maxim* (1934), *The Return of Maxim* (1937) and *The Vyborg Side* (1938) and *Simple People* (1945, released 1956). RT

TRENEV, Konstantin Andreevich (1876–1945) Author and dramatist. Trenev's plays included *The Pugachev Rebellion* (1924), the immensely popular *Lyubov' Yarovaya* (1926), the satirical comedy *The Wife* (1928), *The Clear Ravine* (1931), *The Experiment* (1934) and *On the Banks of the Neva* (1937), one of the first stage portrayals of Lenin. RT

TRET'YAK, Ivan Moiseevich (b. 1923) Commander-in-Chief of Air Defence Forces. Tret'yak, a Ukrainian, joined the Red Army in 1939. He graduated from the Frunze Military Academy (1949) and the General Staff Academy (1959). He held command posts at the Western and Second Baltic Fronts during the Second World War. After a series of promotions he commanded the Belorussian Military District (1967–76), the Far Eastern Military District (1976–84), and was Commander-in-Chief of the Far-Eastern Theatre of War (1984–86). He was a candidate member of the CPSU Central Committee (1971–76) and a full member thereafter. He was a deputy of the Supreme Soviet from 1966. Army General Tret'yak became a Deputy Minister of Defence – Chief Inspector of the Ministry of Defence in 1986 and, when Marshal of Aviation Koldunov was dismissed following the Rust affair in June 1987, Tret'yak replaced him as Commander-in-Chief of the Air Defence Forces. Tret'yak is a close associate of the Minister of Defence, Yazov, and their career paths have been closely interlinked. RA

TRET'YAK, Vladislav Aleksandrovich (b. 1952) Sportsman. The most respected ice-hockey goalminder in the history of the game, he kept goal for the Soviet national side for fifteen years (1970–85). He played for the Central Army Sports Club in Moscow, his team winning six consecutive league titles (1970–76). During his commanding performance for the USSR ice-hockey team against both amateur and then professional sides, they won the world championships ten times, with Tret'yak named the best goalminder of the world championships four times and gaining three Olympic gold medals and one silver. Born in the village of Orudievo in the Moscow Region, Tret'yak retired from competition at the age of thirty-three and became the first Soviet member of the IOC Athletes Commission, founded in 1984. He also devoted part of his foreign earnings from coaching abroad to providing wheelchairs for limbless Soviet ex-Afghanistan veterans. JWR

TRET'YAKOV, Sergey Mikhaylovich (1892–1939) Dramatist, poet, script-writer and literary theorist. Tret'yakov was a prominent figure in the Futurist movement throughout the 1920s in Moscow, and as a member of the *Tvorchestvo* ('Creation') group in the Soviet Far East. He proclaimed the death of the old fiction based on plot and promoted instead a 'literature of fact'. In the journal *The New LEF* (which he edited 1927–29) both proletarian writers and fellow-travellers were attacked. He wrote several plays including *Do You Hear, Moscow?* (1923) and the anti-colonial *Snarl, China!* (1926). Tret'yakov translated

and promoted Brecht's works. In 1939 he became a victim of the Purges. JAEC

TRET'YAKOV, Viktor Viktorovich (b. 1946) Violinist. Tret'yakov was born at Krasnoyarsk. After first studying in Siberia, he graduated from the Moscow Conservatory in 1970 as a pupil of Yuriy Yankelevich, with whom he completed his postgraduate studies in 1973. He was awarded first prize in the All-Union Competition of Musicians and Performers in Moscow in 1965 and was the winner of the International Tchaikovsky Contest in 1966. Since 1970 he has been a soloist with the Moscow Philharmonic. He was made a People's Artist of the RSFSR in 1979 and awarded a State Prize in 1981. GS

TRIFONOV, Yuriy Valentinovich (1925–1981) Son of a founder member of the Cheka, who was arrested and shot in 1937, his position as a member of a disgraced élite family gave him a dual insight into Soviet society. His first very orthodox novel about student life won him the 1950 Stalin Prize, but he later returned to its themes from an entirely different viewpoint. A series of novellas about life among Moscow intellectuals (1969–75) was socially critical and psychologically acute. In *House on the Embankment* (1976) and *The Old Man* (1978) he traced the demoralization of contemporary Soviet society to the history of the ruling élite, going right back to pre-revolutionary times, and drawing on abundant autobiographical experience. GAH

TROTSKY, Lev Davidovich (1879–1940) Trotsky, whose real surname was Bronshtein, was born in Yanovka village in Kherson province in the Ukraine. His parents were Jewish, and his father was a peasant farmer affluent enough to ensure that his son went to secondary school. As an adolescent, Trotsky was interested in literature and, like most Marxists of his generation, gained an interest in politics through Russian populist writings. He left school already attracted by anti-regime attitudes. Joining a Marxist group in Nikolaev, he was arrested and sent into Siberian exile in 1900. He escaped in 1902, emigrating and undertaking adventures he was later to describe in autobiographical sketches.

Trotsky was intellectually adept at soaking up other people's ideas, whether Marxist or not, and interpreting them in his own way. The life of the émigré did not daunt him, and he made for London to assist with the publication of *Iskra*. He supported the *Iskra* group in the controversy with the so-called Economists; he also demanded a centralized and disciplined structure for the Russian Social-Democratic Labour Party, and he did not support concessions in the party to the Jewish Workers' Bund. Yet, like Yu. O. Martov, he decided at the Second Party Congress in 1903 that Lenin's ideas on discipline and centralism were dangerously exaggerated, and he voted with Martov in the debate on party membership qualifications which led to the formation of a Menshevik faction under Martov and a Bolshevik faction under Lenin. The walk-out of the Bundists, however, robbed Martov of victory in elections to the central party bodies.

In 1904 Trotsky published *Our Political Tasks* and attacked the ideas of Lenin's *What Is To Be Done?*; but he never became a committed Menshevik. When the Russian empire was shaken by revolutionary turmoil in 1905, he adopted a different strategy from that espoused by the Mensheviks.

Influenced by Alexander Helphand-Parvus, he suggested that the bourgeoisie in Russia was too weak and untrustworthy to make its own 'bourgeois revolution' and that the absolute monarchy of the Romanovs should be replaced by a 'workers' government'. Such a government would not foster capitalism, a stage nearly all other Russian Marxists felt to be necessary before the 'transition to socialism' could be attempted, but rather would immediately undertake a 'permanent revolution' leading eventually to the achievement of socialism. Even Lenin found this view extremist.

Yet Trotsky argued that large-scale modern industry and its modern working class already existed in Russia even though it lived cheek-by-jowl with the most backward agriculture and an ill-educated peasantry; and that the traditional Russian Marxist revolutionary schedule could be fore-shortened. Trotsky was temperamentally unafraid to stand alone. Tall and inspiring, he was a magnificent orator; and, on his return from emigration in 1905, he moved to St Petersburg where he was chairman of the capital's first workers' council (or 'soviet') in September. The authorities disbanded the soviet and arrested him; but he used his court case to inflame popular opinion against the government. He was sent into Siberian exile. Again he escaped abroad.

The 1905 to 1906 Revolution had witnessed a reunification of the Bolsheviks and Mensheviks at the Fourth Party Congress in 1906; but there were always tensions, and these were exacerbated among the émigrés. Trotsky's ultra-radical strategy was closer to Bolshevism (and to the notions of Rosa Luxemburg) than to Menshevism; but his attitude to party organization was closer to Menshevism: he particularly objected to Lenin's perennial schismatism. He struggled to keep the party unified. But his vanity and hauteur repelled others. He was only a little more trusted than Lenin. Nonetheless in 1908 he skilfully founded a newspaper called *Pravda*, which came to be based in Vienna (and which was not the same newspaper as the Bolshevik *Pravda* set up in St Petersburg in 1912) and he helped to bring about a reunification of the various factions of the Russian Social-Democratic Labour Party at the Central Committee plenum in January 1910. His *Pravda* became the party's main newspaper for a time.

Lenin, however, was insistent on a Bolshevik-dominated party and called a separate Party Conference in Prague in January 1912. Trotsky convoked anti-Bolsheviks to a rival gathering in Vienna in August; but disagreements among this motley assortment of conferees meant that his 'August Bloc' had no durable authority. Writing and publishing became Trotsky's occupation, and he even covered military conflicts in the Balkans as a newspaper correspondent.

At the outbreak of the First World War he moved to Paris and ran an anti-war journal, *Nashe slovo* (Our Word). He condemned the war as imperialist; but, although he had fewer illusions than Lenin about the nationalism of German workers, he took it as axiomatic that they would lead a pan-European socialist revolution. His slogan was a United States of Europe. Trotsky emphasized the threat to civilization posed by the war, and – again unlike Lenin – he detected that the anti-war elements in the Russian Social-Democratic

Labour Party could make more political gains by appealing to society's yearnings for peace than by welcoming Russia's defeat by Germany. Nevertheless, without approving all Lenin's divisive proposals, he became less willing to fall out with him at the Zimmerwald Conference of European anti-war socialists in 1915.

The Russian February Revolution in 1917 found Trotsky in New York. As an anti-war socialist he had difficulties in reaching home, being interned in the Canadian port of Halifax when his ship docked there. He eventually arrived in Petrograd (as St Petersburg had been renamed) in early summer. Since the Bolsheviks were by then calling for a socialist seizure of power and since they already had a mass party of their own, Trotsky opted to join them. He, for his part, no longer wanted unity with a Menshevik leadership which even supplied ministers to join the liberal-dominated Provisional Government.

After the violent street demonstrations in Petrograd in July, Trotsky was arrested for his collaboration with the Bolshevik Central Committee. In August he joined the party and was elected to its Central Committee. On his release he participated actively in the Petrograd soviet, becoming its chairman in September. He backed Lenin's demands for a rising against the Provisional Government. His leading role in the Petrograd soviet's Military Revolutionary Committee in October meant that many practical aspects of the overthrow of the Provisional government were entrusted to him. His oratorical skills were accompanied by organizational capacities of genius. Power was transferred to the Second Congress in the October Revolution of

1917, and Trotsky emerged as Lenin's closest colleague. In the negotiations over the formation of a new government, neither Lenin nor he wanted the Mensheviks and the Socialist Revolutionaries in their coalition, and that view prevailed.

With Lenin as the chairman of the Council of People's Commissars (or *Sovnarkom*), Trotsky was made People's Commissar for Foreign Affairs. This involved discussions with the Central Powers at Brest-Litovsk. Despite being opposed to a separate peace, Trotsky also perceived that the Russian army could not fight on against the Germans; but his policy of 'neither war nor peace' became untenable in January 1918 when the Central Powers delivered their ultimatum. In February 1918 he reluctantly sided with Lenin in agreeing to a separate peace.

Leaving his previous job, Trotsky was appointed as People's Commissar for Military Affairs. His assignment was to form a Red Army. He saw that only a centralized and professional command structure would suffice to win the Civil War, and drew in thousands of officers from the old imperial army – much to the chagrin of many Bolsheviks. Belatedly Lenin gave the necessary political assistance to Trotsky, and Trotsky faced down his Bolshevik critics with the retort that he was attaching a 'political commissar' to each officer in the army. He travelled widely along the war fronts against the Whites between 1918 and 1920. His leadership inspired the men and the officers alike. His organizational aptitude and political vision ensured that he was chosen for the inner subcommittee of the Central Committee, the Politburo, in 1919. Disagreements with Stalin over military strategy and over the appointment of personnel did not halt his progress.

By 1920 Trotsky could see that the country faced economic catastrophe. He urged a limited restoration of private trade as a means of getting peasants to release more grain stocks, but was rebuffed by the central party leadership. His other proposal, which was to transfer Red Army conscripts to jobs in 'labour armies' with the objective of reconstructing industry, was welcomed (even though his demand for trade unions to be rigorously subordinated to the state caused a fierce dispute with Lenin in the winter of 1920 to 1921). But peace did not occur. The Polish-Soviet war broke out, and Trotsky against his better judgement found himself in charge of the invasion of Poland.

The defeat of the Red Army and the continuing economic and social tumult compelled Lenin to advocate the inception of the New Economic Policy (or NEP) from February 1921. This involved a carefully-controlled re-opening of private industrial enterprises and an allowance for peasants to trade their post-taxation grain surplus on the market. Trotsky accepted the NEP, but from 1922 called for greater central state planning of industrial investment and production. This was not outright opposition to the NEP, but an attempt to modify it. Even so, Trotsky's relationship with Lenin was rendered difficult. It was to Trotsky, however, that Lenin turned for help in the controversies with Stalin over Georgia, over bureaucratization in the party and governmental machines and over the state foreign-trade monopoly in 1922.

Their rapprochement was interrupted by Lenin's death in 1924, at which point Trotsky became a contender for the mantle of supreme leadership. In 1923 the crisis in trade between town and countryside had led Trotsky to campaign not only for greater state planning but also for an internal democratic reform of the party. He was castigated as someone who had developed his democratic inclinations only when he was losing power in the party; certainly many of his supporters were unmoved by his request for the party's democratization. Trotsky edged towards participation in a Left Opposition, but by January 1924, as Lenin lay dying, Trotsky had lost the factional struggle.

Friendless at the party's apex, he tried to work loyally in various jobs of state economic administration; but his worries about party policies increased. He argued for a faster pace of industrialization as well as of establishment of collective farms; he also objected to the concentration of Soviet foreign policy on domestic concerns at the expense of fostering a European socialist revolution. Zinov'ev and Kamenev joined him in political dissent in 1926, forming the United Opposition. Defeat for all of them followed in 1927. Suspicion again surfaced that Trotsky, who demanded the extension of democracy to the soviets (short of permitting the re-creation of a multiparty system), was speaking only to further the interests of his own career; and both his past record as a non-Bolshevik and his ineptitude as a marshaller of political support ruined his chances.

The United Opposition was crushed in 1927. Trotsky, who refused to recant, was exiled to Alma-Ata. In 1928 Stalin had him deported. The rest of his life was spent in emigration. He went to Turkey, Norway and, finally, to Mexico. His friends and relatives were persecuted, most of them eventually suffering death or else agreeing to recant. His links with the few remaining Trotskyists did not disappear, and he hoped to set up an anti-Stalin opposition in the USSR. But these brave but frail endeavours were doomed. Show-trials became common. 'Trotskyism' was officially and grotesquely caricatured as a pro-capitalist distortion of Marxism, and Trotsky's adherents were accused of being in league with the Nazis.

Trotsky pondered these developments from abroad. He had come to perceive the authoritarian nature of the Soviet polity only in the 1920s, and his *New Course* of 1923 adumbrated notions about the problems of avoiding bureaucratization and building socialism in a backward peasant country. The astonishing rise to power of Stalin in the 1930s baffled him, not least because he thought him to be a third-rate politician and an insignificant Marxist theoretician. Nonetheless Trotsky's movement into outright condemnation of everything done by Stalin in the First Five-Year Plan came slowly; he perhaps envisaged a reconciliation with a Stalin who was at least embarking on a radical economic course and who, if he got into difficulties, might turn to Trotsky for support. But his vacillations faded as Stalin's grip on power tightened.

Trotsky was forced back into the role of writer, commentator and theorist. He expressed the notion that the October Revolution had been betrayed and that a bureaucratic and essentially conservative, anti-revolutionary stratum had established itself. Stalin, in Trotsky's view, was simply the stratum's figurehead.

Trotsky continued to write hagiographically about the earliest years of Soviet power and believed that a 'workers' state' had been created which was indestructible even by Stalin and his legions of bureaucrats. But profound internal reforms, he thought, were required to restore authority to the Soviet working class. Trotsky urged that such a transformation would be ineffective unless stronger commitment was given to the spread of socialist revolutions in Europe. Socialism in a single country, according to Trotsky, was an impossibility.

The international situation in the late 1930s was dire. Highlighting the dangers of Stalin's pre-occupation with the USSR's internal affairs and recognizing the barbarous potentialities of Nazism, Trotsky formed the so-called Fourth International. He aimed his sallies at the Third International, or Komintern, headed by the party of Stalin in Moscow. A self-proclaimed Leninist to the last, he was in reality always his own man. A brilliant polemicist, a talented writer, a marvellous synthesiser of ideas on politics and culture not only from Russian Marxism but also from other Russian and European heritages, Trotsky was a polymath and socialist of global political stature. He was not a little conceited and was blind to the need to exercise his charm in pursuit of immediate political goals. He had a talent for making personal enemies without knowing he had done so.

Moreover, he had been a ruthless army leader in the Russian Civil War and unconcernedly justified the widespread application of terror. It was therefore ironical that he died by a terrorist act. Stalin's assassins tracked him down in Coyoacan in Mexico in 1940. He was killed by a blow to the head from an ice-pick and died on 20 August. In death he achieved apotheosis among his followers as a doughty and unconditional fighter against all aspects of Stalinism. This was exaggerated acclaim and in any case those followers, in countries throughout the world, have continued to dispute the nature of Trostky's legacy among themselves. In the USSR, at least until 1989, his name was officially anathematized. RJS

TSINTSADZE, Sulkhan Fedorovich (b. 1925) Composer and teacher. Tsintsadze was born in Gori, Georgia. He studied at the Moscow Conservatory, graduating in cello in 1950 and composition in 1953. He was appointed a teacher at the Tbilisi Conservatory in 1963, becoming rector in 1965. He was made a People's Artist of the Georgian SSR in 1961, as well as being awarded several State Prizes. He became a party member in 1966. Although he has composed in different genres, he is noted particularly for his chamber works, which show the influence of Georgian national music. GS

TSIPKO, Aleksandr Sergeevich (b. 1941) One of the boldest and most thoughtful political analysts of the Gorbachev era. A Russian born in Odessa, Tsipko graduated from Moscow University Philosophical Faculty in 1968 and took his candidate's degree there in 1972. In that year he began work at IEMES where he remained – apart from the years 1978 to 1980 when he studied in Poland and took a doctoral degree – until 1986 when he became a consultant in the International Department of the Central Committee. While there he published an impressive series of four articles in the popular science journal, *Nauka i zhizn'*, which argued

that Marx and Lenin were far from guiltless in laying the foundations of Stalinism in the Soviet Union. In 1990 Tsipko left the Central Committee apparatus and returned to Bogomolov's institute as deputy director. In addition to numerous Russian-language publications, he is author of *Is Stalinism Dead?* (New York, 1990). AHB

TSVETAEVA, Marina Ivanovna (1892–1941) Poet and poetic essayist. To many she is the greatest twentieth-century poet of Russia, belonging to no school and yet surpassing the practitioners of various modernist movements like futurism and imagism in her use of neologisms, new verse forms, and metaphor. She speaks in a distinctively female voice, even when adopting a male persona. Her juvenilia have the confidence of a poetic destiny. *Mileposts* (1921) and *Mileposts: I* (1922) contain poetic cycles, which would dominate her later verse: the 'Poems on Moscow' and those dedicated to other poets: Akhmatova and Blok. Her next book, *Separation* (1922), heralds an important theme in her later poetry and includes the longer narrative poem 'On a Red Steed' which is crucial for an understanding of the poet's psychological attitude to her life and craft. Other longer verse narratives written between 1920 and 1923 draw on stylizations of folklore. Her next collection, *Psyche* (1923), continues the sound experimentation which reaches its height in her poems of the Civil War years: *The Swans' Demesne* (1917–21, published in 1957) which celebrates the White Army, and *Craft* (1923, published in Berlin).

After Russia (1922–25, published in Paris in 1928) is arguably the best book by any modern Russian poet.

The variety of voices (anti-bourgeois satire, self-destructive or ironically vengeful 'love' lyrics, elegiac partings, cool female updatings of male myths like Hamlet/Ophelia or Helen of Troy) is matched by the experimental lines of superb imagery and dense sound. Her greatest long poems, *The Ratcatcher* (1925), *Poem of the Mountain* (1924) and *Poem of the End* (1924) were written at the same time while she lived in Prague.

Tsvetaeva wrote mainly autobiographical and critical prose from 1928 until her return to the Soviet Union from Paris in 1939, where she hanged herself in 1941. BH

TSVIGUN, Semon Kuz'mich (1917–1982) A career political policeman, Tsvigun graduated from the Odessa Pedagogical Institute in 1937, spent two years as a schoolteacher and joined the NKVD (later KGB) in 1939. During the Second World War he was an officer in *Smersh*. After the war he was a senior official in the security police in Moldavia (1951–55), where he worked closely with Brezhnev and Chernenko, and later in Tadzhikistan (1955–63, from 1957 KGB Chairman) and Azerbaydzhan (KGB Chairman, 1963–67). As a relative of Brezhnev by marriage and an ally of his, Tsvigun was brought to Moscow in 1967 after Yuriy Andropov had been appointed Chairman of the KGB to be one of the people in a senior position in that organization on whom Brezhnev could rely.

Tsvigun was First Deputy Chairman of the KGB from November 1967 to his death in January 1982, a candidate member of the Central Committee (1971–81) and a full member from 1981. At the time of his death – apparently by suicide – Tsvigun was coming under scrutiny for his involvement in widespread corruption. As Brezhnev's health weakened he was no longer able to offer the same protection as in the past to those close to him. AHB

TSYBIN, Vladimir Dmitrievich (b. 1932) Poet, prose writer, and literary official. Tsybin was born near Frunze of peasant stock, and educated in Moscow. He began as a Cossack poet, but has developed into a highly professional author of personal lyrics and autobiographical prose. GSS

TUKHACHEVSKY, Mikhail Nikolaevich (1893–1937) A truly legendary figure both in life and in death, Mikhail Tukhachevsky ('Tuka') came of a minor landowning family in the Dorogobuzh district of Smolensk province. Moving from school to the First Moscow Cadet Corps, the young Tukhachevsky enrolled in 1912 in the Aleksandrovsk Military School, graduated with distinction in June 1914, and was commissioned into the Semeonov Guards Regiment. His brief front-line service, which brought him six decorations for gallantry, ended on 19 February 1915 when he was taken prisoner. Finally confined in the Ingolstadt fortress for repeated escape attempts, lodged with other prisoners including Captain Charles de Gaulle, Tukhachevsky did break out, passed through Switzerland and eventually returned to Russia in the late winter of 1917.

Throwing in his lot with the Bolsheviks, he joined the party on 5 April 1918, proceeding from the post of military commissar on the Western 'screens' to the Eastern Front and command of the First Red Army on 26 June 1918. Here he carried through the first forced mobilization of ex-Imperial Army officers to staff Red units, bringing the Soviet Republic its first victories with the First Army in the east. At the end of 1918 he moved briefly to command the Eighth Red Army on the Southern Front, then back eastwards to take over the Fifth Red Army for a far-flung offensive, clearing the Urals. On 29 April 1920 he assumed command of the armies of the Western Front and in July-August, in the course of the Soviet-Polish war, undertook his famous but ill-fated 'drive on Warsaw', a reverse which involved him in an envenomed relationship with Stalin and his cronies of the First Cavalry Army, a feud which deepened into hatred and ended in murder.

An ardent proponent in 1920 of the 'strategy of class war' and of an 'International Red Army' to serve world revolution, he was nevertheless in 1921 commanding Red Troops to suppress counter-revolution in Kronstadt and put down peasant rebellion in Tambov. Appointed head of the Red Army Military Academy in August 1921, assistant chief in 1924 and Chief of the Red Army Staff in 1925, as well as a member of the Republic Revolutionary Military Council, Tukhachevsky launched upon serious studies of military theory and simultaneously urged upon Stalin the modernization of the Red Army, a programme encouraged initially by secret Soviet-German military contacts. Shunted off by Stalin to the Leningrad Military District in 1929, he returned to the centre in June 1931 as Chief of Red Army Ordnance (*Nachal'nik vooruzheniya RKKA*), embarking also at that time upon his fundamental work, *New Problems of War* (excerpts of which were first published in 1962). Radical, erudite, dynamic and abreast of advancing technology, Tukhachevsky elaborated the principle of 'combined arms' and, in particular, understood the link between armoured warfare and aviation, fused into his concept of *aviyamotomekhanizatsiya*, connecting military technology and military art in the concept of *glubokaya operatsiya* (deep operational and strategic penetration), an early, indeed the earliest, formulation of 'air-land battle', presently much in vogue. Already in 1929 in his Leningrad command Tukhachevsky had seized upon the importance of parachute troops: his interest in the tank led to the formation of several tank corps by the mid-1930s; his interest also extended to early forms of radar, rocket propulsion and improved naval armament.

With the re-organization of the Soviet military system in 1934 Tukhachevsky emerged as one of the Deputy Commissars for Defence and a year later, on 20 November 1935, was appointed one of the first Marshals of the Soviet Union together with Voroshilov, Budenny, Yegorov and Blyukher. Yet the triumph proved to be short-lived. For all his massive contribution to modernizing the Red Army, Stalin out of vengefulness, suspicion and envy had him marked down for death. Tukhachevsky's ideas had already made their impact with the first modern Field Service Regulations for the Red Army (PU-29); with the new Provisional Field Service Regulations (PU-36) his ideas on 'deep battle' and his innovative operational views received formal codification and detailed exposition, but this alone could not save him. Dingy, dismal death, further disfigured by trumped-up charges of treason, came on 11 June 1937 at the hands of the NKVD. In Tukhachevsky the world

401

of music lost an indifferent would-be violinist; the military world gained a commander of skill and a visionary whose ideas and influence have been only temporarily obscured by Stalin's murderous hatred. The Tukhachevsky legacy flourishes anew. JE

TUNKIN, Grigoriy Ivanovich (b. 1906) Born in the Arkhangel'sk province of peasant stock, Tunkin graduated from a forestry technical school in 1928 and the Moscow Juridical Institute in 1935. He defended a *kandidat* thesis in 1938 on the English parliamentary reform of 1832, and taught briefly at the All-Union Legal Academy before joining the diplomatic service in 1939. At the Ministry of Foreign Affairs he served in succession in the legal section, as Soviet consul in Iran, as counsellor to the Soviet Embassy in Ottawa (1942–44), as deputy head of the Ministry's Second European Section (1944–45), and as head of the First Far Eastern Section (1946–48). He was Minister-Counsellor of the Soviet Embassy in the Korean People's Democratic Republic (1948–51) before returning to Moscow to head the First Far Eastern Section again.

During the early 1950s Tunkin published several legal articles on the Korean problem under pseudonyms. In May 1952 he became head of the legal section of the Ministry of Foreign Affairs, a position he held until August 1965, together with adjunct appointments as head of the Department of International Law at the Moscow Juridical Institute (1949–54), *dotsent* and then professor of International Law at Moscow State University, head of the Department of Legal Disciplines of the Higher Diplomatic School, and professor at the Moscow State Institute of International Relations (1954–63).

In his dual role as legal adviser and scholar Tunkin has played the pre-eminent part in shaping international legal doctrine and practice in the post-Stalin era, his successive works on theory representing the most substantial and original Marxist contribution to the discipline. Shortly after assuming the office of legal adviser in 1952, Tunkin expressed strong disagreement with E. A. Korovin on the issue of two international laws. His view was, and remains, that 'agreement between states' is the basis of international legal rules. Tunkin's approach to international law has constituted the principal juridical foundation of East-West co-operation in the era of peaceful co-existence; the most mature reflection of this is contained in his *Theory of International Law* (1970), published in English in 1974 and many other languages.

Tunkin served in the United Nations International Law Commission (1957–66) and took part in numerous diplomatic conferences, heading the Soviet delegation at the 1958 and 1960 Geneva conferences on the law of the sea, the 1961 Vienna conference on diplomatic intercourse, as well as the 1959 Antarctic treaty conference.

He has been President of the Soviet Association of International Law since it was formed in 1957, on the editorial board of the central legal journals and yearbooks, and was elected to the Hague Permanent Court of Arbitration. A corresponding member of the USSR Academy of Sciences, he continues to lecture and direct the activities of the Department of International Law at Moscow University.

In recent years Tunkin's attention

has turned to the role of power in the international system. His theory of agreement and the concordant wills of states, so central to Soviet concepts of modern international relations, will probably be refined in the Gorbachev diplomacy to reduce the accent on 'struggle' in achieving agreement and enhance the role of co-operation of states. WEB

TUPOLEV, Andrey Nikolaevich (1888–1972) One of the most talented of all Soviet aircraft designers, Andrey Tupolev was the pioneer of both heavy bomber design and the creation of modern passenger aircraft. Born in the Kalinin region, the son of a lawyer, he studied at the Moscow Higher Technical School and then worked at a Moscow aircraft factory. After the revolution, together with Nikolay Zhukovsky, he founded the Central Aerohydrodynamic Institute (TsAGI). During the 1920s and early 1930s Tupolev created a series of all-metal planes, notable among which were the TB-1 and TB-3 heavy bombers, the latter being one of the most advanced planes of its day. In October 1937 Tupolev was arrested, falsely charged with selling aircraft designs to Germany, and, together with many other leading designers, spent several years in a prison design bureau run by the NKVD. Here he developed the Tu-2 bomber, the success of which led to his release from detention in 1943.

In the post-war years Tupolev led the creation of a series of heavy bombers, including the Tu-16 (Badger) and Tu-20 (Bear), and passenger planes, beginning with the Tu-104. While Tupolev was still leader of the design bureau, the supersonic Tu-144 passenger aircraft was developed. Since his death leadership of the design bureau has passed to his son, Andrey Andreevich Tupolev, who continues the tradition of developing advanced bombers and passenger planes. Andrey Tupolev was elected to the Academy of Sciences in 1953. He was made a Hero of Socialist Labour on three occasions (1945, 1957, 1972). He never joined the party. JMC

TURCHANINOVA, Yevdokiya Dmitrievna (1870–1963) Actress. Turchaninova was an actress associated from 1891 with the Malyy Theatre. She played Mme Glumova in Eisenstein's production of *Enough Simplicity for Every Wise Man* (1923) and acted a wide variety of roles in both the classical and Soviet repertoire. RT

TURIN, Viktor Aleksandrovich (1895–1945) Film director. Turin worked in Hollywood (1912–22) and then in Soviet cinema. His films included: *The Slogans of October* (1922), *The Battle of the Giants* (1924), *The Provocateur* (1928), *Turksib* (1929) and *Men of Baku* (1938). RT

TURKIN, Valentin Konstantinovich (1887–1958) Scriptwriter. Turkin wrote the scripts for several films, including: *The Tailor from Torzhok* & *The Station Master* (1925), *The Girl with the Hat Box* (1927) and *The Ghost That Never Returns* (1930). RT

TURISHCHEVA, Lyudmila Ivanovna (b. 1952) Gymnast. One of the two most outstanding women in the history of gymnastics (with Latynina), she competed in three Olympic Games (1968–76), making her Olympic début in Mexico at sixteen and becoming overall champion in 1972. In addition she was a champion of Europe in 1971 and 1973, and of the world in 1970 and 1974, and holder of the World Cup in 1975. Altogether she won more than forty medals in international competition, including twenty-four gold. In recognition of her services to world sport, she received the Olympic Order in 1983. Born in Groznyy, she owed much to her coach Vladislav Rostorotsky for developing her graceful and skilful talents, relying initially on Ukrainian folk melodies to accompany her free-style routine, and then switching (less successfully) to modern music. An active social worker, on retirement from competition, she coached in Rostov and Kiev, where she lived with her husband, the runner Valeriy Borzov. JWR

TVARDOVSKY, Aleksander Trifonovich (1910–1971) Son of a dekulakized peasant, he became a poet and the greatest literary editor of a period when that role was crucial. His long narrative poem, *Vasiliy Terkin*(1941–45), portrayed the simple Russian soldier in idealized but humorous light, and was said to be found in every Red Army knapsack. A sequel, *Terkin in the Other World* (1954–63), satirized the bureaucratic mores of post-Stalin Russia. As chief editor of *Novyy mir* (1950–54 and 1958–70), he played the leading role in securing the publication of much of the most critical literature of the post-Stalin period, notably Solzhenitsyn's *A Day in the Life of Ivan Denisovich* (1962). Under his guidance, *Novyy mir* became a loyal but critical commentator on the Soviet political, economic and cultural scene; some viewed it as being almost tantamount to an official opposition. Its success in this function owed much to Tvardovsky's view that good literature must be honest and fearlessly critical, that it should embody insights derived from the ordinary people and should be written with the aim of educating and forming public opinion. He was elected in 1961 as a candidate

member of the party Central Committee, but his mandate was not renewed in 1966 because of his association with Solzhenitsyn. In his last years, he became increasingly disillusioned with the possibilities of official reform. His *By Right of Memory* (1967–69), which revealed the truth about his father's fate, was forbidden by the censor: Tvardovsky had recourse to *samizdat*, and the work soon appeared in the West. It was not published in the Soviet Union until 1987. Deposed as editor of *Novyy mir* in 1970, he died soon after. At the Eighth Writers' Union Congress in 1986 his name was repeatedly invoked as an example for editors to follow in the new era of *glasnost'*. GAH

TYAZHEL'NIKOV, Yevgeniy **Mikhaylovich** (b. 1928) A teacher and party worker in Chelyabinsk, Tyazhel'nikov was a surprising choice in 1968 as First Secretary of the All-Union Komsomol, and again, in 1977, as head of the Central Committee Department of Propaganda. (The latter position had been vacant for some years since the removal of V. I. Stepakov and A. N. Yakovlev.) Tyazhel'nikov was himself removed from the department immediately after Brezhnev's death, and became Soviet ambassador to Romania. JHM

TYNYANOV, Yuriy Nikolaevich (1894–1943) A Formalist theoretician and scholar, Tynyanov was particularly interested in defining the distinctiveness of poetic language and in analyzing the dynamic of literary evolution. His first major work, on Dostoevsky's parody of Gogol', argues that parody helps literature to change by ridding it of what has become outmoded. During the twenties he also developed the concept of the *dominanta*, as a group of elements in a system (such as a work of literature) which dominate and deform the other elements and which themselves are subject to historical change. In his most sustained investigation of literary evolution, contained in the collection *Archaists and Innovators* (1929), Tynyanov demonstrated that influence does not pass directly through the line of high literature alone but may work indirectly through sub-canonical or antiquated texts. Tynyanov early on believed that literature was not separate from other activities and in a magisterial 1928 article he co-authored with Jakobson he argued that in order to study literature, one must study other systems of discourse that interact with it. In addition to his theoretical work, he wrote historical novels about Kyukhelbaker (*Kyukhlya*, 1925) and Griboedov (*Death and Diplomacy in Persia*, 1927–28); at the end of his life he was working on a large novel about Pushkin. KC

TYRSA, Nikolay Andreevich (1887–1942) Painter and graphic artist. Tyrsa was born in Aralykh. He studied at the Academy of Arts and then at the Zvantseva School in St Petersburg (1905–10). Of the same artistic formation as Bruni and Rudakov, Tyrsa became known for his lyrical landscapes and portraits such as his rendering of Anna Akhmatova (1928). JEB

TYSHLER, Aleksandr Grigor'evich (1898–1980) Painter and designer. Tyshler was born in Melitopol' and, like Rabinovich and Shifrin, attended the Kiev Art Institute in the 1910s. He also came under the influence of Ekster. Enrolling at Vkhutemas in 1921, he experimented with various ideas before arriving at his expressionistic and surrealistic style, exemplified by *Woman and an Airplane* (1927). A founder member of OST, he turned to stage design as a central medium, achieving particular success for his interpretations of Shakespeare. In the 1960s he began to work on wooden sculpture. JEB

TYUKALOV, Yuriy Antonovich (b. 1930) Sportsman. He was the first of the great Soviet rowers. He won a gold medal in the sculls at the 1952 Helsinki Olympics, a gold medal in the double sculls at the 1956 Melbourne Olympics, and a silver medal in the same event at the 1960 Rome Olympics. He was six times European and ten times Soviet champion. Born in Leningrad, he based his training on heavy work loads – some forty kilometres rowing a day. Upon retirement from competition, he devoted his career to art, graduating from the Vera Mukhina Art College in Leningrad, and contributing a number of monumental sculptures to major exhibitions throughout the USSR. JWR

U

UDAL'TSOVA, Nadezhda Andreevna (1886–1961) Painter. Udal'tsova was born in Orel, trained at the MIPSA (1905–9) before living in Paris (1912–13) where she studied cubism. A member of the avant-garde, Udal'tsova, like her husband Aleksandr Drevin, was influenced by Malevich and Tatlin and experimented with abstract painting. A professor at Vkhutemas-Vkhutein (1921–34) she returned to a more Realist style in the 1930s, producing still-lives and landscapes. JEB

UGLANOV, Nikolay Aleksandrovich (1886–1940) A party and government official during the early post-revolutionary period, Uglanov was born into a peasant family, was active in revolutionary politics from the age of seventeen and joined the Bolsheviks in 1907. He took part in the February and October Revolutions and became a member of the Petrograd Soviet; he later served in the Food Commissariat and from 1921 was a member of the local party apparatus in Petrograd, Nizhniy Novgorod (now Gor'ky), and Moscow. From 1928 until 1931 Uglanov was People's Commissar for Labour and from 1927 was a candidate member of the Politburo, but he supported the Right Opposition in internal party disputes and was expelled from the party in 1932. He was readmitted but expelled again in 1936, and died in imprisonment four years later. SLW

ULANOVA, Galina Sergeevna (b. 1910) Outstanding dancer. Peoples' Artist of the RSFSR (1951), Hero of Socialist Labour (1974, 1980).

Ulanova, whose parents were both dancers, was born in St Petersburg; her mother, Maria Fedorovna Romanova, was her daughter's first teacher. As a senior at the Petrograd State Ballet School, Ulanova studied with Agrippina Vaganova.

Graduating in 1928, she joined the Leningrad Theatre for Opera and Ballet (later known as the Kirov). In her first season with the company she danced Aurora in *The Sleeping Beauty*; the following year she was Odette/Odile in *Swan Lake*. Other major roles included the heroine in *Giselle* (1932) and Masha in *The Nutcracker* in 1934. But she was especially known for her creation of roles in new ballets, among them that of Maria in Rostislav Zakharov's *Fountain of Bakhchisaray* (1934) and Juliet in Leonid Lavrovsky's *Romeo and Juliet* (1940).

During the Second World War Ulanova was evacuated with the company to Perm'. In 1944 she joined the Bol'shoy Theatre in Moscow, where she had previously danced as a guest artist. She first appeared in the West in Vienna in 1945, and six years later she danced in Florence. This was followed by performances with the Bol'shoy in Berlin (1954), London (1956), Japan (1957), Paris (1958), the United States and Canada (1959 and 1962). Of her New York début as Juliet, when she was forty-nine years of age, John Martin wrote that she 'transcends in artistic values the youthfulness of nature'.

Ulanova danced as prima ballerina of the Bolshoy until she retired in 1962. Thereafter, she continued to work wtih the company as ballet mistress and coach. Among her outstanding pupils are Yekaterina Maksimova, Nina Timofieva, Lyudmila Semenyaka, and Vladimir Vasil'ev. She has also served on the juries of the international ballet competitions held in Moscow and Varna.

Ulanova has been especially praised for her musicality and for her dramatic power. She approached each of her roles with deep concern for characterization, often developing her interpretation over the years. She told Albert Kahn that 'the value of my work lies in the conviction that the language of the ballet can convey to people great and vital truths about life, about the beauty in life and in the human heart.'

Ulanova's autobiography has been translated into English by S. Rosenberg as *The Making of a Ballerina* (1959). Albert E. Kahn collected his interviews with the dancer in *Days with Ulanova* (1962). SJC

UL'YANOV, Mikhail Aleksandrovich (b. 1927) A tremendously popular actor and cultural figure, Ul'yanov is also an outspoken advocate of *perestroika*; he moved from frequent film and stage appearances as Lenin and Zhukov to the Congress of People's Deputies in 1989 as a deputy from the Communist Party.

Born in the remote Siberian village of Tara, Ul'yanov's introduction to the theatre came when a small Ukrainian theatre company was evacuated there during the war. His strong motivation and considerable talent led him to Moscow by 1946 and, after completing the Shchukin Theatre School, he was invited to join the Vakhtangov Theatre's repertory company. Appearing in over fifty films since 1952 in addition to frequent stage-acting, Ul'yanov's most famous role remains that of the chairman of a village collective farm in *The Chairman* (1964). The film provoked great controversy because of its critical assessment of the (often bureaucratic) difficulties faced by the chairman in rebuilding a farm devastated by the Second World War.

In 1986 Ul'yanov joined forces with director Oleg Yefremov and playwright Mikhail Shatrov to lead a rebellion against the conservative All-Russian Theatre Society and form the more independent Russian Theatre Workers Union (headed by Ul'yanov). Ul'yanov became director of the Vakhtangov Theatre in 1987. He had joined the Communist Party in 1951 and in 1989 was elected one of the Central Committee's delegates to the Congress of People's Deputies in 1989, despite having received forty-seven negative votes. He has since been a forceful critic of those who oppose political change and greater openness. MM

UL'YANOV, Nikolay Pavlovich (1875–1949) Painter. Ul'yanov attended the MIPSA (1889–1902) and exhibited with the Union of

Russian Artists whose orientation towards the Russian countryside and Russian history appealed to him. From 1915 to 1918 he taught at the Stroganov Institute and then, from 1919 to 1922 at Vkhutemas. In the 1930s he made a number of interpretations of Pushkin's life, including *A. S. Pushkin and N. N. Pushkina before a Mirror at a Court Ball* (1937). JEB

UL'YANOVA, Mariya Ilichna (1878–1937) A professional revolutionary and Lenin's younger sister, her career was closely linked with that of Lenin. She worked for the Social Democratic Party from 1898 onward, serving as a secretary to the Central Committee and aide to Lenin among other roles. Exiled to Vologodsky Province from 1912 to 1914, she worked in the Moscow organization of the RSDLP after her release in 1915. After the Bolshevik Revolution, Ul'yanova was an editor of *Pravda* for twelve years and from 1924 onward edited the journal, *The Workers-Peasants' Correspondent*. In 1929 she was appointed to the Lenin Institute to prepare Lenin's letters to his relatives for publication. She also wrote a biography of Lenin. Active in the CPSU, Ul'yanova was a member of the Presidium of the Central Control Commission of the Communist Party from 1932 until her death. In the Soviet period, Mariya Ul'yanova lived with Lenin and Krupskaya, and after his death, with Krupskaya most of the time. NN

URBANSKY, Yevgeniy Yakovlevich (1932–1965) Actor. Urbansky was best known as a film actor but trained at the Moscow Art Theatre. His films included: *A Communist* (1958), *The Ballad of a Soldier* (1959) and *A Clear Sky* (1961). RT

USMANKHODZHAEV, Inamzhon Buzrukovich (b. 1930) Born into the small Uzbek communist elite (his father directed the building of the Great Fergana Canal), Usmankhodzhaev worked mainly in construction and irrigation engineering until he was thirty-five. He became a provincial official in Syrdar'ya and Namangan *oblasti* and spent the years 1969 to 1972 in the Central Committee apparatus in Moscow, before becoming First Secretary of Andizhan *obkom* (1974–78). He then moved to posts at the pinnacle of power in Uzbekistan, Chairman of the Presidium of the Supreme Soviet from 1978 to 1983, and Party First Secretary from 1983 to January 1988. Whilst he held the latter office the 'Uzbek cotton scandal', involving massive falsification of cotton production and bribes paid to conceal it, was being exposed: it had ramifications in Moscow, involving Brezhnev's son-in-law Churbanov, and (some claimed) figures in the Gorbachev leadership. Usmankhodzhaev played a part in further exposures among the Uzbek leadership. Nevertheless he was himself arrested in late 1988 and sentenced to twelve years' imprisonment at the end of 1989. JHM

USMANOV, Gumer Ismagilovich (b. 1932) Soviet politician whose rise to high party office under Gorbachev proved to be extremely short-lived, Usmanov – who is by nationality a Tatar – was born into a working-class family in the town of Chistopol in the Tatar ASSR. After a higher education specialising in agriculture, he taught in an agricultural institute. A Communist Party member from 1953 he worked in the Komsomol apparatus (1953–54) before returning to teaching. He subsequently moved between party and governmental work. From 1966 to 1982 he was Chairman of the

Council of Ministers of the Tatar ASSR and from 1982 to 1989 First Secretary of the Tatar regional party committee. Elected to a Secretaryship of the Central Committee of the CPSU in September 1989, Usmanov held that office only until July 1990. He was a member of the Central Committee of the CPSU from 1986, but failed to be re-elected at the Twenty-Eighth Party Congress four years later. AHB

USPENSKY, Boris Aleksandrovich (b. 1927) Designer. Uspensky was born in Moscow. He is regarded – with Savostyuk with whom he often works – as one of the Soviet Union's leading poster artists. A graduate of the Surikov Institute in Moscow, he has also attracted attention with his graphic interpretations of the ballet. JEB

USPENSKY, Boris Andreevich (Aleksandrovich) (b. 1937) Linguist, semiotician and cultural historian. Uspensky's thesis on the typology of languages preceded works on liturgical pronunciation, general linguistics and the history of the Russian language in the eighteenth century, but he is better known for his semiotic studies (for example on icons, 1971) especially his work on Russian culture written in collaboration with Yu. M. Lotman. He now works mainly on his own, concentrating on early Russian religion, culture, and history. FCMW

USTINOV, Dmitriy Fedorovich (1908–1984) An important Soviet politician over many years who reached the peak of his power in Brezhnev's time, Ustinov made his most important contribution to the Soviet Union during the Second World War when he reorganized and relocated the Soviet armaments industry. Almost his entire career was bound

up with defence and defence industry, and although he was essentially a civilian administrator he was given the title of Marshal soon after he became Soviet Defence Minister in 1976.

Ustinov was born into a working-class family in Samara (now Kuybyshev) and spent a year in the Red Army as a volunteer during his youth. He joined the Communist Party in 1927 and spent the next two years as a manual worker in several different factories. He followed this with the pursuit of a higher technical education, graduating first from the Bauman Higher Technical School in Moscow and in 1934 from the Leningrad Military Technical Institute. For the remainder of the decade he worked in the Leningrad armaments industry and by 1938 he was manager of the Bolshevik Arms Factory.

When the German attack on the Soviet Union took place in June 1941 Ustinov was appointed People's Commissar of Armaments when he was only thirty-two years of age. The Soviet Union had been ill-prepared for the war, but Ustinov displayed impressive energy and ability in reorganizing the defence industry and, in particular, overseeing its evacuation to the area beyond the Urals to prevent it from falling into the hands of the advancing German armies.

Ustinov continued to progress in the Soviet ministerial and Communist Party hierarchy in the post-war era. A full member of the Central Committee from 1952, he remained Minister for Armaments until 1953 when he was appointed Minister of the Defence Industry. From 1957 to 1963 he was a deputy chairman and from 1963 to 1965 First Deputy Chairman of the Council of Ministers, still with supervisory responsibilities for the defence industry. He was brought into the party apparatus by the new Brezhnev–Kosygin leadership in 1965 and, as a Secretary of the Central Committee, had the task of overseeing the military, defence industry and the security organs. From 1965 Ustinov was in addition a candidate member of the Politburo and he was promoted to full membership at the Twenty-Fifth Party Congress in 1976. Shortly after that Congress the Minister of Defence, Marshal Grechko, died suddenly and Ustinov was appointed his successor, even though it was conventional for Soviet defence ministers to be soldiers rather than civilians. Ustinov, however, was a civilian with a quite exceptional knowledge and experience of military affairs and he remained Minister of Defence until his death in December 1984, outliving Brezhnev and Andropov and dying just three months before Chernenko.

Ustinov had continued to be a successful minister in the sense that both the Soviet military and defence industry were granted vast resources and accorded a privileged position in the Soviet economy. The military sector was also recognized to be markedly more efficient than almost all civilian branches of the economy. Ustinov himself was greatly valued by successive Soviet leaders and respected by his Western counterparts. At the Vienna Summit of 1979 Zbigniew Brzezinski (President Carter's National Security Adviser) was impressed by Ustinov's 'quick and shrewd mind'.

In retrospect, Ustinov's achievements under Brezhnev, Andropov and Chernenko are, however, being judged more critically in the Soviet Union itself. It has been increasingly acknowledged that the excessive resources devoted to military build-up damaged the economy as a whole, and as a member of the inner circle of Politburo and Defence Council policymakers Ustinov was one of those responsible for the Soviet military intervention in Afghanistan of 1979 – an action which was finally called off and severely criticized in the Gorbachev era. By the norms of his time, however, Ustinov was a formidably successful politician and his contribution to Soviet victory over the Nazi invaders was his finest hour. AHB

USTVOL'SKAYA, Galina Ivanovna (b. 1919) Composer and teacher. Ustvol'skaya was born in Petrograd. After first studying at the music school attached to the Leningrad Conservatory (1937–39), she entered the main Conservatory as a pupil of Shostakovich, graduating in 1947. After a further four-year period of postgraduate work, during which time she taught composition at the Rimsky-Korsakov music school, she finally left the Conservatory in 1951. Of her compositions in various genres, some are based on ancient Russian chant, resulting in a metrical freedom, while others employ serial techniques. Her work has received little official encouragement or recognition in prizes or state honours. GS

UTESOV, Leonid Osipovich (1895–1982) Light music performer. Utesov was born in Odessa and died in Moscow. Having learnt the violin at an early age, he embarked on an active theatrical life, appearing as actor, instrumentalist, acrobat, singer and conductor. In 1929 he established the first Soviet jazz group, which he called 'Tea-Jazz' (subsequently known as the State Variety Orchestra of the RSFSR) and in which he appeared as conductor, soloist and compère. The group featured in the film *Happy Lads*, with music by Dunaevsky (1932–34). He also did much to publicize traditional Russian songs as well as Soviet pieces. He was made a People's Artist of the USSR in 1965. GS

UTKIN, Iosif Pavlovich (1903–1944) Poet, born in northern China, educated in Irkutsk. Utkin served in the Red Army; he moved to Moscow in 1924, and earned a high reputation for his revolutionary lyrics in the second half of the 1920s, then fell foul of party critics in the 1930s. He died in a plane crash while working as a military journalist. GSS

V

VACHNADZE, Nato (1904–1953)
Actress. Vachnadze was one of the
leading Georgian screen actresses and
her appearances included: *The Horseman from the Wild West* (1925), *The
Living Corpse* and *The Gadfly* (1928),
The Last Masquerade (1934), *The Golden
Valley* (1937) and *The Homeland*
(1940). RT

**VAGANOVA, Agrippina Yakov-
levna** (1879–1951) Pre-eminent ballerina, choreographer, and teacher.
The daughter of an usher at the Mariinsky Theatre, Vaganova graduated
from the Imperial Ballet School in
1897 where her teachers included
Pavel Gerdt, Christian Johansson, and
Lev Ivanov. In addition, she observed
the celebrated Enrico Cecchetti and
his student Ol'ga Preobrazhenska.

Vaganova danced with the Mariinsky troupe from 1897 to 1917. She
was made soloist in 1906 and prima
ballerina in 1915. She was known as
the 'queen of variations' for her
breathtaking leaps and impeccable
technique. Vagnova's major roles
included Odette-Odile in *Swan Lake*,
the Mazurka in *Chopiniana*, the Tsar-
Maiden in *The Humpbacked Horse*, and
Giselle. Vaganova left the stage in
1917 at the height of her career.

Two years later she began teaching
ballet, a career that was to span more

than three decades, contribute to the
survival of classical dance, and form
the basis for the entire system of Soviet
dance education. Her system of
planned instruction was based on
achieving complete equilibrium,
subordinating the dance elements to a
single aesthetic principle, and incorporating soaring elevation. The
system includes elements of academic
ballet, European traditions, and
modern Russian choreography.

From 1919 to 1921 she taught at
Akim Volynsky's ballet school and
from 1921 to 1957 at the Leningrad
Ballet School where she was appointed
director (1934) and professor (1946).
In 1957 the school was named after
her. She served as artistic director of
the Kirov Theatre (1931–37), where
she staged a revival of Michel Fokine's
ballet *Chopiniana* (1931), her own
version of *Swan Lake*, starring Galina
Ulanova (1933), and a new version of
Esmeralda (1935). She taught teachers
at both the Leningrad Ballet School
(1934–41) and the Leningrad Conservatory (1946–51), where she also
headed the choreography department.

Vaganova's writings include *Basic
Classical Dancing* (1934), a widely
translated and classic text in the field.
Her students include Galina Ulanova,

412

Natalya Dudinskaya, and Marina Semenova. scs

VAGINOV (Vagingeim), Konstantin Konstantinovich (1899–1934) A Leningrad poet and prose writer, his early poetry was influenced by the Symbolists and Acmeists (as in the collection *Journey Into Chaos* of 1921), but in the late twenties, after joining Oberiu in 1927, it became more modernist (as in *Experiments in Combining Words by Means of Rythmn* of 1931). He wrote several novels about the Petersburg milieu; the most famous of these, *The Goat's Song* (1927), satirizes his own associates (which included members of the Bakhtin circle). KC

VAGRIS, Yan Yanovich (Vāgris, Jānis) (b. 1930) A Latvian engineer who had made a party career in the cities of Jelgava and Liepaja, Vagris was First Secretary of Riga *gorkom* from 1978 to 1985. He became Chairman of the Presidium of the Latvian Supreme Soviet (1985–88) and, in October 1988, succeeded Boris Pugo as First Secretary of the Latvian Communist Party, at a time of its rising unpopularity, and the rising influence of the Latvian People's Front. JHM

VAINSHTOK, Vladimir Petrovich (1908–1978) Director. Vainshtok directed a number of films including: *The Road to the West* (1928), *The Conquered Land* (1930), *Treasure Island* (1938). RT

VAKHTANGOV, Yevgeniy Bagrationovich (1883–1922) Stage director and actor. Vakhtangov was one of Stanislavsky's pupils at the Moscow Art Theatre. He headed the Student Drama Studio there from 1913 and this became the embryo for the theatre named after him after his death. He developed a theory and style of acting that rejected both the extreme naturalism of Stanislavsky and Meyer-khol'd's reduction of the actor to the role of puppet in the director's hands and owed much to Expressionism. He appeared himself in Dickens' *The Cricket on the Hearth* (1914), Berger's *The Flood* and as the Fool in *Twelfth Night* (both 1919). His most famous productions included Maeterlinck's *The Miracle of St Anthony* (1918 and 1921), Chekhov's *The Wedding* (1920), Strindberg's *Erik XIV* (1921), *The Dybbuk* (1922) for the Habimah Theatre and his last production, a version of Gozzi's *Princess Turandot* (1922). Vakhtangov's methods combined the best of Stanislavsky and of Meyerkhol'd and *Princess Turandot* marked their culmination. Vakhtangov died during the rehearsals and did not live to see the first night, but the production remained in the repertoire of the Vakhtangov Theatre unchanged for many years. RT

VANNIKOV, Boris L'vovich (1897–1962) One of the Soviet Union's early specialists in weapons design and production, Vannikov was People's Commissar for Armaments from 1939. Shortly before the German invasion in June 1941 he was briefly imprisoned after a dispute with Stalin and Zhdanov over mortars and anti-tank guns. Released (in his opinion because the early defeats vindicated his judgement), he returned to head a People's Commissariat for Munitions for the rest of the war. From 1946 he headed a secret 'First Main Administration' attached to the Council of Ministers and concerned with the construction of a nuclear reactor for military purposes. His public appointments resumed in 1953 with the post of First Deputy Minister of Medium Machine Building (also in the nuclear field). He retired in failing health in 1958. JHM

**VANSHENKIN, Konstantin Yakov-
levich** (b. 1925) Poet and literary
official, born in Moscow. He served in
the Second World War, joining the
party in 1953. He found critical
acclaim for the tale in verse *The Heart
of a Mother* (1954), dealing with grief
for a son lost in the war. Vanshenkin
is a prolific author of lyric poetry,
including some famous songs. GSS

VAREYKIS, Iosif Mikhaylovich
(1894–1938) A prominent party
official and one of the principal organizers of collectivization. The son of a
Lithuanian peasant, Vareykis became
a metal worker and took part in the
workers' movement. He joined the
party in 1913, held numerous party
posts in the Civil War and NEP years,
and became known in Baku as 'Tram-
vaykis' because he organized a tram
line there. He was strongly critical of
the Trotsky opposition. He held
various appointments, the first being
head of the Press department of the
Central Committee in Moscow (1924–
26), followed by the secretaryship of
party committees in Saratov province
(1926–28), the new Central Black-
Earth region (TsChO) (1928–34),
and the Voronezh region after the division of TsChO (1934–35). He was
then posted to the Stalingrad region
(1935–37), and the Far East region in
1937. He was a candidate member of
the party Central Committee (1924–
30), and a full member (1930–39).
He was arrested in 1937 after questioning the execution of Tukhachevsky
in a telephone conversation with
Stalin, and was himself executed in
1938. He was rehabilitated in 1956.
RWD

VASIL'EV, Georgiy Nikoaevich
(1899–1946) and **VASIL'EV, Sergey
Dmitrievich** (1900–1959) Erron-
eously known as the 'Vasil'ev

Brothers', they were best known for
their film *Chapaev* (1934), but also
responsible for *Volochaev Days* (1937)
and *The Defence of Tsaritsyn* (1942). RT

VASIL'EV, Pavel Nikolaevich (1910–
1937) A poet, born in north-eastern
Kazakhstan, Vasil'ev led a wandering
life before coming to Moscow in 1929.
His unruly temperament, profligate
talent, and provocatively libertarian
backwoods themes led to his arrest in
1932 and final detention from 1937.
GSS

VASIL'EV, Vladimir Viktorovich
(b. 1940) Leading dancer and choreographer. Vasil'ev studied under
Mikhail Gabovich at the Bol'shoy
Ballet School, graduating in 1958. He
joined the Bol'shoy troupe upon
ation, making a brilliant début as
Danila in *The Stone Flower* (1959).
With his impeccable technique and
exceptional versatility, Vasil'ev
became a leading soloist and excelled
in roles with strong national character.
He has also danced a broad spectrum
of roles from the classical repertoire.

Vasil'ev's major roles have included
Ivanushka in Ivan Radunsky's *The
Humpbacked Horse* (1960), Medjnun in
Konstantin Goleyzovsky's *Leili and
Medjnun* (1964), the title role in Kon-
stantin Boyarsky's *Petrushka* (1964),
and the title role in Yuriy Gri-
gorovich's *Spartacus* (1968).

His choreography has included
Icarus (1971, new version 1976), *These
Charming Sounds* (1978), and *Macbeth*
(1980), in which he danced the
leading role.

Vasil'ev, who often partners his wife
Yekaterina Maksimova, has toured
widely. Recent tours have included a
guest appearance with the Kirov
Ballet in Paris (1988). He has also been
the recipient of many awards and
prizes at international competitions,

and has appeared in films and television programmes. scs

VASILEVSKY, Aleksandr Mikhaylovich (1895–1977) Much less well known but no less important than Marshal Zhukov in fashioning Soviet victories in Europe and in the Far East, the reserved and highly professional Vasilevsky occupies a key position, if only as a vital member of the Zhukov-Vasilevsky command and coordination 'team'. The First World War frustrated the young Vasilevsky's plans to study as an agronomist or possibly a land surveyor. After a crash course at the Alekseevsky military school, in September 1915 he proceeded to the front as an ensign (*praporshchik*) with the 103rd Infantry Division, the Ninth Army, becoming a company commander but taking on the duties of a battalion commander with the rank of *shtabs-kapitan*.

In May 1919 Vasilevsky joined the Red Army, having worked earlier as an instructor in the newly organized 'universal military training' programme (*Vsevobuch*). His first Red command was as assistant section commander in a reserve battalion located in Yefremov, duties involving the 'struggle against kulak-ism and banditry'. In October 1919 he moved to command of a battalion with the Second Tula Rifle Division, subsequently designated Forty-eighth Rifle Division, moving in 1920 to the Eleventh Petrograd Rifle Division (15th Army), taking part in the Soviet-Polish War. For ten years (1921–31), Vasilevsky served as a regimental commander with the Forty-eighth Division, earning a good reputation as a staff officer and for troop training. In May 1931 he was transferred to the Red Army's Combat Training Administration and

accepted as a candidate member of the party in August.

Deeply involved with drawing up regulations for staff work and directives for 'operations in depth', in 1934 Vasilevsky was posted to the Volga Military District as chief of combat training, only to be summoned to Moscow in 1936 to join the first intake to the newly established General Staff Academy. After graduation in 1937 he was posted to the General Staff and in 1938 became a full party member. In May 1940 Vasilevsky was Deputy Chief of the General Staff Operational Directorate, working on Soviet deployment on the northern, northwestern and western axes, plans in which Stalin evidently interfered peremptorily, shifting Soviet strength southwards.

During the war Stalin turned the General Staff into his own work-horse. In August 1941, with Zhukov released from the General Staff, Vasilevsky took over the Operations Directorate, supplying information to the *Stavka* (GHQ) and drafting operational directives. With Shaposhnikov fallen ill in November 1941, Vasilevsky took over the General Staff, formally confirmed as chief in May 1942. But Stalin wanted his men at the front as '*Stavka* coordinators', of which Vasilevsky, acting with Zhukov, became one of the most senior. Between them Zhukov and Vasilevsky planned and coordinated the Stalingrad counteroffensive. The same pattern was repeated at Kursk in 1943, followed by the striking success in the huge Belorussian operations of 1944. In the autumn of 1944 Stalin charged Vasilevsky with the planning for a Soviet offensive in the Far East against the Japanese, but in February 1945 on the death of Chernyakhovsky, Vasilevsky took over his Front command and completed the reduction of Königsberg. Finally made a member of the *Stavka*, Vasilevsky proceeded in June 1945 to the Far East as Commander-in-Chief of Soviet forces ranged against the Japanese Kwantung Army, destroyed in the lightning Manchurian campaign launched on 9 August 1945.

Continuing as Chief of the General Staff after the war, Vasilevsky supervised the postwar re-organization of the Soviet forces, becoming First Deputy Armed Forces Minister in November 1948 and War Minister from March 1949 to March 1953, followed by service as First Deputy Defence Minister (1953–56) and latterly, charged with responsibility for 'military science' (1956–57). In January 1959, reportedly disenchanted with Khrushchev's 'strategic new look', Vasilevsky retired to the Inspectorate, holding his peace for many years. He received his Marshal's star in 1943 and was twice decorated a Hero of the Soviet Union in 1944 and in 1945, honours as well deserved as any. JE

VASNETSOV, Yuriy Alekseevich (1900–1973) Graphic designer. Vasnetsov was born in Vyatka. He graduated from the Leningrad Vkhutein in 1927 before joining Detgiz (Children's Publishing House) as an illustrator. Influenced by the work of Lebedev, Vasnetsov also paid homage to the Russian *lubok* (popular print) and to the folklore of the Russian fair as in his picture *Rainbow-Bow* (1969). JEB

VAVILOV, Nikolay Ivanovich (1887–1943) A plant breeder, scientific administrator, and the Soviet Union's most celebrated geneticist. After his graduation from the Moscow Agricultural Institute in 1911, where he studied with D. N. Pryanishnikov, Vavilov studied plant immunity in England, where he came into contact with William Bateson and R. C. Punnett, two of the founders of genetics. After the revolution he served as professor at Saratov University (1917–21), where he came to public attention for his 'law of homologous series of variations' in closely allied plant species. Touted as the 'Mendeleev of biology' he came to Lenin's attention during the famine for his ambitious proposals for transforming agriculture through scientific plant-breeding.

Following Regel's death, Vavilov transformed his Bureau of Applied Plant-Breeding into the Institute of Applied Botany and New Cultures and became its director (1924–40) (it was renamed the All-Union Institute of Plant-Breeding [VIR] in 1930). There, he set forth a theory of the centres of origin of cultivated plants (1926) and personally led dozens of expeditions throughout the world to collect seeds from these centres for use in selection.

During the first Five-Year Plan, which involved the collectivization of Soviet agriculture, Vavilov rose rapidly in prominence and power. In 1929 he became a member of the Central Executive Committee of Russia (and then of the USSR), the USSR Academy of Sciences, the Ukrainian Academy of Sciences, and the new Lenin All-Union Academy of Agricultural Sciences (VASKhNIL), which he founded and headed (1929–35). In 1930 he became director of the Academy of Sciences laboratory of genetics, transforming it into the Institute of Genetics (IGEN) in 1933, which he directed until 1940.

From 1929 Vavilov helped bring to

prominence the Ukrainian plant breeder, T. D. Lysenko, whose technique of 'vernalization' purported to change permanently the germination time of crops in order to permit extra plantings and harvests. In 1935 Lysenko's attack on genetics as a bourgeois, capitalist, idealist science useless to agriculture led to Vavilov's demotion to vice-president of VASKhNIL and Lysenko's eventual assumption of the presidency. Lysenkoists were able to harass Vavilov and his supporters with the help of the secret police and the party apparatus, but Vavilov sought accommodation until 1939, when he openly broke with Lysenko.

On 6 August 1940 (after the signing of the Nazi-Soviet Pact), Vavilov was arrested while on a collecting expedition in the newly acquired (formerly Polish) Western Ukrainian territory, and shortly thereafter a number of his closest collaborators, including G. D. Karpechenko and S. G. Levitsky, were also arrested. On 9 July 1941 he was found guilty of being a British spy, maintaining links with émigrés, and sabotaging Soviet agriculture. His death sentence was commuted, but he died of malnutrition in a Saratov prison on 26 January 1943. In 1955 he was posthumously rehabilitated and in recent years has been portrayed heroically in Soviet publications. MBA

VAYNONEN, Vasiliy Ivanovich (1901–1964) Choreographer. Vaynonen studied under Vladimir Ponomarev and graduated from the Petrograd Choreographic School in 1919. He was a dancer and then choreographer at the Kirov Theatre from 1919 to 1938. As a dancer he particularly excelled in character roles.

Vaynonen's early choreography was influenced by the experimental work being done in the 1920s, including his participation in the Young Ballet (*Molodoy balet*), founded by George Balanchine in 1921. He later became expert in character and national dances, and incorporated all these elements into his own choreography. His major works included participation in the 1930 production of Dmitry Shostakovich's *The Golden Age*; *The Flames of Paris* (1932), a ballet that established the treatment of heroic, patriotic themes in Soviet choreography; and *Partisan Days* (1937), based on the Russian Civil War.

Vaynonen restaged a number of classical ballets. His version of *The Nutcracker* (1934) became a standard interpretation of the work and he created new versions of *Raymonda* (1938), *Harlequinade* (1945), and *Sleeping Beauty* (1952).

Vaynonen worked as a choreographer for Konstantin Stanislavsky's theatre (1939), at the Bol'shoy Theatre (1946–50, 1954–58), at the Novosibirsk Theatre of Opera and Ballet (1952–53), and in Budapest (1950–51), where he assisted with the development of the Hungarian Ballet and staged both *The Flames of Paris* and *The Nutcracker*.

He was awarded the State Prize of the USSR for both his staging of *The Flames of Paris* and for the interludes of Czech dances in Smetana's *The Bartered Bride* (1948). SCS

VEDERNIKOV, Aleksandr Filippovich (b. 1927) Bass. Vedernikov was born in the village of Mokino. He graduated from the Moscow Conservatory in 1955, and in 1956 he won both the International Schumann Competition in Berlin and the All-Union Contest for the performance of works by Soviet composers. He was a soloist with the Leningrad Kirov

Theatre (1955–58), after which he was transferred to the Moscow Bol'shoy. In 1961 he undertook further training at La Scala, Milan. A member of the party since 1964, he was made a People's Artist of the RSFSR in 1967. The possessor of a deep, mellow voice, he has toured abroad and made a number of recordings. GS

VELIKHOV, Yevgeniy Pavlovich (b. 1935) One of the leading scientists in the contemporary Soviet Union and an influential scientific adviser to the Gorbachev leadership, Velikhov has been a full Academician since 1974, Vice-President of the Academy of Sciences since 1977 and Director of the Kurchatov Institute of Atomic Energy since 1988. He came particularly into the public eye following the Chernobyl' disaster when he was exposed to high levels of radioactivity during a month he spent in the Chernobyl' area investigating the causes and consequences of the accident at that nuclear power station.

An outstanding nuclear physicist who graduated from Moscow University (and also taught there from 1966), Velikhov was already acting as a scientific adviser to Mikhail Gorbachev before the latter became General Secretary. (He accompanied Gorbachev, for example, on his visit to Britain in December 1984.) He has since been a highly important adviser to the Soviet leadership on a broad range of technical matters, including all issues relating to nuclear power, among them the area of strategic weapons and arms control. He has also had special responsibility within the Academy of Sciences for overcoming the Soviet scientific lag in computers and cybernetics.

As early as 1971 (the year in which he joined the Communist Party) Veli-

khov became Director of one of the affiliated institutes of the Kurchatov Institute of Atomic Energy which he now heads. Under Gorbachev he became a candidate member of the Central Committee of the Communist Party (1986–89) and a full member from 1989 to 1990.

Velikhov has been an active public figure in the Soviet Union and one with broad international contacts. He is a co-founder of the International Foundation for the Survival and Development of Humanity, an independent organization with offices in Moscow, Stockholm and Washington which included within its ranks Academician Andrey Sakharov and which also involves prominent Western figures. AHB

VERCHENKO, Yuriy N. A career party official, Verchenko rose through the apparatus of the Komsomol and eventually headed its publishing house, *Molodaya gvardiya*; he then became a secretary of the Moscow City Party committee. In 1970 he became organizational secretary of the Union of Writers, and was confirmed in this post at the Congresses of 1976, 1981, and 1986. He is commonly regarded as the most powerful of all literary officials; his post is probably on the *nomenklatura* of the KGB. GSS

VERESAEV (pseudonym of Smidovich, Vikentiy Vikentievich), (1867–1945) Physician and writer. Veresaev combined his two professions in his *Notes of a Physician* (1901), whose horrific realism goes beyond any prose fiction in Russian. Beginning in 1910 he also wrote literary criticism, the best being the collections *Pushkin in Life* (1926–27) and *Gogol' in Life* (1933). BH

VEREYSKY, Georgiy Semenich
(1886–1962) Graphic designer. Born
in Proskurov, Vereysky studied in
Khar'kov, St Petersburg and Western
Europe before the Revolution, making
his artistic début as an illustrator of
magazines such as *Teatr i iskusstvo*
(Theatre and Art). Chief Curator of
Engravings at the Hermitage from
1918 until 1930, he became known for
his portraits of contemporary writers
and artists such as Alexandre Benois
and Samuil Marshak. JEB

VERNADSKY, Vladimir Ivanovich
(1863–1945) Geochemist, philosopher, administrator. A remarkable
synthetic thinker and an energetic
scientific entrepreneur, Vernadsky
began his career as a mineralogist.
After his graduation from Petersburg
University in 1885, he worked in its
Mineralogical Museum (1886–88)
and studied abroad (1889–90),
writing his master's degree on alumina
in silicates (1891) and his doctorate
on gliding in crystals (1897). A *privat-
dotsent* at Moscow University from
1890, he became its professor of mineralogy and crystallography in 1898.
He was elected a corresponding
member of the Academy of Sciences
in 1908, moved to Petersburg in 1911,
and became a full member of the
Academy in 1912 and director of its
Geological and Mineralogical
Museum in 1914.

In Petersburg he worked actively to
modernize the Academy and increase
its involvement in national development and, after the start of the First
World War, organized the Academy's
Commission for the Study of Natural
Productive Forces (KEPS), serving as
its president (1915–30). During the
troubled years 1917 to 1921 he worked
in the Ukraine where he helped
organize the Ukrainian Academy of
Sciences, served as its first president
(1919–21), and created its Chemical
Laboratory, and also in the Crimea
where he became rector of Tauride
University. After spending four years
in Paris and Prague he returned to
Leningrad in 1926, and subsequently
organized and directed a number of
institutions for the USSR Academy of
Sciences, notably its Biogeochemical
Laboratory (1929–45).

His entrepreneurial activities were
closely associated with the evolution
of his scientific work, which laid the
foundations for modern geochemistry.
His analysis of the chemical elements
of the earth's crust led him to distinguish three thermodynamic zones –
weathering (low temperature and
pressure), metamorphic (moderate
temperature, high pressure), and
magmatizing (high temperature and
pressure) – and six categories of
elements (noble gases, noble metals,
'scattered' elements, rare earths,
radioactive elements, and 'cycling'
elements) based on their role in earth
history, with 'cycling' elements (for
example, carbon, nitrogen, and
oxygen) constituting more than 99%
of the crust. He increasingly emphasized the role of living things in cycling
these elements, processing solar
energy, and shaping the earth's crust,
which he classified into a series of
layers, several of which (granite, sedi-
mentary) he understood as the
product of the layer he called 'the bio-
sphere' (1926).

Radiactive elements also attracted
his special attention. From 1910 he
was active on the Radium Commission and began a systematic search
for radioactive minerals, undertaking
their laboratory study. In 1921 he
organized the State Radium Institute
and served as its director (1921–39),

noting in 1922 that 'we are approaching the great revolution in the life of humanity' when 'man will take control of atomic energy'. In the 1930s he organized and headed various related commissions, including those on heavy water (1934) and isotopes (1939). From 1928 he orchestrated resistance to the Bolshevization of the Academy of Sciences and strongly opposed the purge trials, Stalinism, and Lysenkoism. He may have been spared repression by his powerful students and his involvement in the Soviet bomb project. In recent years he has been lionized in Soviet literature as a scientific and ethical model.

MBA

VERSHININ, Konstantin Andreevich (1900–1973) Former Commander-in-Chief Soviet Air Force. Vershinin played a large role in the evolution of the post-war Soviet Air Force. During the Second World War he commanded the Soviet Air Force on the North Caucasian Front and then the Fourth Air Army. Air operations in the Northern Caucasus, Taman', the Crimea and East Prussia came under his direction. He was appointed Commander-in-Chief of the Soviet Air Force, and Deputy Minister of Defence for the period 1946 to 1949. In the early Cold War years the Soviet Union was vulnerable to strategic air attack and the rapid development of an effective anti-aircraft system became a priority. Vershinin was assigned the key position of commander of the frontier anti-aircraft formation and commander of frontier anti-aircraft defence (1950–53). He was promoted to commander of the Soviet Anti-aircraft Defence Forces (1953–54). In 1957 he regained overall charge of the Soviet Air Force, with the rank of Air Chief Marshal

and became a deputy Minister of Defence. He held this position until 1969. In this period Vershinin developed new operational concepts.

RA

VERTOV, Dziga (pseudonym of Kaufman, Denis Arkad'evich) (1896–1954) Leading Soviet documentary film-maker and the guiding spirit of the Cine-Eye group. Vertov began his film career making newsreels for the Moscow Cinema Committee under the title *Kino-nedelya* (Cine-Week). He also filmed on the agit-trains in the Civil War period and some of the footage was used in his first full-length films *The Anniversary of the Revolution* and *The Battle of Tsaritsyn* (both 1920). Vertov's theory of documentary film-making was first enunciated in the August 1922 manifesto 'We. A Version of a Manifesto' and developed the following year in 'The Cine-Eyes. A Revolution'. These proclaimed that 'the future of cinema lies in the rejection of its present' and argued that 'the cinema eye is more perfect than the human eye' and therefore that cinema was capable of creating a more perfect reality. This new reality was to be realized in the next newsreel series, called *Kinopravda* (Cinema Truth) in a play on the title of the party newspaper. Working with his brother Mikhail Kaufman and his wife Yelizaveta Svilova, Vertov produced a series of stunning full-length documentaries intended to portray 'life caught unawares': *Forward, Soviet!* and *A Sixth Part of the World* (both 1926), *The Eleventh Year* (1928), *The Man with the Movie Camera* (1929) and a series of innovative sound films including: *Enthusiasm* (also known as *The Donbass Symphony*) (1930), *Three Songs of Lenin* (1934) and *The Lullaby* (1937). Vertov's attempts to create a new filmic non-linear narrative form led him to experiments that were all too vulnerable in the rigidifying artistic climate to accusations of formalism and his brilliant career was eclipsed. He ended his life as editor of the newsreel *Novosti dnya* (News of the Day). RT

VESNIN, Aleksandr Aleksandrovich (1883–1959) Painter, architect, and designer. Born in Yur'evets, the most famous of three brothers, all of them architects (**Viktor** [1882–1950]; **Leonid** [1880–1933]), Aleksandr Vesnin studied at the Institute of Civil Engineers in St Petersburg (1903–12). Influenced by Tatlin he supported the conviction, declared at the '5 × 5 = 25' exhibition, that art should be utilitarian. He worked as stage designer, for example, for Aleksandr Tairov's production of *The Man Who Was Thursday* (1923), but gained his real reputation as a Constructivist architect exemplified by his project for the *Leningrad Pravda* building in Moscow (1923–24). He was a member of OSA and co-editor of *Sovremennaya arkhitektura* (Contemporary Architecture) (1926–30). JEB

VEZIROV, Abdul-Rakhman Khalil ogly (b. 1930) An Azeri Komsomol and party official, Vezirov was First Secretary of the Azerbaydzhan Komsomol (1957–60), Secretary of the All-Union Komsomol in Moscow (1960–70), and First Secretary of Kirovabad *gorkom* (1970–75). Demoted to the position of Soviet Consul-General in Calcutta, he went on to be ambassador to Nepal and Pakistan (1979–85). As with Nishanov and Väljas, such absence from domestic politics stood Vezirov initally in good stead: once the troubles in the Nagorno-Karabakh region had discredited the previous leadership, he was summoned to take over the position of First Secretary of the Azerbaydzhan Communist Party. But Vezirov was himself deposed and replaced by A. N. Mutalibov in January 1990. JHM

VIGDOROVA, Frida Abramovna (1915–1965) Prose writer and journalist, born near Mogilev, and educated in Moscow. Vigdorova wrote stories on pedagogical and educational themes, and founded an important *samizdat* genre by bravely recording the trial of Joseph Brodsky in 1964. GSS

VIKULOV, Sergey Vasil'evich (b. 1922) Poet, literary official, and editor, born and brought up near Vologda in a peasant family. Vikulov fought in the Second World War, and joined the Party in 1942. He published lyric verse exclusively on rural themes. In the late 1960s he moved to Moscow, and has since played a prominent part in official literary life, serving on the Presidium of the Union of Writers and other bodies. He became chief editor of the journal *Nash sovremennik* in 1968 and held this post during its emergence as the most dedicated mouthpiece for Russian nationalist sentiments; he handed over to S. Kunyaev late in 1989, retaining his seat on the editorial board. GSS

VIL'YAMS, Petr Vladimirovich (1902–1947) Painter and designer. Vil'yams was born in Moscow. Influenced by Shterenberg, he studied at Vkhutemas (1918–23) and was a member of OST (1925–30). Thereafter he made his name as a stage designer, creating fanciful sets and costumes for many productions at the Moscow Arts Theatre, the Vakhtangov Theatre, the Bol'shoy and other theatres. JEB

VIL'YAMS, Vasiliy Robertovich
(1863–1939) Agronomist, soil scientist. An 1887 graduate of the Petrov Academy, Vil'yams became head of the department of general agronomy and soil science of the Moscow Agricultural Academy in 1894 and remained in that post for the rest of his life. In a series of works (1914–24) he investigated the formation of soils as a process involving the interaction of organic and inorganic components. A convert to Bolshevism at the age of sixty-five, Vil'yams joined the party in 1928 and rapidly rose to prominence during the collectivization of agriculture. He was elected to the Belorussian Academy of Sciences (1929), the USSR Academy of Sciences (1931), and the Lenin All-Union Academy of Agricultural Sciences (1935). In the late 1930s his theories, which emphasized relatively inexpensive techniques and natural fertilizers, won strong political support. He also advocated the universal use of his 'grasslands system' of planting and crop rotation, which was imposed on Soviet agriculture by the government and party with much Stakhanovite enthusiasm and ideological fanfare and remained a source of major controversy through the 1960s. MBA

VINOGRADOV, Oleg Mikhaylovich
(b. 1937) Dancer and outstanding choreographer. A student of Aleksandr Pushkin, Vinogradov graduated from Leningrad Ballet School in 1958. After graduation he joined the troupe of the Novosibirsk Theatre of Opera and Ballet, where he particularly excelled in character parts. From 1963 he also served as assistant choreographer.

Vinogradov then served as choreographer of the Kirov Ballet (1967–72),
as chief choreographer at the Malyy Opera and Ballet Theatre (1973–77), and as artistic director and chief choreographer of the Kirov Ballet (1977–). His ballets have included a broad spectrum of classical and modern works, many of them set to music by Soviet composers. They have been staged throughout the Soviet Union and abroad.

His major ballets have included: *Cinderella* (1964) and *Romeo and Juliet* (1965), with scores by Prokof'iev; *Asel* (1967), with a score by Vladimir Vlasov; a new version of *Aleksandr Nevsky* (1969); a new version of *Coppélia* (1973); *Yaroslavna* (1974), for which he was also librettist and designer; *A Hussar Ballad* (1979), with a score by Tikhon Khrennikov; *The Inspector General* (1980); and *Behests of the Past* (1983). In 1989 the Kirov returned to New York, after an absence of twenty-five years, and presented Vinogradov's *The Battleship 'Potemkin'*. Vinogradov has received numerous awards, including a State Prize (1970) and the Marius Petipa award (1979). SCS

VINOGRADOV, Viktor Vladimirovich (1895–1969) A literary scholar and linguist influenced by Saussure and de Courtenay, he was on the periphery of the Formalists in the twenties. His literary studies comprise largely stylistic analyses of particular authors (notably of Akhmatova, Gogol', Dostoevsky and Pushkin); in his 1923 study of Avvakum's autobiography, he demonstrates how language level is a function of genre. The bulk of his works are devoted to the history and structure of the Russian language and linguistics; he worked on Ushakov's *Interpretative Dictionary*, won a State Prize for his 1947 *The Russian Language*, edited the journal

Questions of Language Study from 1952, and directed work on the Pushkin dictionary. KC

VINOKUROV, Yevgeniy Mikhaylovich (b. 1925) Poet, born in Bryansk, educated in Moscow. He fought in the Second World War, and joined the party in 1952. He represents the 'chamber' tradition in Soviet lyric poetry as opposed to the dominant public declamatory tradition; his work is stylistically restrained and pure. GSS

VINS, Georgiy Petrovich (b. 1928) Secretary of the Council of Evangelical Christian-Baptist Churches, the unregistered Baptist movement in the USSR, from its formation in 1965 until his deportation to America in 1979. He is the son of a Baptist minister who died in a labour camp in 1941. Vins was one of the leaders of the opposition within the Baptist churches to restrictions accepted under state pressure in 1960. He was imprisoned (1966–69 and 1974–79) and was a key organizer of the independent Baptist Council and of clandestine printing presses for religious literature. Since 1979 he has been the Council's overseas representative. MR

VINT, Toomas Endelevich (b. 1944) Graphic artist and painter. Born in Tallin and a graduate of the State Art Institute there, Vint is commonly recognized as a leading contemporary artist in the Baltic states. His work, mainly landscapes, evinces a strong predilection for Art Deco as in *Veresk* (1972). JEB

VIRSALADZE, Simon Bagratovich (b. 1909) Designer. Born in Tiflis, Virsaladze, one of the Soviet Union's leading stage designers, studied in Tiflis, Leningrad and Moscow in the 1920s, acknowledging a particular debt to the method of his teacher Mikhail Bobyshev. He worked for the Bol'shoy (1937–41 and 1945–63) before joining the Georgian Theatre of Opera and Ballet in Tbilisi as chief designer for various productions, such as *Wilhelm Tell* and *Don Juan*. Bright colours, freedom of expression and references to Georgian folk art distinguish his resolutions. JEB

VISHNEVSKAYA, Galina Pavlovna (b. 1926) Soprano. Vishnevskaya was born in Leningrad. After a tumultuous childhood, she studied under Vera Garina in the town of her birth, singing first in operetta (1944), then with the Leningrad Philharmonic Organization. From 1952 she was a leading soloist with the Moscow Bol'shoy and toured regularly abroad. In 1955 she married Mstislav Rostropovich. The soprano part of Britten's *War Requiem* was written specially for her, though she was not permitted by the Soviet authorities to sing at the première in Coventry, while Britten also dedicated to her the song cycle *The Poet's Echo* (to words by Pushkin). Shostakovich's Seven Romances, Op. 127, were likewise dedicated to her. She was made a People's Artist of the USSR in 1966. In 1974 she and her husband left Russia and in 1978 were both deprived of their Soviet citizenship. A superlative performer, her memoirs (*Galina*, London, 1984) are a *sine qua non* for all concerned with Russian and Soviet culture. GS

VISHNEVSKY, Vsevolod Vital'evich (1900–1951) Dramatist, prose writer and journalist. Having volunteered for the front aged fourteen, Vishnevsky went on to pursue a model career as a communist, participating in the Revolution and in every major military event of his lifetime. He claimed to be the military's representative in literature. His major plays, always mass spectacles, include *An Optimistic Tragedy* (1933) about a woman commissar suppressing anarchism in the navy, and *Unforgettable 1919* (1949), an adulatory portrayal of Stalin. In 1933 he was involved improbably in a polemic championing James Joyce. A party member since 1937, he edited the journal *The Banner* from 1944. JAEC

VLADIMIRSKY, Mikhail Fedorovich (1874–1951) An old Bolshevik leader with a wide range of responsibilities. His party membership dated from 1895. A medical student at Tomsk and Moscow Universities, Vladimirsky was exiled in 1896, and emigrated to Germany where he qualified as a doctor. Active in the Moscow uprising in 1905, he was arrested in 1906 and again emigrated – this time to France. He held various posts in the party and government in the Ukraine after the Bolshevik revolution. He was People's Commissar for Health of the RSFSR (1930–34). He served as chairman of the Central Revision Commission of the party from 1927 to 1951, a record period, if one excludes Stalin, for holding a single party post in those years. RWD

VLADIMOV, Georgiy Nikolaevich (real surname: Volosevich) (b. 1931) Literary critic and novelist, whose portraits of working-class life, *The Great Ore* (1961), and *Three Minutes of Silence* (1969) were too frank for the authorities. *Faithful Ruslan*, written 1963–65, circulated in *samizdat* for years before appearing in the West in 1975: it epitomizes the tragedy of the labour camps from the viewpoint of a guard-dog. In 1967 he wrote a personal letter to the Fourth Writers' Union Congress supporting Solzhenitsyn and demanding the abolition of the censorship. In 1977 he

resigned from the Writers' Union, calling it a 'police checkpoint'. He emigrated to West Germany in 1983, and became chief editor of *Grani* (1983–86). GAH

VLASOV, Aleksandr Vladimirovich (b. 1932) Of the Soviet leadership in the late 1980s Vlasov has perhaps the most experience of Soviet ethnic and geographical variety. Born in the Buryat ASSR on the south shore of Lake Baykal, his career was in Eastern Siberia until he was forty. He graduated from the Irkutsk Mining-Metallurgical Institute in 1954, and was engaged in Komsomol and party work in Irkutsk oblast', before becoming second secretary of the Yakut *obkom* from 1965 to 1972. Three years in the Central Committee apparatus in Moscow prepared him for a very different and testing post – that of First Secretary of the Chechen-Ingush *obkom* in the Caucasus, which he held from 1975 to 1984. Vlasov was then First Secretary of the important Rostov *obkom* (1984–86), USSR Minister of Internal Affairs (1986–88) and in October 1988 was named Chairman of the RSFSR Council of Ministers and Candidate Member of the Politburo. JHM

VLASOV, Andrey Andreevich (1900–1946) Russian general. Long the subject of heated debate among western scholars, the career and motives of Andrey Vlasov have recently become the subject of scholarly disputes inside the Soviet Union as well. Entering the Red Army as a private in 1918, Vlasov rose rapidly to the rank of general. After the German invasion, he distinguished himself in the defence of Kiev and during the battle of Moscow his counter-offensive gave the Soviets their first major victory of the war. From Moscow he was sent to the Volkhov front where he was captured in July 1942 following the decimation of his Second Assault Army by the Germans. Shortly thereafter Vlasov emerged as the leader of a Russian anti-communist movement dedicated to the overthrow of Stalin. Although anxious to use him for propaganda purposes, the German authorities did not allow Vlasov's movement to develop. His efforts to establish its independence foundered on German opposition. Radical Nazis opposed any support for the *Vlasovtsy* whatsoever, while Rosenberg's protégés feared that the Vlasov movement would complicate their plans to make use of non-Russian Soviet nationalities. Even those Germans sympathetic to Vlasov had in mind goals very different to his own. Vlasov had no authority over Russian units serving with the Wehrmacht until November 1944, when a 'Committee for the Liberation of the Peoples of Russia' was formed with him at its head. He was authorized to form two divisions from various Russian battalions in the German army and took command of these units from January 1945. The following May, Vlasov surrendered to the Americans, who handed him over to the Soviet authorities. He was tried and hanged in August 1946 along with eleven of his aides.

In the Soviet Union, Vlasov has until recently been dismissed as a traitorous opportunist. Now, however, some Soviet historians are beginning to re-evaluate his motives, both personal and political. WJT

VLASOV, Yuriy Petrovich (b. 1935) Weightlifter. He is that interesting phenomenon – an artistic and political strongman. From being the world heavyweight weightlifting champion, he became a professional writer of some ten books and then outspoken Deputy in the first Congress of people's Deputies. Born in Makeevka, Ukraine, he was sent to the Suvorov Cadet School in Saratov at the age of ten and subsequently entered the Zhukovsky Aircraft Engineering Academy from which he graduated in 1959. Initially a shot putter, he switched to weightlifting and won the gold medal in the 1960 Rome Olympics where he was the first man to break the 200 kg barrier in the snatch, and to surpass the long-standing record set by the American Paul Anderson with a combined total of 537.5 kg. Proclaimed Victor Ludorum of the Rome Olympics, he later won a silver medal at the Tokyo 1964 Olympics, placed second to his Soviet rival Zhabotinsky.

Shortly after, he retired from weightlifting having been four times world, five times national and six times European champion in the heavyweight division, and setting twenty-eight world records. He was a long-standing critic of (drug-induced) 'super-heavyweights'; his own heaviest competition weight was 136 kg (i.e. some thirty kgs less than Zhabotinsky and thirty-four kg less than Paul Anderson). He was one of the first Soviet sportsmen openly to reveal how rife the taking of anabolic steroids was among Soviet weightlifters. His literary work was initially influenced by Hemingway (*Conquering Oneself*, 1964; *White Instant*, 1972; *Salty Joys* 1976), but then more by Bulgakov, and Gogol' and Dostoevsky. In his maiden speech as a deputy in the new parliament in June 1989, he made a bold and emotional attack on the KGB, calling for the removal of its headquarters from Moscow's city centre. JWR

VOINOVICH, V.N., *see* **VOYNO-VICH, V.N.**

VOLKONSKY, Andrey Mikhaylovich (b. 1933) Composer and harpsichordist. Volkonsky was born in Geneva. Of princely origin, he studied piano with Dinu Lipatti in Geneva and composition under Nadia Boulanger in Paris. In 1947 he went to Russia, entering the Moscow Conservatory in 1950 as a pupil of Shaporin, leaving in 1954. In 1955, together with Rudol'f Barshay, he founded the Moscow Chamber Orchestra, followed in 1964 by the ensemble *Madrigal* a unique group specialising in early music. His increasing enthusiasm for serialism and avant-garde Western music, together with criticism of the status quo, led to his expulsion from the Union of Soviet Composers and he emigrated in 1973. GS

VOLOSHIN, Maksimilyan Aleksandrovich (1878–1932) Poet and painter. He lived mainly in Paris before 1917, publishing poetry and essays in the Russian Symbolist journals, then settled finally in the Crimea, where he survived the Civil War and created one of its greatest literary monuments, *Poems on the Terror*, published abroad in 1923. His house at Koktebel has become a resort for writers. GSS

VOL'SKY, Arkadiy Ivanovich (b. 1932) An engineer from the ZIL car factory, Moscow, who became a nationalities administrator. Vol'sky moved into the Central Committee Department of Machine Building in 1969, and was appointed one of its deputy heads (1977–81), and First Deputy Head (1981–83). For the next two years he was assistant to General Secretaries Andropov and Chernenko, returning to head the Machine Building Department from 1985 to 1988.

In July 1988 Vol'sky was sent as a plenipotentiary of the Central Committee and the Supreme Soviet to the restless Nagorno-Karabakh Autonomous *Oblast'* and for most of 1989 was head of a Committee of Special Administration implementing Moscow's direct rule in that territory. JHM

VOROBEV, Arkadiy Nikitich (b. 1924) Weightlifter. He has gone down in world weightlifting as not only the greatest middle-heavyweight in the sport's history, but also as the author of several authoritative books on the sport, a successful national coach and an eminent medical specialist. Born in the village of Mordovo in the Tambov Region, he combined sports training with study, first in coaching, then in sports medicine, graduating from the Sverdlovsk Medical Institute. He competed in three Olympics (1952–60), winning a bronze medal in the light-heavyweight category at the 1952 Helsinki Olympics, and winning gold in the middle-heavyweight division in the 1956 Olympics with a world record of 462.5 kg for the three events, then bettering it at the 1960 Olympics. He was the first Soviet middleweight to win the world championships, which he won five times, and was five times European and ten times Soviet champion, setting a number of world records. Upon retirement from competition in 1960, he became senior coach of the Soviet weightlifting team. His most authoritative book was *Modern Weightlifting Training*, published in 1964. In the early 1970s he turned to sports medicine, becoming Doctor of Medical Sciences, then Professor and eventually, in 1977, Rector of the Moscow Region Physical Culture Institute. JWR

VORONAEV, Ivan Yefimovich (né Cherkasov, Nikolay Petrovich) (1886–c. 1940) Founder of the main Pentecostal church in the Soviet Union. He was a Baptist preacher in Siberia and Manchuria before emigrating in 1912 to America, where he became a Pentecostal. He went to Odessa in 1921, via Bulgaria, where he began the Pentecostal movement. An able preacher and organizer he founded many churches and established an Odessa regional Pentecostal Union in 1924, a Ukrainian Union in 1926 and an All-Union Union in 1927 before being arrested in 1930. After a few months of freedom in 1936 he was rearrested and disappeared without a trace. He is rumoured to have died after camp guard dogs were let loose on him. MR

VORONOV, Gennadiy Ivanovich (b. 1910) The son of a village schoolteacher, Voronov joined the Communist Party in 1931 and after receiving a technical education made a career in the party apparatus. Following a series of party appointments from 1937 to 1955 he became a deputy minister of agriculture of the USSR in 1955, but in 1957 returned to party work as First Secretary of the Orenburg *obkom*. From 1961 he was First Deputy Chairman of the Central Committee Bureau for the RSFSR, a post he held until the bureau's abolition at Brezhnev's instigation in 1966. From 1961 until 1973 Voronov was a member of the top leadership team in the party – as a full member of the Politburo. He was more disposed towards serious agricultural reform than was Brezhnev and in general his relations with Khrushchev's successor were cool. When Brezhnev strengthened his position within the leadership in the early 1970s, he removed Voronov from the Politburo (along with Petro Shelest) in April 1973. AHB

VORONSKY, Aleksandr Konstantinovich (1884–1943) In the twenties a leading figure in literary politics as an editor, critic and theorist. Voronsky came from a family of Tambov priests but joined the Bolsheviks in 1904, and began publishing criticism in the party press in 1911. In 1921 he was recalled by Lenin from Ivanovo-Voznesensk, where he ran a provincial newspaper, to edit the first major Soviet literary journal, *Red Virgin Soil*, which attracted to its pages many prominent fellow-traveller writers, and played a highly formative role in the development of Soviet literature. Voronsky was in the mid-twenties the single most powerful figure in Soviet literature; *inter alia*, he headed the Circle publishing house, co-edited the popular journal *The Searchlight*, and served as mentor to the centrist literary group Pereval. However, as chief patron of Fellow Travellers, he and his ventures became prime targets of attack from self-styled proletarian militants. In 1927 he fell victim to the anti-Trotsky campaign and was dismissed as editor of *Red Virgin Soil*. Although he was spared arrest until 1937, his career was essentially over. He was rehabilitated in the fifties, and a scholarly edition of selected writings was published in 1987. Voronsky is also known for his critical articles and theoretical works of the twenties published in the collections *Art and Life* (1924), *Literary Types* (1926) and *The Art of Perceiving the World* (1928). His theory of literature, which was heavily indebted to Plekhanov, centres around art's task of conveying objective beauty by means of 'immediate impressions'. KC

VOROSHILOV, Kliment Yefremovich (1881–1969) Former Commissar of Defence and Chairman of the Presidium of the Supreme Soviet. Voroshilov, of worker origin, was an underground Bolshevik from 1903 and an active leader in the revolutionary movement. He took part in the 1905 and 1917 revolutions and assisted in the organization of the Cheka. When Stalin was sent to the Tsaritsyn Front in 1918 he chose Voroshilov as his military specialist commander and the close association between the two men dates from that period. Both Stalin and Voroshilov regarded the military specialists supported by Trotsky as counter-revolutionary and had them arrested or sent back to Moscow. Although Voroshilov had no military experience he became one of the senior commanders in the Civil War. Subsequently, as commander of the North Caucasian, then Moscow military districts (1921–25), Voroshilov sided against Trotsky in the debate over the military doctrine of the Red Army. He was appointed as Chairman of the Revolutionary Military Council, and with Stalin's backing in 1925 replaced Frunze as People's Commissar of Military and Naval Affairs. Voroshilov held this post (which became Commissar of Defence) until 1940 and gained the rank of Marshal of the Soviet Union, but appeared to absorb little in these years at the Commissariat. Although he was shrewd he had no head for detail or expert military knowledge. The onus of decision on central military issues, moreover, did not rest with him, but with Stalin.

Stalin's patronage ensured that Voroshilov survived the purges and remained in the high command during the war years. He became Deputy Chairman, then Chairman of the Defence Council of the USSR Council of People's Commissars (1940–41); Commander-in-Chief of the North-western Strategic Sector, then Commander of the Leningrad Army Group (1941). Throughout the war he remained a member of the State Defence Committee and he acted as Supreme Headquarters representative on the Leningrad and Volkhov Fronts. Voroshilov displayed no special talent in these senior posts. He attended the Teheran Conference in 1943. After the war he was made head of the Soviet Control Commission in Hungary (1945–47), a significant political post, and became Deputy Chairman of the Council of Ministers (1946–53). In this period Stalin was suspicious even of Voroshilov; he toyed with the idea that Voroshilov was 'an English spy'. Stalin's death removed this danger and Voroshilov became Chairman of the Presidium of the Supreme Soviet (1953–60). He was a member of the Politburo then Presidium of the CPSU Central Committee (1926–60). Denounced by Khrushchev in 1961 for his alleged sympathy with the 'anti-party group' he was stripped of all his official positions. RA

VOROTNIKOV, Vitaliy Ivanovich (b. 1926) A prominent Soviet politician and full member of the Politburo from 1983 to 1990, Vorotnikov was born in Voronezh and began his working career as an apprentice fitter in 1942. He joined the Communist Party in 1947 and rose through a series of supervisory jobs at a machine-building plant in Kuybyshev before becoming secretary of the plant's party committee in 1955. He moved into the full-time party apparatus of the Kuybyshev region in 1960 and by 1965 was second secretary of the *obkom*. From 1967 to 1971 Vorotnikov was

Chairman of the executive committee of the Kuybyshev regional soviet and in 1971 he moved to his native Voronezh as First Secretary of the regional party committee. In the same year he became a member of the Central Committee of the CPSU.

Vorotnikov's reputation as an efficient industrial administrator led to his being brought to Moscow in 1975 and accorded the post of First Deputy Chairman of the Council of Ministers of the Russian republic. He fell foul of the dominant Brezhnev group within the Soviet leadership in 1979 and was sent to Cuba as Soviet Ambassador. When Andropov became a senior secretary of the Central Committee in 1982 Vorotnikov was brought back to Russia as First Secretary of the Krasnodar' *obkom* and once Andropov became General Secretary Vorotnikov's political career flourished. He was appointed Chairman of the Council of Ministers of the RSFSR in 1983. In the same year he became a candidate member of the Politburo in June and was promoted to full membership in December.

Vorotnikov's relations appeared to be less close with Gorbachev than with Andropov, and Vorotnikov was not an early convert to the need for marketising reform. In 1988 he moved from the Chairmanship of the Council of Ministers of the Russian republic to Chairmanship of the Presidium of its Supreme Soviet, at that time a somewhat less powerful post. When the new and strengthened Chairmanships of the Supreme Soviets of the union republics were later created, Vorotnikov was not a candidate in 1990 for that post in the RSFSR and his political career reached an apparent end when he was at the still relatively young age for a Soviet politician of sixty-four. AHB

VOSS, Avgust Eduardovich (Voss, Augusts) (b. 1916) A Latvian schoolteacher in Siberia before the Second World War, Voss became a party official in Soviet Latvia from 1945. He rose to be Secretary (1960–66) and First Secretary (1966–84) of the Communist Party of Latvia, and continued the Russophile policy of his predecessor, Pel'she. He was President of the Soviet of Nationalities in Moscow from 1984 until his retirement in 1989. JHM

VOYNOVICH, Vladimir Nikolaevich (b. 1932) Poet, dramatist and prose writer. His education was interrupted by the war, and he wrote his first poems when a Red Army soldier and carpenter. One of them became widely sung as the Cosmonauts' Song. His first novellas, published in *Novyy mir* (1961–67), gave a frank and amusing picture of working-class and peasant life, and were attacked by orthodox critics. His *Life and Strange Adventures of Private Ivan Chonkin*, a satire on the Red Army and Soviet conditions generally, circulated in *samizdat* and was published in the West (the first part, without his permission in 1969; later parts in 1975 and 1979). He was excluded from the Writers' Union in 1974 and wrote a documentary satire on it, *The Ivankiad* (1976); he emigrated to West Germany in 1980. In 1988 to 1989 many of his previously banned works, including *Chonkin*, were published in the USSR. GAH

VOYTSIK, Ada Ignat'evna (b. 1905) Popular film actress. Voytsik's roles have included: *The Forty First* (1927), *The Doll with the Millions* and *The House on Trubnaya* (1928), *The Oppenheim Family* (1939) and *Admiral Ushakov* (1953). RT

VOZNESENSKY, Andrey Andreevich (b. 1933) Poet, born in Moscow. He qualified as an architect, and although he has not practised, this element remains important in his poetry as a preoccupation with geometry and a fondness for technological reference. He shot to fame in the early 1960s with dynamic, smartly modernistic lyrics, frequently collected and revised; they include *Parabola* (1960), *The Three-Cornered Pear* (1962), *Antiworlds* (1964), *My Achilles Heart* (1966), *The Oak Leaf like a Cello* (1975) and *The Unaccountable* (1981). He has made one of his long poems, *On the Off Chance* (1972), into a rock opera. Voznesensky has frequently travelled abroad and been translated by leading western poets. After occasional difficulties stemming from his apparent pro-westernism and lack of interest in specifically Soviet themes, since 1985 he has been officially recognized as one of the outstanding poets of his generation and nominated to high office in the Union of Writers. GSS

VOZNESENSKY, Nikolay Alekseevich (1903–1950) Economist and plan official. A party member from 1919, he was the best Chairman of the State Planning Committee Stalin ever had, but this did not save him from arrest and execution for alleged association in the 'Leningrad Affair' after Zhdanov's death in 1948. Born in Teploe, he studied political economy in the newly-founded Institute of Red Professors and lectured there until 1935, when Zhdanov, who had become Leningrad Party Secretary on Kirov's assassination, took him into the local plan department within an Executive Committee chaired by Kosygin. His fortunes fluctuated as Stalin favoured his patron, Zhdanov, or his enemy, Malenkov, when from 1938 to 1941 and from 1942 until his arrest in 1949 he chaired the State Planning Committee. His greatest achievements were in managing the war economy and in a monetary and price reform (1947) which totally stopped war-time inflation and brought equilibrium without rationing (albeit at a low standard of living) to household income and outlay. His swingeing reduction of subsidies in a wholesale price reform introduced on 1 January 1949 would have complemented this in rationalizing central planning, but Stalin reversed the reform as soon as Voznesensky was imprisoned. An Academician since 1943, he had been writing *The Economics of Communism*, but the manuscript was seized in a police search and never recovered. MCK

VUCHETICH, Yevgeniy Viktorovich (1908–1974) Sculptor. Vuchetich was born in Yekaterinoslav. Famous for his severe monuments in Socialist Realist style such as *Partisan* (1937) and *Voroshilov on Horseback* (1937), he was one of the Soviet Union's leading sculptors during Stalin's time. He studied in Rostov-on-Don and at the Institute of Proletarian Visual Art in Leningrad (1926–33), before embarking on his illustrious career. Apart from portraits, he also designed tombstones and allegorical complexes such as *Glory to the Soviet People, Bearer of Peace* for VDNKh (1953). JEB

VVEDENSKY, Aleksandr Ivanovich (1904–1941) Poet, dramatist, and prose writer. Based in Leningrad, he was a founder member, with Kharms and Zabolotsky, of the surrealist Oberiu group (1926–30). He published prolifically in the 1930s as a children's poet, meanwhile writing dramas that were not staged. He was arrested and executed in 1941, and rehabilitated in 1956. GSS

VYALOV, Konstantin Aleksandrovich (1900–1976) Painter. Born in Moscow, Vyalov, after studying at the Stroganov Institute and then Svomas/Vkhutemas (1914–23), made his début as a stage designer for a production of *Sten'ka Razin* in 1924. A leading member of OST (1925–28), Vyalov then favoured a style that might be characterized as Magic Realism. During the 1930s onwards he concentrated on landscapes and naval scenes such as *Divers at Sea* (1936). JEB

VYALYAS, Vayno Iosipovich (Väljas, Vaino) (b. 1931) An Estonian who became First Secretary of the Estonian Communist Party in June 1988. In the early 1950s Vyalyas managed the Komsomol organization at Tartu University whilst taking a history degree there. From 1955 to 1961 he was First Secretary of the Estonian Komsomol and thereafter First Secretary of Tallinn *gorkom* (1961–71), and Secretary for Ideology of the Estonian Communist Party (1971–80). Appointed Soviet ambassador to Venezuela (1980–86) and Nicaragua (1986–88), Vyalyas missed the upsurge of dissidence in his native country, and when someone was needed to revive the declining popularity of communism in Estonia, he could be presented as a politician of some credit. Vyalyas has adopted a policy of careful accommodation with the Popular Front of Estonia, but in March 1990 he was demoted to the chairmanship of the pro-independence Communist Party. JHM

VYSHINSKY, Andrey Yanuarovich (1883–1955) Stalin's principal agent in organizing the trials of the 'enemies of the people' in the 1930s, he designed the Stalinist 'theory of socialist law'. Educated as a lawyer, Vyshinsky joined the RSDLP in 1902, and became a Menshevik; he did not join the Bolsheviks until 1920. Successively lecturer, professor, and Rector of Moscow University (1921–28), he served as head of the higher education section of the People's Commissariat for Education (1928–31). President of the Court in the Shakhty trial in 1928 and the Industrial Party trial in 1930, he was chief prosecutor in the Metro-Vickers trial in 1933, and the major political trials (1936–38). He was noted for his ferocity and ruthlessness, claiming that confessions by the accused were 'the queen of proofs'. He held the post of Chief Procurator of the USSR (1935–39), then deputy People's Commissar (later deputy Minister) of Foreign Affairs (1940–49 and 1953–55), and Minister of Foreign Affairs (1949–53). He was elected a member of the Academy of Sciences in 1939. He was a member of the party Central Committee (1939–55). RWD

VYSOTSKY, Vladimir Semenovich (1938–1980) Poet and actor. Vysotsky was born in Moscow into a military family, and brought up partly in the capital, partly in evacuation during the war, and for a time in East Germany, where his father was posted. He trained as an actor at the Moscow Arts Theatre, but in 1964 joined the newly-founded Taganka Theatre under Yuriy Lyubimov, and remained in the troupe until the end of his life. He played many important stage roles, including Hamlet in the Taganka's production of Pasternak's translation, and Brecht's Galileo. He also appeared in many films. Partly in connection with his work for the stage and cinema he began performing and composing songs in the early 1960s, accompanying himself on the guitar, following the precedent set by Bulat Okudzhava.

By the end of the 1960s he had become the most popular of the guitar poets, and by the end of his life he was the most popular Russian poet of any kind. A few records of his work were issued in the USSR during his lifetime, but his songs circulated mainly on privately-made tape recordings. His premature death from heart failure was due among other things to alcoholism and drug addiction. Soon after his death, his songs and poems began to be published in the USSR; dozens of memoirs about him have appeared, and he has become the subject of a cult whose intensity borders on fanaticism. He is often portrayed as the most talented victim of the Brezhnev years. He was an enormously productive composer of songs.

In the 1960s he was best known for humourous and satirical pieces dealing with the everyday lives of ordinary Soviet citizens – workers, sportsmen, soldiers, and especially criminals, often using sub-standard language. As time went on, the humour tended to be replaced by a passionate individual lyricism, with a note of despair that grew ever more desperate. Vysotsky's funeral was the occasion for one of the most remarkable unofficial displays of public feeling ever seen in the USSR.

His literary stature has not been critically assessed; by some he is dismissed as a superficial figure similar to Western pop superstars, by others revered as the most genuine recent embodiment of the Russian national character and the most honest spokesman for the Russian people during the 'period of stagnation'. GSS

Y

YABLONSKAYA, Tat'yana Nilovna
(b. 1917) Painter. Born in Smolensk, one of the last surviving supporters of Socialist Realism in its original phase (exemplified by her painting *Bread* of 1949), Yablonskaya studied at the Kiev Art Institute just before and after the Second World War. She continues to interpret the lives of the common people, often imbuing her work with a lyrical, contemplative mood, as in *Evening. Old Florence* JEB

YADOV, Vladimir Aleksandrovich
(b. 1929) Director of the Institute of Sociology of the Academy of Sciences of the USSR in Moscow since 1988, Yadov is one of the Soviet Union's leading social scientists. He has spent most of his career in Leningrad where he graduated from Leningrad University in 1952 and took his candidate of sciences degree in philosophy in 1959 and his higher doctorate in 1968. Yadov spent a year in England in 1963–64, studying at Manchester University and the London School of Economics, on leave from the laboratory of sociological research at Leningrad University which he headed from 1959 to 1968. From 1969 to 1975 he was head of the Leningrad branch of the Institute of Sociology of the Academy of Sciences, from 1975 to 1983 a department head in the Institute of Sociological and Economic Problems and from 1984 to 1988 a leading researcher in the Institute of History of Science and Technology in Leningrad.

Yadov, who is a Vice-President of the Soviet Sociological Association, did pioneering sociological research in the Soviet Union in the nineteen-sixties, but the later Brezhnev period did not provide a congenial intellectual environment for the kind of serious empirical sociological research he wished to pursue. It is only in the Gorbachev era that he has been given the official recognition that his work merited, and he accepted an invitation to come to Moscow in 1988 to take over the leadership of the main sociological institute in the country. There have been considerable changes for the better at the Institute of Sociology since Yadov's arrival. Yadov's major books include *Man and His Work* (1967), *Self-Regulation and the Prediction of Social Behaviour of the Individual* (1979) and *Sociological Research: Methodology, Programme, Methods* (2nd edn, 1987). AHB

YAGODA, Genrikh Grigor'evich
(1891–1938) A Soviet political policeman of Jewish origin, Yagoda was deputy head of the GPU as early as 1924 and became head of the security

organs (by which time they had changed their name to NKVD) in 1934. He conducted extensive purges but not enough to satisfy Stalin who replaced him by Yezhov in 1936. Yagoda was given a temporary reprieve as Commissar for Posts and Telegraph (1936–37) but in 1937 was arrested, became a leading victim in the show trial of the 'Anti-Soviet Bloc of Rightists and Trotskyites', and in 1938 was executed. AHB

YAKIR, Petr Ionovich (1923–1982) Historian and human rights activist. He was jailed in 1937 at the age of fourteen for being the son of executed Army Commander Iona Yakir. On his early life see his memoir, *A Childhood in Prison* (1972). Released in 1954, he was enabled by Khrushchev's de-Stalinization to lecture widely about his father. In 1966 he became a dissident in response to the partial rehabilitation of Stalin. In 1969 he was a cofounder and leader of the Action Group to Defend Civil Rights. Arrested in 1972, he broke under interrogation, recanted at a show trial, and was released in 1974. PBR

YAKOBSON, Leonid Veniaminovich (1904–1975) Ballet dancer and leading choreographer. After graduating from the Leningrad Ballet School in 1926, Yakobson danced with both the Kirov (1926–33) and the Bolshoy (1933–42) troupes. He particularly excelled in character roles, such as the Acrobat in *The Red Poppy*.

But it was as a choreographer that Yakobson advanced the development of Soviet ballet. He was a choreographer at the Bol'shoy during his dancing career and at the Kirov Theatre from 1942 to 1950 and from 1956 to 1975. He also did some choreography for the Isadora Duncan School. A follower of Michel Fokine, Yakobson moved away from the rigid conventions of classical ballet and developed freer forms of movement and greater expressiveness. His ballets were thus considered very experimental for their time. He also became known for his choreographic miniatures, including solos and small ensemble dances, such as his celebrated *Vestris*, choreographed for Mikhail Baryshnikov in 1969. On the basis of this aspect of his work, Yakobson founded the Choreographic Miniature Ensemble in 1970.

In 1930 Yakobson was one of four choreographers of the experimental and very controversial ballet *The Age of Gold*, with a score by Dmitriy Shostakovich. He choreographed the Second Act set in a sports arena, which included an impressive acrobatic dance for Galina Ulanova and four cavaliers, of which Yakobson himself was one.

Yakobson's first independent work was *Til Eulenspiegel* (1933), a one-act ballet for which he and Yevgeniy Mravinsky composed a new libretto to the Richard Strauss score. This was followed by *Lost Illusions* (1936), *Romeo and Juliet* (1944), *Capriccio Espagnol* (1944), and *The Stone Guest* (1946).

In 1941 Yakobson choreographed the three-act ballet *Shurale*, using music by the Tatar composer Fardi Yarullin and incorporating some national dancing into the choreography. The story was based on a romantic Tatar legend. War interrupted preparations for staging the ballet which did not have its première until 1950. It received great acclaim and was staged at numerous theatres.

Yakobson's next major work was *Spartacus* (1956), an epic ballet with a symphonic score by Aram Khachaturian. Yakobson's ballet greatly amplified the Spartacus story and he had the dancers not perform on point. This created the impression of a series of animated bas reliefs, recalling Greek and Roman pottery. The ballet was very well received and many times revived. Igor' Moiseev, for instance, produced his own version of the ballet in 1958 and Yakobson himself presented it in a shorter form in 1962 with Maya Plisetskaya.

In 1958 Yakobson created a series of choreographic miniatures which was filmed by Soviet television. He also choreographed ballets to some early avant-garde poems such as Vladimir Mayakovsky's *The Bed Bug* (1962) and Aleksandr Blok's *The Twelve* (1964). In 1974 Yakobson collaborated on the Soviet-American film *The Bluebird*. He was the author of numerous articles on choreography. scs

YAKOVLEV, Aleksandr Nikolaevich (b. 1923) One of the most capable and determined reformers in the Soviet leadership, Aleksandr Yakovlev has been a key figure in the elaboration of domestic reform and of change in foreign policy and a strong promoter and protector of *glasnost'* in the years since 1985. A Soviet politician with unusually strong ties with the intelligentsia, Yakovlev has been a vehicle for transmission of many of their ideas into the highest policy-making circles.

Aleksandr Yakovlev was born into a Russian peasant family in a village close to the ancient city of Yaroslavl'. His father, who received four years of education in a church school, fought in the Civil War; his mother who had only two months' schooling was illiterate.

Yakovlev fought in the Second World War from 1941 until 1943 when he was badly wounded and invalided out of the army in which he had latterly been a company commander. He subsequently attended Yaroslavl' Pedagogical Institute, from which he graduated in 1946. He became a Communist Party member in 1944.

His career as a party official began in 1946 when he joined the apparatus of the Yaroslavl' *obkom*. From 1948 to 1950 he worked on a local newspaper and as a lecturer at the Party School of the Yaroslavl' region before returning to the regional party committee apparatus as a deputy departmental head and then head of department (1950–53).

From 1953 until 1973 Yakovlev worked in the apparatus of the Central Committee in Moscow with the exception of the years 1956 to 1960 when he was granted his wish to have a further period of full-time study. He spent most of that time at the Academy of Social Sciences attached to the Central Committee, from which he graduated in 1960, having also, however (unusually for someone making a party career), been an exchange student at Columbia University, New York, in 1959.

Within the Central Committee apparatus, Yakovlev became First Deputy Head and acting head of the Department of Propaganda from 1965 to 1973. However, a newspaper article which Yakovlev published in late 1972 and which attacked all forms of nationalism and chauvinism, including Russian nationalism, provoked anger in conservative Communist and Russian nationalist circles. Yakovlev was demoted, but given a dignified 'exile' as Soviet Ambassador to Canada for the next ten years.

It was during Andropov's General Secretaryship, and shortly after a visit by Mikhail Gorbachev to Canada, that Yakovlev was brought back to Moscow in 1983. From then on, his rise was astonishingly rapid. His first appointment was as Director (1983–85) of the Institute of World Economy and International Relations (IMEMO). In July 1985, following Gorbachev's election to the party General Secretaryship, Yakovlev became head of the Propaganda Department of the Central Committee, in February 1986 a full member of the Central Committee, in March of the same year a Secretary of the Central Committee, in January 1987 a candidate member of the Politburo and in June of that year a full Politburo member (while retaining his Central Committee Secretaryship).

Yakovlev has, along with Gorbachev himself, been one of the two key formulators of the 'New Political Thinking' during the era of *perestroika*. His open-minded approach to ideological questions has not gone unchallenged by orthodox Marxist-Leninists and it was, to some extent, a compromise between his approach and that of Yegor Ligachev when supervision of ideology was handed to Vadim Medvedev in 1988 and Yakovlev was given overall charge of the Soviet Union's international policy within the Central Committee Secretariat. Although this enhanced still further Yakovlev's already considerable influence on foreign policy, it did not prevent him from being a continuing important voice on domestic politics as well.

Since 1987 Yakovlev has been an active member of the commission set up to examine evidence relating to the repressions of the Stalin years and there has been a steady flow of rehabilitations as a result. He was also

from 1988 to 1990 Chairman of the Commission on International Policy of the Central Committee. In a number of his past writings Yakovlev has given highly critical accounts of American foreign policy since the Second World War, and he has emphasized the need for the Soviet Union to adopt a more multipolar foreign policy rather than place too exclusive a stress on the Soviet-American relationship. It has always been an oversimplification, however, to view him as 'anti-American' and he has described progress in US-Soviet relations as 'the key to avoiding the possibility of a nuclear apocalypse'.

Yakovlev, with his experience of the Central Committee apparatus and his wide range of contacts with reform-minded social scientists, has been an invaluable ally for Mikhail Gorbachev, with whom he has formed since 1983 a close personal and political friendship. He has shown courage and imagination in the pursuit of radical change of the Soviet system and has earned the respect of non-party liberal intellectuals within the Soviet system as well as of party reformers. A member of the Presidential Council from its formation in March 1990, Yakolev did not seek re-election to the Central Committee of the CPSU at the Twenty-Eighth Party Congress and so ceased to be a membeer of the Politburo and Central Committee Secretariat in July 1990. AHB

YAKOVLEV, Aleksandr Sergeevich (1906–1989) Aleksandr Yakovlev was responsible for a large and diverse range of military and civilian aircraft, and was also known as the author of a number of books, including an autobiography, *The Aim of a Lifetime*, published in many editions. Born in Moscow into a relatively prosperous family, he at first built light sporting planes and in 1931 graduated from the Zhukovsky Academy. Between 1940 and 1946 he was simultaneously a chief designer and a deputy commissar of the aviation industry. His many designs include fighters, bombers, vertical take off and landing planes, passenger aircraft (Yak-40 and Yak-42), helicopters and light sporting planes. A party member from 1938, he was made a Hero of Socialist Labour in 1940 and 1957, and was the recipient of six Stalin Prizes, a State Prize and a Lenin Prize. JMC

YAKOVLEV, Boris Nikolaevich (1890–1972) Painter. A Muscovite trained in the traditions of nineteenth-century Russian Realism through his study under Abram Arkhipov and Apollinariy Vasnetsov at the MIPSA, Yakovlev joined AKhRR in 1922 and quickly adapted his style to the Soviet state, exemplified by his painting *Transport Is Returning to Normal* (1923). JEB

YAKOVLEV, Boris Pavlovich (b. 1908) Boris Yakovlev attended the Higher Party School in Moscow (1952–55) after working as a fitter in a factory in the Vladimir region and from 1937 as a party official in Dagestan and Kirgiziya. From 1966 he held posts in the Central Committee apparatus, latterly becoming an instructor in the Propaganda Department. In 1979 he was appointed to head the letters department of the Central Committee, and in 1981 he was elected a member of the party's Central Auditing Commission. SLW

YAKOVLEV, Yegor Vladimirovich (b. 1930) Editor of *Moscow News*, one of the flagships of *glasnost'*, and an outstandingly capable and bold Soviet journalist, Yegor Yakovlev is also the author of some twenty books and over thirty film screenplays. When he was elected to the Congress of People's Deputies in 1989 it was from the list of the Film-Makers' Union.

A Russian by nationality and a reformer and anti-Stalinist of long standing, Yakovlev is the son of a prominent Chekist. His father was head of the Odessa Cheka and later deputy chairman of the Ukrainian Cheka who died in 1937 (perhaps surprisingly for a former Chekist his was a natural death at a time of many executions). Yegor Yakovlev graduated from the Moscow State Historical Archival Institute in the early 1950s, joined the Communist Party in 1954 and worked on a number of different Soviet newspapers, among them *Pravda*, *Leninskoe znamya*, *Izvestiya*, *Sovetskaya Rossiya* and *Zhurnalist*. His nonconformism meant that his normal method of departure from them was by way of dismissal. After he was fired from the magazine for journalists, *Zhurnalist*, of which he had been founding editor since 1967, he went to Prague in 1972 to work on *World Marxist Review*. In 1975 he returned to Moscow to work on *Izvestiya*, but left for Prague again when Chernenko succeeded Andropov. He came back to Moscow when Valentin Falin, at the time head of the Novosti Press Agency, invited him to become editor of *Moscow News* which he took over in August 1986.

This newspaper, which sells over a million copies in all (a majority of them abroad), but has had its sales artificially restricted to 350,000 in the Soviet Union, has become an extremely lively forum for political and cultural debate. It has published news stories which other newspapers have not dared to print and has frequently been the first to extend the boundaries of *glasnost'*. Yakovlev must take the lion's share of the credit for turning *Moscow News* from a propaganda sheet which in the past only purported to be a bridge-building newspaper into a genuine medium of communication between East and West and into a publication which sells out instantly in the Soviet Union. AHB

YAKUBOVSKY, Ivan Ignat'evich (1908–1976) Marshal of the Soviet Union. Yakubovsky was born of Belorussian parents. He completed his officer's training in 1935 in time to take part in the Soviet occupation of Poland. During the war he participated in the Battle of Moscow and later in the capture of Berlin and Prague. He established a reputation both as a distinguished commander of Soviet armoured forces and as a technical innovator. He held senior armoured force commands (1945–53) and was Commander-in-Chief of Soviet Forces in Germany (1960–65), although he was displaced in this post by Marshal Konev during the 1961 Berlin Crisis. In 1961 he became a member of the Central Committee. In 1965 Yakubovsky took over the Kiev Military District and following Malinovsky's death in March 1967 was appointed First Deputy Minister of Defence and Commander-in-Chief of the Warsaw Pact Forces with the rank of Marshal of the Soviet Union. RA

YAKUNIN, Father Gleb Pavlovich (b. 1934) Founder of the Christian Committee for the Defence of Believers' Rights in the USSR. He was ordained at the height of the Khrushchev anti-religious campaign in 1962. Yakunin addressed an open letter to Patriarch Aleksi in 1966, complaining of the hierarchy's subservience to the government, and was dismissed from any official ministry.

In 1975 he wrote with Lev Regel'son to the Fifth Assembly of the World Council of Churches, detailing pressures on religious believers in the Soviet Union. For the next four years, under constant threat of arrest, Fr. Gleb continued to publicize the situation of believers in his country until his arrest in November 1979. He was sentenced to five years strict regime and five years exile. Freed from exile in March 1987, he was finally assigned a parish thirty-five kilometres from Moscow on 11 August of that year, after a wait of twenty years. MR

YAMPOL'SKY, Abram Il'ich (1890–1956) Violinist and teacher. Yampol'sky was born in Yekaterinoslav and died in Moscow. A pupil of the St Petersburg Conservatory, where he studied violin under Sergey Korguev and composition under Yāzeps Vītols and Maksimilyan Shteynberg, he graduated in 1913. From 1913 to 1920 he was active as a performer, teacher and conductor. In 1920, on moving to Moscow, he became assistant leader of the Bol'shoy Theatre Orchestra, and was leader of the 'Persimfans' ensemble (a Soviet Symphony orchestra which performed without a conductor) (1922–23). From 1922 he was a teacher at the Moscow Conservatory, among his pupils being Leonid Kogan. He was made an Honoured Art Worker in 1937 and a Doctor of Arts in 1940. GS

YANAEV, Gennadiy Ivanovich (b. 1937) A Soviet politician who received extraordinarily fast promotion in 1990, Yanaev became in July of that year both a Politburo member and a Secretary of the Central Committee with responsibility for international affairs. Earlier in 1990 Yanaev became head of the official Soviet trade union movement, a post in which he has tried to steer a careful line between supporting the leadership's economic reform proposals and protecting the short-term interests of Soviet workers, a balancing act which involved arguing against a rapid move to a market economy. Yanaev, who has a higher education and a candidate of sciences degree in law, is a Russian by nationality. He was formerly a deputy chairman of the trade union movement and he was elected from the trade unions to the Congress of People's Deputies of the USSR in 1989. He is a member of the Committee of the Supreme Soviet for International Affairs. AHB

YANGEL, Mikhail Kuz'mich (1911–1971) From 1954 Yangel was chief designer of the missile and space launcher design bureau at Dnepropetrovsk. Born in the Irkutsk region, he graduated from the Moscow Aviation Institute in 1937 and then worked in a number of aviation design bureaux. In 1950 he joined the Korolev rocket design bureau. Between 1952 and 1954 Yangel was director of a major rocketry research institute before being appointed to head his own design organization. He was responsible for a series of missiles, including SS-17 and SS-18 ICBMs, and the SS-4 and SS-5 intermediate-range missiles, plus the launchers for many 'Kosmos' satellites. In 1966 Yangel was elected to the Academy of Sciences. A party member from 1931, from 1966 until his death he was a candidate member of the Central Committee. Possibly because of the Dnepropetrovsk association, he appears to have had the patronage of Brezhnev. In 1959 and again in 1961 he was made a Hero of Socialist Labour. JMC

YARIN, Veniamin Aleksandrovich (b. 1940) The youngest member of Gorbachev's Presidential Council when it was appointed in March 1990, Yarin was evidently put there as a spokesman for workers suspicious of the consequences of moves in the direction of a market economy. Yarin, whose background is in construction and metallurgical work, had already made public his concern about the direction being taken by economic reform. He has been an active member of the Congress of People's Deputies (to which he was elected in March 1989) and of the Supreme Soviet. AHB

YAROSLAVSKY, Yemel'yan Mikhaylovich (Gubel'man, Miney Izrailovich) (1878–1943) A party official and Stalinist historian, Yaroslavsky received an incomplete education and gravitated at an early age towards political activity, becoming a member of the Social Democratic Party on its foundation in 1898. He became a political activist during the later Tsarist period, suffering repeated arrest and imprisonment, and from 1917 assumed a prominent role as an editor of party newspapers and a member of the Moscow Military-Revolutionary Committee. After local work in Omsk Yaroslavsky joined the central party apparatus as a Secretary in 1921 and served also as a member of the Central Control Commission (responsible for party discipline), on the board of the Lenin Institute and of various party newspapers, and (from 1925) as chairman of the USSR Union of Atheists, for which he edited *The Godless* and other publications. Yaroslavsky later became head of the party history department of the Higher Party School and wrote or edited several party histories which were

439

authoritative in their time. He is buried in the Kremlin Wall. sLW

YASHIN (Popov), Aleksandr Yakovlevich (1913–1968) A poet and prose writer on rural and kolkhoz themes, he was born into a peasant family in Vologda Province. His prose works of the fifties were prominent in Thaw literature; 'The Levers' (1956) shows how Stalinist conformism became routine, while 'A Vologda Wedding' (1962) describes the grimness of Soviet rural life. KC

YASHIN, Lev Ivanovich (1929–1990) Soccer player. One of the most famous goalkeepers in soccer history, Yashin was born in Moscow. Initially dividing his seasons between ice hockey and soccer, he finally settled for soccer, playing for Moscow Dinamo who won the league title five times between 1954 and 1963 and were Cupwinners in 1953, 1967 and 1970. During his games for the Soviet national side, he won an Olympic gold medal in 1956, a European Championship winners' medal in 1960 and a bronze medal in the 1966 World Cup. He retired from active soccer in 1971 with the unique record of having kept a clean sheet 207 times out of his 438 matches. For a while he coached, then worked full time for Dinamo Sports Society, while concurrently being Deputy Chairman of the Football Section of the USSR Sports Committee. In October 1984 he had his right leg amputated owing to diseased blood vessels. He died on 20 March 1990. JWR

YASTREBOV, Ivan Pavlovich (b. 1911) A member of the CPSU from 1941, Ivan Yastrebov graduated from the Ural Polytechnical Institute in 1936 and worked in industry before entering party service in 1946. He was first secretary of the Perm city party committee (1953–54), and from 1962

worked in the heavy industry department of the CPSU Central Committee, of which he became head in 1984. He was elected a candidate member of the CPSU Central Committee in 1981 and 1986. sLW

YAZOV, Dmitriy Timofeevich (b. 1923) Minister of Defence. Marshal Yazov is an officer of a new school who appears to support the central principles of the process of restructuring instituted by the Gorbachev leadership. His blunt, forthright and critical approach to military issues suited the climate of change in the Soviet Union in the late 1980s and his expertise in personnel-related issues proves valuable in carrying *perestroika* to the armed forces. Yazov appreciates the need for military retrenchment and the opportunities derived from arms control. However, his publications express a traditional military emphasis on the need to maintain military morale and improve combat effectiveness. His interpretation of the 'defensive' character of current Soviet military doctrine, moreover, does not imply a readiness to undertake a radical reconfiguration of Soviet strategy.

Yazov was born of peasant parents in the small village of Yazovo in Omsk province. He was enrolled in a school for infantry officers in Moscow (1941–42) and, once commissioned, fought on the Volkhov and Leningrad fronts. Following the war he served in various command positions before graduating from the Frunze Military Academy in 1956. He graduated from the General Staff Academy in 1967, the same year as Sergey Akhromeev. Yazov assumed command of a senior formation in the Transcaucasus Military District (1969–74) and worked in the Main Personnel Directorate of the

Ministry of Defence (1974–76) before he was transferred to the Far East as the first Deputy Commander of the Far East Military District. He was named commander of the Central Group of Forces in Czechoslovakia in 1979, and a year later was appointed commander of the Central Asian Military District. In this position Yazov could not escape some involvement and possibly had a significant role in the conduct of Soviet military operations in Afghanistan in the early 1980s. He is known to have introduced some innovative techniques for combined arms operations and developed new training techniques for the Soviet armed forces in this period.

In February 1984 Yazov was promoted to the rank of army general and transferred to the more senior command of the Far East Military District. The next change in Yazov's career was crucial; in January 1987 he became Deputy Minister of Defence and head of the Main Personnel Directorate. This was one of the key institutions used by Gorbachev to carry out his *perestroika* of the Ministry of Defence, and a heavy turnover occurred in the senior Soviet command in the brief period Yazov was responsible for personnel. Appointed Minister of Defence in May 1987 over the heads of more senior colleagues, Yazov was confirmed in that post in 1989 by the Supreme Soviet only with much help from Gorbachev after Yazov's responses to questioning had been found unconvincing by many deputies. As Gorbachev sought to calm the concerns of the Soviet military in 1990, Yazov was promoted to the rank of Marshal. A candidate member of the Politburo from 1987 to 1990, he was appointed

to Gorbachev's Presidential Council in March 1990. RA

YEFANOV, V. P., *see* **EFANOV, V. P.**

YEFIMOV, Aleksandr Nikolaevich (b. 1923) Commander-in-Chief Soviet Air Force. Yefimov joined the Red Army in 1941 and served in an Air Assault Regiment during the war. After the war he had command posts in the Air Force. He graduated from the Air Force Academy (1951) and the General Staff Academy (1957). He became Commander of Aviation of the Carpathian Military District in 1965, and First Deputy Commander-in-Chief of the Soviet Air Force in 1969. He held this post for some fifteen years, becoming a Marshal of Aviation in 1975. In December 1984 he replaced Marshal of Aviation Kutakhov as Deputy Minister of Defence and Commander-in-Chief of the Soviet Air Force (Kutakhov died a year later). He became a member of the CPSU Central Committee in 1986. RA

YEFIMOV (Fridland), Boris Yefimovich (b. 1900) Graphic artist, born in Kiev. Although he received no professional training, Yefimov became one of the Soviet Union's foremost caricaturists, beginning his career in 1919 with contributions to newspapers and journals such as *Pravda* and *Krokodil*. From the 1920s onwards he published a number of satirical albums, and his anti-Hitler caricatures of the Second World War enjoyed great popularity with the Russian people. JEB

YEFREMOV, Mikhail Timofeevich (b. 1911) Party First Secretary of a number of powerful Russian provinces (Kuybyshev, Chelyabinsk, Gor'ky) between 1952 and 1965, he became Deputy Chairman of the USSR Council of Ministers (1965–71). He served as Soviet Ambassador to the

GDR (1971–75) and to Austria (1975–86), retiring in 1986. JHM

YEFREMOV, Oleg Nikolaevich (b. 1927) One of the Soviet Union's most outstanding stage directors and leading actors; Oleg Yefremov was one of the founders of the Sovremennik Theatre which under his direction in the 1970s and 1980s was, along with the Taganka, the most innovative of Moscow theatres. Now the artistic director of the Moscow Arts Theatre, he has helped to revive its fortunes after some years in the doldrums. AHB

YEGOROV, Aleksandr Il'ich (1883–1939) Former Chief of the General Staff. Yegorov was born into a lower-middle-class family in Samara Province. He entered the tsarist army as a volunteer and graduated from an Infantry Junker School. By the time of the 1917 revolution he had attained the rank of colonel. He joined, then broke with, the Left Socialist Revolutionaries (1917–18), and was appointed chairman of the Central Board for Prisoners of War and Refugees. Yegorov became associated with Stalin early in the Civil War while in charge of the Tenth Army defending Tsaritsyn. In autumn 1919 he commanded the Red forces of the Southern Front against the White leader Denikin and in 1920 he was the commanding officer of the troops of the South-Western Front. He commanded successively the Kiev and Leningrad Military Districts and the Caucasian Red Banner Army. He was also in charge of troops in the Ukraine, Crimea and the Belorussian Military District at times in the 1920s. In 1931 Yegorov was appointed Chief of Staff of the Workers' and Peasants' Red Army, and in 1935 he became Chief of the General Staff with the rank of Marshal of the Soviet Union. He

replaced Marshal Tukhachevsky as First Deputy People's Commissar of Defence in 1937 and held this post until the following year. However, the reshuffle of posts at this time was the prelude to Stalin's purge of the Soviet high command. Yegorov was an experienced and forward-looking military commander who played an important role in training and equipping the Red Army in the 1930s. This contribution came to an end when Yegorov became a victim of the purge and was shot in 1939. RA

YEGOROV, Yuriy (b. 1954) Pianist. Yuriy Yegorov was born in Kazan'. Having received his first piano lessons as a child, he entered the Marguerite Long-Jacques Thibaud Competition in Paris in 1971, winning a prize. He then studied at the Moscow Conservatory, where his professor was Yakov Zak. He was awarded third place in the International Tchaikovsky Contest in 1974. After several highly successful foreign tours, including the United States in 1978 and England and Europe in 1980, he decided to leave the Soviet Union and now resides in the West. GS

YEL'TSIN, Boris Nikolaevich (b. 1931) Born into a poor peasant family in the Sverdlovsk region, Yel'tsin in recent years has emerged as a formidable politician who was the first in Soviet political life to be rejected by the party leadership and yet make a comeback thanks to popular opinion and electoral support.

Yel'tsin graduated from the Ural Polytechnical Institute, where in addition to specializing in civil engineering he became a member of Sverdlovsk city's volleyball team. He worked in the construction industry from 1957 until 1968, latterly as chief engineer of a housing construction combine in Sverdlovsk. He had joined the Communist Party in 1961 and in 1968 he was co-opted into the party apparatus in Sverdlovsk, eight years later becoming First Secretary of the regional party committee.

Yel'tsin became a full member of the party Central Committee in 1981 and from June 1985 until February 1986 he was a Secretary of the Central Committee. In December 1985 he was appointed to the important post of First Secretary of the Moscow party committee, becoming a candidate member of the Politburo two months later. He was supported for this promotion by Yegor Ligachev – as Ligachev later acknowledged at the Nineteenth Party Conference – even though relations between Yel'tsin and Ligachev were subsequently to become acrimonious. It is likely that Yel'tsin's promotion owed something also to his long-standing acquaintanceship with Ryzhkov whom he had known well in Sverdlovsk.

Yel'tsin's populist style – use of public transport rather than official limousines and rejection of many of the other privileges which traditionally accompanied high party office, together with his struggle against corruption – won him the support of a majority of Muscovites, although his rough treatment of the city bureaucracy alienated many of his subordinates as well as a number of his superiors in the party apparatus. At a Central Committee plenary session to mark the seventieth anniversary of the Bolshevik Revolution in 1987 Yel'tsin made a surprise speech in which he explicitly attacked Ligachev and implictly criticized Gorbachev. He also asked to be relieved of his duties as a candidate member of the Politburo. That wish was readily granted. He

was removed from the headship of the Moscow party organization before the end of 1987 and from candidate membership of the Politburo at the first plenary session of the Central Committee in 1988.

Yel'tsin was demoted to the First Deputy Chairmanship of the State Committee for Construction and, but for the introduction of competitive elections and his support from a broad public, would have vanished into obscurity. However, in the March 1989 election to the Congress of People's Deputies he contested the Moscow constituency and won an overwhelming victory, notwithstanding the strong backing of the party apparatus for his factory-manager opponent. Subsequently he became a member of the Supreme Soviet of the USSR and so gave up his post as the equivalent of a deputy minister. The following year (1990), Yel'tsin – by now a full-time parliamentarian – was elected a member of the RSFSR Supreme Soviet, again with overwhelming popular support (this time from Sverdlovsk).

Gradually Yel'tsin became one of the principal leaders of the opposition in the Soviet Union. His own political position has become more radical and libertarian, even though his style can be authoritarian and in personality he is emotional and impulsive. He has formed an alliance with some of the more radical members of the Moscow intelligentsia, but there is more support for his sometimes over-simple solutions at a man-on-the-street level than in intellectual circles although his standing with the latter rose during 1990.

In 1989 Yel'tsin became one of the leaders of the Inter-Regional Group of Deputies, a ginger group within the legislature favouring faster and more far-reaching reform, and in 1990, following his success in the election to the Supreme Soviet of the RSFSR, he announced his intention to be a candidate for the Chairmanship of the Supreme Soviet of the Russian Republic.

There is little or no reason to suppose that Yel'tsin could have been a more successful leader than Gorbachev, with whom he has frequently been at loggerheads, and although he has criticized the Soviet leader for lack of a long-term strategy for *perestroika*, Yel'tsin has so far failed to offer a coherent alternative one. Nevertheless, Yel'tsin was elected Chairman of the Supreme Soviet of the Russian republic in late May 1990 and has thereby become an increasingly important actor on the Soviet political stage.

Yeltsin's own views have developed under the influence of able advisers and by the summer of 1990 there were signs of a possible new alliance between him and Gorbachev when they jointly set up a team to study how to move more quickly to economic reform. Yel'tsin's undoubted courage and innate stubbornness have made a distinctive and sometimes colourful contribution to the pluralization of Soviet politics. He published a typically defiant and idiosyncratic volume of memoirs, *Against the Grain*, in English in 1990, donating the royalties to the campaign against AIDS (in particular, for the purchase of disposable syringes) in the Soviet Union. AHB

YEMEL'YANOV, Aleksey Mikhaylovich (b. 1935) A Moscow University professor and specialist on agricultural economics who won a hotly-contested election to the Congress of People's Deputies (in the Lenin region of Moscow) in 1989, Yemel'yanov was subsequently elected to the Supreme Soviet (Soviet of the Union) where he is a member of the Committee of the Supreme Soviet for Agrarian Questions and Food. He has emerged as a strong supporter of both political reform and radical economic reform. AHB

YENEY, Yevgeny Yevgen'evich (1890–1971) Set designer. Yeney, who was of Hungarian origin, worked in the Leningrad film studios and was closely associated with the films of Kozintsev and Trauberg from *Mishka versus Yudenich* (1925) to *Hamlet* (1964). RT

YEPISHEV, Aleksey Alekseevich (1908–1985) Former Chief of Main Political Directorate of the Armed Forces. Yepishev worked in the Red Army (1930–38), but most of the senior posts he held in later years were party appointments. He worked for the CPSU Central Committee, among other activities during the war, and became USSR Deputy People's Commissar of Medium Machine Building. After the war the positions he occupied included Deputy Minister of State Security (1951–53), Ambassador to Romania (1955–61), and Ambassador to Yugoslavia (1961–62). In 1956 he took part in the talks between the Soviet and Romanian government delegations on the temporary stationing of Soviet troops in Romania. In 1962 he became Chief of the Main Political Directorate of the Soviet Armed Forces, a post he retained until a few months before his death in 1985. Over this long period Yepishev had an important role in shaping political attitudes and enforcing the party line in the armed forces, in strengthening military discipline and readiness. He wrote extensively on political aspects of the Soviet armed forces. RA

YESENIN, Sergey Aleksandrovich (1895–1925) A poet, born in Ryazan' province, of peasant origin. Yesenin was recognized as an outstanding literary talent by St Petersburg literary circles before the First World War. He welcomed the October Revolution as a spiritual deliverance, especially in the vision of peasant paradise *Inoniya* (1918) and the drama *Pugachev* (1921). Subsequently, however, his life degenerated into scandalous debauchery (*Hooligan's Confession*, 1921; *Tavern Moscow*, 1924), culminating ultimately in suicide. He married and travelled abroad with the American dancer Isadora Duncan (1922–23). He is permanently popular for his sentimental lyrics of village life using religious imagery, his self-pitying and self-dramatizing love poetry, and his personal image as the golden boy gone wrong. GSS

YEVDOKIMOV, Grigoriy Yeremeevich (1884–1936) A sailor who later became a party activist in the underground, Grigoriy Yevdokimov became a Bolshevik in 1903 when he was just nineteen years old. Between 1908 and 1917 he was involved in party work in Omsk, Pavlodar and St Petersburg, where he took part in strikes and was repeatedly arrested and exiled. After the October 1917 revolution he worked in the provinces organizing Soviet rule, and during the Civil War became head of the political department of the Seventh Army which was engaged on the north-western front against Yudenich. From 1922 he was chairman of the Petrograd Trade Union Council and deputy chairman of the Petrograd Soviet, and from 1925 he worked in the Petrograd party committee.

Yevdokimov was repeatedly elected to the party Central Committee, but at the Fourteenth Party Congress in 1925 he sided with the Trotskyist opposition, and for this he was expelled from the Central Committee and later from the party. In 1928 he repented and was readmitted, and in 1931 was appointed to the Central Grain and Cattle Rearing Board, but in January 1935 after Kirov's assassination he was arrested and sentenced to eight years' imprisonment for 'active membership of Moscow Centre counter-revolutionary group'. In 1936 he was retried for membership of the 'Trotskyite-Zinov'evite terrorist centre' and following the court's decision was executed later the same year. SLW

YEVSTIGNEEV, Ruben Nikolaevich (b. 1932) A significant economic reformer, Yevstigneev is one of the deputy heads of the Institute of Comparative International Studies (until 1990 called the Institute of Economics of the World Socialist System) and a member of Leonid Abalkin's State Commission on Economic Reform. Born in Moscow to a Russian father and Armenian mother, Yevstigneev studied at the Moscow Institute of International Relations of the Ministry of Foreign Affairs and subsequently worked in the Institute of Economics of the Academy of Sciences before moving to what is popularly known as the 'Bogomolov institute', of which he became a deputy director in 1989. He is a long-time advocate of economic reform – his numerous publications include *Economic Reform in Socialist Countries* published as long ago as 1968. In the contemporary Soviet Union he is a strong supporter of a decisive move to market relations in the economy. AHB

YEVTUSHENKO, Yevgeniy Aleksandrovich (b. 1933) Born in Zima near Irkutsk, a writer of prose, an actor, film-maker, and photographer, Yevtushenko is primarily known for his poetry. The self-styled heir to Mayakovsky, he has cultivated a dramatic style and read his poems to great crowds, both in the Soviet Union and the West. Although he first published in 1949, he attracted attention only during the Khrushchev thaw with poems such as 'Zima Station' (1956), about a pilgrimage back to his Siberian roots made under the shadow of the anti-Stalinist revelations, 'Babi Yar' (1961), an attack on antisemitism, and 'The Heirs of Stalin' (1962), about the danger of a neo-Stalinist revival. After the furore caused by the publication of his *Precocious Autobiography* in Paris in 1963, and the fall of Khrushchev, Yevtushenko specialized in poetry extolling economic achievements (such as *The Bratsk Power Station* of 1965 which draws a favourable comparison between the future-oriented power station and the ancient pyramids) and anti-Western political poetry, such as 'Beneath the Skin of the Statue of Liberty' (1970). During the eighties, he published a novel using a complex time frame, *Berry Patches* (1981) and directed and wrote a film, *Kindergarten* (1982), set in the war. His 'The Don't-Rock-the-Boaters' and 'Fuku' of 1985 represent early airings of some of the main issues raised during the Gorbachev thaw. KC

YEZHOV, Nikolay Ivanovich (1894–1939) Head of the security forces during the worst years of Stalin's purges, Yezhov succeeded Yagoda as NKVD chief in 1936 but lasted only until 1938 when he was replaced by Beria. The scale of the repression in these two years (and particularly in 1937–38) was so great that it became known as the Yezhovshchina, although Stalin was even more culpable and the prime mover behind the arrests and killings. Briefly a candidate member of the Politburo, Yezhov became Commissar for River Transport after his removal from the NKVD but before long was himself arrested; in 1939 he met the same fate as many of his victims. AHB

YUMASHEV, Ivan Stepanovich (1895–1972) Former Commander-in-Chief of the Soviet Navy. Yumashev entered the tsarist navy in 1912 before serving in the Soviet Navy. In 1921 he was arrested for his part in the Kronstadt uprising, but escaped. After the Civil War he commanded a battleship, a destroyer division and a cruiser brigade. He rose to become Chief of Staff, then Commander, of the Black Sea Fleet. During and after the war (1939–47) he commanded the Soviet Pacific Fleet which took part in the war on the Far Eastern Front and the Soviet occupation of North Korea, Southern Sakhalin and the Kurile Islands. In the period 1947 to 1951 Yumashev was Commander-in-Chief of the Soviet Navy and USSR Minister of the Navy. His last senior post was head of the Voroshilov Naval Academy. RA

YUNAK, Ivan Kharitonovich (b. 1918) Born into a Ukrainian peasant family, Ivan Yunak graduated from an agricultural institute in 1941 and worked in agricultural administration until he became a local party secretary in 1949, five years after he had become a member. He headed the Dnepropetrovsk regional executive committee from 1954 to 1961, when he was named first secretary of the Tula regional party committee. He held this position until 1985 and was a full

Central Committee member from 1961 to 1986. SLW

YUON, Konstantin Fedorovich (1875–1958) Painter. A Muscovite student at the MIPSA under Abram Arkhipov and Valentin Serov (1894–99), Yuon continued the restrained Impressionism of the Union of Russian Artists. He was especially interested in the art and architecture of Old Russia and many of his landscapes were dedicated to the theme of Zagorsk. After the Revolution, he continued as a Realist painter, joining AKhRR in 1925, and adjusting his style to Soviet everyday life as in *Morning in Industrial Moscow* (1949). JEB

YUTKEVICH, Sergey Iosifovich (1904–1985) Film director, teacher and film historian. Yutkevich was a founder member of FEKS and an associate of Eisenstein, Mayakovsky and Meyerkhol'd. His films included: *Lace* (1928), *The Black Sail* (1929), *The Golden Mountains* (1931), *Counterplan* (1932), *The Man with the Gun* (1938), *Yakov Sverdlov* (1940), *The New Adventures of Schweik* (1943), *Skanderbeg* (1954), *Othello* (1956), *Stories about Lenin* (1958), *Lenin in Poland* (1966), *A Theme for a Short Story* (1969), *Lenin in Paris* (1982). RT

Z

ZABOLOTSKY, Nikolay Alekse-evich (1903–1958) Poet, born in Kazan', educated in Moscow and Petrograd. He was a member of the surrealist Oberiu group in Leningrad (1926–30) and active as writer of verse for children; he published *Columns*, a brilliant first collection of lyrics, in 1928, then met great difficulties after party critics condemned the epic *Triumph of Agriculture* (published 1933). He was arrested in 1938, and served five years in the camps. From 1946 he lived in Moscow, working mainly as a translator. His posthumous reputation as a philosophical poet has risen steadily. GSS

ZAGLADIN, Vadim Valentinovich (b. 1927) Zagladin, who has been a leading foreign policy adviser within the Soviet leadership over a lengthy period, was born in Moscow, studied at MGIMO and later taught there. Between 1954 and 1960 he held a variety of editorial posts on newspapers and journals and from 1961 to 1964 was on the staff of *World Marxist Review* in Prague. He moved into the apparatus of the Central Committee of the CPSU in 1964 and became a deputy head of the International Department in 1967. He was promoted to be First Deputy Head in 1975 and held that post until 1988 when he lost those functions but was retained as a part-time adviser to President Gorbachev. Zagladin is noted for his intellectual agility, but was probably too close to Brezhnev as a foreign policy adviser in the 1970s to retain a position of equal prominence in the Gorbachev era. AHB

ZAGONEK, Vyacheslav Frantse-vich (b. 1919) Painter. Zagonek was born in Irkutsk. Graduating from the Academy of Arts he emerged in the 1950s as a master of the lyrical landscape – such as *Cherry Tree in Bloom* (1962–64). JEB

ZAITSEV, Aleksander, *see* **RODNINA, Irina**

ZAKHAROV, Matvey Vasil'evich (1898–1972) Former Chief of General Staff. Zakharov was a volunteer in the Red Guard who took part in the Bolshevik rising in October 1917 and the storming of the Winter Palace in Petrograd. He pursued a career primarily as a staff officer, becoming Chief of Staff of the Leningrad and Odessa Military Districts (1937–41). During the war his posts included Chief of Staff of the North-Western Direction, and Chief of Staff on the Kalinin, Steppe, Second Ukrainian and Transbaykal Fronts. He helped plan and lead major wartime operations, including those in Romania,

Hungary, Austria and Czechoslovakia. His career spanned a variety of positions after the war: Commandant of the General Staff Academy; Deputy Chief of the General Staff and Head of the General Staff Main Board (1949–52); Chief Inspector of the Soviet Army (1952–53); Commander of the Leningrad Military District (1953–57); and Commander-in-Chief of the Soviet occupation troops in Germany (1957–60). He was Chief of the General Staff and USSR First Deputy Minister of Defence in the tense international period 1960 to 1963. He lost these posts, but was reinstated in 1964, and finally relinquished office in 1971. He wrote a number of works on military theory and history. RA

ZAKHAROV, Rostislav Vladimirovich (1907–1984) A choreographer and stage director, Zakharov began his career as a dancer, graduating from the Leningrad Ballet School in 1926 and performing as a soloist until 1929. He then turned to choreography and studied at the Leningrad Theatrical Technicum, from which he graduated in 1932.

From 1934 to 1936 Zakharov was a choreographer at the Kirov Theatre, where he staged his celebrated ballet *The Fountain of Bakhchisaray* (1934). As a choreographer he was known for his utilization of Pushkin themes and his application of realistic principles to ballet. From 1936 to 1956 Zakharov worked at the Bol'shoy Theatre as director of the ballet troupe, choreographer and operatic director, and head of the ballet school. He staged *The Prisoner of the Caucasus* (1938), *Don Quixote* (1939), *Cinderella* (1945), and *The Bronze Horseman* (1949), as well as operas including *Ruslan and Lyudmila* (1937) and *Carmen* (1943).

Zakharov headed the choreography department of the State Institute of Theatrical Arts (1946–84) and was the author of *The Art of the Ballet Master* (1954) and *Thoughts on Dance* (1977). SCS

ZAKHAVA, Boris Yevgen'evich (1896–1976) Stage director and actor. Zakhava was associated with the Vakhtangov Theatre. His roles included Vasiliy Dostigaev in Gor'ky's *Yegor Bulychov and the Others* (1932) and he also acted in Meyerkhol'd's productions of Ostrovsky's *The Forest* (1924), *Give Us Europe!* and *Bubus the Teacher* (both 1925). His production of *Yegor Bulychov and the Others* with Shchukin in the title role was regarded as a significant event in the history of Soviet theatre. His teaching career culminated in his taking charge of the faculty of direction at the State Theatre Institute in 1949. RT

ZALYGIN, Sergey Pavlovich (b. 1913) Prose writer. Born in a village called Durasovka – now part of the Bashkir ASSR – Zalygin moved to Siberia when very young and regards this region as his real homeland. He was trained as an engineer and a hydrologist and in the course of his scientific career worked in different parts of Siberia, in Omsk and Novosibirsk. He is a dedicated campaigner for environmental causes, and played a vital role in the 'Siberian rivers' debate, which led in August 1986 to the suspension of the government decision to divert the Siberian rivers for the irrigation of Soviet Central Asia. When he became a full-time writer, Zalygin moved to Moscow. His fiction stems from the 'village prose' tradition, but it is not circumscribed by it. He has written critically about Stalinism, collectivization and dogmatic Bolshevism. He has also depicted the life of the urban intelligentsia and even the problems of the contemporary woman. Most significantly, his novel *Posle buri* (After the Storm) (1980–85) presents NEP as a socio-political model capable of embracing both nationalist and communist tendencies. Its publication was followed by a vigorous promotion of parallel ideas in the Soviet press.

Zalygin was appointed Chief Editor of *Novyy mir* in August 1986. He is not a member of the CPSU, but has been a secretary of the RSFSR Writers' Union since 1969 and a member of the *buro* of the secretariat of the USSR Writers' Union since 1986. Many official honours have been bestowed upon him; these include the title of Hero of Socialist Labour, the Order of Lenin, and the gold medal of Hammer and Sickle. His most remarkable achievement as Chief Editor has been the publication of Aleksandr Solzhenitsyn's previously banned works. In 1989 he was elected a member of the Congress of People's Deputies of the USSR from the USSR Writers' Union; he is also a member of the Committee of the Supreme Soviet of the USSR on Questions of Ecology and Rational Use of Natural Resources. RHP

ZAMYATIN, Yevgeniy Ivanovich (1884–1937) Fiction writer and essayist. His excellent early works like 'A Provincial Story' (1913) reflect his youth in central Russia in a grotesque narrative style and primitivist view of nature. During the First World War he worked as an engineer supervising the construction of Russian ice-breakers in England where he wrote 'The Islanders' (1918) and 'The Fisher of Men' (1922). His writings in and on literature influenced the Serapion Bro-

thers in the twenties. His stories of survival in post-Revolutionary Petrograd, 'Mamai' (1921) and 'The Cave' (1922) continue the rhythmically repeated images and sounds of his early prose in a more stylized manner. His most famous work, the anti-utopian novel *We* (1920), was published in the Soviet Union in 1988. It combines ferocious humour with the imposition of mathematically-inspired state uniformity. *We* inspired Orwell's *1984*. Zamyatin's 1929 story 'The Flood' continues the Petersburg tradition of murder and rebirth, this time with a female protagonist. Zamyatin emigrated in 1931. BH

ZAMYATIN, Leonid Mitrofanovich (b. 1922) A Russian born in the Voronezh region, Zamyatin joined the staff of the Soviet Ministry of Foreign Affairs in 1946. By 1962 he was head of the ministry's Press Department. From 1970 he was Director General of Tass before becoming head of the International Information Department of the Central Committee in 1978. When that department was abolished and became a section in the Propaganda Department in 1986, Zamyatin left the Central Committee apparatus and became Soviet Ambassador to Great Britain. He was a full member of the Central Committee from 1976 to 1990. AHB

ZARIN', Indulis Avgustovich (b. 1929) Painter. Born in Riga, Zarin' studied at the Rosenthal Art Institute there (1947–52) and then graduated from the Latvian Academy of Arts where he now teaches. His landscapes and revolutionary scenes are distinguished by their colourful, Expressionist manner as in *The Song, Latvian Red Sharpshooters* (1967). JEB

ZARKHI, Aleksandr Grigor'evich
(b. 1908) Leningrad-based film director and scriptwriter. Zarkhi's career is
closely associated with Iosif Kheifits.
RT

ZARKHI, Natan Abramovich (1900–
1935) Scriptwriter. Zarkhi was closely
associated with Pudovkin. He wrote
the scripts for *The Mother* (1926), *The
End of St Petersburg* (1927) and *Victory*
(1938), which was completed after his
death in a car crash. RT

ZASLAVSKAYA, Tat'yana Ivanovna
(b. 1927) Born into a Russian academic family in Kiev, Tat'yana Zaslavskaya began her professional career
as an economist, but today is one of
the Soviet Union's leading sociologists.
She has been a courageous advocate of
radical reform both before and during
the period of *perestroika*. After graduating from the Economics Faculty of
Moscow University in 1950, Zaslavskaya worked until 1963 at the
Institute of Economics of the Academy
of Sciences in Moscow before accepting an invitation from Abel Aganbegyan to join his recently-established
Institute of Economics of Industrial
Production at Novosibirsk. Her
studies became increasingly sociological in their approach and from
1967 she was head of a section of Aganbegyan's institute concerned with
sociological issues.

Zaslavskaya's particular speciality
was agriculture and the problems of
the countryside and in that capacity
she was one of a number of specialists
consulted by Gorbachev from time to
time when he was in charge of agriculture within the Central Committee
apparatus – on the first occasion in
April 1982 when Brezhnev was still
General Secretary. Zaslavskaya
achieved fame abroad and a good deal
of unpleasantness at home when a

paper she presented to a closed
seminar in Novosibirsk was leaked and
published abroad. It gave a highly
critical analysis of Soviet economic
and social institutions along lines
which became almost commonplace
several years later but which were
regarded as highly sensitive before
1985. Zaslavskaya received a party
reprimand from the *obkom*, but in the
longer term her paper strengthened
her reputation as a bold and independent-minded scholar.

During the period of Gorbachev's
leadership of the Soviet Union Zaslavskaya has attained prominence and
has been able to promote both the
discipline of sociology and her own
reformist ideas. She became President
of the Soviet Sociological Association
in 1986 and in 1988 she returned to
Moscow as head of a new Centre for
the Study of Public Opinion which has
subsequently carried out high-quality
survey research on topics that in the
past would have been deemed inad-
missable. Zaslavskaya's publications
include *Migration of the Rural Population*
(co-author, 1970), *The Socio-Economic
Development of the Village* (co-author,
1980), *The Sociology of Economic Life*
(co-author, 1989) and (in English)
The Second Socialist Revolution (1990).

Zalavskaya has been a member of
the Communist Party since 1954, was
a corresponding member of the
Academy of Sciences from 1968 and
has been a full member since 1981. She
was elected to the Congress of People's
Deputies in 1989 on the Academy of
Sciences' list, but declined to be considered for election to the Supreme
Soviet. She is, however, a member of
the Commission of the Soviet of the
Union for Labour, Prices and Social
Policy. AHB

451

ZASLAVSKY, Il'ya Iosifovich (b. 1960) Zaslavsky, a young Jewish member of the Congress of People's Deputies, has made a mark in Soviet political life since his emergence in 1989 as a spokesman for the handicapped. He himself is physically handicapped and he has helped to put the plight of the disabled in the Soviet Union on the political agenda. Zaslavsky, who has a candidate of sciences degree and is a research fellow at the Moscow Textile Institute named after Kosygin, is a member of the Commission of the Supreme Soviet on Veteran and Invalid Affairs. AHB

ZAVADOVSKY, Mikhail Mikhaylovich (1891–1957) Embryologist. A 1914 graduate of Moscow University, Zavadovsky introduced experimental embryology (then called developmental mechanics or dynamics) into Russia. Working at Askanya-Nova and the Moscow Zoo on a wide variety of laboratory and farm animals (notably poultry and sheep) and their parasites, he did innovative and influential research on the role of hormones and vitamins in devlopment and on the reciprocal interaction of developing organs, publishing over 250 works including *Sex and the Development of its Characteristics* (1922), *External and Internal Factors of Development* (1927), and *Developmental Dynamics of the Organism* (1929). In 1923 he created the zoo's laboratory of experimental biology, a world-renowned research centre, and became the zoo's director in 1925. A professor at Moscow University from 1927, he created its department of developmental dynamics (embryology) in 1930 and helped to organize the Institute of Animal Breeding of the Lenin All-Union Academy of Agricultural Sciences, to which he was elected in 1935. The rise of Lysenko and Prezent led to the loss of his laboratory and, in 1948, his professorship. Zavadovsky is reputed to have been the model for the scientist in Mikhail Bulgakov's *Heart of a Dog* (1925). MBA

ZAVADSKY, Yuriy Aleksandrovich (1894–1977) Stage director and actor. Zavadsky worked in the Vakhtangov studio from 1915, and in the Moscow Art Theatre from 1924 to 1931. He ran his own studio from 1924. Between 1932 and 1935 he was Artistic Director of the Central Theatre of the Red Army. In 1940 he was appointed Principal Director of the Mossoviet Theatre. He was also professor at the State Theatre Institute from 1947. His productions included Afinogenov's *Mashenka* (1941). RT

ZAVENYAGIN, Avraamyy Pavlovich (1901–1956) One of the principal industrial administrators of the Stalin period. One of the main characters in Rybakov's *Children of the Arbat* and *1935 and Other Years* is primarily based on Zavenyagin under the name of 'Ryazanov'. Son of a Moscow train driver, Zavenyagin joined the party in 1917. He held various party posts, including that of political commissar of an army division during the Civil War. He was educated at the Mining Institute (Mining Academy) (1923–30), then held important posts in VSNKh, including that of director of the institute for designing metalworks (GIPROMEZ), and head of the iron and steel industry as a whole. He was director of the Magnitogorsk iron and steel works (1933–37); deputy and then first deputy of the People's Commissariat for Heavy Industry (1937–38) and director of the Noril'sk mining and metal combine, which made extensive use of forced labour (1938–41); then, as deputy People's Commissar for Internal Affairs (1941–50), he was responsible for other large projects involving forced labour during the Second World War. In 1953 he became Deputy Minister, then in 1955 Minister, of 'Medium Machine-Building', responsible for the nuclear weapons programme. He was also appointed deputy chairman of the Council of Ministers in 1955. Zavenyagin was a candidate member of the party Central Committee (1934–39 and 1952–56), and made a full member in 1956. RWD

ZAYKOV, Lev Nikolaevich (b. 1923) Zaykov had fast promotion in the political hierarchy during the second half of the 1980s, becoming both a Secretary of the Central Committee and a full member of the Politburo. A Russian by nationality, he was born in Tula and made his career in the military industry in Leningrad. By 1961 he was a factory manager and from 1974 to 1976 general manager of a scientific production association of a military-related industry. In 1976 he became Chairman of the excutive committee of the Leningrad city soviet, a post he held until 1983 when he achieved the more powerful position of First Secretary of the Leningrad regional party committee. After Gorbachev became General Secretary Zaykov was elevated in 1985 to a Secretaryship of the Central Committee even though it was as recently as 1981 that he had become a member of the Central Committee. In 1986 he was made a full member of the Politburo. Within the Secretariat Zaykov has been responsible for overseeing the military and the armaments industry.

For a time Zaykov combined these functions with the First Secretaryship of the Moscow city party organization.

Following the removal of Boris Yel'tsin from that office in late 1987 Zaykov was chosen as his successor, a post he held until November 1989 when he was succeeded by Yuriy Prokof'ev. He retained for a little longer his more senior party offices but he was not one of the Politburo members included by Gorbachev in the Presidential Council established in March 1990.

Zaykov was not re-elected to the Central Committee at the Twenty-Eighth Party Congress and so ceased to be a member of the Politburo and Central Committee Secretariat in July 1990. For the time being he remains a member of the Congress of People's Deputies of the USSR, to which he was elected on the Communist Party list in 1989. AHB

ZELENSKY, Isaak Abramovich (1890–1938) A party official of modest significance during the early post-revolutionary period, Zelensky was a party member from the age of sixteen and a political activist before the revolution. After the October Revolution he became secretary of Moscow city party committee (1920 and 1921–24) and then a Secretary in the central party apparatus (1924) and Secretary of the party's Central Asian Bureau (1924–31). Zelensky served as chairman of the Central Union of Cooperative Societies after 1931; he was arrested in 1938, sentenced to death, and executed. Zelensky was rehabilitated in 1959. SLW

ZEMLYACHKA, (Zalkind) Rosaliya Samoilovna (1876–1947) A revolutionary and party official, Zemlyachka joined the RSDLP in 1896 and was active in the revolutionary movement for two decades prior to the Bolshevik Revolution. She was a party organizer and a party secretary and was arrested several times. After the

Bolshevik Revolution she was a party official with the Eighth and Thirteenth Armies during the Civil War. In 1920 she became a secretary of the Crimean Oblast Committee and in 1922 a secretary of a Moscow Party *raion*. After several other regional party assignments, Zemlyachka was reassigned to work in the Soviet government, in the Workers and Peasants Inspectorate (1926–31), the Commissariat of Transport (1933–34) and then the Soviet Control Commission, which she eventually chaired. She even served as a Deputy Chairman of the Council of People's Commissars (1939–43), the only woman to achieve such a position, before her transfer to the Party Control Committee. She was elected to the Central Committee in 1939 and remained on that body until her death in 1947. NN

ZHABOTINSKY, Leonid Ivanovich (b. 1938) Weightlifter. One of the world's greatest superheavy weightlifters, he was born into a Zaporozhe Cossack family in the village of Uspenska in the Ukraine. Twice Olympic (1964 and 1968), three times world and European, and five times national champion, he established as many as seventeen world records during his competitive career. He was by far the heaviest of the Soviet superheavies, tipping the scales at 165 kg, with a height of 188 cm (neck 51, biceps 48, chest 133, waist 118, thigh 72 and calf 44 cm). His best result was 590 kg for the press, lift and jerk in 1967. JWR

ZHAROV, Mikhail Ivanovich (1900–1981) Actor. Zharov was a versatile film actor whose appearances included: *The Cigarette Girl from Mosselprom* (1924), *Miss Mend* (1926), *Don Diego and Pelagea* (1928), *A Path to Life* (1931), *The Storm* (1934), *Peter the First* (1937–39), *The Return of Maksim*

(1937), *The Vyborg Side* (1939), *Bogdan Khmelnitsky* (1941) and *Michurin* (1949). RT

ZHDANOV, Andrey Aleksandrovich (1896–1948) A prominent figure in Soviet politics in the Stalin era, Zhdanov is most remembered for the harsh cultural policy which he pursued. The son of a school inspector, he joined the Bolsheviks in 1915, took part in the revolution and engaged in political work in the Red Army during the Civil War. From 1934 until his death in 1948 he was a Secretary of the Central Committee; in 1935 he became a candidate member and from 1939 was a full member of the Politburo. Zhdanov was the overseer of ideological affairs from 1944 and he pursued a hard-line policy, dealing especially severely with any signs of Western influence in the post-Second World War period. During the war – from 1941 to 1944 – he was in Leningrad and took a prominent part in the defence of the city. AHB

ZHEIMO, Yanina Boleslavovna (b. 1909) Film actress. Zheimo was closely associated with FEKS. RT

ZHELYABUZHSKY, Yuriy Andreevich (1888–1955) Veteran film director. Zhelyabuzhsky's works included *The Cigarette Girl from Mosselprom* (1924), *The Station Master* (1925) and *Prosperity* (1933). His films have perhaps never been fully appreciated. RT

ZHIDKOV, Yakov Ivanovich (1888–1969) President of the All-Union Council of Evangelical Christians-Baptists from its formation in 1944 until 1966. Brought up in an Evangelical Christian family, he succeeded Ivan Prokhanov as president of the Evangelical Christian Union in 1930. Zhidkov was arrested in 1937. Released by 1943, he helped organize the unification of Evangelical Christians and Baptists. Under his leadership thousands of churches were reestablished in the post-war years, but in 1960 he and the other leaders were forced to announce restrictions on church activity. A split resulted, which has still not been healed, with the dissenters rejecting any form of state control. MR

ZHILINSKY, Dmitriy Dmitrievich (b. 1927) Born in Sochi, Zhilinsky – a leading Soviet painter – graduated from the Surikov Institute in Moscow in 1951 where his main teachers were Chernyshev, Chuykov, Gritsay, and Korin. Close to Favorsky, Zhilinsky draws on many sources of inspiration, including the early Italian Renaissance and Old Russian art. He is know particularly for his portraits of family members and friends, such as Favorsky (1954) and Ivan Yefimov (1954). From 1951 to 1974 he taught at the Surikov Institute. JEB

ZHIRMUNSKY, Viktor Maksimovich (1891–1971) A literary critic and philologist, in the twenties and thirties Zhirmunsky wrote on Russian Romanticism and versification. A former member of OPOYAZ, he disassociated himself from the Formalists in 1924, while continuing to utilize formal analysis in his work. In later years he researched non-Slavic epics and topics in German language and literature. KC

ZHIZNEVA, Ol'ga Andreevna (1899–1972) Actress. Zhizneva was a popular silent film actress whose appearances included: *His Appeal* and *The Tailor from Torzhok* (1925), *The Three Millions Trial* (1926) and *The Ghost that Never Returns* (1930). RT

ZHOLTOVSKY, Ivan Vladislavovich (1867–1959) Architect. Zholtovsky was born near Minsk.

While studying at the Academy of Arts (1887–98), Zholtovsky worked as an architect's assistant and then, in 1900, began to teach at the Stroganov Institute in Moscow. An enthusiast of the Italian Renaissance and also the Baroque, he was largely responsible for the Neo-Palladian style in Russian architecture just before and after the Revolution. In 1923 Zholtovsky helped to design the 'First All-Russian Agricultural Exhibition' in Moscow with Nivinsky, Schchusev, *et al.*, and took part in the competition for the Palace of Soviets (early 1930s). During the Stalin era he designed many 'Italiante' apartments, offices and industrial plants, especially for Moscow. JEB

ZHUKOV, Georgiy Konstantinovich (1896–1974) The outstanding Soviet field commander of the 'Great Patriotic War', Zhukov's name is linked not only with victory over Nazi Germany in 1945 but also with the traditions of Russian military achievement and leadership exemplified by Suvorov, Rumyantsev, Kutuzov and Brusilov. Zhukov began his military service on 7 August 1915, joining the cavalry just a few months short of his nineteenth birthday; the son of an impoverished peasant family, he was an adolescent apprentice furrier in Moscow, a qualified craftsman and, finally, a wartime conscript. Selected for NCO training, Zhukov was decorated for his front-line service, recovered from heavy wounds, passed through the chaotic demobilization of the Imperial Army in 1917, survived a bout of typhus in his home village and, once more fit, volunteered for the Red Army in August 1918, joining the Fourth Cavalry Regiment of the First Moscow Cavalry Division.

Fate steered Zhukov in the direction

of Timoshenko's cavalry brigade and thence towards Budenny's cavalry division, the nucleus of the First Cavalry Army with its 'inner circle' of Stalin, Budenny and Voroshilov. A party member since March 1919, at the close of the Civil War Zhukov elected to stay on in the Red Army, rising to regimental command and attending an advanced instruction course (1924–25), together with Yeremenko, Rokossovsky and Bagramyan. A bright pupil at his village school, as a rising commander Zhukov now devoured professional books and papers, coming into contact with Tukhachevsky and Red Army modernization. In 1933 he took command of the crack Fourth Cavalry Division with its new 'motor-mechanized' component, a mobile strike force which demanded new techniques of training and deployment. Amidst the bloody 'military purge' he took command of the Third Cavalry Corps, defended himself against all charges and in June 1939 at Stalin's behest was ordered to Outer Mongolia to fight off the Japanese incursion on the Khalkin-Gol (Nomohan). In a classic but little known operation, with effective coordination of combined arms using armour and motorized infantry with air support – the model for his future operations – Zhukov inflicted a crushing defeat on the Japanese. A Hero of the Soviet Union and a full General in 1940, Zhukov moved from the Kiev Military District command to the post of Chief of the General Staff in February 1941, inevitably implicating him in the catastrophe of unpreparedness which befell the Red Army in June 1941.

During the war Stalin sent Zhukov into the field. He held Leningrad in a desperate last-ditch defence. He fought the battle of Moscow in tense association with Stalin in the winter of 1941 to 1942. He gave continuous advice to the *Stavka* (GHQ), rising in August 1942 to become First Deputy Defence Commissar and Deputy Supreme Commander-in-Chief (deputy to Stalin himself). With Vasilevsky he planned and coordinated the Soviet counter-offensive at Stalingrad, speeding back to Leningrad to supervise the 'deblockading' operations, returning in the spring of 1943 to coordinate and command at the huge battle of Kursk. Having dealt a devastating blow Zhukov returned to the centre to coordinate the massive defeat inflicted on the German Army in Belorussia, ramming Soviet armies into Poland and on to the river Oder, the prelude to his enormous assault on Berlin itself in April 1945.

In peace Stalin speedily stripped Zhukov of his major commands, demoting him to the Odessa Military District and expelling him from the Central Committee. Virtual banishment to the Urals Military District followed, though Stalin refused to allow Beria to arrest Zhukov on charges of 'conspiracy'. Restored to candidate membership of the Central Committee in 1952, Zhukov bounced back into the military fold on the death of Stalin. Krushchev appointed him as Defence Minister, where he planned the modernization and restructuring of the Soviet armed forces, using his weight with the military in 1957 to lend vital aid to Khrushchev in the struggle with the 'anti-party group'. His reward, however, proved to be abrupt dismissal in October 1957 by the same Khrushchev. Zhukov retained only his party membership and his pension, left now to write his memoirs. In those discreetly edited public versions it is presently possible to refer to Konstantin Simonov's conversations with Marshal Zhukov, adding some new facts but communicating immeasurably more about the man, the commander and the soldier-politician, four times a Hero of the Soviet Union. JE

ZHUKOV, Nikolay Nikolaevich (1908–1973) Graphic artist. Born in Moscow, Zhukov studied in Nizhniy-Novgorod and Saratov before joining the Grekov Studios of Battle-Painting in the 1930s. He is remembered for his sketches of frontline action during the Second World War and for his portraits, for example, of the writer and partisan Petr Vershiga (1950). JEB

ZHURKIN, Vitaliy Vladimirovich (b. 1928) Born in Moscow and a graduate of the Moscow Institute of International Relations (1951), Vitaliy Zhurkin worked as a journalist in radio and television and on *Pravda* before turning in 1965 to diplomacy and the Ministry of Foreign Affairs where he remained until 1968. Since then he has established himself as one of the Soviet Union's leading political analysts. He is a policy-oriented scholar who in 1988 was appointed Director of a newly-established Institute of Europe in Moscow. In the preceding twenty years he worked at the Institute of the USA and Canada, from 1971 as one of the Institute's Deputy Directors. Zhurkin has been not only a prolific writer on international relations but also at times an innovative one in the Soviet context. He was elected to membership of the Central Committee of the CPSU at the party's Twenty-eighth Congress in July 1990. Zhurkin is a Vice-President of the Soviet United Nations Association and of the Soviet Association of Political Sciences. AHB

ZINOV'EV, Aleksandr Aleksandrovich (b. 1922) Philsopher and prose writer. Internationally known in the field of formal logic, he worked at the Institute of Philosophy in Moscow from 1954 until his dismissal following the western publication of his *Yawning Heights* (1976). This and most of his numerous subsequent works mix rambling narrative with social, political and philosophical commentary. His distinctive view of Soviet society, most clearly expounded in *The Reality of Communism* (1981), derives from analysing the 'primary collective', at work- or dwelling-place, as its basic component. An uneven social scientist but a brilliant satirist, he gains his effects by acute observation and by mixing numerous linguistic levels, all of them impregnated with the jargon of Soviet society. He emigrated to West Germany in 1977. GAH

ZINOV'EV, Grigoriy Yevseevich (1883–1936) One of Lenin's closest associates and one of Stalin's most prominent victims, Zinov'ev was born into a lower-middle-class Jewish family in the Ukraine. Active in socialist groups from an early age, he joined the RSDWP in 1901, and in 1903 first met Lenin in Switzerland. Siding with Lenin when the party split at the 1903 Congress, he played a significant part in organizing the Bolshevik faction. Elected to the RSDWP's St Petersburg Committee in 1906 and to the Central Committee in 1907, he returned to Western Europe in 1908 to become Lenin's chief assistant in party organization and propaganda. Elected a member of the first Bolshevik Central Committee in 1912, he was with Lenin in Cracow in July 1914 and moved with him to Switzerland. With Lenin he headed the Central Committee's bureau, edited the Bolshevik newspaper *Sotsial-Demokrat*, and represented the Bolshevik Party at the Zimmerwald and Kienthal conferences of 1915 and 1916. In April 1917, he returned with Lenin through Germany to Russia. There he worked on *Pravda* and in the Petrograd Soviet; and following the July Days he accompanied Lenin into hiding in Finland. In the weeks preceding the October Revolution, he uncharacteristically opposed Lenin. Though a member of the Central Committee's political bureau established to plan the insurrection, Zinov'ev, with Kamenev, publicly opposed the seizure of power as premature; and after the Bolshevik coup he resigned from the Central Committe in protest against Lenin's refusal to form a coalition socialist government. These deviations were soon pardoned, and in December 1917 he became chairman of the Petrograd Soviet. A candidate member of the Politburo from 1919 and full member from 1921, Zinov'ev acquired international prominence as first chairman of the Executive Committee of the Communist Internationl (IKKI) from 1919.

With Lenin's illness and death, Zinov'ev emerged as a major contender for the party leadership, delivering the Central Committee's political report at the Twelfth Party Congress in April 1923 and at the Thirteenth Party Congress in May 1924. Meanwhile he formed a *troika* with Kamenev and Stalin to oppose Trotsky and the 'Left Opposition'. This alliance soon collapsed. In summer 1925, he and Kamenev came out against Stalin and Bukharin over the party's pro-peasant policies. Zinov'ev's 'Leningrad opposition' soon collapsed, and in January 1926 he was dismissed as chairman of the Leningrad Soviet. In spring 1926, he and Kamenev joined forces with Trotsky to form the 'United Opposition'. This led to his removal from the Politburo in July, from the Central Committee and the chairmanship of IKKI in October, and eventually to expulsion from the party in December 1927. Zinov'ev soon recanted and was readmitted to the party in 1928; for four years he worked in the state apparatus. At the end of 1932 he was again expelled for alleged involvement in the Ryutin affair and exiled. Readmitted a year later, he worked on the editorial staff of *Bol'shevik* and spoke at the Seventeenth Party Congress in 1934. Kirov's assassination by a young Leningrad Communist in December 1934 doomed him. In January 1935 he was arrested, tried in secret and sentenced to ten years imprisonment for supposedly organizing an opposition centre in Moscow and for 'moral complicity' in the assassination. In spring 1936 the NKVD reopened the Kirov case, and in August the first of the great purge show trials took place. Together with Kamenev and others, Zinov'ev was accused of collaborating with Trotsky to organize terrorist groups to assassinate Kirov, Stalin and other leaders. On the basis of his and others' confessions, he was found guilty and shot. He was officially rehabilitated in 1988. JB

ZNAMENSKY, Serafim Ivanovich (1906–1942) and **Georgiy Ivanovich** (1905–1946) Athletes. Though virtually unknown outside the USSR, the Znamensky brothers have more athletic tournaments and institutions named after them in the USSR than any other Soviet athletes. They gained fame before the war by dominating

Soviet middle-distance running, from 1500 to 10,000 m. They were born in the village of Zelenaya Sloboda, near Moscow. Usually running together in the same race, they improved national records twenty-three times in the 1500, 2000, 3000, 5000 and 10,000 m. They were the first Soviet runners to break the four-minute barrier in the 1500 m and the 32-minute barrier in the 10,000 m, Georgiy setting the record in the 1500 m and Serafim in the 10,000 m. Largely self-taught, the brothers believed in tempering the body, swimming in icy water, eschewing heating in their living quarters, and running in all weathers. Serafim died at the age of thirty-six in 1942, Georgiy at forty-three in 1946. JWR

ZOSHCHENKO, Mikhail Mikhaylovich (1895–1958) A Leningrader and Serapion Brother, Zoshchenko was an immensely popular prose writer of the twenties and thirties. He is famous for his humorous short *skaz* stories dealing with topical problems which are narrated by urban worker-philistines, and parody sovietese. Even his 1933 novel, *Youth Restored*, is *skaz*-like in its language and composition, although *The Story of a Life* (1935) attempts to be socialist realist. He was criticised for *Before the Sunrise* (1943), and in 1946 he and Akhmatova were attacked by Zhdanov and expelled from the Writers Union, but restored in 1953. KC

ZYKINA, Lyudmila Georg'evna (b. 1929) Mezzo-soprano. Zykina was born in Moscow. Starting life as an amateur singer, she became a soloist with the Pyatnitsky Russian Folk Chorus in 1947, then of the All-Union Radio Chorus of Russian Song in 1951. Since 1960 she has been attached to the Moscow Concert Organization, Moskontsert. She was made a People's Artist of the USSR in 1973. A skilled interpreter of Russian folk-song, often sung by her without accompaniment. GS

Appendix 1

Entries by
Subject and Profession

Agriculture

Bauman, K. Ya.
Belyaev, N. I.
Braun, A. G.
Bresis, V-E. G.
Chernov, M. A.
Chitanava, N. A.
Georgadze, M. P.
Gorbachev, M. S.
Grin'ko, G. F.
Grossu, S. K.
Ignatov, N. G.
Kalin, I. P.
Kalmanovich, M. I.
Kaminsky, G. N.
Kauls, A. E.
Kondratieff, N. D.
Kruchina, N. Ye.
Kubyak, V. M.
Kulakov, F. D.
Kviring, E. I.
Ligachev, Ye. K.
Mesyats, V. K.
Milyutin, V. P.
Movsisyan, V. M.
Nemchinov, V. S.
Nikonov, A. A.
Paskar', P. A.
Ryuytel', A. F.
Sokolov, Ye. Ye.
Trapeznikov, S. P.
Usmanov, G. I.
Vareykis, I. M.
Voronov, G. I.
Yemel'yanov, A. M.
Yunak, I. Kh.

Art, Architecture, and Design

Akimov, N. P.
Alabyan, K. S.
Al'medigen, B. A.
Al'tman, N. I.
Anikushkin, M. K.
Avetisyan, M. K.
Baksheev, V. N.
Barkhin, G. B.
Bazhbeuk-Melikyan, A. A.
Bekhteev, V. G.
Belashova, Ye. F.
Bisti, D. S.
Bogorodsky, F. S.
Brodsky, I. I.
Bruni, L. A.
Burov, A. K.
Byalynitsky-Biruliya, V. K.
Chagall, M.
Chaykov, I. M.
Cheremnykh, M. M.
Chernikhov, Ya. G.
Chernyshev, N. M.
Chuykov, S. A.
Costakis, G.
Deneyka, A. A.
Deni, V. N.
Dmitr'ev, V. V.
Dokuchaev, N. V.
Domagatsky, V. N.
Efanov, V. P.
Ekster, A. A.
Er'ziya (Nefedov), S. D.
Fal'k, R. R.
Favorsky, V. A.

Fedorosvsky, F. F.
Filatchev, O. P.
Filonov, P. N.
Fomin, I. A.
Fonvizen, A. V.
Gabo, N. (Pevzner, N. N.)
Gaponenko, T. G.
Gerasimov, A. M.
Gerasimov, S. V.
Ginzburg, M. Ya.
Glazunov, I. S.
Golosov, I. A.
Golosov, P. A.
Golubkina, A. S.
Goncharov, A. D.
Grabar', I. E.
Grekov, M. B.
Gritsay, A. M.
Gudiashvili, L. (V.) D.
Gumilev, N. S.
Iltner, E. K.
Infante-Arana, F.
Iofan, B. M.
Ioganson, B. V.
Kalashnikov, A. I.
Kandinsky, V. V.
Kaplan, A. L.
Katsman, Ye. A.
Kerbel', L. Ye.
Kibal'nikov, A. P.
Kibrik, Ye. A.
Klutsis, G. G.
Klychev, I.
Komov, O. K.
Konashevich, V. M.
Konchalovsky, P. P.
Konenkov, S. T.

Appendix 1

Sergeev, K. M.
Shiryaev, A. V.
Sizova, A. I.
Slonimsky, Yu. I.
Surits, Ye. Ya.
Tikhomirov, V. D.
Ulanova, G. S.
Vaganova, A. Ya.
Vaynonen, V. I.
Vasil'ev, V. V.
Vinogradov, O. M.
Yakobson, L. V.
Zakharov, R. V.

**Engineers and
Industrialists**

Aleksandrov, I. G.
Aleshin, G. V.
Antonov, A. K.
Artyukhina, A. V.
Baklanov, O. D.
Bardin, I. P.
Batalin, Yu. P.
Belousov, I. S.
Birman, S. P.
Biryukova, A. P.
Bogdanov, P. A.
Brazauskas, A-M. K.
Chubar', V. Ya.
Dmitriev, I. N.
Dolgikh, V. I.
Frolov, K. V.
Gagarov, D. N.
Gol'tsman, A. Z.
Grinevetsky, V. I.
Grum-Grzhimaylo, V. Ye.
Gvakhariya, G. V.
Ivanov, V. I.
Kabkov, Ya. I.
Kadyrov, G. Kh.
Kalmanovich, M. I.
Kamentsev, V. M.
Karimov, I. A.
Khrunichev, M. V.
Kolbin, G. V.
Konotop, V. I.
Korolev, S. P.
Koshkin, M. I.
Kostandov, L. A.
Kosygin, A. N.
Kotin, Zh. Ya.
Kozlov, F. R.

Krasin, L. B.
Krzhizhanovsky, G. M.
Kuybyshev, V. V.
Kviring, E. I.
Lavochkin, S. A.
Lesechko, M. A.
Likhachev, I. A.
Listov, V. V.
Lobov, O. I.
Lobov, S. S.
Lomako, P. F.
Lomov, G. I.
Makhamov, K. M.
Malyshev, V. A.
Masaliev, A. M.
Maslyukov, Yu. D.
Mekk [von Meck], N. K.
Mendybaev, M. S.
Mezhlauk, I. I.
Mezhlauk, V. I.
Musakhanov, M. M.
Mutalibov, A. N.
Nadiradze, A. D.
Nazarbaev, N. A.
Niyazov, S. A.
Novikov, I. T.
Novikov, V. N.
Pervukhin, M. G.
Rudnev, K. N.
Rudzutak, Ya. E.
Ryzhkov, N. I.
Saburov, M. Z.
Sakalauskas, V. V.
Salykov, K.
Serbin, I. D.
Serebrovsky, A. P.
Shakirov, M. Z.
Shalaev, S. A.
Solov'ev, Yu. F.
Sulimov, D. Ye.
Tevosyan, I. F.
Tikhonov, N. A.
Tolstykh, B. L.
Tupolev, A. N.
Usmankhodzhaev, I. B.
Vannikov, B. L.
Vol'sky, A. I.
Yakovlev, A. S.
Yakovlev, B. P.
Yangel, M. K.
Yastrebov, I. P.
Zavenyagin, A. P.

Law

Akulov, I. A.
Alekseev, S. S.
Bisher, I. O.
Boguslavsky, M. M.
Bratus', S. N.
Durdenevsky, V. N.
Gdlyan, T. Kh.
Grabar', V. E.
Ivanov, N. V.
Kalistratova, S. V.
Kolodkin, A. L.
Koretsky, V. M.
Korovin, Ye. A.
Kravtsov, B. V.
Krylenko, N. V.
Krylov, S. B.
Kudryavtsev, V. N.
Kurashvili, B. P.
Laptev, V. V.
Lomov, G. I.
Lukashuk, I. I.
Luk'yanov, A. I.
Lunts, L. A.
Manaenkov, Yu. A.
Murakhovsky, V. S.
Nikonov, V. P.
Pashukanis, Ye. B.
Piskotin, M. I.
Razumovsky, G. P.
Shakhnazarov, G. Kh.
Sheremet, K. F.
Sobchak, A. A.
Strogovich, M. S.
Stuchka, P. I.
Sukharev, A. Ya.
Topornin, B. N.
Trainin, A. N.
Tunkin, G. I.
Vyshinsky, A. Ya.

**Military, Security Police,
and Space Programme**

Akhromeyev, S. F.
Akulov, I. A.
Aliev, G. A.
Altunin, A. T.
Andropov, Yu. V.
Antonov, A. I.
Artemev, P. A.
Bagirov, M. D. A.

Appendix 1

Obukhova, N. A.
Oistrakh, D. F.
Oistrakh, I. D.
Pakhmutova, A. N.
Part, A.
Pauls, R. V.
Petrov, A. P.
Petrov [Krauze], I. I.
Prokof'ev, S. S.
P'yavko, V. I.
Rakhlin, N. G.
Reyzen, M. O.
Rikhter [Richter], S. T.
Roslavets, N. A.
Rostropovich, M. L.
Rozhdestvensky, G. N.
Salmanov, V. N.
Samosud, S. A.
Schnittke, A. G.
Shafran, D. B.
Shalyapin, F. I.
Shaporin, Yu. A.
Shchedrin, R. K.
Shebalin, V. Ya.
Shirinsky, S. P.
Shostakovich, D. D.
Shostakovich, M. D.
Simeonov, K. A.
Slonimsky, S. M.
Sobinov, L. V.
Sofronitsky, V. V.
Solov'ev-Sedoy, V. P.
Spendyarov, A. A.
Svetlanov, Ye. F.
Sviridov, G. V.
Taktakishvili, O. V.
Tchaikovsky, *see* Chaikovsky
Tret'yakov, V. V.
Tsintsadze, S. F.
Ustovol'skaya, G. I.
Utesov, L. O.
Vedernikov, A. F.
Vishnevskaya, G. P.
Volkonsky, A. M.
Yampol'sky, A. I.
Yegorov, Yu.
Zykina, L. G.

Politicians, Political Activists (including Dissidents), and Diplomats

Abalkin, L. I.
Afanas'ev, Yu. N.
Airikyan, P. A.
Akhromeyev, S. F.
Aksenov, A. N.
Aksenov, N. F.
Akulov, I. A.
Aleshin, G. V.
Aliev, G. A.
Altunin, A. T.
Amal'rik, A. A.
Ambartsumov, Ye. A.
Andriyanov, V. M.
Andropov, Yu. V.
Antonov, A. K.
Arbatov, G. A.
Aristov, A. B.
Armand, I. [Ye. F.]
Artem'ev, P. A.
Artyukhina, A. V.
Arutyunyan, S. G.
Arvatov, B. I.
Aytmatov, C. T.
Bagirov, M. D. A.
Bakatin, V. V.
Bakh [Bach], A. N.
Baklanov, O. D.
Batalin, Yu. P.
Bauman, K. Ya.
Bazarov, V. A.
Belousov, I. S.
Belyaev, N. I.
Belyakov, O. S.
Beria, L. P.
Berklav, E. K.
Bessmertnykh, A. A.
Bikkenin, N. B.
Biryukova, A. P.
Bisher, I. O.
Bogdanov, P. A.
Bogomolov, O. T.
Boldin, V. I.
Bonner, Ye. G.
Braun, A. G.
Brazauskas, A-M. K.
Bresis, V-E. G.
Brezhnev, L. I.
Bryukhanov, N. P.

Bubnov, A. S.
Budenny, S. M.
Bukharin, N. I.
Bukovsky, V. K.
Bulganin, N. A.
Bunich, P. G.
Burlatsky, F. M.
Bykov, V. V.
Chakovsky, A. B.
Chazov, Ye. I.
Chebrikov, V. M.
Chernavin, V. N.
Chernenko, K. U.
Chernov, M. A.
Chernyaev, A. S.
Chervonenko, S. V.
Chicherin, G. V.
Chitanava, N. A.
Chornovil, V. M.
Chubar', V. Ya.
Daniel', Yu. M. (pseud. Arshak, N.), *see also* Sinyavsky, A. D.
Dementeva, R. F.
Demichev, P. N.
Dmitriev, I. F.
Dmitriev, I. N.
Dobrynin, A. F.
Dolgikh, V. I.
Drach, I. F.
Dubinin, Yu. V.
Dzasokhov, A. S.
Dzerzhinsky, F. E.
Dzhemilev, M. [Abdulzhemil']
Eykhe, R. I.
Falin, V. M.
Fedorchuk, V. V.
Fedorov, S. N.
Fedoseev, P. N.
Fil'shin, G. I.
Frolov, I. T.
Frolov, K. V.
Frunze, M. V.
Furtseva, Ye. A.
Gagarin, Yu. A.
Gagarov, D. N.
Gamsakhurdia, Z. K.
Gdlyan, T. Kh.
Georgadze, M. P.
Gerasimov, G. I.
Gidaspov, B. V.
Ginzburg, A. I.

Appendix 1

466

Moskalenko, K. S.
Moskvin, I. M.
Movsisyan, V. M.
Mukhitdinov, N. A.
Murakhovsky, V. S.
Musakhanov, M. M.
Mutalibov, A. N.
Mzhavanadze, V. P.
Nasriddinova, Ya. S.
Nazarbaev, N. A.
Neizvestny, E. I.
Nekrasov, V. P.
Nikitin, A. V.
Niklus, M-O.
Nikolaeva, K. I.
Nikonov, A. A.
Nikonov, V. P.
Nishanov, R. N.
Niyazov, S. A.
Novikov, A. A.
Novikov, I. T.
Novikov, V. N.
Ogarkov, N. V.
Oleynik, B. I.
Ordzhonikidze, G. K.
Organov, N. N.
Orlov, Yu. F.
Orlov, Yu. F.
Osinsky, N. [Obolensky, V. V.]
Osipov, V. N.
Panyushkin, A. S.
Paskar', P. A.
Patolichev, N. S.
Pauls, R. V.
Pavlov, G. S.
Pavlychko, D. V.
Pel'she, A. Ya.
Pervukhin, M. G.
Petrov, V. I.
Plyushch, L. I.
Podgorny, N. V.
Podrabinek, A. P.
Poloz'kov, I. K.
Polyansky, D. S.
Ponomarenko, P. K.
Ponomarev, B. N.
Popov, G. Kh.
Popov, V. D.
Pospelov, P. N.
Postyshev, P. P.
Preobrazhensky, Ye. A.
Primakov, Ye. M.

Pristavkin, A. I.
Prokof'ev, Yu. A.
Prunskene, K-D. P.
Pugo, B. K.
Pyatakov, G. L.
Radek, K. B.
Rakovsky, Kh. G.
Rashidov, S. R.
Rasputin, V. G.
Ratushinskaya, I. B.
Razumovsky, G. P.
Revenko, G. I.
Romanov, G. V.
Rokossovsky, K. K.
Rotmistrov, P. A.
Rubiks, A.
Rudnev, K. N.
Rudzutak, Ya. E.
Rusakov, K. V.
Rykov, A. I.
Ryutin, M. N.
Ryuytel', A. F.
Ryzhkov, N. I.
Saburov, M. Z.
Sagdeev, R. Z.
Sakalauskas, V. V.
Sakharov, A. D.
Salykov, K.
Samoilova, K. N.
Semenova, G. V.
Semichastnyy, V. Ye.
Serbin, I. D.
Serebrovsky, A. P.
Serebryakov, L. P.
Shalaev, S. A.
Shakhnazarov, G. Kh.
Shakirov, M. Z.
Shalamov, V. T.
Shaposhnikov, B. M.
Shatalin, S. S.
Shcharansky, A. B.
Shchelokov, N. A.
Shcherbakov, A. S.
Shcherbitsky, V. V.
Sheboldaev, B. P.
Shelepin, A. N.
Shelest, P. Ye.
Shenin, O. S.
Shepilov, D. T.
Shevardnadze, E. A.
Shevchenko, V. S.
Shkiryatov, M. F.
Shlikhter, A. G.

Shlyapnikov, A. G.
Shmelev, N. P.
Shtemenko, S. M.
Shumyatsky, B. Z.
Shvernik, N. M.
Sillari, E-A. A.
Slyun'kov, N. N.
Smidovich, S. N.
Smirnov, G. L.
Smirnov, I. N.
Snechkus, A. Yu.
Sobchak, A. A.
Sokol'nikov, G. Ya.
Sokolov, S. L.
Sokolov, Ye. Ye.
Sokolovsky, V. D.
Solomentsev, M. S.
Solov'ev, Yu. F.
Solzhenitsyn, A. I.
Sorokin, M. I.
Spiridonov, I. V.
Stalin, I. V.
Stankevich, S. B.
Stasova, Ye.
Stepakov, V. I.
Stroev, Ye. S.
Stuchka, P. I.
Sukharev, A. Ya.
Sulimov, D. Ye.
Sultan-Galiev, M. S.
Suslov, M. A.
Sverdlov, Ya. M.
Syrtsov, S. I.
Talyzin, N. V.
Tarasov-Rodionov, A. I.
Tarazevich, G. S.
Tereshkova, V. V.
Tevosyan, I. F.
Tikhonov, N. A.
Titov, V. N.
Tolstykh, B. L.
Tolubko, V. F.
Tomsky, M. P.
Topornin, B. N.
Tovstukha, I. P.
Trapeznikov, S. P.
Tret'yak, I. M.
Trotsky, L. D.
Tsipko, A. S.
Tsvigun, S. K.
Tunkin, G. I.
Tyazhel'nikov, Ye. M.
Uglanov, N. A.

Appendix 1

Shpet, G. G.
Sinyavsky, A. D. (pseud.
  Abram Terts)
Slonimsky, Yu. I.
Smirnov, G. L.
Sokolov, B. M.
Sokolov, Yu. M.
Stankevich, S. B.
Strogovich, M. S.
Surits, Ye. Ya.
Tomashevsky, B. V.
Trainin, A. N.
Tret'yakov, S. M.
Tynyanov, Yu. N.
Uspensky, B. A.
Vinogradov, V. V.
Vladimov, G. N.
Voronsky, A. K.
Yakir, P. I.
Yakovlev, A. N.
Zhirmunsky, V. M.
Zinov'ev, A. A.

Scientists (including the medical profession)

Agol, I. I.
Aleksandrov, A. D.
Astaurov, B. L.
Baev, A. A.
Bakh (Bach), A. N.
Bekhterev, V. M.
Belozersky, A. N.
Belyaev, D. K.
Belyaev, N. K.
Berg, L. S.
Bogomolets, A. A.
Bonner, E. G.
Borisyak, A. A.
Chazov, Ye. I.
Chelomey, V. N.
Chetverikov, S. S.
Chichibabin, A. Ye.
Davidenkov, S. N.
Davitashvili, L. Sh.
Degtyarev, V. A.
Dubinin, N. P.
Efroimson, V. P.
Engel'gardt, V. A.
Fedorov, S. N.
Fersman, A. Ye.
Filipchenko, Yu. A.
Gaisinovich, A. Ye.

Gamaleya, N. F.
Gauze, G. F.
Gershenzon, S. M.
Gessen, B. M.
Gidaspov, B. V.
Glushchenko, I. Ye.
Glushko, V. P.
Grabin, V. G.
Grekova, I. [Ventsel', Ye. S.]
Gromashevsky, L. V.
Gurvich, A. G.
Gvishiani, D. M.
Il'yushin, S. V.
Ipatieff, V. N.
Isachenko, B. L.
Isakova, B. S.
Ivanov, I. I.
Kalashnikov, M. T.
Kaminsky, G. N.
Kapitsa, P. L.
Karpechenko, G. D.
Keller, B. A.
Khadzhinov, M. I.
Kholodnyy, N. G.
Knunyants, I. L.
Kilmogorov, A. N.
Kol'tsov, N. K.
Komarov, V. L.
Korolev, S. P.
Koryagin, A. I.
Koshkin, M. I.
Kotin, Zh. Ya.
Kovrigina, M.
Kozlov, P. K.
Kurchatov, I. V.
Lavochkin, S. A.
Lavrent'ev, M. A.
Lazarev, P. P.
Lepeshinskaya, O. B.
Levit, S. G.
Levitsky, G. A.
Lipsky, V. I.
Lyapunov, A. A.
Lysenko, T. D.
Lyubimenko, V. N.
Medvedev, Zh. A.
Menzbir, M. A.
Michurin, I. V.
Mikoyan, A. I.
Nadiradze, A. D.
Navashin, S. G.
Nesmeyanov, A. N.
Niklus, M-O.

Oparin, A. I.
Orbeli, L. A.
Orlov, Yu. F.
Osip'yan, Yu. A.
Ovchinnikov, Yu. A.
Pavlov, I. P.
Plyushch, L. I.
Podrabinek, A. P.
Prezent, I. I.
Prokof'eva-Bel'govskaya,
  A. A.
Pryanishnikov, D. N.
Sakharov, A. D.
Schmal'gauzen, I. I.
Semashko, N. A.
Semenov, N. N.
Serebrovsky, A. S.
Severtsov, A. N.
Shcharansky, A. B.
Shemyakin, M. M.
Shmidt (Schmidt), O. Yu.
Sisakyan, N. M.
Snezhevsky, A. V.
Sobolev, S. L.
Spirin, A. S.
Staravoytova, G. V.
Sukhachev, V. N.
Talyzin, N. V.
Tarasevich, L. A.
Timofeev-Resovsky, N. V.
Topchiev, A. V.
Tupolev, A. N.
Vavilov, N. I.
Velikhov, Ye. P.
Veresaev [Smidovich], V. V.
Vernadsky, V. I.
Vil'yams, V. R.
Vladimirsky, M. F.
Yakovlev, A. S.
Yangel, M. K.
Zavadovsky, M. M.

Social Scientists (Economists, Political Scientists, Sociologists, Anthropologists)

Abalkin, L. I.
Afanas'ev, V. G.
Aganbegyan, A. G.
Ambartsumov, Ye. A.
Arbatov, G. A.

Appendix 1

Dovzhenko, A. P.
Dzigan, Ye. L.
Eisenstein, S. M.
Ekk, N. V.
Erdman, N. R.
Ermler, F. M.
Faiko, A. M.
Faintsimmer, A. M.
Fedin, K. A.
Ferdinandov, B. A.
Fogel', V. P.
Foregger, N. M.
Gabrilovich, Ye. O.
Galich, A. A.
Gardin, V. R.
Garin, E. P.
Gelovani, M. G.
Gerasimov, S. A.
German, A. B.
Glizer, Yu. S.
Golovnya, A. D.
Gorchakov, N. M.
Gor'ky, M. [Peshkov, A. M.]
Grebner, G. E.
Gubenko, N. N.
Gumilev, N. S.
Il'insky, I. V.
Ioseliani, O.
Ivanovsky, A. V.
Kachalov, V. I.
Kalatozov, M. K.
Kaufman, M. A.
Kazakevich, E. G.
Kedrov, M. N.
Kharms, D. I.
Kheifits, I. Ye.
Khokhlov, K. P.
Khokhlova, A. S.
Khrzhanovsky, A. Yu.
Kirshon, V. M.
Klimov, E.
Knipper-Chekhova, O. L.
Komarov, S. P.
Koonen, A. G.
Kostrichkin, A. A.
Koval'Samborsky, I. I.
Kozintsev, G. M.
Kozlovsky, S. V.
Kuleshov, L. V.
Kulidzhanov, L. A.
Kuzmin, M. A.
Kuz'mina, Ye. A.
Legoshin, V. G.

Leonidov, L. M.
Levitsky, A. A.
Livanov, B. N.
Lobanov, A. M.
Lunacharsky, A. V.
Lunts, L. N.
Lyubimov, Yu. P.
Macheret, A. V.
Makarova, T. F.
Mardzhanov, K. A.
Maretskaya, V. P.
Martinson, S. A.
Massalitinova, V. O.
Mayakovsky, V. V.
Medvedkin, A. I.
Meyerhol'd, V. E.
Michurina-Samoilova, V. A.
Mikhalkov, N. S.
Mikhalkov-Konchalovsky,
   A. S.
Mikhoels, S. M.
Mindadze, A. A.
Moskvin, A. N.
Moskvin, I. M.
Nagibin, Yu. M.
Nemirovich-Danchenko,
   V. I.
Nilin, P. F.
Nilsen, V. S.
Norstein, Yu. B.
Obravtsov, S. V.
Okhlopkov, N. P.
Olesha, Yu. K.
Orlova, L. P.
Otsep, F. A.
Panferov, F. I.
Panfilov, G.
Panteleev, A. P.
Paradzhanov, S. I.
Perestiani, I. N.
Petrov, V. M.
Petrov-Bytov, P. P.
Petrushevskaya, L.
Pogodin, N. F.
Popov, A. D.
Preobrazhenskaya, O. I.
Protozanov, Ye. A.
Pudovkin, V. I.
Pyr'ev, I. A.
Radlov, S. E.
Raikh, Z. N.
Raizman, Yu. Ya.
Raykin, A. I.

Romashov, B. S.
Romm, M. I.
Room, A. M.
Roshal', G. L.
Rozenel' [Lunacharskaya-
   Rozenel'], N. A.
Ryazanov, E. A.
Rzheshevsky, A. B.
Sats, N. I.
Savchenko, I. A.
Semenova, L. N.
Serafimovich, A. S.
Shatrov, M. F.
Shchukin, B. V.
Shengelaya, N. M.
Shepitko, L.
Shklovsky, V. B.
Shkurat, S. I.
Shorin A. F.
Shpinel', I. A.
Shtraukh, M. M.
Shub, Ye. I.
Shukshin, V. M.
Shumyatsky, B. Z.
Shvarts, Ye. L.
Simonov, K. M.
Simonov, R. N.
Smoktunovsky, I. M.
Solntseva, Yu. I.
Sten, A.
Sudakov, I. Ya.
Svashenko, S. A.
Svilova, Ye. I.
Tager, P. G.
Tairov, A. Ya.
Tarasova, A. K.
Tarich, Yu. V.
Tarkovsky, A. A.
Tisse, E. K.
Tolstoy, A. N.
Tovstogonov, G. A.
Trauberg, I. Z.
Trauberg, L. Z.
Trenev, K. A.
Tret'yakov, S. M.
Turchaninova, Ye. D.
Turin, V. A.
Turkin, V. K.
Ul'yanov, M. A.
Urbansky, Ye. Ya.
Vachnadze, N.
Vainshtok, V. P.
Vakhtangov, Ye. B.

Appendix 1

Marchenko, A. T.
Marshak, S. Ya.
Martynov, L. N.
Maslennikov, A. A.
Matveeva, N. N.
Mayakovsky, V. V.
Medvedev, R. A.
Mikhaylov, N. A.
Nagibin, Yu. M.
Narovchatov, S. S.
Nekrasov, V. P.
Nikolaeva, G. Ye.
Nilin, P. F.
Okudzhava, B. S.
Olesha, Yu. K.
Oleynik, B. I.
Oshanin, L. I.
Osipov, V. N.
Ostrovsky, N. A.
Ovechkin, V. V.
Panferov, F. I.
Panova, V. F.
Parnok, S. Ya.
Pasternak, B. L.
Paustovsky, K. G.
Pavlychko, D. V.
Pereverzev, V. F.
Petrushevskaya, L.
Pilnyak, B. [Vogau, B. A.]
Plyushch, L. I.
Pogodin, N. F.
Polevoy, B. [Kampov, B. N.]
Polonskaya, Ye. G.
Polonsky, V. P.
Pospelov, P. N.
Pristavkin, A. I.
Prokof'ev, A. A.
Rashidov, S. R.
Rasputin, V. G.
Ratushinskaya, I. B.
Razgon, L. E.

Rodov, S. A.
Rozhdestvensky, R. I.
Rubtsov, N. M.
Rybakov, A. N.
Samoilov, D. S.
Samoilova, K. N.
Sayanov, V. M.
Seifullina, L. Ya.
Seleznev, G. N.
Sel'vinsky, I. L.
Semenova, G. V.
Serafimovich [Popov], A. S.
Sergeev-Tsensky, S. N.
Shaginyan, M. S.
Shalamov, V. T.
Shchipachev, S. P.
Shefner, V. S.
Shepilov, D. T.
Shkapskaya, M. M.
Shklovsky, V. B.
Shmelev, N. P.
Sholokhov, M. A.
Shukshin, V. M.
Shvarts, Ye. L.
Simonov, K. M.
Sinyavsky, A. D.
Slutsky, B. A.
Smelyakov, Ya. V.
Smidovich, S. N.
Sokolov, A. V. (Sasha)
Sologub, F. K.
Soloukhin, V. A.
Solzhenitsyn, A. I.
Strugatsky, A. N. *and* B. N.
Surkov, A. A.
Svetlov, M. A.
Tarasov-Rodionov, A. I.
Tendryakov, V. F.
Tikhonov, N. S.
Tolstoy, A. N.
Tret'yakov, S. M.

Trifonov, Yu. V.
Tsvetaeva, M. I.
Tsybin, V. D.
Tvardovsky, A. T.
Tynyanov, Yu. N.
Ulyanova, M. I.
Utkin, I. P.
Vaginov [Vagingeim], K. K.
Vanshenkin, K. Ya.
Vasil'ev, P. N.
Verchenko, Yu. N.
Veresaev [pseud. of Smido-
    vich, V. V.]
Vigdorova, F. A.
Vikulov, S. V.
Vinokurov, Ye. M.
Vishnevsky, V. V.
Vladimov, G. N.
Voinovich, V. N.
Volosevich, *see* Vladimov,
    G. N.
Voloshin, M. A.
Voronsky, A. K.
Voznesensky, A. A.
Vvedensky, A. I.
Vysotsky, V. S.
Yakir, P. I.
Yakovlev, Ye. V.
Yashin [Popov], A. Ya.
Yesenin, S. A.
Yevtushenko, Ye. A.
Yuvachev, *see* Kharms, D. I.
Zabolotsky, N. A.
Zagladin, V. V.
Zalygin, S. P.
Zamyatin, Ye. I.
Zhurkin, V. V.
Zinov'ev, A. A.
Zoshenko, M. M.

Appendix 2

Key to Abbreviations and Acronyms

AA Academy of Arts (St Petersburg unless indicated otherwise)

Agitprop [*otdel agitatsii i propagandy*]   Department of Agitation and Propaganda

agit-fil'm [*agitatsionnyy fil'm*]   propaganda film

AKhRR [*Assotsiatsiya khudozhnikov revolyutsionnoy Rossii*]   Association of Artists of Revolutionary Russia (1922–28)

AMN [*Akademiya meditsinskikh nauk*]   Academy of Medical Science

AMO [*Moskovskiy avtomobil'nyy zavod*]   Moscow Automobile Factory

Amtorg [*Amerikanskoe torgovoe aktsionernoe obshchestvo*]   American Trade Joint-Stock Company

AN [*Akademiya nauk*]   Academy of Sciences

APN [*agenstvo pechati Novosti*]   Novosti press agency

ARU [*Ob'edinenie arkhitektorov-urbanistov*]   Association of Architects-Urbanists (1928–31)

ASNOVA [*Assotsiatsiya novykh arkhitektorov*]   Association of New Architects (1923–32)

ASSR [*Avtonomnaya Sovetskaya Sotsialisticheskaya Respublika*]   Autonomous Soviet Socialist Republic

Cheka [*Vserossiyskaya chrezvychaynaya komissiya po bor'be s kontrrevolyutsiey i sabotazhem*]   All-Russian Extraordinary Commission for Combating Counter-Revolution and Sabotage (1918–22)

CMEA Council for Mutual Economic Assistance

COMECON (*see* CMEA)

Comintern [*Kommunisticheskiy internatsional*]   Communist International

CPF Communist Party of Finland

CPSU Communist Party of the Soviet Union

EKO [*Ekonomika i organizatsiya promyshlennogo proizvodstva*]   The Economics and Organization of Industrial Production (Journal)

FEKS Factory of the Eccentric Author

FIG International Gymnastics Federation

GAU [*Glavnoe artilleriyskoe upravlenie*]   Main Artillery Administration

GDL [*Gazodinamicheskaya laboratoriya*]   Gas Dynamics Laboratory
GDR German Democratic Republic
GIPROMEZ [*Gosudarstvennyy institut proektirovaniya metallurgicheskikh zavodov*]   State Institute for Designing and Planning of Metallurgical Plants
GINZ [*Gosudarstvennyy nauchnyy institut narodnogo zdravookhraneniya*]   State Scientific Institute of Public Health
GKNT [*Gosudarstvennyy komitet po nauke i tekhnike*]   State Committee for Science and Technology
GOELRO [*Gosudarstvennaya komissiya po elektrifikatsii Rossii*]   State Commission for the Electrification of Russia
gorkom [*gorodskoy komitet*]   city committee
Gosagroprom [*Gosudarstvennyy agro-promyshlennyy komitet*]   State Agro-Industrial Committee (1985–89)
Gosekonomkomissiya [*Gosudarstvennaya nauchno-ekonomicheskaya komissiya*]   State Scientific-Economic Commission
Gosfil'mofond [*Vsesoyuznyy gosudarstvennyy fond kino-fil'mov SSSR*]   All-Union State Film Archive
Gosplan [*Gosudarstvennyy planovyy komitet*]   State Planning Committee
Gosstroy [*Gosudarstvennyy komitet po deam stroitel'stva*]   State Committee on Construction
ICBM Inter-Continental Ballistic Missile
IGEN [*Institut genetiki*]   Institute of Genetics
IKKI [*Ispolnitel'nyy Komitet Kommunisticheskogo Internatsionala*]   Executive Committee of the Communist International
IMEMO [*Institut mirovoy ekonomiki i mezhdunarodnykh otnosheniy*]   Institute of World Economy and International Relations
IEMSS [*Institut ekonomiki mirovoy sotsialisticheskoy sistemy*]   Institute of Economics of the World Socialist System
IMO [*Institut mezhdunarodnykh otnosheniy*]   Institute of International Relations
IMO International Maritime Organization
INMARSAT International Maritime Satellite Organization
IOC International Olympic Committee
IZO NKP [*otdel izobrazitel'nykh iskusstv (Narodnyy komissariat Prosveshcheniya)*]   Department of the Representative Arts (People's Commissariat of Public Education)
KGB [*Komitet gosudarstvennoy bezopasnosti*]   State Security Committee
Komsomol [*Kommunisticheskiy soyuz molodezhi*]   Young Communist League
KP [*Kommunisticheskaya Partiya*]   Communist Party
LEF [*Levyy front iskusstva*]   Left Front of Art
MAPP [*Moskovskaya assotsiatsiya proletarskikh pisateley*]   Moscow Association of Proletarian Writers

MIG [*samolet konstruktsii Mikoyana i Gurevicha*] (fighter) aircraft (built by Mikoyan and Gurevich)

MIPSA Moscow Institute of Painting, Sculpture and Architecture

MGIMO [*Moskovskiy gosudarstvennyy institut mezhdunarodnykh otnosheniy*] Moscow State Institute of International Relations

MGU [*Moskovskiy gosudarstvennyy universitet*] Moscow State University

Morsvyazsputnik [*Morskaya svyaz'sputnik*] Soviet Maritime Satellite Organization

Narkomzdrav [*Narodnyy komissariat zdravokhraneniya*] People's Commissariat of Public Health

Narkomzem [*Narodnyy Komissariat Zemledeliya*] People's Commissariat of Agriculture

NKVD [*Narodnyy kommissariat vnutrennyikh del*] People's Commissariat for Internal Affairs

NEP [*Novaya ekonomicheskaya politika*] New Economic Policy

Oberiu The Association for Real Art

obkom [*oblastnoy komitet*] *oblast* (regional) committee

OGPU [*Ob'edinennoe gosudarstvennoe politicheskoe upravlenie*] Unified State Political Directorate

OPOYAZ [*Obshchestvo izucheniya teorii poeticheskogo yazyka*] Society for the Study of the Theory of Poetical Language

Orgburo [*Organizatsionnoe byuro*] Organization bureau

ORS [*Obshchestvo Russkikh skul'ptorov*] Society of Russian Sculptors (1925–32)

OSA [*Ob'edinenie sovremennykh arkhitektorov*] Association of Contemporary Artists (1925–31)

OST [*Obshchestvo khudozhnikov-stankovistov*] Society of Studio Artists (1925–32)

Politburo [*Politicheskoe byuro*] Political Bureau (of the Central Committee of the Communist Party)

Proletkul't [*Proletarskaya kul'tura*] Proletarian Culture (organization, 1917–32)

PU [*Polevoy ustav*] Field service regulations
   –29 Field Service Regulations for the Red Army
   –36 Provisional Field Service Regulations

PVO [*protivovozdushnaya oborona*] Anti-Aircraft Defence Forces

Rabkrin [*Raboche-krest'yanskaya inspektsiya*] Workers' and Peasants' Inspectorate

RAPP [*Rossiyskaya assotsiatsiya proletarskikh pisateley*] Russian Association of Proletarian Writers (1925–32)

RKKA [*Raboche-Krest'yanskaya Krasnaya Armiya*] Workers' and Peasants' Red Army (1918–46)

RNII [*Raketnyy nauchno-issledovatel'skiy institut*] Rocket-Propulsion Institute

ROSTA [*Rossiyskoe telegrafnoe agentstvo*]   Russian Telegraph Agency

RSDLP (*see* RSDRP)

RSDRP [*Rossiyskaya sotsial-demokraticheskaya rabochaya partiya*]   Russian Social-Democratic Labour Party (1898–1912; Bolshevik, 1912–18)

RSDWP (*see* RSDRP)

RSFSR [*Rossiyskaya Sotsialisticheskaya Federativnaya Sovetskaya Respublika*] Russian Socialist Federative Soviet Republic

RVSR [*Revolyutsionnyy voennyy sovet Respubliki*]   Republic Revolutionary Military Council (1918–22)

SA [*Sovremenna arkhitektura*]   Contemporary Architecture

SALT Strategic Arms Limitation Treaty

samizdat unofficial copy of unpublished manuscript (literally: self-publication)

SMERSH [*Smert'shpionam!*]   Death to the Spies! (Soviet wartime counter-intelligence)

Sovnarkom [*Sovet Narodnikh Komissarov*]   Council of People's Commissars (re-named, in 1946, Council of Ministers)

sovnarkhoz [*Sovet narodnogo khozyaystva*]   Council of National Economy

Spetsstal' [*Gosudarstvennoe vsesoyuznoe ob'edinenie kachestvennykh i vysokokachestvennykh staley i ferrosplavov*]   State All-Union Association for Quality and High-Grade Alloy Steels and Ferroalloys

SSR [*Sovetskaya Sotsialisticheskaya Respublika*]   Soviet Socialist Republic

STO [*Sovet truda i oborony*]   Council for Labour and Defence

Svomas [*Svobodnye gosudarstvennye khudozhestvennye masterskie*]   Free State Art Studios (in Moscow, unless indicated otherwise)

TASS [*Telegrafnoe Agentstvo Sovetskogo Soyuza*]   Telegraph Agency of the Soviet Union

TRAM [*teatr rabochey molodezhi*]   Theatre of Worker Youth

TsAGI [*Tsentral'nyy aero-gidrodinamicheskiy institute*]   Central Aero-Hydro-dynamical Institute

TsChO [*Tsentral'no-chernozemnaya oblast'*]   Central Black-Earth Region

TsEMI [*Tsentral'nyy ekonomichesko-matematicheskiy institut*]   Central Economic-Mathematical Institute

TsSU [*Tsentral'noe statisticheskoe upravlenie*] Central Statistical Administration

TsUNKhU [*Tsentral'noe upravlenie narodnokhozyaystvennogo ucheta*]   Central Administration for Statistical Survey of the National Economy

UNESCO United Nations Educational, Scientific, and Cultural Organization

Uralmash [*Ural'skiy zavod tyazhelogo mashinostroeniya*]   Ural Heavy Machinery Plant

USSR Union of Soviet Socialist Republics

VAPP [*Vsesoyuznoe agenstvo po avtorskim pravam*]   All-Union Agency for Authors' Rights

Appendix 2

VASKhNIL [*Vsesoyuznaya akademiya sel-skokhozyaistvennykh nauk*]   All-Union Academy of Agricultural Sciences

VDNKh [*Vystavka dostizheniy narodnogo khozyaystva SSSR*]   Exhibition of Economic Achievement

VeCheka (*see* Cheka)

Vkhutein [*Vysshiy gosudarstvennyy khudozhestvenno-tekhnicheskiy institut*]   Higher State Art-Technical Institute (in Moscow, unless indicated otherwise)

VKhUTEMAS [*Vysshie gosudarstvennye khudozhestvenno-tekhnicheskie masterskie*]   Higher State Art-Technical Studios (in Moscow, unless indicated otherwise)

VSNKh [*Vysshiy Sovet Narodnogo Khozyaistva*]   Supreme Council of the National Economy

VTsIK [*Vsesoyuznyy Tsentral'nyy Ispolnitel'nyy Komitet*]   All-Union Central Executive Committee

VTsSPS [*Vsesoyuznyy Tsentral'nyy Sovet Professional'nykh Soyuzov*]   Central Committee of the Soviet Trade Unions

Zhenotdel [*Otdel po rabote sredi zhenshchin*]   Division for work among women

ZIL [*Avtomobil'nyy zavod im. Likhachev*]   Likhachev Automobile Works

ZIS [*Avtomobil'nyy zavod im. Stalina*]   Stalin Automobile Works

Appendix 3

A Guide to the Changing Soviet Institutional Structure

This book is appearing at a time of unprecedented change in the nature and relative strength of Soviet institutions. Something should be said about the structure of the Soviet political system throughout most of the period since the Bolshevik Revolution in 1917 before a brief account is given of Soviet institutions as of the end of July 1990. A concise guide such as this cannot embrace every organization mentioned in the text of the book, but there are certain institutions – such as the Politburo, the party Central Committee, the Council of Ministers or Gosplan – which require some interpretation if the significance of an individual belonging to one or other of them is to become clearer.

The first and most basic point about the Soviet political system is that throughout most of the period since 1917 the organs of the Communist Party have enjoyed a superior power and authority to that of other institutions. There are a few partial exceptions to that generalization. So long as Lenin was alive the ancestor of the present Council of Ministers (or government), *Sovnarkom* (the Council of People's Commissars), did actually function as a government and could reasonably be regarded as the highest policy-making body in the land.

After Lenin's death a tendency which was already detectable in his lifetime became more pronounced – namely for the Politburo and Secretariat of the Central Committee of the party to become policy-making bodies superior to the nominal government and for party bodies at all levels of the system to possess greater authority than the state institutions (particularly the soviets) in the same territorial unit.

A second time when the superior power of the Communist Party could be questioned was the period from 1936 to 1938 when the party organizations themselves were being ruthlessly purged and the security forces – which were, of course, responsible to Stalin personally (who was, among other things, the *de facto* party leader) – had the power of life and death over members of party committees. A glance at the year of death of people whose biographies appear in this book will show a disproportionate number falling in the late 1930s – officials and intellectuals (by and large in the prime of their lives) who had been arrested and executed.

The third period when the superior power of party institutions is far from clear is the most recent stage in the development of the Soviet political system – a stage inaugurated by the elections for the Congress of People's Deputies of the USSR in 1989 and taken a significant step further in 1990 with the creation of a Presidency, a Presidential Council and the holding of competitive elections for the Supreme Soviets in the various republics.

More will be said below about those new institutions, but first attention must be paid to what has been the more typical pattern of relationships over many years. That means beginning with the Communist Party itself. The Communist Party had its origins in the Bolshevik group within the Russian Social Democratic Party; it became a distinctive faction in 1903 and a separate party in 1912. In 1919 it changed its name to Communist Party, although until 1952 it kept the name 'Bolshevik', or the initial 'b', in brackets after 'Communist Party'.

According to the rules of the Communist Party the highest policy-making body is the Party Congress, held every four or five years, but for much of Soviet history the Congress has been manipulated by the party leadership and it adopted policies essentially determined before the Congress began. The Central Committee, according to the party statutes, is the highest policy-making body between Congresses and it has indeed been a body which party leaders have to take seriously. But the Central Committee in Brezhnev's time, for example, rarely met more often than two or three times a year and even though in the Gorbachev era it has met more frequently, it has not been the key policy-making body on a day-to-day and week-to-week basis.

The most powerful individual post not only within the Communist Party but within the Soviet Union has been for much the greater part of Soviet history the General Secretaryship of the Central Committee of the Communist Party (called First Secretaryship of the Central Committee between 1953 and 1966). The highest collective policy-making organ – a kind of Cabinet for the country as well as executive committee of the party – has been the Politburo (renamed Presidium of the Central Committee, 1953–66). Other powerful central party institutions have been the Secretariat of the Central Committee, which has existed throughout the Soviet period, and the Orgburo – concerned, as its name suggests, with organizational matters – which lasted from 1919 to 1952.

The Central Committee apparatus has been divided into a number of departments and, while some of these departments had no equivalent among state institutions, others acted as overseers of ministries and other state bodies. Thus, for example, until the reorganization of the Central Committee departments which took place in the autumn of 1988 (and which reduced the number of Central Committee departments from twenty to nine), the

Administrative Organs Department had the task of overseeing the Ministry of Civilian Aviation, the Ministry of Defence, the KGB, the Ministry of Internal Affairs, the Ministry of Justice, the Procuracy, the Supreme Court and the civil defence organization. Heads of departments of the Central Committee were very important people within the system, although the most powerful politicians of all (after the General Secretary) were the handful of people who were both full (or voting) members of the Politburo and Secretaries of the Central Committee. They each had the oversight of several departments of the Central Committee. They were followed in importance by the other full members of the Politburo and then by candidate members of the Politburo and Secretaries of the Central Committee.

Below the All-Union Central Committee there have been the party organizations of the fifteen union republics and below them regional, city and district party bodies. At the lowest rung of the party hierarchy comes the primary party organization which is formed not on a territorial basis but at the workplace. The Communist Party of the Soviet Union itself has comprised in recent decades a little over six per cent of the total Soviet population and about one adult in ten. The decision-makers within the party have not, as a rule, been the ordinary party members with other jobs to do but those members who are full-time party officials. The individual wielding the greatest power within any given territorial unit – whether a union republic, a region, a town or district – has been the party First Secretary at that particular level of the hierarchy. The First Secretary of the *obkom* (regional party committee) has been a key figure within the Soviet system. Most holders of that office become members of the Central Committee of the party and it is a rank through which a majority of those who over the years become Politburo members have passed.

State institutions can be divided into appointed executive organs, on the one hand, and 'elected' bodies – the soviets – on the other. In the most recent period (see below) the elections have become meaningful, but for much the greater part of Soviet history these were elections without choice. The single candidate in 'elections' to soviets was handpicked by Soviet officialdom, with party organs having a decisive voice. Instructions were even passed down to the local level on the proportion of manual workers, white-collar workers and of women who should be included in the composition of the soviets.

At the top rung of the hierarchy the Supreme Soviet of the USSR was until the implementation of the recent reforms a body which largely rubber-stamped decisions taken elsewhere and which, in any event, met only for a few days each year. At local levels soviets (the organs of local government) had some serious work to do – such as the allocation of housing and many of the functions carried out by local government in the West – but they had no independence from the Communist Party, and party organs could in reality both tell them what to do and could take over many of their functions (known in the Soviet political literature as *podmena*, or 'substitutionism') if local party officials felt so inclined.

The most powerful state institutions have been the ministries. The Ministry of Defence and the Ministry of Foreign Affairs, although they have been accountable not only to the Politburo but also, to some degree, to their party Central Committee supervisory bodies (the International Department in the case of the Foreign Ministry), have been influential institutional actors within the system, the more so because of the Soviet Union's 'superpower' status and global interests. Economic ministries have also wielded a great deal of day-to-day power within their own particular spheres. They have, in a sense, been super-corporations and state monopolist-suppliers of their particular products. Throughout most of Soviet history, there has been a far greater emphasis on the quantity than the quality of production and the ministries have agreed plan targets with Gosplan, the State Planning Committee, which has had a crucial co-ordinating role within the economy. Until 1946 ministers were called commissars and what in the post-war period has been called the Council of Ministers was until 1946 known as *Sovnarkom* (the Council of People's Commissars).

The security organs, or political police, have been all-pervasive instruments of control throughout most of the period since 1917. They have to be recognized under several different names. It was Lenin who created the ancestor of the KGB, the Cheka (Extraordinary Commission for Combating of Counter-Revolution and Sabotage), a body which existed under that name from 1917 to 1922. Thereafter known as OGPU and GPU, the security police subsequently acquired the name NKVD (standing for People's Commissariat of Internal Affairs) in 1934 and kept that title until 1944. These became especially dreaded initials, for it was as the NKVD that the security organs operated during the years of the most ruthless arrests and killings of millions of Soviet citizens. In the post-war period the security police has been known as the MGB (Ministry of State Security) and – from 1953 – as the KGB (Committee of State Security). The head of the KGB, or its earlier equivalents, has generally been close – but also clearly subordinate – to the top party leader or (apart from the period of 'high Stalinism', 1934–53) to the collective leadership of the Communist Party. At some times, but by no means at all, the head of the security organs has himself been a member of the Politburo.

The Council of Ministers – and its inner body, the Presidium of the Council of Ministers – has comprised a group of important Soviet officials. The Presidium of the Council of Ministers has, for example, acted as a kind of court of appeal against decisions on allocation of resources made by Gosplan. The fact remains, however, that the highest court of appeal both on economic matters and foreign policy has been the Politburo. The Chairman of the Council of Ministers (or Prime Minister in Western parlance) has not been the chief executive in the sense in which a majority of West European prime ministers are the most powerful politicians within their countries. Over a period of seventy years in any struggle for supremacy between the Chairman of the Council of Ministers and the party General Secretary, the party leader has won in the end. Yet the Chairman of the Council of Ministers was generally one of the three or four most important leaders in the country, wielding an especially great influence in economic policy.

The most dramatic changes in the Soviet political system since the 1917 Revolution itself have taken place under the leadership of Gorbachev, especially in 1989 to 1990. Important new institutions have been created and other institutions, which bear familiar names, are working in very different ways from in the past. The greatest overall changes have been a significant transfer of power from party to state institutions and the emergence of real accountability of politicians to those below – to their immediate electorate and to the public as a whole – and not only to those above them in a bureaucratic hierarchy. The very rules of the game of Soviet political life are changing at the time of writing, virtually from week to week.

A qualitative change began with the introduction of competitive elections for a new Soviet legislature – the Congress of People's Deputies of the USSR – in 1989. That body consists of 2,250 members of whom 750 were elected from territorial constituencies on the basis of one deputy for every 257,300 voters, 750 from national-territorial constituencies and 750 deputies from 'public organizations' of varying size and significance (including, for example, the Communist Party, the Komsomol, the Academy of Sciences, the industrial trade unions and the Writers' Union). The Congress of People's Deputies elected in turn an inner body, the Supreme Soviet which, unlike the Supreme Soviet of old (which met for only a few days annually) is in session for about eight months of the year. The new Supreme Soviet is, like the old, a bicameral body divided into the Soviet of the Union and the Soviet of Nationalities. But there all resemblance with its predecessor ends. It has a smaller number of deputies (542) and it engages in real debate as, indeed, does the Congress of People's Deputies which is convened for shorter periods. The new Soviet legislature as a whole has become a force to be reckoned with in the political system, not only in its plenary sessions but in its committees which have become serious investigatory and scrutinizing bodies.

A unique institution in the history not only of the Soviet Union but of Russia was created in March 1990 – an executive Presidency – and Gorbachev was elected first *Prezident* by the Congress of People's Deputies, although the Law on the Presidency stipulates that the next election should be by the electorate as a whole. Along with the Presidency, two new institutions were created – a Presidential Council and a Council of the Federation. Both are advisory, but the Presidential Council has now come to look more like a Cabinet than the Politburo which by the Spring of 1990 was no longer meeting as frequently as in the past and which – following the Twenty-eighth Party Congress held in July 1990 – no longer contained the most powerful politicians in the land. The Council of the Federation is designed to give a voice in Moscow to all fifteen union republics in an attempt to avoid the disintegration of the Soviet state which the rise of nationalist sentiment and inter-ethnic tensions have turned into a real possibility. The new 24-person Politburo elected in July 1990 also for the first time includes representatives of all the union republics in this highest executive committee of the Communist Party. The rank of candidate member – whether of the Politburo or the Central Committee – was abolished.

When elections for the legislatures of the various union republics of the Soviet Union took place in 1990 (in most cases directly for the Supreme Soviet, for it was left to the republics themselves to decide whether they wished to have a republican Congress of People's Deputies), another major step towards pluralization and diversity within the Soviet system was taken. But it also threatened to become something more than that, as the parliaments of the three Baltic republics, with Lithuania leading the way, made it clear that they wished to move towards outright independence and there was a possibility of other Soviet republics following suit. The election of Boris Yel'tsin as Chairman of the Supreme Soviet of the Russian republic in late May 1990 raised the possibility of a kind of 'dual power' in the heart of Russia itself, with Yel'tsin attempting to pursue policies which contradicted those of the all-Union leadership headed by Mikhail Gorbachev.

The Soviet system, in other words, was by the spring and summer of 1990 a far cry from that familiar to foreign observers over many years. The 'leading role' of the Communist Party (essentially a euphemism for its monopoly of power) and 'democratic centralism' within it had not only to a large extent ceased to exist in practice, but the former notion was dropped from the Constitution of the USSR. In principle, as well as in practice, the Soviet Union was moving towards a political pluralism such as it had never known before. A competitive party system was in principle accepted in the Spring of 1990 and looked as if it would increasingly become a reality in much of the Soviet Union in the near future.

Thus, whereas high Communist Party office in the past meant real executive authority in the state (whatever Soviet constitutional lawyers may have said, and they have now admitted that the party formerly wielded power and not just influence), no such automatic connection exists today. By the early summer of 1990 there were already Soviet republics in which the most important politician was not the First Secretary of the republican party Central Committee. Lithuania became the first and most obvious case in point.

The Soviet political system is, then, in a period of flux and unprecedented uncertainty. The biographical entries on politicians in this volume reflect the dominance of the Communist Party and its professional apparatus over a period of more than seventy years. They also take account of the changes in the power structure which began to occur in 1989 – foreshadowed, to some extent, by changes engineered from above by Gorbachev in 1987 and 1988, but which have moved in directions that were not at that time fully foreseen or intended.

Accordingly, the weight of particular institutions within the Soviet system is reflected in the emphasis given to them in the political entries; that is an implicit statement about the power of those institutions throughout most of Soviet history and up to the present. It is clearly not a statement about the future, for it seems very likely that institutional change will continue and go beyond what we have seen in 1989 and the first half of 1990. The Soviet Union in the summer of 1990 is already a very different place from what it was a mere five years ago. What it will be like in five or ten years from now is more difficult to predict than ever before.

Archie Brown

Appendix 4

Suggested Further Reading

Robert Auty and Dmitri Obolensky (editors), *Companion to Russian Studies*, vol. 1: *An Introduction to Russian History* (Cambridge University Press: Cambridge and New York, 1976); vol. 2: *An Introduction to Russian Language and Literature* (Cambridge University Press, 1977); and vol. 3: *An Introduction to Russian Art and Architecture* (Cambridge University Press, 1980).

Seweryn Bialer (editor), *Politics, Society and Nationality: Inside Gorbachev's Russia* (Westview: Boulder, Colorado, and London, 1989).

Seweryn Bialer and Michael Mandelbaum (editors), *Gorbachev's Russia and American Foreign Policy* (Westview: Boulder and London, 1988).

Archie Brown, *The Gorbachev Factor in Soviet Politics* (Oxford University Press: Oxford and New York, 1991).

Abraham Brumberg (editor), *Chronicle of a .Revolution: A Western-Soviet Inquiry into Perestroika* (Pantheon Books: New York, 1990).

The Cambridge Encyclopedia of Russia and the Soviet Union (Cambridge University Press: Cambridge and New York, 1982; 2nd (revised) edn, 1992).

Stephen F. Cohen and Katrina vanden Heuvel, *Voices of Glasnost: Interviews with Gorbachev's Reformers* (Norton: New York and London, 1989).

R. W. Davies, *Soviet History in the Gorbachev Revolution* (Macmillan: Basingstoke and London, 1989).

John Erickson, *The Road to Stalingrad* (Weidenfeld and Nicolson: London, 1975).

John Erickson, *The Road to Berlin* (Weidenfeld and Nicolson, London, 1983).

Julian Graffy and Geoffrey A. Hosking (editors), *Culture and the Media in the USSR Today* (Macmillan: London and Basingstoke, 1989).

Max Hayward, *Writers in Russia 1917–1978* (edited by Patricia Blake: Harvill Press: London, 1983).

Jerry F. Hough and Merle Fainsod, *How the Soviet Union is Governed* (Harvard University Press: Cambridge, Mass., 1979).

Jerry F. Hough, *Russia and the West* (Simon and Schuster: New York, 1988; revised edn, Touchstone, 1990).

Gail W. Lapidus, *Women in Soviet Society: Equality, Development and Social Change* (University of California Press: Berkeley and London, 1978).

Nadezhda Mandelstam, *Hope Against Hope: A Memoir* (Collins & Harvill: London, 1971).

Roy A. Medvedev, *Let History Judge: The Origins and Consequences of Stalinism* (revised edn, Oxford University Press: Oxford and New York, 1989).

Zhores A. Medvedev, *Soviet Science* (Oxford University Press: Oxford, 1979).

Alec Nove, *Glasnost' in Action: Cultural Renaissance in Russia* (Unwin Hyman: London and Winchester, Mass., 1989).

Alec Nove, *The Soviet Economic System* (3rd edn, Unwin Hyman: London and Winchester, Mass., 1986).

Nicholas V. Riasanovsky, *A History of Russia* (3rd edn, Oxford University Press: Oxford and New York, 1977).

T. H. Rigby, *Lenin's Government: Sovnarkom 1917–1922* (Cambridge University Press: Cambridge and New York, 1979).

James W. Riordan, *Sport in Soviet Society* (Cambridge University Press: Cambridge and New York, 1977).

Leonard Schapiro, *The Communist Party of the Soviet Union* (2nd edn, Eyre and Spottiswoode: London, 1970).

M. G. Swift, *The Art of Dance in the USSR* (Notre Dame, 1968).

Harold Shukman, *The Blackwell Encyclopedia of the Russian Revolution* (Blackwell: Oxford, 1988).

Victor Terras (editor), *Handbook of Russian Literature* (Yale University Press: New Haven and London, 1985).

Donald W. Treadgold, *Twentieth Century Russia* (7th edn, Westview: Boulder and London, 1990).

Robert C. Tucker, *Political Culture and Political Leadership in the Soviet Union* (Wheatsheaf: Brighton, 1987).

Alexander Vucunich, *Empire of Knowledge: The Academy of Sciences of the USSR (1917–1970)* (University of California Press: Berkeley and Los Angeles, 1984).

Stephen White, *Gorbachev in Power* (Cambridge University Press: Cambridge and New York, 1990).

Appendix 5

New Politburo Members

While this book was in proofs in July 1990 the following people, not covered elsewhere in the book, were elected to the Politburo.

DZASOKHOV, Aleksandr Sergeevich (b. 1934) The Secretary of the Central Committee of the CPSU responsible for ideology and a Politburo member (both positions held only since July 1990), Dzasokhov – an Ossetian by nationality – was born in Ordzhonikidze in the Northern Ossetian ASSR. After a technical education he worked in the apparatus of the Komsomol and then from 1967 until 1986 in the Committee for Solidarity with the Countries of Asia and Africa. From 1986 to 1988 he was Soviet Ambassador to Syria and in 1988 he became First Secretary of the Northern Ossetian regional party committee. A member of the Congress of People's Deputies of the USSR, he is also Chairman of the Committee for International Affairs of the Supreme Soviet. AHB

GURENKO, Stanislav Ivanovich (b. 1936) First Secretary of the Central Committee of the Communist Party of the Ukraine from June 1990 and a member of the Politburo of the CPSU from the following month, Gurenko is a Ukrainian born in the town of Ilovaysk in the Donetsk region. A party

member since 1961, he graduated from the Kiev Polytechnical Institute and pursued a career in industrial management until the mid-1970s when he moved first into the party apparatus and then the Ukrainian government. From 1980 to 1987 he was a deputy chairman of the Ukrainian Council of Ministers. From 1987 until his elevation to the leadership of the Ukrainian Communist Party in 1990 he was second secretary of the party in the Ukraine. AHB

RUBIKS, Alfreds (b. 1935) Latvian by nationality, a Communist Party member since 1958 and First Secretary of the Latvian party since April 1990, Rubiks became a member of the renewed and expanded Politburo in July 1990. Originally a skilled worker, he has spent most of his career in the party, soviet and ministerial apparatus in Latvia. From 1984 until 1990 he was chairman of the Riga city soviet. Rubiks is a member of the Soviet of Nationalities of the USSR. AHB

SEMENOVA, Galina Vladimirovna (b. 1937) A Politburo member and Secretary of the Central Committee of

488

the CPSU since July 1990 (the highest combination of party posts ever held by a woman), Semenova is a relative newcomer to political life. A Russian by nationality, she was born in Smolensk and studied at L'vov University and at the Academy of Social Sciences attached to the Central Committee of the CPSU. Semenova, who has a candidate of sciences degree in philosophy, has been a journalist by profession, working mainly on Komsomol newspapers and journals (1974–80 as editor of *Komsomol'skaya zhizn'*) before becoming editor of *Krestyanka* (Peasant Woman) in January 1981, a post she held until her election to the party leadership following the Twenty-eighth Congress of the CPSU. AHB

SHENIN, Oleg Semenovich (b. 1937) A Secretary of the Central Committee

with special responsibility for the party organization and a Politburo member since July 1990, Shenin – who is of Russian nationality – has belonged to the party since 1962. An engineer by original profession, Shenin studied at the Krasnoyarsk Mining Technical Institute, the Tomsk Engineering-Construction Institute and at the Academy of Social Sciences attached to the Central Committee of the CPSU. From 1955 until 1974 he worked in the construction industry before turning to full-time party functions. From 1987 he was First Secretary of the Krasnoyarsk regional party committee and in 1990 he became chairman in addition of the Krasnoyarsk regional soviet. Since 1989 he has been a member of the Congress of People's Deputies of the USSR. AHB